Best Places
to Stay in
Asia

The Best Places to Stay Series

Best Places to Stay in America's Cities
Kenneth Hale-Wehmann, Editor

Best Places to Stay in Asia
Jerome E. Klein

Best Places to Stay in California
Marilyn McFarlane

Best Places to Stay in the Caribbean
Bill Jamison and Cheryl Alters Jamison

Best Places to Stay in Florida
Christine Davidson

Best Places to Stay in Hawaii
Bill Jamison and Cheryl Alters Jamison

Best Places to Stay in New England
Third Edition
Christina Tree and Kimberly Grant

Best Places to Stay in the Pacific Northwest
Marilyn McFarlane

Best Places to Stay in the Southwest
Gail Barber Rickey

Best Places to Stay in Asia

Jerome E. Klein

Bruce Shaw, Editorial Director

Houghton Mifflin Company · Boston

Copyright © 1988 by The Harvard Common Press

All rights reserved

For information about permission to reproduce selections
from this book, write to Permissions, Houghton Mifflin
Company, 2 Park Street, Boston, Massachusetts 02108.

First Edition

ISBN: 0-395-54549-8 (pbk.)
ISSN: 1048-5457

Printed in the United States of America

Cover design by Jackie Schuman
Maps by Charles Bahne

This book was prepared in conjunction
with Harvard Common Press.

HAD 10 9 8 7 6 5 4 3 2 1

CONTENTS

THE PHILIPPINES   348

Baguio   349
Hyatt Terraces Baguio   350

Batangas   352
Punta Baluarte Inter-Continental   352

Cavite   353
Puerto Azul Beach Hotel   354

Davao City   356
Davao Insular Inter-Continental Inn   356

Manila   358
Century Park Sheraton   359
Holiday Inn Manila   361
Hotel Inter-Continental Manila   362
Hyatt Regency Manila   365
The Mandarin Oriental   367
Manila Hilton International   369
The Manila Hotel   370
The Manila Peninsula   374
The Westin Philippine Plaza   376

SINGAPORE   380

Boulevard Hotel   382
Century Park Sheraton   384
The Dynasty Singapore   386
The Goodwood Park Hotel   388
Hilton International Singapore   390
Holiday Inn Parkview   393
Hotel New Otani Singapore   394
Hyatt Regency Singapore   396
Ladyhill Hotel   399
Le Meridien Singapour   400
Le Meridien Singapour Changi   402
The Mandarin Singapore   403
Marco Polo Singapore   406
Marina Mandarin Singapore   408
Novotel Orchid Inn Singapore   410
The Oriental Singapore   411
Pan Pacific Singapore   414
The Pavilion Inter-Continental   417
Raffles Hotel   419
Shangri-La Singapore   422
Sheraton Towers Singapore   425
The Westin Plaza/The Westin Stamford   427
York Hotel   429

INTRODUCTION

According to an article in the *Consumer Reports Travel Letter* (July 1987), one of the major weaknesses of guidebooks to Asia is the sparse information they provide on hotels. The writer felt the guides do little more than list hotels, or, at best, repeat information found in travel agents' brochures.

This is not another travel guide to Asia. It is, rather, specifically about Asia's hotels and resorts, with a little information about the places they are situated. The book describes, thoroughly, nearly three hundred hotels in sixteen Asian countries.

The hotels and resorts of Asia deserve such a book. Mostly because of the influx of Western travelers, these hotels have in the past few years not only grown in numbers, but have often pioneered new architectural concepts, electronic service systems, and other innovations in hotel management. In so doing, they have sometimes created hotels in ways superior to the finest in Europe and the United States.

According to an annual survey of its readers by *Institutional Investor*, the three best hotels in the world are in Asia: the Oriental in Bangkok, the Mandarin in Hong Kong, and the Hotel Okura in Tokyo (in fifth place is the Shangri-La in Singapore, and in ninth place is the Peninsula in Hong Kong). Among the ten "Great Hotels of the World" described in *Travel & Leisure* (April 1987) are the Regent in Hong Kong, the Oriental in Bangkok, and the Mandarin in Hong Kong. Only one of these ten is in the United States;

the remaining six are among the grand hotels of Europe. In the same month, *Euromoney* published the results of its survey of readers around the world. Their pick of the best hotels in the world came in this order: the Shangri-La, Singapore; the Mandarin, Hong Kong; the Oriental, Bangkok; the Okura, Tokyo; the Regent, Hong Kong; the Savoy, London, the Dolder Grand, Zurich; the Peninsula, Hong Kong; the Imperial, Tokyo; and the Ritz, Madrid. Seven out of the ten are in Asia. And so it goes with other surveys on the subject.

While I agree with the general conclusion of these surveys and others—that many of the top Asian hotels are terrific —I don't believe in fixed evaluations. A great hotelier, the late Alfonso Font, once explained to me that a hotel's reputation hangs on a thin thread. "If the hall porter's wife was cruel to him last night," he said, "at least a dozen of my guests will be unhappy."

I have not, therefore, tried to give you an in-depth critique of each hotel at the moment my wife and I visited it. Instead I have endeavored to give you an honest overview. I tell you about the guest and public rooms, the places to eat, the special amenities, the grounds, the neighborhood. I tell you what is most interesting about the hotel, and even my favorite place in it, if I have one.

Asian hotels are overwhelmingly cognizant of travelers' tastes and compete to satisfy them. During the past three to five years, as new *gran luxe* hotels have arisen, most of the older hotels have been fully renovated, rebuilt, or enlarged. Many have added or enlarged business centers and health centers, always installing state-of-the-art equipment, whether exercise machines or computers. And whereas five years ago you couldn't find an Italian restaurant in an Asian hotel, now there are dozens of them. Even the People's Republic of China is sensitive to its markets. At first the Chinese tried to build and run hotels on their own; now, more experienced, they are becoming partners with the best hotel building and management groups in the world, and their hotels improve day by day.

The fleabag hotels many of us remember from movies featuring Peter Lorre and Sydney Greenstreet still exist in some parts of Asia, but none of them appear in this book. In fact, I've left out any hotel I felt an average American might not be comfortable in, for any of a variety of reasons. But not including a hotel doesn't necessarily mean I don't like it. With the thousands of hotels in Asia, I could not possibly describe all that are worthwhile. But I have tried to include what I feel to be the very best in each place, as well as some of the less expensive hotels that are clean, comfortable, and well situated.

Just because you see such names as Westin, Hilton, Hyatt, Mandarin, Ramada, and Marriott, do not think all the great new hotels are run by major hotel corporations. Most of these are owned by local corporations, sometimes fully, sometimes in partnership with an American, Hong Kong, Japanese, British, French, or Swedish management group. And prepare to be surprised. In Asia, a Holiday Inn or a Ramada may be the best hotel in town.

There are not many fine old colonial hotels left in Asia. I have tried to include the best of them, such as the Oriental in Bangkok, opened in 1877 and now sporting modern additions that tower above the earlier structure, and the famous Raffles in Singapore, built in 1887 and still endeavoring to play its grande dame role, albeit in the shadows of the world's tallest hotel, which is across the street. And then there are the equally famous Manila Hotel, whose seventy-fifth anniversary was recently honored on Philippine postage stamps, and what claims to be the oldest still operative hotel in the world, the Galle Face in Colombo, Sri Lanka, which started business in 1864.

Asian hoteliers manage to be all things to all travelers—Japanese, Americans, Europeans, Middle Easterners, and Australians, among others. Both luxurious and modest hotels provide rooms furnished in traditional Japanese and Indian styles as well as in the Western mode.

There is no doubt that some of the world's most magnificent hotel suites are in Europe and, since recently, in the United States. But Asian hoteliers have proven themselves the masters in providing the suite life. I describe those suites that are exceptional.

Service is also excellent in Asian hotels. In Thailand and Sri Lanka, where labor costs are low, guests have more staff available to serve them than in, say, Japan or Hong Kong. But in the latter places the staff tends to be especially well trained and gracious. In China, where the political and social philosophies discourage subservience to foreigners, service was rough at first. But this is changing. Chinese students of hotel management now learn to welcome guests into their hotels as they would honored persons in their homes—an approach very successful in most of Asia.

Most of the tourist hotels in Asia have restaurants; many have a half dozen or more. These restaurants are often the best in town, and they are sometimes the only ones that serve Western meals. Few hotels neglect the native cuisine, however. In both variety and quality, hotel restaurants in Asia are outstanding.

Asian hotel ventures continue to attract and challenge the imagination of great architects. Between 1916 and 1920, the Imperial Hotel was built in Tokyo from the plans of Frank Lloyd Wright. In 1986, the Westin Stamford and the Westin Plaza in Singapore and the Fragrant Hills near Beijing were built from plans of today's architectural genius, I. M. Pei.

It is interesting how important views have become in the design of new hotels—everywhere, but particularly in Asia. Guest rooms often start on the fifth floor or higher. Restaurants, including revolving dining rooms (see Appendix), are often on the top floor. The world's highest hotel dining room, the Compass Rose, is atop the Westin Stamford of Singapore, more than seventy floors above the earth.

As the Westin Stamford exemplifies, Asia is a place of superlatives in hotel architecture. The largest hotel in the world is the New Otani in Tokyo, with twenty-one hundred rooms and suites. Certainly the most glamorous hotel in India, and possibly in the world, is the Lake Palace in Udaipur, a white marble potentate's palace, two hundred years old, that rises out of a lake. Some of the lobbies in Asian hotels, particularly the newer ones, are not only luxurious, but are also the size of football fields (I list my favorites in the Appendix).

Not all hotels that should be in this kind of book are here. If you discover any you feel should be added, please write to me in care of the publisher and tell me about them. Tell me also if things have changed—for better or worse—at the hotels I describe.

If there is anything else you feel I could do to make this book more helpful to you, let me know. In this way we can together ensure that subsequent editions will be most useful to all travelers in Asia, whether on pleasure or business.

HOW TO USE
THIS BOOK

At the start of each entry I give you a lot of helpful facts, on the following subjects:

Address and Reservation Information. If, after you have worked with your travel agent or corporate travel office and cannot get a reservation, you may want to try on your own. When hotels have cancellations, they sometimes give preference to those on the waiting list who have not involved an agent; this saves them a commission. You may, of course, simply prefer to make your own reservations.

I therefore give not only the address of the hotel but also its phone number and, if it is a resort with a reservations office in a nearby big city, the number there as well. If the hotel has an office or reservations service in the United States, I also give that number. And I give telex, cable, and facsimile information in case you prefer to make your reservation in one of these ways.

The bigger hotels may often be reached at any of several consecutive numbers. This is indicated by a slash; for example, a hotel whose number is listed as 123-4567/70 may be reached at 123-4567, 123-4568, 123-4569, or 123-4570.

Credit Cards. Although most hotels accept all major credit cards, some do not. To prevent unhappy surprises, I indicate which cards each hotel will take.

Who's in Charge? More often than not this information is helpful when you arrive at the hotel or after you return home. It is good to know whom to talk to, and to be able to ask for that person by name. Some like to call or write these people in advance.

The concierge is usually the best person to consult concerning shows, side trips, public events, shopping, or introductions to people you want to meet.

The sales manager or director is most helpful in setting up conferences, seminars, conventions, private meetings, and so on.

Management Company. Since a hotel's name may not tell you who is running it, I provide the name of this company for every hotel not operated independently. If you particularly like—or dislike—the Westin style of management, for instance, you may appreciate knowing that Westin runs Hong Kong's famous Shangri-La.

Rooms and Rates. I list the kinds of rooms as each hotel does. Generally, the terms *double* and *single* refer to the number of occupants. Most rooms have two beds, full-size or larger; a twin room has two twin beds. An executive room includes a large desk and a sitting area.

For the business traveler, a suite provides a private place for meetings outside the bedroom. A "junior suite" is seldom a true suite (two or more adjoining rooms); usually, it is a bedroom with a sitting area adequate for meetings of two to four persons. This area may be set off by a plant stand, ornate screen, or half- or full-height wall, but only rarely can it be completely closed off from the sleeping area. Some hotels are willing to rearrange the sitting area of a junior suite, or the living room of a true suite, as an office, with a conference table, a desk, and even a part-time secretary with a typewriter or desk-top computer.

Special rooms and suites often have fanciful names. Details on amenities may be provided in the text, or you can ask your travel agent or the hotel's resident manager or general manager for a description.

Most, but not all, rooms in the hotels included here have air conditioning, phones, and private bathrooms with showers.

Room rates are accurate, in U.S. dollars, for 1988. All, however, are approximate, since currency values fluctuate, and subject to change. No reference is given to special rates for large users, such as groups, corporations, and travel packagers; contact the hotel sales manager about these. Also, it is well to know that some rooms may be purchased by speculators and sold at higher prices, especially during high seasons or special events such as festivals. If the speculators overbuy, they dispose of the rooms at discount. Travel agents usually know of discounts, off-season bargains, and special rate packages.

Food is not included in the room rate unless indicated.

Number of Rooms and Suites. Some people don't like small hotels, and others don't like large ones. Some like to stay in a hotel with a lot of suites because the clientele is likely to be affluent; others like a place with few suites or none because it is bound to be more down-to-earth or casual. I therefore give the number of rooms and suites and, where they exist, cottages, villas, or bungalows.

Service Charge and Tax For each hotel I indicate the service charge and room tax, if any.

While most hotels add a 10 percent service charge to each bill in lieu of tips, some do not. Even where there is a service charge, a modest tip is usually expected when someone takes particular care in serving you. I indicate the countries in which tipping is never expected.

Most, though not all, governments charge a room tax—ranging from 3 percent to as high as 11 percent. Some levy additional taxes on drinks and food.

BANGLADESH

Bangladesh is a land of mixed moods. It is, at most times, a tranquil place. With its luxuriant tropical forests and lush green croplands, it looks like the fulfillment of a landscape painter's dream. But the country can be turbulent, with monsoon floods, awesome northwesters, devastating cyclones, and tidal surges.

The climate of Bangladesh is tropical, with an average rainfall of eighty inches a year. You can enjoy the country in the rain-drenched monsoon months, in the flower-decked autumn, or in the mellow, sunlit winter.

Nature's bounties are plentiful in this picturesque land, where *shapla* (water lilies) adorn the ripples of the serene lakes, rivers, and ponds. The mighty Himalayan mountain range is the country's northern boundary, and the beautiful, but sometimes tempestuous, Bay of Bengal washes its shores to the south. Three main rivers, the Ganga, the Bramaputra, and the Meghna, have together created the world's largest delta here. Their deposits of silt and rich soil, combined with abundant rainfall and sunshine, make for a fertile land. Mineral resources, particularly natural gas, are plentiful.

This is a populous country, with nearly one hundred million inhabitants, most of whom are Bengalis, although pockets of ethnic tribespeople continue to thrive. Over 80 percent of the population are Sunni Moslems. Though normally as placid and hospitable as the landscape, the people of Bangladesh fought one of the bloodiest wars of independence ever, winning their autonomy from Pakistan in 1971. Freedom is a proud tradition here.

Dhaka, the capital city, has a population of about four million. There is much to see in this "City of Mosques," including the national museum, a Mughal fort, the war heroes' memorial, the old bazaars, and, at nearby Sonargaon, a Buddhist monastery dating from the seventh century A.D. Dhaka is the country's hub, with road, rail, and air services linking it to all regions. Although Bangla is the national language, English is widely spoken and understood in the urban areas.

Dhaka

DHAKA SHERATON HOTEL
1 Minto Road
P.O. Box 504
Dhaka
Bangladesh
Telephone: 505061 or 252911/19
Telex: 642401 SHER BJ
Cable: INHOTELCOR
Fax: 880-2-412972
Reservations:
    In Dhaka call 505061, ext. 640 or 570
    In the USA call 1-800-325-3535
All major credit cards
General Manager: Hermann Simon
Concierges: Mr. Mobarak and Mr. Rozario
Director of Marketing and Sales: M. A. Ashraf
The Sheraton Corporation
Rates (approx.):
    Room $120
    Suite $160–385
300 rooms, 18 suites
Service charge 12.5%; tax 20%

The former Inter-Continental was taken over the by Sheraton Corporation in 1984 and refurbished as one of the world's very fine hotels.

In the heart of the city and only twenty minutes from the international airport, it is a modern, eleven-story hotel with air-conditioned, luxuriously furnished guest rooms and suites. It has beautiful gardens, green lawns, and, in their midst, a large swimming pool. There are flood-lit tennis courts and a giant garden chess set with pieces as big as people. Also available are table tennis, badminton, and squash, and a golf course is just five minutes from the hotel.

The guest rooms are on seven floors of the hotel, two of which were completely renovated in 1987. Among the new features in these rooms are large desks, bedside controls for lighting, radio, color TV, and in-house music, video, and the latest Reuters News. The bathrooms are luxurious, with a generous use of marble and wall-to-wall mirrors.

My favorite spot in this hotel is the Vintage Room, considered the most elegant restaurant in Dhaka. Open for lunch and dinner, it is divided into three separate dining rooms for an intimate atmosphere. Even when it is filled to capacity it doesn't seem crowded. With wood-paneled walls lined with prints of vintage automobiles, it has an Edwardian look to complement its speciality of prime rib steaks, cut at the table to suit the taste of the guest. Another of its specialties is "Chinese fondue," which includes beef tenderloin, fillet of veal, prawns, chicken breast, fish, and Chinese vegetables. The fish served in this room is fresh and excellently prepared.

Another excellent place to eat in this hotel, if you are invited to a banquet or other event held here, is Top of the Park, on the highest floor. The view of the city is delightful at night; in the foreground is nearby Ramna Park.

The informal Bithika Restaurant serves both local and international dishes at all hours.

The Bar, decorated with tapestries by a famous artist, is the best in town. Another fun spot is the open-air Poolside Bar B Que, serving lunch on Thursday, Friday, and Saturday.

Now, for a secret. If you want to be sure of a beautiful view, ask for a room or suite whose last digit is a 3 or a 4 (such as 603 or 604).

CHINA

With an area of 3.7 million square miles (9.6 million square kilometers), this is, after the Soviet Union, the second largest country in the world. It shares frontiers with North Korea, the Mongolian People's Republic, the Soviet Union, Afghanistan, Pakistan, India, Nepal, Bhutan, Burma, Laos, and Vietnam. The population is thought to be between 900 million and 1 billion, making China the most populous country in the world. Some estimates put the population even higher.

The overwhelming majority of the people are the ethnic Chinese, or Han. Among the rest are Mongols, Tibetans, Uighurs, Zhuangs, Koreans, and a number of other minorities.

The origin of China can be traced as far as the second millennium before Christ. Records of its early history exist mainly from the Zhou Dynasty (1122 to 700 B.C.).

The Imperial system was overthrown only in 1911, when the foundations of the People's Republic were established. From the 1920s until 1949, sporadic civil war occurred between the Guomindang (the Nationalist Party) and the Communists, who were finally victorious, driving the Nationalists to set up a truncated regime on the island of Taiwan. The United States and some of its allies boycotted the People's Republic until 1971. In 1972 state-to-state relations were established; full diplomatic relations were set up in 1979.

Western businesses are finding the newly open Chinese

markets as interesting as China itself. Many Western business people work through existing Chinese trade organizations, such as the China Council for the Promotion of International Trade, in Beijing. Some start by contacting the trade counselor at a Chinese embassy; such a counselor, usually from the Ministry of Foreign Trade, can be very helpful. In Washington there is also the National Council for U.S.-China Trade, and in London there is the Sino-British Trade Council. Some prefer to use the services of a Hong Kong agent in doing business with China. Your local commercial bank may be able to put you in touch with an affiliate bank in Hong Kong, which can in turn help you make your business connections.

Only a few of the hotels in China now have business centers, but the few such centers that exist can guide visitors in setting appointments with local officials and business people, and in other procedures.

Because the Chinese have encouraged Western hoteliers to run some of their better hotels, accommodations for visitors are improving rapidly. Still, ideal accommodations are in limited supply.

Getting around by yourself is permitted in Chinese cities, but using the local buses may be difficult. Taxis at the hotels and other places are reserved for the use of foreigners— particularly in Beijing, Shanghai, and Guangzhou—at reasonable prices. It is wise to ask the taxi to wait if you have an appointment; the extra charge is minimal.

Western visitors to China used to complain about the hotel food. Now most are happier, not only because many of the hotels have brought in chefs from Europe and Hong Kong who are familiar with Western tastes, but also because the better Chinese cooks have themselves become chefs. Encouraged by their government, they are competing with the newcomers. Now the native cuisine is usually excellent in their finer restaurants and hotels. Fastidious travelers still bring their own instant coffee, favorite jellies, marmalade, and sauces; however, if your itinerary includes only the grand hotels run by the international hotel groups, you're almost sure to find everything you like.

For shopping, Westerners are generally best served by the stores in the hotels. However, all larger cities have Friendship Stores, where foreigners can buy items of everyday use as well as souvenirs and even fine works of art and antiques. Many of the products available in these stores are difficult or impossible to get in other shops. (It is important to remember that antiques 150 years old or older will not be sold. Even if you manage to acquire any, they cannot be taken out of the country.) The prices in Friendship Stores are equal to prices elsewhere, and payment must be in local currency, not in foreign exchange or special certificates.

Some warnings: Since 1949, tipping has been banned in the People's Republic of China. It is still officially illegal. However, as the Western-managed hotels welcome their regular guests who are used to tipping, the custom is coming into vogue. Some of these hotels have a 10 percent service charge; this will probably become the rule at all Chinese hotels soon. For now, tipping, though banned, is an accepted recognition of exceptional service.

Do not joke or make frivolous remarks at official occasions, including banquets and toasts, and especially not about political leaders. Do not call the country the Republic of China; always use the word *People's*, or just call it China. Do not call Taiwan a country. This brings an immediate reaction, for to your hosts, Taiwan is a province of China. The attitude toward photography is generally liberal, except for military objects. It is rude to take pictures of people without asking, unless they happen to be part of a large scene. Also, it is wise to ask before taking pictures of any wall posters.

Beijing (Peking)

The capital of the People's Republic of China, Beijing is considered the nation's political, economic, and cultural center. It is in the center of Hopeh Province, but it is an independent unit administered by the national government. With an estimated population of well over eight million, it is the second largest city in China, after Shanghai. It has become an important industrial area, the heart of a vast complex of textile mills, ironworks, steelworks, railroad repair shops, machine shops, chemical plants, and factories that build such things as heavy machinery, electronic equipment, aircraft, plastics, synthetic fibers and rolling stock.

Beijing, whose name was formerly romanized as Peking, consists in the main of two formerly walled districts, the Outer City, or Chinese City, and the Inner City, or Tatar City. The twenty-five miles of ramparts and monumental gates that once surrounded the cities have been razed by the Communist government and replaced by wide avenues. Within the Tatar City is the Forbidden City, formerly the emperor's residence, the Imperial City, where his retinue was quartered, and the Legation Quarter. The Forbidden City, now a vast museum, contains the Imperial palaces (two groups of three each) and smaller palaces, all filled with art treasures. The Imperial City is now the seat of the Communist government.

On the southern side of Tatar City is the Tiananmen Square, which contains the monument to the heroes of the revolution, the Great Hall of the People, and the Museum of History and Revolution. Celebrations are held in this square on May Day and the founding date (October 1) of the People's Republic.

Beijing is known for its artificial lakes, its parks, and its temples, which include many of the greatest examples of architecture of the Ming and the Ch'ing dynasties. The fifteenth-century Temple of Heaven, set in a large park, has a massive altar of white marble before which the emperors prayed during the summer solstice. In the Temple of Confucius, built by Kublai Khan, are guarded incised boulders from the Chou Dynasty.

Just outside of Beijing, rivaling these structures, is the Imperial summer palace with its lovely parks.

After 1949, Beijing began to spread well beyond its two core cities, and hundreds of new buildings, hotels, and cultural centers are now in its suburbs. A subway was completed in 1969. The city has an opera, a ballet, and an impressive national library. It has more than twenty-five institutions of higher learning. The Beijing Zoo is famous for its collection of pandas.

In the Tiananmen Square long orderly lines of people are seen waiting to pay their respects at the mausoleum of Chairman Mao, the great Chinese leader.

The restaurants in Beijing are famous for local specialties, such as Beijing Duck and mutton dishes. The restaurants are very busy, and reservations must be made in advance at the hotel desk.

GREAT WALL SHERATON HOTEL
North Donghuan Road
Beijing
People's Republic of China
Telephone: 500-5566
Telex: 20045 GWHBJ CN
Fax: 5001939

Reservations:
  In Beijing call 500-5566
  In the USA call 1-800-325-3535
All major credit cards
General Manager: Tony Zamora
Manager: Max Wilhelm
Director of Sales: Alison Lim
Sheraton Corporation
Rates (approx.):
  Standard room $100
  Superior room $120
  Deluxe room $130
  Junior suite $170
  1-bedroom executive suite $200
  1- or 2-bedroom suite $625+
  Presidential Suite $850
1,007 rooms, 60 suites
Service charge 10%; no tax

This modern and luxurious hotel was opened in 1983 as a joint venture of a Chinese and an American firm. Built with three wings around an impressive cylindrical atrium, it is considered the most complete tourist resort hotel in China today. It is also well situated, only twenty minutes from Tiananmen Square, the center of the city, and about the same distance from the Beijing International Airport.

All of the rooms of the hotel have comfortable king- or queen-sized beds, modern bathrooms, air conditioning, multi-channel color TV, individual temperature control, and smoke detectors. The deluxe Capital and Dynasty suites are on the eighteenth floor of this skyscraper.

The hotel has nine restaurants, several lounges, and a tile-roofed traditional pavilion where tea and pastries are served daily. Most delightful is the traditional Chinese garden with its waterside teahouse and a replica of a section of the Great Wall of China. Another popular spot is the twenty-four-hour Orient Express Coffee Shop. The most exciting place in the hotel is the Cosmos Club, the hotel's lively lounge with entertainment.

My favorite spot is the Yuen Tair Restaurant, on the top floor of the hotel. Enjoy the great views while eating spicy Sichuan pickled cabbage.

A complete resort-style hotel, the Great Wall Sheraton also has a health club, tennis courts, a swimming pool, a billiard room, and its own theater.

Shops in the hotel sell Chinese arts and crafts items and a variety of necessities. There is also a bank and a post office.

Not far from the hotel is the San Li Tun Free Market, where all sorts of Chinese goods can be found, including clothing, pottery, porcelain, and cane furniture.

HUA DU HOTEL
8 Xin Yuan South Road
Chaoyang District
Beijing
People's Republic of China
Telephone: 500-1166
Telex: 22028 HUADU CN
Cable: 5431
Reservations:
In Beijing call 500-2069 or 500-1166-2589
Most major credit cards
General Manager: Liu Zhi Tong
Sales Manager: Kang Yi
Rates (approx.):
Room $35
Suite $70
522 rooms, 19 suites
No service charge; no tax

Established in 1982, The Hua Du Hotel is one of the larger modern hotels in Beijing. It is on the beautiful Liangma River on the west side of North Dong Huan Road, just to the south of the Airport Road.

The rooms, which look out on a traditional Chinese garden, are fairly large, carpeted, and comfortable. Each is equipped with adjustable air conditioning and a ventilation system that keeps the air constantly fresh. Each room also has its own bathroom.

The hotel has a Chinese restaurant and a Western restaurant as well as banquet halls, function rooms, and a bar. The Chinese dining room offers Guangdong and Sichuan fare and, of course, the famous Beijing duck. French cuisine, à la carte and table d'hôte, is served in the Western restaurant.

Other amenities include a souvenir shop, beauty shop, massage room, and clinic, as well as a business center offering telex, photocopy, and other services.

The Hua Du is close to many of the Beijing places of

interest, such as the Ditan (Altar of Earth) Park, the Palace Museum, the Beihai (North Sea) Park, the Tiananmen (Gate of Heavenly Peace) and the Cultural Palace of Nationalities.

KUNLUN HOTEL
21 Liangmaqiao
Chaoyang District
Beijing
People's Republic of China
Telephone: 500-3388
Telex: 210327 BJKLH CN
Cable: 2745
Fax: 5003388 Ext. 82626
Reservations:
   In Beijing call 500-3473
All major credit cards
Chief, Board of Directors: Xu Lian-Quan
General Manager: Zhang Xian-Bing
Concierge: Zhu Xiao-Bo
Sales Manager: Gu Xiao-Feng
Rates (approx.):
   Jan. 1–Mar. 30 $45 double, $65 deluxe
   Apr., June, July, Aug., Nov. $70 double, $90 deluxe
   May, Sept., Oct. $85 double, $105 deluxe
   Suite rates available on request
854 rooms, 74 suites
Service charge 10%; no tax

The tallest hotel in Beijing, the Kunlun rises thirty stories above the Liangman River. It is a truly dramatic and striking modern luxury hotel, with lavish guest rooms and "office suites," used mainly by business people. It has been open since 1986.

At the top of the hotel, on the twenty-seventh floor, is a delightful revolving restaurant serving continental cuisine (there soon will be a helicopter parking apron on top of that). There are seven more restaurants, too, providing regional and national alternatives such as Sichuan, Cantonese, Japanese, and Western cuisines. Particularly popular among these are the Guangdong Restaurant and the pleasant Coffee Shop.

My favorite spot is the hotel lobby, with its gleaming dark marble walls and floors. Displayed on one wall is the world's largest tapestry, portraying the Kunlun Mountains. It is at the entry to the hotel's magnificent open-air atrium.

The hotel seems to have just about everything its guests could want—shopping arcade, function hall, nightclub, health club, tennis court, swimming pool, sauna, beauty salon, massage room. A business club provides secretaries who can work in several languages, as well as telex, facsimile, and other services.

All guest rooms are attractively furnished. Each has its own bathroom, air conditioning, color TV, radio, and refrigerator; the deluxe rooms also have large sitting areas. The suites are decorated in a variety of styles, such as traditional Chinese, European, and Japanese. Each includes one to three bedrooms, a sitting room, a dining room, and a kitchen.

SHANGRI-LA HOTEL
29 Zizhuyuan Road
Beijing
People's Republic of China
Telephone: 831-2211
Telex: 222231 SHABJ CN
Fax: 8021471
Reservations:
   In Beijing call 831-2211
   In Los Angeles call (213) 551-1121
   Elsewhere in the USA call Shangri-La International,
      1-800-457-5050
All major credit cards
General Manager: Al Wymann
Concierge: Benedict Chow
Sales Manager: Nancy Wu
Shangri-La International
Rates (approx.):
   Standard $95 single, $105 double
   Deluxe $120 single, $130 double
   Suites $260–$600
746 rooms, 40 suites
Service charge 10%; no tax

This magnificent complex, opened in January of 1987, is operated by the Shangri-La International organization, in partnership with the Chinese Metals and Minerals Import/Export Corporation of the People's Republic. Shangri-La has ten other fine hotels throughout Asia, some of them among the world's best.

The hotel is situated in western Beijing, near the Negotiations Building, the Exhibition Hall, Beijing University, Ching Hua University, and the zoo.

Consisting of two buildings, the hotel is designed to be of the ultimate service to business visitors to the city. The seven-story West Building has five levels of offices with connecting standard living accommodations; in total, there are seventy-six guest rooms and forty-four offices. All units are air-conditioned, and each office has its own bathroom. The Shang Palace restaurant, where business people may dine with their guests, is on the ground level.

This building adjoins the twenty-four-story Shangri-La Main Building, with six hundred sixty-six guest rooms, two royal suites, and thirty-eight executive suites. The guest rooms, larger here, are elegantly furnished and equipped with air conditioning, color TV with in-house movies, a well-stocked mini-bar and refrigerator, and multichannel in-house music. The suites are magnificent. The Royal Suites are self-contained apartments with four rooms each, including a dining room with a bar and a kitchenette.

The Grand Ballroom of the Shangri-La is complemented by thirteen smaller function rooms that are available for meetings, conventions, private receptions, exhibitions, and banquets, accommodating up to a thousand people total. Special sound and lighting facilities are available, and simultaneous translation can be provided in up to six languages. For small meetings and interviews, the Business Centre of the hotel provides private offices.

One of the more attractive hotel health centers is also here. The Health Club provides separate sauna, steam bath, solarium, and massage facilities for men and women. The hotel's gymnasium has the latest exercise equipment, and a heated swimming pool is available to guests.

This hotel has both Chinese and continental restaurants. The Shang Palace, the largest Cantonese dining room in Beijing, serves excellent food. On the second level of the Main Building, La Brasserie and the Brasserie Bar serve continental-style lunch, dinner, and snacks. On the first level is the Coffee Shop, which serves all meals and snacks. *My favorite spot* is the luxurious Lobby Lounge, with live music and a grand view of the lobby, whose splendid centerpiece sculpture appears to be a tree with gigantic illuminated leaves. There are also, for the night crowd, the Xanadu discotheque and the very popular Peacock Bar. And, finally, The Delicatessen Corner is a nice place to find things to nibble on.

XI YUAN HOTEL
Erligou
Xi Jiao
Beijing 100046
People's Republic of China
Telephone: 831-3388 or 890721
Telex: 22831 XYHCN
Cable: 8766 BEIJING
Reservations:
   In Beijing call 831-4644
All major credit cards
General Manager: Dong Yun
Sales Manager: Zhang You
Rates (approx.):
   Room $60
   Medium suite $100
   Superior suite $189
   Duplex suite $210
   Deluxe suite $360
   Executive suite $720
709 rooms, 63 suites
No service charge; no tax

Situated in Erligou, the western suburb of Beijing, this relatively new hotel (1984) is a sight to see. A V-shaped skyscraper, it has a revolving restaurant sitting on its point.

Considered to be one of the luxury hotels of China, it has a number of other impressive features. One is the magnificent lobby with its high ceiling and unique chandeliers, woven from three thousand plates of six-colored aluminum alloy imported from Japan. The lobby floor is patterned with beautiful marble and granite triangles, giving a terrazzo effect.

Equally impressive is the large fountain in front of the hotel, skirted by flowers, spanned by a pair of beautiful white marble bridges, and full of goldfish. It is particularly lovely at night, when the fountain is lighted.

The hotel also has an especially fine collection of suites, featuring thick Chinese rugs, ornately carved Chinese furniture, and fine ceramic pieces.

Both rooms and suites are well equipped, with refrigerators, color TV, radio, in-house music, air conditioning, and other modern amenities. Computerized telephones in all the rooms provide more than twenty different services at the push of a button.

The hotel has thirteen restaurants, together offering a good variety of choices. The chefs prepare Chinese specialties, such as Shandong, Huaiyang, Sichuan, and Moslem, and Western dishes, including French, British, and Russian.

My favorite spot, the revolving restaurant at the top of the building, is a spectacular place to eat. While you enjoy the food and music in this revolving dining room, you have a panoramic view of the whole ancient and modern capital city of China.

The hotel also has a health club, an indoor swimming pool, a sauna, a barbershop, and a beauty shop, as well as other shops. There is a center for business services, such as telex and photocopying.

There is a two-floor shopping center in the hotel courtyard.

One important tip: The Beijing Zoo, the biggest zoo in China and the home of the famous pandas, is just a few minutes' walk from the hotel.

Guangdong

NAN HAI HOTEL
Shekou Industrial Zone
Shenzhen
Guangdong
People's Republic of China
Telephone: 92888
Telex: 420879 NHHTL CN
Cable: NANHAIHTL CN
Fax: 92440
Reservations:
   In Shekou call 92888
   In Kowloon, Hong Kong, call (3) 681111
   In California call 1-800-622-0847
   Elsewhere in the USA call 1-800-227-4320
All major credit cards
General Manager: B. C. Albert Young
Miramar Group
Rates (approx.):
   Standard single room $40
   Standard twin room $50

Twin room with balcony $74
Family room $92
Executive suite $110
President Suite $185
Chairman Suite $830
371 rooms, 25 suites
Service charge 10%; no tax

Shekou is the fairly new special industrial zone of China, northwest of Hong Kong, which is known for its unending array of electrical equipment factories and oil rigs that attract workers from all over China. It seems hardly a place to go for a holiday.

But the Nan Hai, built for tourists as well as business travelers, is an attraction in itself. Just a forty-five-minute hydrofoil ride away from Hong Kong, the hotel is set in a park of lush tropical green plants. Hong Kong residents in particular find it a welcome weekend escape from their crowded city.

Jointly owned by companies in Hong Kong and the People's Republic, the hotel has nearly four hundred rooms, including a dozen luxurious President Suites with various decor—English (with nice-smelling leather parlor chairs), Japanese (with paper and wooden movable screens), French, and Chinese. Some of the bathrooms include an elevated tub and an "automatic toilet," which makes toilet paper obsolete by spraying water and hot air at the press of a button. From the balconies of the guest rooms, you can look onto the hills of the New Territories of Hong Kong.

The food served at the Nan Hai's ground-floor Chinese restaurant is very good, especially the chef's favorite, double-boiled superior shark's fin soup. Also excellent are the deep-fried stuffed crab balls, sautéed fresh asparagus with sea snail, prawns with Sichuan chilies, and steamed fresh garoupa.

The European dining room on the top floor, which also specializes in seafood, has an excellent menu, with choices like king prawn with mango and stuffed deviled crab.

There is a disco where you can join or watch the locals do a combination of disco and breakdance. There are also a snooker parlor and, of course, a bar.

The grounds include a beach that is nice for strolling, a jogging track, a swimming pool, a mini-golf links, and tennis courts. And there is a sauna for relaxing after the exercise.

For tourists, Shekov offers things to see besides factories, oil rigs, and housing blocks. There is the statue and tomb of the child emperor Zhao Bing, of the Sung dynasty, who at the age of eight drowned after one of his ministers carried him into the sea to protect him from raiders from the north. Another statue overlooks the bay in honor of the imperial commissioner, Lin Tsehsu, known for his battle against the opium trade. Also interesting are the local markets, where hundreds of bikes are parked while the people pick up provisions for dinner.

Despite these attractions, the Nan Hai has been little better than a third occupied since it opened in March of 1986. It is now hoping to increase patronage as business travelers schedule meetings in its conference hall and make the Nan Hai a regular stopping point en route north. In addition to its conference facilities, the hotel has a well-equipped business center providing full secretarial services. The Nan Hai should also benefit from a new law that exempts foreign passport holders from having to wait in Hong Kong for the issuing of their visas. They may proceed directly to the Shekou Industrial Zone and have their visas processed and issued at that port of entry.

ZHONGSHAN INTERNATIONAL HOTEL
2 Zhongshan Road
Shiqi, Zhongshan
Guangdong
People's Republic of China
Telephone: 24788
Cable: 6662
Telex: 44175 ZSIH CN
Fax: 24736
Reservations:
   In Guangdon call 24788-205, 206
MasterCard, Visa, and American Express
General Manager: Zhen Kuen
Sales Manager: Zhen Wei Shu
Rates (approx.):
   Twin room $39
   Double room $28
   Suite $59
   Junior suite $72
   Superior suite $117
   VIP suite $117

Garden suite $169
Deluxe suite $169
Presidential Suite rate available on request
348 rooms, 21 suites
Service charge 10%; no tax

Situated right in the city's center, the Zhongshan International successfully integrates traditional Chinese architecture with the comforts and facilities of a modern hotel.

My favorite spot is the hotel's spacious lobby, whose six magnificent crystal chandeliers are reflected on the rose-magenta marble floor. Most striking as you enter is a white marble mural.

The restaurants are conveniently situated just off the lobby—except for the delightful revolving restaurant, which, on the top floor of the hotel, has a spectacular view of the city and the green hills and farmlands beyond. The three popular and attractive dining rooms are the Chinese Food Restaurant, the Western Food Restaurant, and the French Hall. There are also an exotic-appearing discotheque, a bar, and a café for relaxing drinks and snacks.

All of the hotel's rooms are air-conditioned and equipped with color TVs, refrigerators, piped-in music, and marble bathrooms. The suites are especially attractive, particularly the elegant Presidential Suite, with its interesting and pleasing blending of Oriental and Occidental decors. There are private gardens off the Garden Suite, the Deluxe Suite, and the Presidential Suite.

A multipurpose conference room on the eighteenth floor of the hotel is equipped with a system providing the synchronized translation of speeches into English, Chinese, or Japanese.

Other facilities include a billiard room, a bowling room with four alleys, a majong room, and a swimming pool and sauna. Also within the hotel are a beauty salon and the spacious Shopping Centre, selling high-quality goods.

In the neighborhood of the hotel are a variety of shops providing basic goods for the locals.

Guangzhou (Canton)

Canton, whose name is now romanized as *Guangzhou*, is an ancient city that became a part of China in the third century B.C. Hindu and Arab merchants reached Guangzhou in the tenth century, and the city became the first Chinese port visited regularly by European traders.

In 1511 Portugal secured a trade monopoly, which was eventually broken by the British in the late seventeenth century. In the eighteenth century the French and the Dutch were also admitted. Otherwise, trading was restricted until the Treaty of Nanking in 1842, which, following the Opium War, opened the city to all foreign trade.

Guangzhou was the seat of the revolutionary movement under Sun Yat-sen in 1911. The Republic of China was proclaimed here. In 1927, Guangzhou was briefly the seat of one of the earliest Communist communes in China.

The fall of Guangzhou in late October 1949 signaled the Communist takeover of China.

Guangzhou has a population of well over two million, is the capital of Kwangtung Province, and is a major deep-water port on the Guangzhou River delta.

The city is the transportational, industrial, financial, and trading center of South China. It has shipyards, a steel complex, paper and textile mills, and diversified manufacturing plants.

CHINA HOTEL
Liu Hua Lu
Guangzhou
People's Republic of China
Telephone: 666888
Telex: 44888 CHLGZ CN
Cable: 6888
Fax: 677014
Reservations:
  In Guangzhou call 666888, ext. 2036
  In the USA call China Express at (415) 397-8811 or
     1-800-227-5663
All major credit cards
General Manager: Joachim Burger
Sales Manager: Earbie Chiu
New World Hotels International
Rates (approx.):
  Standard room $63 single, $68 double
  Medium room $75 single, $80 double
  Deluxe room $85 single, $90 double
  Lounge suite $130
  Standard suite $150

Deluxe suite $175
Palace Suite rate available on request
1,017 rooms, 128 suites
Service charge 10%; tax 5%

It was in 1972 that Joachim Burger, then a Hong Kong
hotelier in charge of food and beverages, and now the con-
genial manager of the China Hotel, first visited Guangzhou
to attend its famous Guangzhou Fair and had a rough time
finding hotel accommodations.

The fair drew traders from all over the world, just as this
city had for three millennia. But there were few hotels, and
in the Dong Fang, virtually the only one with modern Western amenities, visiting merchants slept on cots in the corridors and public spaces.

Time passed, and Mr. Burger had no idea that he would
ever go to Guangzhou again. And he had no desire to go,
especially not during the Guangzhou Fair. When Burger
returned in 1981 to help plan a new hotel for Guangzhou,
things were not much better. But change came quickly.
While Burger was supervising the construction of the China
Hotel, the gleaming White Swan Hotel was rising on Shamian Island, on the river. And just as the China Hotel was
completed, the impressive Garden Hotel was being erected.
The city now has five thousand hotel rooms.

The China Hotel is a unique and interesting achievement.
In its strong drive for modernization, China has wisely drawn
upon foreign expertise. The China Hotel is a good example
of this. Perhaps the most ambitious and modern hotel project in the country, the China Hotel is a joint venture between a group of Hong Kong real estate developers and
the Yangcheng Service Development Company of Guangzhou.

Entirely modern in concept, design, and construction,
this eighteen-story hotel is well located, right next to the
Guangzhou Foreign Trade Centre. When it was opened in
June 1984, it was hailed as the most luxurious establishment
of its kind in China.

Each of the nearly twelve hundred well-appointed rooms
is built to the best of international standards, having its
own bathroom, air conditioning, international and local direct-dial telephones, color TV, and refrigerator.

The hotel's dining rooms are, in Guangzhou, a magnificent achievement. This is a city where Western food is
virtually unknown. Joachim Burger, a veteran food and
beverage man, accepted this as a challenge. "Our idea is to

offer as much choice of quality food that we can, to suit the tastes of the many different nationalities who visit the hotel, as well as to provide an excellent standard of cuisine for the people of Guangzhou."

He has apparently succeeded. Seven thousand meals are served every day in the China Hotel's diverse restaurants. During the annual trade fair, the hotel serves thirteen thousand meals daily. The success of its dining rooms contributes substantially to the success of the hotel, which is said by professionals to be the most profitable in China, probably in the five thousand–year history of the nation!

It isn't easy. The hotel must be largely self-sufficient, because there are few local suppliers of foreign food items. For example, its own bakery makes some two thousand rolls at a single baking. And a butchery and smokehouse turn out many varieties of cold cuts, pâtés, salami, sausage, and smoked salmon and mackerel. Such a wide range of Western delicatessen foods has never before been seen in China.

Certainly its busiest Western eating spot is the hotel's spacious Veranda Coffee Shop. A light and airy restaurant that can accommodate nearly four hundred people, it extends around three sides of the hotel's ornate Italian burgundy granite and marble lobby, and its large windows overlook the city.

My favorite spot is the one most popular with gourmets. To reach it you take a scenic ride up an outdoor elevator to the top floor, the eighteenth. The Roof Restaurant offers excellent continental cuisine. An Asian restaurant critic wrote, "by the standards of China only two short years ago (1985), when the restaurant opened, it is miraculous." But, as good as the food is, the view is extra special. From over the rooftops of the city, old Guangzhou is indeed a pleasant sight, especially at night.

The decor is European, with classical arches, a subtle floral wall covering, and subdued moss green as the unifying color. Armchairs are regally styled in French Bourbon designs and upholstered in a silk-rayon blend.

Over the centuries, the Cantonese have devised more imaginative ways of cooking flora and fauna than any of the world's other great chefs. The hotel's Four Seasons restaurant has a noted chef from Hong Kong whose goal is to offer diners as many of these dishes as possible. His kitchen prepares more than one hundred forty different kinds of dim sum, typically Cantonese small snacks, both sweet and savory, such as steamed shrimp dumplings, egg rolls, spare ribs, and tiny pastries that are served at breakfast or lunch. As the restaurant's name suggests, its menus change with the season to take full advantage of Guangdong Province's abundant natural produce. In the spring there is a wealth of fresh vegetables; in summer squashes and melons are at their best, as are fresh lychees, a hard-shelled fruit; in autumn casseroles and snake soup, a Cantonese delicacy are served; in winter there are wild game dishes and rich winter vegetables.

Downstairs is a busy Village Restaurant, which serves simpler, country-style Cantonese cuisine, with its special attraction being the fresh seafood of Guangdong.

The fun eating spot is a gastronomic feature unique to China Hotel called Food Street. It is an arcade of food stalls featuring regional specialities from all parts of China. Here you'll find northern-style dumplings, spicy Sichuan delicacies whose pungent peppers are brought in from Chengdu, and snacks that may be found in the street stalls of Guangzhou, like noodles and congee, a rice gruel, and small dishes of clams, snails, steamed shrimps, and barbecued meats.

The hotel also has a tennis court, a health club with a gymnasium, a sauna, and massage, an outdoor swimming pool, a nine-lane bowling alley, and a disco. And there is the beautiful and tranquil Chinese Garden.

For business people, the hotel offers the services of its comprehensive Business Centre, providing a secretary, a translator, a word processor, a facsimile machine, and a conference room. The hotel's Crystal Ballroom is available for seminars, exhibits, cocktail parties, and banquets.

THE GARDEN HOTEL
368 Huanshi Dong Lu
Guangzhou
People's Republic of China
Telephone: 338989
Telex: 44788 GDHTL CN
Cable: 4735
Fax: 338989, ext. 3232
Reservations:
   In Guangzhou call 338989, ext. 3170
   In Hong Kong call (3) 732-1321
   In the USA call (213) 640-7836, (213) 640-8491, or
      (312) 263-6069
All major credit cards
General Manager: Frank Kam

Director of Sales and Marketing: Joe Ho
The Peninsula Group of Hotels
Rates (approx.):
  Standard room $58 single, $68 double
  Superior room $68 single, $78 double
  Deluxe room $78 single, $88 double
  Standard suite $120 single, $130 double
  Deluxe suite (A) $250 single, $260 double
  Deluxe suite (B) $190 single, $200 double
  Presidental Suite rate available on request
1,050 rooms, 62 suites
Service charge 10%; tax 5%

The Garden Hotel is managed by the famous Peninsula Group, whose flagship hotel is the grand old Peninsula Hotel in Hong Kong. The hotel is a joint venture of the Guangzhou Lin Nan Development Company and the Garden Hotel (Holdings) of Hong Kong. It was designed by Hong Kong architects and built by a local company, the Guangzhou Pearl River Foreign Investment Construction Company.

Two venerable gentlemen are responsible for the initiation of the project—R. C. Lee of Hong Kong, who had always wanted to build the largest five-star hotel in China, and Liano Cheng-zhi of China, who shared his dream. It was also the dream of W. Szeto, a famous seventy-four-year-old architect who desired to design a building in the People's Republic before he retired. In August 1985, after almost seven years of negotiations, planning, and construction, the $115.9 million Garden Hotel held its grand-opening ceremonies.

As befits its name, the hotel is surrounded by large landscaped gardens. The southern portion of the grounds has a large Chinese garden, designed with help from the Forestry and Horticultural Department of Guangzhou. Traditionally Chinese in design, the garden features a cascading waterfall, ponds, and pagodas.

The Garden Hotel is made up of two Y-shaped towers rising above a connecting podium, providing every guest room unobstructed views of the city, gardens, or both. The twenty-four-story Garden Tower has a two-level revolving restaurant on the top; the Hotel Tower is seventeen stories.

Without a doubt, *one of my favorite spots* in the hotel is the magnificent lobby, which is, at this writing, the largest hotel lobby in Asia. Its most striking feature is the intricately carved black marble and gold foil mural above the long reception counter. This gigantic wall sculpture wonderfully illustrates scenes from one of China's most celebrated literary classics, *The Dream of the Red Chamber*, a story of family love and tragedy chosen for its setting in one of the most beautiful gardens on the face of the earth. Crafted by members of the Foshan Arts and Crafts Institute, the mural took more than seven months to complete.

The artists' talents are further displayed on the white marble mural above the hotel's main entrance, which depicts farming life in rural China, and the detailed representation of a kapok tree at the far end of the lobby.

Guarding all who enter the lobby is the Golden Dragon, surrounded by carved corbeils and inspired by those in the Forbidden City of Beijing. A benevolent creature, the Chinese dragon is said to protect all who enter its domain.

Hotel guests wanting some privacy can use their own lounge on the mezzanine, at the top of the elegant carved teak staircase leading from the lobby. The walls of the lounge are hung with eight hand-painted scrolls depicting the twelve Celestial Gods from the cave paintings of the Tang Dynasty.

The hotel is truly a gallery of Chinese folk art, with fine lacquerware from Yangjiang, colorful ceramics from Shiwan, hand-carved wooden screens modeled from traditional temple art, and a replica of the tall statue of the mythical Marshall Liu from the Ancestral Temple in Foshan.

Each of the hotel's more than a thousand rooms and suites are tastefully furnished and designed for comfort. Amenities include luxurious bathrooms; large writing desks; spacious seating arrangements; telephones with direct-dial service to Hong Kong, Macau, and all major cities in China; and individual air-conditioning control. All the rooms also have fully stocked mini-bars, refrigerators, and color TVs with in-house movies.

The fifty-two suites of the hotel are truly luxurious. The deluxe suites, on the top two floors of the Garden Tower, have king-sized beds and sumptuous bathrooms equipped with hair dryers and fancy toiletries.

There is a seemingly unlimited selection of places to eat in this hotel. Featured are the cuisines of both East and West.

From the East, there is the distinctive Cantonese cuisine found in The Peach Blossom and the Lai Wan Market restaurants, and northern Chinese fare at Ming Yuen. Another of *my favorite spots* in this hotel, the revolving Carousel, gives diners a spectacular view of the city of Guangzhou as they choose from an array of alluring regional Chinese specialities at luncheon and dinner buffets.

Western cuisine is represented by the Greenery Coffee Shop and The Cascade, both of which offer a wide variety of international dishes. And a distinguished continental menu, complemented by a superb selection of wines, is presented in the hotel's premier restaurant, The Connoisseur. The fluted columns and graceful arches of the room provide a classic French setting.

Places for drinks include The Tavern, an English pub-style bar, and L'Aperitif, whose ultra-modern rooms are filled with music in the evenings. And from the luxurious armchairs of The China Trader you can overlook the hotel's dramatic porte-cochere entrance, with its colorful fountain.

For business people, the comprehensive Business Centre has rooms that can be used as private offices. The hotel also has a number of function rooms, which can accommodate from thirty-five to three-hundred people, and a dramatic Conference Hall, off the main lobby, which can hold as many as fourteen hundred. It is said to be the largest conference hall in Asia.

The hotel has outdoor, hard-surface tennis courts in the gardens and a large swimming pool and a children's pool on the podium roof. There are also squash courts and a health center with a gymnasium, sauna, and Jacuzzi.

WHITE SWAN HOTEL
One South Street
Shamian Island
Guangzhou
People's Republic of China
Telephone: 886968
Telex: 44688 WSH CN or 44689 WSH CN
Cable: 8888
Fax: 0086-020-861188
Reservations:
   In Guangzhou call 882288
   In New York state, Hawaii, and Alaska call collect
      (212)838-3110
   Elsewhere in the USA call 1-800-223-6800
   In Canada call 1-800-341-8585
All major credit cards
General Manager: Yang Xiao Peng
Sales Manager: Gao Wei Jiang

Leading Hotels of the World
Rates (approx.):
   Superior room $120
   Deluxe room $140
   Suite rates available on request
1,300 rooms, 74 suites
Service charge 10%; tax 5%

What a delightful place for a hotel. The beautiful, modern White Swan rises thirty-four floors above the famous Pearl River on Shamian Island. Its more than a thousand rooms and suites provide dramatic views of the historic island, with its native banyan trees.

Entering the atrium lobby brings a wonderful surprise. A gold-domed pagoda is set at the top of a three-story waterfall, which cascades into the lobby pond. The indoor gardens present a tranquil reflection of Chinese culture, and the sun and blue sky are visible through the glass roof. Near the reception desk, a magnificent traditional jade carving of a two-headed dragon boat welcomes arriving guests. And offering a grand view of all this, and the Pearl River besides, is the River Garden Coffee Shop, where Western and Chinese foods are served from very early in the morning until very late at night.

On the mezzanine, overlooking the lobby, is the pleasant Song Bird Tea Lounge for comfortable buffet breakfasts and lunches, afternoon tea, cocktails and other drinks, salads, roast meat from a cart, and Mexican snacks.

Another beautiful spot for food is the Cantonese Room, the Chinese restaurant on the third floor. One of the culinary sights to see here is the serving of the world-renowned Chinese roast suckling pig.

Besides attractively furnished bedrooms with luxurious bathrooms, the hotel has lovely suites. The most magnificent is the Presidential Suite, which has been occupied by kings, queens, and other leaders from around the world. The suite has windows on every side, so that all of the city can be seen. Fine Chinese antiques accent the contemporary decor, and an indoor garden—on the twenty-eighth floor —is available for strolls. The bathroom has a Jacuzzi, and there is a study-library.

The hotel includes the excellent Business Centre, open every day; the Elizabeth Arden Red Door Beauty Salon; a good shopping arcade; a fully equipped health club and spa; and the River Garden Night Club, adjacent to the pool and garden area and featuring dancing and entertainment.

The hotel's Rolls Royce can meet you at the airport or take you on a comfortable city tour.

Guilin

With a population of over three hundred thousand, this city in the Kwangsi Chuang Autonomous Region of southern China is an important transportation and industrial center. Paper products are made here, and a large tin mine is nearby. Tungsten, manganese, and antimony are found in the area.

Guilin is the China you have seen in landscape paintings. Poets, too, have for thousands of years strived to describe the beauty of this spot.

Guilin nestles in an extraordinary setting of limestone hills, called tower karst. Above the winding Li River and lush plains, they spiral heavenward in fantastic shapes, giving rise to lovely poetic names. The hills are scattered with mysterious caves.

The town has beautiful parks. Visitors also enjoy leisurely cruises on the Li River, past Ming Dynasty mansions. At sunrise you can watch fishermen use trained cormorants to gather the day's catch.

Several fine hotels have been recently built for the tourists who come to enjoy this place of timeless beauty.

GUILIN MANDARIN HOTEL
Bing Jiang Road
Guilin
Guangxi
People's Republic of China
Telephone: 5713
Telex: 48339 GLMAN CN
Reservations:
    In Guilin call 5713
    In Hong Kong call (852) 5-806-8012
    In the USA call (212) 916-0300
American Express, MasterCard, Visa, Diners, Federal
General Manager: Frederic Hsieh
Sales Manager: Joseph W. K. Wong
Rates (approx.):
    Standard room $75 single, $80 double

Superior room $85 single, $90 double
Suites $110–$180
493 rooms, 19 suites
No service charge; tax 15%

First opened on January 1, 1988, this hotel is a joint venture among the Qtuqing Hotel Organisation of Guilin, the Tai Hing (Asia) Promotion Company of Hong Kong, and the Mandarin Realty Company of California. These collaborators have aimed to provide Guilin a tourist hotel that meets high international standards, both in furnishings and service.

The hotel's rooms therefore have private bathrooms with tub showers, mini-bars, international direct-dial telephones, color TV with in-house movies, and piped-in music. There are even bathroom outlets with both 110 and 220 voltage. Four rooms are specially designed for handicapped guests.

The hotel's two restaurants, open from 6:30 A.M. until 11:00 P.M., are the Cathay Restaurant, which features Cantonese cuisine, and the Atrium Coffee Shop (on the second floor), which serves Western fare. There are three bars— the Camel and the Vantagepoint, at the lobby level and on the seventh floor, respectively, and the Poolside Bar, which also serves light snacks.

Most impressive about this new hotel is the magnificent sun-lit atrium lobby, which rises all seven stories of the hotel.

The hotel has souvenir and Chinese art shops, a health center, and a business center, as well as adequate meeting and convention facilities.

Because it is situated right on the bank of the Li River, it has one of the best views of both the river and the city.

HOLIDAY INN GUILIN
14 South Ronghu Road
Guilin
Guangxi
People's Republic of China
Telephone: 3950
Telex: 48456 GLHCL CN
Cable: 6333
Reservations:
    In Guilin call 3950
    In the USA call 1-800-HOLIDAY
All major credit cards

General Manager: Hans F. Zaunmayr
Sales Manager: Toh Tat Leong
Holiday Inn Asia-Pacific
Rates (approx.):
  Economy room $70
  Standard room $80
  Superior room $90
  1-bedroom suite $140
  Presidential Suite $250
250 rooms, 5 suites
Service charge 10%; tax 5%

The new Holiday Inn Guilin, only twenty minutes from the airport, is conveniently situated near the city center on the Banyan Lake Causeway. The view from the hotel is of Banyan Lake, the city, and near and distant mountains, in a constantly shifting kaleidoscope of colors. For the best view, be sure to ask for a room facing north.

The rooms all have individually controlled air conditioning, private bathrooms, refrigerators and mini-bars, radio, color TV with in-house movies, and direct-dial telephones with, on the eighth and ninth floors, extensions in the bathrooms.

The full range of places to eat and drink include the Patio Coffee Shop, next to the lobby, which serves both Western and local dishes and snacks at all hours; the Rendezvous, the main dining room, open for all three meals; and the Chinese Restaurant, which features national specialties. The Skylight Lounge is the hotel's popular watering hole, and the beautiful Golden Cassia Ballroom can hold up to four hundred for cocktails. Three function rooms are available for small meetings and private parties.

The hotel has a health club, a hairdressing salon, and a modest shopping arcade with souvenir, antique, silk, carpet, and necessities shops. Near the hotel is a typical provincial Chinese shopping district; to watch the activity here is fascinating.

LI RIVER HOTEL
1 Shanghai North Road
Guilin
Guangxi
People's Republic of China
Telephone: 2881 5991
Telex: 48470 RUIR CN

Cable: 0044
Reservations:
  In Guilin call 3050
American Express
General Manager: Ye Lin Mua
Sales Manager: Guang Yue Ming
Rates (approx.):
  Standard room $45–$48
  Special room $62
  President Room $500
390 rooms, 3 suites
Service charge 10%; no tax

This modest, inexpensive hotel is well situated, with good views to the south and north. To the south is Elephant Trunk Hill, so named for its shape, and the busy Li River. To the north is a beautiful mountain peak. These views may be had not only from the hotel's dining rooms, but from the guest rooms as well.

The modest rooms all have private bathrooms, air conditioning, telephones, and color TV.

The hotel's shops include one for general merchandise and one for silk, but most interesting is the calligraphy and painting shop. Meals and snacks are available at the Coffee Shop.

The hotel has a variety of other amenities, including a health and exercise center, a reading lounge, a business center, and meeting facilities. Most luxurious is the lobby.

RAMADA RENAISSANCE HOTEL
Yuan Jiang Road
Guilin
Guangxi
People's Republic of China
Telephone: 2411, 2611, or 2692
Telex: 48446 GLGDN CN (HOTEL), or 81252 (Hong Kong Sales), or RAMDA HX
Fax: 5-8450461 (HK)
Reservations:
  In Hong Kong call (5) 239004-5
  In the USA call 1-800-2-RAMADA
All major credit cards
General Manager: Rudolf Bruggemann
Front Office Manager: Lawrence Lui
Director of Sales: Kelvin Poon

Sales Manager: Grace Chan
Ramada International
Rates (approx.):
   Standard room $83 single, $95 double
   Superior room $95 single, $105 double
   Renaissance Club room $116, $126
   Suite $260
334 rooms, 2 suites
Service charge 10%; no tax

Set on the banks of the Li River, this magnificent new hotel opened in mid-1987.

Its vast outdoor swimming pool, heated in the winter, overlooks the river.

Every room has two double beds, a refrigerator with a mini-bar, and international direct-dial telephone. A bedside panel controls the air conditioning, the color TV with in-house movies, and the radio with in-house music channels. The bathroom has a hair dryer, a telephone extension, and marble walls and floors. There is equipment for making your own tea or coffee. Seventy-five of the hotel's rooms and suites offer a view of the Li River and the oddly shaped peaks that flank it.

The hotel's Renaissance Club, occupying two floors, provides extra services and luxuries. The rate for a Renaissance Club room includes a light breakfast, concierge service, and secretarial assistance.

The hotel takes pride in its restaurants. The Continental Restaurant has a European chef, and the palatial Jade Garden, *my favorite spot*, has a staff of Chinese culinary artists. The hotel's main dining room, it has a magnificent view of the river, as does the Piano Bar. The hotel also has a coffee shop and a Japanese dining room.

Other facilities include a vast outdoor swimming pool, heated in the winter and overlooking the river; a health club; and a business center. No shops are in the hotel.

Plans for expansion include the addition of 450 new rooms and suites.

Hangzhou

According to an ancient Chinese saying, "In heaven there is paradise; on earth, Hangzhou." Marco Polo described it as "the most beautiful and magnificent city of paradise in the world." If you see this beautiful city, you will agree.

Its charm is due in good part to the breathtaking spectacle of the West Lake, dotted with a myriad of pavilions, willow trees, old stone bridges, and hundreds upon hundreds of lotus plants.

Hangzhou (formerly spelled *Hangchow*), is the capital of Chekiang Province. With a population of well over a million, it sits on the Jiantang River at the head of Hangzhou Bay, an arm of the East China Sea, and handles the river traffic through its port.

The city has recently developed into a major industrial center. Goods manufactured here now include silk and cotton textiles, pig iron and steel products, automobiles, fertilizers, rubber, paper and bamboo products, pharmaceuticals, cement, chemicals, electronic equipment, machine tools, and processed teas.

Founded in 606 A.D., Hangzhou was from 907 to 960 the capital of a powerful kingdom. Many of the city's most picturesque shrines and monasteries are from this period. The city was the capital of the Southern Sung Dynasty from 1132 to 1276, when it was sacked by Kublai Khan. In this period it had been a center of art, literature, and scholarship—a cosmopolitan city with a large enclave of foreign merchants. Marco Polo felt it to be "the finest and noblest city in the world."

Hangzhou was occupied by the Japanese from 1937 to 1945. It fell to the Communists in 1949.

Its harbor is unique for its exceptional tides, which, rising up to fifteen feet, are often a menace to shipping.

HANGZHOU HOTEL
78 Beishan Street
Hangzhou
People's Republic of China
Telephone: 22921
Telex: 35005/6 HOTCH CN
Cable: 7391
Fax: 22921-2514
Reservations:
   In Hangzhou call 22921, ext. 2114, 2115, or 2116
   In the USA. call (213) 417-3483 or 1-800-457-5050
All major credit cards
General Manager: Wolf Dieter Flecker
Sales Manager: Margaret Chiao
Shangri-La International

Rates (approx.):
  Hillview room $65 single, $80 double
  Gardenview room $75 single, $90 double
  Lakeview room $85 single, $100 double
387 rooms, 47 suites
Service charge 10%; tax 5%

Situated halfway up Beishan Hill, the Hangzhou Hotel has a full view of the beautiful West Lake. The hotel is made up of the modern yet stylish East Building; the majestic, traditional West Building; and, for guests who prefer more privacy, three hillside villas.

Upon taking over the property with a new management team in 1985, Shangri-La International did considerable refurbishing. Modern technological installations were made, including international and domestic direct-dialing for the telephone system, central heating and air conditioning with individual temperature controls in each room, and color TV sets with in-house movies.

The hotel has the best restaurants in town. *My favorite spot* is the Lotus Pond Restaurant, which serves such indigenous Hangzhou dishes as beggar's chicken, vinegar-glazed sweet and sour fish, and braised pork *dong po*.

The Shang Palace restaurant features Cantonese dishes prepared in a wok.

In the Spring Moon Restaurant, European chefs grill two-inch juicy steaks to order. This dining room specializes in what it calls East Meets West Nouvelle Cuisine, the skilled preparation of Oriental foods with Western tastes in mind.

The Cafe Peony is the place for light meals and such reminders of home as hamburgers, pizzas, hot dogs, and pastrami sandwiches. For dessert there is Black Forest cake, Sacher torte, and ice cream concoctions, along with espresso and Irish coffee.

After a meal, a slow, leisurely walk along the shore of the West Lake may inspire some guests, as it has many poets through the centuries. Others may find pleasure in browsing in the hotel's delightful Shopping Cavern, which has a variety of Chinese products. Most interesting is the Silk Shop, which sells an array of silk textiles as well as ready-made garments.

For a nightcap, the spot is the hotel's Garden Bar, which has live entertainment. Or guests may use the mini-bar provided in each room.

To accommodate the business traveler, the hotel offers

the professional services of its Business Centre. It has telex, facsimile, photocopying, offset lithography, and word processing services. The hotel's conference rooms include an auditorium with full stage facilities and a capacity of 560 people.

In the midst of the hotel's extensive landscaped gardens is a large unheated swimming pool, open in summer only.

To see the city on your own, you may rent a bicycle from the hotel. Be sure to get a map from the concierge to such spots as the Tomb and Temple of Yue-Fei, the Yellow Dragon Cave, the Baochu Pagoda, the Jade Spring, and the Botanical Garden—all nearby. Or, take a ride on Beishan Road along the shore of the beautiful West Lake.

Lhasa, Tibet

In the Valley of the River Lhasa, fifteen thousand feet above sea level and surrounded by the Himalayan highlands, is the ancient city of Lhasa.

It was the capital of Tibet, home of the Dalai Lamas. Even today the old city is a tableau of brightly colored prayer flags and temples, ringing bells, and whirling prayer wheels. Along with the exotic aroma of burning juniper, a rich and half-hidden history envelopes the visitor. Llasa is still magical, breathtaking and mysterious. You begin to understand why Tibet is called the Roof of the World, and why this city is known as the Abode of the Gods.

Once isolated and forbidden, as capital of the Tibetan Autonomous Region of the People's Republic Lhasa is open to the rest of the world—to tourists as well as the countless Buddhist pilgrims who flood the city every year.

Has Lhasa been spoilt by this influx of tourists and by the physical changes made during twenty years as part of the People's Republic of China? It certainly is not the city it was as recently as the 1940s. It still does, however, retain its aura of mystery. It is now a city of both old and new. There are enormous steel water towers, gray concrete office buildings, and large Chinese department stores—but around almost every corner you discover the "real city," always a delight.

There are still the narrow streets and alleyways, the courtyards surrounded by wood, stone, or mud-brick homes. You can stand in front of the Jokhang Temple, the holiest place in Tibet, and watch with awe as hundreds of pilgrims prostrate themselves, full length, while ceaselessly chanting *om mani padme hum*. They are there from dawn until sunset.

The Tibetans are delightful. While they take their religious activities very seriously, they always have a broad smile of welcome for the foreigner. They have a great sense of humor, and their infectious outbursts of laughter provide lasting memories.

Getting to Tibet and Lhasa the new way is easy. Two flights arrive daily at the Gonggar Airport, a ninety-minute drive from the city. Or you can get there the old way—by a three-day overland trip from Kathmandu, Nepal.

However you reach Lhasa, you'll feel it was worth the effort. You'll be astonished to see such wonders as the awesome Potala Palace, which rises a thousand feet from the base of a hill. Once the winter home of the Dalai Lamas, it contains elaborate gem-encrusted golden tombs and over a thousand rooms, many of which contain exquisitely detailed murals.

Then there are the monasteries of Sera and Drepung. These miniature villages, fine examples of Tibetan architecture, hold collections of religious paintings, statues, and relics. Drepung once was home to six thousand monks (today there are just a few hundred, including novices). At Sera, most afternoons, visitors may watch the strange sight of the monks' "debate," which looks like a game with all the noise and clapping of hands. In reality, profound questions of Buddhist ideology are being discussed.

Perhaps most memorable, and certainly most entertaining, is the Barkhor Bazaar. Here all manner of curios are sold from the street stalls by smiling, weather-beaten Tibetans, with whom bargaining is a must. You'll carefully check out the silver and turquoise jewelry, prayer flags, rosaries, brass and copper pots and kettles, silver bowls, silk shirts, and so many other things.

High season in Tibet is June through September, but for the nicest weather come in spring or autumn. At these times you'll also find the best bargains in the shops and markets.

HOLIDAY INN LHASA
1 Minzu Lu
Lhasa
Tibet
People's Republic of China
Telephone: 22221
Telex: 68010 HILSA CN or 68011 HILSA CN

Cable: 7391
Reservations:
  In Asia call any Holiday Inn
  In the USA call 1-800-HOLIDAY
Visa and MasterCard
General Manager: Chris Schlitter
Executive Assistant Manager: Hubert Liner
Director of Sales and Marketing: Jill Kluge
Holiday Inn Asia-Pacific
Rates (approx.):
  Economy room $14
  Superior room $38
  Junior suite $64
  Standard suite $80
  3-room suite $97
  Presidential Villas $650
486 rooms and suites
Service charge and tax included

In 1985 the antiquated Lhasa Hotel was taken over by the Holiday Inn corporation, which modernized the building and renamed it the Holiday Inn Lhasa.

The hotel is well situated. On Minzu Lu (Nation Road), it is in the heart of Lhasa's new commercial district, only a five-minute drive from the center of the city. It is right next to Norbulingka, the Dalai Lamas' summer palace, and five minutes from the extraordinary Potala Palace and Barkhor Square.

With nearly five hundred twin-bedded guest rooms and suites and two elegant villas, it is a delightful place for Westerners to stay. All rooms have private baths, color TV with in-house movies, radio with piped-in music, and telephones. And, because of the extreme height of the city, oxygen is piped in to all rooms! Most enjoyable is the view from the windows, of the surrounding Himalayan highlands.

Eating here is pleasant. You can choose from a coffee shop, a Western dining room, and a Chinese dining room. A popular spot is the Lounge Bar, on the mezzanine above the lobby.

My favorite find is the collection of Tibetan sculpture, paintings, and other works of art displayed throughout the hotel.

In the hotel is a Chinese Friendship Store, with fine hand-crafted products from all parts of China.

Running an international-class hotel in Tibet is not easy.

The Holiday Inn Lhasa gets its supplies from Chengdu, three days' drive away. A caravan of four to five trucks is constantly on the road to transport needed supplies. Because there are no gas stations between destinations, one-third of the trucks' cargo space is filled with gasoline.

Shanghai

The name Shanghai dates from the Sung Dynasty (eleventh century), but the town, which became a walled city in the sixteenth century, was unimportant until it was opened to foreign trade by the Treaty of Nanking in 1842. Western influence launched the city's phenomenal growth. The greater part of the city was incorporated into the British concession of Hongkew in 1862. In 1863 the United States and Great Britain consolidated their areas into the International Settlement. The French, who had obtained a concession in 1849, kept it as a separate entity.

The foreign zones were occupied by the Japanese after December 7, 1941. In 1943, the United States and Great Britain renounced their claims in Shanghai, and France did the same in 1946. The city was restored to China at the end of World War II. In May 1949 it fell to the Communists.

Next to Peking, Shanghai is the country's foremost educational center. The city has astronomical observatories, several museums, an opera, a performing arts group, and many research institutes and learned societies.

On the Huangpu River where it flows into the Yangze estuary, Shanghai is in, but independent of, Jiangsu Province. It is the largest city on the Asian continent, with a population estimated at over 12 million. One of the world's great seaports, it handles the major share of China's foreign shipping. It is also the leading industrial city of China, with large steelworks, textile mills, oil-refining and gas-extracting operations, shipbuilding yards, and factories making a variety of light and heavy machinery, electrical and electronic equipment, machine tools, chemicals, pharmaceuticals, turbines, tractors, aircraft, plastics, motor vehicles, and other consumer goods. In addition, Shanghai is the country's major publishing center.

The commercial part of the city, still called the International Settlement, is modern and Western in appearance, with broad streets and spacious boulevards with lots of skyscrapers. Typical Oriental buildings are found only in the original Chinese town, which no longer has walls around it. It is known as the Chapei Quarter.

The city has an international airport, and there is a submarine base in its big harbor.

CYPRESS HOTEL
2419 Hongqiao Road
Shanghai
People's Republic of China
Telephone: 329388
Cable: 9921
Telex: 33288 CYH CN
Reservations:
   In Shanghai call 329323
All major credit cards
General Manager: Yang Yuan-Ping
Sales Manager: Li Chen Lie
Jin Jiang Hotel Group
Rates (approx.):
   Room, high season $60
   Room, shoulder season $50
   Room, low season $29
   Suite $90+
   Others available on request
161 rooms, 4 suites, 69 villas
Service charge 10%; no tax

Situated on the Hongqiao Road in the western district of Shanghai, the Cypress (Long Bai) Hotel is acclaimed for its scenery. It is set in a park with cypress trees, many kinds of shrubs, and numerous varieties of herbaceous flowering plants, some of them rare. Rated a "superior international-class hotel" by an official Chinese directory, it has all up-to-date conveniences.

The hotel's six-story main building has more than one hundred sixty rooms and suites, including the Presidential Suite, where world leaders have resided. Additionally, sixty-seven Western and Japanese-style villas offer full amenities. These villas are most often leased to resident foreign business people or others who are in Shanghai for long periods of time. Another delightful and well-preserved villa, built in the 1920s and almost hidden in the garden, is somewhat in the style of an old English country cottage.

Every guest room in the hotel has a bathroom with marble floors and walls, air conditioning, color TV, a refrigerator, direct-dial telephones, and other modern features.

In July 1987 the hotel opened an extensive recreational center, with an Olympic-size heated swimming pool, a squash court, a gymnasium, a billard room, bowling alleys, sauna bath, a disco, a bar, and a fast-food restaurant.

The hotel's Coffee Shop, on the ground floor, serves Western food and a wide variety of drinks twenty-four hours every day.

Each of the hotel's restaurants has a special theme. The Silk Road Restaurant has a magnificent ten-by-fifty-foot ceramic tile mural depicting East meeting West on the old Silk Road. The decor of the Bamboo Banquet Room cleverly uses many varieties of bamboo. The elegant Villa Restaurant recalls the English countryside, and what is called the Floating Multi-Purpose Restaurant is set in a beautiful garden.

The hotel's cuisine, which draws on Sichuan, Yangzhou, and French styles, has been praised by both guests and food critics. It features creatively prepared items such as as Cypress duck, *hehua jinqian* (minced pork in a lotus shape), and *xueshan wolog* (batter-fried fish).

Seven shops in the hotel feature a variety of items, including old and modern Chinese art objects. There's a hairdresser as well.

The hotel caters to business people. Its Business Centre provides all equipment needed; arranges meetings, such as academic exchanges, technical lectures, and business talks; distributes invitations to meetings and exhibits and provides rooms for such events; and provides translators, interpreters, and even secretaries to accompany business people on their rounds.

My favorite service of the Cypress Hotel is its shuttle bus to the center of the city, leaving six times a day. Fully air-conditioned, the bus makes ten stops: near the consulates, at the Jingan Hotel, at the nearby Shanghai Exhibition Center, at the Jin Jiang Hotel, at the Shanghai Arts and Crafts Center, at the Union Building, at the Peace Hotel, at the Friendship Store, at the Shanghai Mansions, and, finally, back at the Cypress. The service is free to hotel guests; there is a modest charge for others.

HUA TING SHERATON HOTEL
1200 Cao Xi Bei Lu
Shanghai
People's Republic of China
Telephone: 386000
Telex: 33589 SH HTH CN
Cable: 0703

Fax: 550830
Reservations:
   In Shanghai call 386000
   In the USA and Canada call Sheraton Worldwide
      Reservations at 1-800-325-3535 (travel agents only call
      1-800-334-8484)
All major credit cards
General Manager: Walter W. Vickers
Sheraton
Rates (approx.):
   Standard room $95 single, $115 double
   Medium room $105 single, $120 double
   Superior room $115 single, $125 double
   Suite $150 +
968 rooms, 40 suites
Service charge 10%; no tax

Walter Vickers, who began his career at the famous Imperial Hotel in the English coastal resort of Torquay, runs this hotel so well that it is probably one of the top three in China.

With its more than one thousand rooms and fifteen hundred staff members, the Hua Ting Sheraton is Shanghai's first foreign-managed hotel. Mr. Vickers has therefore become an educator: he has trained hundreds of young Chinese men and women, fresh from school, in the hotel business, and at sixty-two he continues the role of headmaster in this herculean task.

Running a Chinese hotel is an interesting and pioneering experience for a Westerner. For example, although the hotel is foreign-managed it uses many Chinese products, including all of the linen and much of the foodstuffs (although the beef is imported from the United States).

Opened in September 1986, the hotel has already had prominent guests, including U.S. Secretary of State George Schultz and Mrs. Shultz, and Steven Spielberg and his film crew.

It is a grand hotel, indeed.

My favorite spot is the lobby, an imposing room with floor, walls, and pillars in new imperial granite, in mottled soft rose and black, combined with an absolutely black granite from India. The ceiling's two round camphorwood relief sculptures, covered in gold leaf, are based on original Tang Dynasty carvings from the Dung Huang caves in Gansu Province. They depict sixteen maidens, eight of whom are playing musical instruments while the other eight dance (eight is a lucky number in China, signifying expanding business and good fortune). Complementing the ceiling reliefs are thirty camphorwood gold-leaf wall panels, one for each of the thirty provinces and municipalities of China. A glass-sided escalator leads to the second floor, as does a beautiful spiral staircase, a master craftsman's dream in granite, brass, and glass. At the foot of the staircase is a lotus pond, with a fountain as well as plants. The ceiling over the lotus pond is three stories high, with glass panels providing natural light.

The hotel rooms are delightfully comfortable, all air-conditioned and with private bathrooms and either king-size or twin beds. Amenities include a telephone, color TV with in-house movies, a radio, and a refrigerator.

For Westerners who need to make the hotel their office while in China, the Business Centre offers typing, photocopying, interpretation, translation, telex, facsimile, and courier services. The secretarial staff is very friendly and helpful. For large events there is the impressive Grand Ballroom, which can seat twelve hundred.

One of the toughest jobs the hotel has accomplished is providing fine dining. It offers the best in Chinese, French, and English cuisine. Among the dining spots is Anton's, specializing in French cuisine and now one of the city's premier restaurants, and Ka Fei Ting, a café offering a wide range of meals around the clock. The English Grill Room features delicious seafoods and charcoal-grilled specialties, and the Guan Yue Tai has a traditional Cantonese menu. The Arcade Cafe offers coffee and pastries from nine in the morning until nine in the evening. And the night spot is Nicole's Disco.

All other amenities are here. The large indoor swimming pool adjoins the Health Club, which has a fully equipped gymnasium as well as sauna, a steam room, and whirlpool and massage services. There are a tennis court, a modern billiard room, and a fully electronic Ten-Pin Bowling Alley.

The hotel has an American-style beauty parlor and barbershop. In the hotel shopping arcade you can find anything from fine silk dresses to locally made jade jewelry.

The staff is ready to help in making sightseeing arrangements.

SHANGHAI HILTON INTERNATIONAL
250 Huashan Road
Shanghai
People's Republic of China
Telephone: 551234

Telex: 33612 HILTL CN
Cable: HILTELS SHANGHAI
Reservations:
  In Shanghai call 551234
  In Hong Kong call (5) 233111, ext. 1115 or 1119
  In New York call (212) 594-4500
  In California call 1-800-445-8667
  In Chicago call (312) 346-2772
  Elsewhere in the USA call any Hilton International or
    Vista International hotel
All major credit cards
General Manager: Heinz J. Schwander
Concierge: Todd Cornell
Director of Sales: Bill Li
Hilton International
Rates (approx.):
  Standard room $110 single, $125 double
  Superior room $125 single, $140 double
  Deluxe room $140 single, $175 double
  Executive Floor room $160 single, $175 double
  Suites $250+
  Others available on request
710 rooms, 67 suites
Service charge 10%; no tax

Fully opened in the spring of 1988, the Shanghai Hilton is forty-three stories high, one of the tallest buildings in the city. It is the first completely foreign-owned property in China.

It is also one of the better-situated hotels in the city, right in the heart of the commercial area. Fronting Huashan Road, it is within a short stroll of Shanghai's busiest and most exciting shopping thoroughfare, Nanjing Road. Just one block north of the hotel, Nanjing Road leads right into Shanghai's teeming downtown.

The nearly eight hundred guest rooms and suites of the Shanghai Hilton International are tastefully decorated in the same luxurious manner as those in the company's other hotels around the world. Each has a sitting area, a large desk, individually controlled air conditioning, a refrigerator with a mini-bar, and international direct-dial telephone. Bedside consoles operate the lights, the color TV with in-house movies, the radio, and taped music.

The hotel's thirty-sixth to thirty-eighth levels are the Executive Floors, which feature luxuriously appointed suites with extra amenities; a separate, speedy check-out desk; and a concierge. Three other floors contain multipurpose rooms, offices by day that can be converted into comfortable bedrooms after hours.

The hotel has a pleasing variety of Chinese restaurants. The Suiyuan dining room serves Cantonese dim sum along with the regional specialties of Shanghai. The opulent Sichuan Court features the spicy cuisine of Sichuan, while the Shanghai Express offers the fare of all regions of China in a casual setting.

Both continental and Japanese meals are offered in the Teppan Grill. Nearby, in the lobby, the Atrium Café provides maximum natural light in a lush garden setting, and is the popular spot for Western food.

For drinks, the quiet spot is the plush Lobby Pavilion, while the "in" spot is the spectacular Penthouse Bar and Lounge, reached by a glass-walled elevator and providing a fantastic panoramic view. The Greenhouse offers poolside drinks and snacks.

The hotel's stately Grand Ballroom can seat up to three hundred fifty guests at banquets or up to five hundred at receptions. It has underground parking for more than one hundred cars.

In addition to the fourth-floor indoor swimming pool, which is heated in winter, there are a health club with a fully equipped gymnasium and saunas, an outdoor tennis court, and two squash courts. In the hotel's Recreation Room there are billiards, snooker, ping pong, and English pub darts.

The hotel has special facilities for the visiting business person. Along with mail, packaging, and courier services, the well-equipped Business Centre has secretaries, interpreters, photocopying machines, and twenty-four-hour telex-cable and facsimile services.

The hotel's shopping center has an airline office, a bank, a barbershop and beauty parlor, a pharmacy, a florist, a bakery, gift shops, and a newspaper kiosk.

The hotel offers sightseeing trips around Shanghai, including half-day and full-day excursions.

SHANGHAI HOTEL
505 Wulumqi Bei Lu
Shanghai
People's Republic of China

Telephone: 312312
Telex: 33002 BTHSG CN
Cable: 0244
Reservations:
   In Shanghai call 312312, ext. 6789
Most major credit cards
General Manager: Zhang Xiao Zhong
Sales Manager: Lu Hi Ming
Shanghai Huating Holding Company
Rates (approx.):
   Double room $40
   Suite $110
594 rooms, 5 suites
Service charge 10%; no tax

This thirty-story hotel, which opened in 1983, is easy to find, for at present it is one of the tallest buildings in Shanghai. Completely designed, constructed, and funded by the municipality of Shanghai, it employs as managers and attendants only graduates of tourist colleges and vocational schools.

Although close to the center of the city, the hotel is in a quiet residential area in the western section, adjacent to two well-known shopping centers on Nanjing Road and Huaihai Road.

The comfortable rooms are decorated with modest and attractive furnishings in traditional Chinese style. All have color TV, piped-in music, telephones, refrigerators, air conditioning, and private bathrooms.

The fifteen dining halls offer good Chinese as well as Western food. Most of the Chinese dishes are prepared in the Guangdong style, others in the styles of Sichuan and Yangzhou.

Seven shops, on the ground floor and the first level above it, feature Chinese souvenirs, handicrafts, silks, paintings, calligraphy, and other native specialties.

The three-story atrium lobby features a spectacular two-story-long chandelier made up of eight Chinese lanterns, one atop another, and a pleasant café.

Tianjin

THE CRYSTAL PALACE HOTEL
You Yi and Binshui roads
Tianjin
People's Republic of China
Telephone: 310567
Telex: 23277 TCPH CN
Fax: (8622) 31051
Reservations:
    In Tianjin call 310567
    In the USA call 1-800-325-5000
    In Canada call 1-800-265-4870
All major credit cards
General Manager: Charles E. Henning
Concierge: Yvette Partridge
Sales Manager: James Kiang
Swissotel
Rates (approx.):
    Room $70–$80 single, $85–$95 double
    Suite $110–$175
318 rooms, 30 suites
Service charge 10%; no tax

Fully opened in October 1987, this beautiful hotel is set on a lake, of which it offers fine views.

The Crystal Palace represents the first Chinese venture by the masters of the art of hotel management. Swissotel runs the Montreux Palace, the Lausanne Palace, and the Hotel La Plaza in Basel; the Hotel Bellevue Palace in Berne; the Hotel President in Geneva; and the Hotel International in Zurich. It also operates hotels in other countries, including the Drake in New York, the Swiss Grand in Chicago, and the elegant Lafayette Hotel in Boston.

This first Chinese Swissotel is designed to offer the best of both worlds, business and pleasure. It has a well-equipped business center consisting of a library with office space, modern equipment, and conference rooms. For pleasure it has truly luxurious guest rooms, a health club, and restaurants featuring Chinese, Japanese, and French cuisine. It even has a banquet hall that can hold up to two hundred fifty guests.

Each guest room has two king-sized or twin beds, a beautiful bathroom with marble walls and floor, a mini-bar, in-house movies, and telephone service with an extension in the bathroom.

Very conveniently situated, the hotel is about ten minutes by car from the city center, twenty minutes from the railroad station, and under an hour from the airport.

HYATT TIANJIN
Jie Fange Road North
Tianjin
People's Republic of China
Telephone: 318888
Telex: 232705 or 23350
Fax: (8622) 310021
Reservations:
   In Tianjin call 318888
   In the USA call any Hyatt Hotel or 1-800-228-9000
All major credit cards
General Manager: George Benngy
Sales Manager: Denis Shea
Hyatt International
Rates (approx.):
   Superior room $90
   Deluxe room $120
   Regency Club room $140
   1-bedroom suite $180
   2-bedroom suite $350
   Presidential Suite $550
450 rooms, 23 suites
Service charge 10%; no tax

Opened in 1986, this was Hyatt's first hotel in the People's Republic of China. Although it is jointly owned by a Hong Kong and a Chinese company, Hyatt agreed to manage it.

The twenty-story Hyatt Tianjin is in the heart of the commercial center of the city, on the banks of the Hai River. Considered one of the more luxurious and modern hotels in China, it is indeed impressive, beginning with its three-story glass atrium lobby and its grand staircase. It also has seven restaurants and bars, including a Japanese restaurant overlooking the river, a café serving Western and Oriental food, a Cantonese restaurant with private dining rooms, a Northern Chinese restaurant with banquet facilities for up to four hundred guests, a relaxing club bar, and a lobby lounge.

My favorite spot, the Tianjin Snack Bar, serves delicious local *shiu mai* specialties, unique Chinese dumplings.

The guest rooms are particularly designed to serve the business traveler. The deluxe rooms include connecting sitting rooms large enough for business meetings and entertainment, with separate entrances to the bathrooms, and built-in white boards for making notes and screening slides or videos. All rooms have international direct-dial telephone, color TV with two channels for in-house movies (in English and Chinese), and mini-bars.

The two top floors are reserved for Regency Club guests, who are served complimentary breakfast and evening cocktails in a private lounge, and are provided all-day concierge service.

The hotel's business center provides secretaries, translators, and interpreterers as well as up-to-date international communications and business equipment.

Throughout the hotel are displayed original works by local artists.

The hotel's Health Spa has hot and cold plunge pools; sauna, steam and Shanghai baths (the Chinese version of Scandinavian hot and cold baths), massage service; and an informal lounge serving fresh fruit juice and other healthful drinks and snacks.

The hotel is a twenty-minute drive from the Tianjin International Airport.

There is no shopping mall here, only a gift shop in the lobby.

Xi'an

Xi'an (Chang An, Hsi-an) has a population in excess of two million. It is the capital of Shaanxi (Shensi) Province, in the Wei River Valley, one of the longest settled parts of China.

Situated on the Lung-hai railroad, Xi'an is an important commercial center in this wheat- and cotton-growing region. It has textile mills, food-processing plants, and factories producing chemicals, cement, motor vehicles, and fertilizer.

The city has such a long history that it is really like a gigantic museum of civilization. Neolithic settlements dating back to 6000 B.C. have been uncovered in this area. Until Xi'an fell into the hands of Turkish and Tibetan invaders in 960 A.D., it was the largest city in the world, the capital of all Chinese dynasties, and a strategic point on the Silk Road.

The city has numerous Tang Dynasty (618–906 A.D.) pagodas, including the seven-story Big Wild Goose Pagoda, containing Bhuddist scriptures brought from India by the Tang Dynasty monk Xuan Zang. Notable too is Xi'an's museum of history, housed in an eleventh-century Confucian temple. It boasts one of China's greatest collections of artifacts, including stone tablets from the Tang Dynasty. The city wall, dating from the Ming Dynasty (1368–1644 A.D.), is still visible in some places. Other historic sites within the city include an eighth-century mosque.

At nearby Qinyong are the famous life-sized terra cotta warriors and horses of the Qin Army, who were lined up by the thousand in 200 B.C. to guard the tomb of Emperor Qin Shi Huangdi. First unearthed in 1974, they are regarded as one of the most valuable archaeological discoveries ever made. Many of the figures are perfectly preserved despite more than two thousand years underground.

Other nearby places to visit include the Banpo Stone Age Village, where houses, pottery, and utensils have been excavated, and the Huaqing Hot Springs, which were used by emperors from the time Xi'an was founded. Visitors today can bathe in these same mineral-rich waters.

The high season at Xi'an is from April 1 until late fall. Winter (low-season) rates go into effect December 1.

BELL TOWER HOTEL
Southwest Corner of Bell Tower
Xi'an
People's Republic of China
Telephone: 718760 or 29203
Telex: 70124 XABTH CN
Cable: 6988 XIAN
Reservations:
    In Xi'an call 718760 or 29203
    In the USA call 1-800-HOLIDAY
All major credit cards
General Manager: Peter Erler
Sales Manager: Alain Tang
Holiday Inn Asia-Pacific
Rates (approx.):
    Standard room $80 single, $85 double
    Medium room $90 single, $90 double

Deluxe room $100 single, $105 double
Suite $110–$160
321 rooms, 4 suites
Service charge 10%; no tax

This new hotel, managed by Holiday Inn, is situated next to the famous Bell Tower of Xi'an and is only ten minutes from the airport.

All of the guest rooms are equipped with individually controlled air conditioning, private bathrooms, radio, color TV, in-house music, refrigerators, and mini-bars. Some of the suites have kitchen units.

For dining, the Tower Cafe Coffee Shop features Western dishes, and the Xi'an Garden Chinese Restaurant serves local and Sichuan dishes. The Lobby Lounge is a cozy place for drinks after a tour, or before or after dinner.

The hotel's club room has a snooker table, dart games, video games, and movies.

GOLDEN FLOWER HOTEL
8 Chang Le Road West
Xi'an
People's Republic of China
Telephone: (029) 32981
Telex: 70145 GFH CN
Fax: 32327
Reservations:
   In the USA call Utell International at (402) 493-4747
      (Omaha) or (212) 245-7130 (New York), or call Trust
      House Forte at (312) 726-5777 (Chicago), (213) 410-
      4960 (Los Angeles), or (212) 481-9000 (New York)
   Elsewhere call any Trust House Forte or Utell office or
      telex SARA Booking Sweden at 17930SARAS
All major credit cards
General Manager: John A. Green
Concierge: Yu Hua
Sales Manager: Ursula Ulterman
SARA Hotels
Rates (approx.):
   Room, low season $80 single, $100 double
   Room, high season $115 single, $135 double
   Deluxe suite $250
205 rooms, 5 suites
No service charge or tax

Known locally as the Crystal Palace, the Golden Flower is the only hotel in Xi'an that meets high international standards. It is a cooperative venture of the Xi'an Tourist Service Company, America's Kowin Group, and the SARA hotel chain of Sweden. It is the only Asian hotel SARA manages (though there will probably be others).

Seven stories tall, the hotel is one of the most visually impressive and architecturally significant buildings to have been constructed in China in recent years. The exterior, completely clad in reflective glass, features bay windows distinguishable only as vertical projections of the plain façade. An open, semicircular staircase leads from the ground to the seven floors, and the two halves of each of the six upper floors are linked by a suspended bridgeway.

All of the guest rooms, decorated in pastel colors, have air conditioning, mini-bars, refrigerators, and radios with in-house music channels.

There are only two restaurants in the hotel, but each is special.

The Jade Restaurant serves some of the best continental cuisine in China. Four foreign chefs use fresh local produce to create a spectacular European buffet.

In the Wan Fu Court, six Sichuan chefs prepare specialties from their native province. The executive chef, Li Cheng Hen, has traveled to many parts of the world, winning awards for his outstanding cuisine.

The place to relax in the evening is the piano bar, called the Drunken Moon. For late-night entertainment and dancing, the hotel offers the only place to go in Xi'an, the Drunken Moon Discotheque.

The hotel provides the kind of services the business traveler and the sophisticated tourist expects. Among them are travel transfers and arrangements; banquet facilities; secretarial and translation services; and telephone, telex, facsimile, and cable services.

HONG KONG

This gem of the Orient, only 399 square miles, has more than five million inhabitants. The most popular travel destination in Asia, it attracts more than three million visitors every year. The number keeps growing, too; to serve all who are expected, over a dozen new hotels are scheduled to open by late 1990.

Hong Kong's existing hotels are among the best in the world. Collectively, they are not only the most comfortable anywhere, but they are unsurpassed in quality of service. And, as you will read on the following pages, there is one to suit every taste or budget.

Spread over 236 small islands and a promontory of the Chinese mainland, Hong Kong is ruled more or less in accordance with British law.

In three treaties resolved between 1841 and 1898, the land was ceded partly in perpetuity and partly by lease set to expire before the year 2000. After numerous negotiations, the British and Chinese prime ministers recently signed a joint understanding on the governing of the territory, which will revert to the People's Republic of China on June 30, 1997. The agreement includes the understanding that Hong Kong's lifestyle and dynamic economy are to be preserved for at least fifty years beyond 1997.

In the early eighties, the impending expiration of the lease, and the changes a new government might impose, greatly concerned the people of Hong Kong. Real estate values fell. Some citizens started planning to move their businesses and residences to other parts of the world. But things have calmed down. Today at least a half dozen new hotels are being built, as are new factories and office buildings. This is certainly a display of confidence in the future.

Hong Kong and the South China coast have been inhabited since ancient times. Archaeological finds date to the neolithic period. But it is the events in China during the last century that have largely shaped Hong Kong's growth.

The modern history of Hong Kong starts with the arrival of the British in 1841. During the latter half of the nineteenth century, Hong Kong developed as the entrepôt for trade with China, attracting both overseas merchants and Chinese immigrants, who shared in the wealth. The population grew rapidly. In 1851, thirty-three thousand people lived in Hong Kong. The collapse of the Ching Dynasty in 1911 brought waves of refugees from political uncertainty, and by 1931 the city had nearly a million inhabitants. When Japanese forces invaded in 1941, there were 1.6 million. But many fled back to China after the invasion, and by the time the British recovered Hong Kong the population was down to about six hundred thousand.

Slowly, Hong Kong recovered. By the 1950s the over two million inhabitants were mass-producing cheap goods and pumping them into the West at competitive prices. As products were upgraded and new markets relentlessly sought, Hong Kong's business community thrived. Today new ideas are still plentiful in Hong Kong, and so is the capital needed to back them.

Hong Kong is now the world's third largest container port and the home for massive shipping firms, the third most important center for gold trading, and, certainly, the financial capital of Asia. The textile and garment industry, the colony's largest, encompasses vast complexes of spinning, carding, and weaving mills that run nonstop twenty-four hours a day. Other industries include shipbuilding; food processing; the manufacture of plastics, electrical and electronic equipment, rubber products, machinery, chemicals, toys, jewelry, furniture, and ceramics; tourism; motion-picture production; insurance; and printing and publishing.

Refugees from political or financial crises are no longer welcomed as they were in the past: illegal immigrants from China are repatriated, and those from Vietnam are returned as soon as is practical. As the population fast approaches six million, the limits to growth seem to be in sight. Still,

Hong Kong's people are among the most affluent in Asia, with a per capita income of well over five thousand dollars.

Tourists know what to do in Hong Kong long before they arrive. Most plan their visit as a shopping expedition, and Hong Kong is ready for them—from Hollywood Road on Hong Kong Island to Nathan Road in Kowloon, and to the many atrium malls on both sides of the harbor, the largest collection of malls of any city in the world.

But there are many things to do besides shop in this vibrant city. Take the Star Ferry for a fabulous harbor ride, the hydrofoil to Macau or Shenzhen, or the cable car to Victoria Peak, where the views are breathtaking. Jog along the waterfront promenade in Kowloon, visit the floating restaurants and see the houseboats at Aberdeen, or stroll the beach at Repulse Bay. Enjoy fine dining and the active night life. And more—much more.

Every hotel has copies of *The Official Hong Kong Guide*. Published by the Hong Kong Tourist Association, the finest organization of its kind in the world, and issued every month, it contains nearly two hundred pages of almost limitless choices. Be sure to ask for your copy.

Important: Make reservations before you arrive in Hong Kong. Do so far in advance for the high seasons, from October to early December and from March to May. As I write this, all hotels in the city are booked solid for three months or more. If you find yourself in Hong Kong without a reservation, check at the airport counter of the Hong Kong Hotels Association, or call the association at (3) 838-380, and they will try to help you. If they can't, you may find a room available in nearby Macau on a weekday, though this is less likely on a weekend. Macau is an hour's hydrofoil trip away from Hong Kong, but a pleasant commute.

Causeway Bay

The old Causeway Bay—in Chinese, Tung Lo Wan (Copper Gong Bay)—has almost disappeared through reclamation. More than a century ago, Jardine's trading company, still Hong Kong's most influential *hong* (company), moved their headquarters from Canton and Macau to this spot. They purchased a large tract, the first plot of land auctioned by the British government after Hong Kong's establishment as a colony, and hewed a whole town out of the rock. They built godowns, offices, workshops, homes, and messes for their employees. The old town has since been replaced by the Excelsior Hotel, the adjacent World Trade Center, and a number of office and apartment blocks, hotels, movie houses, and department stores.

Causeway Bay, on the East Point of Hong Kong Island, pulsates with activity. It is especially lively at night, as its shops and department stores stay open later than those in other areas of Hong Kong, and its bars and nightclubs seem never to close.

Here are at least six major price-fixed department stores and hundreds of shops, ranging from fine boutiques to hair salons. Supper clubs and large restaurants feature lavish musical revues with international talent and floor shows. Food Street, next to The Excelsior, is a complex of twenty-four restaurants offering an extensive variety of Chinese, Western, and other cuisines. For dance aficionados, the discotheques and nightclubs explode with music. For pub crawlers, music and chatter mix with the clink of iced drinks at a number of establishments.

Today Causeway Bay's waterfront is a mass of junks and sampans huddling in the typhoon shelter. The land jutting out into the harbor is Kellet Island, which was an actual island until the causeway was built out to it in 1956. Now it is the headquarters of the Royal Hong Kong Yacht Club, right across from the Excelsior.

The best-known landmark in Causeway Bay is the historic Noon Day Gun, which Jardine's still fires daily at noon from the waterfront opposite The Excelsior (I found people in the hotel checking their watches by it). The firing of the gun has been a tradition since the early days of Hong Kong, more than a century ago, when Jardine's first arrived.

In those days, clippers serving the China trade used to call at East Point to replenish their supplies and to arm themselves against pirates from the considerable stock of ammunition kept by Jardine's. The company also had their own battery and detachment of guards, and it became customary that whenever the Taipan, the company's ship, arrived in or departed the colony, a number of gun salutes were fired. On one occasion, the usual salutes were fired just as the schooner, sailing up the Lei Yun Mun Channel, passed one of Her Majesty's ships, which was flying the broad pennant of the senior naval officer of the port. The gunfire amazed and annoyed the senior naval officer, who was new to the colony and had not heard of the practice.

Jardine's was requested to explain on whose authority it

was permitted to fire salutes. The company replied that the salutes were customary, and that large stocks of powder were kept for the purpose. It is said that Jardine's was then ordered—no one is quite sure by whom—to stop indulging in such gunfire.

As a penalty, and to use up the powder stock, the company was ordered to fire the gun at noon every day thenceforth as a time signal for the colony.

THE EXCELSIOR
281 Gloucester Road
Causeway Bay
P.O. Box 30692
Causeway Bay Post Office
Hong Kong
Telephone: (5)767365
Telex: 74550 EXCON HX
Cable: CONVENTION HONGKONG
Fax: (5)8956459
Reservations:
   In Hong Kong call (5) 890-5859
   In the USA and Canada call 1-800-622-0404
All major credit cards
General Manager: Glen H. Farmer
Concierge: Charles Chang
Director of Sales and Marketing: S. N. Chu
Mandarin Oriental Hotel Group
Rates (approx.):
   Standard room $103
   Superior room $122
   Deluxe room $141
   Deluxe harbor-view room $160
   Business suite $205
   Harbor-view suite $255
   2-bedroom suite $385
   Top suite $575
896 rooms, 30 suites
Service charge 10%; tax 5%

The Excelsior is beautifully situated overlooking Causeway Bay. It is adjacent to the cross-harbor tunnel to Kowloon and to the new subway station. And, important for buyers visiting Hong Kong, it is linked to the Hong Kong World Trade Centre, an integrated complex that has conference facilities for a thousand persons. There are major Japanese department stores in the area, too, such as Daimaru, Matsuzakaya, and Mitsukoshi. Almost all the shops in the blocks near the hotel are open until 10:00 or 11:00 P.M. There is a staggering array of restaurants, pulsating discos, pubs, and bars, and probably the territory's best-kept cinemas. Other hotels are in the Causeway Bay section, such as Park Lane and the Lee Gardens. But they are not on the harbor, nor do they have the abundant facilities of the Excelsior.

Staying at the Excelsior is less expensive than staying at the fine hotels along Salisbury Road, in the Tsimshatsui area of Kowloon, or at those in Hong Kong Central. (For example, the room rates at the Excelsior are almost a third less than the rates at the Mandarin in Hong Kong Central —maybe five minutes away by taxi.) This is probably because Salisbury Road and Hong Kong Central offer more high-quality, name-brand shopping, and most of the hotels in these areas are either newer and fancier or have recently been highly upgraded.

We found the Excelsior to be very comfortable, however. It is well run, by the Mandarin Oriental Hotel Group, which operates two of the best hotels in the world, the Oriental in Bangkok and the Mandarin in Hong Kong Central. The rooms are spacious, clean, and mostly refurbished (though some are a bit frayed). Service is extra special, in the Mandarin tradition. Everyone really *wants* to be of help to you.

The Excelsior is, I found, a truly international hotel. It attracts both business people and tourists, from everywhere. The clientele is not dominated by Americans, Europeans, or any other group. I found the mix enjoyable.

Buyers and other business people enjoy staying at this hotel because the World Trade Centre is in the connected building next door. The hotel also provides extensive meeting and banquet facilities, the well-equipped Business Centre, and a shopping arcade.

For the athlete, all is at hand. An indoor, air-conditioned tennis court is within the hotel, and adjacent to the building is a jogging track.

We enjoyed the comfortable and cozy atmosphere of the Excelsior Grill, which serves superb Western meals at lunch and dinner. If you get there early enough, when the Noon Day Gun is fired, you might be able to get one of the few seats with a view of the Royal Hong Kong Yacht Club and Victoria Harbour.

The Excelsior also boasts a new Italian restaurant, the Cammino, opened early in 1987 on the first floor of the hotel. Its black and pink marble floor, black chairs, and etched glass walls together provide an elegant but relaxing setting where guests can select from a wide range of Italian culinary favorites and fine wines.

Besides opening the Cammino, the hotel has recently renovated the Coffee Shop, with its delightful American and Asian fare, and the Garden Lounge, as well as other public areas.

For an elegant evening I suggest sipping sunset cocktails at the Excelsior's Noon Gun Bar, overlooking the boats of the Royal Hong Kong Yacht Club. Then go to nearby Landau's, which, although still expensive, offers perhaps the town's best value in European cuisine. Finally, you might try a little late-night dancing at the Excelsior's Talk of the Town nightclub, or go to one of the night spots at the Plaza or Lee Garden hotels.

Most fun is to explore the restaurants of nearby Paterson Street and Food Street. The latter, as its name suggests, is devoted to restaurants, with all of the cuisines of Asia available. Its highly respected Peking, Sichuan, and Cantonese restaurants offer such dishes as Thai Bird's Nest Soup and Vietnamese dumplings as well. Afterwards you might like to go to a coffee shop on Paterson Street, where you may select from more than thirty varieties of the brew.

For the summer, I have a trip for you. First, buy some bread, cheese, meats, and wine from a nearby supermarket. Then look for the door next to the parking lot entrance of the World Trade Centre. One flight down is the tunnel that leads under the harbor road to Jardine's Gun. Outside the compound are sampans for hire, and on one of them you may take a leisurely two-hour trip around the boats in the typhoon shelter (by the way, you are expected to bargain for the price of the trip). You dine on what you have brought, or, if you are adventurous, you can purchase food from a food sampan. If you're in luck, you'll encounter the musical sampan with its orchestra's unusual rendition of popular tunes.

If you like to explore on foot, or jog, be sure to ask for your copy of *The Excelsior Hong Kong: Find Your Way Around Causeway Bay*. Not only does this leaflet show you how to get to twenty-four places of interest in the area, but it also has a map of the three subway lines in Hong Kong: the Island Line, which has a station right at the hotel; the Tsuen Wan Line, which takes you under the harbor to the mainland; and the Kwun Tong Line, the mainland extension line.

PARK LANE HOTEL
310 Gloucester Road
Causeway Bay
Hong Kong
Telephone: (5) 890-3355
Telex: 75343 PLH HX
Cable: PARKLANE
Fax: (5) 767853
Reservations:
  In Hong Kong call (5) 890-3355
  In New York state call (212) 725-1510
  Elsewhere in the USA call Distinguished Hotels at
    1-800-R-WARNER
All major credit cards
Managing Director: Chan Chak Fu
General Manager: Kenneth Mullins
Concierge: Henry Kwok
Director of Sales: Andy Siu
Park Lane Hotels International
Rates (approx.):
  Moderate room $115.50
  Superior room $134.70
  Deluxe room $153.80
  Premier room $179.50
  Executive suite $257.00
  Park Lane Suite $321.00
  Presidential Suite (1 bedroom) $770
  Presidential Suite (2 bedrooms) $898
850 rooms, 33 suites
Service charge 10%; tax 5%

The Park Lane Hotel is well named, for the city's Victoria
Park serves as the hotel's front garden.

Guests here hardly know they are in a bustling city. The
park setting, and the activities it encourages, make the place
amazingly serene. You can swim and play tennis on the
grounds, and, of course, jog in the park.

The hotel's larger-than-usual guest rooms have been attractively redecorated. New furnishings include working-
size marble-top desks, three telephones per room, and comfortable sitting areas. The bathrooms, with their marble floors
and walls, are beautiful. Also provided, of course, are such
amenities as color TV and air conditioning.

Two executive floors offer special services for business
people, such as quick check-in, personal valets, and late
check-out. The views from these floors are outstanding.

My favorite spot is the Parc 27 restaurant, on the hotel's top floor (the twenty-seventh). A gallery of edible art, the Parc 27 is especially popular for its buffets and business luncheons. The buffets, presented on enormous marble counters, contain food sculptures, carvings, and montages. The business luncheons feature edible imitations of graphic designs, delicate oil paintings, and gouaches. Though labeled nouvelle cuisine, the food is both delightful and satisfying, particularly the appetizers and the desserts. The decor is pleasant, featuring Italian marble and granite in hues of soft pink and gray. Dinner, served à la carte, is enhanced by the night lights of Hong Kong and Cole Porter or Gershwin melodies from the piano. The (nonedible) murals of harbor scenes, together with the views through the wide windows of Kowloon and the Hong Kong Royal Yacht Club, provide a nautical panorama.

Other restaurants in the hotel include the Parkview Café, open till late at night, and the Promenade, a good spot for breakfast, roast beef luncheon buffet, or à la carte dinner. The favorite place for drinks and sunset cocktails is the rooftop Park 27 Lounge. The Lobby Bar has piano music; the Gallery Bar and Lounge has varying entertainment; and the Starlight Bar has taped music and video.

The Fitness Centre includes a gymnasium, a solarium, a Jacuzzi, saunas, aerobics classes, and massage services.

The hotel's sparkling new Business Centre is on the first floor. Fully equipped with printing, photocopying, secretarial, and telecommunications facilities, it offers superior, personalized business services.

Also for business executives are the function rooms on the top floor of the hotel, sharing some of the spectacular views offered by Parc 27. Because of their decor and views, these function rooms are among the best in the city.

The existence of only four shops in the hotel, all of them featuring fine merchandise, helps make the Park Lane seem like one of the grand hotels of Europe.

NEW CATHAY HOTEL
17 Tung Lo Wan Road
Causeway Bay
Hong Kong
Telephone: (5) 778211
Telex: 72089 CATAY HX
Cable: CATHAYHOTE

Reservations:
  In Hong Kong call (5) 778211
American Express, Visa, MasterCard, Federal
General Manager: Feng Wan Ben
Sales Manager: Tommy Lee
Rates, with continental breakfast (approx.):
  Room $41–$46 single, $46–$52 double
  Suite $79
142 rooms, 2 suites
Service charge 10%; tax 5%

This is a fine, moderate-priced tourist hotel well situated in the center of the Causeway Bay area on Hong Kong Island.

Though the New Cathay is away from the fancier and more popular Nathan Road area, there is plenty to do here. Not far away are the Hong Kong Stadium; Happy Valley, where you can see the horse races; and the Yacht Club of Hong Kong. Right across the street is Victoria Park and, for shoppers, big stores such as Lane Crawford, China Products, and Matsusakaya. Many smaller shops in the area sell electronic equipment, cameras, watches, clothing, and jewelry.

Also in the area are many small restaurants—some very good—serving French, Chinese, Indian, Indonesian, Korean, Japanese, and even fast food.

The rooms are modest but clean and comfortable. All are air-conditioned, and all have private bathrooms, color TV, and refrigerators.

Two convenience restaurants, serving continental and Chinese food, are on the premises, but it is more fun to eat elsewhere.

Hong Kong Central

On Hong Kong Island, this is the financial heart of the colony. Here are the many towering skyscrapers of the financial community, and here is the stock exchange. Here too are the corporate offices of the giant Hong Kong real estate, shipping, and industrial companies. The streets are lined with banks, brokerages, and other offices.

In many of the tall office buildings, the first three or more floors are given over to elegant atrium shopping malls, some of them, like The Landmark, including shops of famous French, Italian, and other designers. Since neighboring buildings are connected with second-level walkways, it is possible to visit five or so gigantic shopping malls without ever going onto the busy streets.

Visitors to Hong Kong Central soon find the older area, around Hollywood Road, where many antique and art shops offer both treasure and trash, all Chinese and all very old, though some pieces look brand-new. Here you may be given a cup of tea, if you appear to be a serious customer, and the bargaining begins.

If you ever saw the movie *Love is a Many-Splendored Thing* or the TV miniseries "Noble House," you'll remember the overwhelmingly beautiful views of Hong Kong from Victoria Peak. Leaving from a station just behind the Hongkong Hilton is the tram to the top of the peak. The thirteen-hundred-foot ride costs about a half dollar.

The embarkation pier of the famous Star Ferry is reached by an underpass in front of the Mandarin Hotel. For about a dime you can ride across Victoria Harbour to Kowloon. One of the world's great bargains, the ride is smooth, and the views from both sides of the ferry are stunning.

FURAMA INTER-CONTINENTAL
One Connaught Road
Central
Hong Kong
Telephone: (5) 255111
Telex: 73081 FURAM HX
Cable: FURAM HONG KONG
Fax: 852 (5) 297405
Reservations:
   In Hong Kong call (5) 229879
   In the USA call 1-800-33-AGAIN
All major credit cards
General Manager: Gerd Koidl
Inter-Continental Hotels
Rates (approx.):
   Standard room $128 single, $141 double
   Superior room $141 single, $154 double
   Suite $308–$410
569 rooms and suites
Service charge 10%; tax 5%

On Hong Kong Island, the Furama Inter-Continental is both conveniently and beautifully situated in the heart of the

Central District, the city's business center. It overlooks the magnificent harbor and, on the other side, the grand Victoria Peak. It is within easy walking distance of both the famous Star Ferry and, in the other direction, the newly opened Hong Kong Stock Exchange and other financial centers of Hong Kong, Asia, and the world.

While it doesn't have overpasses to other buildings and their atrium shopping malls, as does the nearby Mandarin, it does have its own collection of clothing boutiques, tailors, fine jewelry shops, and fancy gift shops, as well as a patisserie and basics such as a drugstore, a florist, and a newsstand.

The Furama also has a good collection of places to dine and to drink. The Rotisserie Restaurant and Lounge, the favorite place for meals, has a charming French chateau decor and, in the evenings, live music.

My favorite spot is La Ronda, Hong Kong's finest revolving restaurant and bar. On the thirtieth floor of the hotel, it provides breathtaking views of the city and its harbor. European as well as Oriental cuisine are featured in the buffet here.

Among the other restaurants in the hotel, The Island is a classic Chinese dining room, specializing in Cantonese dishes. The Furama Coffee Shop, with European, Chinese, and Indonesian selections, serves breakfast and light snacks as well as lunch and dinner. The Lau Ling Bar is a popular spot for business luncheons and relaxing drinks. It features an elegant Oriental decor and live music.

Each of the hotel's guest rooms offers a view of either the harbor or Victoria Peak. Each has individual temperature controls, direct-dial telephone, color TV with a movie channel, radio, multichannel in-house music, a refrigerator with a mini-bar, a hairdryer, and a personal safe. The luxurious suites are ideal for meetings with VIPs and private dining.

An ideal hotel for the business traveler, the Furama has a fully equipped business center, with private offices that can be rented by the day along with complete secretarial, telex, cable, and postal services. The staff can help arrange business appointments and provide translators and interpreters as well.

There are plenty of conference and banquet facilities at the Furama. The collection of eleven function rooms can accommodate any group, from an intimate party to a gathering of fifteen hundred.

THE HONGKONG HILTON
2 Queen's Road
Central
Hong Kong
Telephone: (5) 233111
Telex: 73355 HX
Cable: HILTELS HONG KONG
Fax: (852) 123-40753
Reservations:
   In Hong Kong call (5) 233111, ext. 4
   In New York state and Canada call collect
      (212) 697-9370
   Elsewhere in the USA call 1-800-223-1146
All major credit cards
General Manager: James A. Smith
Concierge: Johnson Chan
Director of Marketing and Sales: Maria Sung
Hilton International
Rates (approx.):
   Standard room $125 single, $136 double
   Moderate room $142 single, $154 double
   Superior room $159 single, $172 double
   Deluxe room $179 single, $192 double
   Harbor-view suite $282
   Tower and corner suites $346
780 rooms, 88 suites
Service charge 10%; tax 10%

I like the Hongkong Hilton because right behind it is the
Peak Tram. The tram provides a great ride to Victoria Peak,
where you'll get the best views of Hong Kong—the views
you'll remember from the movies.

But there are more important reasons for liking the hotel.
First among them is its ideal setting in the middle of the
Central District of Hong Kong Island. The hotel is, literally,
just around the corner from all the major commercial and
financial institutions. Right next to it, in fact, is the skyscraper, recently built to house the Hong Kong and Shanghai bank, that is variously called a monstrosity and an
architectural wonder. This massive collage of glass and pipes
is especially interesting when viewed from the Eagle's Nest
dining room, atop the hotel.

One of the best hotels in the city, the Hongkong Hilton
prides itself in filling the many varied needs of its many
varied guests.

It goes to some lengths. For example, it is the only hotel in Hong Kong to own its own boat—the beautiful and stately 110-foot steel-hulled brigantine *Wan Fu* (Ten Thousand Felicitations). The *Wan Fu* is a reproduction of one of the Royal Navy ships used in the 1840s to chase pirates who preyed upon merchant ships in the South China Sea. An excellent vehicle for sightseeing, island hopping, and beach parties, it is also a unique but comfortable setting for cocktail parties and dinners. A leaflet available at the hotel describes the eight *Wan Fu* cruises. Guests are escorted to the boat at Blake Pier, only a five-minute walk from the hotel.

The Hongkong Hilton is a culinary delight. *My favorite spot*, the top-floor Eagle's Nest, features the best of Chinese cuisine. I enjoyed Beggar's Chicken, which comes with a heavy mallet to break the baked clay in which the bird is encrusted, a souvenir picture of the breaking, and a souvenir key chain with a miniature mallet attached. The wide views of Hong Kong from this dining room are most enjoyable. In the evening there is dancing and music by the Bading Tuason Orchestra.

The hotel has several other good restaurants as well. The Grill, the main dining room, features excellent French cuisine and, in the evening, live piano music. The Jade Lotus serves extensive breakfast and lunch buffets that include Chinese, Western, vegetarian, and spicy Indian dishes. On the lower ground floor, the Den serves Mediterranean buffets at lunch and dinner, along with live music. The Dragon Boat is a favorite spot to meet for a quiet drink or a business lunch of carved meats and salad from the salad bar. Light meals are served all day long at the pool, where the nightly dinner barbecues are especially popular. Cat Street, open until 3:00 A.M., serves both Western and Oriental dishes, from breakfast to late-night snacks.

On the fourth floor, the Health Club has a gymnasium with exercise equipment, saunas, steambaths, Jacuzzis, and a suntanning parlor.

In the second-floor lobby, the hotel's Business Centre is open daily. It offers secretarial, translating, facsimile, telex, and photocopying services; a personal computer; and audio equipment.

The guest rooms are spacious, air-conditioned, and equipped with color TV with in-house movies and announcements of events. The rooms include refrigerators and mini-bars, unique security locks, and some of the best views of the city, the harbor, and Victoria Peak.

The hotel's executive floors each have a lounge that serves

complimentary breakfast, afternoon tea, and evening cocktails. Guests on these floors are provided a concierge and a variety of business services.

More than sixty-five retail outlets of all kinds are on the hotel's ground and first floors. A favorite is the little Gourmet Shop, which sells fresh bread, pastries, cakes, chocolates, and imported specialties.

Be sure to ask for your copy of the hotel's *City Map*. Fitting in a pocket-sized folder, it covers all of Hong Kong Central, Wanchai, and Causeway Bay, and the Tsimshatsui area of Kowloon, across the harbor.

HOTEL VICTORIA
Shun Tak Centre
Connaught Road
Central
Hong Kong
Telephone: (5) 407228
Telex: 86608 HTLVT HX
Cable: HOTELVC
Fax: (5) 476912
Reservations:
  In Hong Kong call (5) 407228, ext. 7301 or 7302
  In the USA call China Express at (415) 397-8811 or
    1-800-227-5663
All major credit cards
Resident Manager: Robert J. Gerber
General Manager: Ray Wong
Front Office Manager: Joseph Chan
Director of Sales: Frederick Leung
New World Hotels International
Rates (approx.):
  Standard room $125
  Superior room $145
  Deluxe room $165
  Standard suite $250
  Harbor-view suite $300
  Penthouse $650–$1,000
540 rooms, 55 suites, 7 penthouses
Service charge 10%; tax 5%

Opened in 1986, this hotel sits right on the edge of Hong Kong's Victoria Harbour. The forty-story building, with its distinctive red stripes, rises above the Shun Tak Centre Macau Ferry Terminal. Because of the hotel's height, some of its views are the most magnificent to be had from any building in Asia.

In addition to the guest rooms and suites, 330 fully furnished apartments are in the building. Set over the apartments, the guest rooms begin twenty-six floors above the attractive gray-marble lobby on the ground floor. More than three-quarters of the rooms have spectacular harbor views, while the rest look out over the fascinating Mid-levels and Peak residential areas of the island.

Each of the rooms has individually controlled air conditioning, a bathroom with marble floors and walls, radio, color TV, piped-in music, international direct-dial telephone, a refrigerator, and a fully stocked mini-bar. Supplies for making coffee and tea are in the room.

The fortieth floor of the hotel has seven beautifully furnished penthouse suites. The thirty-eighth and thirty-ninth house the luxurious Dynasty Club. Guests here are personally greeted and escorted to their rooms. Extra touches include fresh fruit, personalized stationery and matches, bathrobes, and lots of fancy bathroom accessories. A complimentary continental breakfast and, in the evening, complimentary cocktails and hors d'oeuvres are served in the Dynasty Club Lounge on the thirty-ninth floor.

This hotel has a grand collection of restaurants. Dynasty, the hotel's elegant Cantonese dining room, is on the first floor. The marble entrance leads into the main room, decorated in rust and biege, paneled with attractive carved wood, and lit by recessed chandeliers. The ceiling is dominated by a dramatic illuminated mosaic depicting a Chinese maiden dancing in space.

Also on the first floor is the Bocarinos Grill, a European grill room. The Mediterranean decor features ceramic tiles, white stucco walls, and dark wood paneling. Guests order from a menu of traditional meat and seafood dishes as carts bring a selection of salads, breads, and desserts to the table. On Sunday, a sumptuous eight-course brunch is served.

The Cafe Terrace, the hotel's fourth-floor coffee shop, has views of the harbor and the adjacent swimming pool. Lunch and dinner are served both à la carte and buffet-style.

The Interlude, on the first floor, overlooks the hotel lobby. It is decorated in an intimate but high-tech style, in shades of gray and pink with black trim and tinted glass. This is an ideal place for a relaxed lunch, with a choice of roast meats and poultry and a salad bar. The Interlude has live entertainment in the evening and a very good late-night snack menu.

Open from noon until 2 A.M., the ground-floor Lobby Lounge serves light buffet lunches, cakes, pastries, and imaginative coffees and teas prepared at a side table. In the evening there is dancing.

My favorite spot is the pool deck, on the fourth floor next to the Cafe Terrace. Beside the swimming pool and an indoor garden, this is a very attractive place to sunbathe and relax. Cocktails and light snacks are served from 9:00 A.M. until 6:00 P.M.

On the eighth floor are floodlit tennis courts.

On the third floor are the hotel's function rooms, which are used for all kinds of events.

The hotel's Business Centre, on the second floor, is open all day Monday through Friday and Saturday morning. It offers a full range of business services and office facilities.

Shopping is easy for guests at this hotel. The second-floor elevated walkway takes you right to the central business and shopping centers. But even closer, just an elevator ride from your room, is one of the city's largest shopping complexes, the Shun Tak Centre. Adjacent to the hotel, it has one hundred sixty shops and restaurants on three floors.

THE MANDARIN
5 Connaught Road
Central
GPO 2623
Hong Kong
Telephone: (5) 220111
Telex: 73653
Reservations:
  In Hong Kong call (5) 220111
  In the USA call Leading Hotels of the World at
    (212) 838-7874
All major credit cards
General Manager: Jürg E. Tüscher
Concierge: Giovanni Valenti
Sales Manager: Neil Woodcock
Mandarin Oriental Hotel Group
Rates (approx.):
  Standard room $167
  Medium room $203
  Superior room $225
  Corner suite $372
  Standard suite $436

Deluxe suite $494
Presidential Suite $1,250
487 rooms, 58 suites
Service charge 10%; tax 5%

Frequently rated as one of the best hotels in the world (second best in *Institutional Investor* and among the ten best in *Travel and Leisure*), the Mandarin was built in 1963 to serve the business people and financiers of the territory's economic boom. It was designed as an unabashedly sumptuous combination of a Chinese Imperial mansion and an upper-crust London club. Situated in Hong Kong Central's premier business and shopping district, it is only one block from Exchange Square, where the Hong Kong Stock Exchange is, just a few minutes from the huge Bank of China and the Hong Kong and Shanghai Bank, and across the street from both the Post Office Building (locally called the Swiss Cheese Building because all its windows are round) and the pier of the Star Ferry.

From the outside, the hotel appears to be just another tall attractive building among the cluster of tall attractive buildings in this very modern business area. But inside it is different.

The lobby is not overwhelming, as are some of those of a few other fine hotels in Hong Kong. It has an understated but elegant Chinese decor with black marble walls and gilded carvings. Comparatively small and modest, it is always busy. My wife and I enjoyed sitting in the second-floor balcony that surrounds the lobby, people-watching while we sipped cocktails or tea in *my favorite spot*, the Clipper Lounge.

If we had looked carefully we might have seen some celebrities. Ever since it opened, this has been the favorite hotel of visiting British and other European royalty, members of the British Foreign Service, and the business elite. Among the many famous guests have been David Rockefeller, Katherine Graham, and the king of Belgium.

The rooms are not dramatically modern or exciting. They're not supposed to be. They are most comfortable and pleasant, and they are kept that way. The hotel, it seems, is always refurbishing its guest rooms as well as its public areas. The changes are unobtrusive, so as never to disturb loyal guests. The recently redecorated guest rooms are lovely, in a quiet way, with pink Portuguese marble in the bathrooms, and new furniture of teak and burled wood. The style remains in the established decor of the hotel, which it calls Mandarin Chinoiserie.

The Presidential Suites are on the twenty-fourth floor. Especially delightful is the Mandarin Suite, with terraces on two sides, one overlooking the harbor and the other the nearby park and skyscrapers.

To be called the second best hotel in the world requires more than appealing and tasteful decor. Those who claim the Mandarin is so special emphasize the service, which they consider not only exceptional but unique.

When you arrive at the airport, you are met by the driver of the hotel's limousine. Dressed in starched whites, he is friendly and helpful. Before you know it, your baggage is in the trunk and you're comfortably settled in the spacious passenger seats. As you enter the hotel's driveway, you see someone waiting for you. It is an assistant manager, who is immediately joined by a bellman. In a brief time you are checked in, escorted to your room, and served, from a beautiful Chinese porcelain tea set, hot tea and biscuits to freshen you from your long journey.

Behind this formality is a true concern for the needs of each guest. For example, I happened to remark to my wife that the protruding locks on the side of my luggage were a nuisance, always being knocked askew or opened in handling. Overhearing this, a bellman soon brought me some cloth tape, with the suggestion that I cover the hasps with it after packing.

Another time, my wife had been ill at our previous stop, the Mandarin Hotel in Manila. Shortly after we arrived at the Mandarin in Hong Kong, we were asked how she felt and told that a tentative appointment, which we were free to change or cancel, had been set with the hotel's doctor. Before we left, likewise, we were given a can of mosquito repellant to use in the next country on our itinerary, a mosquito-ridden place.

Other guests tell of having tea being brought to their room because someone on the staff had seen them looking tired from a day of shopping. Another tells of buying an antique Chinese garment and finding it needed repair. The sewing was done overnight, and beautifully.

The staff makes an earnest effort to note your likes and dislikes for future visits. If you have tea regularly upon rising the first time, you'll get it the second. If you like to nibble dim sum on your balcony during your siesta, it will be there.

The Mandarin caters to shopoholics, as my wife and I unabashedly are. From the hotel's own two floors of fine shops, you can walk over covered ramps and bridges, never fighting street traffic or the weather, to some of the finest shopping centers in Hong Kong: Alexandra House, Swire House, Prince's Building, Queen's Road Central, and, most elegant of all, the Landmark. This last complex has not only shops and boutiques by famous names from around the world, but, in the center of its atrium, a stage for showing the newest French, American, and Asian fashions. A delightful dining balcony overlooks the stage and the four levels of shops.

There are four fine places to dine at the Mandarin. The modestly priced Mandarin Coffee Shop is far above the level of a typical hotel coffee shop. The favorite restaurant, for most people, is the Mandarin Grill. It is one of the world's truly great grill rooms; 90 percent of its guests are locals. My own favorites, however, are Man Wah, whose decor suggests a small Chinese lacquered treasure box, and the elegant Pierrot, which takes its name from Pablo Picasso's portrait of his son. Luxurious red velvet furnishings and prints by Picasso and other masters set the mood for the classical French meals served at lunch and dinner. Both Man Wah and Pierrot are on the twenty-fifth floor.

On the twenty-fourth floor of the hotel is a complete health center, with a sauna and something I particularly enjoyed—a marble-columned indoor pool that calls to mind a Roman bath.

Wanchai

This less tumultuous section of Hong Kong Island is between Hong Kong Central and Causeway Bay. Those who remember the movie *World of Suzie Wong* may be disappointed when they arrive here.

During the past ten years what formerly was a waterfront red-light area has become a respectable setting for the overflow of office skyscrapers from the commercial Central District.

Yes, there are a few girlie bars and side-street brothels, but most locals and tourists go to what is locally called "the Wanch" for inexpensive Malaysian curry, Thai chili, Italian pasta, Chinese dim sum, a few drinks in a lively pub, or dancing to the music of local orchestras.

Because of extensive land reclamation, the new Wanchai waterfront is becoming an important area. Already situated here are the cultural complex of the Arts Centre and Academy for the Performing Arts, the skyscraper China Resources Building and the Hong Kong Exhibition Centre, and the twin-towered Great Eagle Centre and Harbour Centre. Under construction at this writing is the spectacular Hong Kong Convention and Exhibition Centre.

RAMADA INN HONG KONG
61–73 Lockhart Road
Wanchai
Hong Kong
Telephone: (5) 861-1000
Telex: 82590 RINN HX
Fax: (5) 8656023
Reservations:
  In Hong Kong call (5) 275991 or (5) 275973
  In the USA call 1-800-228-9898
All major credit cards
General Manager: Loy Chung
Front Office Manager: Paul Cheng
Marketing Manager: Daniel Wong
Ramada International
Rates (approx.):
  Superior room $70 single, $79 double
  Deluxe room $79 single, $87 double
  Suite $173
284 rooms, 4 suites
Service charge 10%; tax 5%

This hotel is conveniently situated on Lockhart Road, within walking distance of the Hong Kong Convention and Exhibition Centre and a new Wanchai reclamation. It is just a five-minute taxi ride from both Core Central, the heart of the Central District, and Causeway Bay's shopping and business areas. You need not take a taxi, though, because all forms of major public transport—the Mass Transit Railway, trams, buses, and minibuses—are within each reach.

Attractive, clean, comfortable, and modestly priced, the inn has international direct-dial telephone service, color TV, radio, in-house music and movies, air conditioning, refrigerators, and mini-bars in all its rooms. Tea and coffee makers are also provided, and fruit baskets welcome guests.

Meals are served at Abe's Cafe, drinks at the Captain's Bar.

The full-service Business Centre offers secretarial, translation, interpretation, and courier services along with abundant communications equipment.

Kowloon

The most popular part of the Kowloon Peninsula is the area called Tsimshatsui, at the tip of the peninsula nearest Hong Kong Island.

Tsimshatsui is divided into eastern and western sections. In Tsimshatsui West are the top hotels, like the Peninsula, the Regent, the Hyatt Regency, and the Sheraton, along with many other good hotels. Here too are the Ocean Terminal–Ocean Centre and the New World shopping complexes, among the largest in the world. But most famous of all is Nathan Road, with its long rows of all kinds of shops. Also in the west are the ferry and ocean liner terminals.

Tsimshatsui East has fine hotels, too, like the Shangri-La, the Meridien, and the Holiday Inn Harbour View. It has shops and shopping complexes and a number of restaurants and places of entertainment as well.

Kowloon (Kau Lung) means "Nine Dragons." An ancient Chinese belief has it that dragons live on mountains. Eight of Kowloon's nine lived in the peninsula's eight hills, now flattened and pushed into the sea as reclaimed land. The ninth dragon was the boy emperor Ping, who visited the area eight hundred years ago. His quick-thinking prime minister told him there were in fact nine dragons in Kowloon, as, by legend, emperors *were* dragons.

AMBASSADOR
Nathan and Middle roads
Tsimshatsui West
Kowloon
Hong Kong
Telephone: (3) 666321
Telex: 43840 AMHOC HX
Cable: AMHOCOKL
Fax: (3) 690663
Reservations:
   In Hong Kong call (3) 666321
   In San Francisco call 1-800-227-0840
   Elsewhere in the USA call Utell International at
      1-800-9868
All major credit cards
General Manager: Peter Liu
Sales Manager: B. L. Khouw
Rates (approx.):

Standard room $76 single, $90 double
Medium room $90 single, $105 double
Deluxe room $101 single, $117 double
Suite: $240 or $346
315 rooms, 14 suites
Service charge 10%; tax 5%

One of the best things about the Ambassador is its location. On the corner of Nathan Road at Middle Road, it is right across the street from the Kowloon and the Peninsula hotels, and right at the beginning of the seemingly endless row of shops on Nathan Road.

The modern and spacious lobby is a favorite meeting place. The shopping arcade on the floor above has the usual assortment of tailors, jewelers, and souvenir shops, and a barbershop, beauty salon, travel agency, and medical clinic as well.

The guest rooms are pleasant and modern. Recently refurbished, they have every modern convenience, including air conditioning, color TV, multi-channel radio, international direct-dial telephone service with bathroom extensions, refrigerators with mini-bars, and private bathrooms with showers.

There are a number of places here to eat and drink. The Dynasty offers traditional dim sum service and a view of Hong Kong Harbour. The Caliph Room, open only for dinner, features an international cuisine and also has harbor views. Very popular is the Coffee Shop, open at all hours and the ideal spot for a quick cup of coffee, a light and fast meal, or a late-night snack at the end of a full day running around Hong Kong.

The Lobby Bar is a pleasant setting for a refreshing drink and a chat with friends or business associates.

CARITAS BIANCHI LODGE
4 Cliff Road
Yaumati
Kowloon
Hong Kong
Telephone: (3) 881111
Telex: 39762 CBLOD HX
Cable: BIANCHILOD
Reservations:
　In Hong Kong call (3) 881 111, ext. 206 or 300
　In the USA call (415) 692-9523 or (808) 261-1555

All major credit cards
General Manager: William C. C. Lee
Rates (approx.):
  Room $32 single, $42 double
  Suite $65
88 rooms, 2 suites
Service charge 10%; tax included

This is one of the few small, modern, and clean lodges in the Kowloon area of Hong Kong. On short Cliff Road next to New Man College, it is about a block from the famous Nathan Road, but more than a mile from Nathan Road's busiest area of shops and night spots. The finer hotels around Salisbury Road are also more than a mile away.

For those on a budget, of course, one of the hotel's attractions is its low rates.

All of the guest rooms are pleasant and modern and equipped with air conditioning, private bathrooms, telephones, refrigerators, in-house music, and color TV.

The plain and modest dining room serves both Western and Oriental food, at low prices. For example, a continental breakfast here is approximately $1.80, the American Breakfast is $2.60, lunch is $2.80, and dinner is $5.00.

Services at the hotel include cable, telex, and long-distance telephone; laundry and dry cleaning; limousine; tour arrangements; safe deposit boxes; photocopying; valet parking; and currency exchange.

GRAND HOTEL
14 Carnarvon Road
Kowloon
Hong Kong
Telephone: (3) 669331
Telex: 44838 GRAND HX
Cable: GRANDEL
Fax: (3) 7237840
Reservations:
  In Hong Kong call (3) 667626
All major credit cards
Managing Director: Kenneth Wong
Hotel Manager: Polly Hui
Director of Sales: Allan Chan
Grand Hotel Group
Rates (approx.):

Room $55–$94 single, $62–$101 double
Suite $156–$195
194 rooms, 4 suites
Service charge 10%; tax 5%

This attractive, clean, and reasonably priced hotel lies in the heart of Kowloon's shopping and entertainment district. Transportation to Hong Kong Island is convenient, and most of Kowloon's places of interest are within walking distance.

The lobby, with an attractive Oriental decor, provides delightful views of the crowds passing by. Here a guest relations officer is on duty to help you in any way, including arranging sightseeing tours of any part or all of Hong Kong.

The restaurants in the hotel are pleasant and cozy. The Grand Viking offers a delicious buffet for lunch and dinner, and live piano music in the evening. The Chatterbox coffee shop, open from 7:00 A.M. until midnight, features continental and Chinese dishes and light snacks. At the Target cocktail lounge, you can relax in the Western atmosphere while listening to soft popular music.

The rooms, decorated in pastel colors, are very comfortable and have well-stocked refrigerators and mini-bars. Tea and coffee and supplies for preparing them are also provided.

HOLIDAY INN GOLDEN MILE
P.O. Box 95555
50 Nathan Road
Tsimshatsui West
Kowloon
Hong Kong
Telephone: (3) 693111
Telex: HX56332
Cable: HOLIDAYINN
Fax: (3) 698016
Reservations:
  In Hong Kong call (3) 693111, ext. 299
  In the USA call 1-800-HOLIDAY
All major credit cards
General Manager: Jean Marc Charpenet
Director of Sales: Lawrence Wong
Holiday Inn Asia-Pacific
Rates (approx.):
  Standard room $102 single, $109 double

Superior room $114 single, $122 double
Deluxe room $127 single, $135 double
Standard suite $257
Golden Mile suite $577
Presidential suite $705
600 rooms, 9 suites
Service charge 10%; tax 5%

Yes, there is a Holiday Inn in Hong Kong. One of several Holiday Inns in Asia, this is certainly one of the better ones. Since its opening in 1975, the Holiday Inn Golden Mile has earned no fewer than nine awards for excellence from the company's international headquarters. Its consistently high occupancy rates prompted the opening of a second Hong Kong Holiday Inn, the Harbour View, in 1981.

Hardly like a motel back home, this is a modern sky-scraper hotel, with a great swimming pool, good restaurants, a very attractive lobby, and spacious, pleasant rooms.

All the guest rooms and suites have individually controlled air conditioning, private bathrooms, color TV with in-house movies, refrigerators, mini-bars, and direct-dial telephones. Same-day laundry and valet services and babysitting are available.

My favorite spot is the Baron's Table, where you can watch the chef prepare the mostly German meals as you listen to live piano music. Another popular dining room is the Loong Yuen, which features Chinese cuisine. The Café Vienna is a pleasant hideaway serving Austrian specialties and a variety of other Western and Eastern dishes as well.

As in most hotels in Hong Kong, a number of shops are here, occupying three levels. Their goods range from Chinese jade, gold ornaments, and jewelry to clothing for men and women.

The pride of the hotel is its huge Crystal Ballroom, which has no pillars. Refurbished in 1986, it is available for dinners, dinner-dances, and other private functions.

Guests seem most to enjoy the rooftop swimming pool and the hotel's Health Club, with massage services and saunas.

HOLIDAY INN HARBOUR VIEW
70 Mody Road
P.O. Box 98468
Tsimshatsui East
Kowloon
Hong Kong

Telephone: (3) 721-5161
Telex: HX 38670
Cable: INNVIEW
Fax: (3) 695672
Reservations:
  In Hong Kong call (3) 721-5161, ext. 2541
  In the USA call 1-800-HOLIDAY
All major credit cards
General Manager: Uwe Boeger
Front Office Manager: Edwin Siu
Director of Guest Services: Sian Griffiths
Sales Director: June Chui
Holiday Inn Asia-Pacific
Rates (approx.):
  Standard room $115 single, $126 double
  Superior room $135 single, $145 double
  Deluxe room $154 single, $164 double
  Harbor view room $173 single, $186 double
  Deluxe suite $295
  Harbor view suite $359
  Presidential suite $833
600 rooms, 9 suites
Service charge 10%; tax 5%

With a prime location in busy Tsimshatsui East overlooking the world-famous Victoria Harbour, this hotel is surrounded by shopping centers, commercial buildings, and recreational grounds. More than 60 percent of the rooms have a full view of the harbor. This is an exceptional Holiday Inn, not only because of its setting and view, its lovely guest rooms, and its fine dining rooms, but because of its special service. While looking through the hotel's fan mail, I found this note from a guest: "In lieu of expressing my appreciation with individual gratuities to your staff, I prefer to recognize the entire team. Therefore, please accept my enclosed check of $5,000 as a contribution to your annual staff celebration."

The hotel has a number of places to dine, including the Belvedere, an elegant restaurant specializing in fresh seafood and beef; the Mistral, a Mediterranean restaurant with an authentic European decor; Café Rendezvous and the adjoining Rendezvous Terrace, a coffee and tea lounge featuring an international menu; and the intimate Golden Carp Bar, with a dance floor and live entertainment nightly.

The hotel's function rooms can accommodate up to three hundred people for cocktails, conferences, or banquets.

On the top floor of the hotel is the Sun Court Pool and Health Centre. The pool, open to guests only, is surrounded with comfortable deck chairs and run by a well-trained staff, including lifeguards. The poolside snackbar serves refreshing and nutritious light snacks as well as cooling drinks.

The Health Centre is this hotel's headquarters for the Holiday Inn Asia-Pacific fitness campaign, launched in early 1985. It is equipped with an exercise machine, a bicycle, and a treadmill.

Designed by Don Ashton, the hotel's Business Centre has an extensive range of services and a highly qualified staff. Though tailored to the needs of business travelers, it also is of great service to offices nearby.

You might miss *my favorite spot* in this hotel if I didn't tell you about it. Hidden in the second basement, the Bonbonniere cake shop and confectionary has a selection of homemade cakes, pastries, chocolates, sweets, and breads.

People come from other hotels and the offices in the area to visit the Holiday Inn Harbour View Shopping Arcade. With twenty-seven shops and restaurants, it can certainly be a convenience if business prevents you from exploring Hong Kong's other shops.

THE HONGKONG HOTEL
3 Canton Road
Tsimshatsui West
Kowloon
Hong Kong
Telephone: (3)676011
Telex: 43838 HONHO HX
Cable: HONGHOTEL
Fax: (3) 7234850
Reservations:
   In Hong Kong call (3) 676011
All major credit cards
General Manager: Dieter Loewe
Director of Sales: Dick Wong
Marco Polo International Hotels
Rates (approx.):
   Economy room $71
   Standard room $100 single, $106 double
   Deluxe room $122–$154 single, $128–$154 double
   Studio $154–$173
   Suite $192–$641

744 rooms, 45 suites
Service charge 10%; tax 5%

Well known in the East, this hotel has been a favorite of many experienced world travelers for nearly twenty years. It has a somewhat restrained elegance, definite comfort, and pleasing cuisine.

Even fine old hotels need occasional refreshing, and the Hongkong recently added a veneer of glistening glass, marble, and finely polished wood throughout.

The nearly eight hundred rooms and suites are tastefully decorated, and most have spectacular views of the harbor. They are very comfortable, with king- or queen-sized beds, sofas, settees, writing desks, and well-stocked mini-bars. The Hotelevision channels offer a choice of six movies each evening. The rooms also have direct-dial telephone service and individually adjustable air conditioning.

Virtually every service a guest may require is within the hotel, including a heated, open-air swimming pool, a tropical roof garden (*my favorite spot*), a beauty salon, a barbershop, and a travel agency. There are limousines with English-speaking chauffeurs, a twenty-four-hour babysitting service, and free umbrellas if the weather turns inclement. The hotel will even wrap and mail your packages for you. The Business Centre is well equipped, and there is a selection of function rooms for all events.

The collection of restaurants is very good. The main one, the Bauhunia (named after Hong Kong's national flower) serves sumptuous breakfasts, luncheon buffets, and à la carte continental dinners. There is live entertainment in the evening, a small dance floor, and, best of all, panoramic views of the harbor and of Victoria Peak.

The Chinese words *tai pan* mean "big boss," the unofficial title given to leading businessmen. Tai Pan is also the name of the hotel's premier dining room. This excellent grill offers fresh lobsters from Boston and New Zealand, the finest U.S. beef, and fine wines from around the world. There is live piano music as well.

In the lobby, the Coffee Shop serves all three meals and snacks and is a favorite spot for people watchers.

The fun spot is the Spice Market, where you may sit under the palms and look out over Victoria Harbour as you sample exotic foods of Asia. At lunch and dinner, you may select from a fabulous buffet or a large à la carte menu of authentic local dishes.

The Gun Bar, with a Victorian mood, offers a Pub Lunch-eon featuring exotic curries and a daily roast served from a cart. The Sunday Brunch here is popular. Musicians from around the world entertain after dark, into the early morn-ing hours.

When making reservations, ask about membership in the Tai Pan Club. Privileges include a 20 percent discount on published room rates at all Marco Polo hotels in Singapore and Hong Kong; guaranteed reservations if made seventy-two hours before arrival; upgraded rooms, when available; quick check-in and check-out; complimentary in-house movies; and other amenities.

HOTEL REGAL MERIDIEN
71 Mody Road
Tsimshatsui East
Kowloon
Hong Kong
Telephone: (3) 722-1818
Telex: 40955 HOMRO HX
Cable: HOMRO
Fax: (3) 723-6413
Reservations:
  In Hong Kong call (3) 669996 or (3) 722-1818
  In the USA call 1-800-543-4300
All major credit cards
General Manager: Axel Goerlach
Front Office Manager: Den Lee
Director of Marketing: Ronald Tze
Meridien Hotels International
Rates (approx.):
  Standard room $133 single, $140 double
  Superior room $146 single, $153 double
  Deluxe room $159 single, $165 double
  Meridien Club room $154
  Junior suite $231
  Superior suite $256
  Regal Suite $449
  Presidential Suite $833
551 rooms, 34 suites
Service charge 10%; tax 5%

In the heart of Kowloon's newest and exciting business and entertainment section, this hotel is owned by Regal Hotels International and operated by the French chain Meridien.

Opened in May 1982, it glistens, from the beautiful marble-clad lobby to the guest rooms. Two cultures are well blended here: eighteenth-century French antiques and Louis XVI-style furniture are set harmoniously alongside Chinese works of art.

Designed with luxury in mind, the hotel's guest rooms and suites are tastefully decorated in peach and celadon. Matching chintz bedspreads and curtains add the European touch. All rooms have marble in the bathrooms, and all are fully air-conditioned with independent temperature control. In each room is a color TV, a bedside panel with a six-band radio and a digital alarm clock, a mini-bar and refrigerator, and a range of Hermes toiletries. Two direct-dial telephones and a good-sized work desk are here for the business traveler. The larger suites also have marble Jacuzzi baths. The luxurious Presidential Suite, with two bedrooms on the hotel's fourteenth floor, is magnificently furnished in the French Empire style.

The entire twelfth floor is occupied by the Meridien Club. For extra comfort and service it is ideal, particularly for business travelers. Among the special amenities are complimentary coffee and croissants in the Club Lounge from 7:00 until 10:00 A.M., complimentary cocktails for members and their guests from 5:00 to 7:00 P.M., and free use of the club's Jacuzzi.

For me, the delight of the hotel is its dining rooms. The cuisine is superb and the service impeccable.

At the Restaurant de France the finest of French haute cuisine is flawlessly presented.

Decorated with polished brass and etched glass, La Brasserie is modeled after a fin de siècle Parisian brasserie. This is *my favorite spot*, with delicious French country-style cooking at reasonable prices. The atmosphere is bustling and informal, and hearty appetites are satisfied.

In the midst of the hotel's shopping arcade is Le Grand Café, a coffee shop providing a wide variety of Asian and Western dishes. It is the place for a quick but pleasing meal.

The majestic Regal Seafood Restaurant serves the freshest seafood, including Hong Kong's great specialty, shark fins. Lunch features dim sum, with a choice of the finest Chinese teas. Both locals and guests seem to favor this dining room.

The hotel has two elegant and comfortable lounge bars. La Bagatelle, in the main lobby, has both contemporary and Louis XVI-style furniture. Floor-to-ceiling windows give guests a view of the neighboring park. Le Rendezvous, on the first floor, is a wood-paneled lounge-bar with a collection of original paintings and antiques. Every evening except Sunday there is live music and dancing.

For those who enjoy the night life, in the second basement of the hotel is the Hollywood East Discotheque, which attracts the local jet set and guests alike.

Other facilities include a fully equipped business center, a women's health club, a beauty salon, and five floors of shops. The concierge, with crossed keys on the lapel of his frocked coat, is on hand in the lobby. The guest relations officers, in couturier-designed uniforms and seated at splendid Louis XVI desks, are ready to ensure all guests superlative service.

HYATT REGENCY HONG KONG
67 Nathan Road
Tsimshatsui West
Kowloon
Hong Kong
Telephone: (3) 66232
Telex: HX 43127
Cable: HYATT HONG KONG
Fax: (852) 123-48050
Reservations:
  In Hong Kong call (3) 662321
  In Nebraska call 1-800-228-9001
  In Alaska and Hawaii call 1-800-228-9005
  Elsewhere in the USA call 1-800-228-9000
All major credit cards
Manager: Juergen Wolter
General Manager: Larry Tchou
Concierge: Roger Wong
Director of Sales and Marketing: Colleen Toy
Hyatt International
Rates (approx.):
  Standard room $89 single, $99 double
  Superior room $122 single, $132 double
  Deluxe room $135 single, $145 double
  Regency Club room $180
  Executive suite $321
  Regency Club suites $385
  Presidential Suites $641
706 rooms, 17 suites
Service charge 10%; tax 5%

In the heart of the busiest section of Nathan Road, the Hyatt Regency is one of Hong Kong's older hotels, built about twenty years ago. In July 1985 its managers decided they had a lot of catching up to do with modern times and the competition. They launched a two-year, $20 million renovation program, to transform this popular 723-room hotel beyond recognition.

It wasn't easy. For example, as always in such important matters, the *fung shui*, or geomancer, was consulted (see page 104). He informed the hotel's managers that while it was fine to proceed immediately with the rest of the renovations, work on the main section of the hotel's new lobby, together with its relocated Chin Chin Bar, should be started precisely on February 14. And so it was.

By the end of 1987, the Hyatt Regency Hong Kong had become one of the more luxurious hotels in Hong Kong. The guest rooms are now truly beautiful. Their new color scheme combines earth tones with subtle shades of apricot and celadon. New amenities include central consoles for operating the color TV, radio, air conditioning, and lighting; small safes for guests' valuables; hairdryers in the bathrooms; and writing desks.

The Regency Club opened two new floors at the top of the seventeen-story hotel. They include an expanded lounge, where complimentary breakfast and cocktails are served; a private conference room; and separate restrooms for guests of Regency Club patrons. This Hyatt concept of a "hotel within a hotel" is very popular with business travelers seeking high-quality service. I especially liked the extensive collection of Oriental antiques displayed throughout the Regency Club floors (as well as in other areas of the hotel).

This hotel has now caught up with the other Hyatts around the world in having a fine collection of places to eat and to drink. To Hyatt regulars, the names are familiar.

Hugo's provides excellent continental cuisine well served.

Nathans, open around the clock, is especially popular with Hong Kong's smart, fashion-conscious younger set. Nathans has "moods" rather than mealtimes, five each day, each with a different menu.

The Chinese Restaurant, the Hyatt chain's first, opened late in 1986. It has gained a local reputation for first-class Cantonese cuisine, emphasizing fresh seafood and dim sum.

The long-popular Café, modeled on a typical Parisian street café, offers good service and reasonable prices.

The Chin Chin Bar has been moved, but its atmosphere

is the same. Patrons who want to savor the world of Suzie Wong can still find it here. Off the new lobby, the Chin Chin has a handsome decor combining natural teak paneling with marble from Italy and Spain.

The new lobby is also elegant. It too has teak paneling and marble, along with an elevated ceiling, discrete lighting, lush greenery, and fresh flowers.

The expanded Hyatt Business Centre is off the main lobby. It now offers complete office facilities and services.

There are thirty new shops on the lobby, ground, and basement levels, offering the latest in clothing, jewelry, souvenirs, and so on. This is one area I felt needed renovation, and renovations have been made.

You may want to seek out some of the fine pieces in the hotel's art collection. In the Chinese Restaurant are three large landscape paintings that the hotel commissioned from Wong Chung Fong, a well-known Hong Kong painter. These are complemented by seventy-four Chinese fan paintings from the eighteenth, nineteenth, and twentieth centuries.

In the Café are nine paintings, of a variety of subjects, by the Cantonese Deng Yan Yong (1902–1978). He is widely respected as a leader of twentieth-century developments in Chinese painting.

And in the foyer is a pair of nineteenth-century wooden door guardians, with a lacquer and gilt finish. Three seated figures of the same era, with gilt finish, dominate the main section of the Reception Desk.

If you do not find it in your room, be sure to ask for your copy of *The Hyatt Regency Hong Kong Jogger's Map*—even if you don't jog. It is the best and simplest map we found of Tsimshatsui. Follow it to the Seaside Promenade on the harbor, a popular place for strollers and joggers that offers one of the best views in the area.

THE KOWLOON HOTEL
19–21 Nathan Road
Tsimshatsui West
Kowloon
Hong Kong
Telephone: (3) 698698
Telex: 47604 KLNHL HX
Cable: KLNHOTELHK
Fax: (3) 698698, ext. 8383
Reservations:
   In the USA call the Peninsula Group at (312) 263-6069

All major credit cards
General Manager: Niklaus Leuenberger
Sales Manager: Virginia Wu
Concierge: Paul Ching
Peninsula Group
Rates (approx.):
   Superior double room $69 single, $73 double
   Superior twin room $73 single, $78 double
   Harbor-view or double or twin room $80 single, $85
      double
   Suite $135 single, $155 double
740 rooms, 30 suites
Service charge 10%; tax 5%

When the Kowloon opened in 1986, it represented a new concept in hotel design—to provide top-quality but space-efficient accommodations for budget-conscious modern travelers.

Wholly owned by Hongkong and Shanghai Hotels, this is the second Hong Kong property managed by the Peninsula Group, whose grand old Peninsula Hotel is just in front of the Kowloon Hotel. It is on Nathan Road's Golden Mile, famous for its array of shops and its night life.

The eighteen-story building has 770 guest rooms and suites, tastefully decorated with lighting and colors that make the rather small rooms seem more spacious. The triangular bay windows not only are attractive, but they maximize the amount of available sunlight.

This hotel is an electronic buff's delight. Each guest room is equipped with a computer terminal, called a Telecentre, that provides access to a local map, a current weather report, financial data, and similar information. Incoming messages and the guest's hotel bill can also be checked through the Telecentre. An electronic headboard control panel allows the guest to regulate room temperature, lighting, stereo radio, and television at the touch of the proper button.

State-of-the-art electronic gadgetry is also abundant in the hotel's comprehensive Business Centre, which provides word processors, electronic typewriters, telex, telefacsimile, dictation machines, and all kinds of audio-visual equipment.

On the second floor are most of the restaurants and bars. *My favorite spot* is the Window Café, a split-level restaurant serving international cuisine from 6:30 A.M., with a daily luncheon buffet. The cozy Pizzeria, open for lunch and dinner, serves Italian specialties, including a pasta and salad buffet at lunch. The Middle Row, a warm and convivial lounge bar, is popular for its continental breakfast, roast beef luncheons, and live entertainment in the evening.

In the basement is the Wan Loong Court Chinese restaurant, open from 11:00 A.M. until midnight.

Also in the basement is a shopping arcade, housing more than thirty specialty shops and famous-brand boutiques, including Christian Dior and Celine.

Another nice thing, especially for business people, is the fleet of air-conditioned, chauffeur-driven 250D Mercedes Benz cars. These are available for hire by the hour or day for the trip to the airport, for a business appointment, or even for a personal sightseeing tour of Hong Kong.

THE MARCO POLO HONG KONG
Harbour City
Canton Road
Tsimshatsui West
Kowloon
Hong Kong
Telephone: (3) 721-5111
Telex: 40077 MPHK HX
Cable: MARPOLOTEL
Fax: (3) 7217049
Reservations:
    In Hong Kong call (3) 721-5111, ext. 112
All major credit cards
General Manager: Bruno Simeoni
Concierge: Paul Sin
Director of Sales: John Lai
Marco Polo International
Rates:
    Available on request
441 rooms, 56 suites
Service charge 10%; tax 5%

This hotel is in the heart of Harbour City, which calls itself "the largest shopping and commercial development in Asia." Within the complex are, besides the hotel, more than six hundred shops.

The Marco Polo caters to the business executive. The Business Centre, one of the most complete in the city, is open daily from 9:00 A.M. until 5:00 P.M., and its services are available other times by arrangement with the Guest Relations Officer. The multilingual staff graciously handles any interpreting or translating task. There are private offices, conference rooms, and function rooms, too. Through a package deal, a minimum of fifteen people can have the seminar room, morning and afternoon pastries and finger sandwiches, luncheon at La Brasserie, a message service, and equipment such as a slide projector, a movie projector, video and audio equipment, flip charts, screens, and a blackboard—all for about fourteen dollars per person.

My wife and I felt the rooms to be a bit small, but efficient and pleasant. Even the suites seemed to be more efficient than spacious.

My favorite spot is the hotel's Patisserie, designed in the style of a typical European tea room. It is a good place for lunch, featuring a daily carving and a salad buffet. And the rich continental snacks are irresistible. The Patisserie is outside the hotel proper in Shop 268 of the World Shipping Center, Harbour City.

La Brasserie, on the lower lobby floor, serves all three meals. With checked tablecloths and a pleasant ambiance, it features French provincial cooking.

The Coffee Mill, also on the lower lobby floor, has a colorful Latin American decor and an international menu. Open from 6:00 A.M. until 2:00 A.M., it is an ideal spot for light refreshments and late-night snacks. It also serves a weekend buffet lunch and dinner.

Off the lobby is the Tartan Bar. The Scottish decor includes wood paneling and a collection of tartan wall panels. Drinks are half price during happy hours.

For a discounted room rate and other special privileges, ask about membership in Marco Polo International Hotels' Tai Pan Club (see page 85).

NEW WORLD HOTEL
22 Salisbury Road
Tsimshatsui West
Kowloon
Hong Kong
Telephone: (3) 694111
Telex: 35860 NWHTL
Cable: NWHOTEL
Fax: (3) 699387
Reservations:
  In Hong Kong call (3) 694111
  In the USA call C and C China Express at
    (415) 397-8811
All major credit cards

General Manager: Hans Stettler
Concierge: Peter Chan
Sales Manager: Hugo Miguel
New World Hotels International
Rates (approx.): $ ₁₁ ₈.
  Economy room $59–$68 single, $64–$73 double
  Standard room $92–$106 single, $97–$112 double
  Medium room $100–$115 single, $105–$121 double
  Deluxe room $110–$128 single, $115–$133 double
  Suite $128–$321
691 rooms, 38 suites
Service charge 10%; tax 5%

This recent arrival among the hotels in Tsimshatsui West is a part of the New World Complex, which also contains four hundred shops, apartments, and a huge multilevel garage. Near the Regent Hotel and just across the street from the Sheraton and the Peninsula, the complex faces the famous shopping boulevard Nathan Road. Close by are the Star Ferry and other transportation to all parts of Hong Kong.

First opened in December 1978, this first-class hotel is designed to fill the needs of budget-minded as well as wealthy travelers. No other Asian hotel at this writing has such a wide range of rates starting at fifty-nine dollars.

The New World Development Company used the American talent of Chicago's Skidmore, Owings, and Merrill to design the hotel and the rest of the complex.

Each room has a bathroom, air-conditioning, direct-dial telephone service, a color TV, a refrigerator, and an alarm clock. Available services include babysitting, hairdressing, same-day valet service, package wrapping and mailing, and secretarial services.

In keeping with the hotel's role of being all things to all people, its restaurants are greatly varied. On the fourth floor are four: The Park Lane serves superb continental meals, with jet-fresh seafoods and meats, charcoal-grilled and roasted by a Swiss master chef and his crew. The Panorama, whose floor-to-ceiling windows give a magnificent view of Victoria Harbour, is a lovely spot at sundown. Here are daily carved-meat luncheons and an à la carte dinner menu. The casual Patio Coffee Shop offers Western and Chinese dishes for all meals as well as snacks. A buffet dinner is available daily, and a luncheon buffet is served on Sundays. On the same floor is the Poolside Terrace, set within forty thousand square feet of lush tropical landscaping, including sun decks, fountains, and a fabulous swimming pool. *My favorite spot*, the Poolside Terrace features a light menu and is an ideal place to recover from sightseeing fatigue.

Another delightful place to relax is the eighteenth-floor Penthouse cocktail lounge. Besides panoramic views, it features a special projector that beams twelve hundred tiny rays of light at the ceiling, to look like the Milky Way galaxy.

The fifth-floor New World Sauna (for men only—sorry) is one of the largest health clubs in Hong Kong. The women's New World Fitness and Dance Centre also has saunas, as well as a gymnasium with dance classes and the latest in exercise equipment.

Faces is one of the more exciting discos in the city. Guests can dance, watch from a stand-up bar, or entertain privately in one of six glass-enclosed rooms with individual sound controls.

Well named, the hotel is a new world in all respects.

THE PARK HOTEL HONG KONG
61–65 Chatham Road South
Tsimshatsui West
Kowloon
Hong Kong
Telephone: (3) 661371
Telex: 45740 PARKH HX
Cable: PARKHOTEL
Fax: (3) 739-7259
Reservations:
  In Hong Kong call (3) 661371
  In New York call Utell International at (212) 757-2981
  Elsewhere in the USA call Utell International at
    1-800-223-9868
All major credit cards
General Manager: Dennis Hui
Deputy Manager: Viola Cheung
Rates (approx.):
  Standard room $64 single, $77 double
  Medium room $77 single, $90 double
  Superior room $90 single, $102 double
  Deluxe room $102 single, $115 double
  Junior suite $265
  Deluxe suite $320
450 rooms, 40 suites
Service charge 10%; tax 5%

This comfortable, modest-priced hotel is right in the center of Kowloon's shopping area—an ideal location for those who want to explore the shops on Nathan Road and nearby streets.

The guest rooms are clean, comfortable, and adequately large. Each has its own bathroom, color TV, and refrigerator.

There are ample places to eat in the hotel. The ground-floor Coffee Shop serves quick snacks, a daily buffet lunch, and buffet dinner on Saturdays and Sundays. The Park Chinese Restaurant serves Chinese meals, and, on the eleventh floor, the Poinsettia Room serves European food along with live music in the evening. It also has a comfortable lounge for pre-dinner drinks. At the end of the richly carpeted lobby is the Marigold Bar, with live music in the evening and a happy hour.

The eleventh-floor conference room has all the necessary equipment for conferences and other events as well. The sixteenth-floor Peony Room, with a panoramic view of Hong Kong, is available for all kinds of private functions.

THE PENINSULA
Salisbury Road
Kowloon
Hong Kong
Telephone: (3) 666251
Telex: 43821 PEN HX
Cable: PENHOTE HK
Fax: (3) 7224170
Reservations:
  In Hong Kong call (3) 666251
  In the USA call (213) 640-7836 or (213) 640-8491
    (Los Angeles) or (312) 263-6069 (Chicago)
All major credit cards
General Manager: Eric A. Waldburger
Concierge: Egon Letschka
Peninsula Group
Rates (approx.):
  Room $173–$186 single, $250–$269 double
  Suite $282–$1,667
190 rooms, 20 suites
Service charge 10%; tax 5%

More than a luxurious place to stay, this hotel is an integral part of the community. It is the place to meet, the place to dine, the place to shop, the place to have a cocktail or tea.

It is even a place of history. The Peninsula's site was chosen in 1841—nearly two years before Hong Kong became an official British colony—when a Parsee merchant from Macau bought the land. With others he formed the Hong Kong Hotel Company, which became the Hong Kong and Shanghai Hotels organization, and, later, the Peninsula Group.

Described early on as "the most commodious and best appointed hotel in the Far East, affording unequalled accommodations to travellers and others," the Hong Kong Hotel, as it was first known, opened in 1892. Rates were seventy-five dollars a month for board and lodging, forty-five dollars for lodging alone. The hotel seemed so much a palace that its telegraph address was "Kremlin Hong Kong."

Guests first arrived at the Peninsula, as it is today, in 1927, a year before the hotel actually opened. They were British troops, brought in to protect Hong Kong from a perceived threat from the forces of Chiang Kai-shek. Yet unfurnished, the hotel made a perfect barracks for the companies of Coldstream Guards and Devonshires. During their stay of about a year, they drilled up and down Nathan Road every morning. This, a reporter wrote, "struck terror into the Chinese hearts because the Guards regiment were all over six feet."

The Peninsula was situated on what was then the "unsmart" side of Hong Kong Harbour, for simple and practical reasons. The trains from Europe, via Russia and China, ended their two-and-a-half-week journey at the red brick and mahogany railway station just down the road. And the ocean liners were all quartered at the Kowloon docks, just at the hotel's doorstep. The Pen, as the hotel was nicknamed, soon became the center of of society's whirl, bringing it to the hotel's side of the harbor.

The Peninsula's important role continued through wars and peace. Renovations were necessary to recover from the outrages of the various times: In 1945, after a Victory Ball to celebrate the surrender of Japan, the hotel underwent extensive repairs. Again in 1963, because of the competition from new big hotels like the Hilton, more renovations brought the Pen into the jet age. And in the eighties, with the opening of the ultramodern Regent across the street, the Pen has undergone renovation of both its public rooms and guest rooms. Half the guest rooms at a time have had to close to keep the Pen the best in Hong Kong.

Today, as the flagship hotel of the Peninsula Group, the Peninsula is one of the world's truly grand hotels. It maintains a standard of personal service that has largely disappeared throughout the world. With a loyal and caring staff of six hundred, the hotel maintains a staff-guest ratio of three to one—a ratio rare in European, American, and even Asian hotels. Over seventy members of the staff have been with the hotel more than twenty-five years, several for as long as fifty-five years.

You feel the Pen's sophistication as soon as you arrive at the airport, when the hotel's chauffeur takes your bags and guides you to your Rolls Royce, one of a fleet of nine Silver Shadow IIs.

This feeling continues as you walk between the gigantic marble lions at the hotel's entrance and through the glass doors, which are painted with two fierce, richly attired warriors. Pairs such as these adorn the entrance of every Chinese household, humble or noble, to protect all who dwell within from the evil spirits of the outside world.

Then you enter the lobby. With its elegant columns and regal ambience, this, *my favorite spot*, is famous the world over as Asia's foremost meeting place—for lovers, business people, and high society.

It is a favorite subject of novelists. In *Soldier of Fortune*, Ernest K. Gann tells what it was like in the early fifties:

> The lobby of the Peninsula is a busy place, but the pace is leisurely and the hum of conversation is seldom noticeable above the remote whirring of the overhead fans.
>
> There is a division down the exact middle of the great room and though it is invisible, it is there as surely as if it were wrought of steel. . . .
>
> The division begins at the entrance door and runs straight across to the reception desk, bisecting a wide thoroughfare between the tables. The right side of the lobby is almost invariably pure British and in the mornings is relatively unpopulated except for a few eccentrics who prefer eating their kippers and reading their China Mail in public rather than in the privacy of their rooms. About noon and continuing through the day the space slowly accumulates life, for here the older and more solidly emplaced China hands meet to transact what crumbs of business there may be left for white men in Asia. Or they simply have a quiet tonic and talk about home. Their ladies, too, frequent this space. At late lunch and teatime they are most evident, sitting like wan pink flowers in

bunches of four or five. They almost never join their men and are rarely seen after dark. The waiters on this side are all called "boy" regardless of their age. . . .

The tables are the same on the other side of the barrier and the waiters are the same, but the patrons are of another planet. Some of them are seated at their favorite tables by ten o'clock in the morning where they remain all through the day and a large part of the night. These are the regulars and though they live elsewhere, the Peninsula is their true home, their office, their club and their windows on the passing world. The Chinese sit on this side of the barrier. The Australians and the Indians, the Siamese, the French and the Eurasians all maintain outposts here and mix without prejudice or rancor.

Even with the onslaught of Americans (more than half the hotel's guests now come from North America), little has changed in the lobby. There is still a wrong and a right side, depending who you are, and somehow you sense it, although no one explains it to you. Americans do, at times, sit on the mainly Asian side. But the regulars never sit on the wrong side. Never.

The spaciousness and luxuriousness of the guest rooms reflect a less utilitarian time. They have every convenience: a color TV, a bar and a refrigerator, a hair dryer at the dressing table, personal messages on the TV screen, in-house movies and financial news, and a laser video player with six discs (and more available from the concierge). For the toilette are bathrobes, Georgio Armani toiletries, a sewing kit, laundry detergent, a shower cap—and a bidet, a stall shower as well as a tub, and a telephone in the bathroom. Room attendants greet you with Chinese tea. They will even unpack your things, draw your bath, clean your shoes, and get your clothes cleaned or pressed, at your request, all with astonishing speed.

Guests are mystified by the fact that, although no attendant ever intrudes while they are in the room, they have only to leave for a short time, at almost any hour, to return to find it freshly tidied. (We discovered the secret: When a guest enters the room, an attendant puts a small rubber piece between the jamb and the door. When he sees the rubber dislodged, he enters to tidy the room, replace towels and do whatever else seems necessary.)

On the mezzanine and in corridors off the lobby are Hong Kong's most prestigious boutiques. Whether it be Gucci's or Loewe's or another designer's line, a fine jewelry shop, or a tailor who can create a suit made to measure in a few days, the very best is here.

The Peninsula has several of Hong's Kong's finest restaurants.

The most famous is Gaddi's, named after the first Swiss general manager of the Peninsula, Leo Gaddi. Opened in 1953, it has gained an international reputation for being not only the finest restaurant in Hong Kong but one of the best in the East. Gaddi's is exceptional for both its fine French cuisine and its impeccable service, directed by the maître d'hôtel of nearly twenty years, Rolf Heiniger (who has an uncanny memory—he remembered us between visits two years apart). The luxurious decor features crystal chandeliers, custom-made by Christofle of Paris, and priceless Chinese antiques.

Chesa is reminiscent of a rustic Swiss inn. The menu features authentic Alpine specialties and dishes inspired by other European cuisines as well.

The recently refurbished Verandah Grill, the hotel's main dining room, includes a gleaming copper grill. The menu features, besides grilled specialties, fresh seafood and continental dishes for breakfast, lunch, and dinner. The luncheon buffet is very good and extensive. The Verandah Lounge-Bar, with Regency-style furniture and sweeping colonnades, leads to a light and gracious room where guests can enjoy a cup of tea with snacks and pastries. Open until 2:00 P.M., this is a most relaxing spot.

The Spring Moon Chinese Restaurant provides elegant Cantonese meals in luxurious surroundings at lunch and dinner.

The Inagiku Japanese Restaurant displays the beauty and simplicity of Japanese culinary arts in an authentic setting.

The Club is a sophisticated night spot with discotheque dancing.

The hotel's one and only *gran luxe* suite is the Marco Polo. Well over two thousand square feet, it is being refurbished at this writing, at a cost of one million dollars. When completed, it will resemble the spacious living and dining room of a grand manor house in Europe. Guests here will have twenty-four-hour private valet and a chauffeur-driven Rolls Royce.

Keeping up with the times and the competition, the hotel will have a business center and a health club by the end of 1988.

These changes are part of the $49 million facelift announced in August 1987. The plans call for the erection of two towers and a change in the hotel's famous U-shaped façade, which I suspect will be protested by many old-time guests.

Eighty percent of the hotel's business is repeat. No wonder.

Imperial
580 HK
& 880. HK
Eaton

THE PRINCE HOTEL
Harbour City
Canton Road
Tsimshatsui West
Kowloon
Hong Kong
Telephone: (3) 723-7788
Cable: HTLPRINZHK
Fax: (3) 7215545
Reservations:
   In Hong Kong call (3) 723-7788 or (3) 731-8318
   In the USA call Utell International at 1-800-9868
All major credit cards   *1-800-223-9868*
General Manager: William A. Reich
Marco Polo International Hotels
Rates (approx):
   Standard room $74 single, $80 double
   Superior room $100 single, $106 double
   Deluxe room $108 single, $115 double
   Suite $179
350 rooms, 51 suites
Service charge 10%; tax 5%

Along with its sisters, the Hongkong Hotel and the Marco Polo Hong Kong, the Prince is situated in the gigantic Canton Road complex that includes Harbour City, a popular shopping, commercial, and residential center with more than one thousand retail stores, restaurants, and services under one roof.

This hotel is ideal for the no-nonsense guest wanting everything within easy reach. Adjacent to the spectacular waterfront, it overlooks not only the harbor but also the greenery of Kowloon Park. The Kai Tak airport is only a twenty-minute drive away. You can walk directly from the hotel into Harbour City, and from there air-conditioned walkways take you to two of Hong Kong's other major shopping complexes, the Ocean Centre and the Ocean Terminal. For the business traveler, the hotel is virtually at the center of Kowloon's commercial district, and only about fifteen minutes, by the Star Ferry, from Hong Kong Island's central business area. For the tourist, the hotel is close to the MTR, Hong Kong's modern underground railway, which takes visitors to famous sights. The main railway station is close by, making possible trips into the People's Republic of China.

The large, ultramodern guest rooms have either one queen-size or two double beds. Many have a good view of the attractive Kowloon Park. Each has a roomy sitting area, a big desk, a mini-bar and refrigerator, a color TV with current movies on the Hotelevision channel, international direct-dial telephone, individually controlled air conditioning, and a pleasant bathroom. Besides the usual toiletries, sewing kit, magazines, and English-language newspaper, a bath-robe is provided in the suites. Guests may use the swim-ming pool of the neighboring Hongkong Hotel.

Opened in 1984, the Prince was built especially for busi-ness travelers. For their needs, the Businessmen's Corner is just off the gleaming marble lobby. This center can handle all secretarial, translating, and photocopying requirements, and it offers the latest telecommunication services. The ho-tel also has three function rooms available for conferences, training seminars, or private parties.

The Rib Room, the hotel's main restaurant and grill room, is a luxurious setting for lunch or dinner. It is on the third floor, at the top of the sweeping staircase from the lobby. At the butcher's counter, you may select from cuts of U.S. Angus or Kobe beef or the finest New Zealand lamb. The delightful Sunday and holiday buffet brunch costs about ten dollars. The business lunch, available Monday through Saturday, costs about eight and a half dollars.

With its red tiled floor and Moroccan arches, the Coffee Shop is a pleasant place to enjoy breakfast, lunch, or dinner, or a snack any time.

In addition to popular drinks, the Tavern, with a Victorian decor, serves what it calls Super Sandwiches—and they are. This is a very pleasant lunch-time meeting place for business executives.

The Lobby Lounge, with a spacious modern decor, over-looks busy Canton Road. During the late afternoon and evening a pianist entertains.

My favorite spots here are actually outside the hotel. They are the Ocean Centre and the Ocean Terminal, which to-gether have not only a thousand shops, but three movie houses and two discotheques as well. It's like having both the great Harrod's and Bloomingdale's next door!

For a discounted room rate and other special privileges, ask about membership in Marco Polo International Hotels' Tai Pan Club (see page 85).

THE REGENT
Salisbury Road
Tsimshatsui West
Kowloon
Hong Kong
Telephone: (3) 721-1211
Telex: 37134 REG HX
Cable: REGENTEL
Fax: (3) 7231410
Reservations:
   In Hong Kong call (3) 721-1211
   In the USA call Regent International Hotels at
      1-800-545-4000
All major credit cards
General Manager: Rudolf Greiner
Concierge: Herbert Croft
Director of Sales: Rose Kettle
Regent International Hotels
Rates (approx):
   Room $152–$220
   Suite $240–$400
531 rooms, 30 deluxe suites, 43 junior suites
Service charge 10%; tax 5%

On spectacular Victoria Harbour in Tsimshatsui West, the Regent opened in October 1980. The most luxurious hotel in Hong Kong, it is always at least 90 percent occupied. It is also a major tourist attraction.

Arriving guests enter a tree-lined driveway that opens into a large cobblestone piazza. Parked here is the Regent's fleet of twelve sleek slate-gray Daimlers, ready to fetch a guest arriving at Kai Tak, Hong Kong's international airport, or to take someone on a shopping tour.

Walking through the large glass front doors, you feel like a French Louis entering his court at Versailles, or the maharajah of Jaipur entering his palace. You face a forty-foot-high glass wall at the end of the most magnificent hotel lobby you have ever seen. Through this glass wall is an incomparable view of Hong Kong Island.

This view of Hong Kong is not just an architectural stroke of genius. Before the hotel was built, a *fung sui* man was brought in. He is an Oriental geomancer whose responsibility is to determine the most auspicious location for a building, its doors and windows, and even its furniture. He exorcises evil spirits, helps select a patron god, and erects shrines behind the structure where the god can be properly honored.

The entire hotel staff was involved in selecting a god. After some discussion they chose Kuan Ti, who is known for his dedication to loyalty and righteousness. He also had good references for the job: he serves as the patron god of the Hong Kong police department. So, every day joss sticks are lighted at the shrines of Kuan Ti, and a lamp burns perpetually at each of his shrines.

The geomancer also had to make sure that the nine dragons of Kowloon had enough room to pass from the peninsula's hills to the harbor for their daily baths. He had the architects design a glass-walled main floor (glass is not considered an obstruction) so the spirit creatures can reach the water.

The geomancer advised wisely. When I first entered the Regent I stood speechless, overwhelmed by the glistening marble floor of the expansive lobby; the magnificent wide, winding marble staircase; and, most of all, the fantastic view through the windows of the world's most dramatic harbor.

Seventy percent of the hotel's rooms also have this view. The rest look out on the cobblestone piazza and a landscaped pool terrace.

Arriving in your room is an adventure in itself. After escorting you there, the assistant manager returns with tea, chocolate pralines, and a platter of Oriental and Western fruits.

The rooms and suites offer luxury in contemporary style. All have air conditioning, refrigerators, international direct-dial telephone, color TV, and built-in sound systems for AM-FM and in-house music. There are multivoltage plugs for European and U.S. appliances, and three telephones per guest room—one next to the bed, one on the desk, and one in the bathroom.

The bathrooms, of rose marble and glass, are beautiful. Each has an enclosed shower and a sunken bathtub. Luxurious terry cloth bathrobes and slippers and a selection of toiletries are provided.

Each floor has its own butler service, reached by pressing a call button next to the bed or desk. There is a butler for each suite and for each group of three or four rooms. Although all food comes from the main kitchen, a butler's service pantry is on each floor.

The hotel's health club is so popular that it has recently been expanded from four to six private rooms. In each is a deep, solid granite Jacuzzi, clad in Brazilian marble, and a walk-in steam sauna-shower. A heat lamp has been added over the massage bed. For only forty dollars, guests can spend about an hour and a half luxuriating here.

The swimming pool, at 2,102 square feet, is the largest in Hong Kong. Since it is on the third floor, swimmers have a view of the harbor.

For business travelers, the elaborate Business Centre offers secretarial services and an extensive reference library on Hong Kong and local business resources.

As do many of the hotels in Hong Kong, the Regent has its own shopping mall, which includes a number of fine boutiques. And just next door is the gigantic New World Centre, one of the largest shopping centers in Asia, with over four hundred stores ranging from souvenir emporiums to fine jewelry shops. The Regent shops are more elegant, but those in the New World Centre are fun.

In describing the Regent as one of the ten great hotels in the world, George Lang wrote in *Travel and Leisure* (April 1987) that "if the *Guide Michelin* were to come to Asia, at least two of the Regent's four restaurants would get two or three stars." Although that venerable guide has never given more than two stars to a hotel dining room—and those only to three hotel dining rooms in Paris—Lang, I feel, is correct in his enthusiasm. *My favorite spots*, the Plume and the Lain Ching Heen, are magnificent restaurants.

You are welcomed at the Plume with champagne-mir, champagne with a kir-like splash of myrtille. Then, hot Indian *na'an* comes to table from a tandoori oven; you spread it with pâté de foie gras with peppercorns. The daily menu is a single page, but it is a page of extraordinary offerings. And more than ten thousand bottles of wine are in the cellar.

At the water's edge, the Lain Ching Heen has a great view (as does the Plume) and its own Chinese miniature garden. The Chinese cuisine is among the best in Hong Kong.

There are other very good and less expensive places to eat in the Regent. My usual favorite is the Harbourside, which has an unobstructed view of passing vessels of all kinds, the jogging track and waterside promenade, and Hong Kong Island across the bay. Here you can get as little or as much as you want to eat whenever you want it.

For those who like steak, the excellent Steak House features U.S. prime beef and has a sumptuous salad bar.

The mezzanine lounge has live entertainment in the evenings, and the Lobby Lounge offers drinks with a view.

Just a five-minute walk from the hotel, at the peninsula's extremity, are the Star Ferry piers. I found the ride to Hong Kong Island one of the most delightful and inexpensive sea voyages I've ever had. Near the piers is the Ocean Terminal. More than a docking place for ocean liners, this modern complex, with the neighboring Ocean Centre, is said to be one of the most comprehensive shopping malls in the world. It takes at least a full day to visit all the shops.

The walk to the harbor area along Salisbury Road is itself enjoyable. You pass the famous old Peninsula Hotel (see separate entry), the Hong Kong Planetarium, and the Science Museum.

Nathan Road starts just across from the Regent. The bustling heart of Tsimshatsui, this street stretches for miles, though the first mile has most of the shops, restaurants, and nightclubs.

According to Rudolf Greiner, the Regent's manager, the hotel's average guest is a high-level business executive most likely from the world of fashion, banking, investment, or diplomacy. Almost half the guests come from the United States, almost a quarter from Europe. During the Christmas season, the Regent attracts many American visitors who "like to be pampered Regent-style." There is a big party on Christmas Day, when the hotel is completely occupied.

SHANGRI-LA HONG KONG
64 Mody Road
Tsimshatsui East
Kowloon
Hong Kong
Telephone: (3) 721-2111
Telex: 36718 SHALA HX
Fax: (3) 7238686
Reservations:
  In Hong Kong call (3) 723-3336
  In the USA call 1-800-228-3000
All major credit cards

General Manager: J. David Hayden
Concierge: Sam Chan
Director of Marketing: Michael Andrea
Westin Hotels and Resorts
Rates (approx):
  Superior room $170 single, $185 double
  Deluxe room $190 single, $205 double
  Harbor-view room $245 single, $260 double
671 rooms, 48 suites
Service charge 10%; tax 5%

My most memorable impression of the Shangri-La is its lobby, which is of breathtaking proportions. Two stories high, it is decorated with gleaming marble imported from Carrara, Italy; sparkling, gigantic crystal chandeliers from Austria; a large graceful fountain; and two fantastic murals commissioned from the British artist Malcolm Golding. Entitled *Shangri-La Valley*, they depict Golding's personal idea of paradise: dark, forbidding mountains, a mystical red palace, multicolored blossoms, and a myriad of small birds and animals. At high tea (3:00 to 6:00 P.M.), the Lobby Lounge is *my favorite spot*. Here you can watch the busy flow of traffic across the lobby floor, all below the immense murals of Shangri-La.

One of the more delightful and elegant hotels in Hong Kong, the Shangri-La is situated right on the Tsimshatsui East waterfront, overlooking Victoria Harbour. From my windows I could watch the ships of all sizes, as well as joggers and strollers on the waterfront promenade.

The guest rooms, furnished with either a king-size or two double beds, are very comfortable and spacious; they are said to be among the largest in Hong Kong. Some have wide bay windows to afford magnificent views of the city and its harbor. All have bedside controls for radio, lighting, and even the drapes. Also provided are air conditioning, color TV, twenty-four-hour in-house movies, two direct-dial telephones for both local and overseas calls, an alarm clock, and a mini-bar. The spacious bathrooms have walls and floors of luxurious marble. Chinese tea is brought to the room immediately upon a guest's arrival.

On the twenty-first floor is Club 21, for the traveling VIP. Special privileges exclusively for guests here include complimentary limousine rides to and from the airport, fast check-in and check-out, free valet service, and personalized stationery.

The eleventh floor of the hotel is special, too: It is reserved for nonsmokers. There are no ashtrays, and none of the room attendants smoke. No tobacco odors linger anywhere.

My favorite dining spot is the Margaux, on the mezzanine. With spectacular views of Victoria Harbour, it is beautifully furnished in teak and brass and decorated in dusty peach and powder blue, with velvet patchwork on the dining chairs and heavy, modern curtains to match. Berndorf silver, Wedgwood china, and Waterford crystal make up the table settings. Superb continental cuisine is elegantly served at dinner, table d'hôte, and lunch.

On the basement floors are more exciting dining rooms. The Shang Palace, lavishly decorated in red and gold, serves dim sum at lunch and Cantonese specialties at dinner. Nadaman, decorated with bamboo screens, stepping stones, and bonsai, is a quiet spot for lunch or dinner. The specialty of this Japanese dining room is *kaiseki*.

A popular spot is the hotel's Coffee Garden (on the mezzanine, it isn't really a garden). Breakfast and luncheon buffets are served here, and kosher meals are available on request. There is a nonsmokers' section.

Westerners enjoy the Steak Place, open every evening on the mezzanine.

Also on the mezzanine is the Music Room, which offers drinks and, every Tuesday, live American pop music of the fifties and sixties.

The Tiara Lounge, on the twenty-first floor, is a delightful bar with live piano music and a spectacular view.

The Shangri-La Health Club has separate saunas, massage rooms, locker rooms, and lounges for men and women, and a swimming pool, a Jacuzzi, a solarium, and an exercise room for general use.

SHERATON HONG KONG HOTEL AND TOWERS
20 Nathan Road
Tsimshatsui East
Kowloon
Hong Kong
Telephone: (3) 691111
Telex: (780) 45813
Cable: SHER HONG KONG
Fax: (852) 123-48227
Reservations:
   In Hong Kong call (3) 732-6773
   In the USA call 1-800-325-3535
All major credit cards

Hotel Manager: Des Pugson
General Manager: Bernd Loeke
Concierge: Andy So
Director of Sales: Debra Pettitt
Rates (approx.):
  Standard room $103
  Standard Towers room $112
  Superior room $128 single, $138 double
  Superior Towers room $150 single, $160 double
  Deluxe room $147 single, $158 double
  Deluxe Towers room $175 single, $185 double
  Suite $173–$1,026
922 rooms, 113 suites
Service charge 10%; tax 5%

This is a big hotel, and a very good one in the perfect spot.

At the corner of Kowloon's Nathan and Salisbury Roads, the Sheraton Hong Kong has a magnificent view of Victoria Harbour. From a harbor-view room or restaurant, you can watch the passenger liners, container ships, oil tankers, barges, ferries (including the famous Star Ferry), and, occasionally, traditional Chinese junks as they pass by.

The Sheraton is also at the beginning of Kowloon's famous Golden Mile of exciting shops and night life. And, surrounding the hotel are commercial complexes providing office space for local and international business concerns. Across the street are two of the best hotels in Hong Kong.

The hotel has fine guest rooms, all fully air-conditioned, with private bathrooms, color TVs, radios, international direct-dial telephone service, mini-bars, and refrigerators. The Reuter World Report, channeled through the TV sets, gives the news in full color, with constant updates all day long.

Opened in 1983 and upgraded in 1986, the Sheraton Towers has 128 guest rooms with their own express elevator and elegantly decorated lounge. Guests here are provided concierge and butler service; international newspapers and journals; personalized stationery; two-hour laundry service; complimentary breakfast, afternoon tea, and evening hors d'oeuvres; and free use of the rooftop pool and health club.

Even VIPs are happy here. The split-level Presidential Suites have floor-to-ceiling windows that offer full views of the harbor. Each contains a study, a bar, a lounge, a dining area, and a fully equipped kitchen. The exquisitely decorated bedrooms are reached by a spiral staircase from the lounge. Each suite also has a marble Jacuzzi.

The hotel has a rooftop swimming pool, heated in the

winter, and a Health Club complete with sauna and massage facilities.

The Sheraton is a business person's ideal. Its Business Centre offers postal services, full- and part-time secretarial services, offices and conference rooms, telex and cable facilities, photocopying, telecommunications, access to the View Data financial information service, and much more.

The hotel also provides transportation to and from the airport or to any local destination, an airport representative to meet you, speedy check-out, a twenty-four-hour currency exchange, laundry and valet services, babysitting, a beauty shop and a barbershop, a medical clinic, and a number of other services. It is almost a city in itself.

There is more than ample choice of places to eat.

My favorite spot is the Pink Giraffe, at the top of the hotel. Overlooking Victoria Harbour, this elegant restaurant features fine international cuisine and live entertainment from around the world. At night thousands of tiny lights twinkle on the ceiling.

The Coffee Shop and the Sidewalk Cafe offer casual meals, including very satisfying meaty hamburgers and creamy milkshakes.

The Grandstand Grill, with a decor reminiscent of Hong Kong's Happy Valley race track a century ago, is best known for its U.S. prime beef.

At Someplace Else, in the first basement, lunch or dinner is arranged in a humorous pattern, such as a happy face or an animal shape, on each plate. The menu is a delightful mix of American, Italian, Mexican, Chinese, and Japanese cuisines.

The newest dining room in the hotel is Unkai, offering traditional Japanese cuisine by chefs from Osaka. It has a large à la carte menu, *teppanyaki* counters, a sushi bar, a private room, and three tatami rooms, in which diners sit on mats on the floor.

Places for drinks are the Great Wall Bar, on the ground floor overlooking busy Nathan Road, and the relaxing top-floor Sky Lounge, which has the same spectacular views as the Pink Giraffe.

The Sheraton's banquet and convention facilities range from small rooms with terraces to the large Silver Ballroom. With the hotel's state-of-the-art audio-visual equipment, business conferences and seminars are successfully staged here.

Within the hotel, too, is a six-story mall with more than eighty shops.

My wife and I like the Sheraton's two bullet-shaped, anodized aluminum and glass elevators, custom-built in Japan, which slide up and down the hotel's exterior (a third glass elevator operates within the building, to and from the shopping mall floors). From the elevators are spectacular views of Hong Kong Island and Victoria Harbour.

Cheung Chau Island

HOTEL WARWICK
East Bay
Cheung Chau Island
Hong Kong
Telephone: (5) 981-0081
Telex: 74369 FEORG HX
Cable: FAREASTGROP
Fax: (3) 7853342
Reservations:
   In Hong Kong call (5) 417031 or (5) 415921
   In the USA call New York Warwick at (212) 247-2700,
      Warwick Seattle at (206) 443-4300, or Warwick
      Denver at (303) 861-2000
All major credit cards
General Manager: Herbert Williams
Sales Manager: Audrey Pok
Warwick International Hotels
Rates (approx.):
   Ocean-view room $70 Oct.–May, $77 June–Sept.
   Mountain-view room $63 Oct.–May, $70 June–Sept.
   Suites $207– $1,630
66 rooms, 4 suites
Service charge 10%; tax 5%

Few of the three million yearly visitors to Hong Kong take the time to go island hopping. I'm sure most don't even know Hong Kong's outlying islands exist. But those who have taken the time to visit them like them.

Cheung Chau is probably the best one to visit if time is short. A tiny island, just one square mile, it is about three-quarters mile west of Hong Kong. There is regular ferry service from Central Hong Kong by the Yaumatei Ferry; the trip lasts an hour.

Everything on the island is reached by foot. Since the

roads are really lanes or alleys, no motorized vehicles are permitted.

The only hotel on the island, the Warwick serves both international and local guests. Just a seven-minute walk from the ferry pier, it is ideally nestled between Yung Wan beach and Kwun Yam Wan beach.

All rooms and suites are air-conditioned and have private bathrooms with showers, color TVs, radios, and telephones.

The hotel's restaurants all face the open bay, the beaches, and the lush green hills. The Bayview Restaurant specializes in Chinese cuisines and fresh seafood prepared to the guests' tastes. The Bayview is as popular with foreign tourists as with the locals.

My favorite spot is the Terrace Café, a place to have a snack or a drink and really relax.

For drinks, both the Cave Discotheque and the Cave Bar are popular.

The hotel has a swimming pool with a swim-up bar and a recently renovated patio where tourists like to have a meal, even if they are just visiting the island for the day. From here is a beautiful view of the bay, the beaches, and the hills.

The busy fishing village on the island has an interesting market for noodles and dry fish products. Boat building is a thriving industry, and visitors enjoy seeing junks being built as they have been for centuries, entirely from the memory of the master boat builder. The sheltered bays are picturesque anchorages for hundreds of junks and sampans.

There are seven temples on the island. The most ancient, more than two centuries old, is the Taoist Temple dedicated to Pak Tai, the god of the fishermen. On the eastern side of the island is Cheung Po Tsai, a pirate's cave.

INDIA

With a population of more than six hundred million, this is the second most populous country in the world. It occupies more than a million and a quarter square miles, from the Arabian Sea on the west to Burma on the east. India's border also touches, from west to east, Pakistan, a small portion of Afghanistan atop the state of Jammu, Kashmir, China, Nepal, Sikkim, Bhutan, and Bangladesh. The country comprises twenty-one states and nine union territories. New Delhi is the national capital.

Agriculture supports 70 percent of the Indian people. Vast quantities of rice are grown wherever the land is level and water is plentiful. Cotton, tobacco, and jute are the main non-food crops. There are large tea plantations. India perhaps has more cattle per capita than any country in the world, but traditional stock-raising practices and the Hindu stricture against the killing of cows detract from their economic value.

Coastal fisheries and, to a lesser degree, inland fisheries are important; so are pearling grounds. Light manufacture, especially of cotton, woolen, and silk textiles and jute and leather products, have been greatly expanded in recent years.

Modern cities include cosmopolitan Bombay and Bangalore; Delhi, Old and New; and Chandigarh, the city planned by Le Corbusier.

India's climate varies from intense tropical heat in the

south to snows that permanently cover the peaks on its northern frontiers.

The origins of Indian civilization are shrouded in the mists of time. The principal ideas and beliefs that have helped shape Hindu culture are derived from ancient texts like the Rigveda. India, however, is a secular state—a home to many religions besides Hinduism, some of which originated here.

Both Buddha, the "Awakened One," and Mahavirs, the "Brave One"—founders of Buddhism and Jainism, respectively—lived and preached here in the beginning of the fifth century B.C. The first incursion of the Islamic world came in 712 A.D., when part of India's northwest was captured by Arab invaders. The Sikh religion traces its history to the fifteenth century and to Guru Nanak, the first of its ten gurus. Christianity came to India with Saint Thomas the Apostle a few years after the Crucifixion.

For visitors, India offers much to see and to do. Make your plans carefully. If you wish to explore western India, Bombay is your entry. Calcutta is the entry to the mysteries of the east. If you want to see the India of yore, with its spices, tea, silk, and ivory, Madras is the ideal starting point. For art and architecture and all things historical, the imperial city of Delhi is the place to begin.

Bangalore

This city of nearly two million people is set three thousand feet above sea level in the state of Karnataka in south-central India. Founded in 1537, it became the administrative seat of Mysore in 1831. Today it is the region's transportation hub and major industrial center. Electronics and aircraft industries, textile mills, and many other kinds of manufacturing are here. A well-planned city with wide streets and many parks, Bangalore has also become famous as a place for retirement.

About an hour and a half from Bombay by air, Bangalore has one of the best climates in India. Because it is so high above sea level, it is spared stifling heat, even during the monsoon season.

If you saw the film *A Passage to India* you may recognize the two-billion-year-old hills that David Lean nonchalantly blasted to make his Marabar Caves. Bangalore is a center of movie making in India; about ten films a month are made here. If you are lucky, you may see film stars at your hotel, or even some actual filming on the grounds.

Because of its wide, tree-lined streets, the city reminds some of Paris. Bangalore also has grand colonial buildings and the splendid post-Raj parliamentary headquarters, the Vidhan Soudha, which declares above its main entrance: "Government Work is God's Work."

Not to be missed are the extensive botanic gardens at Lal Bagh, the Hindu temples, and, especially, Tippoo's Palace, an eighteenth-century wooden pavilion used by Sultan Tippoo as his summer residence.

Bangalore is renowned for its beautiful cottons, woolens, and silks, and they are bargains at the markets. Rosewood, teak, and lacquerware souvenirs are also well-priced. And there are stylish leather shoes, belts, and bags, all very inexpensive. Some of the best spots to shop are the Government of India Emporiums, where you won't be taken for a ride. Prices are set, so there is no bargaining.

Bangalore's name means "boiled beans," but don't let this mislead you. The local food is delicious.

HOLIDAY INN BANGALORE
P.O. Box 174
28 Sankey Road
Bangalore 560 052
India
Telephone: 73354 or 79451
Telex: 845354 MACH IN
Cable: MACHARLES
Reservations:
  In Bangalore call 79451
  In the USA call 1-800-HOLIDAY
All major credit cards
Chairman: C. B. Pardhanani
Assistant General Manager: Kumar Chandran
Sales Manager: Farida Mody
Holiday Inn Asia-Pacific
Rates (approx.):
  Standard room $50 single, $60 double
  Executive suite $65 single, $70 double
  Deluxe suite $155
  Presidential Suite $200
161 rooms, 28 suites
Service charge 10%; tax 10%

Attractively situated with beautiful views of the Bangalore Golf Club, this hotel is within easy reach of downtown Bangalore and less than a mile from the airport. It is one of the top Holiday Inns, beautifully constructed, with a very impressive atrium lobby.

Among the fine places to eat and drink here is the Ambrosia, the hotel's main dining room, which features Indian and continental cuisines. The Bamboo serves regional specialties, and the Lanai Coffee Shop is open twenty-four hours. There is also the Sundowner Bar, and nicest of all is the open-air Barbeque.

The inn has a swimming pool and a well-equipped health club. Available services include safe deposit for valuables, currency exchange, tour planning, same-day laundry service, car rental, secretarial service, and babysitting. A large function room can be divided into smaller rooms. There are only two shops, selling flowers and books.

All of the guest rooms are spacious and have individually controlled air conditioning, color TV with in-house movies, radio, telephones, and refrigerators. Either king-sized or twin beds are available.

My favorite sight in this hotel is the "twin atrium," two large areas of the lobby sharing an intricately designed stained-glass roof and glass elevators that look like space capsules. Surrounded by flora, fountains, and cascading water, the atrium is like a grand hall of the future set in a lush tropical garden.

TAJ RESIDENCY
14 Mahatma Ghandi Road
Bangalore 560 001
India
Telephone: 568888
Telex: 845 8367
Cable: RESIDENT
Reservations:
    In Bangalore call 568888
    In the USA call the Taj Group at 1-800-I LUV TAJ
All major credit cards
General Manager: N. R. Daruwalla
Sales Manager: P. M. Baliga
Taj Group of Hotels
Rates (approx.):

Room $38 single, $46 double
Suite $88 single, $100 double
180 rooms and suites
No service charge; tax 10%

This is a very comfortable hotel. It isn't too big, and it is very nicely furnished. I especially enjoyed relaxing in the lobby, with its big wicker chairs and fine thick carpets.

The hotel is centrally air-conditioned. All rooms have telephones, attached bathrooms with showers, in-house music, and color TV with in-house movies. The balconies bloom with yellow and orange bougainvillaeas, and the rooms are decorated in colors of the garden. All the beds have patchwork quilts, in the same design but in various colors.

Catering to the business executive, the hotel has the finest convention facilities in town and a complete business center.

Restaurants here are several. The charming Memories of China serves Sichuan and Hunan dishes. The Southern Comfort coffee shop, decorated in a garden theme, features specialties from South India and the rest of the world. My favorite, for its elegant, nostalgic decor, is the Jockey Club, named in tribute to Bangalore's racing tradition. Guests choose from a club-style menu with continental specialties at lunch and dinner.

The hotel is close to the city's shopping and entertainment areas and only a ten-minute drive from the airport.

WELCOMGROUP WINDSOR MANOR
25 Sankey Road
Bangalore 560 052
India
Telephone: 79431 or 28031
Telex: 0845-8209
Cable: WELCOTEL
Reservations:
    In Bangalore call 79431 or 28031
    In the USA call Sheraton at 1-800-325-3535
Most major credit cards
General Manager: S. S. Dhawan
Sales Manager: M. Mehrotra
Welcomgroup Sheraton
Rates (approx.):

Deluxe room $55 single, $62 double
Regency Room $61 single, $70 double
Stuart Room $71 single, $80 double
Manor Room $79 single, $88 double
Luxury suite $208
Deluxe suite $250
Presidential Suite $334
128 rooms, 12 suites
No service charge; tax 10%

You might not guess it when you see it, but this hotel was built in 1982. Constructed in a colonial style, in white brick with arches, columns, and bay windows, the distinguished building recalls the India of a half century ago.

Each room and each magnificent suite are immaculately designed, with elegant window sashes, drapery that sweeps to the floor, discreet touches of gilt, and the soft glow of bracket lamps. Each has stereophonic music and other recorded programs on four channels, individual room-temperature control, and private bathrooms with tub showers. Each of the suites has a different decor, and each has a name, such as Auckland, Hastings, or Trafalgar, rather than a number.

The places to dine and to drink are delightful. The formal Wellington Room features European cuisines as well as regional foods of India. It has its own bar and a dance floor.

My favorite spot is the Royal Afghan, the pavilion on the lawn by the swimming pool. It is famous for serving the best tandoori (meats roasted in the style of the Northwest frontier) in the city.

Other spots to eat include the Nelson Room, a twenty-four-hour restaurant, and the Royal Derby, an English-style pub.

The Deccan Lounge is the hotel's business center. Besides typing, photocopying, a library, and so on, it offers a board room, a bar, a lounge, and a restaurant, all exclusively for guests who pay the somewhat higher Executive Club rates.

The hotel has three function rooms: the House of Lords, a banquet area that can be turned into small meeting rooms; the Westminster Room, for board meetings and other small gatherings; and the Regency, with a capacity of two hundred and a terrace to handle an overflow.

Also within the hotel are a beauty parlor, a barbershop, and a curio shop.

This is a lovely place to stay, with superb service and fine food.

Bombay

Bombay is India in miniature. The Western influence is obvious in the skyscrapers; imposing office buildings, old and brand-new; department stores; rows and rows of shops; electric trains; London-type buses; and streets jammed with traffic. But this is very much a city of the East. Its labyrinth of alleys and close-packed tenements surround the crowded bazaars that give flavor and names to its various neighborhoods.

For decades Bombay has been the commercial and industrial capital of India. This bustling metropolis is the most cosmopolitan in the nation. Its ethnic mix gives it color and vibrancy as in no other part of India.

There is much to see in the city: the Prince of Wales Museum; the Flora Fountain; the Fort area, including the Churchgate and Nariman Point, which constitutes the commercial hub of the city; Marine Drive; Malabar Hill, with its Hanging Gardens; Kamala Nehru Park, in a wide and graceful sweep around the Backbay area; and the Mahalakshmi Race Course, said to be the finest of its kind in the entire world.

On the outskirts of Bombay is the Borivli National Park, with its lion safaris and the ancient Kanheri Caves. And across the harbor, by launch trip, are the famous Elephanta Caves.

LEELA PENTA HOTEL
Near Bombay International Airport
Bombay 400 059
India
Telephone: 636 3636
Telex: 011-72339 PNTA-IN or 72204 PNTA-IN
Fax: 636 0606
Reservations:
　　In Bombay call 636-3636
　　In the USA call (212) 239-8810 or 1-800-225-3456
All major credit cards
Vice President, Operations: Pramod Mathur
Sales Manager: Renu Malhotra
Managing Director: Vivek Nair
Penta Hotels
Rates (approx.):
　　General room　$95 single, $102 double
　　Superior room　$110 single, $118 double

Executive suite $157
Deluxe suite $315
Presidential Suite $550
252 rooms, 31 suites
No service charge; tax 7%

Only a short distance from Bombay's Sahar International Airport, the modern Leela Penta looks like a gigantic accordian just off the highway. Its gardens overflow with fragrant temple flowers, while bougainvillaea adorn the parapets in a riot of color. The majestic areca palms, groves of bamboo, and variety of creepers together create a tropical paradise. In the midst of all this is the Blue Lagoon, the hotel's pool, with flood-lit tennis courts close by.

The hotel was opened in April 1987, fulfilling a dream of Captain C. P. Kirshnan Nair's. He had come to Bombay in 1947 with his wife, Leela, in the hopes of fulfilling another dream, that of Leela's—to set up a factory for the manufacture of beautiful laces. (This is how the famous Leela Lace came into being. Today Leela Fashions can boast of two of the world's famous labels, Liz Claibourne and Calvin Klein.) On land they had purchased as the site of a lace factory, the Nairs ended up building, in collaboration with the Penta organization, one of the most exciting hotels in Bombay.

As you enter the hotel, you see lotus lilies on the lobby's pond. You smell the perfume of the blood-red champak blossoms in the reception area, at the feet of an impressive antique figure of a Ganesh *murti*. Nearby, on another level, imposing bronzes of Vishnu and Shiva stand like sentinels.

The hotel's decor blends the contemporary and the traditional. Glazed Italian marble sets off tastefully selected Indian artifacts. Ivory-inlaid doors complement etched Belgian glass screens.

Each spot is special. At the Orchid Lounge, tiny lights glow softly as the pianist plays. The curtains and the upholstery, both with an orchid motif, were woven at the Nairs' looms in Cannanore, on the southwest coast.

In the hotel's lobby are two more retreats: Bonaparte's, a swanky and sophisticated split-level bar with music video to dance by, and the Indian Harvest restaurant, which has an age-old *haveli* decor with silver and burnished brass.

My favorite spot at this hotel is the Waterfall Cafe, whose large French windows look out on five waterfalls cascading over rocks into a garden pond. International specialties are served here around the clock.

Other places to dine include the Chef's Table, which features French haute cuisine, and the Great Wall of China, whose Chinese dishes are exquisite.

The guest rooms are luxurious. The Botticino marble–fitted bathrooms have, among other nice things, single-lever hot and cold mixers for the basins and showers. All amenities are provided, including toiletries, hair dryers, color TV with in-house movies, air conditioning, four-channel in-house music, international direct-dial telephone with extensions in the bathrooms, mini-bars, and refrigerators.

The hotel's fully equipped Fitness and Racquet Centre has, besides the free-form swimming pool with a water slide, squash and badminton courts with a glass wall to protect onlookers.

The Business Centre offers word processors, telex, secretarial services, and offices and conference rooms. The hotel's state-of-the-art Conference Centre and Convention Centre can accommodate up to six hundred people, its ballroom up to twelve hundred.

The hotel also houses nearly a dozen shops. Particularly interesting are A. Salaam's jewelry shop and the Sonshil India Enterprises handicrafts shop.

TAJ MAHAL INTER-CONTINENTAL
Apollo Bunder
Bombay 400 039
India
Telephone: 91 (22) 202-3366
Telex: 11-3832 TAJB IN or 11-6175 TAJB IN
Cable: PALACE
Fax: 022-2872711
Reservations:
  In Bombay call 202 2524
  In the USA call 1-800-I LUV TAJ or 1-800-33-AGAIN
    (travel agents call 1-800-327-0200)
All major credit cards
General Manager: Subir Bhowmick
Sales Manager: Pankaj Baliga
Inter-Continental Hotels
Rates (approx.):
  Regular room $100 single, $113 double
  Deluxe room $117 single, $125 double
  Executive suite $250
  Large suite $333
  Special suite $417

Deluxe suite $500
Super-deluxe suite $583
650 rooms, 48 suites
No service charge; tax 7%

It is simply called the Taj, but simple it is not. As you come upon it, you see two hotels: the grand old palatial structure built in 1904, and, next to it, a twenty-four-story tower that looks as if it were imported from Miami Beach. There's a special softness to the old Taj that the new Taj can never capture.

But the original Taj Mahal and its tower are together one of India's landmarks. Compared by some with its mighty namesake, the Taj was truly conceived out of love, and it has been nurtured for eighty-five years by people who made it one of the grand hotels of the world. When it celebrates its centennial in 2004, many feel the Taj will still be as beautiful as it was upon its opening.

Jamsetji Tata, the founder of the Taj, born in 1839, was no Conrad Hilton. He wished to build the finest hotel in the East as a gift to the city he loved. He was ahead of his time: In 1888 he made sure the Taj would have its own laundry, an aerated water bottling plant, electroplating for its silver, a Mora silver-burnishing machine, a crockery-washing plant, and elevators. He traveled to the capitals of Europe and bought only the best.

His pride was contagious. There is a story that the French architect, after working months on his drawings, went to France to rest. When he returned he found the hotel completed, beautifully, in every minute detail—with one exception. It was placed on the site back to front! The native contruction team had set the entrance facing a narrow back street instead of the magnificent Bombay harbor.

So the Frenchman shot himself in the head. (Sixty-nine years later, the management made partial amends: They placed the entrance to the New Taj tower on the seafront.)

The hotel was completed at a cost of £5 million in 1904. Tata, like his architect, did not live to attend the opening ceremonies.

Tata's pride apparently continues to infect the present managers. They have meticulously kept up the grandeur of the old Taj, and rewrought its magic in the new. Shortly after it opened an Indian journalist wrote, "The New Taj is not another ice-cube hotel you find everywhere in the world. Tradition has not been forsaken."

Bombay, metropolitan and cosmopolitan as it is, is a dead

city at 10:00 P.M. For many, a weekday evening's entertainment is hanging around the foyer of the Taj, then walking a mile, it seems, to the other end of the hotel, people
watching en route. After the Taj, Grand Central Station
resembles a quiet park.

Today the Taj Mahal, like Bombay, is a fine combination
of East and West—of Old World charm and panache and
present-day sophistication and splendor, gracefully joined
on the waterfront of India's premier metropolis.

My favorite spot is the chic Apollo Bar, twenty-four floors
above Bombay, where you may enjoy "a cocktail in your
hand and the city nightscape at your feet." Next door is
the Rooftop Rendezvous, which is said to provide the finest
continental meals in Bombay. The service is impeccable,
and the view of the city spectacular.

Other restaurants in the Taj include the Golden Dragon,
one of the finest Chinese restaurants in Asia outside China;
the Shamiana, a twenty-four-hour coffee shop, decorated
with Indian folk art motifs, where you may order anything
from a cappuccino to wiener schnitzel; and the Tanjore,
offering regional foods of India. For snacks and drinks there
are the Sea Lounge, overlooking the harbor, and the old
Harbour Bar. The Blow Up is a discotheque club, of which
hotel guests are considered temporary members.

The hotel's abundant facilities include a health and exercise center, a swimming pool, a business center, and plenty
of meeting rooms.

WELCOMGROUP SEA ROCK
Land's End
Bandra
P.O. Box 9831
Bombay 400 050
India
Telephone: 642 5454
Telex: 011-71230
Cable: SEAROCK
Reservations:
  In Bombay call 642 7196, 642-9400, or 642-5454, ext. 202
    or 268
  In the USA call ITC at (212) 986-3724 (telex: 426083)
All major credit cards
General Manager: C. B. Narang
Sales Manager: David Appasamy
Welcomgroup

Rates (approx.):
  Deluxe room $67 single, $75 double
  Superior room $70 single, $78 double
  Executive Chamber $78 single, $86 double
  Executive Club room $102
  Executive suite $150–$170
  Deluxe suite $235
  Presidential Suite $315
380 rooms, 20 suites
Service charge 10%; tax 7% room, 15% food

Perched on idyllic Land's End, in suburban Bombay over-looking the Arabian Sea, is an ideal hotel for the business traveler. It has ample leisure facilities, and it is conveniently situated, too—not far from the center of town and about fifteen minutes' drive from the airport.

The hotel's pride is its three floors of rooms furnished especially for the convenience of the business traveler, with all the services a busy decision-maker may need. For guests on these floors, the Executive Club office provides secretarial, photocopying, courier, and other business services. A lounge adjoins the office. Breakfast and cocktails are included in the Executive Club rates.

Also for business travelers is the hotel's first-floor Business Centre, which offers offices, meeting rooms, word processors, telefacsimile, and other facilities to all the hotel's guests. A comprehensive business library contains vital information on Bombay's businesses and business associations. The hotel's various conference rooms can accommodate as many as three hundred fifty persons. For big events, outside terraces can accommodate up to two thousand.

The hotel's restaurants are so good they have become the favorites of local executives and their guests as well as of frequent travelers.

I have two *favorite spots* here. One is the Palace of the West Empress, a revolving restaurant at the top of the hotel that serves excellent Chinese meals in the recreated pleasure palace of a Ming emperor's beautiful lover. The views are outstanding.

My other *favorite spot* is the Lobster Pot, which, strangely, is Bombay's only seafood restaurant. The decor is Mediterranean, with fishermen's lamps that dim and brighten and a violinist to serenade diners. Offerings include mussels and lobsters from Goa, prawns and fried potatoes from nearby Danda, and delicious pink salmon, smoked in an oakwood fire, sliced very fine, and stuffed with a shrimp salad.

The Earthen Oven serves rich-flavored barbecued meats and breads baked in clay ovens, the robust fare of the tribespeople of the northwest frontier.

At the Vega diners can watch the preparation of vegetarian foods in the glass-fronted kitchen while enjoying live Indian music.

The bright and cheerful Oceanic coffee shop is open twenty-four hours a day. It's great for a quick bite, or even a substantial meal.

The Kanakona Bar is a good spot for a lunch-time or sunset drink. The view is delightful, for the bar overlooks the hotel's swimming pool and the Arabian Sea.

For late-night dancing there is the high-tech Cavern, an underground discotheque.

The Mind and Body Temple is a health and exercise center offering aerobics and yoga for classes; a turkish bath, a sauna, and a Jacuzzi; and *shiatsu*, Japanese accupressure to rejuvenate travel-weary bodies. There are also tennis and squash courts, billiards, and an ocean-side swimming pool with several sun decks overlooking the Arabian Sea. The children have their own pool. The hotel can arrange for guests to play golf at a nearby course.

Two major shopping areas near the hotel, called Hill Road and Linking Road, have stores appropriate to this prestigious residential area. The hotel itself has fifteen shops, selling handicrafts, rugs, and jewelry, among other things.

Cochin

MALABAR HOTEL
Willingdon Island
Cochin 682 009
India
Telephone: 6811
Telex: 885 661 MLBR IN
Cable: COMFORT
Reservations:
  In Cochin call 6811
  In the USA call the Taj Group at 1-800-I LUV TAJ
All major credit cards

General Manager: G. Mohamed
Sales Manager: A. V. Sivaraman
Taj Group of Hotels
Rates (approx.):
  Room $42 single, $50 double
  Superior room $54
  Deluxe suite $146
35 rooms, 2 suites
No service charge; tax 10%

Stunningly situated on an artificially created island, the Malabar Hotel has possibly the best view of the Cochin harbor, its beautiful backwaters, and its picturesque surroundings. Watching the long rice boats with their woven wicker roofs pass by, you almost feel as if you are on a boat, too.

Yet the hotel is not remote. It is within walking distance of the railway terminal, by a small bridge, and ten minutes' drive from the airport.

The red-tiled building appears from the outside older than it is. It blends well with the world around it.

Inside, the recently renovated rooms are well appointed, with attached bathrooms, telephones, in-house music, color TV with in-house movies, and air conditioning.

The very attractive Rice Boats dining room is actually furnished with a rice boat, with tables inside it. Continental, Indian, and local specialties and served here. The Sao Gabriel bar has an elegant marine decor. Outside, the hotel holds barbecues on the lawns.

The hotel's only shop, the Malabar Chest, sells handcrafted goods, souvenirs, and necessities.

In and around Cochin there is plenty to see: the sixteenth-century Jewish synagogue; the Dutch Palace; the Saint Francis Church, built in 1510, where Vasco da Gama was buried, and the Bolghatty Palace.

All parts of the district of Kerala can easily be seen on side trips from Cochin. The waterborne city of Allepey, its canals filled with straw-roofed boats, looks almost like Venice. At the Periyar Game Sanctuary visitors can see the big game from a motor launch. Interesting, too, are the tea plantations at Peermade, Munnar, and Annamallais; and Tripunithura, with its array of Hindu temples and palaces.

Goa

On the Arabian Sea, Goa is made up of three noncontiguous former Portuguese colonies that were seized by India in 1961.

With a population close to a million, Goa has 1,430 square miles. It has three ports on the Malabar Coast—Agoada, Marmagao, and Panjim. Its chief products are rice, cashew nuts, and coconuts.

The Moslems conquered Goa in 1312, but by 1370 it was part of the Hindu kingdom of Vijayanagar. A hundred years later the Moslems took Goa again, and in 1510 the Portuguese took it from the Moslems. Old Goa, the Portuguese capital, was a prosperous port city in the late sixteenth century.

Goa has sixty-five miles of palm-fringed beaches and regions of great beauty, including marvelous cathedrals and Hindu temples and towns with quaint Latin squares.

FORT AGUADA BEACH RESORT
Singuerim
Bardez
Goa 403 515
India
Telephone: 75017
Telex: 194291TAJIN
Cable: FORT AGUADA GOA
Reservations:
  In Goa call 403 515
  In the USA call the Taj Group at 1-800-I LUV TAJ
All major credit cards
General Manager: Salil Dutt
Sales Manager: P. M. Baliga
Taj Group of Hotels
Rates (approx.):
  Room, regular season $54 single, $61 double
  Room, Christmas season $63 single, $71 double
  88 rooms, 32 cottages
No service charge; tax 7% food, 10% drinks

Acclaimed as one of the finest beach resorts in India, Fort Aguada overlooks the golden Calangute Beach.

The rooms are in both the main hotel block and the cottages on either side of it along the hillside running down to the sea. All rooms face the sea. All have telephones, color

TV with in-house movies, in-house music, and bathrooms. The rooms in the main block are air-conditioned.

The Seashell Restaurant serves Indian, continental, and Goan specialties. For less formal dining there are the Alphonso de Albuquerque Shack, for grilled meat and Goan dishes, and the Saint Francis Xavier Shack, for Chinese food (at dinner only). The Anchor Bar serves cocktails, Goan wines, and snacks.

The resort includes a freshwater swimming pool and facilities for boating, water-skiing, parasailing, windsurfing, tennis, badminton, squash, and volleyball. The air-conditioned games room has billiards, table tennis, cards, chess, and a library. The health club offers a gymnasium, hydrotherapy, and a sauna.

TAJ HOLIDAY VILLAGE
Singuerim
Bardez
Goa 403 515
India
Telephone: 7514/17
Telex: 194291 TAJ IN
Cable: FORTAGUADA GOA
Reservations:
    In Goa call 7514/17
    In the USA call the Taj Group at 1-800-I LUV TAJ
All major credit cards
General Manager: Salil Dutt
Sales Manager: P. M. Baliga
Taj Group of Hotels
Rates (approx.):
    Room $54 single, $62 double
100 rooms in 33 cottages
No service charge; tax 7% food, 10% drinks

This casual resort is made up of a cluster of cottages, some air-conditioned and some not, facing the beach near Fort Aguada Beach Resort. The cottages range from single rooms to three-room family units. All rooms have telephones and attached baths.

The Beach House, a rustic eating house adjoining the Beach Bar, serves Goan and Portuguese cuisine. Other restaurants are close by in town.

There is a swimming pool with a swim-up bar, and a wading pool for children.

WELCOMGROUP CIDADE DE GOA
Vainguinim Beach
Dona Paula
Goa 403 004
India
Telephone: 3301/3307
Telex: 194-257 DONA IN
Cable: WELCOTEL
Reservations:
  In Goa call 3308
  In Delhi call 301-4127
  In the USA call ITC at 1-800-325-3535 or, in New York, (212) 986-3724
All major credit cards
President: N. J. de Souza
Sales Manager: I. B. Cardoso
Sheraton International
Rates (approx.):
  Room, Oct. 1–Dec. 15 $54 single, $62 double
  Room, Dec. 16–Feb. 28 $62 single, $69 double
  Room, Mar. 1–June 10 $46 single, $54 double
  Room, June 11–Sept. 30 $39 single, $46 double
  Suite $154
101 rooms, 4 suites
No service charge; tax 12% food and drinks

Nestling against a hillside beside the exclusive Dona Paula area of Goa is a beach resort designed to resemble a Portuguese town. Run by Sheraton International for the Welcomgroup hotel chain of India, it has plazas, promenades, and patios, and restaurants and fiestas just like those in Portugual.

You enter Cidade de Goa (City of Goa) through an impressive gateway to arrive at a portico where park benches and frosted street lamps give the appearance of a town square. You then enter the Salao do Mar, a spacious lobby with beamed ceiling and trompe l'oeil murals.

The guest rooms are typically Iberian, with white walls and wicker furniture. Every room has a beautiful view of the sea. Each has air conditioning, color TV, a refrigerator, an attached bathroom, in-house music, and so on. The Da-mao rooms are in the Gujarati style, with terra cotta on the walls, mirror-work furnishings, and *takhat* (sleeping platforms).

In the heart of this make-believe city is the Taverna, the lobby bar beside a grassy patio. Musicians fill the evenings with the strumming of their guitars.

The delightful restaurant Praca d'Alfama has balconies and muted street lamps like those in a Portuguese town square. The restaurant serves Goan, Portuguese, and Indian dishes, including *vindaloo*, oysters, lobster, and king prawns.

The hotel's recreational facilities include two swimming pools overlooking the Arabian Sea, with Lagoa Azul, the pool-side restaurant open for all meals and snacks and featuring live band music in the evening. Also available are tennis and table tennis, chess, cycling, a video room, and indoor games. There is a private beach for sunbathing. The calm waters are ideal for windsurfing, sailing dinghies, riding water scooters, and boating. The health club offers saunas, steambaths, massage, and a gymnasium.

Most fun are the theme parties and other events arranged by the hotel. There are Goan nights with typical Goan music and folk dances, moonlight beach barbecues, river cruises and buffets, "beach-o-theques," and even special evenings in ancestral Goan homes.

For meetings and conferences, the hotel's Sala de Banquette can hold up to 180 persons, theater-style.

The hotel's small shopping area consists of Conchita, a boutique; Kasmir Treasure, a gift and carpet shop; and Loja Cidade, a necessities shop.

Jaipur

The capital of Rajasthan in western India, this transportation and commercial center has a population of nearly seven hundred thousand. Founded in 1728, it is known for the color of its houses as the Pink City, and is surrounded by a twenty-foot crenulated wall. An unusual feature of an Indian city this size is its excellent system of wide and regular streets.

Popular with visitors are its teeming bazaars, worth visiting even if you don't care to shop. If you want, though, you can haggle over colorful muslins and silks, tie-dyed saris, or old silver. There's also filigree jewelery, enameled plates and pendants, and precious and semiprecious stones. Most famous is the "Jaipur Blue" pottery and lacquerware.

The best example of the Rajasthani stone carvers' skill is the Hawa Mahal, the Palace of the Winds, whose broad pyramidal façade is honeycombed with windows and projecting balconies of latticed screens through which the ladies of the Zenana were able to observe life on the broad avenues of Jaipur without being seen.

It might be fun to take an elephant ride to Amber, the capital of the principality before Jaipur was built. Most interesting is the palace inside its fortress.

Other places to visit are the City Palace Museum and the museum of the Rajasthani arts and crafts in the Ramnivas Gardens.

There are many stories about this ancient city, but one of the more interesting is of modern times. The ruling family, an enlightened group, liked to do the unusual. In 1959 the maharani decided to step out of her palace and rub shoulders with her people to win an election. She was subsequently listed among the world's ten most beautiful women, along with Vivien Leigh.

RAMBAGH PALACE HOTEL
Bhawani Songh Road
Jaipur 302 005
Rajasthan
India
Telephone: 75141
Telex: 0365-254 RBAG IN
Cable: RAMBAGH
Reservations:
   In Jaipur call 75141
   In the USA call 1-800-I LUV TAJ or 1-800-33-AGAIN
All major credit cards
General Manager: Vikram Singh
Taj Group of Hotels
Rates (approx.):
   Deluxe room $79
   Garden suite $119 single, $138 double
   Deluxe suite $178 single, $198 double
   Royal Suite $277 single, $316 double
60 rooms, 45 suites
No service charge; tax 6%

So regal is this setting that Michael Korda shot the movie *Queenie* here in 1987.

The hotel was built in 1727 as a palace for the scholar-prince Maharaja Sawai Jai Singh II, who lent his name to what has been declared India's best-planned city. His crowning achievement, the Rambagh Palace, is a building of delicate cupolas and fretted screens set amidst sprawling, splendidly landscaped lawns.

Modern economies changed the destiny of the building. Since it could no longer be maintained in its grand state as a regal residence, Prince Man Singh sadly decided to keep it alive by making it a hotel.

The Rambagh Palace Hotel opened in 1957, staffed by servants of the royal family. Since the Taj Group took over its management in 1972, the hotel has offered a rare combination of princely living and professional hotel service.

It is still very much a palace. Many precious art pieces decorate the luxurious suites and special rooms. Magnificent remnants of the past include the mirror-mosaic peacock of the Peacock Room, and its baroque bathroom; the exquisite blue pottery, glass vases, and gilded family portraits of the Maharani Suite, and its bathroom with twelve shower heads at different levels; the elaborately framed European oil paintings of the Maharaja Suite; the silk embroideries; and the golden dragons, mirror-work bamboos, and ceramic "China men" of the Oriental Room.

You live like a Maharaja even in a regular guest room. All the rooms are beautifully furnished in the colorful Rajasthani style. In fact, except for the magnificent dining room, whose decor is eighteenth-century French, and the Oriental Room, the hotel is a beautiful blend of native Indian styles.

The Rambagh Gardens show their centuries of continuous care. Mohammed Abdul Ghaffar Khan, who was sent to horticultural school in England by Prince Man Singh, is head among twelve gardeners. *My favorite spot* is the Rose Garden, whose colors are riotous. The gardeners also arrange the traditional *guldastas* (bouquets) in the palace and the displays of fruit from the orchards.

In the Polo Bar you can sip a drink amidst trophies and mementos won by the late Maharaja's polo team, which was called "the most celebrated in the twentieth century."

The Suvarna Mahal dining room serves continental, Indian, and Chinese meals.

You can play tennis, squash, or golf at the hotel, or you can cool off in the indoor swimming pool. The health club offers a gymnasium, with separate sections for men and women; a steam room, a sauna, and a whirlpool; and a massage room.

Even business people find the hotel to their liking. It has five conference rooms and all necessary services.

The hotel's shopping arcade has a whole Rajasthani bazaar under one roof.

Jodhpur

Jodhpur, or Marwar, is a city and former principality in Rajasthan state in northwestern India.

Jodhpur's foundations were laid in 1459 by Rao Jodha, chief of the Rathore, a Rajput clan who claim descent from Rama, the hero of the Ramayana epic. A high stone wall, nearly six miles long, still protects the city. Within the wall is an imposing fort on a low range of sandstone hills, high above the surrounding plains. From the fort you can look down on the old and new parts of the city, which lies at the foot of the hills.

The city is an important marketplace for wool, and manufactures here include textiles, and electrical and leather products.

Among the important things to see are—

• The Mehrangarh Fort—its museum and its palace. The palace is intricately adorned with long, carved panels and latticed windows of exquisite design in red sandstone.

• The Jaswant Thada, a royal crematorium in imposing white marble, built in 1899.

• The Government Museum, in the middle of the Umaid Public Garden.

• The Girdikot and Sardar Markets, near the Clock Tower. The narrow lanes are lined with tiny shops of all kinds, offering Rajasthani textiles, handicrafts, clay figurines, camels and elephants, marble curios with inlay work, and silver jewelry.

• The Umaid Bhawan Palace, now a fabulous hotel.

WELCOMGROUP UMAID BHAWAN PALACE
Jodhpur 342 006
Rajasthan
India
Telephone: 22316, 22516, or 22366

Telex: 552 202 UBP IN
Cable: PALACE
Reservations:
  In Jodhpur call 22316
  In New Delhi call 301-0101
  In the USA call ITC at (212) 986-3724
All major credit cards
General Manager: Shiv Hazari
Sales Manager: Alok Jain
Welcomgroup
Rates (approx.):
  Normal room, May–Sept. $33–$37 single, $37–$41
    double
  Normal room, Oct.–Apr. $45–$50 single, $52–$58
    double
  Royal chamber, May–Sept. $47
  Royal chamber, Oct.–Apr. $70
  Suite C $77
  Suite B $116
  Suite A $154
58 rooms, 8 suites
No service charge; tax 6% food

Truly one of the most magnificent hotels in the world, the
Maharaja Umaid Singh's palace at Jodhpur was once one
of the largest private residences in the world. Designed by
English architects and built between 1929 and 1944, it is a
splendid example of the art deco style, with Hindu details.
This architectural triumph is constructed of hand-chiseled
sandstone blocks put together without mortar, by a unique
system of interlocking. Although it was financed out of the
Maharaja's personal funds, the romantic structure was built
as part of a public works program to relieve the distress
caused by a famine.

Its site on Chittar Hill, a rock outcropping on the opposite
side of Jodhpur from the historic fort of past Marwar princes,
was chosen for astrological, not practical, reasons. Half a
million donkey-loads of earth had to be brought in to form
a flat base upon which to build the palace, and a twelve-
mile railway was constructed to carry the creamy pink Sur-
sagar sandstone from the quarry. Providing a water supply
was equally difficult in this desert region. Four thousand
artisans worked fifteen years to complete the palace.

It is a sight never to be forgotten. Covering three and a
half acres in twenty-six acres of landscaped grounds, the

sprawling, domed edifice is heavily decorated with sculptures of birds, wild pigs, and horses. It is a fantasy brought to life—an Englishman's fantasy of the sort of palace a maharaja would want.

Each of the hotel's rooms has its own bath and dressing area, and a few have parlors as well. The art deco furnishings are reminiscent of some of the movie palaces built in the United States in the thirties.

The Regal Suites (Suites A in the rates list) were formerly occupied by Maharaja Umaid Singh and Maharani Badan Kanwar. Designed by S. Norblin, a Pole, they are perhaps one of the finest examples of art deco architecture. Most magnificent is the maharani's bathroom; the bathtub is carved from a single piece of pink marble, and the walls and floors are covered with other fine marbles.

Life-sized paintings and color-tinted photographs of Jodhpur maharajas are in the rooms and in the halls. Throughout the palace is the current maharaja's art collection, which includes antique clocks, miniature paintings, trophies, and fine pieces of china and glass.

In the palace are about twenty public rooms, among them a banquet hall, a movie theater, and a ballroom.

My favorite spot is the central hall, crowned with a spectacular, 105-foot inner dome (the central dome of the palace's exterior rises eighty feet above this). From the lobby sweep twin staircases, made from a million square feet of the finest marble.

The billiard room features an inlaid wooden base for the billiard table and, covering the wall, a collection of prints showing Derby winners through the years.

It is truly a regal experience to dine in the elegant Marwar Hall, with its high ceiling, ornate columns and arches, chandeliers, and red-turbaned waiters. Served here are excellent continental and Indian meals, with many Rajasthani specialties.

The Risala dining room is less formal, and Dal Badal is for those who prefer eating outdoors. Drinks are available at the Trophy Bar.

For the sports enthusiast there are tennis and squash courts and an underground swimming pool, its hand-painted tiles displaying underwater scenes on the walls and the signs of the zodiac on the floor. His Highness's lakeside hunting lodge is available for rent. Pleasant for a stroll are the fifteen acres of gardens.

Three shops in the hotel offer Rajasthani handicrafts, antiques, jewelry, and postcards and film. Very close to the hotel is a row of eight art galleries and handicrafts shops, which will ship purchases anywhere.

The hotel staff is happy to arrange parties, group dinners, and sightseeing trips. At parties on the ramparts of the Mehrangarh Fort, Rajasthani music and colorful folk dances are followed by a lavish barbecue under the stars. Special dinners are held under the hotel's century-old desert tent or even on the illuminated lawns of the palace garden. Even more exciting is an overnight trip in the maharaja's saloon train car to the desert city of Jaisalmer. With teak paneling, rosewood furniture, and silver fittings, this parlor car provides princely comfort.

Perhaps the most wonderful part of this desert palace is its impressive staff of one hundred fifty red-turbaned staff members, some of whom have served the maharaja's family almost since their birth.

Madras

In southeast India on the Bay of Bengal, Madras is the capital of the state of Tamil Nadu. It is a commercial and a manufacturing center with large textile mills, chemical plants, and tanneries. Exported from here are leather, peanuts, and cotton.

The city is mostly built around Fort Saint George, a British outpost completed in 1640. Soon after the fort's construction Madras became an important British trading center. The French captured the city in 1746, but two years later the British took it back.

The site of the University of Madras, the city is culturally rich. Among the most exciting places to visit is the famous Kapaleswarwar Koil Temple, with its gigantic lotus pool. For museum buffs, not to be missed are the archives in Fort Saint George, the Government Museum, and the National Art Gallery; in the last is a fascinating collection of old bronzes, paintings, and rare manuscripts. Also here is the sixteenth-century Portuguese Cathedral of Saint Thomas the Apostle, where the saint is supposed to have been buried. Other places to see include the Madras High Court Buildings, the Moore Market, the People's Park, and the Hindu temple of Parthasarathy.

The Marina, a famous and delightful shore drive, borders one of the longest beaches in the world.

TAJ COROMANDEL HOTEL
17 Nungambakkam High Road
Madras 600 034
India
Telephone: 474849
Telex: 41 7149 TAJM IN
Cable: HOTELORENT
Reservations:
  In Madras call 474849
  In the USA call the Taj Group at 1-800-I LUV TAJ; or
    call Leading Hotels of the World at 1-800-223-6800 or,
    in New York, (212) 838-3110 (call collect)
All major credit cards
General Manager: M. B. Patel
Sales Manager: A. V. Sivaraman
Taj Group of Hotels
Rates (approx.):
  Standard room $58 single, $65 double
  Deluxe room $75
  Small suite $113
  Deluxe suite $167–$280
240 rooms and suites
No service charge; tax 7% food, 10% drinks

A picturesque white skyscraper, the Taj Coromandel works at keeping its reputation as the best hotel in southern India.

In the heart of the busy city, it is a modern hotel popular with the business traveler. All of its rooms have air conditioning, telephones, attached bathrooms, color TV with in-house movies, and piped-in music.

The decor is delightfully native. In the public areas are a terra-cotta horse, an ancient temple lamp, a sitar, a canopy, hand-carved frames at doors and windows, and other features that echo the locale.

Similarly decorated is the Mysore restaurant, which offers traditional dishes from all parts of India. In the evening, a classical Indian dancer performs.

The Pavilion coffee shop, beside the hotel's large swimming pool, is open around the clock. There's always someone here enjoying the snacks, savories, and good cheer.

For a change of scene, the Golden Dragon features Sichuan cuisine.

The Fort Saint George bar has a colonial decor reminiscent of the city's seventeenth-century fortress, for which it is named.

The hotel has many amenities: a health club, a beauty salon, laundry service, and necessities shops.

New Delhi

The capital of India, New Delhi is set on the bank of the Jumna River in north-central India. This modern city was constructed between 1912 and 1929 to replace Calcutta as the capital of British India. The city was inaugurated in 1931.

With a population of more than three hundred thousand, New Delhi is an important transportation hub and trade center. It has textile mills, printing plants, and a number of light industrial facilities.

The city has broad, symmetrically aligned streets that provide vistas of historic monuments. Between the main governmental buildings a broad boulevard, the Raj Path, leads from a massive war memorial arch, built in 1921, through a great court to the resplendent sandstone and marble Government House, formerly the viceroy's palace.

In the southern section of the city is the prayer ground where Mahatma Ghandi was assassinated in 1948.

Adjoining New Delhi is the city of Delhi, or Old Delhi, with its population of nearly four million. It is enclosed by high stone walls, erected in 1638 by Shah Jahan when he made Delhi the capital of the Mughal Empire. Within the walls he built the famous Red Fort—so called for its walls and gateways of red sandstone—that contained the imperial Mughal Palace.

From 1921 to 1931, Delhi was the interim capital of British India.

Just south of the Red Fort, on the banks of the Jumna, is Rajghat, where Gandhi's body was cremated. Rajghat is now one of the most revered shrines in India.

In northwest Delhi, beyond the old walls, are residences, hotels, clubs, and the University of India. An amphitheater, built in 1911, marks the site of the ceremony in 1877 in which Queen Victoria was proclaimed the empress of India.

Within the fifty square miles south of New Delhi are more

important dynastic remains than exist in any other area of the country.

HYATT REGENCY DELHI
Bhikaiji Cama Place
Ring Road
New Delhi 110 066
India
Telephone: 609911
Telex: 031-62779 HYT IN or 031-61512 HYT IN
Cable: HYATT NEW DELHI
Fax: 609880
Reservations:
  In New Delhi call 609911, ext. 2939, 2940, or 2941
  In the USA call 1-800-228-9000
All major credit cards
Managing Directors: S. K. Gupta, S. K. Jatia
Vice President, Hotel Operations: Karl-Werner Diefenbach
Guest Services Manager: Meena Bhatia
Director of Sales: Nandini Verma
Hyatt Hotels and Resorts
Rates (approx.):
  Deluxe room $104 single, $140 double
  Regency Club room $140 single, $156 double
  Suite $160–$560
512 rooms, 23 suites
No service charge; tax 7% food, 10% drinks

The Hyatt Regency Delhi has successfully served both business travelers and tourists since mid-1983. *Travel Times*, the monthly travel magazine published by the *Times* of India, named it one of the country's ten best hotels.

About fifteen minutes from both the airport and the center of the city, the Hyatt Regency is in New Delhi's exclusive residential and commercial district. The ten-story hotel has the sparkle and efficiency of a Hyatt property, yet the decor and feeling of an Indian hotel. Its architecture, inspired by the Golden Gupta period in India, is clean and modern.

Costing $40 million, the hotel has three duplex Presidential Suites, four deluxe suites, ten superior suites, and six executive suites. Most luxurious of the Presidential Suites is the Victorian, split over the sixth and seventh floors. It has three bedrooms, a living room and separate dining room, a pantry, a terrace garden, and a private sauna and Jacuzzi, in addition to personal valet service. The smaller, two-bedroom Kalamkari and Rajasthani suites offer similar comforts. The Kalamkari, like the Victorian, is within the confines of the Regency Club, a private area for executives with sixty rooms, five suites, a lounge, and a conference room.

All the guest rooms are modern and attractive, with light touches in the Indian motif. All have individually controlled air conditioning, color TV with in-house movies, radio with multichannel in-house music, direct-dial telephone service, refrigerators, mini-bars, and private bathrooms with showers.

As is the case with Hyatt hotels around the world, the Hyatt Regency Delhi offers a good selection of places to eat and drink. There are four restaurants, a bar, a lounge, and a pool-side snack bar.

Valentino's is *my favorite spot*. With an art deco decor, it features Chef Riccardo Parlanti's Italian *nuova cucina* and, in the evening, live music. Valentino's is on the hotel's mezzanine and is open for lunch and dinner. Formal dress is requested and tables should be reserved.

Pearls serves authentic Sichvan and Haka dishes at lunch and dinner.

Aangan offers northern Indian cuisine at lunch and dinner. The Ghazal singers entertain at dinner.

The Cafe Promenade, open twenty-four hours a day, is on the ground level overlooking the landscaped pool area. It serves continental and Indian foods.

A popular spot is the Cafe Express, in the lobby, which serves a fast breakfast and refreshments through the day. Live piano music adds to the pleasant atmosphere.

On the mezzanine level another pianist plays at the Piano Bar.

The recently opened Oasis Discotheque has a unique glass dance floor over water, 153 lights, 3,200 watts of music, two gigantic video screens, three TV monitors, and a fog machine. Locals as well as hotel guests enjoy the electronically produced thunder, flashes of lightning, and pounding music until the early morning hours.

The Hyatt Fitness Centre includes a swimming pool, a gymnasium, saunas, massage rooms, and steam rooms; some of the facilities have separate sections for men and women. Two hard-surfaced tennis courts are adjacent to the pool. The nine-station workout setup is the only one of its kind in India. The staff can provide all kinds of help and instruction, including yoga classes.

The Hyatt Business Centre is well staffed and well equipped.

THE OBEROI
Dr. Zakir Hussain Marg
New Delhi 110 003
India
Telephone: 363030
Telex: 3829, 63222, or 62218
Cable: OBHOTEL
Fax: 360484
Reservations:
  In New Delhi call 363030
  In the USA call 1-800-223-1474, 1-800-223-0888,
    (212) 682-7655, or (212) 841-1111
All major credit cards
General Manager: Sunil Chandra
Sales Manager: Renu Kapoor
Oberoi Hotels
Rates (approx.):
  Standard room $120 single, $132 double
  Others available on request
350 rooms, 33 suites
No service charge; tax 7% food and drinks

A special place, the Oberoi opened in 1965 as India's first luxurious modern hotel. It recently completed a multimillion-dollar renovation of its guest rooms, restaurants, and other public areas.

The hotel is conveniently situated about twenty minutes from the airport and only ten minutes from Connaught Place, New Delhi's main shopping and commercial area. While some rooms overlook the lush greens of the Delhi Golf Course (which guests may use for a nominal fee), the others have views of the historic tomb of the Mughal emperor Humayun. Nearby are several important monuments; the Delhi Zoo, housed within the ruins of a fort; and various museums and cultural centers.

The lobby is marked by extensive use of polished granite, comfortable leather Chesterfield sofas, an illuminated Tree of Life, and bronze sculptures by Amar Nath Sehgal, winner of the United Nations Peace Medal.

The guest rooms, redecorated in pastels, feature spacious writing desks, international direct-dial telephone service, mini-bars, in-house music and movies, and some of the most luxurious bathrooms in India, created of polished granite. Each floor has its own butler service. The butlers welcome guests into their rooms and coordinate their needs with the hotel's other departments, such as laundry, valet, and food and beverage services.

The hotel's newly designed Executive Centre has a comprehensive range of facilities, including secretarial services, facsimile, word processors, photocopying, and global courier service. An elegantly furnished office and a conference room are available.

The restaurants and bars are luxurious. The Taipan, on the top floor, has been judged to have the best Sichuan food in India. Favorites include smoked duck, fried chicken in honey sauce, and bird's nest soup. The walls display original nineteenth-century Chinese watercolors and polished teak lattice screens. The Taipan is open for lunch and dinner.

Also on the top floor is *my favorite spot*, the Connaught Bar, whose wide windows permit a magnificent view of the Delhi skyline. On one side is a mirror-paneled wall that reflects the gentle rose and beige hues of the interior. Open from 7:00 P.M. until 2:00 A.M., the bar features a live band and dancing.

La Rochelle offers a buffet lunch and French dinners. Here favorites include roast guinea fowl with cranberry sauce on creamed leeks; lobster medallions, prawns, mussels, and fillets of sole in a saffron and pastis sauce; and some choice Caspian caviar. Hand-cut crystal and fine crockery are on the tables, and on the walls are sketches of La Rochelle, a town at the estuary of the Charente River on the west coast of France.

Esmeralda is a new pool-side restaurant, where lunch and dinner are served.

At the Palms, on the lobby level, sunshine pours in through transparent domes. Palms fringe the fountains and dapple the patterned black and white marble floor. This pleasant spot, with an excellent soup and salad bar, is open around the clock for snacks and meals.

Also on the lobby level is the Club Bar, overlooking the pool.

The Health Club, equipped with the latest fitness facilities, is for the exclusive use of hotel guests. It has a gym with separate sections for women and men.

The hotel's shopping arcade has been redesigned to resemble a ritzy Parisian shopping boulevard.

Do take time to look at the works of art displayed throughout the public areas and guest rooms. The hotel has one of the finest collections of engravings, aquatints, lithographs, and mezzotints of the eighteenth and nineteenth centuries.

TAJ MAHAL HOTEL
One Mansingh Road
New Delhi 110 011
India
Telephone: 3016162
Telex: 031-66874 TAJ DIN or 031-4758 TAJ DIN
Cable: TAJ DEL
Reservations:
   In New Delhi call 3016162, ext. 2611
   In the USA call Leading Hotels of the World at
      1-800-223-6800 or, in New York and Alaska,
      (212) 838-3110 (collect)
All major credit cards
General Manager: Ravi Dubey
Sales Manager: Deepa Misra Harris
Taj Group of Hotels
Rates (approx.):
   Twin or double $98 single, $106 double
   Suite $270–$355
272 rooms, 28 suites
No service charge; tax 7% food, 10% drinks

Made of the beige, hand-chiseled Dholpur sandstone that
is used on the façades of most of New Delhi's buildings,
the Taj Mahal is one of the city's finest hotels. It is well
situated, in a prime residential area within walking distance
of the main shopping, entertainment, commercial, and governmental centers.

Entering the hotel is a delightful experience. Your car
brings you up a slope to the main entrance, where a short
flight of marble steps leads to the double glass doors. Inside,
the lobby looks like a court of the great Mughals. Pure,
untainted white marble accentuates the vast proportions,
while the raised formal seating area, converging with three
majestic central domes, creates a *takhat*, an elevated and
revered place. The domes are colored royal blue, wine red,
and golden yellow—blue to symbolize the past, red to symbolize the present, and yellow for the future. The white of
the surroundings unites all these.

Nearby is a marble lotus pool, its *jaali* work, or lace-like
traceries, by the Makrana artisans whose forefathers helped
to build and embellish *the* Taj Mahal. Crystal and brass
candalabra (*jhad*) have been faithfully reproduced from miniature paintings of the past.

A second, sunken lobby, off the main lobby, is also designed in blue, red, yellow, and white. Its grand staircase with marble balustrades, the ceramic *jaali* screens on its windows to diffuse the light, and the brass planters hung from its ceiling at both ends are magnificent. No wonder the lobbies are *my favorite spots* here.

The guest rooms are the quintessence of comfort and tranquility. The "campaign-style" teak furniture, with clean lines and brass fittings, is copied from British military designs inspired by the troops' need for furniture that could be easily collapsed or disassembled for stowing and carrying. Because the rooms are unusually large, they provide space for comfortably seating at least five people. In the single rooms are queen-sized Murphy beds, unique in India.

The hotel has five restaurants:

The Haveli dining room, open for lunch and dinner, offers *kadai* specialties from Peshawar. The decor is *haveli*, and Indian musicians and dancers perform at night.

The rooftop Casa Medici provides Italian meals and a breathtaking cityscape. Open for lunch and dinner, it features dancing at night.

The House of Ming, appointed with exquisite pieces of blue and white Ming porcelain, serves authentic Cantonese and Sichuan dishes.

Open around the clock, Machan serves international foods, including unusual specialties from the jungle areas of Southeast Asia. Like a real *machan*, a jungle treetop residence, it overlooks trees on the hotel's grounds.

The Captain's Bar serves continental breakfast and flambés as well as drinks. A pianist performs at night.

The Emperor Lounge serves tea and light snacks.

The Taj Mahal also has a disco, called the Number One, and a patisserie, where everything is tempting.

The hotel's Business Centre is open twenty-four hours a day. Also for business executives is the Chambers, a members-only club.

The beautiful swimming pool, with underwater lighting, is set in a garden along with a snack bar. Adjacent to the pool is a health club with separate sections for women and men. The club has a yoga center, gymnasiums, sauna and steam baths, and massage rooms.

TAJ PALACE HOTEL
Two Sarda Patel Marg
Diplomatic Enclave
New Delhi 110 021
India

Telephone: 3010404
Telex: 031-62761 TAJS IN or 031-62756 TAJS IN
Fax: 11-3011252
Reservations:
  In New Delhi call 3010404
  In the USA call Leading Hotels of the World at
    1-800-223-6800; or call Utell Worldwide at
    1-800-223-9868 or, in New York, at (212) 757-2981
All major credit cards
General Manager: S. P. Warty
Front Office Manager: Vikramaditya Ranawat
Sales Manager: Gitanjali Aiyar
Taj Group of Hotels
Rates (approx.):
  Standard room $96 single, $108 double
  Executive suite $200
  Deluxe suite $280
  Deluxe suite with terrace $320
  Luxury suite $440
  Presidential Suite $480
400 rooms, 34 suites
No service charge; tax 7% food and drinks

This is another Taj hotel of palatial proportions. Situated in the prestigious diplomatic enclave, it is on the main road, just ten minutes from both the airport and New Delhi's commercial center.

Set in six acres of manicured gardens, the Taj Palace is a magnificent sight to behold as you approach it.

But even more exciting is the view as you enter the hotel. The lobby is a huge expanse of polished marble, tastefully furnished in an Indian style. Huge canopies with a mango-leaf motif cover the ceiling. Below them, comfortable seats overlook the pool and the colorful gardens. Every evening a three-piece ensemble plays here. Teas and dainty snacks are served all day.

In the guest rooms, amenities include color TV with in-house movies, direct-dial telephone, radio with in-house music, refrigerators, fresh fruit and soft drinks, daily newspapers and a few magazines, and sometimes flowers. In the suites guests get more: bathrobes and slippers, baskets of soaps, all kinds of toiletries, flowers daily, personalized stationery, and five different daily newspapers. All rooms have purified, iced drinking water.

The hotel's comprehensive Business Centre, on the mezzanine, includes four meeting rooms, a conference room with a big, round table, and an impressive board room. The exceptionally well-planned convention center, with a separate entrance, has nine salons that can accommodate from fifty to five hundred people.

The health club offers steam baths, saunas, whirlpool baths, a gymnasium with all the latest keep-fit gadgetry, yoga classes, and a variety of massage services. Open every day, it serves both men and women.

My favorite spots in this hotel are its imaginative and beautiful places to eat.

The most exciting, the Orient Express, seats only thirty-six people at tables and forty-two at a bar. A real dining car, it is named for the train whose last run from Paris to Istanbul in 1976 ended a century of European elegance in rail travel. The splendor of the famous line is recreated in this continental dining room, with its soft lighting and nightly crooner. Lunch and dinner are four-course, and diners dress up.

The Tea House of the August Moon is set in a courtyard complete with pond, bridge, and bamboo grove. Painted dragons adorn the restaurant's ceiling. Served here are authentic Sichuan, Beijing, and Cantonese dishes including dim sum.

At Handi meat and vegetables are transformed into flavorful, aromatic stew through long simmering in a *handi*, a large earthenware or metal pot with a tight-fitting lid. This dining room offers a choice from twelve *handi* dishes, all originating in the outpost town of Patan in Gujrat. There is a buffet at lunch and live music in the evening.

The Isfahan, open twenty-four hours a day, is named for the city of Isfahan, Persia's capital and center of art and culture during the Middle Ages. Great craftsmen migrated from Isfahan to Delhi in search of the tempting benefits offered by the mighty Mughal emperor Akbar. As a result, the sophisticated and highly stylized art of Persia blended with its vivid Indian counterpart. The cuisine of Isfahan reflects this combination, too.

On the first floor, overlooking a terrace garden, is the well-named Quiet Place. This lounge, with its soft background music, is perfect for unwinding or for business discussions.

The Taj Palace has its own shopping arcade, called the Collection. There is also a small, fine shopping center at Malcha Marg, a short walk from the Taj Palace. Delhi's maining shopping area, at Connaught Place, is a ten-minute drive away.

WELCOMGROUP MAURYA SHERATON
Diplomatic Enclave
New Delhi 110 021
India
Telephone: 301-0101
Telex: 031-61447
Cable: WELCOTEL
Reservations:
  In New Delhi call 301-0101
  In the USA call 1-800-325-3535
All major credit cards
Resident Manager: Pawan Verma
General Manager: Anil Channa
Sales Manager: Shadhi Vandrewala
Sheraton International
Rates (approx.):
  Deluxe room $101 single, $109 double
  Executive Club room $112 single, $121 double
  Executive Dynasty room $123 single, $150 double
  Deluxe suite $215
  Luxury Suite $269
  Presidential Suite $423
  Tower Club room $123 single, $150 double
  Tower Club suite $215
500 rooms, 20 suites
No service charge; tax 7% food

Bernie, a two-year-old female Saint Bernard, greets guests of the Welcomgroup Maurya Sheraton every morning as they arrive in the lobby. She is hardly what you would expect in these luxurious accommodations in the heart of India's capital. But this hotel is unusual in many ways.

A favorite spot of mine is the hotel lobby, which is modeled after the *chaitya*, or Bhuddist prayer hall, at Karla, near Bombay. Four pillars support a two-tiered domed roof that rises over two stories. Great beams of teakwood form a rib-cage structure on the dome's interior. Following a tradition started in the second century B.C. in *chaitya* halls cut from rock, a three-thousand-square-foot mural adorns the ceiling. Entitled *The Great Procession*, it was painted by Krishen Khanna over a period of more than two years. The mural portrays a *yatra*, a pilgrimage or procession, and attempts to incorporate all of Bhuddist Indian life and philosophy.

Native elements are featured elsewhere in the hotel's architecture and decor. The building's exterior is faced with Dholpur stone, in the tradition of Mauryan Buddhist *stupa* architecture. Replicas of Ajanta frescoes embellish the guest rooms and public areas. Superb works of Indian art are placed in the lobbies on all six floors, suspended from ceilings, and positioned in the gardens and elsewhere on the grounds.

The guest rooms, and particularly the suites, are luxurious. Each of the Presidential and Luxury suites commemorates a famous character in Mauryan history. For example, the Fa-Hien Suite is named after a Chinese chronicler who traveled through the vast Mauryan empire. Hand-painted screens, silk panels, Chinese lamps, and burnished copper re-create an aura of the ancient Orient. The Firdausi Suite, named after a famous Sufi poet, is reminiscent of exotic Persian splendor. Here are cool marble floors to set off the rich Persian rugs, and jewel-like touches of turquoise, purple, and green.

The exclusive Tower Club houses suites and executive guest rooms ideal for the business traveler. Here also are a separate check-in desk, a private lounge, a well-equipped business center, a bar, a library, private dining rooms, conference facilities, and a small health club.

The hotel has a splendid variety of places to dine or drink. The Bukhara, one of India's best-known restaurants, is sparsely decorated to recall the rugged life of India's frontier. Tandoori-style meats are served hot and succulent off the skewer.

Bali-Hi, on the rooftop, specializes in Chinese cuisine. In the evenings it offers candle-lit dining and dancing, at lunch a wonderful Chinese and continental buffet.

French cuisine is served in the Takshila, also on the rooftop.

The Pavilion restaurant, open twenty-four hours a day, overlooks the hotel's solar-heated outdoor swimming pool. Drinks and food are also served at the pool side.

The Mayur dining room features *dum pukhit*, the unique cuisine of the Nawabs. Called the "nouvelle cuisine of royal fare," it uses very little oil and is very aromatic.

Srinagar

This city of nearly five hundred thousand is the historic capital of Kashmir.

Set in the Vale of Kashmir on the Jhelum River, Srinagar is one of the most famous and beautiful summer resorts of the East. There are many canals, and transportation is chiefly by boat.

Things are changing, however. In place of the famous hand-woven cashmere shawls, machine-made silks, woolens, and carpets are now manufactured here. Other products include plywood and cement.

The city was founded in the sixth century. Extensive Buddhist ruins are nearby.

Control of Kashmir has been contested by India and Pakistan since India's partition in 1947. Srinagar is now the capital of the state of Jammu and Kashmir, the Indian sector of the territory.

ALEXANDRA PALACE GROUP OF HOUSEBOATS
P.O. Box 66
Dal Lake
Srinagar 190 001
Kashmir
India
Telephone: 73186, 72028, or 79427
Cable: CARNES
Reservations:
  In Srinagar call 73186
  In the USA call Molly Schiff at Geeta Tours,
    (312) 262-4959
All major credit cards
General Manager: Yousuf Karnai
Rates (approx.):
  Room $23 single, $35 double
  Suite rate available on request
45 rooms, 9 suites
No service charge; tax 10%

Moored to the banks of Dal and Nagin lakes in the Kashmir valley are six floating "palaces." With their gaudy exteriors, they look like oversized fringed surreys.

Inside, however, they are comfortable and elegant. Each deluxe houseboat is fitted with all modern facilities. It has several bedrooms with private baths, a kitchen, a drawing room, a dining room, a garden, a back porch for relaxing and watching the scenery, its own servants, and a *shikara* (water taxi).

Thomas Moore called Kashmir the Asian Switzerland, a combination of Alpine grandeur and exotic Eastern charm. The picturesque valley of Kashmir, its floor between five and six thousand feet in altitude, is some eighty miles long and twenty-five miles wide. Snow-capped ranges surround it.

The city of Srinagar (whose name means "city of wealth") is most beautiful in the spring, particularly when viewed from a height. The Jehlum River bisects the city; eleven bridges connect the two parts. Srinagar is an excellent base for excursions to all parts of the Kashmir valley.

Dal and Nagin lakes have been called the "pair of blue eyes of the fair city of Srinagar." Five-mile-long Dal Lake has islands and floating gardens, and offers swimming, surfing, and boating. Nagin Lake, with its very clear water, is the favorite for water-skiing. Equipment can be rented at the Nagin Club, which also has facilities for bathing and boating.

A visitor who stayed on the Alexandra Palace wrote: "To us, this is heaven. This is where you are made to feel like the lord or lady of the manor and live a life of quiet ease in the dream world unique to Kashmir. Your boys will whip up a batch of hot doughnuts as quick as look at you, keep your dinner hot until midnight, fill your fridge with grog and the sideboard with fruits and nuts."

Another wrote: "The daffodils, forsythia, almond blossoms, wildflowers, and budding willows give us hints as to how beautiful this valley can be. The peaks of the snow-capped mountains are visible to add to the grandeur. . . . We will always remember our stay in this houseboat."

Be sure to request a deluxe houseboat, which will have septic facilities and other amenities Westerners usually require. For a spring or early summer visit, reserve well in advance.

Udaipur

THE LAKE PALACE
Pichola Lake
Udaipur 313 001
India
Telephone: 23241
Telex: 33 203 LPAL IN
Cable: LAKEPALACE
Reservations:
   In Udaipur call 23241
   In the USA call the Taj Group at 1-800-I LUV TAJ

All major credit cards
General Manager: Deepak Dutt
Sales Manager: P. M. Baliga
Taj Group of Hotels
Rates (approx.):
  Room $50 single, $58 double
  Suite $167–$208
80 rooms, 6 suites
tax 7% food, 10% drinks

What a palace!

Built more than three centuries ago as a maharani's summer residence, the Lake Palace is now one of the world's most dramatic hotels. A white marble structure that seems to have risen out of the calm waters of Lake Pichola, it looks like a fairy tale come to life.

All the rooms and suites are superbly appointed, with things that the maharani never enjoyed, like piped-in music and color TV with in-house movies.

Each of the five large suites offers something special. The Khush Mahal has stained-glass alcoves, through which the sun shines in intricate patterns. The Sajjan Niwas has a collection of Rajasthani miniature paintings and a grand view from its private terrace. In the Kamal Mahal, the windows are decorated with lotus-patterned inlay work. The Sarvaritu, with a dressing room separate from the bedroom, opens out to the pool. The modern Udai Prakish, finally, has a large terrace overlooking the pool.

Among the places to dine and to drink are Jalkiran, a pleasant terrace café; Neel Kamal, which serves both Indian and continental meals; and the Amritsagar Bar, with a regal decor.

The majestic Chandra Prakash Room seats about fifty people for a meeting and about thirty-five for a reception —more if the adjoining terrace is used.

There is entertainment—such as colorful Rajasthani folk dances, puppet shows, and musical recitals—in an open-air theater. Some guests like to go on private picnics arranged by the hotel on lovely nearby islands. Others just like to row, or fish, or swim.

My favorite spot is beside the beautiful lily pond in the hotel's courtyard. The pond has a tiny marble island in its center, reached by a white marble walk from the irregular white marble banks.

There is much to see in the nearby town of Udaipur, including the City Palace (now a museum), the imposing palace of Udai Singh, and the yellow sandstone Jag Mandir Palace. Important to see also is the Saheliyon-Ki-Bari Park, a display of Hindu landscaping on a princely scale.

Not too far away are two great lakes. Sparkling Rajsamand Lake has the history of Mewar cut into its embankment stones. Jaisamand Lake, one of Asia's largest artificial lakes, reflects the famous Temple of Shiva, which sits on its banks.

A number of other imposing temples are nearby, including the carved marble Eklingji Temple.

INDONESIA

Indonesia has more than three thousand islands extending more than three thousand miles along the equator from the Malaysian mainland toward Australia. In total, the islands occupy 735 thousand square miles. The archipelago forms a natural barrier between the Indian and the Pacific oceans.

Each of the larger islands has a central mountainous area flanked by coastal plains. Indonesia has more than a hundred active volcanoes, and earthquakes are frequent, although rarely severe.

The animal life of Indonesia forms a connecting link between the fauna of Asia and that of Australia. Elephants are found in Sumatra and Borneo, tigers as far south as Java and Bali, and marsupials in Timor and Irian Barat. Crocodiles, snakes, and richly colored birds are everywhere.

The republic has a population of 140 million. The most important of the islands, economically, are Java, Bali, and Sumatra. The capital is Jakarta, on Java.

The country's tropical climate, abundant rainfall, and fertile volcanic soil provide rich agricultural yields. Rubber is the most valuable export crop; others include sugar cane, coffee, tea, palm oil, tobacco, and coconuts. Rice is the major food crop; others are maize, yams, soybeans, peanuts, cassava, and fruits. Fish are abundant in both the ocean and inland waters. The country has great timberlands, from which teak, sandalwood, ironwood, camphor, and ebony are cut. A leading producer of petroleum, Indonesia is said to have a sixth of the world's supply of tin as well. Bauxite, nickel, coal, manganese, gold, and silver are also mined. Besides agriculture and lumbering, industry consists of a small amount of light manufacturing.

The country has suffered invasion and turmoil since the early Christian era, when traders and Hindu and Buddhist monks began arriving from India. By the end of the eighth century, kingdoms having a close relationship with India had grown in Sumatra and Java. The spectacular Buddhist temples you may see in Borobudor date from this time.

In the fourteenth and fifteenth century Arab traders discovered Indonesia, and by the end of the sixteenth century Islam had become the dominant religion.

Westerners discovered the area in the early sixteenth century when the Portuguese, lured by the spice trade, establishing trading posts in Indonesia. The Dutch arrived in 1596, and the English followed in 1600. In 1610 the Dutch pushed out the Portuguese, who kept but one outpost in the eastern part of Timor, and in 1623 the Dutch overcame the English. The Dutch East India Company thence controlled the area until 1799, when the Dutch government took over the islands, calling them the Dutch East Indies. During the Napoleonic Wars, from 1811 to 1814, they were occupied by the English.

In the nineteenth century, the native people began to demand their land from the Western occupiers. In 1906 and again in 1908, the native rulers of Bali fought suicidal wars against the Dutch.

Sukarno founded the Indonesian Nationalist Party in 1927. It gained power during World War II, when the Japanese occupied the islands. In August 1945, when the Japanese surrendered, Sukarno declared Indonesia an independent republic. For four years the Nationalists fought the Dutch for control of the islands. With pressure from the United Nations, the independent Republic of Indonesia was established in 1949. Sukarno was elected president.

The ousting of the Dutch ruined the economy and brought soaring inflation. To retain his power, Sukarno dissolved the parliament in 1960 and reinstated the constitution of 1945, which authorized the running of the country by a single and independent executive.

Supported by the army and the Communist Party, Sukarno attempted to expand his sphere of control: He took Netherlands New Guinea from the Dutch in August 1963, and he battled the new Federation of Malaysia for Malaysian territory on Borneo from 1963 to 1966.

During these years Sukarno became hostile toward the United States and courted the friendship of Communist China. In 1965 he withdrew Indonesia from the United Nations.

In September 1965 the Communists attempted a coup against the army. The army, led by General Suharto, defeated the effort. Suharto gradually assumed the powers of Sukarno, who was kept on as a symbolic leader.

Helped by massive student demonstrations against Sukarno, the new government finally gained full control. In 1966 General Suharto ceased the country's war against Malaysia, reestablished close ties with the United States, and reentered the United Nations. In 1967 Sukarno was completely removed from power, and in 1968 Suharto was elected president.

Bali

With a population of more than two million, this island occupies twenty-two hundred square miles. It is in eastern Indonesia, just east of Java across the narrow Bali Strait.

Although relatively small, Bali is densely populated. Culturally and economically, it is one of the most important of the Indonesian islands.

Largely mountainous, with active volcanoes, Bali has a fertile southern plain. The Balinese are skillful farmers. Rice, their chief crop, is grown with the help of an elaborate irrigation system. Vegetables, fruits, coffee, livestock, and processed foods are important products.

Tourism is also an important business.

The people are noted for their artistic skill, particularly in wood carving, for their physical beauty, and for their elaborate culture.

BALI HYATT
P.O. Box 392
Sanur, Denpasar
Bali
Indonesia

Telephone: (0361) 8271
Telex: 35127 HYATTDPR
Cable: BALIHYATT
Fax: (0361) 71693
Reservations:
  In Indonesia call (0361) 8271, ext. 85014
  In Alaska or Hawaii call 1-800-228-9005
  Elsewhere in the USA call 1-800-228-9000
All credit cards except Carte Blanche
General Manager: Pierre U. Stacher
Director of Sales: Utut Irawan
Hyatt International
Rates, with continental breakfast (approx.):
  Superior room $70 single, $85 double
  Deluxe room $80 single, $95 double
  Regency Club room $95 single, $115 double
  Junior suite $200
  Duplex suite, 1 bedroom $400
  Duplex suite, 2 bedrooms $470
387 rooms, 11 suites
Service charge 10%; tax 5.5%

The "Island of the Gods," Bali is known as a tropical paradise. The Bali Hyatt's setting, on the white sands of Sanur Beach, is the Bali of everyone's dreams. Amid thirty-six acres of luxuriant tropical gardens, the hotel is surrounded by palms, with high volcanic peaks in the distance. Representing the best of Balinese architecture, the building blends harmoniously with the natural surroundings.

You enter an open lobby with a soaring thatched roof. Then to one of the air-conditioned rooms, each with a private bath and shower, all designed in Balinese style with grass mattings, temple hangings, intricately carved teak and bamboo furniture, and hand-blocked batiks. The bay windows and secluded balconies in all the rooms offer views of tropical gardens, golfing greens, Sanur Beach and the Indian Ocean, or Bali's sacred volcano, Gunung Agung.

For a few dollars more, the hotel's Regency Club offers extra amenities, ranging from a daily basket of fresh fruits and a newspaper to all kinds of fancy soaps and other toiletries. The Regency Club rooms are a bit larger and have the best views of the sea or the gardens.

The hotel has a variety of restaurants: The Ming Cafe, open twenty-four hours a day, has everything from snacks to full meals. Its extensive buffet breakfast is a great start to the day. At the beach is the Pizzeria, with a selection of pizza and pastas. Then there is the Fisherman's Palace, right next to the pool. Drinks and snacks are available at the sunken Pool Bar. For gourmets, the Spice Islander Restaurant features fine continental and Indonesian meals. But *my favorite spot* is under the stars at the Purnama Terrace, where you may enjoy authentic Indonesian dinners along with Balinese dances and other performances.

After dinner, you may want to dance the night away in the elegant Matahari Bar and Discotheque. Or you may prefer the quiet of the Piano Bar, on an open-air terrace just off the lobby.

The hotel's shops feature handmade Balinese arts and crafts items as well as necessities.

The athletic enjoy a jogging track that winds across Sanur Beach and through the tropical gardens. There are also tennis courts, a three-hole golf course, and bicycles for hire. After the exercise, a Finnish sauna and massage are available.

This is the perfect place for those who love being in, on, or by the water. The most popular pastime seems to be lying around the pool and, on occasion, diving in and swimming up to the sunken bar for an exotic thirst quencher. While many guests thus relax, some are aboard the windsurfers, others are sailing on two-person dinghies or outriggers, and still others are water-skiing or exploring the many coral reefs off Sanur Beach. Some guests like to charter a boat and go fishing in Bali's ocean waters, known for their variety of game fish, including barracuda, Spanish mackerel, and yellowfin tuna. Others prefer a more tranquil trip around the outlying islands on one of the hotel's two pleasure cruisers.

There are other tranquil activities, too, such as collecting shells on the beach or just strolling through the lush landscape of hibiscus, bougainvillaea, frangipani, and lotus ponds.

Be sure to explore the rest of the island. To help you, the Hyatt Bali offers its forty-page *Guide to Bali*. Get your copy at the assistant manager's desk if you do not find it in your room.

You'd think business is forgotten here. Not so. This hotel caters to business travelers and proves to be an ideal setting for conferences, meetings, and conventions. A full range of secretarial services is available, and the function rooms employ the latest in audio-visual technology.

HOTEL BALI OBEROI
Legian Beach
Jalan Kayu Aya
P.O. Box 351
Denpasar
Bali
Indonesia
Telephone: (0361) 51061
Telex: 35125 OBHOTL IA
Cable: BALIOBEROI
Fax: (0361) 71791
Reservations:
   In Bali call (361) 51061
   In the USA call Oberoi Reservations at 1-800-223-1474,
       Leading Hotels of the World at 1-800-223-6800, or
       Loews Hotels at 1-800-223-0888
All major credit cards
General Manager: Kamal Kant Kaul
Sales Manager: Sri Pitono
Oberoi Hotels International
Rates (approx.):
   Lanai cottage $85 single, $95 double
   Private villa $180
   Presidential Villa $265
   Istana Suite $290
60 cottages, 15 villages
Service charge 10%; tax 5.5%

This is Bali as you have always expected it to be. The Hotel
Bali Oberoi is not a resort hotel; it is a resort. Spread over
some thirty-five acres, it was formerly a private club. Guests
stay in delightful lanai cottages or villas surrounded by
bougainvillaea, hibiscus, and frangipani on the hotel's mile-
long private beach.

   Even though it is only a few miles from the airport and
conveniently situated for taking in all the major sights of
the island, the Bali Oberoi is astonishingly secluded and
peaceful. And the gracious, charming staff gives such discreet and polished service you are almost unaware of it.

   The hotel's size is also nice. When fully occupied it has
only one hundred fifty guests—just enough to be fun, never
enough to feel crowded.

   Each of the fifteen private villas has its own garden courtyard and private balcony overlooking the beach. The bedrooms are fully air-conditioned, and each bathroom has a

luxurious sunken tub. The magnificent Presidential Villa even has its own private swimming pool.

The Istana Suite is designed as a traditional Balinese residence for a royal family, yet with all modern conveniences. It has three air-conditioned bedrooms, a large living area, and a delightful fountain in a private garden courtyard.

The sixty lanai cottages are also luxurious. Each has a balcony opening onto a flower-filled garden, a direct-dial telephone, a refrigerator, a mini-bar, three-channel radio, in-house music, and a spacious bathroom. There is laundry and valet service and room service for snacks, iced drinks, fresh fruit, and full meals.

But it is better to dine in the beautiful and lively places outside your room. The lovely, open-air Frangipani Cafe, on the beach front, serves light snacks and those delicious Balinese iced fruit drinks. More formal is the Kura Kura dining room, which is a delightful Balinese setting for fine international cuisine.

In the picturesque amphitheater, *my favorite spot*, you can enjoy a romantic candle lit dinner while you watch an intricate Balinese dance.

You may like to hide away in the garden Kayu Bar and play a game of chess, an Indonesian passion. You'll have no trouble finding a partner. Or you may want to just relax and observe, as you sip a cool cocktail.

There are miles of almost empty beaches to stroll on, the warm sea to splash in, and gorgeous sunsets to admire.

The hotel's swimming pool is surrounded by gardens, with a pool-side bar, chess hut, pool table, and ping-pong table. There are tennis courts with lighting for evening play, and, not far away in the mountains, a magnificent eighteen-hole golf course. Old movies play in the evening, in the conference room just off the lobby.

At the hotel's Health Club you can enjoy, among the usual services, a traditional Balinese massage with soothing herbal oils.

Amidst all this pleasure, business isn't forgotten. The hotel's Bale Banjar Executive Conference Room is a perfect venue for meetings, seminars, lectures, and business parties.

HOTEL CLUB BUALU
P.O. Box 6
Nusa Dusa
Bali
Indonesia

Telephone: (0361) 71310
Telex: 35231 BUALU ND
Cable: HOTEL BUALU
Reservations:
  In Bali call (0361) 71310
  In the USA call Utell International at (212) 757-2981 (in
    New York) or 1-800-223-9868
All major credit cards
Director: Rodolfo Giusti
Keraton Hotels International
Rates (approx.):
  Deluxe room $55–$65 single, $60–$70 double
  Suite $90–$100
50 rooms, 6 suites
Service charge 5%; tax 10%

Near the white sand beaches of Nusa Dua, Bali's new tourist
resort, and about ten minutes from the airport, this is the
first hotel opened by Keraton Hotels International. Directed
by two experienced Italian hoteliers, Keraton is developing
a management program for small Southeast Asian hotels
that are to offer the same kinds of rooms, facilities, and
services as in big hotels, but at a much lower price. Many
guests feel Keraton has succeeded here.

Although the nonathlete is certainly not neglected, the
Hotel Club Bualu is a great place for sports enthusiasts.
Available here are a swimming pool, two tennis courts,
horseback riding, windsurfing, surfing, snorkeling, outrigger sailing, bicycle riding, volleyball, table tennis, jogging
tracks, and scuba diving.

The hotel's scuba-diving program is especially well developed. The Dive Shop has a compressor, forty well-main-
tained air tanks, a complete range of other equipment, and
two dive boats—a native outrigger for up to six divers and
a very comfortable Zodiac for up to eighteen divers. The
hotel gives free boat transport and diving instruction in the
amazing reef area in front of the hotel; the cost for equipped
divers is only ten dollars, for two air tanks. A six-day class
is $150, with the first lesson free in case you find you don't
like scuba diving.

The hotel's fifty lovely rooms are in six two-story Balinese-
style buildings, surrounded by glorious tropical gardens.
All have air conditioning, radio, telephone, and an antique
decor. An exclusive line of Balinese materials was designed
for the upholstering, ceramics, and baskets. Many little surprises at this hotel—such as a choice of pillows, compli-

mentary fruit baskets, bathrobes, and Javanese umbrellas —make you feel pampered.

The Benoa Harbour dining room, decorated with ship models and other things nautical, serves Indonesian and European meals. Prices are very reasonable: a full meal costs between nine and fifteen dollars.

Right on the beach is the Bintang Lava Pizzeria, serving pizza and other Italian specialties. A full meal here costs between five and nine dollars.

By the swimming pool, in the garden, is the Pancoran Grill, featuring grilled meat and seafood. A meal costs only seven to eleven dollars.

Tropical drinks are served at the Bird Cage Lounge, in the lobby. The lounge is exquisitely decorated with Javanese bird cages, Balinese bird woodcarvings, and antiques.

The service at the Hotel Club Bualu is very personal and special. As soon as you arrive from the airport—and the hotel picks you up and returns you there free of charge—you are personally greeted by the recreation manager or the guest services manager. They and their assistants are the concerned kind of people who will sit with you in the bar or the dining room and find out what you'd like to do and how much money you can spend, then arrange for transportation—by anything from a bike to a limo.

NUSA DUA BEACH HOTEL
P.O. Box 1028
Denpasar
Bali
Indonesia
Telephone: (0361) 71210
Telex: 35206
Fax: (0361) 71229
Reservations:
    In Bali call (0361) 71210
    In the USA call 1-800-247-8380 or 1-800-247-6794
All major credit cards
General Manager: Paul A. Blake
Sales Manager: Putu Netra Switrajava
Aerowisata Hotels
Rates (approx.):
    Standard room $70 single, $80 double
    Superior room $75 single, $85 double
    Deluxe room $80 single, $90 double

Executive room $95 single, $115 double
Suite $150–$1,200
425 rooms, 25 suites
Service charge 10%; tax 5.5%

The Nusa Dua Beach Hotel was the first to open in this beautiful new resort. Built at a cost of $30 million, it was completed in December 1982.

The builders' objective was to build an ultramodern hotel that would harmonize with Indonesia's natural and cultural environment. They succeeded. Designed to reflect the traditional Balinese village with its *puri* (central palace), *bale banjar* (community center) and *menara kulkul* (watchtower), the hotel is set on 850 acres of tropical park lands. There are whispering coconut palms, brilliant blossoms, reflecting pools, fountains, and cascading water.

The four stories of rooms and suites all have air conditioning and private balconies. From most are spectacular views of the beach, the island of Nusa Penida, or Gunung Agung, Bali's highest volcano. All rooms contain traditional Balinese art pieces.

The hotel includes large family studios, spacious one- and two-bedroom suites, and two stunning Presidential Suites, each with a private swimming pool and personal staff. These last are expensive, but you get what you pay for.

There are three restaurants within the hotel complex: The formal Kertagosa Restaurant, serving Oriental and international specialties, features live entertainment and dance music. The open-air Lumba-Lumba Restaurant adjoins the pool and the beach front. *My favorite spot*, it specializes in charcoal-broiled lobster, crab, and shrimp and other succulent seafood dishes. In the lower lobby you'll find the Warung Bali Coffee Shop, open around the clock. Informal and air-conditioned inside with a terrace as well, this very popular place serves a wide selection of European, Indonesian, and Oriental specialties.

There are also three bars here: the Kertagosa Cocktail Lounge, on the lobby level; the Lobby Bar, also on the lobby level and overlooking the terraced gardens, the pool, and the beach; and the pool-side Jukung Bar.

For entertainment there is the Disco, near the car park, or the Budaya Open Stage, at the pool garden. The latter, a traditional Balinese open-air theater, presents cultural performances along with buffet dinners every Monday and Friday evening.

You'll keep busy here. The hotel has two all-weather

tennis courts, two squash courts, bicycles, a jogging track, and table tennis. The Health Center includes an astounding amount of equipment, everything from an abdominal conditioner to a thigh and knee machine and much more. Water sports include snorkeling, windsurfing, and sailing. The game room has video film shows, chess, backgammon, and so on. And you can explore the island with help from the easy-to-read map of Bali provided by the hotel.

Business people's needs are handled with many types of equipment and services. The Keraton, a beautiful convention hall modeled after the palaces of Central Java, can hold as many as five hundred people and can be divided into smaller rooms.

You will enjoy this resort. President and Mrs. Reagan did in 1986, when they stayed in one of the Presidential Suites en route to the Tokyo Summit Meeting of the Seven Major Nations.

Jakarta

Jakarta, the capital of Indonesia, on the northern coast of West Java, is a teeming metropolis of six million people. It is a city of many contrasts, where urban and provincial, traditional and modern, coexist harmoniously.

Founded in 1572 as the small harbor town of Sunda Kelapa, it was renamed Jayakarta, "City of Victory," by the Moslems in the 1500s. In 1619 the Dutch renamed the city Batavia.

Jakarta's charm is the result of its checkered history and mixture of cultural heritages. The winding streets and quaint red-tiled houses in the old sector are reminders of the days when the Dutch were in charge. Historical buildings like the Stadhuis, restored as the City Museum; the Old Supreme Court Building; the Portuguese Church, now a museum; the Merdeka Palace; and the massive National Mosque are landmarks of the city's past.

Other places of interest are the Jakarta Museum, the Satria Mandala Museum, the Maritime Museum, and, in the center of the city, the National Monument (MONAS). This three hundred–foot obelisk, topped with the shape of a flame said to be coated with twelve hundred troy ounces of gold, has at its base a historical museum and a meditation hall.

Taman Mini, a twelve thousand–acre park, displays the diversity of plant life and architecture in Indonesia's twenty-seven provinces. There is a fantastic orchid garden, a bird park with an aviary, and a pretty lake.

Modern Jakarta is the country's center of government, commerce, and industry. It has an extensive communications network with the rest of the nation and the outside world, and the modern Soekarno-Hatta International Airport.

HOTEL BOROBUDUR INTER-CONTINENTAL
Jalan Lapangan Banteng Selatan
P.O. Box 329
Jakarta
Indonesia
Telephone: 370108
Telex: BDO JKT 44156
Cable: BOROBUDUR JAKARTA
Fax: 62-21-359741
All major credit cards
General Manager: Behrouz Tamdydi
Concierge: Sudharsono
Marketing Director: Ratna Krisman
Inter-Continental Hotels
Rates (approx.):
  Special room $110 single, $120 double
  Standard room $115 single, $125 double
  Superior room $120 single, $130 double
  Junior suite $180
  Alpine Suite $180–$230
  Diplomatic Suite $350
  Presidential Suite $600
941 rooms, 231 suites
Service charge 10%; tax 5%

This hotel is a skyscraper of Indonesian marble, sparkling crystal, and polished teak. Set in twenty-three acres of landscaped grounds, it is the most impressive hotel in Jakarta and the biggest in the Southern Hemisphere. It is named after the Bhuddist Borobudur Temple, famous for the hand-carved stone reliefs around its base. One of these reliefs is reproduced in the hotel's large reception area, where also stand statues of nymphs copied from the temple's wall.

The hotel is proud of its dining rooms, for which beef is flown in from the United States, and other foods from Europe, every day. *My favorite spot* is the Toba Rotisserie, where the elegant decor is highlighted by the warmth of burnished copper over the cooking area and counter. Other dining rooms include the Keio Japanese Restaurant; the Nelayan Seafood Restaurant, specializing in subtly flavored Oriental seafood specialities; and the Bogor Brasserie, a pleasant coffee shop looking out on the garden and popular at lunch time with people from Jakarta's bustling business community. Other places to eat are the Poolside Snack Bar and, overlooking the garden, the palm-fringed Pendopo Lounge.

With its spacious park grounds, the Hotel Borobudur Inter-Continental is much like a country club in the midst of a big city. There are jogging trails, tennis courts, squash courts, a small golf course, Olympic-sized swimming pool, a small wading pool, and a health club.

This is a popular hotel for business people, both local and traveling. Besides the Business Center, which can supply everything from instant translation services to a private office for a few hours or a few days, it has convention facilities for as many as twenty-three hundred people. The ballrooms, with their crystal and star-like glass chandeliers, are elegant.

The many shops on the premises include a beauty salon, a barbershop, a newsstand, a gift shop, a florist shop, a jewelry shop, a drugstore, airline offices, and a travel agency.

The recently added Garden Wing is made up of magnificent suites, each with a large, fully equipped kitchen; even a dishwasher and a microwave oven are included. In the living rooms and bedrooms hang paintings, based on carvings in the Borobudur Temple, by the artist Hatta Humbali. The suites are simply decorated with fine natural fabrics, marble, and teakwood.

JAKARTA HILTON INTERNATIONAL
Jalan Jendral Gatot Subroto
P.O. Box 3315
Jakarta
Indonesia
Telephone: 583051, 588011, or 587981
Telex: 46673 or 46698 HILTON IA
Cable: HILTELS
Fax: 62-21-583091
Reservations:
   In Jakarta call 583051, 588011, or 587981, ext. 3003,
      3004, 3005, or 3006
   In the USA call 1-800-223-1146

All major credit cards
General Manager: Michael Schuetzendorf
Concierge: Reinhard Noya
Sales Director: Rudy Setiawan
Hilton International
Rates (approx.):
   Superior room $110 single, $125 double
   Garden Tower room $140 single, $155 double
   Studio suite $210
   Alcove suite $275
   Executive suite $345
   Presidential Suite $675
   Garden suite $460
   Penthouse Suite $1,750
664 rooms, 77 suites
Service charge 10%; tax 5%

The Jakarta Hilton International is part of a complex started in 1971, when the PT Indobuildo company purchased a parcel of land, with rice paddies and huts, nestled around a river bend. In 1974 the company opened the Indonesian Bazaar, with the authentic Balinese Theatre, and the Batak Village group of shops—all of which surrounded a picturesque artificial lake. Also built were Executive Lanais, meant to be home to thousands of newcomers to fast-developing Indonesia, and the Executive Club, for the foreigners' social activities and sports.

The Jakarta Hilton opened in 1976 with 396 bedrooms and suites. It grew in 1983, when the Garden Tower, with 213 new hotel guest rooms, was added to the complex (along with two thirty-story towers of apartments, new sports facilities, and a shopping center).

My favorite spot in this hotel is the spectacular lobby. Replicating the interior of the Sultan's Palace in Yogyakarta, Central Java, it is highlighted by a magnificent antique carved wooden screen that separates the lobby from the Kudus Bar.

The hotel's original guest rooms, first decorated in an Indonesian style to please the expected tourists, have been redesigned to accommodate business travelers (who now make up 99 percent of the hotel's visitors). The rooms in the Garden Tower have even more modern amenities, including king-sized beds, writing desks, color TV, international direct-dial telephone, and electronic door locks. The spacious marble bathrooms include both tubs and shower stalls. Still, all the furniture is made in Indonesia—the upholsteries by home weavers in West Java—and colorful batik panels hang on the walls.

Try to get a peep at the pièce de résistance of the Garden Tower extension—the top-floor Penthouse Suite. Below a helipad, it is designed to serve a visiting statesman, stateswoman, or corporate chief executive. With an unobstructed view across the entire city of Jakarta, the Penthouse has three bedrooms, a study, a music room, a lounge, a large dining area, and even a soundproof room with communications equipment. It has a private elevator, a private butler, and a private swimming pool. The suite is surrounded by a large terrace with colorful bougainvillaea.

The hotel has several places to eat and drink:

The Taman Sari, named after the Sultan of Yogyakarta's summer retreat in Central Java, features haute cuisine and "Indonesian nouvelle cuisine" at lunch and dinner.

The low-priced Peacock Cafe coffee shop, open twenty-four hours a day, serves local and international fare and has a special dessert counter. The daily buffet is $8.80, and the menu features items from $1.50 to $10.25.

For a quiet escape, the Garden Lounge features not only cocktails but Devonshire tea, which is served along with scones, wafer-thin cucumber sandwiches, and muffins.

The Kudus Bar, off the grand lobby, offers live musical entertainment at night.

Outside the hotel but within the complex is the Sriwedari Gardens restaurant. The light, healthful cuisine here includes both local and international fare. It is a fun place: Friday evening features live jazz; Saturday is Hawaiian Night; and Sunday brings the Hilton Hoedown, starring the Crude Oil Cowboys. On the weekends, food stalls supplement the barbecue and buffet offerings. A meal here costs about six and a half dollars.

The hotel's Executive Business Centre offers secretarial and translation services; twenty-four-hour telex, facsimile, and photocopying services; an IBM word processor; and a UPI news tape.

There are two fitness centers, one in the Hilton Executive Club and the other in the Garden Tower. Both have plenty of the latest equipment. Also available are a 1,500-meter jogging track, with distance markers; three squash courts; and nine flood-lit outdoor tennis courts. Both the Executive Club and the main hotel have large outdoor swimming pools and children's pools.

At no extra charge for "executive lady travelers," the hotel offers the Lady Jakarta Hilton program. It includes accommodation on the nonsmoking fifteenth or sixteenth floor, or on a regular floor, the fourteenth. The Lady Jakarta rooms have floral wallpaper in pastel hues, queen-sized beds, quilted batik bedspreads with scatter cushions, special toiletries, hairdryers, scales, robes, and the latest editions of *Vogue* and *Travel and Leisure*. The room price includes daily tea at the Garden Lounge.

MANDARIN ORIENTAL
Jalan M. H. Thamrin
P.O. Box 3392
Jakarta
Indonesia
Telephone: 321307
Telex: 61755 MANDA JKT
Cable: MANDAHOTEL
Fax: 62-21-324669
Reservations:
  In Jakarta call 321307
  In the USA call (212) 752-9710, (213) 649-1634, or
    (312) 346-7663
All major credit cards
General Manager: A. G. P. Laird
Concierge: J. Berhitoe
Director of Sales and Marketing: Carlo R. H. Gomez
Sales Manager: Herdy Sayogha
Mandarin Oriental Hotel Group
Rates (approx.):
  Room $105 single, $115 double
  Suite $220–$600
455 rooms, 19 suites
Service charge 10%; tax 5.5%

The Mandarin Oriental is situated right in the middle of Jakarta, just across from the city's Welcome Monument, whose lighted multicolored fountains are a colorful sight at night.

The hotel is very popular with business people, not only for its location and its Business Centre but also for its staff, who seem really concerned that all goes well for visitors to their hotel and city.

The guest rooms, like those in the other Mandarin Oriental hotels, are elegantly furnished and spacious. With built-in teak closets, silk lampshades, and hand-batiked quilts, their decor is delightfully Indonesian. Their windows are insulated to block out all the street noises. Bedside consoles control the air conditioning, radio, multichannel in-house music, and color TV with in-house movies. All rooms have refrigerators and mini-bars. The extra large bathrooms, surfaced with a local cream-colored marble, are equipped with bathtubs, showers, telephone extensions and radio speakers, and usually double wash basins.

Dining and wining is pleasant in all the hotel's restaurants:

The Marquee Coffee Shop is *my favorite spot*, for its cheerful atmosphere and nice view of Jakarta. The walls are decorated with white timber screens and panels of blue hand-painted tiles to match the blue patterned carpet. White cane furniture with sky blue upholstery, brass, and crystal lamps create a charming ambiance.

The richly furnished Club Room, with an extensive wine list, serves lunch and dinner in the grand French style.

The Spice Garden features 160 hot and spicy Sichuan specialties.

The Clipper Lounge is a popular place for meeting friends or business associates over drinks or a light meal. The deep beige chairs are attractive against the dark wood paneling. During the evening a group plays light background music.

The Captain's Bar is the favorite spot of local businessmen. Sports films are shown at midday, when four-course lunch is served at a fixed price. In the evening a jazz band plays.

Although the hotel has no gardens, on the fifth-floor Pelangi Terrace is a hexagonal open-air swimming pool. Drinks and snacks are served at the pool side and under big, resort-style umbrellas.

Athletic guests also enjoy two air-conditioned squash courts, on the twenty-seventh floor, and the hotel's fitness center. The center's state-of-the-art equipment, imported from the United States, includes weight machines, free weights, and a variety of aerobic pieces such as exercise bicycles, treadmills, and rowing machines. A trained staff is always at hand, and six health classes are offered during the day. At 5:45 A.M. enthusiastic runners gather in the lobby for any of three different runs in the hotel's environs.

An ideal hotel for the business traveler, this is also a pleasant place for the tourist to stay.

Surabaya

The city of Surabaya is on the northeast corner of the island of Java, directly opposite the neighboring island of Madura. The city's population is about two and a half million, about the same as Singapore's. This makes it the largest city of East Java and the second largest city, after Jakarta, of all Java.

Over centuries the city has grown southward from the port area, the oldest part of the city, and from the surroundings of the Kail Mas River. During the past few years a new residential suburb, called Darmo, and a large industrial estate, at Rungkut, have been established in the southeast.

A hub of trade, finance, and manufacturing, Surabaya is also a major base for the Indonesian navy and a center for shipbuilding and repair. It isn't a place to visit for its dance, music, art, and other cultural life. What historical sights there are to see involve the period from 1945 to 1949, when the nation was fighting for its independence. The major monument, Tugu Pahlawan, was built in memory of those who died at that time. There are many statues to military figures, particularly General Sudirman and Bung Tomo. There are no monuments to heroes of earlier times, although some streets are named for them.

Visitors do enjoy seeing the harbor, the port, and some important streets (*jalans*), especially Jalan Pemuda and Jalan Tunjungan. On Pemuda is an enormous Dutch-built residence, now the official home of the governor of East Java. Almost opposite it is a Bhuddist statue known as Joko Dolog ("Guardian of Young Teak") and nicknamed the Fat Boy. Erected in 1236 in honor of the last king of a Javanese kingdom, the statue was brought here by the Dutch three hundred years ago. The Fat Boy is believed to have curative powers, and if you visit him on a Thursday evening or Friday you'll see people asking him to cure their ailments and resolve their worries.

Also on Pemuda is the Mitra Theatre Complex, a Dutch colonial building now housing a movie theater as well as offices.

Jalan Tunjungan is the city's main shopping area. Although Jakarta has a number of modern shopping centers such as Ratu Plaza and Duta Merlin, none equal this street in the variety and quality of shops.

Other things to see in town are the Heroes Moument, the flower markets, the zoo, the Ampel Mosque, and the

Museum Emp Tantular, with archaeological and technological displays. Opposite the zoo, the museum has helpful,
English-speaking guides but no labels in English.

HYATT BUMI SURABAYA
124–128 Jalan Basuki Rakhmat
Surabaya 60271
Indonesia
Telephone: 470875 or 470503
Telex: 34316 HYATT SIA
Cable: HYATT SURABAYA
Fax: 0062-31-470508
Reservations:
  In Surabaya call 470875
  In Jakarta call (021) 376008
  In the USA and Canada call 1-800-228-9000
All major credit cards
General Manager: Thomas John
Sales Manager: Harold Lumangkun
Hyatt International Hotels
Rates (approx.):
  Standard room $70 single, $80 double
  Superior room $85 single, $95 double
  Deluxe patio room $90 single, $100 double
  Regency Club room $125 single, $140 double
  Superior suite $185
  Executive suite $175–$260
  Presidential Suite $700
268 rooms and suites
Service charge 21%; tax 5%

The Hyatt Bumi Surabaya is in the heart of the city's business district, near the excellent Tunjungan Shopping Centre.
The most up-to-date convention center in the city, it is only
twenty minutes by taxi from the Juanda Airport.

All guest rooms are nicely furnished in the efficient Hyatt
style and well-equipped with amenities such as color TV,
in-house movies, air conditioning, private bathrooms, direct-dial telephone, radio, purified drinking water, and mini-
bars. The top two of the hotel's ten floors house the Regency
Club. Very popular with business travelers, the higher-priced
rooms here include extra services and amenities.

The hotel has several places to eat: The always popular
Hugo's, familiar to those who stay at Hyatt's around the
world, features roast prime rib of beef served from a silver

trolley and, unique in East Java, nouvelle cuisine. Salads and flambés are prepared at your table. Other restaurants in the hotel are Ceshiang, serving Chinese meals, Shima, serving Japanese food, and the Arumanis Terrace, open twenty-four hours a day. Here also are a pool-side snack bar, the Kecapi piano lounge, and the Harbour Tavern Bar.

For business travelers and others, this hotel is an oasis in a city where air conditioning, king-sized beds, and first-class dining rooms can't be taken for granted.

Ask for your copy of the *Hyatt Hotel's Guide to Surabaya*, a very helpful forty-eight-page booklet with maps.

Japan

A country of more than 120 million people occupying only about 144 thousand square miles, Japan is an archipelago off the coast of East Asia; its capital is Tokyo. Comprised of four main islands, Hokkaido, Honshu, Shikoku, and Kyushu, Japan also has many smaller islands stretched in an arc between the Sea of Japan, the East China Sea, and the Pacific Ocean. Honshu, Shikoku, and Kyushu surround the Inland Sea. All the islands are mountainous. The highest and most famous peak, on Honshu, is Mount Fuji, elevation 12,388 feet. There are rushing short rivers, forested slopes, irregular and lovely lakes, and small rich plains.

The arable land in Japan is intensely cultivated. Farmers use irrigation, terracing, and multiple cropping to coax rich crops out of the soil. Chief crops include rice and other cereals, vegetables, and industrial crops like mulberry trees for feeding silkworms. Livestock is also raised. Fishing is highly developed, and the annual catch is one of the biggest in the world.

In the late nineteenth century Japan was rapidly and thoroughly industrialized. Textiles were a leading item, and vast quantities of light manufactured goods were produced. In the 1950s and 1960s the production of heavy machinery grew. Today Japan is a leading producer of ships, motor vehicles, steel, textiles, and, of course, electronic equipment.

The Japanese believe their Empire was founded in 660

B.C. by the emperor Jimmu, a lineal descendent of the sun goddess and ancestor of the present emperor. By A.D. 400, Japan was inhabited by numerous clans or tribal kingdoms ruled by priest-chiefs. Initial contact with the West began in the mid-1500s, when a China-bound ship from Portugal landed in Japan, but, in the 1600s, fearing conquest by the Europeans, the Japanese expelled all foreigners and severely limited further contact. This isolationism persisted until the mid-1800s. Renewed relations with the West also signaled vast changes in Japanese government, law, and society and transformed Japan into a world power. Westerners are vividly familiar with Japan's post-World War II history: Following the explosion of the atomic bombs over Hiroshima and Nagasaki in 1945 and Japan's surrender to Allied troops, the Empire was dissolved, and the country was demilitarized. In 1947 a new constitution was adopted, and the emperor publicly disclaimed his divinity. In 1952 Japan again assumed full sovereignty and has been ruled by conservative governments desiring to maintain close, cooperative relations with the West. Its open, democratic society is very appealing to travelers.

The Japan National Tourist Organization is truly dedicated to helping tourists. It has a unique service called Japan Travel-Phone. If you need any help in getting around or finding some place, just go to the public phone booth nearby and dial 106 (in Tokyo and Kyoto you have to deposit a 10-yen coin, which is returned; this is a free call everywhere). Speak slowly and distinctly in English and say, "Collect call, T.I.C." You will be connected to an English-speaking person who will help you. Make the call any time between 9:00 A.M. and 5:00 P.M.

Japan can be very expensive, as you will note in reading some of the room rates and costs for meals on the pages that follow. But, according to the people at Westin Hotels and Resorts, Japan can be as inexpensive or as expensive as you would like it to be—not unlike any large Western nation.

The point they make is that most travelers do not take the time to plan and to research. They give eight recommendations:

1. Contact a travel agent, who is usually an excellent resource in helping the traveler find bargains throughout Japan.

2. Contact a Japan National Tourist Organization (JNTO) office. There are offices throughout the United States and

Canada, and they can be helpful in suggesting ways for you and your family to reduce costs, if that is your objective.

3. Secure a Japan Rail Pass. Available to all foreign visitors who have visas, this can be one of the most relaxing and inexpensive ways of seeing and getting around Japan.

4. Get off the beaten path. Traveling costs less outside the big cities, just as in most other countries.

5. Shop at department stores. Those in Japan generally have excellent selections and are used to serving and shipping for foreigners.

6. Use free travel help at the hotel or the JNTO travel phone to get help from trained people.

7. Set your budget, and tell it to your travel agent, who can help you keep within it.

8. Be realistic. Japan, like the United States, France, England, and other popular countries, has developed a wide range of services available to visitors, and, of course, the luxury services are priced accordingly.

Hiroshima

With a population of about one million, this is the capital of the Hiroshima prefecture on southwest Honshu, located on Hiroshima Bay. It is an important commercial and industrial center where textiles, sake, ship components, automobiles, tools, furniture, machinery, and canned foods are produced. Here, too, are markets for agricultural and marine products. Founded in 1594 as a castle city on the Ota River delta, it is divided by the river's seven mouths into six islands that are now connected by eighty-one bridges.

On August 6, 1945, Hiroshima was the target of the first atomic bomb ever dropped on a populated area. Almost thirteen thousand people were killed and 90 percent of the city was leveled. Today, most of the city has been rebuilt, and it is a splendid, modern city. The most important structure in the city today is Peace Memorial Park. Visitors also favor Hiroshima Castle and Hijiyama Park.

ANA HOTEL HIROSHIMA
7–20 Naka-Machi
Kaka-ku
Hiroshima 30
Japan

Telephone: (082) 241-1111
Telex: 652751 ANAHIJ J
Fax: (082) 241-9123
Reservations:
  In Hiroshima call (082) 241-1111
  In the USA call Robert F. Warner:
    in New York State call (212) 725-1510; elsewhere in
    the USA call 1-800-858-4849
All major credit cards
General Manager: Masaru Matsubara
Sales Manager: Mikiya Awai
ANA (All Nippon Airways) Hotels
Rates (approx.):
  Standard room $57 single, $105 double
  Superior room $61 single, $108 double
  Deluxe room $64 single, $111 double
  Suite $203–$1,080
431 rooms, 8 suites
Service charge 10%; tax 10%

A comfortable and modern hotel in the heart of the International City of Peace, as Hiroshima is now called, the ANA Hotel Hiroshima is a twenty-two-floor structure. Its exceptional height provides views of Peace Memorial Park, Hiroshima Castle, the Atomic Bomb Dome, and Miyajima Island. The hotel's management is dedicated to its theme of international harmony. Every facet of the service reflects this feeling.

Each of the hotel's rooms is equipped with color TV carrying the CATV news channel, a refrigerator, direct-dial telephones with an extension in the bathroom, a tub/shower combination, and controlled air conditioning.

The hotel provides Western, Chinese, and Japanese dining rooms. On the hotel's first floor is the hotel's coffee shop, the Boulogne, open from 7:00 A.M. to midnight. The hotel's Tea and Cocktail Lounge is open from 9:00 A.M. to 11:00 P.M. On the fifth floor is the Japanese restaurant, the Unkai, open for breakfast and lunch, and the Chinese dining room, the Tao Li, open for lunch and dinner. The top floor is the location for the Castle View restaurant, affording diners the opportunity to take in views of the city. The Star Dust bar lounge and the main bar, the Vega, are also found on the top floor and are known for their views as well.

The health club, Santeloi, is located on the sixth floor. Its features include a training gym, a sauna, and a heated indoor swimming pool, open from noon to 9:00 P.M.

Banquet and conference facilities are found on the third floor. Manyo Hall, used for large international conferences, is equipped to provide simultaneous interpretation in four languages.

Ibusuki

IBUSUKI KANKO HOTEL
3755 Juni-Cho
Ibusuki City 891-04
Kagoshima
Japan
Telephone: (099) 322-2131
Telex: 786711 IKHJ
Cable: IBUSUKI KANKO
Fax: (099)322-2882
Reservations:
  In Ibusuki call (099) 322-2131
  In Tokyo call (03) 563-0136
All major credit cards
President: Yohachiro Iwasaki
General Manager: Kouichi Yamamoto
Sales Manager: Osamu Shimpuku
Nikkou Hotels International
Rates (approx.):
  Standard room $68 single, $81 double
  Superior room $84 single, $98 double
  Deluxe room $101 single, $115 double
  Suite $236
631 rooms, 7 suites
Service charge 10%; tax 10%

The Ibusuki Kanko Hotel claims that it is the biggest resort hotel on the Pacific coast. It rises ten stories above the ground and goes three floors underground. The north side of the hotel faces the sea, and, on the south side, there is a large, landscaped garden with a pond, palm trees, and pools. Actually in the national park of Kirishima and Yaku, the hotel is in the heart of a tropical setting where flowers bloom year round.

The Ibusuki hot springs make this a popular spot. The beach, similar to Hawaii's Waikiki but less crowded, is considered a natural sauna where people take sand baths, said to be effective as both a cure for illness and as a beauty treatment.

A favorite area is the Jungle Promenade, where more than three thousand tame tropical birds are found living in the trees. Guests of the hotel are able to soak in the more than fifty hot spring pools among the tropical surroundings of the first Jungle Bath ever built in Japan. Five thousand guests can dine and watch the Japanese and Polynesian folk dances in the Restaurant Theater found in this jungle complex.

The Sky Lounge on the top floor of the hotel, open from 7:00 A.M. to midnight, serves Western-style à la carte dishes and drinks. The lounge provides a magnificent panorama of the entire city, Kinko Bay, and the Osumi Peninsula on the opposite shore. You can see the peaks of Mount Kirishima and Mount Kaimondake, where honeymooning couples go to plant a pair of trees in the Honeymoon Memorial Planting Garden—more than sixty thousand pairs of trees are already in place.

The Main Dining Room of the hotel serves French and other continental cuisines in a luxurious setting. Breakfast and dinner are served poolside, as is lunch during the summer months. The main lobby is the location for the coffee shop, the Tapa Room, open from 7:00 A.M. to 6:00 P.M. The Chirin Midnight Snack Bar is open from 7:30 P.M. to 1:00 A.M. and serves beverages and Japanese food such as *onigiri* (rice balls) and *udon* (noodles). The Okonomi Japanese dining room, featuring à la carte sushi, tempura, and local dishes, is open for breakfast and dinner.

The hotel's guest rooms and their bathrooms are modern and spacious and have the necessary amenities. The hot springs are taxed separately at 150 yen (about one dollar).

Ito

On the eastern shore of the Izu Peninsula, Ito is noted as a port with an abundance of marine products and as a shopping and amusement center. It has a number of good restaurants, many featuring seafood, and celebrated hot springs. Many of Japan's writers and poets have written about Ito (or gone there to write while relaxing). The town has many literary monuments attesting to the fame of its writers.

Izu Peninsula abounds with the natural splendor of mountains and coastlines. Standing on the Amagi Range, which rises the full length of the peninsula, one can view Mount Fuji, the Hakone Mountains (Japan's South "Alps"), and the notable Seven Izu Islands. East Izu has complicated coastlines formed from lava and dotted with lovely crinums. South Izu has a graceful pastoral setting that blends with shores ranging from the simple to the rugged.

On the coast north of Ito is Atami, one of Japan's largest hot spring resorts. It is called the "Naples of the Orient" because of its enchanting night cityscape. The Atami Spa, with about three hundred fifty springs, has been famous for centuries. Izu Shrine, with a long history, is an international tourist attraction.

Majestic Mount Fuji can be seen from practically anywhere on the Kawana estate. A scenic drive can take one closer to it as well as past the natural gardens of Oniwa and Okuniwa.

KAWANA HOTEL
1459 Kawana
Ito
Shizuoka Prefecture 414
Japan
Telephone: (055) 745-1111
Telex: 392-7565 KATEL J
Cable: KATEL ITO
Fax: (055) 745-3834
Reservations:
   In Tokyo call (03) 562-3771
   In the USA call Robert F. Warner: in New York State
      call (212) 725-1510; elsewhere in the USA call
      1-800-792-7637
All major credit cards
General Manager: Yoshiharu Yoneyama
Concierge: Tastuo Kato
Sales Manager: Mamoru Murakami
Hotel Okura Chain
Rates (approx.):
   Standard room $140 single, $160 double
   Deluxe room $213
   Suite $467–$1,600
140 rooms, 4 suites
Service charge 10%; tax 10%

Hailed by many as one of the very best hotels in the world, the elegant Kawana Hotel is the pride and joy of Baron

Okura, who conceived the Okura Hotel in Tokyo. The Kawana Hotel is a two-hour ride by train from downtown Tokyo, and it is a golfer's paradise. Its two eighteen-hole courses, including the Fuji Course with marvelous views of Mount Fuji in the distance, were designed by C. H. Allison, famed for creating hazardous sand traps.

Situated on the coast of the Izu Peninsula in the scenic Fuji-Hakone-Izu National Park, this is one of Japan's great luxury resort hotels. Many of the guests enjoy ocean cruising, fishing, and sightseeing trips. There are three swimming pools, two tennis courts, a billiard room, and a card room. Four banquet halls are capable of accommodating one thousand participants in the conferences or conventions held at the hotel. Diners can enjoy two European-style restaurants, a country-style house, Japanese restaurants, and two bars.

Kobe

A port city with more than 1.5 million residents, Kobe is the capital of Hyogo prefecture of south Honshu, Japan, on Osaka Bay. Known for its shipbuilding yards, vehicle factories, iron and steel mills, sugar refineries, and rubber, chemical, and food-processing plants, it also has seven colleges and universities and many temples and shrines. The city was heavily bombed during World War II, but it has since been rebuilt.

Known as one of the most modern and largest ports in the world, Kobe has been developing since 1868. From Port Island Northern Park you can see the big container ships come and go. Views of Mount Rokko can be enjoyed through the windows of the foreign homes, called *ijinkan*. A lot of old residential buildings are along the Kaigan-dori and Nakattotei, including the Port Tower, the pier for passenger boats to Setonaikai. There is a sightseeing boat that offers one-hour cruises around the port.

KOBE PORTOPIA HOTEL
10-1, 6-Chome Minotojima Nakamachi
Chuo-Ku
Kobe City 650
Japan
Telephone: (078) 302-1111

Telex: 5622-112 KOPTEL J
Cable: PORTOPIA KOBE
Fax: (078) 302-6877
Reservations:
  In Kobe call (078) 302-1111
  In California call 1-800-525-4685
  In Hawaii call 1-800-926-4522
  Elsewhere in the USA call 1-800-NIKKO-US or
    1-800-221-4862
All major credit cards
President: Tsutomu Nakauchi
General Manager: Ichiro Yoshimura
Sales Manager: Tadao Watanabe
Nikko Hotels International
Rates (approx.):
  Single room $57–$95
  Double room $135–$169
  Suite $338–$1,350
540 rooms, 10 suites
Service charge 10%; tax 10%

This is a luxurious new hotel located on Port Island, just off the Kobe shore. Thirty-two floors high and equipped with an exterior see-through elevator, this is the tallest hotel in western Japan. As a result, the guests enjoy views from every room, including sights of Seto-naikai, or the Inland Sea; the expansive Rokko mountain range; and a panorama of Kobe by night. The rooms are tastefully appointed and are fully equipped with the latest amenities.

The Portopia Club is a gorgeous salon for the exclusive use of the hotel's executive guests. In a comfortable setting overlooking the sea, its features include recreation rooms, a heated swimming pool, a gymnasium, tennis courts, and sauna. The pool, sauna, and gymnasium are available to all hotel guests on request.

Dining facilities are abundant. The first floor is the location for the Shofukuro Japanese restaurant, offering Japanese cuisine; the Hiraiso-Shushi, offering fresh seafood from the Inland Sea; the Yawaragi-Tempura an Eels, which features deep-fried tempura; and La Belle Cour Tea Lounge, which is at the water's edge and is connected to the main lounge. Guests love to watch the waterfall from this location.

On the second floor is the Tajima-Teppan-yaki, specializing in delicious Kobe beef and fresh seafood from the Inland Sea; St. Malo Coffee House, offering snacks, drinks, and a great bakery; and L'Estacade Bar, providing live piano music.

The upper floors house Shukei-en Chinese restaurant on the twenty-ninth floor, featuring the Canton dishes of Hong Kong chef Wai Lo; the Plein d'Etoiles (Full of Stars) Sky Lounge on the thirtieth floor, which has a sweeping view of Kobe by night and provides nightly entertainment by first-class entertainers; and Alain Chapel French restaurant on the thirty-first floor, run by Chapel, an outstanding practitioner of nouvelle cuisine.

The hotel is less than an hour's drive from Osaka International Airport and a ten-minute drive from the Shin-Kobe station. Be sure to get your copy of the *Kansai Walking Map* issued by the hotel.

Kyoto

The capital of the Kyoto prefecture on south Honshu, Kyoto is a busy city located on the Kamo River, which uses Yado as its port. Kyoto is famous for its cloisonné, bronzes, damascene work, porcelain, and lacquer ware. Its renowned silk industry dates from the year 794. Its industries include food processing, copper rolling, and the manufacture of spinning and dyeing machinery, precision tools, electrical equipment, and cameras.

Founded in the eighth century, Kyoto lost its political power in 1192 to Tokyo; however, for centuries this delightful city has been the cultural center of Japan. Rich also in historic interest, Kyoto is the site of the tombs of many famous Japanese. Old palaces, shrines, and monuments as well as fine parks and gardens add to the beauty of the city. Among the many historical sights are the Old Imperial Palace built in 794 by Emperor Kwammu, which was destroyed and rebuilt many times (the present structure was built in 1858); and the Nijo Castle, built in 1603 by Tokugawa Ieyasu, which served as the residence for visiting shoguns. The interior of Nijo Castle is considered far more flamboyant than that of the Old Imperial Palace.

A religious center, Kyoto is noted especially for its ancient Buddist temples and its Heian shrine (a Shinto holy place with a fifty-nine-foot-high statue of Buddha).

Among the interesting temples to visit are the Higashi-Honganji Temple, a Buddhist temple erected in 1602; the Kinkakuji Temple, the "Golden Pavilion," built in 1397, which has one of Japan's finest gardens; the Ginkakuji Temple, the "Silver Pavilion," built in 1479, which also has a celebrated garden; the Nishi-Honganji Temple, of the Shinshu sect, one of the finest in Kyoto; the Saihoji Temple, the "Moss Temple," established in 1339, which is famous for its garden covered with a thick carpet of more than fifty varieties of moss; the Kiyomizu Temple, dating from 794 (this structure was built in 1633), which has a magnificent panoramic view of Kyoto from its platform and is surrounded by beautiful cherry and maple trees; the Ryoanji Temple, with its unique garden consisting of only fifteen small ricks set on a background of white sand; and the Chioin Temple, which was originally built in 1211 and rebuilt in 1639, with an eighty-ton bell that is the largest in the nation, and beautiful pictures on screens and panels in the reception rooms.

There are four big festivals held in Kyoto annually. The Gion Festival originated in the ninth century, and on July 17 and 24 there is a procession of twenty floats throughout the city. The Aoi Festival, "the festival of the hollyhocks," is on May 15 with a procession showing the grandeur of old court life. The Jidai Festival, "the festival of ages," is held on October 22; it was first observed in 1850 to celebrate the eleven hundredth anniversary of the founding of Kyoto, with a colorful procession of thirteen groups representing great events in Kyoto's history. Daimonji is held on August 16, when a fire is lit in the form of the figure meaning "great"; this is the oldest and biggest of the city's five traditional fires of various designs on the hillsides surrounding Kyoto.

ANA HOTEL KYOTO
Nijojo-Mae
Horikawa-dori
Nakagyo-ku
Kyoto 604
Japan
Telephone: (075) 231-1155
Telex: 5423181 ANAHK J
Fax: (075) 231-5333
Reservations:
  In Kyoto call (075) 231-1155
  In the USA, call Robert F. Warner: in New York state
    call (212) 725-1510; elsewhere in the USA
    call 1-800-792-7637
All major credit cards

Property Manager: Masumi Ito
General Manager: Shigeru Ito
Concierge: Nagami
Sales Manager: Anazawa
ANA Hotels
Rates (approx.):
  Standard room $56 single, $102 double
  Superior room $66 single, $125 double
  Deluxe room $92 single, $145 double
  Suite $197–$986
303 rooms, 9 suites
Service charge 10%; tax 10%

Located next to Nijo Castle, one of Kyoto's delightful landmarks, this modestly priced hotel is attractive both inside and outside. The large windowed wall in the lobby actually gives one the impression of being outdoors. Watching the waterfall through this window makes any time spent in the lobby more relaxing.

The rooms are spacious and comfortable and are well supplied with such amenities as toothbrush and razor as well as both green and plum teas. When reserving your room, ask for one on the castle side, which has an especially nice view. The suites are located on a separate floor of the hotel, and three of them are decorated in Japanese style. Try to see the majestic Castle Suite, which has beautiful ceilings, furnishings, and views.

Catering to the traveling business person's needs, the ANA Hotel Kyoto has a business service center and a health and exercise center, featuring a swimming pool and sauna. Called the Santeloi, this is Kyoto's first urban health spa, an exclusive swim-and-sauna membership club. The spa lounge is truly marvelous.

The restaurants are varied and attractive. On the first floor is Cozy, a coffee shop with a view of the garden, open from 7:00 A.M. until midnight. Also on the first floor are the Unkai Japanese restaurant; the Kamon, with five private rooms featuring Kyoto-style dining; and Karin, serving Chinese cuisine at lunch and dinner. Drinking establishments on the first floor are the comfortable Koto Lounge, which faces a Japanese garden with a cascading waterfall; and Castle Gate, a luxurious bar off the lobby open from 5:00 P.M. to midnight.

An attractive shopping arcade is found in the basement of the hotel, where the Traditional Arts and Crafts Gallery has interesting handicraft displays and exhibitions.

This hotel is an hour by car from Osaka International Airport and five minutes from the Hankyu Line's Shijo-Omiya Station.

KYOTO HOTEL
Kawaramachi Oike
Nakagyo-ku
Kyoto 604
Japan
Telephone: (075) 211-5111
Telex: 5422-126 KYOTEL
Cable: KYOHO KYOTO
Fax: (075) 221-7770
Reservations:
   In Kyoto call (075) 233-2333
   In Tokyo call (03) 265-6625
   In New York call (212) 758-8975
   In Los Angeles call (213) 488-9917
   In San Francisco call (415) 398-4259
All major credit cards
President: Masashi Takahashi
General Manager: Shoji Arai
Concierge: Yasuko Kawakatssu
Sales Manager: Soichiro Miyata
Nikko Hotels International
Rates (approx.):
   Economy room $51 single, $88 double
   Standard room $61 single, $125 double
   Deluxe room $75–$112 single, $169–$202 double
   Japanese-style suite $155
   Western-style suite $404
507 rooms, 12 suites
Service charge 10%; tax 10%

Situated at Kawaramachi and Oike Streets, Kyoto Hotel is on the Takase River near the mist-covered Higashiyama mountains. Some of the city's finest shops are adjacent to the hotel, while only minutes away are castles, temples, museums, and galleries.

Built in 1888 as the Tokiwa Hotel and later renamed, the Kyoto Hotel is proudly celebrating its centennial. Enjoying its reputation as the best hotel in the city, this venerable building has lodged many famous guests over the years, such as the Duke of Windsor, the Crown Prince of Russia, baseball player Babe Ruth, and many actors and actresses, including Joan Collins, Marlon Brando, and John Wayne (who made a movie in the 1950s about Commodore Perry, whose negotiations in 1854 reopened Japan to the West). In times gone by special bands announced the arrival and departure of dignitaries or other prestigious foreign guests, and today the hotel still marks such occasions with a display of *sayonara* banners.

The rooms in the hotel, even the economy rooms, are attractive and spacious, with, of course, the more expensive being more luxurious. All have air conditioning and heat, color TV—with an English-language channel, radio, mini-bar, and facilities for making green tea. Summer kimonos and slippers are also provided.

Dining and drinking establishments in the hotel are exceptional. The first floor houses the Edinburgh, the main dining room, which is open from 7:00 to 10:00 A.M. Fresh-baked muffins and Western-style breakfasts are available here. In the basement you can eat lunch or dinner at Tohlee, a Chinese restaurant. Grace, a European-style smorgasbord open from 5:00 to 10:00 P.M., is also located in the basement. For five thousand yen (about thirty-two dollars), you can choose all you want from more than thirty dishes.

The second floor is the location for several establishments. The Ikegami sushi bar serves lunch and dinner. The Bianca Restaurant and Coffee Shop is open from 10:00 A.M. until 11:00 P.M. The Isecho Japanese restaurant is open for breakfast, lunch, and dinner. The Lounge Bar, a combination coffee lounge and bar, offers beverages, cakes, ceremonial green tea, and Japanese sweets, and is just the place to write postcards and relax. The Target Club is also located on the second floor; open from 5:00 P.M. to midnight, the club offers piano entertainment for a small cover charge.

On the ninth floor is Tokiwa, a Japanese steak house that features *teppanyaki* steak at lunch or dinner. Tables are available, but if you sit at the counter you can watch the chef prepare your meal in front of you. My favorite place is Restaurant Français La Mer, specializing in the cuisine of southern France.

Five convenience shops, an art gallery, and a pottery shop are also located in the hotel. And while Kyoto Hotel has no sports facilities, for a modest fee guests can use the Higashiyama Tennis Club, about an hour's drive away, or the Seamax Sporting Complex, fifteen minutes away by subway.

Only a five-minute walk from the Kyoto Hotel is a covered

arcade containing small boutiques, souvenir shops, inexpensive restaurants, a supermarket, a Japanese public bath, and many other places including a self-service coin laundry. Local restaurants serve *okonomiyaki*, an inexpensive and enjoyable meal of hot crêpes and cream. The supermarket stocks food items rarely seen in markets back home, from local vegetables and fruits to octopus.

The hotel has some printed pieces you should be sure to ask for. One is the Kyoto Hotel leaflet, which gives information about local castles, shrines, museums, parks, gardens, and other points of interest. Another is the sightseeing map of Kyoto, which has sketches and explanations in English and Japanese. There is also an easy-to-follow map you can request from the concierge, *Inexpensive Restaurants within Five Minutes Walking Distance from the Kyoto Hotel*.

Kyoto Hotel is about an hour's drive from Osaka Airport and about twelve minutes from the Kyoto Station.

KYOTO TOKYU HOTEL
Horikawa-Gojo
Shimogyo-ku
Kyoto 600
Japan
Telephone: (075) 341-2411
Telex: 5422-459
Cable: KYOTOTOKYU TEL
Fax: (075) 341-2488
Reservations:
   In Kyoto call (075) 341-2411
   In the USA call Robert F. Warner: in New York State
      call (212) 725-1510; elsewhere in the USA call
      1-800-792-7637
All major credit cards
General Manager: Joji Yanagihara
Sales Manager: Koichi Watanabe
Tokyu Hotel Chain
Rates (approx.):
   Economy room $62 single, $108 double
   Other room $89–$99 single, $122–$151 double
   Suite $361–$526
433 rooms, 6 suites
Service charge 10%; tax 10%

In the city's center, Kyoto Tokyu Hotel is a very pleasant and comfortable modestly priced lodging. Within walking distance to public transportation, the hotel is close to major shopping and places of historical interest, including the famous Nishihongan-Ji Temple, which can be seen from some of the guest rooms. The lobby and plaza open onto a beautiful, traditional Kyoto garden. There is an outdoor swimming pool in an attractive courtyard, which has imposing stone walls penetrated by little waterfalls.

Dining and drinking establishments include the main bar, a popular rendezvous; Mishima-Tei, a sukiyaki restaurant featuring seasonal Kyoto cuisine prepared by the staff of one of Kyoto's oldest and most famous restaurants; the Mitsuwa Kobe steak restaurant; the Tankuma Kyoto specialty restaurant; and La Riviere, specializing in French dining.

The hotel also houses nine banquet halls available to small gatherings as well as international conferences.

The hotel is about an hour's drive from Osaka International Airport and about five minutes from the Kyoto Station.

MIYAKO HOTEL
Sanjo Keage
Higashiyama-ku
Kyoto 605
Japan
Telephone: (075) 771-7111
Telex: 5422-132 MIYAKO J
Cable: MIYAKO KYOTO
Fax: (075) 751-2490
Reservations:
   In Kyoto call (075) 771-7111
   In Tokyo call (03) 572-8301
   In the USA call Miyako Hotels at 1-800-336-1136, or
      Westin at 1-800-228-3000
All major credit cards
General Manager: Ryuzo Harada
President: Kazue Niwa
Sales Manager: Toshio Nomura
Miyako Hotel Kintetsu Chain
Rates (approx.):
   Standard room $134 single, $138 double
   Medium room $155 single, $159 double
   Deluxe room $224 single, $228 double
   Suite $586–$2,069
477 rooms, 6 suites
Service charge 10%; tax 10%

The Miyako, a ninety-year-old institution, is set on sixteen acres of lush, landscaped gardens on a wooded hillside, located at the northern foot of Mount Kacho, a peak in the Higashiyama range. The vicinity includes well-known religious sites such as the Heian Shrine, the Nanzenji Temple, the Shoren-in Temple, and the Chio-in Temple, as well as the grand Kyoto National Municipal Museum of Art. Though away from the hustle and bustle of the city center, the Miyako is still situated so guests may enjoy the attractions of this former capital without going too far from the hotel.

The celebrated Dr. Togo Murano, a member of the Japan Art Academy, designed the Miyako's main building, which is eight stories high, as well as the Miyako's seven-story Garden Wing and the Kasui-en, an elegant arbor-type annex that opened in spring 1988.

The hotel has a large banquet hall, capable of serving one thousand diners, and fourteen other large and small function rooms. The new annex adds many desirable facilities: a large ballroom, more function rooms, spacious guest rooms, a fitness club, a continental restaurant, a steak house, a night lounge, and a shopping gallery of fine shops as well as boutiques.

You may choose Japanese- or Western-style accommodations; both are luxurious. It is fun for Westerners to reserve a secluded Japanese-style suite, including Japanese bath and central heating, and to try living in true Japanese style. All the rooms have air conditioning and color TV.

The hotel offers a number of dining options. *My favorite spot* is the Grand View Restaurant, featuring continental cuisine and a breathtaking view of the city. Be sure to request a copy of the leaflet available from this restaurant identifying each of the mountains, buildings, and shrines you can see from your table.

Other dining facilities include the Circular Room, a tranquil lounge with a view, featuring specialty dishes; the Sukiyaki Shabu-Shabu Gagoromo, specializing in Ohmi beef sukiyaki or *shabu-shabu*; the Shisen, a Chinese restaurant featuring Sichuan-style dishes and Chinese wine; the Hamasaku, a Japanese restaurant serving shrimp tempura and Kansai cuisine; the Miyako Coffee Shop, serving Western snacks; the Tea Lounge, a quiet lounge offering homemade cakes, cookies, and refreshments, as well as ceremonial tea and evening cocktails; and the Seven Stars Bar, serving snacks as well as drinks.

In addition to the leaflet you can get from the Grand View Restaurant, two other free leaflets are available to guests.

The Ten Best Gardens in Kyoto is a map and story sheet that can guide you on a walking tour of the city. *The Shinmonzen Street Shopping Guide* is a booklet describing Kyoto's favorite shopping boulevard, particularly its fine jewelry, antique, art, and furniture shops. The last page of this booklet has a map, in English and Japanese, showing all the major tourist attractions as well as all the major hotels in Kyoto. At the bottom of the map is a message for the taxi driver, so all you need to do is point to the place on the map you want to see.

WESTIN KYOTO TAKARA-GA-IKE PRINCE HOTEL
Takaragaike
Sakyo-ku
Kyoto 606
Japan
Telephone: (075) 712-1111
Telex: 542-3261 KYTPRHJ
Cable: TAKPRINCE KYOTO
Fax: (075) 712-7677
Reservations:
   In Tokyo call (03) 209-8686
   In New York call (212) 889-5928
   In Los Angeles call (213) 689-4800
   Elsewhere in the USA and in Canada call
      1-800-228-3000
All major credit cards
General Manager: Eiju Ohshima
Concierge: Kohki Umeda
Sales Manager: Masaru Takemoto
Westin Hotels and Resorts
Rates (approx.):
   Twin room $180 single, $200 double
   Double room $200 single, $220 double
   Suite $467–$533
   Royal Suite $1,200–$1,333
322 rooms, 21 suites, 7 Royal Suites
Service charge 10%; tax 10%

One of Japan's newest hotels (it opened October 9, 1986), the Takara-ga-ike (pronounced "Taka-aura-guy-ee-kay") Prince Hotel is located next to Kyoto's International Conference Center. Dr. Togo Murano, who also designed Kyoto's Miyako Hotel, gave the Prince an attractive circular design that blends in discreetly with surrounding natural scenery.

The rooms are luxurious and spacious, with approximately 475 square feet. The suites are also very large, the regular suites up to 850 square feet and the Royal Suites up to 1,704 square feet. Well equipped, each room has a refrigerator, color TV, individual thermostat and air-conditioning controls, large windows with panoramic views, and large beds designed especially with the Western traveler in mind.

The hotel is so sumptuous because it was built to house the seven summit leaders (and their spouses and principal staff members) for the 1986 summit conference involving the governments of the United States, Japan, Great Britain, Germany, France, Canada, and Italy. Kyoto was initially selected because its International Conference Center was one of the country's few locations suitable for the large, prestigious gathering. When the site for the summit was changed from Kyoto to Tokyo, building plans for the Kyoto facility were not drastically altered.

The result is a hotel with some unique features. There are seven guest floors, each designed for one of the seven nations, and each with forty-six rooms. Each floor has one Royal Suite, measuring more than fifteen hundred square feet. Also featured are extraordinary security measures, extra-spacious rooms, and ultra-luxurious interior designs. There are also seven different reception halls and a grand ballroom that can accommodate two thousand guests.

My favorite spot is the Japanese Tea House, also designed by Dr. Murano and set in a tasteful garden. Each of its three rooms is traditionally equipped, including a sunken *kotatsu*, providing comfortable seating. The largest room accommodates ten to twenty guests, the middle-sized room four to eight, and the tea ceremony room up to four guests. The tea house may be reserved for traditional dining from 11:00 A.M. to 9:00 P.M. Complimentary tea demonstrations are given in the tea ceremony room from 9:00 A.M. to 5:00 P.M.; tea and Japanese confections are supplied at a moderate charge. Be sure to request the tea house booklet, which explains the tea ceremony as well as the history of tea's introduction to Japan from China in the eighth century.

Dining facilities at this hotel are excellent. French cuisine, prepared under Chef Adrien Alexandre, is served in Beaux Sejours Restaurant, open from 7:00 A.M. to 9:00 P.M. for all three meals. Lunch and dinner are available at the Sushi

Restaurant, where *nigiri-sushi* is prepared while you watch; and at the Tohen, a Chinese restaurant specializing in authentic dishes served by chefs from Beijing. The Tempura Restaurant, open at 7:00 A.M. for a Japanese-style breakfast, has private rooms or seats at a counter as well as open restaurant dining. The hotel's Main Bar is open from noon to midnight, offering a dimly lighted setting.

Other facilities available at the hotel include a wedding hall, a photo studio, a beauty salon, a souvenir shop, and a business service center.

Niseko

HOTEL NIKKO ANNUPURI
480-1, Niseko Aza
Niseko-machi
Abuta-Gun
Hokkaido 048-15
Japan
Telephone: (013) 658-3311
Telex: 957207 NHIANP
Fax: 0136-58-3317
Reservations:
    In Niseko call (013) 658-3311
    In the USA call 1-800-221-4862
All major credit cards
President: Fujito Omuro
Sales Manager: Tokko Ujiie
Nikko Hotels International
Rates (approx.):
    Apr. 1–July 15 and Sept. 1–Nov. 30 $84–$105
    July 16–Aug. 31 $98–$119
119 rooms, 2 suites
Service charge 10%; tax 10%

This resort hotel opened in early 1986 at the foot of the island of Hokkaido's famous Niseko Annupuri International Ski Area. A great ski resort in winter, it is also an all-season resort with six tennis courts and with a nearby championship golf course. And to help soothe athletes' tired muscles, there is even a huge Japanese-style bath.

The Lilac Dining room is the place to eat in the hotel, and there is the Lavender Bar Lounge. Other facilities include a drugstore, a pro shop, and a ski rental shop. Excellent shops next to the hotel satisfy shoppers' needs.

The views are delightful. From the side of the dining room you can see Mount Annupuri and from the front side you can get a good view of Mount Konbudake.

The hotel is a two-hour-and-twenty-minute ride from the Chitose Airport and a two-hour drive from Sapporo City.

Okinawa

This Japanese island in the western Pacific Ocean has an area of only 454 square miles, yet its population is in excess of two million. It is 350 miles southwest of Kyushu and a part of the Okinawa prefecture. The largest of the Okinawa group of islands in the Ryukyu Island archipelago, it is a long, narrow, irregularly shaped island of volcanic origin with coral formations in the south. The northern part is mountainous, rising to 1,657 feet, with a dense cover of vegetation. Sugar cane, sweet potatoes, and rice are Okinawa's principal crops, and fishing is naturally important.

The island, site of some of the largest U.S. military bases in the western Pacific, was seized by the Allies during World War II as the last step in the Pacific war before invasion of Japan's home islands. U.S. army and marine forces landed on Okinawa on April 1, 1945, suffering heavy losses, and offshore navy vessels were damaged or sunk by Japanese suicide planes and one-man rocket missiles. Organized Japanese resistance continued until June 21, 1945, and in August of that year Okinawa was placed under U.S. military control, which continued until 1972, when control reverted to Japan.

With its subtropical climate, the island today is an attractive area for beach resorts.

SHERATON OKINAWA HOTEL
1478 Kishaba
Kitanakagusuku-Son
Okinawa 901-23
Japan
Telephone: (098) 935-4321
Telex: J79828
Fax: (098) 935-3546
Reservations:

In Okinawa call (098) 935-4321
In the USA call 1-800-324-3535
All major credit cards
General Manager: Nicholas Bahouth
Executive Assistant Manager: Cary M. Gray
Sales Manager: Hiro Toyama
Sheraton Corporation
Rates (approx.):
   Standard room $65 single, $85 double
   Superior room $80 single, $100 double
   Deluxe room $95 single, $120 double
   Junior suite $300
   Deluxe suite $435
301 rooms, 7 suites
Service charge 10%; tax 10%

The hotel is nestled on the top of Kishaba Hill and occupies
five acres of gentle, rolling park land. Nearby are the Southeast Botanical Gardens, the historic Nakagusuko Castle, the
city zoo, and a seaside amusement park. Also nearby, and
reason alone to come here, are the Okinawan beaches, which
are broad and clean. There is excellent swimming and every
kind of water sport.

The hotel rooms and suites are comfortable, spacious,
and well equipped with the amenities, and many have panoramic views of the East China Sea and the vast Pacific.
What is especially nice is that each room opens onto a large
balcony with ocean or hillside views, providing an ideal
spot for breakfast or sunset cocktails. All rooms and suites
have individually controlled air conditioning, color TV, a
radio, refrigerator, and coffee- and tea-making supplies.

The dining rooms are excellent. *My favorite spot*, the Castle
Grill, has the finest French cuisine; its decor makes you feel
that you are dining in an ancient Japanese castle as you
overlook the East China Sea. The Genji Restaurant serves
a varied selection of Japanese delicacies, including traditional tempura, sukiyaki, and *teppanyaki*, and Okinawan
favorites. A popular garden view spot, the Mingei Cafe,
serves everything from light snacks to complete meals and
is open from 7:00 A.M. until 11:00 P.M.; Mingei Cafe features
delightful home-baked pastries. Cocktails and live music
are featured at the Castle Lounge, and the Den, the hotel's
disco, is open from 7:30 P.M. until midnight.

A seasonal outdoor swimming pool, a beauty salon, a
sauna, a steam bath, a massage service, and a gift and
specialty shop are on the premises.

Osaka

A city with over three million people and the capital of Osaka prefecture, Osaka is in southern Honshu on the Osaka Bay, at the mouth of the meandering Yodo River. A major transportation hub and port, Osaka occupies one of the longest settled sites in western Japan and has been important as a commercial center for fifteen hundred years. In the sixteenth century General Hideyoshi built a powerful castle here. Though destroyed by fire in the 1800s, the castle has been reconstructed and still towers above the city. The commercial area developed near the castle while industry, including food processing, printing, and manufacturing of chemicals, textiles, and steel, concentrated on the waterfront. Osaka is still the focal point for a chain of nearby industrial cities. More than eight hundred bridges are in Osaka, which is called the City of Rivers.

Besides the Hideyoshi castle, other notable landmarks include the Buddhist temple Shitennoji, the oldest temple in Japan, founded in 593, and Temmangu, a Shinto shrine founded in 949. As early as the fourth century imperial palaces were built here; the magnificent moated castle, Osaka-jo, is truly worth seeing. Osaka's parks and gardens are noted for their exceptional beauty.

An important cultural center as well, the city is well known for its Noh and Bunraku puppetry theaters. There are also museums of fine art, ceramics, history, and technology as well as Japan's first concert hall for classical music. In all seasons are festivals with floats and fireworks, and spring produces a tremendous show of cherry blossoms.

In striking contrast to Osaka's ancient past is its manmade island, Technoport, devoted to research and development in the high-technology industries. Visitors will truly enjoy its futuristic subterranean city of shopping arcades and malls.

Osaka's airport is also futuristic and is becoming one of the great international airports of the world.

ANA-SHERATON HOTEL OSAKA
1-3-1, Dojimahama
Kita-ku
Osaka 530
Japan
Telephone: (06) 347-1112
Telex: 5236884 ANAEOS J

Fax: (06) 348-9208
Reservations:
   In Osaka call (06) 347-1112
   In the USA call Robert F. Warner: in New York state
      call (212) 725-1510; elsewhere in the USA call
      1-800-792-7637
All major credit cards
Property Manager: Kazuhiro Takeuchi
General Manager: Yoshimi Michigami
Concierge: Mikio Omori
Sales Manager: Minoru Yamazaki
ANA Hotels
Rates (approx.):
   Standard room $79 single, $131 double
   Superior room $85 single, $151 double
   Deluxe room $99 single, $171 double
   Suite $237–$1,314
500 rooms, 26 suites
Service charge 10%; tax 10%

The hotel design is supposed to symbolize the twenty-first-century theme of this international city, and it is indeed a modern structure both outside and in. On the hotel's south side and in sharp contrast to the busy city is the slow-flowing Jojima River, reflecting a portion of the city's history as a city of waterways. It is a stone's throw from the Midosuji, the main boulevard through the Osaka business center. The hotel overlooks the city's unique land-locked island, Nakanoshima.

The main lobby combines modern architecture with a natural setting. Water trickles down a six-story rock sculpture behind the hotel's main stairway and in the courtyard, rising to the skylight on the sixth floor, water splashes over a raintree, which is the focal point of this picturesque lobby.

There are a number of delightful spots to be discovered in this hotel. One is the rooftop patio, a perfect spot for a morning rendezvous or a leisurely after-swim sunbath. Next to the patio is the Garden Room, providing another quiet setting for conversation or for a get-together. On the fifth floor of the hotel is a naturally lighted swimming pool and a sauna and lounge for men.

The guest rooms are all furnished in soft, warm tones, each having a mini-bar and cable TV.

For the business traveler, the guest service department offers a business center and a travel staff. There is a guest relations staff to handle the needs of all hotel guests.

The dining is varied. In the hotel's lobby is a lounge, the Glass Umbrella, which is surrounded by water. My favorite is the two-level Cafe in the Park on the first and second floors overlooking the gardens; Cafe in the Park serves a wide selection in coffee-shop style. The second floor has the excellent Rose Room, the hotel's French restaurant, and the charming Library Bar with a cozy fireplace. On the sixth floor are the Unkai, the Japanese dining room, and the Karin, the Chinese restaurant. In the basement is the Cellar Bar and the Wakamizu, the Japanese noodle house.

Well located, the hotel is ten minutes by car from the Shin Osaka Station and a half hour from the Osaka International Airport.

HOTEL NIKKO OSAKA
7, Nishinocho
Daihoji-machi
Minami-ku
Osaka 542
Japan
Telephone: (06) 244-1111
Telex: 522 7575 NHIOSA
Cable: HOTELNIKKOOSAKA
Fax: (06) 245-2432
Reservations:
   In Osaka call (06) 244-1111
   In the USA, call Nikko Hotels at 1-800-NIKKO-US or
      1-800-645-5687, or call Loews International
      1-800-223-0888
All major credit cards
President: Tsuneo Komatsu
General Manager: Kanji Ohashi
Concierge: Shizuo Inoue
Sales Director: Yoshihisa Hoya
Nikko Hotels International
Rates (approx.):
   Standard room (west wing) $115 single, $135 double
   Standard room (east wing) $131 single, $151 double
   Executive Floor room $145 single, $164 double
   Deluxe room $223 single, $243 double
   Suite $250–$1,314
648 rooms, 7 suites
Service charge 10%; tax 10%

At thirty-two stories, the impressive, white Hotel Nikko Osaka towers over Osaka's Midosuji Avenue on the Shinsaibashi, one of the city's main business thoroughfares. This is a delightful area, because Midosuji Avenue is one of the more elegant boulevards in Japan. Two famous department stores, Daimaru and Sogo, are in front of the hotel. Behind the two stores is the popular Shinsaibashi shopping street, with a large collection of shops selling everything from high fashion to the traditional Japanese crafts. The American Village, called America-Mura, and the European Village, called Europe-Mura, are two trendy areas near the hotel on either side of Midosuji Avenue. Further down the boulevard you will come to the Kabuki Theatre, and at the opposite end is the interesting Electric Science Museum.

While all the rooms are beautiful, particularly attractive are the rooms on the twenty-seventh floor, called the Hanae Mori rooms, named for the world-famous fashion designer who decorated them, using soft pastels and rich fabrics. Of course most magnificent is the hotel's Imperial Suite; ask if you can take a look at it. The twenty-eighth through thirtieth floors have guest rooms and suites reserved for dignitaries.

My favorite spot is the Jet Stream on the thirty-second floor of the hotel. This sky lounge is the place for refreshment after a day of business or sightseeing. The view of Osaka at night is breathtaking. The hotel has three other lounges. On the first floor is the Tea Lounge, a spacious and bright place for meeting friends and getting snacks or refreshments. The Lobby Lounge and the Vol de Nuit, the bar lounge with live entertainment, are on the second floor.

Dining facilities include the Serena coffee shop on the second floor, offering light dining early until late. On the third floor is the hotel's Les Célébrités, featuring international cuisine in an elegant setting. Also on the third floor are the Ich Teppan Yaki Restaurant, featuring meats and seafood prepared while you sit at the counter and watch; the Benkay Japanese restaurant with its sukiyaki, sushi, and full-course Japanese meals; and the Toh-Lee restaurant, featuring authentic Chinese cuisine.

Beneath the hotel is the White Avenue Shopping Arcade, and on the level below that are the White Avenue restaurants, featuring coffee shops, snack bars, and a disco. The subway entrance is here, too. And although the hotel has no swimming pool or fitness center, it has published the *Guide for Joggers*; ask for a copy of this map.

NEW OTANI
4, Shiromi 1-chome
Higashi-ku
Osaka 540
Japan
Telephone: (06) 941-1111
Telex: 5293330 OTNOSK
Fax: (06) 941-9769
Reservations:
  In Osaka call (06) 941-1111
  In Tokyo call (03) 221-2696
  In California call 1-800-252-0197
  Elsewhere in the USA call 1-800-421-8795
All major credit cards
General Manager: Hiroshi Kohda
Concierge: Yoshihiro Kurahashi
Sales Manager: Shinsuke Tajima
Utell International
Rates (approx.):
  Single room $88–$97
  Twin room $111–$141 single, $129–$158 double
  Double room $117–$141 single, $135–$158 double
  Large twin room $129–$158 single, $147–$235 double
  Suite $352–$1,764
  Japanese suite $294
610 rooms, 12 suites
Service charge 10%; tax 10%

Another of Japan's brand-new state-of-the-art hotels has arrived and is doing very well. Its doors opened September 1, 1986, with a staff of six hundred. The hotel, beautifully designed and situated, is part of the new Osaka Business Park, which is developing into the city's new center for commerce as well as pleasure. The hotel caters to the needs of travelers using this business park, and to assist them the hotel offers a fully equipped business center.

The pleasure of being in the hotel begins as you enter. The open four-story atrium here is both impressive and dramatic in scale, yet intimate in feeling.

The hotel prides itself on the room decor. A team of international designers selected subdued colors and sophisticated interior designs and blended them with traditional Japanese taste. In addition to having the standard amenities offered by a top hotel, you can enjoy some special features. For example, you may open the windows for fresh air if you wish. You can light your room automatically by inserting your room key in a key box beside the room door. And you will enjoy the basket in your bathroom containing a selection of toiletries, including Lanvin shampoo and rinse. Because the hotel overlooks the historic Osaka Castle and its beautiful surrounding park land, you will enjoy scenic views both from your room and the hotel's exceptional restaurants.

There are so many places to eat in this hotel that you may have difficulty selecting one. In the Sakura, Chef Simada blends the best of East and West. The Keyaki (Teppan Grill) is where the choicest Kobe beef and the freshest seafood is prepared while you watch, and every seat offers a spectacular view of Osaka Castle. The Four Seasons lounge, on the eighteenth floor, serves light refreshments during the day and is a piano bar at night, with a grand view of the lights of Osaka and Osaka Castle. Trader Vic's offers cuisine from around the world. Taikan-en serves Chinese dishes cuisine created by Chef Chu Chuing Fa. In the Shiromi Master Chef Tamura Hidemi presents his inventive Japanese cuisine. The Azalea, open from 7:00 A.M. until midnight, is a full-service restaurant offering light lunches, full-course dinners, or just a cup of coffee. The Shiromi Lounge features tea and cocktails. The lobby lounge is a popular place for social meetings and conversation; light refreshments are served, and during the evening a harpest performs.

As a special service for its guests, the hotel has arranged for complimentary Aqualiner water bus service Monday through Friday (except holidays) between the hotel and Yotsubashi Railroad Station in downtown Osaka. This fifteen-minute bus ride eliminates concern about traffic and is a unique and thoroughly relaxing way to get around Osaka's miles of winding rivers and 808 bridges.

The hotel has a number of health and fitness facilities. On the fourth floor is its Fitness Club, featuring the women's Esthetic Salon, massage rooms, tanning rooms, a Finnish sauna, a Jacuzzi hot tub, and lounges. The hotel also has four tennis courts and indoor and outdoor pools. Ask for a copy of the jogging map showing four courses on the nearby castle grounds. All of these give you a feeling of being in a resort rather than in a major city hotel.

For convenient shopping, there is the Plaza Chateau shopping arcade, which features a variety of shops and exclusive boutiques from around the world.

There are also nineteen banquet halls in the hotel.

OSAKA HILTON INTERNATIONAL
8–8, Umeda 1-chome
Kita-ku
Osaka 530
Japan
Telephone: (06) 347-7111
Telex: 524-2201 HILOSA
Cable: HILTELS Osaka
Fax: (06) 347-7001
Reservations:
  In Osaka call (06) 347-7111
  In Tokoyo call (03) 344-9361
  In the USA call Hilton Reservation Service
    1-800-445-8667
All major credit cards
General Manager: Richard Chapman
Senior Assistant Manager: Takashi Nawa
Director of Sales: Hideyuki Satoh
Hilton International
Rates (approx.):
  Single room $105–$158
  Double room $128–$191
  One-bedroom suite $262–$460
  Two-bedroom suite $591–$624
  Deluxe two-bedroom $1,183
  Japanese-style room $263
553 rooms, 39 suites
Service charge 10%; tax 10%

One of Hilton International's spectacular new hotels is this super-modern building in Osaka. In the heart of the city's dynamic Umeda business district, this thirty-five-story tower is a landmark in a city of gleaming skyscrapers. Conveniently situated, it is directly opposite the Osaka Station, a short walk from department stores, shopping centers, and entertainment areas, and only a twenty-five-minute drive from the airport. Pedestrian walkways connect the hotel with major train and subway networks, allowing the visitor easy access to any area of the city or to places such as Tokyo, Kyoto, or Nara. This is an ideal spot for the business visitor or tourist.

This hotel has a dramatic lobby. In the center is a sculpture of hundreds of birds in flight, suspended in a four-story atrium. This forty-six-foot-long display of stainless steel and aluminum origami was created through the use of computer graphics by artist Rob Fisher. Beneath the mobile is a magnificent multi-hued, Thai-made carpet creating the illusion of a cloud-covered stream finding its way down the valley of the foyer. Completing the stunning effect is an enormous example of the *shakkai* gardening concept, or "borrowed scenery," in the form of a riotous display of daisies and chrysanthemums at the foot of a living persimmon tree. Created by a master of the *sogetsu* school, the display is changed seasonally.

Having opened in September of 1986, this hotel had an immediate 100 percent occupancy rate, with only 30 percent of its guests from outside of Japan. It is the second tallest building in the city, a 476-foot structure of curvilinear concrete, glass, and silver porcelain tiles, only exceeded by the 492-foot-high Twin Tower Building near the Osaka Castle. Skyscrapers are new to this city; as recently as 1953, the tallest building was only twelve stories high.

Near the hotel, and an important part of the Umeda district of the city, is the area's Ume-Chika (Umeda Shopping Center); the largest underground commercial center in the world, it accommodates half a million shoppers on an average day. One of the Ume-Chika tunnels connects with the first basement level of the Hilton, where visitors can dine in any of a dozen restaurants, purchase almost anything, and even shop duty-free.

Adjacent to the hotel is the Hilton Plaza, an eight-story-high collection of boutiques representing some of the world's most prestigious couturiers, perfumeries, and jewelers. The ground level of this plaza has a massive rotunda topped with a skylight featuring another soaring mobile of orange and silver free-form panels, reflected in the glass wall that separates the mall from the hotel.

Osaka is very much a business city, long called the City of Merchants. The Hilton caters to the business traveler and has designated its thirty-first through thirty-third floors as its Executive Floors, designed to serve the captains of industry from around the world who flock to this city to wheel and deal. The business center on the ground floor is open six days a week, thirteen hours a day, offering services and state-of-the-art equipment. There are eleven conference rooms on the fourth and tenth floors, and the Golden Key Club, on the tenth floor, is for private corporate members. The fitness center, increasingly considered a necessity to the business traveler, is on the seventh floor with sauna, massage room, gym, pool, and tennis court. A very helpful jogging map of the area offering two routes, a short and a long one, is available to any guest.

The rooms are delightfully spacious, larger than many Japanese hotel rooms, and are well equipped. Each has a color TV with English-channel and multilingual broadcasts and in-house movies, direct-dial telephones, private bath with shower and tub, individual climate control, a mini-bar and refrigerator, and an alarm clock–radio. The hotel also provides delicate touches, such as placing fresh flowers and a clean *yukata* (cotton dressing gown) daily in every room. The shoji-screened windows provide views of the old *shita-machi* downtown, an area of woodblock-gray roofs, wandering lanes, and woven bamboo gates.

Ask if you can see the Imperial Suite. The eighteen-hundred-dollar-a-day suite has Givenchy bed and bath linens, silk-papered walls, black lacquered dining room and kitchen furniture, and Japanese antiques.

Most of the hotel's restaurants are on the second and third floors. The Karuta, named for an ancient card game, is the popular-priced coffee shop open from 7:00 A.M. to 1:00 A.M. Nearby is Lipo (named for the hard-drinking Chinese poet Li Po), a cocktail piano bar serving buffet lunch on weekdays. The Seasons is the hotel's fine dining room; Dynasty is a sophisticated Chinese restaurant; and Genji serves sushi, tempura, and *teppanyaki* from its counters and *kaiseki* meals in its dining room.

The lobby is the location for the In Place, a popular rendezvous before an evening out. Continental breakfast is available here from 7:00 A.M., and afternoon tea is accompanied by piano music.

My favorite place is found on the thirty-fifth floor. Windows on the World, the Hilton's spectacular sky lounge, offers fantastic views of Osaka. The art glass panels that separate the tables and frame the windows are notable, too. Osaka has long been a center of the glass industry, and artist Stephen Gormley has etched its history onto the glass by heat and moulding techniques. There are 110 different designs, all worth examining. Lunch and afternoon tea are served, and Windows on the World is open until 1:00 A.M. for drinking and dancing.

THE PLAZA
2-2-49, Oyodo-Minami
Oyodo-ku
Osaka 531
Japan
Telephone: (06) 453-1111

Telex: 5245557 PLAOSA J
Cable: PLAZAHOTEL OSAKA
Fax: (06) 454-0169
Reservations:
　In Osaka call (06) 453-1111
　In the USA call Leading Hotels of the World: in New
　　York call (212) 838-3110; elsewhere in the USA call
　　1-800-223-6800
All major credit cards
General Manager: Hiroshi Ohno
Concierge: Shigeo Mizui
Sales Manager: Sodao Muranaka
Leading Hotels of the World
Rates (approx.):
　Standard room　$80 single, $120 double
　Superior room　$100 single, $160 double
　Deluxe room　$125 single, $230 double
　Japanese-style suite　$230
　Western-style suite　$270–$530
　Presidential suite　$930
　Imperial Suite　$1,530
535 rooms, 13 suites
Service charge 10%; tax 10%

The lobby in this hotel is truly elegant. There is a sparkling chandelier, paintings by Marc Chagall and Pablo Picasso, a bas-relief by Ryokichi Mukai, and extraordinary pieces of traditional Oriental arts and crafts.

Business travelers favor the Plaza because of its convenient location, being only fifteen minutes from the airport and close to Osaka's commercial center. Catering to these visitors, the hotel provides a business center, twenty-four-hour room service, and experienced assistance in arranging conferences and exhibitions. There is even a special VIP penthouse on the twenty-third floor. Since it opened in October 1969 the Plaza has been a popular gathering place for business and social activities, ranging from international conventions to wedding receptions and private parties. There are twenty-one banquet rooms and two grand ballrooms.

My favorite spot is Le Rendezvous, a gourmet restaurant on the top floor under the supervision of Louis Outheir, owner and chef of L'Oasis, a three-star restaurant in France; and Stephane Raimbault, chef de cuisine. Le Rendezvous is the only member in all of Asia to be listed in *Traditions et qualite*, the highly respected French epicurean association directory.

On the hotel's fourth floor are four more restaurants, surrounded by a large Japanese garden. They include Belvedere, a continental-style dining room; Hanagiri, providing Japanese-style cuisine; Sui-en, with Chinese cuisine; and Yodo, the popular *teppanyaki* place. Also on this floor is the Bluebell Bar, a British pub adjacent to Yodo and convenient for pre-dinner drinks.

There are three other drinking establishments, the Marco Polo off the main lobby, offering a great view; the Vista cocktail and dance lounge, on the twenty-third floor, also providing a great view of the city; and the adjacent Sundowner Bar.

There is no health or exercise center, but the hotel has an outside swimming pool on the fifth floor. There are also three Japanese-style suites on this floor, as well as Kochian, the Japanese tea ceremony room.

In the first-level basement there is a shopping arcade; the Umeda is walking distance from the hotel; and the Symphony Hall of Osaka is across the street.

All rooms are spacious and air-conditioned, and have color TV, mini-bars, refrigerators, Japanese tea service, and the Japanese *rukata* and other amenities.

ROYAL HOTEL
5-3-68 Nakanoshima
Kita-ku
Osaka 530
Japan
Telephone: (06) 448-1121
Telex: J63350 ROYAL HTL
Cable: ROYALHOTEL OSAKA
Fax: (06) 444-6570
Reservations:
  In Osaka call (06) 448-1121
  In the USA call Preferred Hotels Worldwide (in
    Chicago (312) 953-0505, elsewhere in the USA 1-800-
    323-7500) or SRS Hotels (in New York (212) 593-2988,
    elsewhere in the USA 1-800-223-5652)
All major credit cards
President: Chusuke Takahashi
Managing Director: Takanori Kasai
Concierge: Hiroshi Matsuoka
Director of Room Sales: Haruki Hayashi
Preferred Hotels Worldwide
Rates (approx.):

Tower room $160 single, $220–$313 double
East wing room $140 single, $160–$227 double
West wing room $113 single, $180 double
Suite $333–$2,333
1,247 rooms, 53 suites
Service charge 10%; tax 10%

One of Japan's larger hotels, the Royal Hotel is a splendid example of how big is not necessarily bad. This hotel is truly dedicated to the highest level of comfort and service. The hotel opened in 1936, its west wing in 1965, the east wing in 1973, and the east annex in 1987. Considered the unofficial state guest house in Osaka, it has had the honor of providing accommodations for successive generations of U.S. presidents, heads of state from other countries, Japan's royal family and prime ministers, and many other dignitaries. Yet, it has a wide range of rooms available, some at modest rates for Japan, and has accomplished its objective of being everyone's hotel.

Visitors to the Royal Hotel are always struck by the beauty of the building, proving that the designer accomplished his objective. In 1960 architect Isoya Yoshida was asked to design a functional hotel, but he envisioned an oasis where people could find refuge from the hectic pace of the "concrete jungle all around," a combination of light, water, and greenery offering "the providence of nature, soothing to the senses." Yoshida, one of Japan's greatest architects, keyed his entire design to the Heian period. The effect begins with the hotel's exterior, which from a distance presents a uniform bronze appearance, but closer inspection reveals an elegant yet simple arrangement of tiles, much like the *kasuri* pattern used in classic kimono fabrics.

Upon entering, visitors are captivated by the interior. The luxurious wall-to-wall tapestry carpet is woven entirely by hand in the *manyo* pattern of different colored leaves beautifully depicting Japan's four seasons. The columns have gold-lacquered bird patterns done in the style of the Fujiwara era, harmonizing with the carpet.

The lobby's main lounge, which incorporates natural and man-made elements in the Heian motif, gives one the feeling of being in the nearby Japanese garden with its refreshing waterfall. Chandeliers hang from the ceiling two floors above. These light fixtures are made of two hundred fifty thousand crystals threaded onto forty-five thousand steel threads and produce a cloud-like effect. Paintings on the lounge walls depict scenes from the tales of Genji, portraying the daily life of Heian nobles.

The lounges in the different wings of the hotel, the Grand Banquet Hall, and indeed all the public rooms are visually splendid. The Royal Hotel was twice presented with a Building Contractors Society award for its design, first in 1967 when the main wing was completed and again in 1975 for construction of its east wing.

The beauty of the public areas extends into the hotel's rooms. Each room is soundproofed and equipped with a comfortable semi-double or double bed, individual climate control, refrigerator, English-language cable TV, direct-dial and bathroom telephones, message alert, hi-fi radio, and an ice water supply.

Business visitors enjoy special treatment here. About one hundred twenty rooms, on the twenty-third through twenty-seventh floors of the east wing and the fourteenth floor of the west wing, have been set aside for executives. The service staff is available twenty-four hours a day. There is an executive salon in the first floor lobby, open from 8:30 A.M. to 6:00 P.M. except Sundays and holidays, for business travelers who require business information or assistance. This salon has a wide diversity of services and equipment.

The dining facilities are excellent and varied. There are four Japanese-style, two Chinese, an Italian, a gourmet French, and European-style restaurants. There are two sushi shops, a *teppanyaki* grill, and a coffee shop. Of these restaurants, Chambord, serving French cuisine, is considered one of Osaka's finest dining rooms; on the twenty-ninth floor, it also provides a fine view of the city. Restaurant Beau Rivage, on the seventh floor of the new east annex, has a Mediterranean look with a terrace full of light, water, and vegetation. The spacious Coffee House Corbeille, on the first floor, offers fast service for modest prices. I also like the Japanese tea parlor, Tsuruya Hachiman, on the first basement level, serving traditional Japanese cookies, cakes, *zenzai* (sweet red bean soup), and other delights.

An exciting cultural school—the only hotel-sponsored school in Asia I know of—provides classes on Japanese painting, Western painting, dyeing, calligraphy, engraving, seal engraving, ceramics, cooking, and Japanese embroidery, often taught by authorities in these crafts. Called Ecole de Royal, the full-fledged school also arranges field trips, tours, parties, and much more.

The hotel also offers a swimming pool, the Royal Health

Club, a babysitting service, and a comprehensive shopping arcade.

Tokyo

This city of twelve million has been described variously as baffling and refreshing, futuristic and anachronistic, polluted and pristine, charming and blighted, invigorating and enervating, provincial and cosmopolitan, and all these descriptions are accurate. Greater Tokyo consists of an urban area divided into twenty-three wards, a rural area with farms and mountain villages, and the Izu Islands stretching to the south of Tokyo Bay. The administrative, financial, educational, and cultural center of Japan, Tokyo is also a major industrial hub surrounded by many suburban manufacturing complexes. Among its diverse industries are metalworking, machine building, food processing, printing and publishing, oil refining, and the manufacture of automobiles, steel, electronic apparatus, transport equipment, cameras, chemicals, optical goods, furniture, leather products, and textiles.

The world's first monorail for public transportation operates between downtown Tokyo and the nearby Haneda International Airport. The city's transportation system includes "bullet trains" that travel at more than three hundred miles an hour between Tokyo and Osaka.

The present city was founded in the twelfth century as the village of Edo (or Yeddo). In 1457 Ota Dokan completed his castle at Edo. The castle passed in 1590 to Ieyasu Tokugawa, the founder of the Tokugawa line of shoguns. In 1868 the last Tokugawa shogun surrendered to the imperial forces, and the capital of Japan was moved from Kyoto to Tokyo, when the city was given its present name. The famous landmarks in Tokyo include the Meiji and Hie shrines; the Sengakuji, Gokokuji, and Sensoji temples; and the Korakuen, a seventeenth-century landscaped garden.

Tokyo's shopping and entertainment area is known as the Ginza; the Marunouchi quarter is the business center. One of the world's foremost educational centers, Tokyo has nearly one hundred fifty institutions for higher learning. There are many museums and more than two hundred parks and gardens. Heavily bombed during World War II,

Tokyo required extensive rebuilding and now is one of the most modern cities in the world.

The collection of Tokyo hotels on the pages that follow is a small selection from its many hotels, most of which are up to date and comfortable. I have included, of course, the best and newest among our collection, as well as some of the older fine hotels and a number of the popular and more modestly priced hotels. In general, however, Tokyo hotel prices are fairly high.

Most hotels in Tokyo offer a free walking map that you should read as soon as you arrive. *Tokyo: Where to Go, What to Do, and How to Get There!* is published four times a year; a big guide, it includes a central city map of Tokyo inside its back cover.

ANA HOTEL TOKYO
12–33 Akasaka 1-chome
Minato-ku
Tokyo 107
Japan
Telephone: (03) 505-1111
Telex: 2424625ANAETH J
Fax: (03) 505-1155
Reservations:
  In Tokyo call (03) 505-1111
  In the USA call Robert F. Warner:
    in New York state call (212) 725-1510;
    elsewhere in the USA call 1-800-792-7637
All major credit cards
Property Manager: Hiroshi Matsuoka
General Manager: Yu Murakawa
Concierge: Fumio Hashimoto
Sales Manager: Yukinobu Saeki
ANA Hotels
Rates (approx.):
  Standard room $122 single, $164 double
  Superior room $171 double
  Deluxe room $184 double
  Suite $263–$1,314
900 rooms, 33 suites
Service charge 10%; tax 10%

A striking white thirty-seven-floor skyscraper that opened in 1986, the hotel is at Ark Hills. Considered the true heart of the city of Tokyo because it is at the crossroads of Aka-saka, Roppongi, Toranomon, and Kasumigaseki, Ark Hills is a new and exciting district, where international business, culture, and high society come together. This lovely All Nippon Accommodations hotel is considered to be the crown jewel of the chain's collection of fine hotels throughout Japan and the Pacific area. Elegance is apparent the moment you enter the dramatic atrium lobby filled with sunlight, waterfalls, and living trees. The natural, open effect pervades the entire hotel, including the guest rooms. Every room has a view either of Mount Fuji, the Imperial Palace, or Tokyo Bay. This is possible because the hotel was designed in the shape of a triangle. Whether you select a guest room, a Japanese tatami suite or a Western suite with its regal decor, each has its own thermostatic control, a well-stocked refrigerator, and a mini-bar. There are cable TV movies in English.

The traveling executive is pampered here. The thirty-fourth floor has special executive rooms with executive privileges. An executive lounge serves complimentary drinks and, in the morning, complimentary continental breakfast. The second floor provides a well-staffed and equipped business center.

Guests will enjoy the Japanese garden and the outdoor garden pool, and for the men there is a sauna. The second floor is the location of Le Marche, where high-fashion name brands and a fine selection of gift items are available.

The variety of dining and drinking facilities at ANA Hotel Tokyo is excellent. On the second floor, open from 6:00 A.M. until 2:00 A.M., is the Cascade, the hotel's quick-service coffee shop, and on the same floor is the Atrium Lounge, the lobby spot for cocktails and light savories or coffee and dessert, open from 9:00 A.M. until 10:00 P.M. There are four dining rooms together on the hotel's third floor: Le Patio, featuring Mediterranean cuisine at all three meals; the Karin Chinese restaurant, serving Cantonese and Sichuan specialties and dim sum at lunch and dinner; the lovely Rose Room, which features continental cuisine served with French flair; and Unkai, the Japanese dining room facing a beautiful Japanese garden. In the Di Vinci main bar you may have drinks and light dishes from 11:00 A.M. until midnight. On the thirty-seventh, the top floor of the hotel, are the view dining and drinking spots, the Akasaka *teppanyaki* restaurant; the Osaka Tsuruya, featuring Kansai cuisine; and the Astral Sky Bar, open until 2:30 A.M.

CAPITAL TOKYU HOTEL
10-3, Nagata-cho 2-chome
Chiyoda-ku
Tokyo 100
Japan
Telephone: (03) 581-4511
Telex: J24290 THCCAP
Cable: CAPITOL TOKYUTEL
Fax: (03) 581-5822
Reservations:
  In Tokyo call (03) 581-4511
  In the USA call Robert F. Warner:
    in New York state call (212) 725-1510;
    elsewhere in the USA call 1-800-R WARNER
All major credit cards
President: Kazuo Saito
General Manager: Mitsugi Nakajima
Concierge: Kenji Katoh
Sales Manager: Noriyoshi Ohta
Tokyu Hotel Chain
Rates (approx.):
  Single room $153–$207
  Double room $190–$240
  Executive suite $453
  Deluxe suite $1,667
460 rooms, 18 suites
Service charge 10%; tax 10%

The Capital Tokyu Hotel is operated by the Tokyu Hotel Chain, a company whose name, Tokyu, means Tokyo Express. This giant firm began by running the commuter railroad serving Tokyo's southwestern metropolitan area. Once named the Tokyo Hilton, this hotel is Tokyu's flagship, located in the Akasaka section of Tokyo, only minutes away from the city's center and next to a centuries-old shrine. The hotel has both Western- and Japanese-style bedrooms, though even the Western rooms contain traditional Japanese features, such as sliding shoji screens.

For dining there are six popular restaurants, including the Genji, a Japanese restaurant featuring sushi, tempura, *shabu-shabu*, and *teppanyaki* served by kimono-clad waitresses. The Tea Lounge offers breakfast and is later open for cocktails and relaxing. The hotel's Star Hill Restaurant is one of the most popular Chinese restaurants in the city, featuring lunch from 11:30 A.M. until 3:00 P.M. and dinner from 5:00 until 10:30 P.M. Tropical drinks are very popular and are served at the Tea Lounge, the Misao Lounge, the Garden Cafe, the Lipo Bar, and at the pool. For a dinner, show, and dancing there is the hotel's Pearl Ballroom.

Other services include a business center and convention and meeting facilities, as well as a swimming pool and a few shops, and the Ginza shopping district and the Roppongi restaurant street are only ten minutes away by taxi.

CENTURY HYATT
2-7-2 Nishi-Shinjuku
Shinjuku-ku
Tokyo
Japan
Telephone: (03) 349-0111
Telex: J29411
Cable: CENHYATT
Fax: (03) 344-5575
Reservations:
    In Tokyo call (03) 349-8181
    In the USA call 1-800-228-9000
All major credit cards
General Manager: Yasuo Sekiguchi
Sales Manager: Hiroshi Sato
Concierge: Junko Koizumi
Hyatt International
Rates (approx.):
    Standard room $120 single, $145 double
    Superior room $170 double
    Deluxe room $190 double
    Suite $300–$2,000
800 rooms, 20 suites
Service charge 10%; tax 10%

The Century Hyatt in Tokyo is the first Hyatt hotel in Japan. This is a deluxe twenty-eight-story, eight-hundred-room facility situated in Tokyo's Shinjuku district, the most exciting shopping area in Tokyo. The hotel is noted for its seven-story-high atrium lobby with magnificent crystal chandeliers, and for its many dining and function rooms, including twenty-three banquet halls and private dining rooms used for everything from international conferences and seminars to private parties.

The bedrooms and suites are beautifully furnished either in Western decor or Japanese style. They are supplied with many amenities, including fancy soaps, shampoo, rinse, a tooth brush, a razor, and three sizes of towels, as well as slippers and a *yukata* (a Japanese set of pajamas). In the suites, bathrobes are also provided.

The business traveler likes this hotel because of its popular Regency Club floor, a deluxe hotel within the hotel, and its efficient business executive center as well.

My favorite spot is the penthouse swimming pool on the twenty-eighth floor, open from 10:00 A.M. to 9:00 P.M. Overnight guests pay a fifteen-hundred-yen (ten-dollar) entrance fee. (Other visitors must pay fifty-five hundred yen.) In addition to the pool and its view of the city, this facility provides luxurious suntan corners, a warm room, a shower corner, and an attractive powder room.

The dining rooms in this hotel are delightful. The first floor is the location for the Jade Garden, a Chinese restaurant. The master chef was born in Shanghai and was trained by a student of the personal chef of the last princess of China. Traditional imperial Chinese cuisine is featured here. The lobby lounge on the second floor is centered under the huge Austrian crystal chandeliers of the lobby's seven-story atrium; this lounge is a favorite spot to meet friends and enjoy coffee, tea, and French pastries.

The third floor has two restaurants. Kamogawa is a quiet, restrained Japanese dining room serving classical cuisine prepared with fresh seafood and produce; its tempura corner is very popular. Hugo's is an international steak and seafood house overlooking a park; *teppanyaki* is grilled on a hot plate for guests to watch.

Other places to eat include the Boulogne, serving American and European cuisine for all three meals; the Caterina, an informal terrace-style restaurant featuring salad and dessert bars; Miyako, a Japanese sushi pub; the Tradewind Pub; the Rhapsody night lounge on the twenty-seventh floor, featuring popular jazz vocalists and musical groups as well as a breathtaking view of Tokyo; the Eau de Vie bar; and the Samba Club Regency, a popular discotheque.

The most exciting restaurant is Chenonceaux, a dining room on the twenty-seventh floor, offering authentic French cuisine and wine from its ten-thousand-bottle cellar. This elegantly decorated establishment also offers an astonishing view of Tokyo at night.

There are so many places to dine and drink that the Century Hyatt has published its own catalog, *The Restaurant and Bar Guide*. Another printed piece available, called *A Bird's Eye View of Shinjuku*, is a detailed map with lots of information on Tokyo's banks, churches, embassies, airlines, hotels, and amusements.

GINZA TOBU HOTEL
14-9, Ginza 6-chome
Chuo-ku
Tokyo 104
Japan
Telephone: (03) 546-0111
Telex: 252-3388 GNZTOB J
Fax: (03) 541-4136
Reservations:
   In Tokyo call (03) 546-0111
   In the USA call Ramada Renaissance at 1-800-228-9898
All major credit cards
President: Kaichiro Nezu
General Manager: Eiichi Kasai
Sales & Operations: Takahisa Nagashima
Ramada Inc.
Ramada Renaissance
Rates (approx.):
   Single room $87–$113
   Double room $147–$200
   Twin room $147–$233
   Suite $253–$1,000
205 rooms, 11 suites
Service charge 10%; tax 10%

Opened in October 1987, the Ginza Tobu Hotel is located on a major Ginza thoroughfare, the major shopping district of Tokyo, right in the city's premier commercial center. It is within walking distance of the Imperial Palace, the Kabuki theater, the Marounuchi offices, and a number of other major attractions.

All of the guest rooms have twin or large double beds, individually controlled air conditioning, bedside control panels, TV, stereo radio, in-house movies, mini-bars and refrigerators, an international direct-dial telephone system, and hair dryers in the bathrooms. The tenth floor of the hotel, called the Ramada Renaissance Club, has twenty-three deluxe rooms and extra services aimed at the business traveler; the top (eleventh) floor is the executive suite floor.

There are three basement floors in the hotel, two of which are for parking. The first basement level has two dining rooms, the Losier Dor, which features French cuisine, and the Ginza Muraki, a Japanese restaurant serving *kaiseki*, *shabu-shabu*, and tempura. The Korin bar on this level has live piano entertainment. The Cafe Restaurant, on the first (or lobby) floor of the hotel, is a twenty-four-hour restaurant serving Mediterranean cuisine, featuring fresh seafood and a salad bar.

Just off the lobby is the hotel's travel and business center to handle the needs of traveling business executives, featuring secretarial services, telecommunications, and interpreters to provide translations for such needs as reports, letters, and contracts.

HOTEL OKURA
2-10-4, Toranomon 2 chome
Minatu-ku
Tokyo 105
Japan
Telephone: (03) 582-0111
Telex: J 22790
Cable: HOTELOKURA
Fax: (03) 582-3707
Reservations:
    In Tokyo call (03) 582-0111
    In the USA call Leading Hotels of the World at 1-800-
        223-6800, John A. Tetley at 1-800-421-0000, or
        Distinguished Hotels at 1-800-R-WARNER
All major credit cards
President/General Manager: Tasuro Goto
Director of Sales: Hiro Suzuki
Hotel Okura Chain
Leading Hotels of the World
Distinguished Hotels
SAS Associated Hotels
Rates (approx.):
    Single room $145–$212
    Double room $174–207 single, $200–$233 double
    Twin room $141–$212 single, $168–$237 double
    Deluxe twin room $309–$329
    Japanese room $217–$427
    Suite $388–$604
    Royal Suite $1,248–$1,380
    Presidential Suite $1,708
    Imperial Suite $2,300
910 rooms, including 67 suites
Service charge 10%; tax 10%

The world-renowned Hotel Okura celebrated its twenty-fifth anniversary in spring 1987. Surveys of international travelers by leading business publications indicate the Okura's high status: *Euromoney* readers selected the Okura as the best hotel in Tokyo and as the fourth best hotel in the world; international bankers surveyed by *Institutional Investor* rated the Okura as the third best in the world; and Britain's *Business Traveller* readers declared it the world's seventh best hotel. This is the hotel selected to accommodate President Reagan and his principal staff members while attending the 1986 Western Nations Summit Conference. The Okura is dedicated to its business; Iwajiro Noda, the hotel's ninety-year-old honorary chairman, reveals the hotel philosophy: "I always tell my staff to make our accommodation, cuisine, and service better than anyone else's, even by a razor-thin margin. This razor-thin margin makes a big difference."

Built on the grounds of Baron Kishichiro Okura's estate, the traditional-style buildings are surrounded by classical Japanese gardens. The hotel is a short distance from the Imperial Palace, in the heart of Tokyo, and serves as an ideal business base. On convenient Embassy Row, close to the Marunouchi business center as well as the Akasaka-Roppongi area noted for its night life, Hotel Okura is perfectly situated. Next to the hotel is the Okura Shuko-kan Museum, housing the late baron's art collection, including national treasures and important items of culture.

The main lobby, one of the many beautiful spaces in the hotel, is striking. The famous Okura lanterns are designed in the manner of ancient jewels discovered in fifth-century Japanese tombs. Silk orchid-patterned wall coverings are combined with soft-hued Takoishi stone panels from Japan's Gumma prefecture. Sections of the lower walls are fitted with delicate shoji panels, reflecting the movement of wind-stirred bamboo leaves from the garden below.

All the guest rooms are attractive and very comfortable (the Presidential, Royal, and Imperial suites are extraordinary), and guests of the seventh-floor Japanese-style rooms can see the Okura's winding river garden, landscaping with a thousand-year-old tradition dating back to Japan's ancient imperial court in Kyoto. It is said courtiers would sit at the bank of a winding stream in which floated cups of sake, and before they could drink they would have to compose a poem. Also on the seventh floor is the Chosho-an Tea Ceremony Room, an authentic example of traditional tea-ceremony architecture. Guests can enjoy tea in traditional floor-seated style or, if preferred, in conventional chairs.

The Chosho-an room has a splendid view of the winding river garden.

The Okura has eight outstanding dining facilities, including La Belle Epoque, a twelfth-floor restaurant that serves French cuisine in an art nouveau setting with excellent views and is open for lunch and dinner. The Continental Room on the tenth floor has a selection of ninety European dishes on its menu. Toh-ka-lin, a Cantonese restaurant on the sixth floor of the main building, has more than two hundred dishes on its menu. Yamazato, on the fifth floor of the main building, serves all varieties of Japanese cuisine for all three meals. The Orchid Room, also on the fifth floor, features fresh seafood in an opulent setting of silk wall coverings, shoji panels, and Okura lanterns.

Open from 5:30 A.M. until 1:00 A.M., the Camelia Corner, a coffee shop noted for its fast service and takeout section, is located on the first floor of the south wing. The Terrace Restaurant, open from 8:00 A.M. to 9:00 P.M., serves everything from simple fare to full dinners in a garden atmosphere with visiting birds.

On the top floor of the Okura is the Starlight Lounge; with windows on three sides it provides views of much of Tokyo. In addition to drinks, light meals are served from 11:30 A.M. to 5:00 P.M., after which the lounge remains open for cocktails and views with live music until midnight. There are two other bars, the Highlander on the first floor and the Orchid Bar on the fifth.

The executive service salon, adjacent to the lobby of the main building, is open from 8:30 A.M. to 7:00 P.M. daily, except Sunday and national holidays. It is probably the finest hotel business center in the world, providing exceptional services and facilities for the business traveler. One of its most valuable services is in the area of business research. The Data Bank of Nohon Keizai Shimbun provides a variety of facts, including financial, industrial, and other economic statistical data, retrieved news of business performance, macroeconomic factors, and political factors. International economic news is given via the video system in the main room of the salon by Kyodo News. The salon library is the largest I've seen in a business center. It has over four hundred volumes on culture and world business, including major indices.

The salon serves cocktails from 5:30 until 7:30 every evening, except Sunday and holidays. Some executives invite business associates, others unwind with a drink and read a current periodical or book or watch English TV programs via Sound Multiplex Television. There are luncheon meetings for executive guests and other business people scheduled each month. Informed speakers from many fields deal with topics of interest to the international business world. When registering in the salon, hotel guests are told about the next luncheon meeting.

The Okura health club is expertly staffed by physicians, nurses, nutritionists, and trainers. Facilities include a sunroom-style indoor heated pool, a steam bath, an informal pool-side restaurant, and a members' salon. The hotel's large outdoor swimming pool, in a garden setting, is open from mid-June through mid-September.

The hotel has two attractive shopping arcades with a total of thirty interesting shops and boutiques. The main building arcade is on the hotel's first floor, and the south wing arcade may be reached by an underpass from the lobby of the main building to the floor below the south wing lobby.

HOTEL SEIYO GINZA
1, Ginza
Chuo-ku
Tokyo 104
Japan
Telephone: (03) 535-1111
Telex: 252-3118 HSYG J
Fax: (03) 535-1110
Reservations:
In Tokyo call (03) 535-1120
In the USA call The Grande Collection of Hotels: in New York call (212) 841-1500; elsewhere in the USA call 1-800-243-1166
All major credit cards
General Manager: Tokuya Nagai
Concierge: Momoko Ohno
Sales Manager: Shigeki Sakita
K.K. Hotel Seiyo Management
Rates (approx.):
Suite $254–$434 single, $334–$1,667 double
80 suites
Service charge 10%; tax 10%

Seiji Tsutsumi, one of the richest men in Japan, who heads the group that runs the Seibu department store chain, could find no hotel to please his tastes, so he spent seventy million dollars to build this luxury residential hotel. An expensive lodging designed for the kind of people who can afford it, the Seiyo Ginza, which opened in March 1987, is deliberately small, with only twelve floors. Its highly polished white ceramic tile exterior is a highly visible landmark on the Ginza. It provides a superior level of service and rightly compares itself with the Plaza Athenee or the Ritz of Paris, the Connaught or Claridge in London, or the Pierre, Carlyle, or Mayfair Regent in New York.

During your entire stay you have a personal secretary who handles dinner reservations, hires interpreters for business appointments, arranges for special purchases, and so forth. Guest rooms have a lot of useful buttons to press, such as the one to call your personal concierge. Two buttons, "Do Not Disturb" and "Maid Service," are linked to the hotel's computer system so they can be responded to properly.

The rooms have been designed by different architectural firms, giving each suite a unique appearance. Individual humidity and temperature controls, as well as a selection of seven different types of pillows, ensure the guest's comfort. Each room is equipped with a private safe, despite Tokyo's reputation as one of the most crime-free cities in the world. Ample audiovisual components, including TV, amplifier, and tuner, are provided, and sound can be piped into the bathroom. Guests also have access to the hotel's library of two hundred video tapes. The rooms have walk-in closets and well-supplied bathrooms that are among the largest available in Japanese hotels, each having a separate shower stall with steam bath.

There are four fine dining rooms. On the second floor is the French restaurant, the Pastorale; it is open for lunch and dinner and has one of the largest wine cellars in Japan. Akio Kamata, its grand chef, was trained by Roger Verge of France. It is an expensive restaurant: dinner for two, with a modest amount of wine, can cost six hundred dollars for a couple.

On the first basement level is the Bar and Ristorante Attore. Open for lunch and dinner, it serves the cuisine of Northern Italy. On the same floor is the Cafe Intra, a casual place for dining that is open from 8:00 A.M. to 11:00 P.M. It is less expensive that the Attore; for about nine dollars you can get a dish called Carmen Dip-in, made with chorizo sausage, egg, and red pepper cooked in tomato, served with a dipping sauce and asparagus.

The Prelude Lounge, on the second floor near the Pastorale and open from 7:00 A.M. to 11:00 P.M., serves continental breakfast and afternoon tea. Primarily a place to entertain clients or use as a meeting place before or after dinner, the lounge serves seasonal hor d'oeuvres in the evenings with the drinks.

The entire third floor, the Salon la Ronde, provides facilities for private groups or receptions.

The hotel has no swimming pool, but it does have a fitness room for light exercise.

IMPERIAL HOTEL
1–1, Uchisaiwai-cho 1-chome
Chiyoda-ku
Tokyo 100
Japan
Telephone: (03) 504-1111
Telex: 222-2346 IMPHO J
Cable: IMPHO TOKYO
Fax: (03) 504-1111
Reservations:
  In Tokyo call (03) 504-1111 or telex 222-2367 IMPRSV J
  In the USA call Leading Hotels of the World:
    in New York and Alaska call collect (212) 838-3110;
    elsewhere in the USA call 1-800-223-6800
All major credit cards
President and General Manager: Ichiro Inumaru
Sales Manager: Kiyohito Minoshima
Leading Hotels of the World
Rates (approx.):
  Main building room $150–$200 single, $177–$227
    double
  Tower room $160–$280 single, $187–$307 double
  Deluxe main building room $240–$280 single,
    $267–$307 double
  Deluxe tower room $240–$280 single, $267–$307
    double
  Suite in Main Building $400–$4,000
  Suite in Tower $400–$933
1,140 rooms, 76 suites
Service charge 10%; tax 10%

With its century of service and innovation, Tokyo's Imperial Hotel has set the trend for the international-class hotel in Japan. In the late 1800s, when Japan was reopened to the West, foreign advisers, diplomats, dignitaries, tourists, and business people began traveling regularly to this country, and providing Westerners with Western-style accommodations became a matter of proper courtesy and prestige as well. Construction of the Imperial Hotel was completed in 1890, but it was several years before the hotel was financially successful. In 1915, when it could no longer keep up with demand and a new building was needed, American architect Frank Lloyd Wright was selected. Though considered heretical, Wright's revolutionary theories produced a superior structure, which suffered no damage in the Great Kanto Earthquake. Long after World War II the Wright-designed Imperial still enjoyed a reputation as one of the world's most romantic and exotic hotels, but by the late sixties the hotel was again slated for renovation. A section of Wright's original structure has been relocated to Meiji Mura, near Nagoya.

Reopened in 1970, the main building of the present Imperial set a standard of luxury and service aimed at accommodating the large numbers of Western business travelers. For its ninetieth anniversary, in 1980, the Imperial Tower was opened. The first building in Japan to create within itself a complete, integrated, and thoroughly contemporary urban environment, the thirty-one-story Imperial Tower is more than just a hotel annex. The tower has, in addition to hundreds of rooms and suites, a rooftop swimming pool and sauna, four floors of name-brand shops, an entire floor of Western and Japanese restaurants, fourteen floors of international business offices, and full facilities for banquets and other functions.

The tower's 363 guest rooms and suites, together with those in the main building, bring the Imperial's room count to 1,140, making this one of Tokyo's largest hotels. The guest rooms are spacious, larger than the average room of any hotel in Tokyo. Rooms have solid wood furniture, plush carpeting, and attractive draperies, and the bathrooms in the tower rooms have the most modern, luxurious facilities, including oversized bathtubs. All of the guest rooms have great views of downtown Tokyo, Tokyo Bay, and the Imperial Palace. The wide bay windows of the tower rooms are made with special "half-mirror" glass that lets in ample sunlight, but reflects more than a third of incoming heat, thus keeping the rooms cool in the summer.

With the addition of the floor of restaurants in the Imperial Tower, the hotel now has one of the largest variety of fine hotel dining rooms in the city. The Fountainebleau, open for lunch and dinner, serves classical French haute cuisine and is the most elegant of the dining rooms presided over by award-winning executive chef Nobuo Murakami; the Fountainbleau is considered to be one of Asia's most respected French kitchens. Prunier, another elegant dining room, features continental style seafood prepared by chef Masaki Tsuchida for lunch and dinner. Les Saisons, a delightfully furnished dining room, serves contemporary French food, presented with chef Kunio Fukasawa's Japanese flair for artful arrangement, at all meals. Cycles, open from 6:00 A.M. until 1:00 A.M. daily, is the coffeehouse of the hotel, where the pastries served are truly tantalizing. Another refreshing spot is Salon de Thé, featuring freshly brewed coffees and teas from around the world.

Other dining rooms include La Brasserie, serving continental cuisine at lunch and dinner, and the Rainbow Room. This last restaurant originally opened in 1985 as the Imperial Viking and was Japan's first smorgasbord restaurant. When the "viking" concept was copied throughout Japan, this facility was renamed, and it now offers French and Scandinavian buffets. Serving all three meals, it is open from 7:00 A.M. to 10:00 P.M. For Japanese dining there are the Nadaman, Isecho, Kitcho, Nakata, Ten-ichi, and Sushigen restaurants, and the Chinese dining room is called Peking. The hotel also has three tea chambers, Toko-an, where guests may enjoy an authentic tea ceremony from 10:00 A.M. until 4:00 P.M.

The lounges and bars are all excellent places to refresh and relax. Among them are the Old Imperial Bar, the Rendez-Vous Bar and the Rendez-Vous Lounge (both in the lobby), and the Rainbow Lounge, noted for its grand views of Hibiya Park, the Imperial Palace, and the lights on the Ginza.

The swimming pool and sauna, on the tower's nineteenth and twentieth floors, respectively, are open year-round. The pool and the floors are heated in winter, and at night there is a great view of Tokyo from the pool.

The executive service lounge provides place to have business meetings, read news media from around the world, or use the latest office equipment and secretarial services.

When the Imperial Hotel Arcade was established more than sixty years ago, it was the very first shopping arcade in Japan, and it is still one of Japan's finest. Just added to it is the Imperial Plaza, a new shopping complex occupying four floors of the tower. With its magnificent decor and collection of international designer shops, it is comparable to the Landmark in Hong Kong or the Trump Tower shopping atrium in New York.

Be sure to walk around the hotel grounds and the area. To help you with this, ask for *The Imperial's Imperial Palace Jogging Map*. You don't need to jog to enjoy the sights it guides you past.

KEIO PLAZA INTER-CONTINENTAL HOTEL
2-1 Nishi-Shinjuku 2-chome
Shinjuku-ku
Tokyo 160
Japan
Telephone: 81 (3) 344-0111
Telex: KOPTEL J26874
Cable: KEIOPLATEL TOKYO
Fax: (03) 344-0247 or (3) 345-8269
Reservations:
   In the USA call 1-800-33-AGAIN
All major credit cards
General Manager: Sadao Suzuki
Inter-Continental Hotels
Rates (approx.):
   Special room $140 single, $153 double
   Standard room $150 single, $163 double
   Superior room $180 single, $200 double
   Standard suite $333
   Superior suite $1,333
1,485 rooms and suites
Service charge 10%; tax 10%

This is one of the tallest skyscraper hotels in Tokyo. In the heart of the west side of Tokyo's Shinjuku district, the Keio Plaza is close to the nation's biggest shopping and entertainment district as well as the New Metropolitan Center. The elegantly decorated lobby has some unique objects, such as the light-as-air cobweb chandeliers floating over the marbled area.

Guest rooms have big picture windows providing a wonderful view of Tokyo and, weather permitting, of Mount Fuji. Color TV in every room offers Tokyo's multichannel TV broadcasts and in-house movies, and the hotel can arrange for closed-circuit broadcasts as well. Among the pleasant amenities are a *yukata* (nightgown), slippers, a hot server, a telephone receiver in the bathroom, and a direct-dial telephone for local and overseas calls.

There are ten lounges throughout the Keio Plaza. Among them is the Cocktail and Tea Lounge, an off-the-lobby rendezvous open from ten to ten. Its south tower counterpart is the Duet, a quiet spot for serious talk. At night, the Polestar Skybar, on the forty-fifth floor of the main tower, has a magnificent view. The Bar Brilliant, on the second floor of the south tower, seems to be popular with the business set, while "Let's" is an informal spot for a convivial gathering. Each of the lounges is different in mood and decor. Some feature piano or guitar music at night.

The Keio Plaza houses nineteen international restaurants. *My favorite spot* is the Sky Restaurant Ambrosia, on the forty-fourth floor of the main tower, which combines the best in continental haute cuisine with an outstanding view of Tokyo. The second floor of the main tower is the location for several delightful dining rooms. Here you find steaks at the Medallion grill; sea food at Prunier; variety at the Coffee House Jurin, open twenty-two hours a day; and delicate Cantonese cuisine at Nan-En. For Japanese food there are five restaurants, whose offerings cover the gamut of Japan's national cuisine, from sukiyaki to *teppanyaki* to noodles and *kaiseki ryori*. For example, the classically elegant Miyama dining room on the forty-fifth floor of the main tower serves haute cuisine, and the rustic Ashibi offers country-style food at its seasonal best. For dancing and entertainment with dinner, the plush Consort Supper Club has a floor show with its meals.

The hotel often hosts groups from around the world in its fifth-level convention complex, where the spacious Concord Ballroom and Eminence Hall are located. The hotel also has a number of other small and medium-sized rooms for various functions such as intimate dinners, cocktail receptions, or business seminars.

A spacious shopping arcade also provides travel services, shoe shines, medical and dental services, packing and shipping, and so forth.

Guests may use the outdoor pool on the seventh floor garden terrace of the hotel and the adjacent sauna. There is a health club across the street where guests may use the indoor track, gymnasium, indoor pools, and squash courts at a special discount rate.

Here's an interesting and comforting item about the Keio Plaza: 580 staff members belong to to a fire-fighting team, and 144 of them have passed the Tokyo fire department's primary fire-fighting test. Members of the volunteer team undergo training as many as ten times a year by fire department instructors, and twice a year they take part in joint training exercises.

MIYAKO HOTEL TOKYO
1-1-50, Shiroganedai 1-chome
Minato-ku
Tokyo 108
Japan
Telephone: (03) 447-3111
Telex: 242-3111 MYKTKYJ
Cable: MIYAKO TKY
Fax: (03) 447-3133
Reservations:
  In Tokyo call (03) 447-3111
  In the USA call (212) 661-3210
Access, Barclay, Choice, Discover, and Eurocard
General Manager: Yukio Saeki
Concierge: Masamichi Tanaka
Sales Manager: Suestugu Ito
Miyako Hotel Kintetsu Chain
Rates (approx.):
  Standard "A" room $109 single, $136–$143 double
  Standard "B" room $122 single, $143 double
  Superior room $156 single, $163 double
  Deluxe room $183 single or double
  Executive suite $407
  Royal Suite $678
  Imperial Suite $814
500 rooms, 10 suites
Service charge 10%; tax 10%

The Miyako is a twelve-story structure on five-and-a-half acres of exquisitely landscaped Japanese gardens. It was designed by architects Minoru Yamasaki, planner of the Century Plaza in Los Angeles and the World Trade Center in New York City, and Togo Murano, designer of many fine Tokyo hotels, member of the Japan Art Academy, and chief architect of Tokyo's National Guest House restoration program. In a lovely part of the city, the Miyako is almost surrounded by beautiful shrines, such as the Kakurin-ji Temple, the Genssho-ji Temple, the Shoman-ji Temple, and the Zuisho-ji Temple. Not far from the hotel, just above the nearby expressway, are the French, West German, Finnish, Iranian, South Korean, and Cuban embassies, all on the edge of the Arisuggawa Memorial Park.

The rooms, which are all fire- and earthquake-proofed, are spacious and equipped with private bath and shower, radio, color TV, and air conditioning.

Wining and dining is a pleasure here. The Grill Room is

open for all three meals and provides a garden view, as do the Japanese and Chinese restaurants. Salon Cafe Miyako, open from 8:00 A.M. until 1:00 A.M., is especially good for snacks, drinks, and relaxing. The Silver Hill Coffee Shop, open from 6:30 A.M. until 11:30 P.M., is a good place for modestly priced dining or coffee. *My favorite spot* in the hotel is the Crystal Lounge, in the front of the lobby, which is ideal for meeting people or just relaxing.

The health club of the hotel has an indoor swimming pool, sauna, and steam baths. It is fully equipped and has supervised men's and women's athletic programs. There is an arcade with elegant shops. On a balcony overlooking the pool is the pool-side lounge, a tea-time favorite open from noon until 11:00 P.M.

The free *Walking Map* shows the routes by which you may explore this beautiful area of Tokyo. Be sure to take your camera along.

The hotel is less than half an hour from the Haneda Airport, the Tokyo City Air Terminal to Narita Airport, and the Tokyo Central Railway Station. There is a complimentary hotel bus to nearby railway stations for the loop-line, subway lines, and the monorail to Haneda Airport. In the evening the bus goes to the Ginza shopping districts.

ROPPONGI PRINCE HOTEL
2–7, Roppongi 3-chome
Minato-ku
Tokyo 106
Japan
Telephone: (03) 587-1111
Telex: 242-7231 RPNPRH J
Fax: (03) 587-0770
Reservations:
   In Tokyo call (03) 587-1111
   In New York call (212) 889-5928
   In Los Angeles call (213) 689-4800
   Elsewhere in the USA call 1-800-542-8686
All major credit cards
General Manager: Makoto Orihara
Prince Hotels
Rates (approx.):
   Standard twin room $122 single, $132 double
   Standard double room $135
   Deluxe twin room $152
   Deluxe double room $148

Twin suite $329
Double bed suite $263
204 rooms, 12 suites
Service charge 10%; tax 10%

The Roppongi Prince Hotel is a small, delightful lodging that for Tokyo is also modestly priced. A modern structure whose striking lobby features brilliantly conceived lighting, it is an attractive V-shaped building with a very unusual V-shaped swimming pool inside. In fact, the pool is *my favorite spot*. It was designed by innovative Japanese architect Kisho Kurokawa, who also designed the entire hotel, including its eight restaurants and bar. At the heart of its plaza pool deck is a dramatic live tree. The architect achieved his intention of creating restfulness and a comfortable ambiance. The hotel roof has a solar mirror that directs sunshine down to the pool. Adjacent to the pool, where swimwear-clad guests may go, is the Hibiscus Coffee Shop, serving salads, fruit cocktails, and light snacks.

Other dining establishments include the Moon Grow Restaurant, which features continental cuisine and is one of Tokyo's more elegant dining rooms. The Da Zoretta a Roma serves authentic Italian dishes in a bright café-bar style overlooking the hotel pool. For Japanese dining there are the Edo Tempura, the Ichibei Sushi, and the Iikura Steak House restaurants. Guests also enjoy the decor of the Windsor main bar.

The hotel is only five minutes from the Ginza, twenty minutes from the Haneda International Airport, and about ninety minutes from Narita International Airport. Right across the street is the IBM headquarters building.

SHERATON GRANDE TOKYO BAY HOTEL
1–9 Maihama
Uraysu-shi
Chiba-ken
Tokyo 160
Japan
Telephone: 03-443-6881
Fax: (03) 346-9788
Reservations:
    In Tokyo call 03-264-4270
    In the USA call 1-800-325-3535
All major credit cards
Sheraton Corporation

Rates (approx.):
  Room $164 single, $187–$374 double
  Suite $383
800 rooms and suites
Service charge 10%; tax 10%

I had to include this hotel even though it was not open when I prepared this book. There's one very good reason: it is directly adjacent to Tokyo's Disneyland, which is celebrating its fifth anniversary. Certainly a place to stay if you bring the kids along, and I know that some adults enjoy Disneyland as much or more than the kids—particularly as a place to let off steam and relax after a hectic week or so of business negotiations.

But even if there were no Disneyland next door, this would be a special hotel. Sheraton has planned it as Tokyo's first "resort hotel." The hotel is set on two and a half acres of landscaped gardens overlooking Tokyo Bay. The Japanese landscape artist Shodo Suzuki created an exciting and dramatic Japanese garden surrounding the S-shaped hotel. There is a Grotto Bar right behind a waterfall that forms a background for the outdoor pool, and the gardens are laced with meandering waterways.

There is an interesting mix of accommodations in the rooms and suites, including the more luxurious Sheraton Towers, favored by business travelers and affluent vacationers. If you want to have more traditional quarters, you may stay in a Japanese Inn with authenic *furo* baths. Every room has a mini-bar and refrigerator.

The hotel has a superb array of places to eat and to drink, presenting international, Japanese, and Chinese cuisines; some restaurants feature entertainment as well. On the top of the hotel, certain to be *my favorite spot*, is the Sky Lounge and Restaurant, which promises to serve elegant meals above panoramic views. What a great spot for an overview of the colorful Disneyland at night!

In the hotel's own Japanese gardens, barbecued fare is served in secluded huts beneath the waterfall. There is also a coffee shop and twenty-four-hour room service.

Within the hotel area there are plenty of activities for the sports-minded. A fully equipped sports complex has an indoor and outdoor swimming pool, five tennis courts (four indoor and one outdoor), a sauna and aerobics facilities. There's a shopping arcade, with a barber and a beauty salon on the lower levels.

This is a place for conventions and conferences. There

are over thirty thousand square feet of meeting and banquet space. The Fuji Ballroom can handle 2,500 people at a reception, and the Kegon Ballroom has a capacity of 450. The hotel also has a Seminar Room and a Board Room for getting down to business. There are top-floor meeting rooms designed to keep participants from being annoyed or tempted by other hotel activities.

There is a shuttle bus service from the hotel to Tokyo Disneyland and Narita and Haneda airports as well as central Tokyo. By car, the hotel is forty minutes from Narita, thirty minutes from Haneda and twenty-five minutes from the Tokyo Station.

SHINAGAWA PRINCE HOTEL
4-10-30 Takanawa 4-chome
Minato-ku
Tokyo 108
Japan
Telephone: (03) 440-1111
Telex: 242-5178 SHAPRHJ
Cable: SHINAPRI
Fax: (03) 441-7092
Reservations:
   In Tokyo call (03) 440-1111
   In New York call (212) 889-5928
   In Los Angeles call (213) 689-4800
   Elsewhere in the USA call 1-800-542-8686
All major credit cards
General Manager: Shigeru Kurosu
Sales Manager: Hideo Nonaka
Prince Hotels
Rates (approx.):
   Room $49 single, $79–$82 double
1,273 rooms, no suites
Service charge 10%; tax 10%

This is the hotel for the economy-minded visitor to Tokyo. It has two ultramodern towers and is close enough to Tokyo's principal rail and subway lines to make moving around the city very easy. It has become a favorite for families because so much is so close. Within the complex right outside the hotel doors is an entire recreation village. Among the many different places within the complex are the Prince's Ice Arena, a year-round indoor skating rink that has hockey games and ice-show extravaganzas; the Bowling Center, which has 104 lanes under one roof; the Takanawa Tennis Center, which has nine indoor courts open throughout the year that can be reserved on request and also has lockers and showers available; the Gold Hall, for exhibitions, sports events, and shows; and a summer swimming pool. Also in the complex is a gymnastic exercise center and the fantastic Prince Delica supermarket for beautiful fresh food.

The hotel has thirteen restaurants, offering a variety of Western, Japanese, and Chinese foods. The lounges range from a very relaxing piano bar to a lively beer hall.

This is a fun place for the family on a budget or for the younger business person. It is only fifteen minutes from the Ginza, twenty minutes from the Tokyo International Airport at Haneda or the Tokyo City Air Terminal for Narita. It takes only fifty minutes to go to Tokyo Disneyland by car.

The rooms are modest and small, but so is the price.

SHINJUKU PRINCE HOTEL
1-30-1 Kabuki-cho 1-chome
Shinjuku-ku
Tokyo 160
Japan
Telephone: (03) 205-1111
Telex: 232-4733 SHIPRH J
Fax: 03 205-1952
Reservations:
  In Tokyo call (03) 205-1111
  In New York call (212) 889-5928
  In Los Angeles call (213) 689-4800
  Elsewhere in the USA call 1-800-542-8686
All major credit cards
General Manager: Shokei Hasegawa
Sales Manager: Fusao Shagawa
Prince Hotels
Rates (approx.):
  Standard twin room $95
  Deluxe twin room $125
571 rooms, no suites
Service charge 10%; tax 10%

The Shinjuku is the bustling new business center of Tokyo. One of the more impressive buildings in this area is the twenty-five-story red brick Shinjuku hotel. The guest rooms of the hotel, which are modern and comfortable, begin on the tenth floor. Below that, occupying space from the hotel's second basement to the eighth floor, is the trendy PePe Promenade, where you will find a number of boutiques, fashionable shops, and fun places to eat, such as the Piccadilly Circus for ice cream, the Makena for coffee and cake, the Pousse Cafe for light cocktails and canapés, and the Fumizuki Restaurant for Japanese food.

Another place to enjoy shopping is the American Boulevard, a fashionable complex popular for its range of seasonable wear and sportswear. Young adults favor this shopping area, and a lot of American-made products and clothes are available. Among the places to eat are the Captain Sandwich House, the West-Side Snack, and the Strike Curry Shop.

The hotel has a number of restaurants including the Chatelaine Restaurant with soft music; the Chatelaine Top Lounge, on the hotel's top floor with a magnificent view; the Trianon Steak Restaurant, the hotel's main dining room; the Fumizuki Japanese restaurant; the Restaurant Bayern, with German food and beer, and the Alitalia, with Italian food, wine, and live music.

The Shinjuku subway station is just a five-minute walk away from the hotel, providing easy access by train and subway to central Tokyo. The Ginza is only twenty minutes away by car. It is a half hour from here to the international airport at Haneda and ninety minutes to the one at Narita.

SUNSHINE CITY PRINCE HOTEL
1–5, Higashi-Ikebukuro 3-chome
Toshima-ku
Tokyo 170
Japan
Telephone: (03) 988-1111
Telex: 272-3749 SUNPRHJ
Cable: SUNPRH J
Fax: (03) 983-0115
Reservations:
   In Tokyo call (03) 988-1111
   In New York call (212) 889-5928
   In Los Angeles call (213) 689-4800
   Elsewhere in the USA call 1-800-542-8686
All major credit cards
General Manager: Tsunenari Okuyama
Sales Manager: Michihide Kobayashi
Prince Hotels

Rates (approx.):
  Standard twin-bed room $72 single, $108 double
  Deluxe twin-bed room $105 single, $131 double
  Deluxe double-bed room $145–$151
  Suite A (business) $329
  Suite B (family) $296
1,166 rooms, 10 suites
Service charge 10%; tax 10%

In 1987, yet another exciting complex was completed in Tokyo. Called Sunshine City, it is Tokyo's newest and most complete business, shopping, and entertainment center. It is not in the heart of the city, but only twenty minutes from the Ginza, about a half hour from the international airport at Haneda, and eighty minutes from the airport at Narita. In the middle of this multifaceted complex is the brand new Sunshine City Prince Hotel. Thirty-eight stories high, it is the second tallest building in the complex.

The tallest building of this complex, the Sunshine 60 Building, is the second-tallest building in Asia (the tallest is the seventy-three-story Westin Stamford Hotel in Singapore). Its special elevator, which goes to the top, the sixtieth floor, is said to be the fastest elevator in the world, traveling 1,968 feet per minute. The entire trip to the top takes thirty-five seconds! At the top is a glass-enclosed observatory giving visitors a thrilling panoramic view of Tokyo. You can even see the entire Kanto Plain and Mount Fuji from here.

Other structures within the Sunshine City complex include the World Import Mart, Japan's comprehensive import promotion center with offices, exhibition halls, wholesale center, conference rooms, and, on its ninth floor, a group of theme restaurants. Occupying the tenth and eleventh floors is the world's highest aquarium, Sunshine International Aquarium, with some of the world's rarest fish. Also on the tenth floor is the Sunshine Planetarium, a completely computer-controlled facility, the first of its kind in Japan. Adjacent to the World Import Mart is the Cultural Center, with its theater, exhibition halls, art gallery, museums, gymnasium, and meeting rooms. Under the Sunshine City Prince Hotel is the Alpha shopping and restaurant complex, occupying four levels beneath the Sunshine 60 office tower and the Sunshine Public Square. It contains 220 speciality shops on three of the levels and an entire floor of restaurants. Also within the complex is the Sunshine City Mitsukoshi, a full-sized unit of the famous department store chain.

The Sunshine City Prince Hotel is large, modestly priced, and full of nice things. For example, all of the 1,166 rooms have feather quilts to provide extra comfort. There is an entire floor reserved for ladies only, and there is a non-smoking floor. This first-class international-style hotel also has some Japanese-style guest rooms as well.

The hotel has eight dining rooms offering a variety of cuisines. The Trianon Restaurant, occupying the entire fifty-ninth floor of the Sunshine 60 Building, features French dishes. It has the same breathtaking views as the observatory on the floor above and makes dining an especially enjoyable experience, particularly at night, when the city lights are fantastic. Other dining rooms include Alitalia, an Italian restaurant; the Bayern, the German cuisine and beer room; the Musashino sushi restaurant; the Kokiden Chinese restaurant; the lobby lounge for drinks and light snacks; and the Windsor, the main bar where music accompanies drinks.

The hotel has convention and meeting facilities. Hotel guests may use the health and exercise facilities in the Culture Center of Sunshine City, where on the fifth through seventh floors are the gymnasium, a swimming pool, and a jogging track.

TAKANAWA PRINCE HOTEL
3-13-1, Takanawa
Minato-ku
Tokyo 108
Japan
Telephone: (03) 447-1111
Telex: 242-3232 TAKPRHJ
Cable: PRINSOTEL
Fax: (03) 446-0849
Reservations:
   In Tokyo call (03) 447-1111
   In New York call (212) 889-5928
   In Los Angeles call (213) 689-4800
   Elsewhere in the USA call 1-800-542-8686
All major credit cards
General Manager: Hiroshi Ebihara
Sales Manager: Yuji Miyake
Prince Hotels

Rates (approx.):
  Single room $112
  Double room $151
  Suite $263–$986
402 rooms, 16 suites
Service charge 10%; tax 10%

NEW TAKANAWA PRINCE HOTEL
3-13-1, Takanawa
Minato-ku
Tokyo 108
Japan
Telephone: (03) 442-1111
Telex: 242-7418 PHTAKA J
Cable: PRINSOTEL
Fax: (03) 444-1234
Reservations:
  In Tokyo call (03) 442-1111
  In New York call (212) 889-5928
  In Los Angeles call (213) 689-4800
  Elsewhere in the USA call 1-800-542-8686
All major credit cards
General Manager: Hiroshi Ebihara
Sales Manager: Yuji Miyake
Prince Hotels
Rates (approx.):
  Single room $125
  Double room $151
  Suite $296–$361
968 rooms, 32 suites
Service charge 10%; tax 10%

The two hotels are on a lush, green estate linked by some of Tokyo's grandest Japanese gardens. Sitting on a hilltop amid ponds and flower and plant-bordered paths, these two popular-priced hotels are in the city's center. The guest houses on the estate are special attractions of the hotel, particularly for those planning meetings, parties, or other events. One is the Kihinkan (which means "guest house"), a Meiji-era annex to the hotel, and the other is the Prince Kaikan, an independent, formal stone building located between the two hotels in the garden center. There are another eight banquet halls, lounges, and ballrooms in both hotels as well.

Both hotels have many restaurants. The Takanawa Prince

has its Le Trianon French restaurant, the Katsura Steak House, the Kokiden Chinese restaurant, the Patio coffee shop, the Wakatate tempura restaurant, the Matsukaze sushi restaurant, the Takanawatei Shippoku Cuisine, the Chatelaine tea salon, the Komyo cocktail lounge, the Prince Royal main bar, and the Nite Spot Member's Club.

The New Takanawa Prince has nine more, including the Beaux Sejours French restaurant, the Tohri Chinese restaurant, the Shimizu Japanese restaurant, the Marmolada Italian restaurant, the Edelweiss Parlor, the Asama main bar, the Momiji Lounge, the Shumei Japanese-style room, and the Ean Japanese tea house.

The Takanawa Prince has two swimming pools, and the new hotel also has its own swimming pool. There is a business service room in the new hotel as well as boutiques and a souvenir shop, where items ranging from the Prince Hotels' original articles to traditional craft items of pottery, porcelain, ceramics, and jewelry are available.

Even if you do not attend any events that would bring you into the Hiten Main Banquet Hall, the Uzushio Entrance Hall, or the Sakura Reception Hall, you should visit just to see the dramatic decor of these rooms. Particularly dazzling are the seven-color chandeliers designed by Togo Murano, the famous interior designer whose work is seen throughout the New Takanawa Prince. By the way, the name Hiten refers to celestial nymphs floating on azure skies and was suggested by the famous Japanese novelist Yasushi Inoue.

The hotels are about ninety minutes from the New Tokyo International Airport at Narita, about twenty minutes from the Tokyo International Airport at Haneda, and about fifteen minutes by taxi to the Ginza.

TOKYO HILTON INTERNATIONAL
6-2, Nishi-Shinjuku 6-chome
Shinjuku-ku
Tokyo 160
Japan
Telephone: (03) 344-5111
Telex: 232-4515 HILTON J
Cable: HILTELS TOKYO
Fax: (03) 342-6094
Reservations:
   In Tokyo call (03) 344-51111
   In the USA call any Hilton Reservation Service or
      Hilton International or Vista International hotel

All major credit cards
Managing Director: Richard E. Handl
General Manager: Yutaka (Dan) Nakamura
Concierge: Nobuyoshi Shimada
Sales Manager: Takemitsu Itoh
Hilton International
Rates (approx.):
  Queen-bed room $140 single, $160 double
  King-bed room $167 single, $193 double
  Twin-bed room $153 single, $173 double
  Queen-bed room with sofa $187 single, $213 double
  Suite $200–$1,600
836 rooms, 53 suites
Service charge 10%; tax 10%

The Tokyo Hilton International opened in 1984 after the Hilton lost its contract to manage what is now called the Capitol Tokyu, on the other side of town. The present Hilton is managed by Hilton International and is owned by Nippon Hilton, a joint venture between Hilton and twelve Japanese insurance and finance companies. This is the largest Hilton International Hotel in the Asia and Pacific region and is in the new Shinjuku district of Tokyo. A thirty-eight-story building with distinctive brick color and a gentle S-curve, this is one of Japan's tallest structures. It overlooks Shinjuku Central Park and is minutes away from the heart of the business and entertainment area. Two blocks away is the Metropolitan Expressway, as is the Shinjuku Station, which has twelve rail lines.

Located in the western part of Tokyo, Shinjuku has actually been a center for lodging and entertainment since the Edo period (1603 to 1867). Recent planned decentralization has resulted in a stunning new high-rise environment, making Shinjuku the business and entertainment center of the city. The area is noted for its large department stores, open-air plazas, pedestrian malls, and multilevel walkways, producing a twenty-first-century setting reflecting Japan's astonishing industrial achievement. Fortunately much of the fine old areas still remain, including the Meiji Shrine and the Shinju-ku Gyoen National Garden. In eastern Shinjuku (Kabuki-cho) are the theaters, nightclubs, bars, and restaurants in a maze of tiny back lanes and alleys.

The hotel's guest rooms and suites provide views of Shinjuku Central Park and business district, as well as Mount Fuji in the distance. The comfortable, well-appointed rooms are among the largest in Tokyo and are equipped with all the conveniences of a deluxe hotel, including direct-dial telephones, mini-bars, individual climate controls, and color TVs with in-house movies and an English-language channel. The rooms have the best in Western design combined with unique Japanese features, such as shoji screens. I especially enjoy the special care taken for the comfort and enjoyment of hotel guests. A "happi-coat" and a robe and slippers are neatly set at the foot of the bed. And there is a beautiful flower arrangement and fresh fruit on a lacquer tray. I call this "endless fruit," because whatever you eat is replaced exactly by the next maid.

It is worthwhile to note that the Hilton uses the bank exchange rate and has no handling charge for exchanging guests' dollars to yen. And here is a tip on making reservations: for extra space request one of the wedge-shaped rooms, numbers 9, 10, 24, and 25 on floors eight through thirty-eight.

The top three floors have special VIP services designed for the traveling executive, including separate check-in, upgraded rooms and accessories, a separate concierge, and a private lounge with complimentary continental breakfast, snacks, and cocktails.

Other facilities include the glittering Kiku Ballroom, which can accommodate one thousand guests, and eighteen additional function rooms with audio-visual aids. The fifth floor houses the fitness center, with an indoor pool under a skylight roof, a pool-side snack bar, sauna and massage facilities, and a well-equipped gymnasium. Two outdoor tennis courts with coaches are available on the sixth floor. In the basement there is a shopping arcade, including a duty-free shop. The hotel's business center is on the ground floor and has a well-stocked reference library and a small meeting room. There are even wedding facilities in the hotel, including a Shinto wedding ceremony room.

The Hilton International takes special care everywhere with its dining rooms, and this hotel is no exception. The Imari, called Tokyo's showcase dining room, has grills, the freshest of seafood, and fine vintage wines in an elegant setting. Musashino has several small Japanese dining rooms featuring the national cuisine, and the Dynasty serves a variety of Chinese regional foods. Popularly priced informal meals are available in the Sakura, which has glass wall panels giving views of the spectacular lobby below. Just off the lobby is the Marble Lounge, for drinks, light meals, and snacks. St. George's Bar has draft beer in an English pub setting. The place for drinks before or after dinner is the sophisticated Black Pearl Bar, which is open until midnight.

Two free hotel publications are available to guests, a jogging map and the most helpful *Shopping around Shinjuku*.

TOKYO PRINCE HOTEL
3-1, Shibakoen 3-chome
Minato-ku
Tokyo 105
Japan
Telephone: (03) 432-1111
Telex: 242-2488 TYOPRH J
Cable: HOTEL PRINCE, TYO
Fax: (03) 434-5551
Reservations:
  In Tokyo call (03) 432-1111
  In New York call (212) 889-5928
  In Los Angeles call (213) 689-4800
  Elsewhere in the USA call 1-800-542-8686
All major credit cards
General Manager: Toshihiro Haba
Sales Manager: Hideo Iwasawa
Prince Hotels
Rates (approx.):
  Standard twin-bed room $125 single, $138 double
  Deluxe twin-bed room $138 single, $177 double
  Deluxe double-bed room $177
  Suite $394–$1,117
484 rooms, 18 suites
Service charge 10%; tax 10%

Located in a quiet and convenient area at the foot of the Tokyo Tower and overlooking the lush green gardens of Shiba Park, the hotel is close to most things in this world's largest city. It is only five minutes by car from here to the Ginza and thirty-five minutes to Tokyo Disneyland. It is only twenty minutes to the airport at Haneda and ninety minutes to the airport at Narita.

The hotel's rooms are modest, comfortable, and clean, and there is a swimming pool and a jogging course.

The Tokyo Prince has a good mix of restaurants, including Beaux Sejours, a fine French dining room with a garden view; the informal Porto Coffee Shop; the Marronnier Chinese restaurant; the Gotoku Sushi restaurant; the Fukusa tempura restaurant; the Prince Villa restaurant, with garden view; the Petrea restaurant; the Garden restaurant; and the popular informal meeting place, the Pikake Tea Salon. There are also two bars and a lounge.

WESTIN AKASAKA PRINCE HOTEL
1–2, Kioi-cho, Chiyoda-ku
Tokyo 102
Japan
Telephone: (03) 234-1111
Telex: 232-4028 AKAPRH J
Cable: PRINCEAT TOKYO
Fax: (03) 262-5163
Reservations:
   In Tokyo call (03) 234-1111
   In New York call (212) 889-5982
   In Los Angeles call (213) 689-4800
   Elsewhere in the USA call Westin Reservations at
      1-800-228-3000 or Prince Hotels at 1-800-542-8686
All major credit cards
General Manager: Taro Kobayashi
Resident Manager: Masaru Tanaka
Sales Manager: Tomoki Koyanagi
Prince Hotels
Westin Hotels and Resorts
Rates (approx.):
   Standard twin-bed room $125 single, $174 double
   Medium twin- or double-bed room $148 single, $200
      double
   Other room $174–$256
   Suite $460–$559
   Business suite $223–$256 single
   Japanese suite $526–$559
637 rooms, 124 suites
Service charge 10%; tax 10%

This striking, ultra modern forty-story structure is called Kenzo Tange's triumph, because in creating it this architect established a standard that many believe will set the tone for hotel design throughout the world. Tange believed, "A hotel is a major place for social communication. In this environment, people should be made to feel important and have control of space. As a result, interior design should be simple and elegant and have the use of subtle color schemes." Tange's selection of a V-shape structural design gives the hotel a core and two wings, enabling every guest room to have a spectacular view of Tokyo. The hotel has been described as dramatic, surprisingly beautiful, and an architectural masterpiece. Among Tange's other notable projects are the National Gymnasium for the 1964 Olympics held in Tokyo; a palace for King Faisal at Jeddah, Saudi Arabia; and the Cannes Festival Hall and Congress Center in France.

Ideally located, the Akasaka Prince is in the heart of Japan's governmental, business, and cultural districts. Situated between the Imperial Palace and the Omiya Palace, the hotel is within sight of the three-hundred-year-old East Garden of the Imperial Palace on the east side of the hotel. To the southeast are Nagata-cho, the seat of the Diet, Japan's legislative branch of government, and the Prime Minister's residence; Kasumigaseki, the location of most of Japan's major government offices; and the Ginza, Tokyo's famous shopping and entertainment center. West of the hotel is the 180-acre Meiji Shrine, a monument to Emperor and Empress Meiji. The shrine has wonderful things to see, such as the garden with one hundred varieties of irises, a treasure house of objects from the Meiji reign, and a huge torii gateway lined with seventeen-hundred-year-old cypress trees. To the west and north of the hotel is the well-known Shinjuku Garden. Nearby are the National Stadium, the baseball stadium, and seven theaters, including the National Theater and the Tokyo Kosei Nenkin Kaikan Hall. Two minutes away are the major subway stations; five minutes away is the Kasumigaseki entry ramp of the Shuto Expressway; and ten minutes away is the Tokyo JNR Station. The Ginza is fifteen minutes away by car; Marunouchi is ten minutes; and Kasumogaseki is five minutes away. Nagatacho is five to ten minutes away by foot.

The lobby of the Westin Akasaka Prince is glistening white marble—not only the floors and countertops but the grand piano as well. The only contrast comes from the large flower arrangement set part way up the grand white marble staircase. An example of ikebana, traditional Japanese flower arranging, these fresh flowers are provided by the Sogetsu School.

The regular guest rooms, at 395 square feet, are among the largest in Tokyo. The rooms have extra-long beds, color TVs, refrigerators, and spacious living areas, bathrooms, and adjacent powder rooms. Each room has a comfortable couch near the large windows, something you usually find only in larger suites. The decor is modern, and the rooms are totally soundproof and have individual controls for air conditioning.

Eight guest floors serve the needs of business guests, with a centrally located meeting room on each floor. These rooms can accommodate from five to forty people for everything from brief meetings to luncheons. The hotel has an executive service center that is open from 8:00 A.M. to 9:00 P.M. weekdays and from 8:00 A.M. to 3:00 P.M. on weekends and holidays.

Royal Floor Service is provided on the thirty-fifth through thirty-ninth floors. Visiting executive guests are invited to the weekly cocktail party held for them in the white-leather Royal Pacific Lounge on the twentieth floor.

The hotel has a grand ballroom that can accommodate twenty-five hundred people. There are facilities for simultaneous translation for international conferences as well as stage equipment, lighting, and special sound systems.

The twelve restaurants and lounges in the hotel each has its distinct character. The favorites are Le Trianon, the French restaurant occupying seven private rooms in the Akasaka Prince Guest House, open for lunch and dinner; and the Napoleon Lounge on the floor below in the guest house, open from 11:00 A.M. to 11:00 P.M. Both are elegant. My favorite restaurant is the Blue Gardenia, on the top floor; this is a continental dining room with a 360-degree view of Tokyo. The Potomac, an American-style coffee shop on the third floor, has a grill-type menu and fast service. The first basement level is the location for the Ohmi steak house, the Kioi Japanese restaurant, the Kiri for tempura, and the Tachibans for sushi. In the lobby is the Marble Square, serving specially blended coffees and teas as well as cocktails and hors d'oeuvres. The Top of Akasaka is a cocktail lounge open from 11:00 A.M. to midnight, noted for its view; the Fountain Terrace Parlor serves excellent sodas and desserts in its fashionable quarters in the first basement near the grand marble staircase.

Toyohashi

HOLIDAY INN TOYOHASHI
141 Fujisawa-cho
Toyohashi-shi 440
Aichi Prefecture
Japan
Telephone: (0532) 48-3131
Telex: 4322 126
Cable: Holidex: TYJJA HX13489B
Fax: (0532) 46-6672
Reservations:
　In Toyohashi call (0532) 48-3131
　In Tokyo call (03) 496-9325
　In the USA call 1-800-HOLIDAY
All major credit cards
Director: Azuma Umemura
General Manager: Yasuhiko Yoshida
Concierge: Kuniko Samata
Sales Manager: Mr. Otha
Rates (approx.):
　Holiday Double room　$49 single, $69 double
　Holiday Double Deluxe room　$63 single, $83 double
　Family Twin room (with two double beds)　$76 single,
　　$96 double
　Holiday Twin room (with two double beds)　$83
　　single, $103 double
144 rooms, no suites
Service charge 10%; tax 10%

Toyohashi is a small city of three hundred thousand in central Honshu, on Tokyo Bay. It is the main center of Japan's patent medicine industry and has factories that produce cotton and rayon yarn and pulp.

The Holiday Inn is part of an exciting complex called Holiday Square. It has, in addition to the inn, indoor and outdoor swimming pools, tennis courts (free rental of tennis shoes is available), the Holiday Theatre, the Holiday Hall, an Olympic Sports Centre, a McDonald's, a Kentucky Fried Chicken, a Hawaiian Pool, a sixty-lane Bowling Centre, a bank, a cake shop, a restaurant (the Royal Host), and an ice-skating rink. Right now, construction is under way to add a thirty-two-story hotel building with 362 rooms and

35 suites, a convention hall, a health club, another swimming pool, a Holiday Garden with a small church, a restaurant on the thirty-first floor with a panoramic view, and a view lounge on the thirty-second floor. Also being added is an international Cultural Centre with an English school and a Chinese school, all scheduled to open in 1989.

The inn has two specialty restaurants, a coffee shop, and a bar. Special meals are available that are low in calories, cholesterol, sugar, and salt.

If you have forgotten any of your toiletry items, the hotel will provide them without charge. One Japanese custom that is still widely practiced is the removal of shoes when entering a building and putting on slippers. In this Holiday Inn, shoes are worn almost everywhere, but Japanese slippers are provided in all guest rooms.

The hotel provides an information desk in the lobby, staffed by Louise Castle, a British employee, to offer assistance to English-speaking guests. The hotel also provides a free jogging map of the area.

It takes just over two hours to get here from Tokyo and less than two hours from Kyoto. The Holiday Inn is ninety minutes from Nagoya International Airport and only ten minutes from the town's industrial area. The port, the station, and the city center are only five minutes away.

KOREA

Korea is on a peninsula in East Asia occupying about eighty-five thousand square miles. Seoul was the traditional capital until 1948, when two separate regimes were formally established: the Republic of Korea in the south, with a population of more than 35 million and Seoul as its capital, and the Democratic People's Republic in the north, with a population of more than 17 million and Pyongyang as its capital. In 1972 the two regimes agreed to establish machinery to work for unification. Unfortunately, despite efforts of the United Nations, the United States, and others, unification is no closer today than it was then.

Korea has abundant natural resources and a varied economy. The country once had vast timber sources, but the south is now largely deforested, the result of illegal cutting after 1945 and damage during the Korean War (1950–53). Most of what remains is in the north. The country has great mineral wealth—again, most of it in the north. Of the peninsula's five major minerals—gold, iron, coal, tungsten, and graphite—only the last two are found principally in the south. Rice is the main crop throughout Korea. Cattle are raised in the south, but chiefly as beasts of burden. The fishing waters off Korea are among the best in the world. Korean ships have extended their range into the Atlantic and Arctic oceans, where they catch tuna for canning and export.

The postwar economy was aided by large amounts of

foreign aid and the governments' intensive economic development programs. In the south consumer goods industries now dominate, but heavy industry has also been established. A great variety of products are manufactured, including electrical equipment, chemicals, ceramic goods, and plywood.

Chinese and Japanese influences have been strong throughout Korean history, but the Koreans, descended from Tungusic tribal peoples, are a distinct racial and cultural group. Their documented history begins in the twelfth century B.C., when a Chinese scholar, Ki-tze, founded a colony at Pyongyang. After 100 B.C. the Chinese colony of Lolang, established near Pyongyang, had a strong influence on the tribes of the peninsula. The kingdom of Koguryo, the first native Korean state, started in the first century A.D. and by the fourth century had taken over Lolang.

After centuries of rule under various kingdoms and invasions, the country was annexed by Japan in 1910. In World War II, at the Cairo Conference in 1943, the United States, Great Britain, and China promised Korea its independence. At the end of the war Korea was divided into two zones as a temporary measure, with the Soviet troops in the north and Americans south of latitude 38 degrees north. In 1948 the separation became permanent when two separate regimes were formally created.

Off the coast of the Korean peninsula are about thirty-four hundred islands, only a tenth of which are inhabited. About two thousand are clustered off the jagged western part of the southern coastline. Among these are both large limestone deposits, glistening white, and black volcanic rock formations. Resorts have been established near the lime caverns.

All four seasons are enjoyable in Korea, but spring and autumn are short, summer and winter long. In summer, the rainy season usually comes in June and July. Below-freezing weather begins the middle of November and usually ends by the end of February.

Before arriving in Korea, be sure to read about the people and their culture—especially their arts and their love of the native trees and plants (the pine tree, honored for its ability to stay green through the harsh Korean winters, is their favorite). Two helpful books, both published in English in Korea, can be obtained in most of the hotels serving a Western clientele. They are *Welcome to Korea: Comprehensive Guide to the Land of Morning Calm* (Travel Press) and *This Season in Korea* (Intraco).

Seoul was chosen to host the 1988 Summer Olympics (the twenty-fourth). Korea is the second country in Asia, after Japan, to play host.

The Seoul Sports Complex, where most of the games are held, lies across the Han River in the southern part of Seoul. The complex has an indoor swimming pool, gymnasiums, a baseball field, and other facilities, with a combined capacity of two hundred thousand people. The subway goes to the complex in less than a half hour from downtown. Equestrian events are held in Kwach'on, one of Seoul's satellite cities. Yachting is held in Pusan, the harbor city. Rowing and canoeing are on the Han River. T'aenung, in the northeastern part of Seoul, has the shooting range.

To accommodate athletes and journalists, the Olympic Village and the Press Village were constructed near the Seoul Sports Complex. The Olympic Committee chose the *Hodori*, the Korean tiger, as the official mascot to welcome visitors from around the world.

All accommodations described here are in the Republic of Korea, which registers one hundred sixty tourist hotels. The Korean Tourist Association, a governmental agency, classifies these according to price as deluxe, first-class, second-class, and third-class. Even within a given class, however, rates vary greatly. For example, the charge for a room with twin beds and bath ranges from $78 to $200 in a deluxe hotel to $23 to $34 in a third-class hotel.

Some of the hotels have *ondol*, or Korean-style, rooms. Guests leave their shoes at the door and step onto the elevated floor, heated in winter and cooled in summer by ducts running below. Mattresses are laid right on the floor, and the bedding and decor are Korean. As with Western-style guest rooms, a private bathroom adjoins each *ondol*.

Most tourist hotels include one or more bars and cocktail lounges, a variety of restaurants, and on-site recreational facilities such as tennis courts and swimming pools.

In all these hotels there is a 10 percent value-added tax on rooms, meals, and other services, but foreign travelers are exempted from paying it. A 10 percent service charge is added to all bills, so tips are not required.

The past few years have seen an exceptional effort to improve hotel accommodations in the Republic of Korea. Today Seoul especially offers a wide selection of deluxe hotels, and many more of first-class rank. Pusan, Kyongju, and Chejudo Island all have their share of better hotels now.

Despite the construction of ninety-eight new hotels before the Olympic games, a shortage of rooms was predicted.

The Seoul Olympic Organizing Committee reserved 70 percent of the rooms in major hotels, and 90 percent of the rooms in new hotels, for the official Olympic participants.

For more information on Korean hotels, call the Seoul office of the Korean Tourist Association at (02) 757-2345. The people there are very courteous and helpful.

Cheju

HYATT REGENCY CHEJU
3039-1, Saekdal-dong
Seogwipo-si
Cheju-do 590-40
Republic of Korea
Telephone: (0642) 32-2001
Telex: NAMJU K66749
Fax: 32-2039
Reservations:
    In Cheju call (064) 32-2001
    In Korea call (02) 797-7819/20
    In the USA call 1-800-228-9000
All major credit cards
General Manager: Edward N. Tai
Concierge: J. W. Kim
Sales Manager: D. H. Kim
Hyatt Hotels and Resorts
Rates (approx.):
    Standard room $74
    Superior room $93
    Deluxe room $108–28
    Ondol $98
    Suite $195–$650
224 rooms, 18 suites
Service charge 10%; no tax for foreigners

Cheju is a delightful island resort south of the Korean peninsula. It is about thirty minutes' flight from Pusan, about an hour from Seoul, and about an hour and a half from Osaka, Japan.

The island has acquired a number of descriptive names, such as "The Island of the Gods," "The Emerald Island," and "The Hawaii of Korea." This is because of its beauty, which ranges from the lofty Mount Halla to the famous female divers who make their living gathering seafood and other marine products from the depths of the East China Sea.

An extinct volcano, Halla is the highest mountain in the Republic of Korea, with a huge crater on its peak. On its slopes are the beauties of nature—forests, caves, and exquisite waterfalls. Two of the most spectacular waterfalls are Chongbang, which spills directly into the sea, and Chonjeyon, sometimes called "the Niagara of Korea."

Most visitors are attracted to the unique natural rock formations, such as Dragon Head Rock, Cholbuam Rock, and Haenyo, found throughout the island. Each bears a primitive resemblance to a man or animal and over time has become the subject of a variety of mysterious or romantic legends.

Even better known, perhaps, are the Tol-Harubang (Stone Grandfather) figures, carved from the native lava rock. They are believed to have once been important in the shamanism that is still practiced on this island.

Near the Kimnyong village fifteen miles from Cheju City are the Manjang and Snake caves. The seven-mile Manjang Lava Tube is the longest series of connected caves in the world. Formed by hot gases forced through the molten rock millions of years ago, it is home to twenty thousand bats.

Favorite activities for visitors to the island include deep-sea fishing, pheasant hunting, hiking, golfing, horseback riding, swimming, and just walking on the white coral beaches.

The first Western-style hotel on this picturesque island, the Hyatt Regency opened on March 1, 1985, in a spectacular setting on an escarpment overlooking the Pacific Ocean. It has a dramatic eight-story atrium lobby, one of *my favorite spots* in this resort hotel. The sunlight floods the interior of the building from the top of the atrium. Tropical plants and other greenery decorate the lobby and surround its splendid waterfall. This building is connected by enclosed walkways to a casino, a recreational room filled with video and other games, and a library.

All of the hotel rooms, on eleven floors, have individually controlled air conditioning and heating, private baths and showers, piped-in music, radio, color TV, in-house movies, mini-bars with refrigerators, international direct dialing, and private safes.

The hotel offers a wide variety of other amenities, such as indoor and outdoor swimming pools, tennis courts, a children's playground, a beauty shop and a barbershop.

Choongmoon Beach, only a few steps from the hotel, is very popular among the guests for lounging, sunning, and swimming.

Up to five hundred people can attend a reception in the ballroom, which is often partitioned for smaller gatherings. The hotel's modern conference rooms are soundproof, and a simultaneous translation system is available.

The Health Club has a fully equipped gymnasium as well as sauna, steam, and massage facilities, tennis courts, and a jogging track. The indoor pool is lined with volcanic rock and surrounded by waterfalls and tropical plants. The outdoor pool has its own sunken Grotto Bar.

The restaurants provide delicious choices. There is continental cuisine at Dagmar's, and Japanese delicacies at the tranquil Umibe, which has its own Japanese garden. Haewon features pheasant specialties and other Korean dishes. A great spot to relax is the exotic Island Lounge, which is surrounded by fishponds, waterfalls, and tropical foliage.

For some, the most excitement is at the luxurious Regency Casino, which is open twenty-four hours a day. Here they have the choice of playing blackjack, roulette, poker, or baccarat. Others like to dance away the night at the dazzling Moonlight Club.

Be sure to ask for your copy of the hotel's attractive brochure, *Guide Map of Cheju Island*. It shows you where to go and what to see to enjoy this beautiful island.

Kangwon-do

DRAGON VALLEY HOTEL
130, Yongsan-ri
Toam-myon
Pyongchang-gun
Kangwon-do
Republic of Korea
Telephone: Hweung-gye (03746) 2168 or 2169
Telex: TWINDRA K 24270
Fax: (02) 548-2458
Reservations:
   In Yong Pyeong call Hweong-gye (0374) 32-5757
   In Seoul call 548-2251/4
Visa, Diners, American Express, MasterCard
General Manager: Park Myong-soon

Sales Manager: Kang Taejim
Rates (approx.):
   Two-person *ondol* $37
   Three-person *ondol* $68
   Four-person *ondol* $90
   Five-person *ondol* $120
   Twin room $83
   Suite A $165
   Suite B $270
10% service charge and tax included
191 rooms, 14 suites

With the only international-sized ski run in Korea, the Yongpyeong Ski Resort is crowded from early December to late March every year.

It has ten lifts in all and night lighting on the main slope, which at the top is nearly four thousand feet above sea level. There is a ski school, and a snowmobile and a medical team are on constant alert.

Only a few hours' drive from Seoul in Kangwon-do province, this lushly forested resort has facilities for many warm- as well as cold-weather sports. It has a very nice seven-hole golf course with Western turfgrass, a first in Korea, and an artificial lake with an island green. Mount Sorak is close by, and Kyongpodae Beach is only a half-hour's drive away. At the beach are more accommodations provided by the Yongpyeong resort: a youth hostel with *ondol* rooms for families and bunk beds for students and groups, and a condominium.

Overlooking the Tongpyeong Resort is the Dragon Valley Hotel, a first-class tourist hotel that was expanded and re-built from what had been the Juwha Hotel for skiers. The Dragon Valley has mostly Korean-style rooms, as well as Western-style rooms and some suites. Within the hotel are the Cafe Chalet, a restaurant and coffee shop, and Doraji, the hotel's Korean Restaurant. Here, too, is the Lobby Lounge, *my favorite spot* for a drink by the fireplace.

The Ski Haus, an annex to this attractive hotel, has more restaurants, a sauna, a health club, an indoor swimming pool, a bakery, some function rooms, and a souvenir shop. The restaurants here include a cafeteria called Gelände, a coffee shop called Avec, and Highland, a superb steak-house, all on the second floor.

The Valley Center, the resort's entertainment complex near the hotel, has still more restaurants, a supermarket, a billiard room, a game room, a ski shop, a souvenir shop, a delicatessen, a bakery, and even a pizza house.

HOTEL SORAK PARK
74-3, Dorak-dong
Sokcho-shi
Kangwon-do 210-20
Republic of Korea
Telephone: (0392) 34-7711
Telex: SPHOTEL K24142
Reservations:
  In Seoul call (02) 753-2585, 753-2867, 753-2868, or
    (0392) 347711
  In Kangwon-do call 753
American Express, Diners, MasterCard, Visa
President: Kyung-Joon Kim
General Manager: Seung-Pyung Kim
Sales Manager: Bong-Nam Cho
Rates (approx.):
  Double room $77
  Twin room $85
  Triple room $90
  Ondol $90
  Deluxe twin room $90
  Junior suite $130
  Park Suite $220
  Royal Suite $680
121 rooms, 10 suites
Service charge 10%; no tax for foreigners

This hotel is at the edge of Soraksan National Park, well known for its temples, waterfalls, peaks, hiking trails, mineral water, and hot spring. The park is lovely in all four seasons. In the fall, the views of the maple trees are magnificent. In the winter, the park is a snow-covered wonderland, comparable in beauty to the Swiss Alps.

The hotel has a coffee shop, Korean and Japanese restaurants, and a Western grill room. On the second floor are two delightful traditional tea rooms, one Korean and the other Japanese.

The basement of the hotel is a fun place, with a very popular nightclub, a game room, a beauty salon and barbershop, and a casino room. The hotel claims its casino is the best in Korea and comparable to those in Las Vegas and

Monte Carlo, though it is definitely more modest in scale.

My favorite spot is the hotel's unique garden. Here many of the more beautiful flower and plant species of the Sorak mountain range have been collected for the guests to see. It is easy to forget time while you are here.

The view of Mount Sorak from the hotel is a memorable delight, especially while you are enjoying the hotel's barbecue in the garden.

Some fun things to do outside the hotel include visiting the nearby souvenir shop or the dried fish shop downtown, or enjoying, if you like such things, raw fish at the shop in the Daepo port. Ask Young-Nam Ahn, the front-office manager, about other interesting places to visit.

Kyongju

KYONGJU TOKYU HOTEL
410, Shinpyong-Dong
Bomun Lake Resort
Kyongju
Republic of Korea
Telephone: (0561) 2-9901-16
Telex: 54328 KJTOKYU K
Fax: (82) 561 42-9916
Reservations:
  In Seoul call (02) 753-2386
  In the USA call Pan-Pacific Hotels at (213) 452-7736 or,
    except in Hawaii or Alaska, 1-800-4040
All major credit cards
General Manager: T. Hirokawa
Sales Manager: Seong-Ho Koh
Pan-Pacific Hotels
Rates (approx.):
  Room $88
  Standard *ondol* $90
  Deluxe *ondol* $165
  Junior suite $112
  Standard suite $176
  Deluxe suite $200
  Royal Suite $530
303 rooms, 15 suites
Service charge 10%; tax 10%

This first-class resort hotel overlooks the tranquil shores of Lake Bomun. The lake is at the eastern edge of Kyongju City, the ancient capital of Korea's Shilla Dynasty (57 B.C. to 935 A.D.).

For archaeology and history buffs, Kyongju City offers a wealth of mementos from its rich and intriguing past. There are the Sokkuram Buddhist cave sculptures, the dramatic Bulguksa Temple, the royal tombs, and magnificent monuments, pagodas, and ruins wherever you look. The hotel can arrange tours for you through the city, which has been designated a UNESCO excavation site.

The large, newly developed Bomun Lake Resort offers a variety of water sports, an eighteen-hole golf course, twenty tennis courts, and recreation of a traditional Korean village.

All of the hotel's spacious rooms face the lake. All have individually controlled air conditioning, attractive furnishings, telephones, radios, and a choice of taped music. The Korean-style (*ondol*) rooms are lavish.

There is a pleasant selection of places to eat. The King's Arm, overlooking the lake and the hotel's gardens, features international and Korean cuisine. The Hojeon is an authentic Japanese restaurant, and the Café Terrasse is popular for its fresh-brewed coffee, English tea, soft drinks, and afternoon cocktails. After a day of exploration, most guests like to relax in this informal lobby lounge. A *favorite spot* is the Hobanjanj Korean Pavillion, which serves international foods in a rather whimsical lakeside pavilion. Traditional banquets are often held in the top-floor function room; it's fun to peek in.

And there are the King's Arm Bar, down a few steps from the lobby, and the Seven and Eleven, a nightclub that features music and dancing until 4:00 A.M.

Don't be startled if you see a giant white duck sailing on the lake. If you look closer you'll see it really is a cruise boat designed to look like a duck. The hotel would be pleased to arrange for you to enjoy a trip on it.

Pusan

This city of nearly 3 million people is Korea's largest port. Lying at the head of the Naktong River basin, it has served as the main southern gateway to Korea from Japan, which, during its rule over Korea (1910 to 1945) developed this excellent harbor.

Pusan's factories make woolen, cotton, and silk textiles; iron and steel; tires; plywood; frozen seafood; fishing nets; and wigs. Nearby hot springs have made Pusan an important resort city as well.

Historic landmarks include the Kyongbok Palace (1394), the treasure-filled Changdok Palace (1488), and the Toksu Palace (1593), home of the National Museum and Art Gallery.

T.I. Kim, concierge at the Westin Chosun Beach, strongly suggests that first-time visitors go to the Pusan International Market, in the heart of downtown.

PUSAN TOURIST HOTEL
12.2-GA
Dong Kwang-Dong
Jung-Gu
Pusan
Republic of Korea
Telephone: (051) 23-4301-9 or (051) 23-5251-60
Telex: PSHOTEL K53657
Cable: PUSAN HOTEL
Fax: (051) 244-1153
Reservations:
   In Pusan call (05) 23-4301, ext. 330 or 331
All major credit cards
General Manager: Bong-Tae Choi
Concierge: Jung-Hak Kim
Sales Manager: Ho-Gyung Hyung
Rates (approx.):
   Single room $32
   Double room $49
   Ondol $46
   Twin room A $51
   Twin room B $49
   Suite A $78
   Suite B $65
   Royal Suite $171
273 rooms, 20 suites
Service charge 10%; no tax for foreigners

This is a pleasant and inexpensive tourist hotel in the center of the city. Although the modern, fifteen-story building is situated right between Yongdusan Park and the city hall, a short walk takes you to Songdo Beach or the Pusan Big Bridge, which leads to the island park of Tae Jong Dae.

Other attractions are also close by. The international pier is a five-minute drive away, and the airport is a thirty-minute drive, as are the beautiful Bomosa Temple and the Gum Gang Won Park with its zoo. Other beaches, and even the Dong Rae Hot Spring, are less than a half hour from the hotel. If you plan to go anywhere by taxi, the concierge will write instructions for the driver on a small card with the heading (in Korean and English), "Please guide our guest to the following place. Thank you." A map is printed on the opposite side.

The bedrooms are clean and orderly, each having a bathroom. The hotel staff is very friendly and helpful.

There are several places to eat in the hotel: the Rose Garden Main Grill, the Lilac Coffee Shop, and the Chinese Restaurant. The Bakery Shop features French confections.

On the fifteenth floor of the hotel, the Sky Bar provides a magnificent view of Pusan, especially at night, when you see the lights not only of the city but also of the ships in the harbor. The Night and Disco Club, in the hotel's basement, has a disco on the first level and a nightclub below it.

Other amenities include the Sauna and Health Club, offering exercise equipment and sauna and massage services, and the Game Room, for those who like to challenge the one-armed bandits.

Except for the barber's, no shops are in the hotel. But since it is in the center of the busy city, nearby are a number of shops featuring native handicrafts or duty-free goods. The concierge will guide you to find what you want.

THE WESTIN CHOSUN BEACH
737, Woo-1-Dong
Haeundae-ku
P.O. Box 29
Pusan 607-04
Republic of Korea
Telephone: (051) 742-7411/20
Telex: CHOSUNB K53718
Cable: WESTCHO
Fax: (051) 742-1313
Reservations:
  In Pusan call (051) 742-7411/20
  In the USA call 1-800-228-3000
All major credit cards
General Manager: Andrew N. Jones

Concierge: T. I. Kim
Sales Director: Jhong-Bae Lee
Westin Hotels and Resorts
Rates (approx.):
   Superior $82
   Deluxe $96
   Premier $105
   Suite $250+
353 rooms, 16 suites
Service charge 10%; no tax for foreigners

This lovely Hyatt resort is on the popular Dong Baek Peninsula, right at the beautiful Haeundae Beach. It is the only hotel in Pusan that meets high international standards.

The guest rooms are beautiful, featuring Korean fabrics and artwork even where the furniture is Western. All rooms have an ocean view, and full-length windows to enjoy it. All have private baths, individually controlled air conditioning, color TV, radio, and telephones.

The hotel offers several dining choices. *My favorite spot*, the Ninth Gate, serves excellent continental meals. Kuromatsu is a Japanese restaurant, and the Dong Baek Restaurant serves all three meals every day. For night life there is the dramatic Xanadu, a sophisticated entertainment lounge. At the Beach Street Pub you may play a game of darts or watch televised sports while having a refreshing drink.

Shops within the hotel include a pottery shop, a handicraft shop, a gallery, a sundry shop, a beauty parlor, a barbershop, and a photo shop.

In the lower level of the hotel is a very good fitness center. It's complete array of workout equipment includes exercise bicycles, a treadmill, a jungle gym, a pulley, and dumbbells. Separate facilities for men and women feature sauna, whirlpool, cold tub, and showers. Aerobic classes are held on weekdays. The outdoor pool is open in season.

Seoul

Sprawling in the Han River basin, the city of Seoul is flanked by rocky, wooded mountains rising sixteen hundred feet above sea level. The river flows east to west, forming a barrier to the south of the old city, although modern Seoul has spilled far beyond the Han.

Because its topographical advantages made the city a natural fortress, the founders of the Yi Dynasty selected Seoul to be the Korean capital at the end of the fourteenth century. Seoul has been the center of Korean politics, economics, transportation, and culture ever since.

Seoul's population, only one hundred thousand at the beginning of the Yi Dynasty, had reached about 10 million by the end of 1985, with an annual growth rate of 3.2 percent. By creating new jobs, the rapid economic growth that started in the 1960s brought a massive influx of people from the rural areas.

Today Seoul is among the five most populous cities in the world. But in spite of its size the city always gives the impression of being manageable and safe. In many spots it is a sparkling architectural gem; in others it retains the charm of another era.

Proud of their heritage, Koreans have carefully preserved Seoul's major architectural masterpieces. The downtown core is broadly demarcated by the course of the old city wall, which, with its gates (including the famous South Gate and East Gate), has been fully restored in the sections that remain. Within this boundary are the great royal palaces, peaceful and quiet havens from the din and bustle of the city outside.

Seoul is still growing. Offices and housing, transportation facilities, and recreational facilities are going up all over the town.

On Youido, an island created by filling in part of the Han River, new office buildings and apartments have been rising for more than fifteen years. Now Youido is known as a prestigious business address, an exclusive residential area, and, with its chic clubs and restaurants, the new center for night life. Here is found the National Assembly Building, the Korean Stock Exchange, the studios of Korea's major broadcasting companies, and, rising above them all, the sixty-three-story Daehan Life Insurance Building, Korea's highest skyscraper.

Seoul's modern subway system, which took fourteen and a half years to build, is the seventh longest in the world. It carries five million passengers daily, who find that twenty minutes is plenty of time to get downtown from any of the suburbs.

Taxi service, for those who prefer it, is among the cheapest in the world.

The Han River Development Project, begun in 1982, has improved the shoreline and its roads, recreational parks, and green areas. The freeway system has also been improved dramatically in recent years, speeding traffic from the Kimpo International Airport to the Seoul Sports Complex, site of the Olympics, within forty minutes.

Although these and other projects have helped the city cope with its growth, Seoul remains a centralized city whose more important and interesting places can be enjoyed on foot. Major financial, shopping, entertainment, and business centers are concentrated within the downtown core. Several of Seoul's leading hotels and department stores are also within the hub, as is the trendy Myong-dong district, the place to see and be seen, to shop for clothing of original Korean design, or to just have a cup of coffee in a smart café.

Seoul symbolizes the progressive outlook of a people determined to build a harmonious urban community. This ancient "Phoenix City of the Orient" has been reborn as a modern metropolis.

HOTEL LOTTE DOWNTOWN
1, Sogong-Dong
Chung-Ku
C. P. O. Box 3500
Seoul 100
Republic of Korea
Telephone: (02) 752-3758
Telex: LOTTEHO K23533/5
Cable: HOTELOTTE
Fax: (02) 752-3758
Reservations:
　　In Seoul call (02) 771-10
　　In the USA call 1-800-22-LOTTE, 1-800-323-7500, or
　　　　1-800-223-5652
All major credit cards
Chairman: Kyuk-Ho Shin
General Manager: Toshiji Isaka
Concierge: Se-Kwon Kim
Sales Manager: Yang-Dong Song
Rates (approx.):
　　Standard room　　$140 single, $152 double
　　Superior room　　$143 single, $155 double
　　Executive room　　$162 single, $172 double
　　Suite　　$216–$2,045
1,352 rooms, 120 suites
Service charge 10%; no tax for foreigners

In a skyscraper in the heart of Seoul is the luxurious Hotel Lotte Downtown. The thirty-eight story ultramodern structure fits in well with the Seoul of today, a jigsaw puzzle of modern skyscrapers and venerable palaces, art galleries and temples, cultural centers and open-air markets. Representative of the contrasts one finds everywhere in Korea, the Hotel Lotte Downtown is a striking collage of Western and Eastern cultures, providing a unique atmosphere of hospitality and creative vitality.

Plans for the hotel, which opened on March 10, 1979, started in 1973, when the miraculous growth and prosperity of Korea attracted international attention. Kyuk-Ho Shin, the chairman of the Lotte Group (which ran large department and other retail stores) envisioned a hotel in Seoul that would rival the greatest of the world. With the heavy influx of business people and tourists, he believed, Seoul needed a hotel-shopping complex that could well serve the needs of a cosmopolitan and discerning clientele.

During the five years of planning and three years of construction, people and materials from the four corners of the earth were mobilized. The hotel includes Korea's only high-rise exterior glass elevator, a year-round, indoor swimming pool, and *thirty-one* restaurants. The Businessman's Corner includes the services of a friendly staff and four telexes.

Work on the hotel has never stopped. By the end of 1987, the 376-room New Wing Tower was completed next to the original Hotel Lotte. Its larger rooms are tailored to please the VIP, providing extra privacy and conveniences such as limited-access elevators, executive floors, and an exclusive duty-free shop. Adjacent to the hotel is Korea's largest and most modern shopping center, on the eighth floor of which is the Lotte Duty Free Shop, with boutiques featuring names such as Gucci, Hermes, Dunhill, Christian Dior, Lanvin, and Fendi. Connecting the hotel and the shopping center is an underground passage lined with 148 specialty and souvenir shops.

From the opulent Royal Suite to the simpler but exotic standard double room, all of the hotel's rooms have bright decors that let you know you are in a land of excitement. All of them, on the sixth to the thirty-fourth floors in the main hotel and the fifteenth to the thirty-fourth floors in the new wing, have superb views of the entire city and the surrounding mountains. All rooms are air-conditioned, have color TV and radio, alarm clocks, mini-bars and refrigerators, and luxurious bathrooms with telephones. The hotel staff is adept at providing skilled but unobtrusive service.

Among the popular restaurants here are La Coquilla, which serves excellent seafood and Italian specialties; Prince Eugene, which transports the diner to the elegant world of eighteenth-century Vienna; Mu Gung Hwa and Po Suk Jung, Korean dining rooms; Toh Lim Palace, noted for its sensational Pekinese dishes; and Benkay and Momoyama, which serve Japanese specialties. Less formal are the Cafe Gardenia, which serves waffles and pancakes on the Lotte Plaza, the Cafe Peninsula, with its generous servings of popular Oriental, American, and European dishes, and the Sky Cafeteria, on the hotel's top floor.

Among drinking spots are *my favorite*, the Lobby Lounge, where both exotic cocktails and teas are served against a spectacular wall painting inspired by Korea's famous waterfall at Sorak Mountain; Bobby London, an authentic-looking English pub where you can enjoy fish and chips and a game of darts; and the more sophisticated Windsor Bar, an international meeting spot by day and a piano bar at night.

For night life, take a ride on the glass elevator to Annabelle's. Overlooking the city from the thirty-seventh floor, this club offers live entertainment in the evening and becomes a swinging discotheque after midnight.

In Jamsil, a stylish suburban hub across the Han River and close to the venue of the 1988 Seoul Olympics, the new sister to the Hotel Lotte Downtown. The Hotel Lotte Jamsil is a 511-room state-of-the-art complex that opened in April 1988. Sharing a single roof with the hotel are two department stores, a theme park, and an atrium-style market and sports center.

With guest rooms on the sixth to the thirtieth floors, the hotel wing has a cafeteria and a coffee lounge on the first floor, and Korean, Japanese, Chinese, and Western dining rooms on the second. On the third floor are ten small and medium conference rooms and a ballroom that can accommodate fifteen hundred people; on the fourth and fifth are the sauna, the sauna lounge, and the pool. On the top floor, the thirty-first, is the Viking Restaurant, with fantastic views of all of Seoul and of the Olympic areas as well.

A second wing features the Disney-like Theme Park, with some sixty attractions, many of which are original. Although the park is still under construction at this writing, we are promised there will be nothing like it in the world. It is designed for children, but I suspect that people of all ages will be lured into it.

Below the Theme Park, on two levels, are bowling alleys and an ice rink.

The third wing of the complex is a six-level Sports Center, with a parking garage beneath it. Featured in the center are a golf clinic, squash courts, a track, a bowling alley, two pools (one for members, one for hotel guests), a sauna with lockers and a lounge, a coffee shop, and a cafeteria.

Also part of the complex are two Lotte department stores, featuring everything from haute couture to fresh produce. One of the department stores will be the largest in the Orient, complete with a theater (for fashion shows, cooking demonstrations, and the like) and a duty-free shop. The smaller store will have tennis courts on its roof.

HOTEL SHILLA
202, 2-Ga, Jangchung-Dong
Chung-Gu
Seoul 100
Republic of Korea
Telephone: 233-3131
Telex: SHILLA K24160
Fax: 233-5073
Reservations:
    In Seoul call 233-3131, ext. 310
    In the USA call Hotel Shilla at 1-800-221-2094 or
        Leading Hotels of the World at 1-800-223-6800
Most major credit cards
General Manager: Bong-Shik Kang
Concierge: Kun-Jong Baik
Sales Manager: W. T. Baek
Rates (approx.):
    Standard room $138
    Superior room $150
    Deluxe room $188–$238
    Suites $275–$2,750
636 rooms, 74 suites
Service charge 10%; no tax for foreigners

Just ten minutes from the Seoul Olympic Stadium, the Shilla is in twenty-three acres of peaceful wooded gardens on the slope of Mount Namsan in the heart of Seoul. It is twenty minutes from the Kimpo International Airport.

The hotel takes its name from Korea's Shilla Dynasty (57 B.C. to 935 A.D.), which, by uniting the three kingdoms of Shilla, Korguryo, and Paekche in 668 A.D., unified the peninsula for the first time and thereby retarded China's aggression. This unification created a society and culture that formed the mainstream of subsequent Korean history.

The Shilla Dynasty is best remembered for its contributions to Korean art and culture. The Hotel Shilla is designed to combine the elegance of ancient Korean architecture with modern world-class luxury. The best example of this blend is *my favorite spot*, the ornate and luxurious lobby. The golden chandeliers are in the style of the resplendent belts worn by the Kings of the Shilla Dynasty. The ornamental relief patterns, or *wadang*, on the lobby walls are reproduced from ancient Korean renderings of the lotus flower. The ceiling is thirty-nine feet high, giving both a sense of openness and views of the lobby from the second and third floors.

The hotel offers outstanding views of its surroundings as well. From the Japanese and Korean restaurants, the coffee shop, the east side of the French restaurant, and all rooms on the east or back side of the hotel, the view is of Mount Namsan.

But the most interesting view is from the west side, including rooms at the front of the hotel, the west side of the French restaurant, and the executive floor lounges. From these you look down on the former state guest house, Yeong Bin Gwan.

Translated literally, this means "the big house (gwan) welcoming (yeong) esteemed guests (bin)." Built in 1967 in traditional Korean style and staffed by the Shilla organization, this building housed nearly forty heads of state before it was purchased in 1973 as part of the site of the Hotel Shilla. Currently it contains two hotel banquet rooms and an international buffet restaurant, Shangri-La, offering beautiful views of the exquisite surrounding gardens at lunch and dinner.

The newest dining room is La Fontana, Seoul's most spacious Italian restaurant, which opened in May 1987. Luigi Fadda, of Milan, is the chef. La Continentale is a French dining room on the twenty-third floor, where Chef André Bertrom offers sixty-eight different dishes. Azalea, a coffee shop, features Western items from 6:30 A.M. until 2:30 A.M. and a grand view of the gardens. Other restaurants include Sorabol, a Korean dining room, and Palsun, a Chinese restaurant, both on the second floor, and the third-floor Atiake, a Japanese dining room, and Teppan Yaki, with lovely views to dine by.

On the first floor of the hotel is Rainbow, the main bar,

with a grotto decor and popular piano and violin music at night. A favorite spot is the Lobby Lounge, featuring a piano and string quartet in the evening. The Pointe is a new high-tech discotheque on the first basement floor.

The Shilla became the Headquarters Hotel for the Summer Olympics '88 and all rooms, except for a few rooms occupied by long-term guests, were reserved for the members of the International Olympic Committee.

The Shilla is the pioneer in the no-tipping rule in Korea. When the company operated the state guest house, they felt that the Western custom of tipping was un-Korean and pushy. They substituted a 10 percent service charge, still in effect, and began dismissing any employee known to accept a tip (they also introduced a profit-sharing plan for all employees). Pleased with the Shilla model, the Korean Ministry of Transporation in 1977 instituted a 10 percent service charge to replace tipping throughout the travel and tourism industry.

The tipping rule can be a problem. When the King of Qatar was a guest, his staff obtained the names of some seventy people who had a hand in caring for him and his entourage, and as he departed they turned over seventy envelopes, each containing from a hundred to a thousand dollars and inscribed, with an employee's name. After two weeks of meetings the directors decided it would be an insult to return the money, so they put it in a fund for educational assistance of the employees' children.

Because the hotel is a favorite of business travelers, the sixteenth and eighteenth floors are reserved for them. A delightful lounge on each of these floors serves complimentary continental breakfast, tea and coffee, and cocktails with snacks. Also for business people is the first-floor Business Center, providing a full range of services and equipment.

The hotel has two tennis courts and a full-service health club, with a weight and exercise room, saunas, hot tubs, a jogging course, indoor and outdoor pools, and medical services.

Adding to the beauty of the landscaped grounds is the collection of sculptures: 106 created by Choi Jong Tae and 39 by other well-known sculptors. Sponsored by the Gana Gallery, this is the first display of its kind in Korea. Be sure to obtain a copy of the magnificent book *Open-Air Sculpture Exhibition*, in English and Korean, as your souvenir of this unique sculpture garden.

HYATT REGENCY SEOUL
747-7 Hannam-Dong
Yongsan-Ku
Seoul 140
Republic of Korea
Telephone: 798-0061/9 or 798-1601/9
Telex: K24136/K24537
Cable: HYATTSEOUL
Fax: 798-6953
Reservations:
   In Seoul call 794-2282
   In the USA call 1-800-228-9000
All major credit cards
Chairman: Akira Nozaki
General Manager: Arthur H. Holliger
Sales Manager: Rick Masuda
Hyatt Hotels and Resorts
Rates (approx.):
   Standard room $121 single, $131 double
   Superior room $129 single, $139 double
   Deluxe room $159 single, $169 double
   Regency Club standard room $164-$173
   Regency Club deluxe room $190-$200
   Junior suite $237
   Corner/Executive suite $264
   Regency Club suite $269–$295
   Deluxe suite $457
   Royal Suite $1,000
604 rooms, 37 suites
Service charge 10%; tax 10% (may be exempted with
tourist visa)

The Hyatt Regency Seoul, a luxurious resort hotel set in
eighteen acres of beautiful gardens at the foot of Mount
Namsan (South Mountain), offers a fine panoramic view of
the city and the Han River.

The surroundings are refreshingly clean and uncrowded,
comfortably away from the congestion of downtown Seoul.
Yet the hotel is only seven minutes by car or taxi from the
downtown commercial district, and twelve minutes from
the new commercial center of Yoido Island. It is also within
easy walking distance of Itaewon, which earns its fame as
a shopper's paradise as well as one of the Seoul's most
popular evening entertainment spots.

The hotel, which opened in the spring of 1978, has since
1985 been engaged in ambitious renovation projects. In 1986

the hotel opened its new Silhouette Buffet and Silhouette Lounge on the twentieth floor. In 1987 it upgraded rooms and suites and opened a new café, a delicatessen, a shopping arcade, more restaurants and bars, and, to wide acclaim, the comprehensive Hyatt Fitness Center. Included in the center's features are an indoor and an outdoor swimming pool, a women's spa, a men's sauna, a gymnasium, an aerobics studio, and squash courts. There are also walking and jogging tracks and two tennis courts on the property.

The hotel's Business Centre offers twenty-four-hour telex, facsimile, secretarial, and international courier services, and helps track down manufacturers and services through its cross-reference files of all these organizations in Korea. It also provides conference facilities and printing and photocopying services.

The seventeenth and eighteenth floors of the hotel are the home of the Regency Club, which includes a conference room, a lounge, a concierge, and a host. This is an ideal spot for executive travelers to conduct business meetings, make calls, and so on.

The hotel has five restaurants. Western specialties are featured at Hugo's. The Japanese dining room, Akasaka, features sushi, sashimi, and tempura. Buffet-style lunch and dinner are popular at the Silhouette, which features continental, Japanese, and Korean cuisines. In the evening it is pleasant to relax in the Regency Bar and listen to music in a cozy cosmopolitan setting.

My favorite spot, on a weekend evening in summer, is the poolside, where you can join in a friendly American barbecue.

Each of the guest rooms and suites has individually controlled air conditioning and heating, international direct-dial telephone service with a bathroom extension, in-house music, radio, TV, a mini-bar with a refrigerator, and an alarm clock.

KING SEJONG HOTEL
61-3, Chungmuro 2-Ga
P.O. Box 2583
Chung-Ku
Seoul 100
Republic of Korea
Telephone: 776-1811
Telex: K27265

Cable: HOTESEJONG
Fax: 755-4906
Reservations:
  In Seoul call 776-1181
  In California call 1-800-622-0847
  In Nebraska call 402-493-4747
  Elsewhere in the USA call Utell International at
    1-800-44-UTELL or 1-800-227-4320
All major credit cards
President: Chang Gun Choo
General Manager: Sung Kwang Kim
Concierge: Jae Sung Park
Sales Director: Je-Eun Yoo
Rates (approx.):
  Superior single $100
  Moderate double $100
  Deluxe double $109
  Moderate twin $109
  Deluxe twin $115
  Super deluxe twin $136
  Ondol $119
  King Sejong Suite $180
  Royal Suite $217
250 rooms, 15 suites
Service charge 10%; no tax

Close to major businesses and entertainment, the King Sejong is in the heart of downtown Seoul. It is situated at
Taegye-ro, the southern approach to Myong-dong, one of
Seoul's largest shopping areas. The lovely Mount Namsan
can be viewed from its windows. And the Kimpo International Airport, to which the hotel provides free bus service, is just thirty minutes away.

The rooms are comfortable and pleasant and have modern, international-class amenities, including mini-bars and
color TV with cable movies. Best of all, all rooms and suites
have views. You may select the mountain view on one side
or the panoramic city view on the other.

On the lobby level are a coffee shop, lounges, a shopping
arcade, and a bar.

The American-style Oak Room has a plush green decor
and a full-wall picture window. Serving Western meals, it
is the favorite spot for business luncheons and dinners.

The Soojeong Coffee Shop, with its comfortable wicker
chairs, is *my favorite spot*. It has seasonal food festivals four

times a year, each celebrating a local product. In the spring it might be strawberries; in the fall it might be apples. American-style buffet breakfasts are lavish here, and light beverages and meals, to the accompaniment of piano music, are available through the late evening.

There is a fully equipped Health Club with not only a fair-sized gymnasium, but the special delights of cool mineral and radon baths, Jacuzzi, and sauna. The club also has its own TV lounge.

The hotel has an Executive Service to accommodate the communication and clerical needs of business people.

You'll find a wide range of exotic drink concoctions at the hotel's popular Dynasty Bar.

A favorite of the local people is Eun Ha Soo, a buffet restaurant serving traditional Korean foods, with many kinds of kimchi and *bul-go-ki*. On the fourth floor, it provides a panoramic view of Mount Namsan and the city.

For a sample of Seoul night life try the Napoleon, the hotel's dramatically decorated night club, on the third floor.

THE RAMADA INN OLYMPIA
108-2, Pyung Chang-dong
Jongro-ku
Seoul
Republic of Korea
Telephone: 353-5121/7 or 353-5151/7
Telex: RAMADA K 23171
Cable: RAMADA
Fax: 353-8118
Reservations:
   In Seoul call 353-5121
   In the USA call 1-800-272-6232
American Express, Visa, Diners, MasterCard
President: Wang Sik Kim
General Manager: Peter Schnyder
Sales Manager: Yong Nam Cha
Ramada International Hotels
Rates (approx.):
   Standard $87 single, $113 double
   Deluxe $125
   Business suite $225
   Royal Suite $625
310 rooms, 11 suites
Service charge 10%; no tax for foreigners

This hotel is attractively situated on the edge of Bukak Park, a national park, and more than half its guest rooms and all its restaurants overlook the unbroken vista of tree-covered hills. Although in the midst of this spectacular scenery, the hotel is only a ten-minute taxi ride from the heart of the city (you can also use the hotel's free shuttle service, leaving every hour to downtown Seoul). The Kimpo International Airport is only a half-hour away, and the hotel staff is on hand at the airport to help when you arrive and depart.

This Ramada Inn is special: For one thing the water, drawn from the hotel's own well, is very good. For another, the staff is constantly available to meet every need.

The rooms are also nice, from the luxurious executive suites, where private meetings may be held, to the standard twins. All have radio, color TV, in-house video, and mini-bars.

The dining rooms, a total of seven, feature a variety of cuisines, as apparent from their names: the Manduo Chinese Restaurant, the Viking Buffet, the Losanne Western Grill, the Shimiz Japanese Restaurant, the Manhajang Korean Restaurant, the Baden Baden Coffee Shop, and the Venus Lobby Lounge. For drinks, there are the Rose Karaoke Bar and the Olympia Night Club.

My favorite spot for either lunch or dinner is the Viking, where you can eat as much as you please while enjoying views of the garden and waterfalls and the tree-covered mountains in the background.

Other amenities include a shopping mall, with a gift shop, a pharmacy, a beauty salon, and a barbershop; and the Fitness Centre, with saunas for men and women, an indoor pool, and a poolside bar. There is also a jogging course, which seems to be a popular meeting place for guests.

RAMADA RENAISSANCE HOTEL
676 Yeogsam-dong
Gangnam-ku
Seoul
Republic of Korea
Telephone: (02) 553-5414
Telex: K 28318
Fax: (02) 553-8118
Reservations:
  In Seoul call (02) 553-8580
  In the USA call 1-800-228-9898 or 1-800-272-6232
Most major credit cards

Executive Manager: David H. Chung
Ramada International Hotels
Rates (approx.):
  Rooms $86–$138
  Korean suite $325
  Standard suite $308
  Superior suite $432
  Royal Suite $1,232
  Presidential Suite $2,200
500 rooms, 15 suites
Service charge 10%; no tax for foreigners

Well situated for the commercial guest, this Ramada hotel is in the heart of Seoul's fastest-growing commercial district, Tehran Street, Yeogsam. It is close by the Olympic Stadium, the Korea Exhibition Centre, the new Trade Centre, and the Olympic Freeway.

The rooms and suites all have air conditioning, color TV, video, radio, piped-in music, and bedside controls for all of these. Other amenities include refrigerators, mini-bars, nice-sized work desks, and modern bathrooms with hair-dryers and telephones. For those who want to feel like VIPs, the hotel's Ramada Renaissance Club occupies two floors offering sixty-eight larger rooms and more services.

There are six restaurants: Korean, Japanese, Chinese, and continental dining rooms; a coffee shop; and a buffet restaurant. Popular is the pool-side lounge and bar.

The hotel also has a business center, a sauna, a swimming pool, a tennis court and a shopping arcade.

SEOUL HILTON INTERNATIONAL
395, 5-ka, Namdeanum-ro
Chung-ku
Seoul 100
Republic of Korea
Telephone: 753-7788
Telex: K26695 KHILTON
Cable: HILTELS SEOUL
Fax: 754-2510
Reservations:
  In Seoul call 778-1351
  In New York state call collect (212) 697-9370
  Elsewhere in the USA call 1-800-223-1146
All major credit cards
General Manager: Christian Schuecking

Sales Manager: Jee-heung Yoo
Hilton International Company
Rates (approx.):
  Room $139 single, $167 double
  Executive Floor room $176 single, $211 double
  Ondol $139 single, $167 double
  One-bedroom suite $235
  Corner suite $256
  Two-bedroom suite $352
  Parkhill Suite $704–$939
  Vista Suite $875–$1,100
  Namdaemum Suite $1,387
712 rooms, 67 suites
Service charge 10%; No tax for foreigners

Situated near the South Gate, a great treasure of the Republic of Korea, and adjacent to the Daewoo Centre, this twenty-three-story hotel overlooks downtown Seoul and Mount Namsan. The Kimpo International Airport, to which the hotel provides shuttle bus service four times daily, is only thirty minutes' drive away and the main railway station is within five minutes' walk.

My favorite spot is the atrium lobby. Its centerpiece is Henry Moore's dramatic, forty-six-foot-high bronze sculpture called *Large Reclining Woman 1982*, one of seven cast by the eminent British sculptor. Sitting prominently on a marble stand facing the lobby lounge, it is the focal point of the three-story atrium. This, along with a central staircase, huge bronze pillars, American oak paneling, and an Italian marble fountain, is the sight you see when you enter the Seoul Hilton.

Each of the rooms of the hotel is decorated with works of Korean arts and crafts. Each has a window that opens, and a typical Korean *changmun*—a wood and paper sliding window covering—which is just as pretty from the outside as from the inside. The design is repeated in the wardrobe doors, and the same wood is used for the doors to the guest rooms.

A specially designed stacking chest made in Korea takes the place of the conventional chest of drawers. It serves a dual purpose, as a cabinet for the color TV, which tucks away neatly when not in use, as well as for clothing. The colors in the guest rooms are celadon and burgundy. Bedside lamps are copies of Koryo-style porcelain.

All of the rooms have mini-bars, executive writing desks, bathrobes, and international direct-dial telephones. The twentieth floor is reserved for nonsmokers. On the two top floors are the executive rooms and suites; a private lounge where complimentary breakfast, afternoon tea and coffee, and pre-dinner drinks are served; and a concierge.

The fine collection of restaurants offer great variety. *My favorite* is The Seasons. One of the more tastefully decorated dining rooms in town, it is airy, with well-spaced tables and comfortable chairs and banquettes. Fine china, glassware, and cutlery add to its elegance. The haute cuisine duplicates the best of Europe—not an easy task, since some necessary ingredients must be imported. Available are such grand dishes as baked bisque of lobster armagnac, soufflé of lobster with saffron sauce, and fillet of snapper in chablis, as well as superb roast beef and tasty lamb and veal dishes. Overwhelming are the crêpes, soufflés, cakes, and mousses at dessert time.

The other excellent restaurants include The Genji, with five dining rooms serving sashimi, sushi, tempura, *teppanyaki*, and other Japanese delicacies; the inexpensive Garden Cafe and Orangerie, with its generous buffet; the Phoenix, serving Cantonese cuisine, and Il Ponte, a new Italian restaurant.

For drinks there are the Palm Court Lounge, the Seasons Lounge, and the Oak Room bar and lounge, where buffet luncheons are served. The Rainforest disco is open until early morning.

The hotel's convention center—the largest in Korea, with a capacity of thirty-five hundred—has been the setting for meetings of the World Bank and the International Monetary Fund. It has no pillars to block the view of the stage, and it can be divided into three smaller sections. Its state-of-the-art audio-visual equipment includes simultaneous translation facilities.

Open to members and hotel guests at modest rates, the Seoul Hilton Executive Health Club includes an extensive gymnasium, sauna, massage, an indoor heated swimming pool, and a scientifically designed jogging track.

Be sure to ask for two very helpful leaflets published by the hotel—the *City Map*, which folds into a pocket-sized holder, and the *Jogging Course*, which shows two routes through neighboring Namsan Park, where you can get a cable car to the top of picturesque Mount Namsan.

SEOUL PLAZA HOTEL
23, 2-ka, Taipyung-ro
Chung-Ku
Seoul 100
Republic of Korea
Telephone: (02) 771-22
Telex: K26215, K24244
Cable: PLAZAHL SEOUL
Fax: (02) 756-3610 or (02) 755-8897
Reservations:
  In Seoul call (02) 771-22
  In the USA and Canada call Loews Representation
    International at 1-800-223-0888 or, in New York, at
    1-800-522-5455; or call Prince Hotels at 1-800-223-2094
    or, in New York, at 1-800-542-8686 or, in Los
    Angeles, at 1-800-223-2094
All major credit cards
General Manager: Pyong-Chin Min
Sales Manager: Jung-Mok Yang
Rates (approx.):
  Superior room $115
  Deluxe room $130
  Executive room $180
  Business room $280
  Residential Suite $280
  Plaza suite $380
  Presidential Suite $800
  Royal Suite $800
540 rooms, 14 suites
Service charge 10%; no tax for foreigners

The Seoul Plaza opened at the end of 1976 under the management of the Prince Hotel chain of Japan. In 1980 the owner took over and ran the hotel independently, striving to give it an elegance of appearance and service.

Since 1984 they have carried out a very successful program of renovation, starting with the rooms and suites. By 1987 the private dining rooms had been given a facelift, and an American style dining room was opened on the twenty-second floor.

Because business travelers are a main concern, a comfortable worktable has been installed in each room. Other amenities include independent heating and air-conditioning control, color TV, a mini-bar, and a telephone extension in the bathroom.

Dining is also an important concern, so ten different cuisines are featured among the dining rooms.

My favorite, for its elegant decor, fine wine, and French food, is the Elysée. On the top floor, it offers fine views of the city at lunch and dinner.

Among the other restaurants, the newly opened Asadal, on the fourth floor, serves delicacies of the Korean court cuisine in an antique setting with a view of the garden. On the third floor, award-winning chefs at the Tao Yuen provide traditional Chinese meals. Also on the third floor, the Kotobuki, with separate rooms for Japanese sushi, tempura, and tatami, is open for all three meals. So is the El Toro Steak House, on the second floor; It features the best beef in Seoul, charcoal-grilled to order. Finally, the popular Place Coffee House, on the second floor overlooking City Hall Plaza, serves foods from around the world from 6:30 A.M. until midnight.

For drinks, the Fontana Lobby Lounge is open from 8:00 A.M. until 10:00 P.M.; it also serves light meals and snacks. The Chateau Main Bar, with stone-block walls and soft lighting, is a favorite place for quiet rendezvous. Decorated with rough red bricks, stained glass windows, and Old World crystal chandeliers, the Continental Plaza Pub combines the best of German wine cellars and English pubs. Most delightful is the top-floor Skylark Lounge, open from 11:00 A.M. until 11:00 P.M. and providing a spectacular view of the city.

The hotel has a completely equipped Businessman's Center in the lobby and a fine shopping plaza.

For sightseeing, just a few steps from the hotel is Doksu, Palace of Virtuous Longevity. Originally a villa for a king's grandson, it became the royal family's residential palace in the era of King Kojong. The hotel's free shuttle bus stops at various other sights in Seoul, including the Dongdaemun (East Gate) Market.

SHERATON WALKER HILL
San 21, Kwangjang-dong
Sundong-ku
C.P.O. Box 714
Seoul 133
Republic of Korea
Telephone: (02) 453-0121 or (02) 453-0131
Telex: WALKHTL K28517

Cable: WALKER HILL
Fax: 4526867
Reservations:
　In Seoul call (02) 453-0121 or (02) 453-0131
　In Tokyo call (03) 584-0632/3
　In the USA call 1-800-325-3535
All major credit cards
General Manager: Y. C. Sung
Sales Manager: Jay Hahn
Sheraton International
Rates (approx.):
　Superior room　$125
　Deluxe room　$130
　Suite or villa　$280–$3,000
692 rooms, 78 suites, 26 villas
Service charge 10%; no tax for foreigners

What a hotel!

Of all the hotels in Seoul, the Sheraton Walker Hill has the most magnificent view of the expansive Han River, with its surrounding mountains in the background. The view is particularly gorgeous in the spring and fall, but also breathtaking after a fresh snowfall. To enjoy it, ask for one of the 270 rooms with a river view from the Tower, or one of the 230 riverside rooms in the annexes and villas.

The lobby of the hotel is also the most spectacular in Seoul. Polished teak columns reach to a glass roof. A waterfall cascades into a sunken pool. And there are the bells, which have a story:

The beautiful, twenty-ton bronze Emillie Bell in Kyongju is probably the most famous legacy of the ancient Shilla Dynasty. Legend has it that the bell was silent, and remained silent in spite of frequent recastings, until the Chief Priest dreamt that the bell would ring only if a child born in the year, month, day, and hour of the dragon was offered to the fiery metal.

A child was found, and the bell was again melted down. As the infant was thrown into the molten metal her tiny voice was heard crying "Emi! Emi!" (Mother! Mother!). It is said that, even today, when the bell is struck it can be heard up to forty miles away, always crying "Emi . . . ! Emi . . . !"

Replicas of this famous bell hang in the lobby of the Sheraton Walker Hill. I have it on good authority that, although they were cast with the same method and skill, no infant had to be sacrificed.

The Sheraton Walker Hill is like a small city within a big city. Although it is situated on 139 completely private, beautifully landscaped acres, it is only twenty minutes by freeway from downtown Seoul. A hotel shuttle runs every half hour to take guests to places of business, entertainment, or culture.

You enjoy the feeling of luxury even as you enter your room. Oriental antiques rest on fine imported wool carpets. The splendid views from the large windows are set off by tasteful objets d'art—perhaps a beautifully worked vase, or a golden hand-painted screen. Amidst these are a color TV, in-house movies, piped-in music, and other useful amenities.

The dining choices are appropriate for this kind of hotel, ranging from gourmet entrées at the Celadon Room to Western favorites at the Cascade Cafe, right beside the lobby waterfall. In the Convention Center are the Korean restaurant Ondal, the Japanese restaurant Sekitei, and the Chinese restaurant Golden Dragon, with a magnificent view of the Han River and the remains of an ancient Korean fort set on one of the surrounding hills. Superb buffets are the specialty at the Summit restaurant, on the sixteenth floor of the main building.

But the fun place to go is the Kayagum, a 720-seat theater-restaurant. Dinner here is accompanied by the exciting Honey Bee Revue, featuring some one hundred performers in a variety of colorful Korean dances. International stars perform here, too. You might just catch a show from Las Vegas, Paris, London, or New York.

And there's the Casino Walker Hill. Open twenty-four hours a day, it is said to be unique in the Orient, offering a variety of gambling games found in few places outside Atlantic City and Las Vegas. There's blackjack, roulette, dice, baccarat, and *Tai-sai*, with over a hundred multilingual croupiers.

In the penthouse of the hotel's Convention Center is the Walker Hill Art Center, featuring changing exhibitions, lectures, and folk performances.

For business and social events there are seventeen function rooms and the Grand Ballroom. The posh Board Room is equal to that of any corporation.

For leisure, walks around the landscaped grounds are fun. There are also tennis courts, a golf driving range, large indoor and outdoor pools, a poolside lounge and bar, and a men's and women's health center with saunas, massages, and Jacuzzi. There is also a good variety of shops.

In its early years, when the Sheraton Walker Hill was simply a hotel with a very nice hilltop restaurant, it was a favorite spot of American GIs. Some of them return to this hotel today to show their wives how beautiful the area can be in times of peace.

Be sure to ask for your copy of the hotel's booklet, *Sports and Leisure Information*. This way, you'll be sure to miss nothing!

WESTIN CHOSUN
C.P.O. Box 3706
Seoul 100
Republic of Korea
Telephone: (82-2) 771-05
Telex: K24256 or K28432
Cable: WESTCHOSUN SEOUL
Fax: (82-2) 752-1443
Reservations:
    In Seoul call (82-2) 771-05
    In the USA call 1-800-228-3000
All major credit cards
General Manager: Giovanni Angelini
Concierge: Kwan-Ho Chung
Senior Sales Manager: Carole Alexander
Westin Hotels and Resorts
Rates (approx.):
    Superior room $130
    Deluxe room $140
    Corner suite $280
    Royal Suite $550
    Presidential Suite $900
477 rooms, 22 suites
Service charge 10%; no tax for foreigners

This deluxe twenty-story hotel, managed by Westin since 1979, is in the heart of Seoul. The hotels' symbol is the Temple of Heaven, a pagoda-like temple, designated a national treasure, in the hotel's side garden on what was once Korea's "most sacred ground." The temple was built in 1897 as the place where Yi Dynasty kings and nobles came to worship their ancestors.

This hotel caters primarily to business travelers, and for

them it is conveniently in the center of the downtown business district. For this clientele, the Executive Business Center offers twenty-four hour telex and facsimile service, multilingual secretaries, and private office space. Five function rooms on the top floor are available for meetings and other events.

The hotel claims its 350-square-foot guest rooms are the largest in Seoul. They are also designed to serve the business traveler's needs: each is fitted with a free-standing desk and international direct-dial phones at the desk and the bed.

The hotel building, from a bird's-eye view, is basically a triangle with slightly concave sides, providing various views. Room windows open.

The hotel has the usual Westin fine collection of dining spots. The Ninth Gate features French and continental cuisine, and the Cafe Royale is an American-style dining room with prompt service. Yesterday, with an Old World decor, serves Oriental and continental dishes. The Galaxy has a daily international buffet, and the Sushi-Cho serves authentic Japanese food. The Lobby Court, popular for tea, coffee, juices, and cocktails, is a calm spot to unwind.

Xanadu, named after an ancient pleasure pavilion built for the mighty Kublai Khan, is the hotel's entertainment spot. The decor is plush, in autumn tones. A London disc jockey orchestrates the sound, color, and lighting effects, which culminate in nightly laser shows.

The hotel has a fitness center and a swimming pool, open in season, with a pool-side barbecue—a favorite treat when it is available.

The hotel shopping arcade includes more than forty shops, of all types.

Be sure to ask for the hotel's helpful folding map of Seoul. Pocket-size, it is very useful, and it is free.

Taejeon City

YOUSOUNG TOURIST HOTEL
480, Bongmyong-dong
Chung-gu, Taejeon City
Chungchungnamdo 300-31
Republic of Korea

Telephone: (042) 822-0611-5, (042) 822-0711-5, or
   (042) 822-0811-5
Fax: (042) 822-0041
Reservations:
   In Taejeon call (042) 822-0611-5
   In Seoul call (02) 273-3379
Visa, American Express, Diners, MasterCard
President: Moon-Byung Park
General Manager: Che-Bork Lee
Sales Manager: Sang-Tae Yedm
Rates (approx.):
   Western room $53
   Ondol room $53
   Junior suite, *ondol* or Western $57
   Other suite $73
140 rooms, 8 suites
Service charge 10%; no tax

The story goes that the Yousoung hot spring was discovered
more than fifteen hundred years ago, at the time of the
Paekje Kingdom. Until the end of the Yi Dynasty in 1910,
the spa was visited by the royal family for its therapeutic
and restorative properties. The somewhat alkaline waters
with a natural radiant heat promoted a remarkable sense
of well-being. One of the Orient's finest, the hot spring has
a well spring temperature of 153 degrees Fahrenheit (53
degrees Celsius).

There's more here than the hot spring. Near the hotel is
a golf course and the entrance to the Kyeryongsan National
Park and the Tonghak-sa Temple. Kongju and Puyo, capitals of the ancient Paeje realm, are not far away. Worth
seeing, too, are the imposing figures of Buddha at Nonsan
and Popju-sa, as well as such places as the Independence
Hall and the Hyonchung-sa Shrine. Most pleasurable is a
scenic drive in the area of the Taechong Dam.

The hotel is Korea's first resort spa with overall computerized efficiency, including a direct-dial digital telephone
system and computer-monitoring of heat, air conditioning
and water purity. Certainly a place for the health-minded,
this is also a good setting for seminars, banquets, and other
special occasions, as well as just relaxation.

The comfortable guest rooms are available in nine different styles. Water from the hot spring is piped into each
room.

In the Health Club men and women may enjoy separate
sauna facilities, the country's largest indoor hot spring pool,

a fully equipped gym, a massage service, and a lounge with video, cocktails, and meal service. An outdoor pool is also fed by the hot spring.

The hotel has a fine dining room, a French coffee house, and a cocktail bar. Most delightful is the Sky Lounge of the Khans Club on the top floor. For entertainment there is the four hundred–seat nightclub, Casanova. It features a complete laser show plus musical performances by popular entertainers.

A shopping arcade features mostly local products.

If you want to know what time it is back home or anywhere else in the world, look at the big wall clock–map behind the reception desk in the lobby.

Taejeon is two hours by train from Seoul.

MACAU

The name of Macau is derived from that of a Chinese goddess, known as A-Ma or Ling Ma. The village where Macau now stands was previously known to the Chinese as Hou Kong or Hoi Keang.

According to legend, a junk sailing across the South China Sea on a clear day found itself in a sudden storm. Everybody on board was about to give up hope when an attractive woman, who had boarded the ship at the very last moment, stood up and ordered the elements to calm down. Miraculously, the sea became calm. The junk arrived safely at Hoi Keanj. Then the young woman went ashore and walked to the nearby Barra Hill where, with a glowing light and sweet perfume, she ascended into heaven. At this spot a temple was built in homage to her.

Centuries later, when Portuguese sailors landed and asked the name of the place, the natives replied "A-Ma-Gao" (Bay of A-Ma) and so the peninsula got its name. In modern usage Amagao was shortened to Macau. The city's name in full is actually "City of the Name of God, Macau. There is None More Loyal." In Portuguese, "Cidade do Nome de Deus de Macau, Nao Ha Outra Mais Leal."

Macau was officially founded in 1557 during the period of exploration by Prince Henry the Navigator and other Portuguese. In 1513 Jorge Alvares became the first Portuguese to set foot in southern China. Eventually traders consolidated their activities at Macau.

Macau was the base for the introduction of Christianity

into China and then Japan. By the 1600s other nations, particularly the Dutch, began trying to take Macau.

In 1841, the British settled in Hong Kong, and the economic importance of Macau declined as that of Hong Kong developed. Macau is still regarded as an important distribution center for rice, fish, piece goods and other Chinese products. It has an active manufacturing and exporting business, mainly of textiles and garments, toys, electronics and artificial flowers.

It is a small area. The peninsula is 2.5 miles in length and 1.04 miles wide, with a total of 2.1 square miles. With the islands of Taipa and Coloane the territory, still under Portuguese rule, totals 15.5 square miles, and has about four hundred thousand inhabitants.

The Macau–People's Republic of China border was officially opened to foreign tourists in 1979; since then, an increasing number of foreign visitors have passed through the Macau Border Gate (Portas do Cerco) to visit China. Day tours can be made inexpensively from Macau.

There are many tourist sights in Macau, but gambling seems to be the major attraction. There are the Lisboa Tourist Complex, with a two-story casino open twenty-four hours a day; a two-deck casino on the floating Macau Palace; the Casino Jai-Alai; and the Oriental Casino. They are said to offer the widest range of casino games in the world. And, of course, most of the hotels also have their own casinos.

Found here too is Jai-Alai, greyhound racing, harness racing (which started in 1980), and, usually during the third weekend in November, the Grand Prix, the Far East's Gala motorcycle and Formula III car racing event.

There is also the Crazy Paris Show nightly at the Mona Lisa Hall in the Hotel Lisboa and well as the Paris Night Club at the Hotel Estoril. These and other hotels have bars, discotheques, nightclubs, and supper clubs.

Shopping is very popular. Jewelry (particularly gold), Chinese antiques, porcelain, pottery, electric gadgets, and knitted wear are among the most popular items purchased. And there are flea markets best left to the knowledgeable. For assurance and guidance use the shopping guide published by the Department of Tourism. The main shopping area is along the Avenida do Infante D. Henrique and Avenida Almeida Ribeiro.

Macau's historic structures include the remaining façade of St. Paul's Basilica (built in 1635 by Roman Catholic Japanese artisans and burned in 1835), a fascinating example of late Italian Renaissance architecture, with a mixture of western and Oriental motifs. There is St. Domingo's church and convent, founded in 1670, the fort and chapel of Guia (1626), the fort of Sao Paulo de Monte (sixteenth century), and statues to da Gama and Luis de Camoes. There are a number of temples, including the Temple of Kun Iam, built six hundred years ago with a small gold lacquer statue of Marco Polo. He doesn't look as he did in the movies! Be sure to take a tour or, if on your own, get a guide from your hotel or the tourist office.

HOTEL BELA VISTA
8, Rua do Comendador Kou Ho Neng
Macau
Telephone: 573821
Telex: 88734 HOMA OM
Cable: VISTA
Fax: (853) 594622
Reservations:
   In Macau call 573821
All major credit cards
General Manager: Adriano Pinto Marques
Rates (approx.):
   Room $18 single, $25–$30 double
   Suite $38–$40
17 rooms, 3 suites
Service charge 10%; tax 5%

This is a modest-priced hotel situated in a garden at the top of a steep flight of steps. It has a restaurant situated in a veranda with a grand view over the Praia Grande Bay. Inside is an impressive marble staircase with wrought iron railings.

The rooms cannot be called luxurious, but each has an air-conditioning unit and color TV, and most rooms have balconies with views either of the bay or of the town.

It was once called Boa Vista, which means good view, and the present name is not much different—it means nice view. The view of the China Sea, the majestic mountains, the old bridge of Macau and Taipa, and the waters below with their junks, tankas, and sampans and China in the background, is indeed good, and nice, to see.

It is an authentic Colonial Hotel, opened at the end of the last century by an English couple, Capain Eillim Edward Blake and his wife Catherine. It was they who gave it the

Boa Vista name. It was purchased in 1948 by three Chinese ladies, the present owners.

HOTEL LISBOA
Avenida da Amizade
Macau
Telephone: 77666
Telex: 88203 HOTEL OM
Cable: HOTELISBOA
Reservations:
  In Macau call 77666
All major credit cards
General Manager: Pedro Lobo
Rates (approx.):
  Old-wing room $15–$20 single, $40–$60 double
  New-wing double room $48
  New-wing twin room $66
  Suite $80–$200
750 rooms and suites
Service charge 10%; tax 5%

When you see the Hotel Lisboa at night it reminds you of Las Vegas, with its round buildings, all the bright lights, and the fancy spires atop each of the hotel's wings.

Actually, the Hotel Lisboa, despite its modern look today, is the Territory's oldest luxury hotel, as well as the largest. In recent years it has been extensively refurbished and has added a lot of new attractions and facilities, making it a self-contained hotel-casino complex.

There are two casinos, which never close. They offer their guests everything from roulette (with European odds) to blackjack and baccarat, and well as the Chinese games of Big and Small and Fantan.

A lot of attention is paid to the cuisine in a variety of dining rooms. *My favorite spot* is the A Galera Gourmet Restaurant, an elegant wood-paneled dining room offering fare that, according to the management, is "a synthesis of the best of Macau's colonial heritage, spiced by the East." There are nine other places to eat in the hotel, including the Japanese Restaurant, the Chinese Restaurant, the popular Coffee Shop, and the spacious Portas do Sol Restaurant and Night Club, where you can see what is called the "Crazy Paris" show.

The suites are quite attractive and spacious and the rooms

are good-sized and nicely furnished. There is twenty-four-hour room service.

The hotel has a large swimming pool with cabanas, a billiard room, a children's playground, and a bowling center with four alleys.

The most popular spot is the shopping arcade in the New Wing, which offers essentials as well as duty-free shopping. However, you'll find that shopping is better in Hong Kong.

There are convention and meeting facilities in the hotel.

HOTEL PRESIDENTE
Avenida da Amizade
Macau
Telephone: 553888, 71822
Telex: 88440 HPM OM
Reservations:
   In Macau call 71723 or 552737
All major credit cards
General Manager: Chuk-keong Wong
Concierge: William Leung
Sales Managers: John Fung, Christian Lio
Rates (approx.):
   Room $55–$68
   Junior suite $122
   Executive suite $180
   Presidential Suite $256
333 rooms, 6 suites
Service charge 10%; tax 5%

The Hotel Presidente is the newest hotel in Macau. It is a twenty-one-story modern facility facing Porto Exterior (the Outer Harbor), and many of the rooms have spectacular views across the harbor of the islands of Taipa and Coloane, and of the Pearl River and the Taipa Bridge.

While the hotel does not have a casino of its own, it is within easy walking distance of all of Macau's casinos as well as the entertainment, business and shopping areas of Macau.

This is a comfortable place, with all of its guest rooms and luxury suites air-conditioned and having en-suite bathrooms. There are direct-dial telephones and color TV, and twenty-four-hour room service.

The hotel has three restaurants offering a variety of cuisines, and the Skylight Nightclub and Disco has an international cabaret and floor show.

A lovely garden plaza was recently built at the back of the hotel.

HOTEL ROYAL
2–4, Estrada da Vitoria
Macau
Telephone: 552222
Telex: 88514 ROYAL OM
Reservations:
  In Macau call 78822
  In Hong Kong call (5) 422-033
All major credit cards
General Manager: Yoji Saito
Dai-ichi Hotels
Rates (approx.):
  Room $36–$46
  Suite $75–$140
380 rooms and suites
Service charge 10%; tax 5%

The Hotel Royal is a member of the Japanese hotel group Dai-ichi, which operates a number of hotels in Japan and in Guam and was the second international hotel chain to open a hotel in Macau.

Nearly twenty stories high, close to shops and the business area, the hotel overlooks the city, the China Sea and Mainland China. It also looks directly down on the Vasco da Gama Gardens, named for the Portuguese explorer.

The hotel claims the only indoor swimming pool in Macau. It also offers its guests a well-equipped health club.

There are four places in the hotel to drink and dine. The most popular cuisine is Chinese, served either in the Royal Peking Restaurant, which features Northern cuisine, or, in another dining room, the succulent fare from Southern China. European cuisine is served in the Vasco da Gama Room. There is a pleasant coffee shop for tasty snacks on the run. And, of course, there is a Japanese restaurant.

There is a duty-free shop, beauty salon, and florist as well as a travel agency in the hotel.

HYATT REGENCY MACAU
Taipa Island
Macau
Telephone: 27000

Telex: 88512 HY MAC OM
Reservations:
  In Hong Kong call (3) 661311 or (3) 662321, ext. 381
  In Alaska and Hawaii call 1-800-228-9005
  Elsewhere in the USA call 1-800-228-9000
All major credit cards
General Manager: Ian Duncan
Hyatt Hotels and Resorts
Rates (approx.):
  Standard room $71
  Superior room $83
  Deluxe room $96
  Junior suite $180
  Deluxe suite $256
  Special suite $359
  President Suite $641
335 rooms, 21 suites
Service charge 10%; no tax

The Hyatt Regency is immediately across the Taipa Bridge, which goes from the Macau peninsula to Taipa Island. It is well-situated, five minutes from the main entertainment area of the Territory, and next to the Macau Trotting Race Track.

This hotel is pretty much a resort in itself, with the spacious and beautiful circular pool (surrounded by landscaped gardens) popular during the day and the Green Parrot discotheque popular at night. That is, they are popular for those who can stay away from the twenty-four-hour casino, which features more games than I ever heard of, including fan-tan and *dai sui.* There is jai alai every night, and the Canidrome and Trotting Club have regular meetings attended by the punters.

The Macanese friendliness is particularly apparent at the Hyatt Regency, especially when dining, whether you are enjoying a leisurely buffet in the stylish A Pousada Café restaurant or relaxing over tea in the spacious Atrio Lounge.

The gourmets enjoy the O Pescador's Portuguese specialties. And there is authentic *teppanyaki* cuisine in Kamogawa, the Japanese restaurant. *My favorite spot* is the Green House, with its lush garden setting. It is just the place to relax with an aperitif.

Like many Hyatts, this hotel has a Regency Club, an entire floor with its own concierge service and an exclusive lounge where complimentary breakfasts and evening cocktails are served.

In June of 1986, the Hyatt opened Macau's first complete health and recreational complex on three acres of land linked directly to the hotel. The facilities in this complex include the largest swimming pool in the Territory, a swim-up bar, four lighted tennis courts, two air-conditioned squash courts, a multipurpose court for badminton, basketball or volleyball, a putting green, a jogging track, and a children's playground.

The complex is in a three-story building set in a landscaped garden. It also contains a fitness center with the most modern of exercise equipment as well as a sauna, Jacuzzi, steambath, cold plunge, massage and suntanning facilities, a beauty clinic and a hair salon.

The Flamingo, a delightful restaurant in the center, has optional courtyard dining and an open kitchen where you can see the preparation of the Macanese and Portuguese specialties.

THE MANDARIN ORIENTAL MACAU
Avenida da Amizade
P.O. Box 3016
Macau
Telephone: 567 888
Telex: 88588 OMA OM
Reservations:
   In Macau call 567 888
   In the USA call Leading Hotels of the World at
      1-800-663-0787
All major credit cards
General Manager: Gian Carlo Balenieri
Concierge: Tyrone Lee
Sales Manager: Danny Lam
Director of Sales and Marketing: Richard Ng
Mandarin Oriental Hotel Group
Rates (approx.):
   Standard room $75
   Superior room $88
   Deluxe room $100
   Dynasty room $115
   Suite $177–$770
406 rooms, 32 suites
Service charge 10%; tax 5%

The superb new Mandarin Oriental Macau stands at the seawall of the enclave's Outer Harbor, close to the arrival terminal, the big casinos, and the shopping district. It is the finest hotel in Macau, run by the same group that runs the world's highest-rated hotel, the Oriental in Bangkok, and the fabulous Mandarin in Hong Kong.

The Grand Staircase, with its red lacquer railings and decorations, dominates the magnificent lobby. Handsome handmade teak furniture decorates the lobby.

Each of the hotel's spacious guest rooms and suites has uninterrupted views over the South China Sea to the neighboring island of Taipa, or north to the wooded hillside of the Guia fortress.

Guest rooms are elegant and spacious and designed to maximize comfort. Tastefully decorated soft pink or green with Portuguese fabrics and natural teak, the rooms have individually controlled central air conditioning, mini-bars, radio, and multichannel in-house music. In addition, each has a dressing table and an executive writing corner. The bathrooms are marble, spacious and full of interesting amenities. There is color TV, direct-dial telephone and twenty-four-hour room service as well as same day laundry and dry cleaning.

The hotel's thirty-two suites have balconies, bars, and separate guest closets. The largest suites, the Oriental and the Macau, are over two thousand square feet, and each has a lounge with dining room, two bedrooms and bathrooms, a pantry, and a guest closet.

As with all Mandarin Oriental hotels, this has a fine selection of places to dine. The Grill on the second floor, with a sea view, features grilled meats and seafood served among elegant Portuguese decor. The Dynasty, also on the second floor, is open at lunch and dinner to serve Cantonese cuisine. The Cafe Girassol is on the first floor of the hotel and also has a sea view. It is a coffee shop serving Portuguese and other continental specialities. The Caravela Lounge overlooks the Main Lobby. Here light snacks and beverages are served all day. On the third floor is the Poolside Terrace, which has grilled steaks, light snacks, and barbecue items during the day. The Bar da Guia on the first floor has stylish Portuguese decor and a display of paintings of historic racing cars. In the evening a trio entertains.

On the second floor is the hotel's gambling room, the Oriental Casino. It's the newest in town and very popular.

The Mandarin is run in the style of a resort hotel, so it has good sports facilities. There are two tennis courts, a large swimming pool, two air-conditioned squash courts and a Health Center complete with a sauna and massage services.

Here, *my favorite spot* is on the terrace of the room, having breakfast with a view of the South China Sea.

POUSADA DE SAO TIAGO
Avenida da Republica
Macau
Telephone: 78111
Telex: 88376 TIAGO OM
Reservations:
  In Macau call 78111
  In Hong Kong call (5) 261 288
All major credit cards
General Manager: H. Reinhard Steffen
Guest Relations: Ginnie Cheang
Sales Manager: Winnie Fok
Rates (approx.):
  Superior room $91
  Deluxe twin $104
  Honeymoon Suite $123
  Da Barra Suite $160
  Other suite $240
20 rooms, 3 suites
Service charge 10%; tax 5%

What a delight! The Pousada de Sao Tiago reminds you of the wonderful pousadas of Portugal. It is a small deluxe hotel constructed within the walls of a 350-year-old fort. Called the Fortress of St. James of the Barrier, it was named for the patron saint of the Portuguese army.

All is beauty outside of this inn (for it really is an inn, not a hotel): The gnarled trees left standing in the courtyard are several hundred years old. Inside, the furnishings reflect the past. All the rooms and suites are set with seventeenth-century items including mahogany tables, hand-painted tiles, and leather chairs that were created in Portugal just for this inn.

This is an ideal spot for such a place. The fortress, built in 1629, was constructed to have a truly spectacular view of China across the narrow channel. It was built on a broad platform, raised from the sea on a twenty-one-foot-thick wall. This platform held dwellings for sixty men. There was also a cistern carved into the solid rock that could store three thousand tons of water. The fort's bronze cast cannons were made by the famed Asian armorer Manuel Bocarro, who operated a foundry that supplied the Ming Court in Peiking as well as the lords of Japan.

Over the years, and certainly in the last few decades, the fort became a ruin. In 1978 the Department of Tourism of Macau decided to create a hotel on the site. It took a great deal of imagination, $2.6 million and three years.

Some very unusual things were done. Most interesting is the entrance of the old fort, now used as the entrance to the inn. It is a tunnel cut 350 years ago through the solid rock. There are granite steps, worn smooth from the traffic of the Portuguese soldiers who walked there. These stairs rise to a moss-covered wall, turn left, and continue along the wall up another flight right into the lobby. It is beautiful. Water flows down the wall and is led by two gutters, one on either side of the tunnel, to the entrance. The architect pointed out that the water flow is more than a decorative thing. "In winter," he says, "its humidity gives relief from our dry climate, and in summer it cools down the inn."

Another architectural ploy is the use of the ancient cistern to feed the bubbling fountain that rises at the outside deck of the inn's coffee shop. The wine cellar was once a secret room to store munitions. A bar and a reading room have been built around a two-centuries-old camphor tree in the central courtyard.

Prepare to do a little bit of sacrificing for the sake of a feeling of seventeenth-century authenticity. There is no elevator and you won't find a refrigerator in your room. You can't get room service after midnight, and TV reception is not good. But, don't fret—the service is fantastic. What hotel in Asia, or anywhere else, has 100 employees to serve the guests of 23 rooms? Four to one!

The rooms are luxurious. Every room is different in structure and in furnishings, and the bathrooms are covered with marble brought here from Portugal. While only the best rooms have views of the Chinese fishing boats in the harbor, all rooms have tranquil and pleasant views.

There's a story about the inn's St. James Chapel. It was built in 1740 and restored when the inn was built. Soldiers stationed here believed that their patron saint would leave the chapel every night and take his turn at patrol of the ramparts. The legend goes that every morning there was mud on the boots of the statue of St. James. A soldier was assigned to polish the boots every morning.

With so few rooms, it is wise to reserve them well in advance, especially for the months of April, July, and August, and also October, when some of those attending the Canton Trade Fair relax at this inn. In November the Grand Prix is held at the Macau race track and the inn is filled, as it is around Christmastime.

There is much to enjoy around this inn, including a swimming pool and a solarium and, *my favorite* spot, the landscaped gardens.

Care is taken with the cuisine as well. The Bar Cascata, which seats only twenty-five, offers fine wines, iced beer, and mixed drinks. For a light meal or a fine-blended coffee the place is the Café da Barra, where you can sit inside or outdoors. The gourmet with an appetite should dine at the Restaurante Fortaleza, where a splendid menu of Portuguese and continental dishes is available.

MALAYSIA

This southeast Asia nation has a population in excess of 13 million and occupies more than 128 thousand square miles. It consists of two parts, West Malaysia on the Malay Peninsula and East Malaysia on the island of Borneo. The two are separated by the South China Sea.

North of West Malaysia is Thailand, to the east is the South China Sea, and to the south is Singapore, separated by the narrow Johore Strait. On the west is the Strait of Malacca and the Andaman Sea.

East Malaysia has the South China Sea on its north as well as the Sulu Sea. On the east is the Celebes Sea and to the south and west is Kalimanta, which is the Indonesian Borneo. The capital of Malaysia is Kuala Lumpur.

Both East and West Malaysia have mountainous interiors and coastal plains. Being close to the equator, Malaysia has a tropical, rainy climate. About three-quarters of the country is forest, and many parts have not been explored.

There is a great ethnic variety among Malaysia's peoples. About two-fifths are Malays and almost as many are Chinese. About a tenth are Indians and Pakistanis and the rest belong to sixteen indigenous ethnic groups. Conflict between the two major groups has been a large part of the country's history.

The country is one of the world's leading suppliers of tin and rubber. Other large exports are timber and forest products, palm oil, and iron ore. Most of the people earn their livelihood working at subsistence agriculture, with rice the staple food. Fish furnishes most of the protein. Industry, mostly processing and light manufacturing, is located mostly in West Malaysia.

While the people are friendly, the laws are tough. Tourists should be aware that the death penalty is mandatory for those dealing in certain quantities of drugs, no matter your nationality. There are large fines for littering in public places. Driving is on the left side of the road, seat belts are compulsory, and speed limits enforced. Tipping is generally not expected or required.

Malaysia is a Muslim monarchy, and respect for its traditions and customs is expected.

Johor Bahru

Johor Bahru is the capital of the Johor state, on the southern end of the Malaysian Peninsula, opposite Singapore. The city has a population of more than one hundred fifty thousand. It is connected with Singapore by a causeway across the Johore Strait.

This city is, for the most part, a trade center for the state of Johor, which has extensive rubber plantations and raises rice, copra, pineapples, gambier and palm products. In 1914, Johor became a British protectorate. Until 1948, when it entered the Federation of Malaya, it was one of the Unfederated Malaya States.

After the hustle and bustle of Singapore, this smaller town offers a true Asian contrast, with quieter traffic and inexpensive shops selling Malaysian products.

Among the places to visit is the Istana Besar, built in 1866, which is the site of all royal events and is famous for its fine gardens. The Sultan Abu Bakar Mosque, overlooking the Straits of Johor, is one of the finest in Malaysia. The Royal Mausoleum, where all the Sultans of Johor have been buried, has interesting tombs.

One of the most delightful things to do is to stroll along the waterfront in the cool of the evening. The town is lively at night. You can taste real Malaysian food at such places as the Tepian Tebrau stalls in the Jalan Abu Bakar on the seafront, and the hawker stalls next to the main market and the Tun Abdul Razak Complex.

The nightclubs, pubs, and music lounges are popular, attracting visitors for the evening from Singapore.

HOLIDAY INN JOHOR BAHRU
Jalan Dato Sulaiman
Century Garden
K.B. No. 779
80990 Johor Bahru
West Malaysia
Telephone: 07-323800
Telex: MAc0790
Cable: HOLIDAYINN
Fax: (07) 318884
Reservations:
  In Johor Bahru call 07-323800
  In Kuala Lumpur call 03-248-1066
  In the USA call 1-800-HOLIDAY
All major credit cards
General Manager: Beppi Forster
Sales Manager: Marianne Lim
Holiday Inn Asia-Pacific
Rates (approx.):
  Standard room $48 single, $56 double
  Deluxe room $52 single, $61 double
  King Leisure room $56 single, $65 double
  Suite $82, $108, and $281
185 rooms, 13 suites
Service charge 10%; tax 5%

The Holiday Inn Johor Bahru is the first international hotel in this city, and it provides the comforts pleasing to Americans while keeping the exotic touches of the East.

It is well located, with Jalan Dato Sulaiman at the front of the hotel, just off the Jalan Tebrau, the city's main thoroughfare. It is only eighteen miles from the Sultan Ismail Airport and only a fifteen-minute drive from Singapore.

It is next door to the longest commercial and entertainment complex in Malaysia. Called the Holiday Plaza, the complex is designed for a lot of activities—shopping, eating, entertainment, and sport. It has shops on three floors, an office tower, a movie, a medical center, a nightclub, banking and financial services, a children's playground and an assortment of food places. Here Americans are suprised to find McDonald's and Kentucky Fried Chicken. Among the other shops here is Mr. Mom's Cookies, "the nuttiest cookies in town." Yes, they've caught on here, too.

The rooms in this hotel are comfortable, with all rooms and suites having individually controlled air conditioning and a private bathroom with a pulsating massage shower head, radio, color TV with in-house movie channel, mini-bar and refrigerator.

The array of eating places includes the Meisan Szechuan restaurant; the Boulevard Coffee House and Restaurant, serving everything from quick snacks to candlelight dinners with European cuisine; the Red Baron cocktail lounge, with live entertainment in the evening; and the Millenium Disco, with the latest in sound and light. There is a pool-side snack bar and a rooftop garden for barbecues and outside parties.

Kota Kinabalu

Kota Kinabalu, also called Jesselton, is the modern capital of Sabah (North Borneo), which lies on the northeastern tip of the island of Borneo. Kota Kinabalu has a population of about fifty thousand and is on a small inlet of the South China Sea. It was founded in 1899.

Borneo is a hilly rolling country with mountain ranges rising to six thousand feet. In its central highlands stands the highest peak in southeast Asia, the majestic Mount Kinabalu, which rises to 13,455 feet.

Sabah is probably the most primitive area of Malaysia. Some of the tribes that live here were once headhunters, but now they get along well and are friendly to tourists. In fact, they even have their own tourist association, which guides visitors to the unique sights, including a bat cave (where tourists watch tribesmen collect nests for their famous bird's nest soup), excursions to rubber plantations and local villages, and a ride on a jungle train, where passengers share their seats with friendly monkeys.

There is the town of Tanjong Aru, which literally extends into the sea with a "floating village" built on stilts in the still water. Here Sunday is market day, when farmers bringing their produce accompanied by their wives in local costume can be seen at Tuaran, four miles from Tanjong Aru.

HYATT KINABALU INTERNATIONAL
Jalan Datuk Alleh Sulong
88994 Kota Kinabalu
Sabah
Malaysia
Telephone: (088) 221234
Telex: HYATKK MA 80036

Cable: HYATTKI
Fax: 60/88/225972
Reservations:
  In Kota Kinabalu call (088) 221234, ext. 2041 or 2042
  In the USA call Hyatt International at 1-800-228-9005
All major credit cards
General Manager: Lawrence Lau
Sales Manager: Emily Lai
Hyatt International
Rates (approx.):
  Standard room $74 single, $90 double
  Superior room $80 single, $96 double
  Deluxe room $88 single, $104 double
  Regency Club room $108 single, $124 double
  Suite $160–$500
315 rooms, 20 suites
Service charge 10%; tax 5%

This Hyatt is in the heart of Kota Kinabalu's business, shopping, and entertainment district. It overlooks the South China Sea, and is only fifteen minutes away from the Kota Kinabalu International Airport.

The rooms are, as in all Hyatts, good-sized and well-equipped with color TVs, direct-dial telephones, air-conditioning controls, mini-bars, private baths with showers, and an assortment of amenities. Most of the hotel's rooms and suites have balconies so that views of the town and the ocean can be enjoyed.

My favorite place is the five-story atrium lobby you enter when you arrive. It has tropical shrubs, palms and trees and a fountain in the center surrounded by orchids in bloom. Cascading creepers from the guest room balconies overlooking the atrium give it an out-of-doors feeling. The lobby is furnished with comfortable rattan chairs upholstered in light orange and cream, blending well with the rust color floors. During the day, the whole atrium is flooded with sunlight from a skylight. Drinks are served in the lobby's Bambaazon Bar at one end, and light snacks are available at the Cafe Terrace at the other end of the atrium.

Also at the lobby level is the Semporna Grill, considered one of the finer dining rooms in town, It is noted for its fresh seafood, U.S. beef and selections of continental and local specialties, and an array of spectacular desserts. It is named after Semporna, a fishing town on the east coast of Sabah, famous for its rich fishing grounds. It has a view overlooking the sun terrace of the swimming pool and the nearby Tunku Abdul Rahman National Park Coral islands. This grill is open from 7:30 P.M. until 10:30 P.M. A pianist accompanies the dining.

Also on the lobby level is the Phoenix Court, named for the legendary bird still revered by the Chinese. This Chinese dining room serves dim sum for breakfast and specializes in both Cantonese and Szechuan cuisines served at lunch and dinner. At the entrance are three aquariums where you can see live tiger prawns, a variety of fish, and lobsters. You can pick your meal right there.

A delightful spot is Tanjung Ria, the twenty-four-hour café at lobby level that overlooks the sea and nearby Gaya island. The decor features local handicrafts and furnishings by the indigenous tribes of Sabah. Handwoven rattan mats hang on the walls. Of note is the dining room's dessert menu and, for the children, a delightful menu they can color. Older guests are given daily newspapers to read as they enter.

On the hotel's fourth floor is the VIP setup, known in all Hyatts as the Regency Club. For a modest additional charge more spacious accommodations and fuller services are provided.

Much is found in this hotel, including the Business Centre, an outdoor swimming pool, a valet shop for laundry and dry cleaning, the Delicatessen for baked delicacies and take-out gourmet items, a fitness center, a nightclub, and a uni-sex saloon.

And here's something really special: a late-night hair salon and in-room massage for female executive guests!

Kuala Lumpur

Kuala Lumpur was established in the late 1850s as a settlement of Chinese tin miners in the muddy surroundings of the Gombak and Klang rivers in Maylasia. Its name tells of its beginnings—it means "muddy confluence."

From the humble mining outpost it once was, Kuala Lumpur has become a busy international city where the clean lines of modern buildings contrast with older and more ornate examples of indigenous and colonial architecture.

This city of a half-million people is green and gracious, multiracial yet harmonious, where Malaysian smiles and hospitality are very evident.

There is much of interest to the visitor in Malaysia's capital city. The Museum Negara provides an excellent introduction to Malay culture, with handicrafts from all over the country. The Railway Station is a very popular spot for taking pictures because of the domes and minarets that make up its typically Moorish architecture. The Malayan Railways headquarters building opposite reflects Moorish styles important in the early development of the city. They were both built in 1855 on the Jalan Hishamuddin.

The national mosque, named the Jame Mosque, breaks the modern skyline with its intricately designed domes and minarets. It sits at the point where miners developed the original outpost.

The Chan See Shu Yuen Temple, on the Jalan Maharaja Lela, is made up of courtyards and pavilions and surrounded by elaborate sculptures depicting the Taoist faith.

The most photographed landmark in the country is the Sultan Abdul Samad building, headquarters for the Malaysian judicial system. Its attraction is its dramatic Moorish architecture.

The Lake Garden, just beside the museum, is the city's best known natural landmark, enjoyed by strollers and picnickers.

Fun to visit are the many colorful markets in the city. Your hotel's concierge will tell you where to find them.

Just north of the city are the famous Batu Caves, where, at the top of 242 steps, a Hindu shrine is set deep in limestone cliffs. Here, too, is the beautiful Templer's Park, twelve hundred hectares of unspoiled countryside.

FEDERAL HOTEL
35, Jalan Bukit Bintang
P.O. Box 10829
55100 Kuala Lumpur
Malaysia
Telephone: 03-248-9166
Telex: MA 30429 FEDTEL
Cable: FEDEROTEL
Fax: 03-243-8381
Reservations:
  In Kuala Lumpur call (03) 248-9166 or (03) 248-8144
  In California call 1-800-525-4685
  In Hawaii call 1-808-926-4522
  Elsewhere in the USA call Nikko Hotels 1-800-221-4862
    or Utell International at (212) 757-2981 or
    1-800-223-9868

All major credit cards
General Manager: Noel Hawkes
Sales Manager: Theresa Wong
Nikko Hotels International
Rates (approx.):
  Standard room $52 single, $61 double
  Deluxe room $65 single $74 double
  Junior Suite $87
  Suite $109
450 rooms, 24 suites
Service charge 10%; tax 5%

Certainly one of the more delightful hotels in Kuala Lumpur, the Federal Hotel is right at the heart of the metropolis, in the area called the Golden Triangle. It is on Jalan Bukit Bintang, which bustles from the activity of people from many offices, shopping complexes, restaurants and other public places.

The Federal looks newer than it is. It had its beginning shortly after the "Merdeka" independence from England, when it was established as the first international-class hotel in Kuala Lumpur and was used to accommodate visiting dignitaries and heads of state.

Today, its brand-new updated counterpart, The Prince Hotel in Jalan Imbi, is linked to it by a covered walkway that connects the Federal's Kontiki Poolside Restaurant to the Prince Hotel's Ballroom. Guests at the Federal may use the facilities of the deluxe sister hotel and vice versa, giving them the choice of six places to eat and drink, two health centers and two discotheques.

With Japanese and Singaporean business people comprising a large portion of its present clientele, the Federal also has luxurious suites, such as the Japanese Suite and the Malaysian Suite, designed for the more discerning traveler. All hotel rooms are up-to-date, fully air-conditioned, and have color TV and video movies.

The local people like this hotel and use it for their banquets and other events. With indoor and outdoor stadiums nearby, visiting sports groups use the hotel's facilities.

The eating and drinking places are attractive. The Mandarin Garden, designed with an ancient palatial decor, is noted for its Cantonese and Sichuan cuisines and popular dim sum. Waitresses wear the traditional *cheong sam*. Up on the fifteenth floor is one of *my favorite spots*, the Sky Room, which is the place for a candlelight dinner along with a floor show featuring international talent. It provides

French and other continental cuisines along with a selection of wines. *But my very favorite spot* is on the eighteenth floor of the hotel. It is the Revolving Bintang Lounge, the only revolving restaurant in Malaysia. It has breathtaking views of the city and features lively entertainment every night.

The hotel's coffee shop, The Trumpet Cafe, is on the ground floor and serves Malaysian and Western dishes. A favored spot for light snacks and refreshments, it is flanked by greenery and has an excellent view of the Bukit Bintang.

At the Kontiki Poolside restaurant the daily buffet luncheon offers forty choices and has a picturesque Polynesian setting. In the evening there's fresh seafood and meat barbecue. Also overlooking the pool is the posh Lobby Bar, and more secluded is the hotel's Piano Bar.

On the hotel's mezzanine is the Federal Club, which is called the "boogie wonderland of K.L. City." You can mingle with the locals in some lively action and entertainment.

On the ground floor is the Federal Health Centre, which offers massage, sauna, steam and Turkish bath facilities, and the Federal Bowl, with an eighteen-lane bowling center. Reserve your alley.

HOLIDAY INN CITY CENTRE
P.O. Box 11586
Jalan Raja Laut
50750 Kuala Lumpur
West Malaysia
Telephone: (03) 293-9233
Telex: MA 28130
Cable: HOLIDAYINN
Reservations:
  In Kuala Lumpur call (03) 293-9233
  In the USA, call 1-800-HOLIDAY
All major credit cards
Resident Manager: Gordor Koh
Sales Manager: Jasmine Lee
Holiday Inn Asia-Pacific
Rates (approx.):
  Standard room $40 single, $40 double
  Deluxe room $48 single, $52 double
  King Leisure $55 single, $62 double
  Executive suite $73
  Deluxe suite $93
  Presidential Suite $167

237 rooms, 13 suites
Service charge 10%; tax 5%

The eighteen-story Holiday Inn City Centre is located along-side the Gombak River, right where the city had its beginning. It is within easy walking distance of the city's commercial, entertainment and shopping district.

The rooms and suites are modern, and each has a private bathroom (with showers having automatic massage shower heads), individually controlled air conditioning, color TV with in-house movies, self-dial telephone, refrigerator, and mini-bar.

It is very much a business person's hotel, having a business service center and five small function rooms for events, as well as the Dewan Raja Laut Ballroom, which can accommodate up to two hundred for banquets.

The hotel also has a squash court and a health center. There is a massage service and other services include babysitting, laundry service and twenty-four-hour room service. There is a swimming pool and a shopping arcade that includes a hair salon, a drugstore, a florist and a travel agent. The outdoor pool has a swim-up bar.

Within walking distance are several very good shopping complexes, including Yaohan, The Mall and the Pertama Complex.

The Meisan Szechuan Restaurant has good Chinese dinners. The Kapitan Bar is a pleasant spot and has evening entertainment.

My favorite spot is the Benteng Coffee Shop, which has a nice view of the garden and always has beautiful, tempting cakes on display. The Benteng Coffee Shop is very popular locally, mostly because of the interesting variety of its menu. It offers nine appetizers, nine soups, six salads, twenty-six local and Western entrées, and fifteen desserts. A specialty is a selection of ten different mouth-watering noodle dishes, such as Shrimp Dumpling Noodles, Braised Fresh Noodles in a Claypot and Stewed Tendon Noodles. It is open twenty-four hours a day, and it's a very popular place for a late-night supper, served from 10:30 P.M. until 8 A.M., featuring local dishes of luscious *nasi lemak* and Teochew porridge. In the afternoon, high tea is served, featuring delicate pastries, finger sandwiches and those lovely cakes.

HYATT SAUJANA HOTEL AND COUNTRY CLUB
Subang International Airport Highway
P.O. Box 111
46710 Petaling Jaya
Malaysia
Telephone: (03) 746-1188
Telex: MA 37967 SKMJV
Fax: (60) 3-746-2789
Reservations:
    In Kuala Lumpur call 03-746-1188
    In the USA call 1-800-228-9000
    In Nebraska call 1-800-228-9001
    In Alaska, Hawaii call 1-800-228-9005
All major credit cards
General Manager: Maurice Holland
Concierge: Ms. Nirmala
Director of Sales: James Low
Hyatt International
Rates (approx.):
    Standard room $53 single, $62 double
    Superior room $62 single, $71 double
    Deluxe room $71 single, $80 double
    Suite $173
223 rooms, 8 suites
Service charge 10%; tax 5%

Opened in 1987, the Hotel Saujana is called Malaysia's "first business resort." It is the kind of hotel popular in the United States, offering the best of two worlds: an escape from the city for a relaxed pool-side break or escape to the golf course, or a place for business, offering top-level conference and meeting facilities. It is only a mile and half from downtown Kuala Lumpur and just five minutes away from the Subank International Airport.

In addition to two eighteen-hole championship golf courses, the hotel has tennis and squash courts, a fitness center, a jogging track, and an outdoor swimming pool in its own landscaped gardens.

The rooms and suites are designed to reflect Malaysian decor. Each has individually controlled air conditioning, private bath with shower, radio, minibar and refrigerator, color TV, piped-in music, international direct-dial telephone, and other Hyatt-style amenities.

As in most other Hyatts, there are two floors given over to the Regency Club, which offers more luxurious accommodations and amenities for a higher rate.

My favorite spot is the Senja Restaurant, the unique specialty dining room that overlooks the lake, with boats moored alongside. There is live music; it is an elegant setting for dinner.

The Suria Cafe serves Malasian, Nyonkan, and Western foods on an outdoor terrace, by the refreshing fountain of the Malacca Countryard, or in the indoor dining room, air-conditioned and elegant.

Other popular spots are the pool-side snack bar and the Bayu Lounge for drinks and simple repasts.

KUALA LUMPUR HILTON
Jalan Sultan Ismail
P.O. Box 10577
Kuala Lumpur 50718
Malaysia
Telephones: (03) 242-2122
(03) 242-2222
Telex: MA 30495
Cable: HILTELS Kuala Lumpur
Fax: (03) 2438069
Reservations:
  In Kuala Lumpur call (03) 242-2122
  In the USA call (212) 697-9370
All major credit cards
General Manager: Jan A. Oudendijk
Front Office Manager: Khoo Chee Choo
Director of Sales: Mohd Zain Puteh
Hilton International
Rates (approx.):
  City-view room $56 single, $64 double
  Mountain-view room $62 single, $70 double
  Executive suite $160
  Junior suite $92
589 rooms, 42 suites
Service charge 10%; tax 5%

The high-rise Kuala Lumpur Hilton is superbly located, overlooking the Selangor Turf Club race course and equally distant from the National Art Gallery. It is less than five minutes from the heart of the city's downtown.

The guest rooms all have floor-to-ceiling bay windows that offer superb views, and you pay slightly more for a view of the Central Mountain Range than you do for that of the city. Both are delightful—the mountains during the day and the cityscape at night.

The rooms are modern and fairly spacious, and the soft pastel colors are both attractive and restful. All rooms have separate dressing areas, and are well-equipped with individually controlled air conditioning, color TV with in-house movies, direct-dial telephones, writing desks, and self-service mini-bars. There is twenty-four-hour room service. The bathroom has a marble sink, a range of toiletries and a shower with a long bathtub, and a bidet.

As in most Hilton International hotels, this hotel has two Executive Floors with upgraded facilities designed to please the traveling business person. Guests in these rooms have a butler service, early morning tea or coffee, complimentary continental breakfasts and cocktails, two private lounges, and a special express check-in and check-out service. There are specially designed rooms available for the handicapped.

There are ample choices for dining and wining. *My favorite spot* is the gourmet Melaka Grill. It is decorated in the style of a nineteenth-century Eastern seaport. It has beautifully prepared Western specialties ranging from choice grilled meats to sophisticated dishes, with a good selection of wines. The fun time is at lunch on Wednesdays, when a fashion show is served along with the meal. This room is open daily from noon until 2:30 P.M.

The Planters' Inn is a twenty-four-hour restaurant that serves continental and local specialties in a setting reminiscent of a traditional rubber planter's home. Here the variety is staggering, from bountiful breakfast buffets to set meals, à la carte menus and even a high tea during the afternoon. It even has the locally popular all-night assorted porridge menu.

There is the Pizzaria, which is a delightful poolside restaurant serving pizzas and pastas. It has a wine bar and a salad bar. You may dine at this charming outdoor Italian "restorante by the pool" in casual comfort and be serenaded by Italian love songs. It is open from noon until 10:30 P.M. There is a pool-side barbecue every Thursday evening and a seafood buffet every Friday evening.

Another favorite spot of ours is the Club Bar. It is like a typical English pub with a pub-style luncheon served Monday through Friday. The Pub Lunch features assorted cold cuts, a carved specialty, a hot pie, garden fresh salad, fruits and desserts. It offers a selection of magazines, newspapers and pub games for its guests. It is open from noon to midnight.

Others may prefer something more Malaysian: in the Aviary Bar you may have your drink amidst lush tropical foliage and an aviary of exotic jungle birds. Live entertainment is furnished by a jazz quartet, a trio, or a solo singer. It is open from 11 A.M. until 1 A.M. except on Saturdays, when it closes at 2 A.M.

For more nighttime excitement there is the elegant Tin Mine Disco Club, which has a cover charge of about ten dollars. It has laser lights, a smoke machine, and a private champagne room and backgammon area. This room is open from nine in the evening until two in the morning.

The hotel has a shopping arcade that occupies two floors and includes a travel agent, a beauty salon and barber shop, a drugstore, car rental, a newsstand, a medical clinic, and a number of specialty shops offering arts and crafts and designer fashions.

There's plenty for those wanting sports facilities—four squash courts and two floodlit tennis courts, as well as the Pro Shop, where equipment can be rented or purchased. There is the Clark Hatch Physical Fitness Center, with a fully fitted gymnasium, sauna, Turkish steam bath, and massage. For joggers, the hotel provides a map of the city's jogging routes (on request). You can arrange horseback riding or golf at the Royal Selangor Golf Club.

Being a Hilton International, the hotel has a business center that provides a full range of secretarial services, word processing, facsimile, photocopying, worldwide courier service, typewriter rental, packing services, interpreters and a twenty-four-hour telex.

The nearest shopping spot to visit is the small Malaysian handicraft center called Karyaneka. It is in Jalan Raja Chulan, just a stone's throw from the hotel. This area is a quaint village made up of fourteen houses of uniquely Malaysian architecture. Each house exhibits and sells the traditional handicrafts belonging to a particular Malaysian state.

A ten-minute taxi drive from the hotel is the Central Market, which is worth seeing and photographing. It has a collection of exhibitions, cultural performances and a lot of specialized shops. About an eight-minute walk from the hotel are the complexes of Kuala Lumpur Plaza, Sungei Wang Plaza, the Bukit Bintang Plaza, and others. In addition to a variety of shops and designer boutiques, these centers each has a resident department store. Duty-free shopping is available at Hartamas in the Kuala Lumpur Plaza.

PETALING JAYA HILTON
2 Jalan Barat
Petaling Jaya 46200
Selangor
Malaysia
Telephone: (03) 755-9122 or (03) 755-3533
Telex: PJHLTN MA36008
Cable: PJ HILTON PETALING JAYA
Fax: (03) 553909
Reservations:
   In Petaling Jaya call (03) 242-2222, ext. 421
   In the USA call Hilton Reservations at 1-800-445-8667
All major credit cards
General Manager: Ricardo M. Tapia
Executive Assistant Manager: En Mohd Ilyas
Sales Director: Mazhar Khan
Hilton International
Rates (approx.):
   Superior room $56 single, $64 double
   Deluxe room $64 single, $72 double
   Executive Floor room $72 single, $80 double
   Suite $120
385 rooms, 10 suites
Service charge 10%; tax 5%

The Petaling Jaya Hilton is situated in the center of Malaysia's major satellite town, midway between the Subang International Airport and the capital city of Kuala Lumpur, and within easy reach of both.

Surrounded by attractive suburbs and a number of shopping, sports and recreational centers, it is also close to the main industrial complexes. This makes it an ideal location for the business visitor and a somewhat quieter setting for the tourist.

Petaling Jaya means "Tree of Success" in Malay. This was once a tiny mining town on the outskirts of Kuala Lumpur. Today, it is a thriving modern town in which visitors find a glittering blend of domes, minarets, spires, and steeples—which together reflect the many cultures that make up present-day Malaysia.

Seen from the hotel is the magnificent Darul Ehsan Marble Arch, which marks the border between the State of Selangor and the Federal Territory of Kuala Lumpur. The arch is Moorish in style and flanked by ancient war cannons, and is floodlit at night.

Petaling Jaya has an excellent golf course and a range of good restaurants, nightclubs and shopping centers. This is a perfect base for exploring the picturesque old towns in this part of Malaysia.

Each of the hotel's rooms has views over the town of Kuala Lumpur and of a distant mountain range. Elegantly furnished with rattan and local wood, the rooms are decorated in pastels and make use of attractive batik fabrics. Each has a writing desk, direct-dial telephone, color TV with in-house movies, refrigerator and mini-bar, and individually controlled air conditioning. The hotel has a Hilton Executive Floor providing upgraded accommodations and services for a modestly higher fee. Although designed for the business traveler, many tourists enjoy these more spacious and more fully serviced rooms.

The main dining room of the hotel is the Paya Serai. Light and airy, it overlooks the landscaped gardens, pool, and terraces. Here, buffet breakfasts and lunches are served as well as an extensive à la carte menu of local and international cuisines. In the evening, it becomes more elegant, featuring charcoal grills.

The Toh Yuen Restaurant serves Chinese cuisine in an elegant setting that recreates a classic "Peach Garden" of ancient China. In the Nipponkan, Japanese food is served in an authentic surrounding of stone lanterns and tiny Japanese gardens. The Anggerik Lounge is furnished with kampong-style window frames and brass ceiling fans that capture the ambiance of earlier times. This is the favored spot for a quick breakfast, a pot of tea, or refreshment at sundown. The Epitome Club/Disco is the place for carvery and salad lunches, Happy Hour drinks, and for lively evening entertainment.

The large Kristal Ballroom can accommodate over five hundred for banquets, and it can be partitioned into three separate rooms.

The outdoor swimming pool is the only one in the area and is set amidst gardens with palm trees, creating a tropical setting. There are occasional Malaysian cultural performances on the terrace. The Physical Fitness Center, complete with a fully equipped gymnasium, sauna, massage, whirlpool and steam bath, is open from early morning until late evening. Nearby—not on the hotel grounds—are golf, squash and tennis facilities. Check with the assistant manager to make arrangements to use these facilities.

The Executive Business Centre has, in addition to the usual services and facilities, a reference library and a twenty-four-hour news service. There is a shopping arcade with all convenience shops and souvenirs. Nearby are the Asia Jaya Shopping Complex and the Jaya Shopping Complex. The assistant manager will give you easy directions.

Be sure to get a free copy of the *Joggers Map*, whether you jog or not. It helps you in walking around the area.

THE REGENT OF KUALA LUMPUR
Jalan Sultan Ismail
Kuala Lumpur 50250
Malaysia
Telephone: 242-5588
Telex: MA 30486 REGENT
Cable: REGHOTEL K.L.
Fax: 241-5524
Reservations:
  In Kuala Lumpur call (02) 242-8845
  In Hawaii and Alaska call 1-800-626-2626
  Elsewhere in the USA call Regent International at
    1-800-545-4000
All major credit cards
General Manager: Karl-Heinz Zimmermann
Front Office Manager: Krishna Badhur
Director of Sales and Marketing: Nicholas Curtis
Regent International Hotels
Rates (approx.):
  Deluxe room $75
  Grand deluxe room $87
  Executive suite $166
  Deluxe suite $228
298 rooms, 41 suites
Service charge 10%; tax 5%

The Regent of Kuala Lumpur is one of the fine top-level hotels managed by the Hong Kong hotel organization, Regent International Hotel Group. This hotel is in the heart of the city of Kuala Lumpur, in the central business district. It faces the city's most popular shopping complex.

The main lobby of the hotel has a decor of subdued and understated elegance, with rich use of Malaysian woods. It

Kuala Lumpur 309

sets the theme and tone for the decor throughout the hotel and its guests' rooms. All of the rooms and suites are tastefully furnished and have individually controlled air conditioning, color TV, direct-dial telephones, mini-bars, and in-house feature films.

The Business Centre is designed to meet the needs of business executives, with its full services and equipment. The Sports Club has three air-conditioned squash courts, a tennis court, a sauna steam bath, qualified masseurs, and a spa and herbal bath. A complete gymnasium managed by Fitness International is on the hotel's fifth floor.

There is fine dining and entertainment in the six dining rooms and restaurants. The Suasa Brasserie has both continental and French cuisines, and is a favorite in the city for fine dining. The Payang Coffee House on the lower lobby serves local fare from Malay to Chinese and Indian, and some say it has the best buffet lunch and dinner in town. The hotel's Ranch Grill is noted for its steaks, seafood grills, and fresh salads.

My favorite spot is at the poolside restaurant called Treetops, especially the popular barbecue on Wednesday nights or the brunch on Sundays. The Regent Court on the second floor features Cantonese and Sichuan cuisines. The Garden Lounge has light entertainment amidst the cool, tropical setting of an indoor garden.

The Lake Gardens, just ten minutes' drive from the hotel, has a most interesting jogging circuit complete with exercise stations for the serious jogger. The hotel Guest Relations officers will help you get there. If you wish to jog around the city, ask for the Regent's *Jogger's Map*. It has an approximately 2.8-mile route within the city starting at the hotel. This guide is useful even if you are not a jogger.

SHANGRI-LA HOTEL
11 Jalan Sultan Ismail
50250 Kuala Lumpur
Malaysia
Telephone: (03) 232-2388
Telex: SHNGKL, MA 30021
Fax: (03) 230-1514
Reservations:
　In Kuala Lumpur call (03) 232-2388, ext. 1260/5
　In Los Angeles call 213-417-3483
　Elsewhere in the USA call Shangri-La International at
　　1-800-457-5050

All major credit cards
General Manager: Dario A. Regazzoni
Concierge: Sharim Jantan
Director of Marketing: Lewis Bloom
Shangri-La International
Rates (approx.):
  Superior room $72 single, $82 double
  Deluxe room $80 single, $90 double
  1-bedroom executive suite $144
  1-bedroom specialty suite $220
  2-bedroom specialty suite $300
  1-bedroom Royal or Malaysia Suite $800
  2-bedroom Royal or Malaysia Suite $880
722 rooms, 36 suites
Service charge 10%; tax 5%

The Shangri-La Hotel of Kuala Lumpur is ideally located in the city's "Golden Triangle," the heart of the business and entertainment district of "K.L." Apart from its convenience for shopping and sightseeing, the hotel has panoramic views from both the front and back. On one side is the glittering modernity of the city, on the other is the beauty of the Buki Nanas forest reserve.

The hotel is only forty minutes from the airport and the race track is only a five-minute walk from the hotel. It will be converted into a park in 1989.

The thirty-three-story skyscraper hotel is a sight to see both outside and inside. It has beautifully landscaped gardens and cascading greenery. As you step into the lobby, you see magnificent marble, deep-piled carpets and lush tropical foliage.

Within a year of its opening, the readers of *Executive Travel Magazine* selected the Shangri-La as one of the winners in a poll on the "Best Hotel in the Rest of the World." The Shangri-La claims to have the largest guest rooms in the city. Each room has a large executive desk, color TV, in-house movies, international direct-dial telephone, refrigerator and mini-bar, individual temperature control, twenty-four-hour room service, and attractive marble bathroom. The rooms and suites all are kept supplied with garden-fresh flowers. The thirty-six custom-designed suites are located on the upper floors, having the best views of the city.

The dining rooms are good. The Shang Palace has delectable Chinese cuisine ranging from shark fins to dim sum, all prepared by a team of Hong Kong chefs. The Nadaman, the Japanese restaurant, with traditional decor, has separate counters for sushi, tempura, and *teppanyaki*.

My favorite is the Restaurant Lafite, a prestigious dining room with French Provincial decor as the setting for its continental cuisine. Here is the spot for a candlelight dinner. Lovely, too, is the twenty-four-hour Coffee Garden in a setting overlooking extensive landscaped gardens, fringed by tropical gardens. The menu includes Malay, Chinese and Indian dishes.

The Lobby Lounge is the spot for relaxing and drinks. In the evening, there is piano music. The views from its windows are breathtaking.

The hotel has a fully equipped Health Center with a gymnasium, sauna, Jacuzzis, and expert massage. The hotel also has a swimming pool and squash and tennis courts.

At night, guests find the setting they want either in the quiet of the Pub, an English bar, or Club Oz, the dynamic and exciting music and dancing spot.

The Shangri-La prides itself in being a combination of "a premier businessman's hotel and a ritzy resort hotel." To help the business guests, it has what it claims to be the best-equipped convention facilities of any hotel in town. The ballroom can accommodate up to two thousand and there are thirteen other function rooms with the latest audio-visual systems, eight simultaneous language translation channels, press rooms and electronic voting panels. The hotel has a fully equipped business center as well.

Dario Ragazzoni, the general manager, a Swiss hotelier, let me see some of his fan mail from satisfied guests. He came here from the Regent in Bangkok, where he earned an excellent reputation and is earning the same here. No wonder the hotel wins awards and comes out so well in polls.

Kuantan

HYATT KUANTAN
Telok Chempedak
25050 Kuantan
P.O. Box 250
Pahang Daruk Makmur
Malaysia

Telephone: (09) 525211
Telex: HTTKN 50252
Cable: HYATT KUANTAN
Fax: (09) 507577
Reservations:
  In Kuantan call (09) 525211, ext. 720 or 722
  In the USA call Hyatt International at 1-800-228-9000
All major credit cards
General Manager: Joseph Nietlisbach
Sales Manager: Chan Lai Hoong
Hyatt International Hotels
Rates (approx.):
  Standard room $44 single, $52 double
  Superior room $52 single, $64 double
  Deluxe room $60 single, $72 double
  Regency Club room $80 single, $92 double
  Executive suite $120
  Presidential Suite $220–$260
185 rooms, 11 suites
Service charge 10%; tax 5%

Hyatt found one of the most beautiful of the Malaysian seaside resorts in which to establish this attractive complex.

The Hyatt Kuantan is right on the beach, ten minutes from Kuantan town. Teluk Cempedak Beach is on the east coast of the Malaysian peninsula, 163 miles east of Kuala Lumpur and 208 miles north of Singapore. By car, it is about four hours from Kuala Lumpur and five and a half hours from Singapore.

Malaysia's exotic East Coast is known for its serenity, charm and traditional crafts. The Hyatt Kuantan, with its decor, and setting has captured the best of this serene atmosphere. Lapped by warm, inviting waters, cooled by gentle breezes and swaying casuarinas, it is the ideal resort hotel.

My favorite spot is the lobby, delightfully open and decorated with local batik and Malaysian redwood. Part of its decor is the impressive view of the bay. Another beautiful spot is the aquamarine pool, right next to the beach. It has an island bar not only serving drinks but super ice cream creations.

All of this resort's guest rooms are exotically furnished with colorful batik and stylish rattan furniture as well as all the modern facilities needed to provide the comforts desired by the international traveler. But as with nearly every Asian hotel, the needs of the business visitors are not forgotten.

This resort is often host to conferences and seminars, and has function rooms to accommodate from ten to three hundred persons.

My favorite spot to dine is the Kampong Cafe Restaurant, built on stilts and overlooking the South China Sea. Here is served spicy Malaysian delicacies, as well as a choice of Western dishes and seafood specialties. And most wonderful is that it is possible to eat and relax here any time during the day's twenty-four-hours.

On the beach there is The Sampan, a rustic fishing boat converted into a bar. It's a wonderful place to enjoy the sunset and drinks. The Verandah, which really is the hotel's verandah, is on a comfortable breezy corner overlooking the ocean. This is a lovely spot for cocktails or pre-dinner drinks. For an evening of serious dining there is Hugo's, the hotel's fancy dining room. The cuisine is exceptional, the ambiance is most elegant, and the sweeping view of the bay is magnificent.

And for those wishing a lively end of the evening into morning there is the Chukka discotheque, with the stimulating music of Juliana's of London.

During the day, if lying around gets boring, guests have a choice of tennis, squash, sailing, fishing, jogging and even jungle-trekking. Be sure to ask for the *Hyatt Kuantan Jogger's Map*. If you don't jog, stroll the recommended route. You'll see most of the estate and have a pleasant day. The tennis courts (three of them) are lighted for night play. There is also scuba diving, snorkeling and golf available in the vicinity.

The Executive Business Centre is open Monday through Friday from 9 A.M. until 5 P.M. and has full services and equipment. The Health Centre opens daily at noon and closes at midnight. Its facilities include sauna, steambath, and massage.

The hotel's Regency Club is on the fourth floor, offering special VIP services and facilities for a modest additional rate.

Another place to enjoy, right at the hotel, is the Botanical Garden. The golf course is just past it, where the Kuantan River enters the sea.

RAMADA BEACH RESORT KUANTAN
152, Sungai Karang
26100 Beserah
Kuantan
Pahang
Malaysia
Telephone: (09) 587544
Telex: MA 50307 RAMAKU
Reservations:
  In Kuantan call (09) 587544
  In Kuala Lumpur call (03) 242-3968
  In the USA call 1-800-2-RAMADA
All major credit cards
General Manager: Frank Liepmann
Director of Sales: Jimmie Ng
Ramada International
Rates (approx.):
  Standard room $44 single, $52 double
  Superior room $56 single, $64 double
  Deluxe room $64 single, $72 double
  Suite $140
158 rooms, 4 suites
Service charge 10%; tax 5%

Opened at the beginning of 1987, the Ramada resort is on one of the most beautiful stretches of the Beserah Beach. The hotel is fifteen minutes from Kuantan town and twenty minutes from the Kuantan airport. And the harbor is only ten minutes from the hotel.

Set on four and a half acres of landscaped grounds in Sungai Karang, it offers all of the desired resort facilities. There are glass-backed squash courts—the only ones on this coast—with a sauna and a whirlpool, a gym, a swimming pool, and a billiard room.

There are also the Executive Centre, the Health/Exercise Centre, and the Library Lounge, on the hotel's first floor. All four of the hotel's suites are on the second floor.

A complete range of dining facilities includes the Nankai, the only Japanese restaurant on this coast; the Segara, a continental and Chinese dining room; and Cafe Bayu, a twenty-four-hour coffee shop. In the recreation area, the Refreshment Centre serves light snacks and drinks, as does the Pengkalan Poolside. For the night crowd, there is the Dewi Discotheque.

The rooms are attractive and equipped with color TV, individually controlled air conditioning, in-house video channels, international direct-dial telephones, refrigerators and large bathrooms with luxurious fittings.

The hotel has conference facilities with audio-visual and stage facilities.

Be sure to ask for your copy of the hotel's map of Kuantan. With it you'll know where to find the places to go and see in Kuantan, including its riverfront Esplanade, the various industrial areas to the north and west of the town, and the fishing village at Tanjong Lumpur, across the Kuantan River.

Malacca

About halfway between Kuala Lumpur and Singapore, this is the oldest city in Malaysia. The story goes that about six hundred years ago a refugee prince by the name of Parameswara sought sanctuary in a modest fishing village. He was so pleased that he decreed a city be built there to honor his hosts, and he named it Malacca, taken from the local Melaka trees. Founded in the Malay Kingdom, it was for centuries the center for gold, ivory, tin, spices, and silks.

It fell under a succession of so-called protective influences—first the Chinese, then, in the sixteenth century, the Portuguese, followed by the Dutch in 1641 and the British in 1824.

There's much to see in Malacca. You can visit the oldest Chinese Temple in Malaysia—the Cheng Hoon Teng—and behind this is Bukit China Hill, one of the oldest and largest Chinese burial grounds outside of China. There are early Portuguese churches—one once held the remains of Saint Francis Xavier. The Porta de Santiago is the gateway of the original Portuguese port. There are also the Tranquerah Mosque and the comprehensive Malacca Museum.

This area—the east coast of West Malaysia—has hundreds of miles of unspoiled, golden beaches dotted with small villages. The offshore islands are miniature tropical paradises with many romantic legends attached to them.

The city was on the decline until about 1900, when world demand for rubber, tin, and coconut increased. Although thriving today, it is not as important as it was in the past. It is becoming, however, increasingly attractive to the traveler.

One typically outstanding attraction is the old fortress, which stands south of the river on a small hill. The old, thick walls are gone, but many of the Dutch warehouses, the city hall and the ancient churches have survived.

Under the guns of the old fort is the quarter where the foreign traders lived. Now the quarter is completely inhabited by Chinese, complete with temples and cemetery. These Chinese have become the true Malaysians of this area through intermarriages.

The main shopping area is filled with a variety of retail establishments ranging from huge stores to colorful and busy bazaars. Prices at the shopping complexes are fixed, but bargaining is expected at small retail shops and roadside stalls. The bigger shopping centers are found on Jalan Munshi Abdullah, Jalan Bunga Raya, Jalan Hang Tuah, and Jalan Bendahara.

Before exploring on your own, visit the Malacca Tourist Information Centre on Jalan Kota (telephone (06) 225895). Get a copy of the *Malacca Map and Guide*, which is easy to use and very interesting.

RAMADA RENAISSANCE HOTEL MELAKA
Jalan Bendahara
P.O. Box 105
75720 Malacca
Malaysia
Telephone: (06) 248888
Telex: RAMADA MA 62966
Cable: RAMADARENA
Fax: 06-249269
Reservations:
   In Malacca call (06) 248888, ext. 323
   In the USA call 1-800-228-9898 or 1-800-2-RAMADA
All major credit cards
General Manager: Werner R. Schmidt
Sales Manager: Noel Chai
Ramada International
Rates (approx.):
   Standard room $47 single, $56 double
   Superior room $60 single, $69 double
   Deluxe room $69 single, $77 double
   Suite $150–$343
284 rooms, 16 suites
Service charge 10%; tax 5%

To really enjoy the ancient city of Malacca it might be a good idea to check in at the Ramada Renaissance Hotel, because this twenty-four-story modern structure is right in the heart of old Malacca. From here it is easy to explore the city on foot or by trishaw.

This is the most recent international-class hotel to open in Malacca and is a good choice for either the business traveler or tourist. All of the rooms and suites have striking bathrooms, radios, color TVs, in-house video, international direct-dial phones, and mini-bars. Two of the floors are designated as non-smoking. There is the Renaissance Floor on the 23rd level, which provides more luxurious accommodations and services for a modestly higher rate (about $100 for double accommodations). Guests of the floor have access by special elevator keys. There is a lounge where cocktails and hors d'oeuvres are served and a concierge is on duty to serve the floor guests.

The hotel does try to serve well those having events and meetings. The Bunga Raya Convention Hall seats one thousand, and there are four other seminar rooms and the fully equipped Businessmen's Centre.

My favorite spot is the hotel lobby. It is imposing with two grand chandeliers, created in Austria in the shape of Japanese lanterns. In the center is a delightful multispray fountain. The marble floors glisten as they beautifully reflect the chandeliers.

Another lovely spot is the pool and Malacca Garden on the ninth floor of the hotel. On the pool terrace is the Poolside Bar and Restaurant, with lush plants around it. While snacking or dining you have a panoramic view of the town. You may eat or drink here from 8 A.M. until 7 P.M.

The Taming Sari is the grill room of the Ramada; it offers international cuisine accompanied by light music. "Taming Sari" is the name of a famous sword of a powerful warrior of the mid-fifteenth century and it is believed to have special magical powers. It is open for dinner only, from 6:00 until 10:30 P.M.

Summerfield's is the spacious open-air coffee shop of the hotel, open 24 hours to serve a wide range of local and international items. It is very popular and modestly priced.

Long Feng means "Dragon" and "Phoenix." It is a Chinese belief that the two together bring peace, harmony, and oneness, and this Chinese restaurant is indeed a peaceful spot to enjoy Cantonese cuisine. The decor is harmonious thanks to the use of hand-painted scenes of nature. It is open for breakfast, lunch and dinner.

Another great spot to visit is the hotel's Fanosa Lounge. It is named after Malacca's famous fortress, built in 1511 by the Portugese to defend their newly occupied port. A replica of the fort is built into the bar.

For the night crowd, the hotel has the Stardust Discotheque, which is open from 8 P.M. until 2 A.M. every night. With a DJ, it offers the latest sounds and blasts of pulsating lights.

Of course, being the complete facility that it is, the hotel has a health center with a gymnasium, massage, Jacuzzi, steam and sauna, and squash courts.

Be sure to get a copy of the hotel's *Malacca Town Map* free of charge at the information desk. It is very helpful and can fold easily into your pocket.

A tip on something special we had not had since my wife and I were at the Tour d'Argent in Paris: When at the Taming Sari grill room you may want to order Canard Rouennais a la Taming Sari, or, in French, *Canard Pressé*. Just as in the Tour d'Argent in Paris, you get a certificate as proof you have eaten it. It is, as you've figured out, pressed duck, and the machine used to press it is the only one of its kind in Malaysia.

Penang

Great things come in small packages. Certainly that can be said about the little fifteen-by-ten-mile island of Penang. Off the west coast of Malaysia, it is a tropical paradise, an island of palms. *Pulau Pinang* (the Pearl of the Orient): when you say golden shores are lapped by gentle blue waters, you are right. It is charming, dignified, quiet, and truly beautiful, with lush foliage of giant palms and luxurious ferns, flowering trees and shrubs. Colorful gardens, fruit orchards, and rich rice and coconut groves abound. There are fairy-tale beaches and bays and fishing villages, rocky headlands, and hills rising to almost three thousand feet, from which can be seen range after range of mountains in the Kedah section on Malaysia's mainland. One magnificent view is that upon entering Penang's natural harbor through either its North or South Channel.

George Town is the official name of the city, although it is always referred to as Penang, just as the island is called Penang although its official name is Prince of Wales Island.

The city is on the northeast side of the island, right on the sea. It has a population of well over a quarter million. The streets are broad and tree-lined, the houses tropical in design and spacious, with white walls, red roofs and lovely gardens. Many of them, especially on Northam Road, are occupied by people who have retired to paradise.

Penang was the first British settlement in Malaysia, ceded to the East India Company by the Sultan of Kedah in 1785. It was acquired to provide protection and serve as the supply point for cargo ships on their way to and from the ports of China. It is now the leading port of Malaysia, the third most important in the country for transoceanic shipments, and it is the commercial center of northern Malaysia.

The people of the island are mostly a mixture of Malay, Tamil (Indian) and Chinese plus a smattering of Westerners. The whole island has a total of about a million people. Malay is the official language and Chinese a major one. Most residents, and certainly business people, speak English.

The best buys in George Town include Malaysian handicrafts and the usual assortment of articles made in Far Eastern countries, curios, cheap "luxury" goods, and antiques. The main shopping district is the Penang Road/Burmah Road and Loboh Campbell area. Off the main shopping areas, along Rope Walk, are several junk shops worth visiting. The shops are usually open from about 10 A.M. until 10 P.M.

Sights can be seen by walking or riding around the city. Among the places worth visiting are the Acheen Street Mosque, one of the oldest in Penang, built by Syded Sheriff Tengku Syed Hussain Aidid who came to the island in 1792 from Sumatra. This architecture has an Egyptian look, a radical change from the Moorish architecture of most mosques. The Khoo Kongsi in Cannon Square is the most picturesque of the clan-temples in Malaysia, with richly carved ornamentation on the roof, walls and pillars reflecting the art and architecture of ancient China. Others to see are the Kapitan Kling Mosque (1820), the Sri Mariamman Temple (1883), the Kuan Yin Temple (1880, the oldest in Penang), St. George's Church (1818), the first Anglican Church in Malaysia, Penang Museum and Art Gallery, the Cathedral of the Assumption, Logan Memorial and High Court, the Cheong Fatt Tze Mansion (fine porcelain and antiques collections), the Clock Tower (erected in 1897 in conjunction with Queen Victoria's Diamond Jubilee), Fort Cornwallis (1808–10), the Municipal Council Building on the Esplanade, and the Dewan Sri Pinang, the multipurpose auditorium building.

Outside of town try to see the Butterfly Farm, which opened in 1986. It is the world's largest butterfly farm with three thousand living specimens of more than fifty species. It is in Teluk Bahang. See also the Kek Lok Si at Air Itam, the largest Buddhist Temple complex in Malaysia and one of the finest in southeast Asia. Started in 1890, it took more than two decades to build. The Natukkotai Chettiar Temple at the Jalan Waterfall is the largest Hindu temple in Penang. In front of the shrine is a peacock given to Subramaniam by his mother. And at Lorong Burmah is Wat Chaysmang-kalaram, a Buddhist temple of Thai architecture, the world's third largest reclining Buddha, 108 feet long. And you'll find, at Jalan Mesjid Negeri, the State Mosque (completed in 1980 after four years of work). It is immense and can hold five thousand worshippers. Other places to see are Penang Hill, the Youth Park, the Snake Temple, the Botanic Garden, the Air Itam Dam and the Forest Recreation Park.

The Shangri-La Group of Hotels in Penang has an ex-cellent booklet called *Shangri-La's Penang*. With a copy in hand you'll know what to see and do in and out of George Town.

GOLDEN SANDS HOTEL
Batu Feringgi Beach
P.O. Box 222
Penang 11100
Malaysia
Telephone: 04-811911
Telex: GOSANDS MA 40627
Cable: GOLDSANDS PENANG
Fax: (04) 811880
Reservations:
  In Penang call (04) 811799
  In the USA call 1-800-457-5050
  In Los Angeles call (213) 551-1121
All major credit cards
General Manager: Brian Hladnik
Sales Manager: Sunny Khoo
Shangri-La International
Rates (approx.):
  Standard room $55 single, $65 double
  Superior room $66 single, $78 double
  Deluxe room $76 single, $88 double
  Suite $156–$250
395 rooms, 6 suites
Service charge 10%; tax 5%

Located on the the Shangri-La International's own private stretch of fabled Batu Feringgi beach, the Golden Sands is a dramatic sight, designed as it is in the form of a sweeping arc enclosing a unique, free-form swimming pool. It is the ideal resort hotel for both family travelers and business people.

The rooms are typical of Shangri-La's special concern. Each room and suite has a private balcony, private bathroom, color TV with an in-house movie channel, central air conditioning with in-room controls, and direct-dial phones. Two rooms are designed for guests who are handicapped.

One of *my favorite spots* is the Hawaiian-style swimming pool. It is attractively designed, with boulders, coconut palms, and a tiny island to make it look like a lagoon.

Nearby is a wading pool with what is called a slippery dip or wet slide, which appeals to both young and old.

It's a very resorty resort; there are unlimited activities. You can go for a jungle walk, watch a snake charmer perform or have your fortune told by the hotel's resident palmist.

You may take a power boat cruise, sign up for cooking, napkin folding or fruit- and vegetable-carving classes. Or you may compete in tennis, squash, or volleyball matches arranged by the hotel. Nearby are all kinds of seaports to see, and you can arrange to go fishing, windsurfing, and even para-sailing. Or you may go for a round of golf at the nearby eighteen-hole golf course (about a twenty-minute drive from the hotel).

In addition to twenty-four-hour room service, there are three dining rooms and three bars. A favorite is the Grill, which has been changed from a very formal dining room into a delightfully casual spot. What is exciting about this place is the all-you-can-eat salad bar and a wide selection of appetizers. Most popular is a reasonably priced steak dinner.

My favorite spot is the hotel's Bunga Raya Restaurant, which overlooks the open sea. It is a Penang-style dining room serving local specialties. There is a selection of authentic Chinese, Malay and Indian dishes.

The Coffee House is open around the clock and has excellent views of the swimming pool, the landscaped gardens and the beach. Light and airy, this partially open-air restaurant is the spot for a leisurely meal or a light snack. I like the local desserts, such as *longan*, lychee, *pengat pisang* or *ais kacang* with a dollop of ice cream as a topping.

Swimmers may enjoy drinks at the picturesque Kuda Laut pool-side bar. *My favorite refreshment spot* is the Sunset Lounge at sunset. With its rattan chairs and tables and views of the pool, tropical garden, and setting sun, it is ideal for pre-dinner drinks. A resident band provides background music.

Malam Pulau Pinang or Penang Night is the big festive event at the hotel when you enjoy a evening of eating on the beach in front of the hotel. There is an endless feast of local specialties, with hawker-stalls set up to serve such delicacies as *penang assam laksa, char koay teow, mee rebus, satay,* and *nonya kuith* under the palm trees. If you're lucky, it will be a star-studded or moonlit night. The highlight of the evening is the performances of local dancers and singers.

The hotel is more than a holiday resort. It has facilities for company meetings, conventions, banquets, and exhibitions. The hotel's Orchid Room can hold up to a hundred people for a banquet.

Although the hotel does not have a business center, it does offer a complete range of secretarial services and equipment for meetings and other business executives' needs.

To have been completed by June 1988 is an addition to the property that will add 85 new guest bedrooms, a spectacular new glass-fronted ballroom overlooking the grounds and the pool, and a lovely Malay-style beachfront restaurant that will have breakfasts, barbecue lunches, and theme dinners. There will also be a second swimming pool in the Hawaiian lagoon style and a unique twenty-person outdoor Jacuzzi.

HOLIDAY INN PENANG
11100 Batu Ferrignhi
George Town
Penang
Malaysia
Telephone: 04-811601-612
Telex: MA 40952
Cable: HOLIDAY INN
Reservations:
  In Penang call 811977
  In the USA call 1-800-HOLIDAY
All major credit cards
General Manager: Jean Ricoux
Sales Manager: Barbara Stewart
Holiday Inn Asia-Pacific

Rates (approx.):
   Standard room $64 single, $69 double
   Superior room $73 single, $82 double
   Penthouse studio $113
   Garden studio $113
   Balcony suite $145
   Executive suite $163
152 rooms, 10 suites
Service charge 10%; tax 5%

On this very popular and beautiful beach, the Holiday Inn offers comfortable accommodations and good services at reasonable rates. As at all the beach resorts in Malaysia, there is much to do, including windsurfing, sailing, fishing, and scuba diving. For the less active there is always swimming and sunbathing at the hotel's half-Olympic-size swimming pool or at the beach.

Among the recreational activities set up by the staff of the hotel for the guests are the jungle walk, a tropical bicycle ride, and pool-side activities. At the watersports center you may arrange for catamaran sailing, canoeing, para-sailing, and water-skiing. There are coaches to teach you tennis or windsurfing at regularly held clinics.

All of the hotel's rooms and suites have color TV with three local channels and one for in-house video programs. There are mini-bars, refrigerators, and other amenities in the rooms.

The hotel has recently renovated and expanded its meeting facilities, which have all vital audio-visual and standard technical equipment. There is a staff to handle details for conferences, seminars, and other meetings.

The Coffee House on the ground floor features traditional Malaysian cuisine. Delicacies here include fried *koay teow, teow, prawn mee, nasi goreng, satay,* or *ice kacang.* It is open from 6 A.M. until midnight. European favorites are available, and there is a lavish breakfast buffet starting at 10:30 A.M. On the lower ground floor is the Baron's Table, serving steaks and continental cuisine. Dinner is from 7:00 P.M. to midnight daily except Sunday. The Meisan Terrace restaurant overlooks the beach and features Sichuan cuisine. Featured is duck prepared in a variety of ways. Dinner is served from 6:00 P.M.

The Lobby Lounge is open from 4:00 P.M. until midnight. The New Image Band entertains at night, except on Monday.

Much happens at and around the pool. There is a pool

volleyball game every evening if enough team members are recruited from the guests. A pool-side bar opens early, at 8 A.M. And this is the favorite spot to check out the sunsets.

PENANG MUTIARA BEACH RESORT
Jalan Telok Bahang
Penang 11050
Malaysia
Telephone: (04) 804306, (04) 804315, (04) 804336, (04) 804339, or (04) 804358
Telex: PMBR 40822
Fax: (04) 803470
Reservations:
    In Penang call (04) 804336 or (04) 804339
    In New York state call (212) 838-3110 collect
    Elsewhere in the USA call Leading Hotels of the World at 1-800-223-6800
All major credit cards
General Manager: Werni Eisen
Sales Manager: Anthony Ang
Mandarin Singapore International
Rates (approx.):
    Deluxe room $98
    Junior suite $140
    Presidential Suite $1,200
Other suites available
443 rooms, 48 suites
Service charge 10%; tax 5%

This resort hotel will be ready for you late in 1988. The Penang Mutiara Beach Resort is to be a world-class hotel in Teluk Bahang, the finest beachfront on Penang Island.

In the grand style of the Mandarin Singapore hotels, it is to have luxuriously furnished rooms, each with a picturesque view of the fishing boats on the ocean. Standing twelve stories, the hotel is on an eighteen-acre estate.

It is a beautifully designed property. On arrival the guest sees a rich blue ceramic flooring at the Porta Cochere, at the entrance. The main lobby is surrounded by glass, giving beautiful views of the gardens and the ocean. All is white —the polished marble lobby floor, the textured walls providing a setting for the bright Malay–patterned rugs and *kain songket* (Malaysian gold-embroidered fabric). There are two pools, with the concierge's desk between them.

Next to the lobby is the Palmetto Lounge, where guests may enjoy a panoramic view of the ocean while tea or cocktails are served. There are glass walls on all three sides and stained-glass chandeliers are above, in the shape and style of the Wau Bulan (the Malaysian Moon Kite). There are two grand staircases, flanked by waterfalls, which lead from the Palmetto Lounge to four dining areas at the garden level.

The Garden Terrace is a twenty-four-hour coffee shop serving all meals al fresco (outdoors) or in air-conditioned gazebos. The House of Four Seasons is a Chinese Restaurant, serving Oriental cuisine in a decor like that of a luxurious home, with Chinese artifacts, screens, and panels. Tsuru-No-Ya is the Japanese Restaurant, entered through a traditional Japanese garden. It has *teppan yaki* tables, tatami rooms, and a sushi bar.

La Farfalla is the elegant Italian grill room, with chandeliers of faceted crystal and silk panels hanging from rose-hued mirror ceilings. Next to it is the Puppetry, a secluded bar whose decor features shadow puppets depicted on etched and carved mirrors.

In the lower lobby is the Study Discotheque, run by Juliana's of London, with the decor of a built-in library.

A short walk across the hotel gardens and you get to the Catch. This promises to be the delightful fresh seafood dining room of the resort.

Something to see is the Mutiara Ballroom, which is designed to resemble a Malaysian palatial state room. It can accommodate up to five hundred people.

All guest rooms have an ocean view. Each room is spacious, about 560 square feet, including the balcony. There are native materials, including hardwood floors and wooden louvres, a wicker sofa and chair, and a ceiling fan (the rooms have individually controlled air conditioning). The bathrooms, with separate shower and toilet compartments, have double-wide vanity counters and oversized tubs. There is color TV with flight information, a direct-dial telephone, a well-stocked bar and refrigerator, a hair dryer, and a safe-deposit box.

The recreational facilities include two outdoor swimming pools, four tennis courts, four squash courts, a health club complete with gymnasium, sauna and steam baths, massage rooms, and a Jacuzzi. There's a roller-skating rink and volleyball, netball, and badminton courts. There are jogging tracks and a luxurious clubhouse.

In the hotel's arcade is to be a full range of shops for pleasure and necessity.

The hotel's Marina Club has its own yachting facilities and landing pier for visiting yachts.

RASA SAYANG HOTEL
Batu Feringgi Beach
P.O. Box 735
Penang 10790
Malaysia
Telephone: (04) 811811
Telex: MA 40065 RASTEL
Cable: RASAYANG PENANG
Fax: (04) 811984
Reservations:
    In Penang call (04) 811811
    In Los Angeles call (213) 551-1121
    Elsewhere in the USA call 1-800-457-5050
All major credit cards
General Manager: Rudolf Staudinger
Assist Sales Manager: Victor Koi
Shangri-La International
Rates (approx.):
    Standard room $52 single, $62 double
    Superior room $68 single, $80 double
    1-bedroom suite $230
    2-bedroom suite $370
    4-bedroom suite $800
320 rooms, 13 suites
Service charge 10%; tax 5%

The Rasa Sayany Hotel is situated on the beautiful and unspoilt Batu Feringgi Beach. Spread over twelve acres, this lovely Shangri-La-run hotel is on land that rises into a plush green hill on one side; on the other, it slopes down gently, covered by neat lawns and tropical trees until it meets the beach. It is only forty-five minutes from the international airport, about twenty minutes to the city center, and thirty-five minutes to rail and sea terminals.

The rooms are pleasant and the suites are spacious. They are all air conditioned with individual control and have attached bathrooms. Each has a color TV with in-house video entertainment, piped-in music, direct-dial telephone, refrigerator, and mini-bar. The sea-facing rooms (superior) are built with private balconies, and the mountain view rooms (standard) are special in that they have hip-baths.

The thirteen suites are all elegant, but the best is the Tranquil Suite. It comes complete with a dining room, kitchenette, bar, lounge and four spacious bedrooms, each with an outstanding view of the ocean. Its two levels are joined by a spiral stairway. The other suites offer a choice of decor for which they are named—the Malay, Chinese, Indian, Thai and Japanese suites.

My favorites spots, partly because of their views, one of the garden and the other of the pool, are the Feringgi Grill and the Coffee Garden. The grill has a Western ambiance and the decor of a mock Tudor English pub, and it features French nouvelle cuisine. A mealtime there is the light jazz music of a resident band. Only dinner is served, starting at 7:00 P.M. The coffee shop is a twenty-four-hour inside-outside dining room, which is very pleasant and the most popular in the hotel. The hotel also has the Furusato Restaurant, which is said to be the best Japanese dining room on the island. It has all the expected Japanese specialties— sushi, tempura, *teppanyaki* and *yaki-tori*.

The bars are lovely spots. The Feringgi Bar is next to the grill and opens at 4 P.M. and closes at midnight. It's a popular spot before and after dinner next door. By the beach is Tepi Laut, a quaint thatched-roof bar, good for drinks and light snacks.

Cinta is the plush and sophisticated discotheque in the hotel run by Juliana's of London. Some call it the hottest night spot on Penang. Things go wild there in sound and light until early morning.

For the sports enthusiast, there are many choices. The hotel has a putting green, tennis, squash, table tennis and volleyball. There are two swimming pools and ocean sports include waterskiing, boating, sailing and fishing. The hotel's Health Club has facilities including massage, sauna, *o-furo* (a Japanese hot bath), and a mini gym. Hiking on the nearby hills or jogging along the beach are popular. For joggers or walkers, it is delightful to take the road skirting the coastline from the hotel to the fishing village, a distance of about five and a half miles to and fro, with views of the Straits of Malacca.

You can get an education here, too. There are courses and demonstrations in napkin folding, culinary and local handicrafts, and other subjects. An active place, the hotel offers a variety of competitions. There is a huge outdoor chess set as well as darts and amusement machines. The hotel has a modest shopping arcade.

The hotel has had successful conventions because of its ample facilities (for up to six hundred people). There is the Executive Centre, with full secretarial and telex services.

SHANGRI-LA INN
Magazine Road
P.O. Box 846
George Town
Penang 10300
Malaysia
Telephone: (04) 622 622
Telex: MA 40878
Fax: (04) 626526
Reservations:
  In Penang call (04) 622622
  In the USA call 1-800-457-5050
Most major credit cards
General Manager: Eric Lim
Sales Manager: Stephen Cheah
Shangri-La International
Rates (approx.):
  Standard room $46 single, $52 double
  Superior room $56 single, $62 double
  Suite $112–$504
442 rooms, 16 suites
Service charge 10%; tax 5%

This eighteen-story hotel is perfectly situated in the heart of the city at the Komtar Complex, which is in the prime commercial center of downtown George Town. Komtar is an exciting and very comprehensive development that combines civic, administrative and commercial functions. It contains all of the state and federal government offices as well as the big GAMA Supermarket Department store.

The hotel is the tallest building in town, and from the fifth floor up there are excellent views in every direction.

All of the rooms are luxurious in decor and have individual air conditioning, color TV with in-room movies, multi-music channels, refrigerators, mini-bars, international direct-dial telephone, and twenty-four-hour room service.

The restaurants include the Shang Palace, which serves Cantonese cuisine, and the Coffee Garden, which serves both local and Western cuisine. The Lobby Lounge and Bar serves cocktails and pre-dinner or after-dinner drinks to the accompaniment of live music. The Poolside Bar and Terrace serves cooling drinks as well.

There's a swimming pool and a fully equipped Health Centre. For those who wish to play golf, there is an eighteen-hole championship course at Bukit Jambul Country Club that can be played by hotel guests for a special green fee. Tennis and squash can be arranged, too.

The hotel provides a shuttle service to take guests to beautiful Batu Feringgi Beach, where they may enjoy the facilities of the three Shangri-La International resorts at the beach—the Rasa Sayang, Golden Sands, and Palm Beach hotels.

The hotel is well used for business meetings, conventions, private receptions, and banquets. The main ballroom can accommodate up to nine hundred, and there are seven smaller function rooms with a full range of audio-visual equipment. There is also the well-equipped Professional Business Centre.

The hotel has a second-floor discotheque featuring music by Juliana's of London.

The hotel is within easy walking distance of all major banks, insurance companies, business houses, and department stores, and right next door to federal and state government offices. Be sure to get your free copy of the hotel's booklet entitled *Within Walking Distance.* . . . Not only does it describe everything within walking distance of the hotel, it has a very helpful three-dimensional-style map of Penang.

Sarawak

Formerly a British colony, Sarawak is now one of the Malaysian states. It is on the northwestern coast of Borneo.

In 1838, Sir James Brooke, a retired British army officer, landed in Borneo and helped the reigning sultan suppress unruly rebel tribes. As a reward, he was made the first rajah of Sarawak. Brooke was the first white man in history to become a rajah. His descendants retained control of Sarawak until 1946, when it was ceded to the British.

Kuching is the capital city and a river port eighteen miles from the sea. Founded in 1839, it now has a population of about 75,000. On its waterfront are markets heaped with fish and tropical fruits. Sarawak is a big producer of pepper, and the tramp steamers can be seen being loaded with this spicy cargo. The small shops all have signs in Chinese. The Palace (Astana) was built by Sir Charles Brooke, the second rajah.

This small town has many Hindu temples, Muslim mosques, and a truly picturesque bazaar. Its famous museum has an excellent collection describing the lives, history, and arts of the people of Sarawak. The Dayaks, for example, inhabit "long houses," with the entire village living under the same palm-leaf roof.

The most exciting time to be in Sarawak is June 1, the Dayak Festival Day. A cockerel is killed and offered to the gods. There are war dances, cockfights, and blow-pipe competitions and demonstrations.

DAMAI BEACH RESORT
P.O. Box 2870
93756 Kuching
Sarawak
Malaysia
Telephone: (082) 411777
Telex: DAMAI MA 70081
Fax: (082) 428911
Reservations:
   In Sarawak call (082) 411777
   In the USA call 1-800-HOLIDAY
All major credit cards
General Manager: Peter Mueller
Resident Manager: Shamshir Salleh Askor
Sales Manager: Diana Tong
Holiday Inn Asia-Pacific
Rates (approx.):
   Superior room $48
   Deluxe room $57
   Superior room with meals $79 single, $96 double
   Deluxe room with meals $87 single, $104 double
   Suite $153–$283
202 rooms, 13 suites
Service charge 10%; tax 5%

This resort run by Holiday Inn is situated at Teluk Bandung Beach, at the foothills of Mount Santubong, and it overlooks the South China Sea. It is a bit more than twelve miles from the town of Kuching.

It is only twenty minutes by coach from the airport to a jetty, and from there it is an interesting thirty-minute ride by ferry down the Sarawak River to the hotel's landing dock.

An attractive tropical resort, Damai Beach has chalets, studios, and guest rooms spread over ninety acres of land, flanked by an undulating tropical rain forest. The rooms are varied in design and are on a hillside leading down to the pool and the beach. All rooms have private baths, showers, and hair dryers. They are fully air conditioned and have direct-dial phones and color TV with in-house video.

Among the activities enjoyed by guests are jungle trekking, fishing, water-skiing, windsurfing, and sailing. There are two all-weather tennis courts and two squash courts, and under construction is an eighteen-hole golf course. The big swimming pool has a sunken bar and a Jacuzzi.

Many of the nearby tropical rain forests are national parks. Found in them are abundant varieties of birds, butterflies, flowers, and wildlife.

The Mango Tree Terrace is adjacent to the swimming pool and serves a variety of local and international dishes. Cafe Satang, the main air-conditioned restaurant, is open for breakfast, lunch, and dinner and features Malay, Chinese, and Western cuisines with the accent on seafood.

HOLIDAY INN KUCHING
Jalan Tunku Abdul Rahman
P.O. Box 2362
93100 Kuching
Sarawak
Malaysia
Telephone: (082) 423111
Telex: MA 70086
Cable: HOLIDAYINN
Fax: (082) 426169
Reservations:
    In Kuching call (082) 423111, ext. 1115,
    or (082) 250277
    In the USA call 1-800-HOLIDAY
All major credit cards
General Manager: Peter E. Mueller
Sales Manager: Diana Tong
Rates (approx.):
    Standard room $56 single, $65 double
    Deluxe room $65 single, $73 double
    Superior room $65 single, $73 double

King Leisure room $73 single, $83 double
Suite $142–$417
303 rooms, 17 suites
Service charge 10%; tax 5%

Sarawak's first and only international-class hotel was enlarged in August of 1985. The hotel is well situated, in the center of the city on the banks of the picturesque Sarawak River. And it is only about fifteen minutes from the airport.

Most the hotel's rooms have panoramic views of the river, and all are equipped with the latest amenities, including direct-dial phones. There are individually controlled air conditioning, color TV, radio, and deluxe private bathrooms. One of the hotel's floors is reserved for nonsmokers, another for women.

The Meisan Sichuan Restaurant, with a unique two-level octagonal architecture, serves spicy Chinese specialties. The Orchid Garden coffee shop is always open for meals or snacks. The Serapi restaurant specializes in continental and Western cuisine and is considered one of the best dining rooms of its kind in town.

A delightful spot is the Rajang Bar, which has a view of the Sarawak River. The Poolside Pavilion is a traditionally styled lounge next to the open-air swimming pool. For the night crowd there's the colorful and exciting Aquarius Discotheque.

The hotel has a business center for executives, with secretarial services, office equipment, and a reference library as well as full communication services. There is a health center with a Finnish sauna, and a floodlit tennis court.

The hotel also has a beautiful ballroom, called Dewan Asajaya, which can seat up to four hundred fifty for dinners and eight hundred theater-style. There are smaller function rooms as well.

Be sure to get your copy of the hotel's own *Jogger's Map*. There are four different routes mapped out around the city, ranging from twelve minutes to a half hour. It serves as an excellent walking map for sightseers as well. You'll note that within easy walking distance is the town's main bazaar, a few of the outstanding temples, and the Sarawak Museum.

NEPAL

For many years Nepal was best known because it has the world's highest peak, Sagarmatha, better known as Mount Everest. Although Everest still captures the imagination of mountain climber and tourist alike, there are many other attractions in this ancient land.

The beautiful Kathmandu Valley, surrounded by green hills and towering mountains, with the majestic Himalayas against its northeastern background, forms the heart of the kingdom of Nepal. The valley is home to three cities of great historic interest—Kathmandu, Patan and Bhaktapur. All have ancient monuments, relics and architecture.

Nepal is a kingdom with over 13 million inhabitants occupying about fifty-four thousand square miles in Central Asia. It is bordered on the north by the People's Republic of China (the Tibet region) and on the other three sides by India. The chief ethnic group, the Newars, were probably the original inhabitants of the Kathmandu Valley. The population overall today represents a long intermingling of Mongolians, who mostly came from Tibet, and Indo-Aryans, who came from the Ganges plain in the south.

The majority of the people are farmers, and two-thirds of the nation's income is from their work. Rice is the main crop. Other foods raised include wheat, barley, pulses, and oilseeds. Cash crops include jute, tobacco, opium, indigo, and cotton. The forests provide sal wood and commercially valuable bamboo and rattan. Livestock raising is second to crop farming in the economy.

Transportation and communications difficulties have hindered the growth of industry and trade. Tourism is the chief source of foreign income, along with subsidies from the Indian government and the pensions the native Gurkhas get from their service in the British Indian Army.

Kathmandu

This city, with a population of well over a hundred thousand, is the capital of Nepal and is in the central part of the nation at about forty-five hundred feet above sea level. It is on an ancient trade and pilgrim route from India to Tibet, China, and Mongolia. Kathmandu became independent in the fifteenth century and was captured in 1768 by the Gurkhas, who made it their capital. The late eighteenth century brought the British, and it was made a British resident seat.

It was once called Kantipur. The present name is derived from Kasthammandap, an imposing pagoda near Durbar Square.

Most capital cities, even those that are ancient, have new sections as well as old quarters. Not this city. Kathmandu and the entire valley remain much as they have been for centuries.

There is much to see. There are about a dozen Rana palaces, which have the only Western-style architecture in Nepal. Each is an immense white-walled building, designed in the elaborate style of the French royal palace at Versailles. Most are now adapted into office and business buildings. The largest has fifteen hundred rooms and was once used by the prime minister. It is now the government's secretariat.

Durbar Square is noted for its Taleju Bhavani temple, whose gateway is guarded by a huge figure of Hanuman, the monkey god. On the other side of the square is the temple of Kumari Devi, one of the strangest sights in the country. The temple is occupied by a young woman who is worshipped as a living goddess. The girl is selected at the age of nine or ten and replaced when she enters adolescence. The selected goddess may often be seen on her balcony, but photographs are not permitted. It is a beautiful temple, with profusely carved wooden balconies and lat-ticed windows.

Other sights include the temple of Kastha Mandap, which is said to have been built from the timber of a single tree. Another place to see is Hanuman Dhoka, the traditional seat of royalty, with its multiroofed temples and palaces all intricately carved.

EVEREST SHERATON HOTEL
P.O. Box 659
New Baneswork
Kathmandu
Nepal
Telephone: 220567, 220614, 220288, or 220389
Telex: 2260 HOTEVS NP
2546 SHERAT NP
Cable: MALARI
Reservations:
  In Kathmandu call 220567
  In the USA call Sheraton at 1-800-325-3535
All major credit cards
General Manager: Albert Lo
Sales Manager: Samanta J. Tuladhar
Sheraton Hotels
Rates (approx.):
  Room $80–$100 single, $88–$128 double
  Junior suite $130
157 rooms, 6 suites
No service charge; tax 15%

The Everest Sheraton is near the Tribhuvan International Airport of Nepal and minutes away from the center of the city of Kathmandu. And, most exciting, it was constructed so that guests would have a 180-degree view of the Hi-malayas.

The rooms are all nicely furnished, and the theme suites reflect the culture of the country. In fact, lovely touches of Nepaliana are everywhere.

Most delightful is the selection one has from among the nine restaurants and bars. The Downtown dining room claims to have the "best of the West" in its food and decor. Among its proud examples of American cuisine are steaks and hamburgers, New Orleans specialties and Mexican se-lections.

My favorite spots are on the seventh floor, where you have panoramic views of the Himalayas and of Kathmamdu City while you drink and dine. One spot is the Far Pavilion, which has an *Arabian Nights* decor and features Mughal, Tandoori, and Dumphuk cuisines. Also on the seventh floor is Bugles and Tigers, a bar lounge with the decor of a Gurkha officers' mess. In honor of the ultra-brave Gurkhas there are some pretty potent concoctions served. If you have courage you might ask for a "Victoria Cross" or an "Act of Valour."

For authenticity in Tibetan, Manchurian, or Chinese food—served in elegant surroundings—eat at Sherpaland on the seventh floor. Here you may want to order "The Manchurian Steamboat" or the "Sherpa Sama."

Great for the views is Ropes, a terrace restaurant and bar that has truly fabulous views and barbecues. This establishment is written about in some guides to great international bars.

The Early Bird is the best spot to watch the sunrise, if you are an early riser. You look over 180 degrees of the Himalayas, while you have breakfast of fresh hot breads and preserves, and coffee, tea, or juice. You can even get the early-morning news here.

At pool side you can get, in addition to beautiful tans, hearty snacks and generous drinks. The Himalayan Tavern has an interesting array of drinks. Among them are Mad Carew, Kathmandu Sunset, and the Hillary Conquest. The popular Happy Hour is from 6:00 P.M. to 7:00 P.M. For house guests and members only is Pumpkins, "the only five-star discotheque in town." Reputations is the name of the coffee lounge with surprising snacks.

The hotel facilities include tennis, a swimming pool, a beauty parlor, a health club, conference halls, and banquet rooms.

The hotel has a courtesy coach that runs to and from the center of town every hour from 9:00 A.M. to noon and from 2:00 P.M. to 8:00 P.M. It is free.

Note: The rooms with the best views are on the fifth and sixth floors, facing back.

HOTEL DE L'ANNAPURNA
Durbar Marg
P.O. Box 140
Kathmandu
Nepal

Telephone: 221711
Telex: NP 2205 AAPU
Cable: ANNAPURNA
Reservations:
   In Kathmandu call 221711
   In the USA call Utell International at 1-800-223-9868
   In New York call (212) 757-2981
All major credit cards except Diners
Managing Director: Sahadev Rana
Acting General Manager: U.S. Jamwal
Front Office Manager: Balaram K.C.
Rates (approx.):
   Standard room $70 single, $85 double
   Junior suite $135
   Deluxe suite $185
159 rooms, 4 suites
No service charge; tax 15%

The Annapurna has served its guests well since its opening as a modern hotel in 1965. The hotel of today is much enlarged.

It is modern indeed, with all of its rooms individually air-conditioned and with private modern bathrooms.

The dining rooms are attractive and varied. You may have Nepalese or continental cuisine in the Arch Room. Chinese cuisine is the feature of the Arniko specialty dining room. The Ghar-E-Kabab features Indian cuisine. The very popular Coffee Shop features a choice of international dishes.

There is twenty-four-hour room service at this hotel for meals and drinks, and drinks are served from the bar to those sitting around the pool—the largest hotel swimming pool in Nepal.

The hotel has its own bakery and pastry shop and same-day laundry and dry cleaning. There is a business center, a health club, sauna, tennis courts and a billiard room.

The hotel is located right in the center of the city of Kathmandu, so shopping and business areas are close to the hotel. There is also shopping in the hotel's arcade.

The hotel has, in addition to the Business Centre, ideal conference and seminar facilities served by the Business Centre staff.

The hotel is next to the Royal Palace, and it is a five-minute walk to the heart of the old town.

Pokhara

FISH TAIL LODGE
Pokhara Valley
Near Phewa Lake
P.O. Box 10
Pokhara
Nepal
Telephone: 20071 or 20072
Telex: NP 2205 AAPU
Cable: ANNAPURNA
Reservations:
  In Pokhara call 20071
  In the USA call Utell International at 1-800-223-9868
  In New York call (212) 757-2981
All major credit cards except Diners
Executive Director: Sahadev Rana
Manager: Tony D'Souza
Front Office Manager: Balaram K.C. at the Hotel De
  L'Annapurna
Rates (approx.):
  European plan $30 single, $43 double
  American plan $52 single, $87 double
  Modified American plan $44 single, $71 double
47 rooms, no suites
No service charge; tax 12%

This lovely lodge is situated on an island fifty feet off the shore of Lake Phewa, and is only five minutes from the airport. Guest are received and transported to the lodge on its own shuttle-float.

The hotel's lovely rooms, each with a private bath, and the lodge's central dining room and bar are all within four picturesque round structures that blend well with the beautiful landscape. *Every* window has a view of the mountains. The breathtaking views are something you do not get used to easily even after a few days.

The cuisine in the hotel dining room is varied, including continental, Nepali, and Indian specialties. Dancers perform while you dine.

It is easy to get to Pokhara on one of the daily flights of the Royal Nepal Airlines from Kathmandu. The flight takes thirty-five minutes, and the mountain views are magnificent. You can have a scenic ride in a coach or car from Kathmandu. It is a five-hour trip.

PAKISTAN

Although Pakistan was founded in 1947, its history can be traced to at least twenty-five hundred years before Christ, when a highly developed civilization flourished in the Indus Valley. Through the centuries a variety of civilizations came and contributed their cultures and peoples. Around 1500 B.C. the Aryans overwhelmed this region and influenced the Hindu civilization, whose center moved further east into the Ganges Valley. Later, around 500 B.C., the Persians occupied the northern regions.

The Greeks came in 327 B.C. under Alexander the Great. In 712 A.D. the Arabs, led by Mohammad Ben Qasim, landed somewhere near Karachi and ruled the lower half of Pakistan for two centuries. During this period Islam influenced the life, culture, and traditions of the people. The Muslims came in the tenth century A.D. and ruled almost the whole subcontinent up to the eighteenth century, when the British took over. They ruled for nearly two hundred years. From a struggle beginning in 1940, Pakistan emerged as a soverign state on August 14, 1947, when the British Indian Empire was partitioned into two independent states, India and Pakistan.

Pakistan is a republic, with almost 75 million people occupying more than three hundred ten thousand square miles in southern Asia. Islamabad is its capital. India is on the east, the Arabian Sea is on the south, Iran is on the southwest, and Afghanistan is on the west and north. The country is hot and dry, with desert conditions in most of the area. The Indus River is the lifeline of the nation.

There is a modest bed tax per person per night. In Karachi it is fifty rupees and in Lahore it is twenty.

Karachi

This city was once the federal capital of Pakistan and is still its largest city, chief seaport, and hub of commerce and industry. Early in the eighteenth century it was only a fishing village. Today its nearly four million people, mostly immigrants, have made it into one of the most prosperous cities of the East.

Its harbor on the Arabian Sea is one of the finest on the subcontinent, and the Karachi airport is the largest in Asia. The city itself is sprawling and flat. The spacious, carefully laid-out thoroughfares are bordered with narrow, crowded bazaars that operate in the shadows of modern commercial and government buildings.

The longest of these boulevards is Bunder Road, which is the biggest business and shopping district. Here camels mingle unconcernedly with the people who walk under them and cars that drive around them.

Karachi is not the greatest for sightseers, although there are some imposing buildings to be seen. The High Court and the National Assembly buildings are two of the city's finest modern structures. Frere Hall, one of the oldest buildings, is now the National Museum. The while marble mausoleum at the northern end of Bunder Road is that of Mohammed Al Jinnah, the principal founder of Pakistan. For visitors, it is striking to see the footpath dentists, hairdressers, fortune-tellers, and faith-healers all doing business next to modern buildings.

HOLIDAY INN KARACHI
P.O. Box 10444
9 Abdullah Haroon Road
Karachi
Pakistan
Telephone: 520111 or 522011
Telex: 25466 HIK PK or 28035 HIK PK
Cable: HOLIDAYINN

Reservations:
  In Karachi call 520111
  In the USA call 1-800-HOLIDAY
All major credit cards
General Manager: Winfried Loffler
Rooms Manager: Barkat Mitha
Marketing Manager: Tahir Masood
Holiday Inn Asia-Pacific
Rates (approx.):
  Standard room $80 single, $95 double
  Executive Club room $90 single, $105 double
  Suite $140–$335
219 rooms, 10 suites
No service charge; tax 7.5%

This full-service, international-class Holiday Inn is in the city center, right next to the United States Consulate. About a twenty-five-minute drive from the Karachi International Airport, it has a complete variety of services for business travelers and tourists. There is a swimming pool with a snack bar, and the Executive Club with facilities for meeting business guests; there are squash and tennis courts, a sauna and a fitness room. There is a business center with cable and telex facilities and Reuters Financial Services.

The hotel has the neat Holiday Inn–style rooms, and there is twenty-four-hour room service.

The restaurant and bar facilities are good. The hotel's gourmet dining room is the Sherezade Restaurant on the first floor, which serves lunch and dinner, buffets, and à la carte continental and Pakistani cuisine. It has a fine view of the pool.

Suzie Wong is the Chinese restaurant on the ground floor of the hotel, which is open for lunch and dinner. The Nadia Coffee Shop, also on the ground floor, is open twenty-four hours. There is a patisserie and a delicatessen.

Juliana's Reflections, on the ground floor, is the only discotheque in Karachi. It is open only on Thursday evenings.

The hotel has a liquor license, which permits it to serve non-Muslim guests drinks in their rooms.

All of the rooms have air conditioning, color TV, mini-bars, refrigerators and private baths. And all have a lovely view of the Frere Garden of Karachi.

KARACHI SHERATON HOTEL
Club Road
P.O. Box 3918
Karachi
Pakistan
Telephone: 521021
Telex: 25255 ASHER PK
Reservations:
   In Karachi call 521221 or 526289
   In the USA call 1-800-325-3535
All major credit cards
Resident Manager: Hafeez Malik
Front Office Manager: Sohail Pasha
Sales Director: Bilal Saeed
Sheraton Hotels
Rates (approx.):
   Standard room $75 single, $86 double
   Moghul Court room $98 single, $109 double
   Suite $126–$458
446 rooms, 60 suites
No service charge; tax 7.5%

When this hotel opened in July 1982, it was compared with the best luxury hotels around the world.

As you enter the lobby you see under the massive glittering chandelier the hotel's sunken twenty-four-hour coffee lounge, called Fanoos. The lobby and its ceiling and the lounge are spectacular.

There is a VIP floor, where the two- and four-bedroom suites are situated. They have panoramic views of the Karachi metropolis. All fourteen suites on this floor have spacious lounges and dining areas with separate pantries. The king-sized beds have overhead canopies, and handwoven carpets in the rooms blend with the Oriental decor of teak and brass. The large bathrooms are onyx-tiled with gold fittings.

The Royale Suite of the hotel is fascinating. It has eight rooms—a master bedroom, three other bedrooms, a study, a large drawing room and a dining area, an equipped kitchen, spacious bathrooms, walk-in closets, tinted-mirror paneling, intricate woodwork, big-screen color TVs, and much more.

On the seventh and eighth floors of the hotel are the ninety-five rooms of the Moghul Court. They have been created especially for the high-earning, expense-account executive. The Moghul Court lounge serves tea, coffee, juices, and fruits at no extra charge. There is a newspaper rack with all the important periodicals, and there is a twenty-four-hour butler service.

Facing the swimming pool at the mezzanine level are the fourteen private duplex suits of the Shalimar Court. These suites are occupied by long-staying guests throughout the year.

The Darbar is the hotel's banquet area. It can accommodate up to fifteen hundred people. It is the first in the nation to provide a simultaneous translation system. There are other meeting rooms as well.

Le Marquis is the gourmet dining room with elegant French decor, and piano music during dinner. The Lotus Court features authentic Chinese cusine. The Al Bustan serves Pakistani food specialties, and the Fanoos Lounge provides twenty-four-hour service with a wide variety of Arabic and continental dishes. The hotel's Maekada Lounge is the only place in Karachi serving expresso, capuccino, and other freshly brewed coffees.

The hotel has a well-equipped business center with telex, secretarial, and photocopying services. There is a shopping arcade.

The hotel's Health and Recreation Club is exceptional. It has the latest equipment and facilities, including an all-purpose gymnasium, Jaccuzi, saunas for men and women, steam room, massage, shower, chilled bath, Jogmaster, and aerobics. It has everything from ankle pulleys to an Ergo-meter (a heavy-duty bicycle exerciser with scientific instruments permitting physiological measurements at exercising intervals) and a Hydraulic Rowing Machine. There's an outdoor freshwater swimming pool, a play pool, and floodlit tennis.

The hotel is just fourteen miles from the airport and close to the commercial banking and residential areas of Karachi.

Lahore

Lahore, with over two million people, is the second largest city in Pakistan and is the capital of the province of Punjab, the picturesque "land of the five rivers."

Said to have been founded by Loh, the son of Rama Chandra, the legendary hero of Ramayana, it is recorded to have been a dependency of the great ruler Lalitaditya in the eighth century A.D. Between 1021 and 1023 A.D. this city was occupied by Mahmud Ghaznavi. Lahore, as we know it today, reached its peak during the reign of the Mughal rulers, particularly during the time of Akbar the Great. The Mughals gave the city some of its finest pieces of architecture (you can still see their masterpieces preserved in their original grandeur). Then began its decline.

Reigning from 1849 to 1947, the British brought life back to the city by harmoniously combining the Mughal, Gothic, and Victorian styles of architecture in a number of important buildings, such as the High Court, Government College, the Central Museum, National College of Arts, Montgomery Hall, the Tollinton Markets, the Punjab University (old campus), and the Provincial Assembly.

When Pakistan came into being in 1947 the city took on a new look, and many new buildings were constructed. These included modern shopping centers, the Fortress Stadium, the New Campus of Punjab University, the Al-falah Building, and many more, but the real elegance and beauty of Lahore lies in the buildings created during the days of the imperial Mughals.

Especially notable are the palace and mausoleum of emperor Jahangir and the Shalimar Gardens (probably you've heard of the perfume named for them), just outside of the city. Only three sections of the original seven sections of the gardens remain. They had symbolized the divisions of Islamic paradise.

Lahore's museum of Indian antiquities is among the most noted in the east.

Other sights to be sure to see are the Lahore Fort; Badshahi, the world's largest mosque; Wazir Khan's Mosque, built in 1634 A.D. with world-famous mosaic tile decorations; the tombs of Anarkali and Noor Jehan ("Light of the World"). Empress Noor Jehan, wife of the Afgan Prince of Bengal, was taken captive when her husband was killed and was wooed and won by Jehangir, becoming his empress in 1611.

The Mall is the main shopping place and has a plaque dedicated to Rudyard Kipling.

The city is a little over an hour by air from Karachi. It has a blossoming film industry. The city is at its best during the winter season, from October to March.

HILTON INTERNATIONAL LAHORE
87 Shahrah-e-Quaid-e-Azam
The Mall
Lahore
Pakistan
Telephone: 69971 or 310281
Telex: LH44678 HILTN PK
Cable: HILTELS LAHORE
Reservations:
  In Lahore call 62294
  In the USA call Hilton Reservation Service at
    1-800-445-8667
All major credit cards
Owner: B. Avari
General Manager: J. P. Mainardi
Bell Captain: Lehrasib
Sales Manager: Daud Mazhar
Hilton International Hotels
Rates (approx.):
  Room, January–March $70 single, $82 double
  Room, April–August $86 single, $97 double
  Room, September–December $93 single, $102 double
  Junior suite $175
  Executive suite $292
  Presidential Suite $380
190 rooms, 15 suites
No service charge; tax 7.5%

The Hilton International Lahore is in the heart of the city, within walking distance of the commercial and shopping areas and the Provincial Assembly. It is just opposite the Zoological Gardens, with the newly constructed Pakistan Arts Council on one side.

It occupies a five-and-a-half-acre garden site. Each of the hotel's rooms and suites have private balconies. They are different in that each room has an Oriental-style sitting alcove, mirrorwork details and native onyx in the bathrooms.

Every room has air conditioning with individual controls, a direct-dial telephone, a radio, color TV with in-house movies in English, taped music, a mini-bar and a refrigerator. There are rooms equipped for the handicapped. There are outstanding views of the main street and the Zoological Gardens from all three floors.

The rooms with the best views are 45 to 49, 51, 53, 55, 57, 58, 59, 61, and 63 on all three floors.

All of the things sightseers enjoy are within minutes of the hotel. Business guests have all needed facilities, including the fully equipped and staffed Executive Business Centre, situated in the main lobby. The business secretary on duty arranges for all kinds of services, sets appointments, and provides business information. The center is open from 9:00 A.M. to 6:00 P.M. on Saturday through Thursday. It is closed on Friday and on public holidays. For meetings, the hotel has facilities in rooms holding from fifteen to five hundred persons.

The Punjab Terrace Club—"for runners and walkers alike"—offers a variety of activities. A swimming pool on the SP floor is chilled in summer and heated in winter. It is a part of the health complex. There are also a steam bath and physical training equipment.

There are light refreshments and snacks or full meals at the Poolside restaurant, and on the same floor there are the barbershop and the beauty parlor. People use them while waiting their turn on the exercise machines or in the steam bath or massage parlor.

In addition to the Poolside restaurant, there is Kim's Coffee House for informal dining. For formal dining and gourmet meals there is the Fort Grill. Refreshments are served in the exotic Anarkail Bar and Lounge in an elegant sunken section of the hotel lobby. There are a few shops in the hotel, offering the basics.

PEARL-CONTINENTAL HOTEL LAHORE
Sharrah-e-Quad-e-Azam
P.O. Box 983
Lahore
Pakistan
Telephone: 69931
Telex: 44877 PEARL PK
Cable: PEARLCONT LAHORE
Reservations:
   In Lahore call 69931 or 67931
   In USA call Utell International at 1-800-223-9868
All major credit cards
General Manager: Bob J. DeLange
Concierge: Orgeus Cornelius
Sales and Marketing Manager: Zafar Iqbal Shour
Rates (approx.):
   Room $82–$94 single, $81–$103 double
   Suite $168–$252

200 rooms, 14 suites
No service charge; tax 7.5%

Lahore's Pearl-Continental is set close to the city's commercial center and the main government offices, and is only a fifteen-minute drive from the airport. It is set in a twelve-acre estate, with lush tropical gardens. In these gardens are two grass tennis courts, a large swimming pool, a hard tennis court with flood lights, a Pitch 'n Putt six-hole golf course, table tennis, exercise equipment, tetherball, and a super jogging track. And there are a children's playground and such games as Frisbee, darts, carom board, chess, cards, and Scrabble.

The hotel has an attractive lobby and dining rooms. They have all been recently spruced up, and a good job was done. For example, the newly renovated Brasserie dining room has the ambiance of an exotic polo lounge and is ideal for business lunches and family dinners. All meals are available here. The Coffee Shop provides snacks, light meals, and drinks twenty-four hours a day, and has great ice cream concoctions.

La Terrazza is the hotel's newly created à la carte barbecue restaurant. Here you can get a charcoal-grilled Pakistani or continental dish served in the beautifully illuminated garden next to the pool. It is the relaxing place to dine.

The hotel has a number of banquet and events rooms, which can hold up to five hundred fifty. Larger groups opt for the beautiful gardens, where events can be catered for groups up to twenty-five hundred.

All of the guest rooms and suites have direct-dial telephones, color TV with in-house movies, radio, taped music channels, and mini-bars. Room service is available twenty-four hours.

There is a ground floor shopping arcade and telex and postal services available.

THE PHILIPPINES

The Republic of the Philippines is a nation of more than seven thousand islands separating the Pacific Ocean from the South China Sea. Covering 1,147 miles north to south and 598 miles east to west, there are three main island groups. Luzon, to the north, is the biggest island. The Visayas, in the center, have the most islands. Mindanao and the Sulu chain comprise the southern group.

It was in 1521 that Ferdinand Magellan is said to have discovered Samar, a central island. Forty-four years later the Spaniard Miguel Legaspi landed at Cebu. Proclaiming sovereignty over the entire archipelago, he named it after his patron, King Philip II of Spain. Introducing the Catholic religion helped put the Spanish imprint on the people. Throughout the period, armed conflict and resistance to colonialism troubled the islands.

At the turn of the century, the U.S. Navy defeated the Spanish fleet inside Manila Bay, and soon a revolutionary Philippine Republic was born. It was short-lived. By 1902, the United States was in control. In 1946, after more conflicts, the nation became independent and the republic was born.

Filipinos are basically of Malay stock with some Chinese and Spanish ancestry. There are over a hundred linguistic, cultural, and ethnic groups in the country. Today's population is about 54 million, and about 10 million live in metropolitan Manila.

The country's national language is Filipino, which is based on the Tagalog dialect. English is widely spoken. It is the basic tool of instruction in schools and is used in business, industry, and government. This makes the Philippines the largest English-speaking country in Asia and the third largest in the world.

The Philippines has a tropical climate, with relatively high humidity, mild temperatures, abundant rainfall, and gentle winds. The wet season is from June to October, and the cool dry season is from November to February. The hot dry season follows in March though May, when both temperature and humidity reach maximum levels.

Manufacturing is concentrated in metropolitan Manila, near the nation's prime port, but there is considerable industry on Cebu, Negros, and Mindanao. Important products are processed foods, chemicals, cement, textiles, metalware, tobacco products, wood and cork products, beverages, wearing apparel, and electrical machinery. The major exports are foods, lumber, and minerals. The major imports are machinery, transportation equipment, fuels and lubricants, and base metals.

Baguio

Baguio is the summer capital of the Philippines because of its cooler climate in the summer months. A one-hour flight from Manila, the town is set high on pine-covered hills. The city has many government buildings, and it is noted for the wood carvings of its Igorot aborigines. It is also a mountain resort within beautiful pine forests, and is the center of major gold and copper mining areas.

It was originally settled by the Spanish and was developed soon after American occupation. By 1913 roads were built to connect the town with main highways.

Below Baguio is the fishing village of San Fernando, which is built on stilts right out over the water. The beach is lined with papaya and stately palm trees. From this South Seas–style village it is a long yet easy climb by car to Baguio, which is about five thousand feet above sea level.

Visitors enjoy taking day trips to see the attractions in the area. Particularly interesting are the amazing Banaue

Rice Terraces, sometimes called the "eighth wonder of the world." These terraces were carved out of the mountainside thousands of years ago by the members of the Ifugao tribes without the aid of metal tools. If put end to end these terraces would reach halfway around the world. You will see Ifugao tribesmen here, clad only in loincloths and carrying spears.

In Baguio itself, one of the more popular attractions is the colorful market. Among the items on display and for sale are straw hats, rattan objects, silver filigree, carved masks, wooden bowls, fine embroidery, and soft *piña* cloth, which is woven by hand from the fiber of the pineapple plant.

HYATT TERRACES BAGUIO
26 South Drive
Baguio City 0201
Philippines
Telephone: (422) 5670/80
Telex: 27202 HYATT PH
Reservations:
   In Manila call 817-2847 or 817-3046
   In the USA call Hyatt International at 1-800-228-9000
All major credit cards
General Manager: Heinrich L. Maulbecker
Concierge: Monina Selga
Sales Manager: Liza M. Tatco
Hyatt International
Rates (approx.):
   Deluxe room $39 single, $42 double
   Corner suite $51
   Regency Club room $49 single, $52 double
   Regency Club suite $61
   Executive suite $90
   Penthouse Suite $216
293 rooms, 52 suites
No service charge; tax 13.5%

This attractive Hyatt hotel is an architectural showcase in the midst of the city, on a beautiful landscaped property atop the dramatic Cordillera Mountains. It is just over forty-five minutes by plane, but five hours by bus, from Manila. The hotel is in the plush residential area of the city and an easy ride to the Baguio Convention Center and downtown shopping, or to the Loakan Airport.

Yes, it does have an atrium lobby, as do many other Hyatts. Here, every kind of activity seems to start at the Atrium Plaza, where early risers greet each other at the Kaili Cafe-Restaurant. At twilight guests are found together at the Fireplace Bar drinking and listening to soft music. Afterwards, the choice for dinner is the Hanazono Restaurant, for Japanese cuisine, or the Copper Grill, for a candle-lit gourmet dinner in a truly elegant setting.

You don't have to leave the hotel to have an exciting evening. You can choose the vibrant life at the Gold Mine Discotheque, or you can try your luck at blackjack, roulette, Big and Small, or baccarat at the hotel's casino.

There is much to do during the day as well. Baguio offers two of the finest golf courses in the country, tennis, horse-back riding, boating, and hiking. There are an indoor swimming pool and sauna, and a game room with a choice of chess, balut, backgammon, or cards.

Guests enjoy the hotel's arranged sightseeing trip to the Easter Weaving School, the City Market, the Philippine Military Academy, the People's Park, Burnham Park, Mines View Park, the Lourdes Grotto, and the Crystal Cave. Be sure to ask for the Hyatt Terraces Baguio map folder, which not only has an easy-to-follow illustrated map of the city but has details about the town, the restaurants, shopping, and other attractions as well. It is free.

The hotel's rooms are very attractively furnished and have balconies with panoramic views. The suites are truly elegant, some with fireplaces, as befits a mountain resort. The Regency Club is on the sixth floor of the hotel, offering more luxurious accommodations and services for about ten dollars more per room. The rooms are spacious and have color TV, direct-dial telephones, private baths, and potable hot and cold tap water.

For groups, the hotel arranges great theme parties. The most famous of these and the most exciting is the fake ambush for a group of guests put on by the nearby "head-hunters." When they "attack" the bus and the Igorot natives in loincloths surround it, not all guests are sure it is just a show. They are soon convinced, however, when the natives take their "captives" to a clearing at the forest edge, with the Bakekang Falls as a backdrop, and present them with a sumptuous feast of prawns, chicken, pork barbecue, and assorted vegetable and fruits. Of course, by the time the evening is over the guests realize that the "native head-hunters" who "captured" them were members of the hotel staff.

Batangas

PUNTA BALUARTE INTER-CONTINENTAL
Catalagan
Batangas
Philippines
Telephone: 63 (2) 8159711 or 893653
Telex: RCA 23314 ICH PH
Cable: INHOTELCOR
Reservations:
  In Batangas call 893653
  In the USA call Inter-Continental Hotels at
    1-800-33-AGAIN
All major credit cards
General Manager: H. Schnuppe
Inter-Continental Hotels
Rates (approx.):
  Standard room $50 single, $59 double
  Superior room $60 single, $69 double
  Suite $105–$135
165 rooms and suites
Service charge 10%; tax 13.5%

The Punta Baluarte Inter-Continental resort is at Calatagan, near Batangas, the capital of Batangas Province in southwest Luzon. The town is an important port on Batangas Bay; it has a large oil refinery; and it is the center for the surrounding fertile farm area noted for its fruits, cacao, and coffee.

Punta Baluarte is about two and a half hours travel time from Manila, in the lush, green rural area of Batangas. Nearby, from the Tagaytay Ridge, you may have a breathtaking view of the famous Taal Volcano. Once an ancient stronghold, Punta Baluarte sits snugly at the spot where the Pacific Ocean and the China Sea join. Exotic frangipani trees line the road, which takes you to the bougainvillaea-packed grounds of the Punta Baluarte Inter-Continental.

Once there, you have the choice of living in a *nipa* bungalow, a *bicol* house, a studio, or a cabaña—all nestled on hillsides, linked by winding stone pathways sloping toward the sea. The decor is native rattan, reflecting the Filipino ambiance.

My favorite spot is the magnificent Calatagan Golf Club, an eighteen-hole championship golf course designed by Robert Trent Jones. Fun, too, is horseback riding along trails teeming with wildlife. Guests may explore the tropical marine life by deep-sea diving, or fishing from the hotel's motor banca. There's a speedboat for water-skiers, a twenty-five-foot Balboa for experienced sailors, and windsurfboards or native motor bancas.

It is a pleasure to walk down a trail to the tropical free-form swimming pool and its lounge. Next to the Pagapas Coffee Shop is a saltwater pool as well. If you're an early riser, you'll want to watch the sunrise while you breakfast at the Pagapas Coffee Shop and enjoy the fresh island fruits, *tapa* (dried beef), and *kapeng barako* (Batangas brewed coffee).

You can watch or even take part in a variety of activities, like darts, billiards, table tennis, pelota, badminton, tennis, or even polo or cockfighting.

There are several choices for dining. One is the Mulawin Clubhouse Restaurant, which features exotic dishes and international cuisine. *My favorite* and most memorable way to eat here is having a moonlit dinner by the sea at the Beach Barbecue. Here you can listen to the whispers of the swaying palms and the sounds of love songs accompanied by guitar music while you enjoy the native *inihaw* (grilled seafoods).

The drinks are creative. Try the Punta Baluarte Dynamite or a spicy Bloody Mary at the Pagapas or Mulawin Bar.

Each of the hotel rooms has a refrigerator well-stocked with soft drinks and beer. There is a small selection of liquor in the room for a nightcap.

The hotel has other facilities, such as rooms and outdoor places for meetings or banquets or conferences. There is laundry and valet service and there is a barrio store selling native handicrafts.

Cavite

Cavite is a city of about eighty thousand situated on a small peninsula in Manila Bay. It has been important as a naval base and trade center since the days of the Spanish.

In the Spanish-American War it was captured by Admiral George Dewey on May 1, 1898. The United States established a major naval base at Sangeley Point just opposite the city proper. At the outset of World War II this base was bombed by the Japanese and virtually destroyed.

Cavite is about thirty-six miles southwest of Manila, facing the South China Sea, and about a ninety-minute drive from the city on the newly opened coastal road from Roxas Boulevard.

PUERTO AZUL BEACH HOTEL
Ternate
Cavite
Philippines
P.O. Box 7773-M
Airmail Distribution Center
MIA, Pasay City
Metro Manila
Philippines 3117
Telephone: 574731/40
Telex: 64546 AZUTEL PN
Cable: TERNATEL
Reservations:
  In Cavite call 574731/40
  In Manila call 571373 or 571377
Most major credit cards
General Manager: Rigo Hartmann
Sales Managers: Teresa A. Regino and Brenne Frias
Sulo Group of Hotels and Restaurants
Rates (approx.):
  Standard room $52 single, $57 double
  Moderate room $57 single, $62 double
  Superior room $65 single, $70 double
  1-bedroom executive suite $130
  2-bedroom executive suite $180
  Presidential Suite $190
340 rooms and suites
Service charge 10%; tax 13.5%

Puerto Azul is one of Asia's more spectacular complexes. It is a complete resort established on 8,148 acres of lush hills and forests, hugging a beach coastline and overlooking the magnificence of Corregidor and the South China Sea.

The hotel is only part of the resort. In addition there is the separately owned Puerto Azul Beach and Country Club, which you may explore as a guest of the hotel. In fact you should, for it has a stunning shell-shaped clubhouse and a truly magnificent large free-form swimming pool by the sea, with forty rooms in thatched cottages on the beach. It has a spectacular eighteen-hole Gary Player golf course and a nine-hole par three links on Camandag Beach. And there's much more.

Another part of this resort estate is Mira Hills. You may end up buying a home and living here! You have two options—the Mira Hills Subdivision or the Ocean Villa Condominiums. When I was there the condo villas were all sold, but plans were announced for another group to be built soon. They are well designed and comfortable and have magnificent views.

The hotel is something special, too. Its 340 rooms and suites are in seventeen buildings clustered around the hotel's administration building, and all have panoramic views of the golf course, the beach, the mountains, and the sea through wide picture windows or from private lanais. The rooms have a resort ambiance created through the use of wicker, shells, and cheerful fabrics.

My favorite pastime was riding the jeepneys, which continuously travel from the residential buildings to the various places on the estate. Jeepneys are the colorfully adorned minibuses that crowd the streets of Manila and are packed to overflowing with passengers traveling around the city. There is no more colorful public transportation vehicle in the world. At Puerto Azul, they are just as colorful but never crowded. They have an interesting history. They started after World War II when the U.S. Army sold its used jeeps to civilians who made eccentrically decorated public buses out of them.

The grounds are the joy of the place. The surrounding woodlands are ideal for hiking, nature walks, biking, bird watching, horseback riding, and picture taking. There are seven coves offering all kinds of water sports. Guests are issued cards enabling them to use the wonderful facilities of the Puerto Azul Beach and Country Club. The hotel is popular with business people as well as golfers and beach lovers. It has spacious ballrooms and function rooms used for conferences and conventions.

My favorite spot is La Parilla, situated on a terrace overlooking the mountains, the hills, and the golf course. It is ideal for al fresco dining, and it features barbecued and grilled specialties. On Saturdays, guests enjoy a performance of Filipino songs and dances. La Parilla is open from 6:30 A.M. until 10:00 P.M.

The Ninofranco Restaurant is the formal dining room, open from Tuesday through Sunday to serve continental and seafood specialties.

The Mardicas Bar is an attractive cocktail lounge by day and a discotheque at night. It is open at 10:00 A.M. and sometimes closes at midnight or later—depending on the mood of the guests.

While you are here, I suggest that you ride in an outrigger across the bay to the fortress island of Corregidor. If you recall what happened there during World War II, you'll find it interesting.

Davao City

Located in southeast Mindanao, at the mouth of the Davao River on the Davao Gulf, Davao City is the chief commercial center and port of Mindanao. The city serves a prosperous region that produces hemp, coffee, cacao, and timber.

During World War II the city and the port were seized by the Japanese, who used it as a base of operations against the Dutch East Indies. In 1945, after most of the Philippines had been liberated, Japanese forces clung stubbornly to the city and its recovery required heavy fighting.

Davao has a land area of 748 square miles, making it one of the largest cities in the world. About an hour and a half from Manila by jet, this booming business city has vast and colorful lands where Christian settlers and Muslim sultanates coexist in harmony.

You've probably enjoyed fruit from this area. It is the home to multinational fruit farms that export luscious bananas, pineapples, and other tropical fruits that eventually bear such names as Chiquita, Del Monte, and Dole.

The city has remained rural and rustic. A tour of it from the hotel will take you to a weaving center operated by Mandaya tribeswomen, to a Buddhist temple, or to a Mosque. You will visit an orchid farm and see the city fruit market loaded with exotic fruits you may have never seen before. Then you should take time to bargain for some of the native crafts.

DAVAO INSULAR INTER-CONTINENTAL INN
Lanang
P.O. Box 144
Davao City 9501
Philippines
Telephone: 76051/61

Telex: ITT 48209 DAVINS PM
Cable: DAVINS PM
Reservations:
   In Davao call 76051/61
   In the USA call Inter-Continental Hotels at
      1-800-33-AGAIN
All major credit cards
General Manager: John O'Carroll
Concierge: Romeo S. Montenegro
Sales Manager: Rosie C. Dayao
Inter-Continental Hotels
Rates (approx.):
   Minimum $39 single, $45 double
   Moderate $41 single, $48 double
   Superior $43 single, $50 double
   Suite $120
147 rooms, 6 suites
Service charge 10%; tax 13.7% room, 4.2% food, 8.7%
   drinks

The hotel is by the beach overlooking the Davao Gulf and
Samal Island. Only five to ten minutes from the airport, it
is set on very pretty grounds, with palm trees, beautiful
landscaping, and a large circular swimming pool.

The rooms are nicely furnished, roomy, and fully air-
conditioned. There are five restaurants and bars. Among
them is La Parilla Grill, which serves charbroiled steaks and
seafoods. The fancier Mandaya Restaurant features international cuisine.

In addition to swimming in the pool, there are tennis and
an array of watersports. The hotel has room service and
laundry and valet services as well.

Business guests will find excellent meeting facilities, including seven function rooms and a grand ballroom that
can hold up to 750 for conferences.

Hotel-run theme parties are very popular and include one
favorite called Fiesta Filipiniana, which is set among the
nipa huts. There is a Hawaiian luau with a roasted pig, and
a number of other fun events. The hotel offers a number
of sightseeing excursions through a local tour organization.
Among them is a tour of Davao; a full-day tour of three
nearby islands; a trip to see the world famous Philippine
Eagle, the second-largest bird on earth; a four-day trek to
the peak of the highest mountain in the Philippines, Mount
Apo; a banana plantation tour; and a visit to a cockfight.

(They love cockfights in this country. It is jokingly said that Filipino males take better care of their cocks than their wives!)

Manila

Manila is the capital and the metropolitan center of the Philippines. It is the chief port and the center of all governmental, cultural, industrial, and commercial activities. It is, as well, the center of manufacturing of the country, with large metal fabrication, automobile assembly, and textile and garment industries.

Once the proud city of Sulayman, Manila now has within its borders four key cities and thirteen towns and municipalities. It was already flourishing as a Malay settlement when the conquistadores decided to establish the capital of Spain's empire in the Pacific here. For the next three centuries it was the noble and loyal city from which the Spanish governor-general ruled.

Today Manila is one of the biggest and busiest cities in Asia, with more than 8 million residents, and its people hope it will become an increasingly important center for international trade.

The areas of Manila offers an intriguing blending of old and new. Established in 1571 and developed by Spanish missionaries, it was once a walled city with many churches. The grandeur remains, except that most of the walls and turrets are gone. On the Pasig River are the remains of the old city, and much has been done to restore some of its old walls and gates.

The city, which for a number of centuries was under the control of the Spanish (except from 1762 to 1764, when the British occupied it), is no stranger to violence. In 1898 it was seized by U.S. forces after the Battle of Manila Bay. In World War II the city was occupied by the Japanese. The battle in 1945 to recover it reduced the old walled city to rubble, destroying many fine seventeenth-century buildings; only the Church of Saint Agustin (1606) was spared. In 1968 an earthquake killed more than three hundred people and damaged many buildings, and in 1972 the city was damaged by flooding.

There is much for visitors to see and enjoy in this city. The wide boulevard on the curve of Manila Bay was once named for Admiral Dewey. It is now called Roxas Boulevard, and it is a grand boulevard indeed. It is fun to discover some of the city's streets with American names, such as Nebraska and Tennessee streets.

Near the mouth of the Bay is Corregidor, scene of a vicious battle between the Japanese and American forces. Bataan is on the peninsula opposite Corregidor, and people go there by boat for swimming and picnics.

Among the many sights to see in Manila are the Rizal Monument, Cuartel de Espana, Plaza Cervantes, the Supreme Court Building, Santo Tomas, Quezon Memorial, Santiago Ruins ("Shrine of Freedom"), remains of the old city, Intramuros, Rizal Avenue, and, of course, the grand Roxas Boulevard.

Most interesting is Makati, an area where a number of the fine modern international hotels are located. This is sort of a modern suburb of the city, with fine shops, restaurants, skyscrapers, and stunning residential areas (and even the stock exchanges). Makati also has the American Military Cemetery and Memorial, the National Museum on Herran Street, the Cultural Center of the Philippines, and the Luz Gallery.

Rizal Park, with its monument to the Philippine national hero, Dr. Jose Rizal, is a favorite spot for Manilan families on Sunday afternoons, and on almost any day it is a good spot to enjoy the famous sunset over Manila Bay.

CENTURY PARK SHERATON
Vito Cruz and M. Adriatico
Malate
P.O. Box 117
Manila
Philippines
Telephone: 506041 or 596041
Telex: 40489 SHERMLA PM
Cable: CENPARK MLA
Fax: (632) 521-3413
Reservations:
   In Manila call 506041
   In the USA call Sheraton Hotels at 1-800-325-3535
All major credit cards
General Manager: Peter H. Stevens
Sales and Marketing Manager: Leny Roco Fabul
Sheraton Hotels
Rates (approx.):
   Standard room $83 single, $89 double
   Superior room $88 single, $94 double

Deluxe room $93 single, $99 double
Suite $160–$700
500 rooms, 96 suites
Service charge 10%; tax 13.64%

This delightful Sheraton hotel is in the heart of Manila's business district, as well as in the cultural, entertainment, and shopping area. It is only fifteen minutes from the international airport and Makati. Furthermore, it is within easy walking distance of the Philippine International Convention Center and the Rizal Memorial Sports Complex.

The building is twenty stories high, and the rooms have balconies overlooking Manila. As in the high-quality Sheraton hotels, every room is well furnished and equipped. Each has color TV, refrigerator, mini-bar, telephone with bathroom extension, radio and taped music selections, tub shower, and individually-controlled air conditioning. The luxurious Park Tower suites have kitchens.

Very much the hotel for the guest in Manila on business or pleasure, it has facilities for all. For the business traveler, it has the Businessman's Center, which is open from 9:00 A.M. to 6:00 P.M. Monday through Saturday, with secretarial services, typewriters, and cablegram, telex, and facsimile facilities available from 7:00 A.M. to 11:00 P.M. There is a physical fitness center with separate men and women's gyms. Massage services are available there or in the guest rooms at any hour. There are also steam bath and sauna facilities. There is a half-acre swimming pool on the hotel grounds, and tennis and golf are nearby.

The hotel has five meeting and board rooms, a ballroom accommodating up to eight hundred for receptions, and ultramodern audio-visual equipment.

I have two *favorite spots* in this hotel, and one of them is the very pleasant lobby. It is a full acre in size and rises six stories to a glass roof. To best enjoy it, be seated in the Atrium Lounge. You can enjoy cocktails to the accompaniment of a string orchestra in late afternoon. In fact, you may enjoy coffee liqueurs or ice coupes any time between 11:00 A.M. and 10:00 P.M.

The other *favorite spot* of mine is the Top of the Century, the cocktail lounge on the nineteenth floor that has one of the best panoramic views of Manila. It's just right for music and martinis, Monday to Sunday 5:00 P.M. to 1:00 A.M. Come and enjoy the sunset.

The main dining room of the hotel is Sud, with an elegant south-of-France decor. Creative continental cuisine is featured here at lunch and dinner. On the upper lobby level is Aoi, the Japanese dining room, offering a choice of misono, tempura, and robata counters, or teppan and à la carte selection. There are private rooms in tatami decor. Lunch and dinner are served.

Another delightful spot is the Cafe in the Park, at the Atrium lobby, which offers from 6:00 A.M. until 2:30 A.M. a snack or a meal. There are à la carte menus for all meals as well as a daily breakfast and lunch buffets and occasional food festivals.

The Palm Grove is at the free-form swimming pool, and it supplies tall drinks and snacks from 10:00 A.M. until 6:00 P.M.

Adjacent to the lobby is the Kachina Lounge, which is the showcase for the top bands and singers of the Philippines. It is open from 8:00 P.M. until 2:00 A.M. For more night life, there is the Cellar Disco, where disc jockeys belt out the sound in a room filled with kaleidoscopic lights from 8:00 P.M. until 3:00 P.M.

The Harrison Plaza Commercial Center is just across from the hotel. It is the largest single-roof air-conditioned shopping complex in the Philippines. This two-story building has 137 specialty stores, including branches of the city's two largest fine-quality department stores, Rustan's and Shoemart. In it, too, are four cinemas and eight restaurants and snack bars. The Designer's Alley on the second floor shows fine apparel by the leading designers of the Philippines.

Be sure to ask for the delightful *Jogger's Guide* prepared by the hotel. It has an attractive pictorial map, very helpful not only for joggers but for anyone who wishes to explore the area within a few blocks of the hotel. When you see this map you realize how much there is to see and to do nearby.

HOLIDAY INN MANILA
P.O. Box 138
3001 Roxas Boulevard
Pasay City 3129
Metro Manila
Philippines
Telephone: 597961/80
Telex: 63487 HOLIDAY PN
Cable: HOLIDAYINN
Fax: 585211

Reservations:
  In Manila call 580131
  In the USA call 1-800-HOLIDAY
Most major credit cards
General Manager: Gerhard Kropp
Sales Manager: Romy Jakosalem
Holiday Inn Asia-Pacific
Rates (approx.):
  Moderate room $85 single, $90 double
  Superior room $100 single, $110 double
  Suite $150–$180
311 rooms, 24 suites
Service charge 10%; tax 13.7% room, 4.2% food, 8.7%
  drinks

On Roxas Boulevard, twenty minutes' drive from the Manila International Airport, this hotel lies directly across the street from the Philippine Convention Complex, and it has spectacular views of Manila Bay. To be sure to enjoy them from your room, ask for a room in the left wing of the hotel.

Fairly new and modern, the hotel has comfortable and nicely furnished rooms. It also has a good collection of places to dine and to drink.

The Baron's Table serves continental cuisine in an Old World ambiance, featuring an eight-piece string ensemble at dinner time. Next to it is the intimate Baron's Bar. The Cafe Vienna serves a variety of Filipino and European dishes throughout the day. The Delicatessen Corner is the spot for inexpensive, light snacks, and it sells homemade items to take out. The Paseo del Sol is the snack bar at the swimming pool and near the Health Club. The El Camarote Cocktail Lounge has live entertainment at night.

Cognizant of the business traveler's needs, the hotel has its Business Centre, and for conference or convention facilities it has the Ambassador's Sala and the Embassy Ballroom.

HOTEL INTER-CONTINENTAL MANILA
Ayala Avenue
Makati
Metro Manila
P.O. Box 731
Philippines
Telephone: (2) 8159711
Telex: RCA 23314 ICHPH

Cable: INHOTELCOR MANILA
Fax: 8171330
Reservations:
  In Manila call 8159711
  In the USA call Inter-Continental at 1-800-33-AGAIN
All major credit cards
General Manager: Eric A. P. Pruffer
Concierge: Francisco Maristela
Sales Manager: Marissa B. Aquino
Inter-Continental Hotels
Rates (approx.):
  Moderate room $96 single, $106 double
  Deluxe room $116 single, $126 double
  Suite $150–$1,000
400 rooms and suites
Service charge 10%; tax 13.7%

Even though the Hotel Inter-Continental Manila first opened its doors in 1969, it is called "the grand old lady of Makati," because it was the first of the international-class hotels to open in Manila's Makati district.

This fourteen-story hotel is only eight miles (or about ten minutes) from the Manila International Airport. It has, because of its location, attracted business visitors to Manila, and over the years it has developed an exceptional array of services and facilities that are required by this type of clientele.

For example, most impressive is the Manila IHC Guest Relations Department, with a staff of four. They attend to everything, including checking in every arrival and compiling guest history cards to make possible unique personalized service.

There is, too, a state-of-the-art Business Centre that provides secretarial services, offices for rent, translation, copying, computers, facsimile machines, telex and cable facilities, global courier service, and almost anything else a business executive might need.

The hotel has introduced digital telephones that permit international direct dialing. There is a non-smoking floor for the health-conscious traveler as well.

In March 1988 the hotel completed a major portion of its renovation program. Part of the project are new suites designed to please the upper levels of business and leisure travelers. The most outstanding among these will be the Presidential Suite, which is to have four rooms as well as a Jacuzzi, an authentic Finnish sauna with a massage table in the bath area, a dining room with a table for twelve, and a living room with a baby grand piano.

The hotel continues to have a 90 percent repeat guest occupancy. The hotel has instituted a VIP program for its regular guests that even includes a complimentary haircut and shave or hairstyling in the hotel's barber-beauty salon.

The dining choices are many, but the top choice is the Prince Albert Rotisserie, the really fancy dining room, offering continental cuisine as well as the speciality of the house, roast prime rib. Within the elegant restaurant is the Salon Carlos P. Romulo, named after the famous Philippine statesman. This private dining room was so named by the International *Chaine des Rostisseurs*, of which the late diplomat was an active member.

One of the most popular eating places in the hotel is the Jeepney Coffee Shop. It is one of the busiest spots in Manila every morning. It is home to the 365 Club, a regular group of opinion leaders from the newspaper, government, and business sectors of the city who discuss national issues over endless cups of coffee. It is said that this is where the press gathers the next day's news.

The overflow crowd of executives on the run who cannot fit into Jeepney's Coffee Shop will be found at La Terrasse having a more relaxed buffet breakfast and, later, lunch. This is where Manila's elite meet in the afternoon to plan fund-raising projects over tea and pastries.

My favorite spot is higher up, on the top floor of the hotel. It is the Bahia Restaurant, which attracts a sizeable crowd for the generous and sumptuous luncheon buffet (reserve your table). It is especially grand at dinner. A quartet serenades while the guests enjoy the panoramic view of Makati's skyline. Most popular are the seafood specialties, but the favorite is the Mongolian barbecue, which is cooked to the guest's specifications. It was first served here a few years ago, and now dining rooms all over Manila serve somewhat less successful imitations.

Open until two in the morning is the hotel's Le Boulevardier, the lounge featuring current hit bands. Manila's yuppies have made the place their own.

Some seek the seclusion of the Gambrinus Cocktail Lounge, which is a lovely spot for a lunch of choice roasts with salads and cold cuts.

The kids aren't forgotten here. On Sundays the rooftop dining room, Bahia, has a kiddie show put on by a fellow called Mr. Magic.

The active night crowd, too, has its spot. It is the Where Else discotheque. And sitting-around-the-pool people can make a day of it because of the Soly Sombra Pool Snack bar, serving casual meals and tropical thirst quenchers.

The hotel's rooms and suites are fully air-conditioned, and there are color TV, an in-house music channel, and mini-bars. There is twenty-four-hour room service. On the lobby level, there is a shopping arcade with boutiques, gift shops, beauty salons, and travel and car rental services.

HYATT REGENCY MANILA
P.O. Box 2462 Manila
2702 Roxas Boulevard
Pasay
Metro Manila
Philippines
Telephone: 8312611 or 8312621
Telex: 63344 ETPHYA PN
Cable: HYATT MANILA
Fax: (63) (2) 8187372 or (63) (2) 8179742
Reservations:
   In Manila call 8312611
   In the USA call Hyatt International at 1-800-228-9000
All major credit cards
General Manager: Perfecto F. Quicho
Sales: Rene Henson
Hyatt International
Rates (approx.):
   Standard room $64 single, $72 double
   Superior room $72 single, $80 double
   Deluxe room $80 single, $88 double
   Regency Club room $97 single, $107 double
   Suite $250
265 rooms, 31 suites
Service charge 10%; tax 13.7%

If you have visited this hotel, but not recently, you are in for a pleasant surprise. All of the rooms and suites have been renovated, and the elegance of the restaurants and the bars has been enriched.

The hotel is well situated, right on Roxas Boulevard with a view of Manila Bay, and only eight minutes by cab from the Manila International Airport and fifteen minutes from the Makati Commercial Center. It is ten minutes from the popular Ermita tourist area and near the Philippine International Convention Center and the Cultural Center of the Philippines.

One of *my favorite spots* in the hotel is the lobby. The magnificence of its unique gigantic crystal chandeliers is beautifully reflected on the highly polished marble of this spacious area. It is a grand room.

All of the hotel's rooms and suites have balconies, giving every guest an opportunity to enjoy the famous Filipino sunset over Manila Bay. All rooms are also fully air-conditioned, with thermostats, direct-dial phones with bathroom extensions, color TV, and iced potable tap water among the Hyatt-style amenities. There is a Regency Club floor, offering upgraded accommodations and services for a higher fee.

Another *favorite spot* is the Bistro, which is the café-restaurant on the mezzanine that overlooks the lobby. It is open from 7:00 A.M. until 11:00 P.M.

Hugo's, the dining room on the ground floor, is known for light continental cuisine and features charcoal-grilled steaks, fresh seafood, and tempting desserts. A string quartet provides semi-classical music. It is open for lunch and dinner on weekdays and for dinner only on Saturday. It is closed on Sunday.

A scenic Japanese bridge and garden lead to the Tempura-Misono, the picturesque room on the ground floor, that serves Japanese cuisine at lunch and dinner.

The two bars are the Calesa Bar on the ground floor, which serves cocktails as show bands and guest soloists entertain, and the Gallery, an intimate lounge adjacent to the lobby. Both are open from 10:00 A.M. until 2:00 A.M.

Alive with laser lights and the latest in sound is Isis, the hotel's popular disco at the penthouse level, with its own express elevator. It is open from 9:00 P.M. until 3:00 A.M.

The hotel's Business Center, on the ground floor, is open from 8:00 A.M. until 7:00 P.M. on weekdays and until 5:00 P.M. on Saturday; it is closed on Sunday. A lot more than a place for secretarial and communications and copying services, it has translation, interpretation, and temporary employment services, word processing, and computerized business information.

There are not many shops in the hotel, but those in it are excellent, including two with native handicrafts, an art gallery, and a sportswear shop. But, I must admit, *my favorite* is the Sugar Plum Patisserie with its collection of freshly-baked breads, pastries, and rich chocolates at reasonable prices. It is open from 8:00 A.M. until 9:00 P.M. on the ground floor. Also excellent is the Bistro, on the mezzanine; it has an ice cream corner with sixteen fabulous flavors and a selection of rich toppings.

THE MANDARIN ORIENTAL
Makati Avenue
Makati
Metro Manila
Philippines
Telephone: (2) 8163601
Telex: MANDA PN 63756
Cable: MANDAHOTEL
Fax: (2) 8172472
Reservations:
   In Manila call (2) 8163601
   In the USA call Leading Hotels of the World at (212)
      752-9710 (New York) or (213) 649-634 (Los Angeles),
      or call Utell International at (212) 245-7130
All major credit cards
General Manager: Nigel B. B. Roberts
Front Office Manager: Josephine Pacheco
Director of Sales and Marketing: Marita Marcos
Mandarin Oriental Hotel Group
Rates (approx.):
   Deluxe room $115 single, $130 double
   Executive room $150 single, $160 double
   Suite $220–$1,250
470 rooms, 20 suites
Service charge 10%; tax 13.7%

Typical of the Mandarin Oriental hotels in Asia, this is an elegant place. Situated as it is in the heart of Manila's commercial and business district, it is certainly one of the most beautiful and comfortable hotels in the city. My enjoyment began before I even arrived at the hotel, when my wife and I were picked up by the hotel's limo and whisked to the hotel in no time.

The first place you see is the dramatic and beautiful hotel lobby. This circular room has an exquisite blend of the elegant and the indigenous, finished with gray marble walls and lush green carpeting. The centerpiece and main object of art is a sculpture of three statues representing the three main islands of the Philippines, created by Filipino sculptor José Alcantara.

Seen from the outside, the hotel is an impressive white skyscraper surrounded by landscaped gardens with a free-form pool and swaying palm trees.

The rooms and suites are luxurious and comfortable. The decor is tasteful, and there are bedside TV-radio-light controls that are most convenient (and fun). The rooms and the suites are spacious, and the large marble bathrooms are a pleasure to use. There are mini-bars and international direct-dial telephones.

For those who enjoy the attention of a personal butler and the pleasure of a private pool and garden on the rooftop, the spot to stay is the Mandarin Suite. One of the world's best hotel suites, it is an ideal place for work and pleasure in an elegant Oriental environment. While we were there we saw a delightful Philippine fashion show presented in the suite's immense living room.

Even those staying at other hotels, and local residents as well, come to the hotel to enjoy its beautiful dining rooms. *My favorite* is the Brasserie at L'Hirondelle. The wood-paneled walls with magnificent blue and white tile inserts provide the elegant decor for French cuisine and fine wines. Also on the main floor is one of the prettiest hotel restaurants I've seen, the Tivoli. It has an impressive continental menu and it is the preferred venue for businessmen and entrepreneurs.

The Carousel Bar is a lively spot, with a band offering lively renditions of contemporary music. The Marquee is a cozy spot for light meals, selected Filipino specialties, snacks, and pastries. You'll find yourself in this lovely room more often than you might expect. The Clipper Lounge is popular, too. It is the spot for buffet lunches, for afternoon high tea, or for a drink before dinner. The live classical music is a pleasant and restful background for the day or evening. While relaxing you can people-watch into the lobby.

I was surprised by the amount of space given over to the Business Centre of the hotel. Open daily, it is a comprehensive office having every kind of service, equipment, and information a business person arriving in Manila could need.

Impressive, too, are the seven function halls of the hotel, serving every need from a conference to a banquet. The magnificent ballroom can hold up to a thousand people for cocktails.

The hotel has a beautiful, free-form pool, and the pool side is great for an al fresco breakfast, lunch, or a snack and refreshing cold drinks. The Health Club has fully equipped weight rooms, sauna, and professional massage services for men and women.

For tennis, squash, or golf, the hotel can arrange for guest memberships in Metro Manila's exclusive sports and country clubs.

An important note: The best views are from rooms on the tenth to eighteenth floors of the hotel's Wing C. Here you may have a view of the Makati skyline, which is especially beautiful at night, and in the distance the hills of Antipolo can be seen.

About a ten-minute walk from the hotel are major department stores, boutiques, shops, restaurants, theaters, and galleries. There is no shopping arcade in the hotel, but there is a boutique that has a wide range of locally made products, and a magazine stand.

MANILA HILTON INTERNATIONAL
P.O. Box 4430
United Nations Avenue
Ermita
Manila
Philippines
Telephone: 573711
Telex: ITT 40773 HILTON PM
RCA 27538 HLTN PM
Cable: HILTELS MANILA
Reservations:
  In Manila call 597415
  In the USA call 1-800-HILTONS
All major credit cards
General Manager: Wolfgang Schack
Sales Manager: Judy Lopez
Hilton International
Rates (approx.):
  Superior room $63 single, $72 double
  Deluxe room $72 single, $82 double
  Suite $114–$258
406 rooms, 17 suites
Service charge 10%; tax 13.7%

The Hilton is well located both for tourists and for business visitors to Manila. It is in the heart of the business, shopping, and entertainment district. Here you are only a three-minute walk from Manila Bay, right next to Luneta Park and the ancient walled city of Intramuros. Right across United Nations Avenue is the Ermita Shopping area, and nearby are the Manila Metropolitan Theater, the Jai-Alai Fronton, the National Museum, City Hall, government offices, and assorted historical spots. The hotel is about twenty minutes by taxi from the Manila International Airport.

A lively hotel, it has the Casino Filipino in the basement for card games, roulette, and slot machines. The casino is open from 1:00 P.M. until 4:00 A.M.

Off the lobby, open from 8:00 A.M. until 11:00 P.M., Mondays to Saturdays, is the Businessmen's Center, with every needed kind of business service, equipment, and information available.

The hotel also has rooms with facilities especially for the handicapped. An entire floor is reserved for non-smokers. Free transfer to the Makati Commercial Center can be arranged with the Guest Relations Officer.

The hotel has a swimming pool, and sauna and massage are available. Jogging is at the nearby Rizal Park, and tennis courts are available at the Rizal Memorial Stadium, five minutes away by taxi. On the fifth floor is the Poolside Terrace, in the garden next to the pool. Light refreshments and meals are served from 11:00 A.M. until 6:00 P.M.

The Rotisserie is an elegant lounge and grill room that serves U.S. beef and gourmet dishes at lunch on weekdays and dinner every night, on the third floor. Also on this floor is the Toh Yuen dining room, serving authentic Chinese meals prepared by cooks from Hong Kong. Lunch and dinner are served daily, and dim sum is offered every Sunday from 9:00 A.M. until 3:00 P.M.

Open from 6:00 A.M. until midnight on the ground floor is the popular Café Coquilla for meals and snacks. There are a lavish breakfast buffet from 6:00 until 10:00 A.M. Monday to Saturday and family brunch on Sunday.

On the ground floor, too, is the Lobby Bar, which has a lunch buffet on weekdays and cocktail lounge entertainment after dark. It is open from 11:00 A.M. until 1:00 A.M. The Hilton Patisserie is open from 7:00 A.M. until 7:00 P.M. and serves snacks and refreshments as well as selling fresh bread and pastries.

THE MANILA HOTEL
Rizal Park
P.O. Box 307
Manila
Philippines

Telephone: 470011
Cable: MANILHOTEL
Telex: ITT 40537 MHOTEL PM
ETPI 63496 MHOTEL PN
RCA 22479 MHC PH
Fax: 471124
Reservations:
  In Manila call 470011
  In the USA call Robert F. Warner at 1-800-R-WARNER
    or Utell International at 1-800-44-UTELL
All major credit cards
General Manager: Frans Schutzman
Concierge: Cherry Bustamante
Sales Managers: Ma-Anne Felix and Annie Convocar
Rates (approx.):
  Deluxe room $95 single, $105 double
  Superior deluxe room $110–$130 single, $125–$145
    double
  MacArthur Club room $160
  Suite $165–$1,500
570 rooms, 56 suites
Service charge 10%; tax 13.7%

In 1987 this hotel celebrated its seventy-fifth anniversary. It was not only an important event for the hotel and its loyal guests through the years, but also for the nation, which issued a postage stamp in honor of the event. The hotel has had an important role in the history of the Philippines.

When Ernest Hemingway was asked by a local reporter during his visit to Manila in the 1930s to define a good narrative, he replied: "It is a good story if it is like the Manila Hotel."

Events started in 1912 when the hotel first opened its doors with a parade of automobiles led by Commissioner William Howard Taft, with cannons, gongs, fireworks, and brass bands playing the music of John Philip Sousa.

The biggest event in the 1920s in Manila was the arrival of the Prince of Wales aboard the H.M.S. Renown. Sent on a goodwill mission by his father, King George V, the Prince himself decided to make a stop in Manila to play polo. A grand reception was given in his honor at the hotel. He was said to be charming and courteous and was thoughtful enough to give each person who served him a set of gold cuff links when he left.

In the thirties the flow of celebrities continued. Most noticed among them were Dorothy Dix, the American columnist on manners, and Douglas Fairbanks, Jr. Several policeman were stationed at the lobby entrance to hold back crowds when Fairbanks was a guest.

The most splendid years of the hotel were 1935 to 1941, when Gen. Douglas MacArthur lived there. President Quezon appointed General MacArthur his military advisor. The general's demands included a salary equal to that of the governor-general (the then highest-ranking American in the Philippines) and a residence approximating the comforts and grandeur of the Malacanang Palace. His request was granted, and, later, as commanding general of the American Forces in the Pacific, he found his second home in the seven-room Penthouse Suite of the Manila Hotel. MacArthur and his wife, Jean, made the Manila Hotel their home for six years.

During the war years, Japanese military men occupied the hotel. The MacArthur Penthouse was converted into the quarters of Japanese Premiere Hideki Tojo and, later, General Yamashita.

During the war General Yamashita was to see the devastation of his penthouse. The hotel did survive the war and witnessed Philippine independence, formally declared on July 4, 1946.

During the frenzied fifties and sixties, the hotel had a steady flow of the famous. Presidents, actors, statesmen, and entertainers were its frequent guests. The most ardently courted guest who ever stayed at the hotel is said to have been the first Miss Universe, Armi Kuusela.

One of the biggest political events here was the October 1966 Asian Summit Meeting on the Vietnam War. Among the guests then were Pres. and Mrs. Lyndon Johnson, Sec. of State Dean Rusk, Pres. Park Chung Hee of Korea, Pres. Nguyen Van Thieu of Vietnam and his defense minister, Prime Minister Kitticachorn of Thailand, Prime Minister Richard Holt of Australia, and Prime Minister Keith Holyoake of New Zealand. For their stay, the hotel furniture was temporarily moved from the suites, which were refurnished for these dignitaries.

In the seventies the hotel was neglected and began to deteriorate. Finally, in October 1977, it was reopened with an elegantly refurbished old wing standing in front of a brand new eighteen-story tower. Once again the flow of celebrities came, including royalty from far and near, heads of governments, magnates and moguls, tycoons, sheiks, superstars, world-class fashion designers, and entertainers—all of them looking for and finding the fabled romance of the East. And so it goes today.

The Manila Hotel is on Manila's main boulevard, about twenty minutes from the Manila International Airport and five minutes' walking distance from the South Harbor. It is close to shops, boutiques, art galleries, restaurants, and nightclubs.

The rooms and suites are spacious and have Filipino decor. There are individually controlled central air conditioning, radio, color TV, telephone with bathroom extensions, refrigerators, and about everything else for guests' comfort.

The hotel has thirteen meeting rooms, with the new Fiesta Pavilion the largest. It can seat eighteen hundred theater-style. The facilities include six-channel simultaneous translation equipment, slide and movie overhead projectors, screens, and tape recorders. The Executive Services Center is the model of a service center for the traveling business person. It includes a lot of very special things, such as fast printing services, all communications systems, and a well-stocked library of up to date information on the Philippines.

One place to be sure to visit is the hotel's Archives Rooms, which is filled with mementos and awards collected over three-quarters of a century.

There is a health club with men's and women's gyms, steam bath and massage service, two all-weather tennis courts, a game room, squash courts and a pro shop, and a large swimming pool. Called the Bay Club, this is one of the most sophisticated and comprehensive sports and health clubs in a hotel. It is open from 10:00 A.M. until 6:00 P.M.

On page six of the *For Your Information* booklet in your room is a map of the area. Designed for the use of joggers, it tells you of everything within walking (and jogging) distance of the hotel.

I saved the best until last—the hotel's places to eat, drink, and be entertained. *My favorite* among them is Maynilá where you may enjoy Filipino meals served continental-style in elegant turn-of-the-century art nouveau ambiance, while enjoying a nightly Filipino cultural show. A large room, it seats over two hundred.

Another favorite is the Champagne Room, called "Asia's most elegant dining room." It is a French specialty restaurant, with an eleven-man violin ensemble. The Cowrie Grill has a unique look, with its walls covered with shells reflecting an amber glow (there are thousands of them, representing the islands of the Philippine Archipelago). This is the spot for steaks and seafood for lunch and dinner. Café Ilang-Ilang is a most pleasant place to have snacks or meals. From its picture windows you have a view of the pool and the lawns along the bay.

Another view spot is the Sea Breeze Grill, where you may enjoy the famous golden Manila Bay sunsets. Open for dinner, it provides barbecues, seafood, and a salad bar. It is set in the midst of lush tropical gardens, so it is closed during the rainy season.

The newest, and very lovely, dining room is Roma Ristorante Italiano, which has been declared the town's finest Italian dining room. It features homemade pasta, regional fish and meat dishes, Italian wines, and an amazing array of appetizers.

One of the finest and biggest hotel lobbies is that of this hotel, with its stately pillars and arches. The vaulted ceilings are accentuated with Old World brass chandeliers. In the Lobby Lounge there is a breakfast buffet and a business lunch. There is a concert pianist every evening. For drinking, there is the Tap Room Bar, with its beautiful Tiffany-style bay window, and the Après, the discotheque with pizzazz.

THE MANILA PENINSULA
Makati and Ayala avenues
Makati
Metro Manila
Philippines
Telephone: 8193456
Telex: 22507/22476 PEN PH
Cable: PENHOT MANILA
Fax: (632) 815-4825
Reservations:
   In Manila call 8193456
   In the USA call Preferred Hotels Worldwide at
      1-800-323-7500 or Steigenberger Reservations System
      at 1-800-223-5652
Most major credit cards
General Manager: Manfred Timmel
Resident Manager: Jacques A. Warnez
Sales and Marketing Director: Vickie Perez de Tagle
Peninsula Group
Rates (approx.):
   Deluxe room $110 single, $125 double

Super deluxe room $125 single, $140 double
Suite $230–$950
535 rooms, 21 suites
Service charge 10%; tax 13.7%

This Manila unit of the Peninsula Group of hotels was built
in 1978 to meet the need for five-star accommodations for
delegates to the International Monetary Fund Conference.
It has ever since maintained the high standards under which
it was established.

My favorite spot in this Peninsula hotel is what you see
when you enter—the lobby. It is extraordinary. You walk
through the glass portals, onto the gleaming marble floor,
and look up to a ceiling four stories above. The hotel has
two eleven-story wings that are entered from this lobby.
The warm, friendly feeling of the lobby is fostered by the
decor: an emerald green carpet with bright leaf patterns and
shiny, brass-topped tables. In the lobby lounge you see a
businessman sipping a beer, pre-dinner guests having cocktails, or some guests just enjoying an early dinner or a light
snack. Some just sit and watch.

This lobby never sleeps. The clink of coffee cups and iced
drinks is heard until the very early hours of the morning.
Open twenty-four hours, it serves light snacks and refreshments to all, including insomniacs who wish to pass away
the hours in peace.

In 1983 an upper lobby was opened on the hotel's mezzanine. The view from here is just as breathtaking. Another
innovation of recent years is the hotel's series of symphonic
concerts held right in the lobby. The acoustic qualities of
the lobby permit the audience to believe it is listening to
the music of Mozart and Chopin, Tchaikovsky and Bach in
one of the concert halls of London or New York. These
concerts are presented one Sunday a month from September to December by the Manila Symphony Orchestra.

The hotel's rooms and suites, including the spacious ten-
room Presidential Suite (with its own sauna), are all well-
appointed. Every room has a fully stocked refrigerator, color
TV, radio, in-house sound system, and large desk.

The hotel has a large range of amenities, including a
swimming pool, a tropical garden, a business center and
several gourmet restaurants.

The restaurants range from a Spanish-style coffee shop,
La Bodega, to the Chesa, a chalet-style restaurant serving
Swiss specialties, to the Old Manila Grill Room. Bars include
the Tipanan cocktail lounge, overlooking the garden area,

and the Bar, a popular spot for business and social gatherings with a Venetian-inspired decor.

A unique feature of the hotel is its helicopter landing pad on the roof, with direct access to both the Presidential Suite and the eleventh-floor elevator lobby.

There are three levels of shopping arcades in the hotel, which include a medical and a dental clinic. The Manila Peninsula Cake Shop is here, too, selling its famous homemade chocolates, bread, cakes, sausages, and delicatessen items.

The hotel has no tennis, golf, or bowling facilities, although use of such facilities elsewhere can be arranged.

Very important: Be sure to get your copy of a little leaflet entitled *Your Way Around Makati*. It is an easy-to-follow map of Makati's shopping arcades, major banks, insurance firms, museums, churches, airline offices, and lots more. It is very useful for walkers or joggers.

THE WESTIN PHILIPPINE PLAZA
Cultural Center of the Philippines Complex
Roxas Boulevard
P.O. Box 1146
Manila
Philippines
Telephone: 8320701
Telex: 40443 FILPLAZA PM
Cable: PHILPLAZA MANILA
Fax: 832-3485
Reservations:
   In Manila call 8320701
   In the USA call Westin Hotels at 1-800-228-3000
All major credit cards except Carte Blanche
General Manager: Paul Ross
Sales Manager: Joe Hickman
Westin Hotels and Resorts
Rates (approx.):
   Moderate room $85 single, $100 double
   Superior room $90 single, $105 double
   Deluxe room $95 single, $110 double
   Pool-view room $110 single, $125 double
   Suite $250–$2,000
675 rooms, 50 suites
Service charge 10%; tax 13.5%

This is an exciting hotel built in an exciting place in Manila right on Manila Bay, not far from the business, shopping, and entertainment center of the city. It is a part of the Cultural Center of the Philippines Complex, along with the $100 million Philippine International Convention Center, the Philippine Center for International Trade and Exhibitions, the Folk Arts Theatre, and the Manila Film Center and Design Center. The hotel and all of the complex structures were built on land reclaimed from Manila Bay. So were the beautifully landscaped gardens surrounding the Westin Philippine Plaza and its magnificent swimming pool.

Done in vibrant colors that reflect the country's rich culture and heritage, the guest rooms are luxurious and world-class. They are also a showcase of Philippine-made materials and ingenious local craftsmanship. Textured capiz shell is used for the lamps, Romblon marble for the tabletops, and unmatched narra for paneling and furniture. There are bedcovers and headboards with native designs and comfortable rattan chairs. Each room and suite has a private lanai with breathtaking views of Manila Bay and the city.

The rooms are well equipped with modern amenities, including color TV, radio, direct-dial telephone, alarm clocks, well-stocked refrigerators, mini-bars, and individually controlled air conditioning.

The Westin is Manila's only seaside resort, featuring extensive health facilities: a putting green, a lagoon-like swimming pool, and a twenty-four-hour health club with a gym, sauna, Jacuzzi whirlpool bath, and massage service.

On the southern side of the hotel are four Mateflex-surfaced tennis courts that are floodlit for evening games and are surrounded by spectator stands which can hold twelve hundred people. These courts have had tournaments during the past years with celebrities like Ilie Nastase, John Newcombe, Yvonne Goolagong, and Martina Navratilova. The courts open at 6:00 A.M. and close at 10:00 P.M.

The Westin Philippine Plaza's swimming pool is unique in a couple of ways. It is free-form and has an island bar and kiosk in the center. Swimmers may slide into the pool from two water slides. Over to one side is a five-hole putting green. Here, hotel guests and members of PlazaSpa, the hotel's private membership health club, can practice their golf.

The PlazaSpa is fully equipped with sophisticated facilities, from an exercise bicycle to the latest hydraulic rowing machine. And the hotel's compound includes a jogging trail by the sea.

One of *my favorite spots* in this hotel is the two-story lobby that overlooks the exotic gardens and Manila Bay, which is a joy to see at sunset. The lobby has reflecting pools, trees, and a waterfall, which creates the ambiance of an outdoor plaza within the hotel. And surrounding the lobby are a number of fine shops, the most magnificent of which is the jewelry shop of Fe S. Panlilio, truly one of the world's great gemologists. You must visit her shop and see perhaps the most creative jewelry in the world. Mrs. Panlilio has sold fine pieces to the rulers and great of the world, and it was she who selected the stone for the engagement ring of Princess Diana.

Another *favorite spot* of mine is the Imperial Suite, on the top floor of the hotel. It is truly one of the world's most magnificent suites. The foyer alone is enough to see, with its Philippine furnishings, a water fountain at its center, and tropical plantings. I hope you can manage to get a peek at it. It used to be a favorite place for Mrs. Marcos, and her shell collection is in the music room.

This hotel has a great selection of places to eat and to drink. Perhaps the most elegant is the turn-of-the-century dining room called Abelardo's, which serves an excellent candlelit dinner from 7:00 until 11:30 P.M. Pier 7 Steak and Seafood Restaurant serves an international buffet at lunch and an à la carte dinner featuring grilled specialties, and there is a large salad bar. At night there is a strolling string quartet.

Open from 6:00 A.M. until midnight is a coffee shop called Café Fiesta. It features a breakfast buffet, and special at lunch is U.S. rib of beef. The Lobby Court, the lounge in the lobby, serves cocktails and snacks accompanied by semi-classical piano and jazz music. It is open from 10:00 A.M. until midnight.

Called Treasure Island is the restaurant-bar in the middle of the swimming pool. Don't worry, you don't have to swim to get there. There is a picturesque bridge leading to it. It is open from 7:00 A.M. until 10:00 P.M.

Lost Horizon is the discotheque, with a sunken galleon interior and the latest in sound and lighting equipment and live disco music, open from 7:00 P.M. until 2:00 A.M.

Not to be missed is the Phistahan Dinner and Cultural Show on the grounds of the hotel. It is a spectacle of songs, dances, and rituals. It begins with a unique torch-lighting ceremony at sundown and is followed by a sumptuous dinner buffet—a very colorful event on Sunday, Wednesday, and Friday with dinner at 7:00 P.M. and the show at 8:00 P.M. Make reservations, for only 120 may be seated.

Peek in at the Grand Plaza Ballroom if you can. Its Venetian chandeliers are magnificent. It is the largest five-star ballroom in the country and can hold up to two thousand people theater-style. There are twelve other function rooms in the hotel.

For business people, the excellent Business Centre is open from 8:00 A.M. until 8:00 P.M. every day including Sunday. It has an executive boardroom, a Reuters newswire, a library, and an efficient staff ready to provide a range of business services.

SINGAPORE

Singapore is quite a bit in a very small area. It is a republic with a population of two and a half million occupying 225 square miles, consisting of the island of Singapore (210 square miles) and about sixty small adjacent islands. It is in southeast Asia at the southern tip of the Malaysian Peninsula. Singapore City is the capital, the largest city, and the chief port, and is on the southern shore of the island. Gradually the distinction between Singapore and Singapore City is disappearing as the entire island becomes urbanized.

Singapore was originally called Temasek, which means "Sea Town." According to legend, Sang Nila Utama, a prince of the Sri Vijaya Empire, which ruled the region between the seventh and fourteenth centuries, landed at Temasek. Upon seeing a strange beast, which he mistook for a lion, he renamed the place Singa Pura, which means "Lion City."

With the arrival in 1819 of Sir Stamford Raffles, Singapore became a trading post of the British East India Company. Five years later full sovereignty over the island was ceded. In 1826, Singapore joined Penang and Malacca to form the Straits Settlements. Originally administered from Penang, the Straits Settlements were governed from Singapore after 1832. The island grew in importance, particularly after the opening of the Suez Canal in 1869.

World War II brought three years of occupation by the Japanese. Shortly after British administration was restored in 1946, Singapore became a crown colony.

In 1959 the colony became a state with an internal government. Singapore joined the Federation of Malaysia in 1963, but subsequently became an independent and sovereign republic, with membership in the United Nations and the British Commonwealth, two years later.

From a fishing community of mostly Chinese, Malays, and Indians in the 1800s, Singapore has grown into a modern metropolis with skyscapers and a highly successful economy. Today 76 percent of Singaporeans are Chinese, 15 percent Malay, and 7 percent Indian. The remaining 2 percent of the population is made up of Eurasians and residents from around the world.

There are four official languages—Mandarin, Malay, Tamil, and English. English, the language used for business and administration, is widely spoken and understood.

Singapore is a parliamentary democracy with voting rights for adults aged twenty-one or more, and its laws are based on the British judicial system. The republic is headed by a president and governed by a parliament and cabinet.

The country has no major natural resources, but it has developed a deep-water harbor, making good use of an industrious labor force and an important geographic location. The goal of the government is to foster Singapore's economic development as a regional service and prime financial center in this part of the world.

The port is the second busiest in the world; it is used by more than three hundred shipping lines. Gigantic supertankers and container ships, sleek passenger liners, fishing trawlers, and traditional wooden lighters all share the busy waters of Singapore.

It is one of the world's major oil refining and distribution centers and is also a major world supplier of electronic components and a leader in shipbuilding and repair.

Singapore has established itself as an important financial and insurance center of Asia. The country's financial status was enhanced by the launching of the Singapore International Monetary Exchange (SIMEX) in 1984, with a mutual offset link with the Chicago Mercantile Exchange (CME).

Arriving at Singapore's Changi International Airport, I soon discovered it is one of the world's most sophisticated. Millions were invested in its passenger terminal, which has a capacity to handle five thousand passengers during peak hours, and some 10 million passengers a year. And it is still growing, with a second terminal just about completed.

Singapore is attracting more tourists every year. Its central location within Asia, its excellent facilities, exceptional cleanliness, fascinating cultural contrasts, and tourist attractions are the reasons. Almost three million visitors come to Singapore each year, making it one of only six countries in the world to receive more visitors annually than its resident population.

To protect its residents and its visitors, Singapore has some tough, no-nonsense rules. Drugs are not permitted, and finding them can result in a prison sentence the offender's home country can do nothing about. There are tough litter and street laws, too. The streets are exceptionally clean, and you do not jaywalk!

There is excellent shopping, with many atrium malls in office buildings and hotels. The wide, attractive Orchard Road has many international boutiques and shops.

The Old World is well preserved here, too. There are three well-kept sections of the old city: Chinatown, Little India, and Arab Street. Visitors enjoy exploring and shopping in these areas. Being a compact city, Singapore is easy to get around, and the taxis are inexpensive with a modest surcharge during the rush hours.

The Singapore Tourist Promotion Board (STPB) does an excellent job of helping tourists. At your hotel be sure to ask for your free copy of the 176-page *Singapore Official Guide* prepared by the STPB. It has helpful maps and commentary.

Singapore is a hotel guest's paradise. At this time there are more rooms than can be filled. Anxious to be well established in this growing metropolis, which may assume some of Hong Kong's business when China takes back that city, hotel chains and investors have built luxurious hotels in this city. Right now, you can get real bargains and have a large number of hotels from which to select.

BOULEVARD HOTEL
200 Orchard Boulevard
Singapore 1024
Telephone: 737-2911
Telex: RS 21771
Cable: BOUTEL
Reservations:
   In California call 1-800-922-1344
   Elsewhere in the USA call 1-800-247-6435
All major credit cards
General Manager: Alfred G. B. Lew
Sales Manager: Peter H. M. Yip
Goodwood Group

Rates (approx.):
  Superior room $67.50 single, $77.50 double
  Deluxe room $77.50 single, $87.50 double
  Business class room $87.50 single, $102.50 double
  Suite $115–$150
528 rooms and suites
Service charge 10%; tax 3%

The Boulevard Hotel is a spanking modern hotel providing excellent service and affordable luxury. It is sparkling, cosmopolitan, and perfect for its location on Singapore's fine shopping boulevard, Orchard Road. Its neighbors are luxurious private residences, elegant boutiques, and exclusive shops.

Its atrium lobby is impressive and dramatic. The rooms are attractively furnished with a light and pleasant decor and color scheme. Many of the hotel rooms and suites feature pantry counters and kitchenettes, which are especially useful to those intending a long stay. Some bedrooms have large lounge areas and working desks. *My favorite spot* is the atrium lobby with its magnificent sculpture work. Here angled lamps cast a cozy glow over leather sofas, luxuriant ferns, and exotic orchids.

Another favorite spot in the hotel is the Pooldeck, which has two swimming pools and places to relax while you are served a tropical fruit juice or a light snack.

The Manhattan is the hotel's gourmet dining room, where you can get a hearty meal with a steak and salad or well-prepared seafood. Here, the dessert trolly is very tempting. For more casual dining, there is the Cafe Carousel. You may also enjoy traditional Japanese fare at the Gajoen Restaurant or Northern Indian food at the Mayarani. For music and drinks, try the more intimate Alcove Lounge or the vibrant My Place discotheque.

Very much a business person's hotel, it has set aside seventy well-appointed and extra large business-class rooms overlooking the pool. They are ideally furnished for business travelers, who also enjoy the use of the Business Centre and Lounge facilities and complimentary breakfasts. The Business Centre is a good one, offering everything from a secretary who handles telexes, typing, photocopying, and other "girl Friday" duties, to the latest of office equipment.

The Boulevard has four meeting rooms of varying sizes for different functions, from a lavish dinner for over two hundred people to a workshop seminar for ten.

CENTURY PARK SHERATON
16 Nassim Hill
P.O. Box 89
Tanglin Post Office
Singapore 1025
Telephone: 732-1222
Telex: RS33545/21817 CPSSIN
Cable: CENPARK SINGAPORE
Fax: 732-2222
Reservations:
   In Singapore call 732-1113 or 235-6560
   In the USA call 1-800-325-3535
All major credit cards
Resident Manager: Yoshimasa Kabata
General Manager: Guido Jonas
Front Office Manager: Sam Tay
Director of Sales: William Tan
Sheraton Hotels
Rates (approx.):
   Standard room $77
   Superior room $86
   Deluxe room $105
   Cabaña $105
   Suite $105–$476
460 rooms, 31 suites
Service charge 10%; tax 3%

The Century Park Sheraton is a lovely hotel set on Nassim
Hill, amidst lush foliage and greenery in one of Singapore's
most exclusive residential areas. Built on a gentle ridge, this
fourteen-story building is a slim structure that can be seen
from a distance.

The hotel was started in 1976 as the Tanglin Hotel and
purchased by Tan Sri Khoo Teck Puat before it was completed. This Singapore financier and hotel magnate named
it the Connaught Hotel. At the end of that same year, All
Nippon Airways purchased the hotel. It finally opened in
the beginning of 1979 and since then has been very successful, with one of the highest occupancies in the city.

What is outstanding about this hotel is its decor. It was
created by a Danish designer, Bent Severin, who said that
this hotel is a statement of "classical grace and charm."

This classical grace is discovered immediately upon entering the hotel's lobby, which is an expanse of cream-
colored serpenggiante marble set off dramatically by a
generous use of warm and ornately-molded teak wood

paneling. Sixteen ten-foot high Corinthian columns with tall, bell-shaped gold capitals subtly define the expanse and create a feeling of luxury and elegance. The mood is further enhanced by numerous sparkling, finely-prismed crystal chandeliers set against intricately coffered ceilings, and an original Vulcan de Arelier Aubusson tapestry that dominates the elevator lobby area.

As magnificent as the hotel was from the start, all of the rooms by 1986 had been fully refurbished and enriched with luxurious refinements. The program was not a whim. The hotel conducts quarterly surveys on guests' preferences on such items as room color, desk positioning, furniture upholstery, and new services desired. So what you see is what the guests requested.

Each room has a private bathroom and full amenities, such as a mini-bar, color TV, in-house movies, direct-dial telephones, and individually controled air conditioning. There is also a nonsmoking floor.

The interests of nonsmokers are taken seriously in this hotel. There is, for example, a nonsmoking area in the Cafe-in-the-Park, the hotel's elegant twenty-four-hour coffee-house.

Because business persons have found the hotel so much to their liking, the hotel has constructed a full-service business center. It not only has communications and secretarial and printing services, but it provides for the rental of an office on an hourly or daily basis. The Business Centre is open from 8:00 A.M. until 7:00 P.M. from Mondays through Fridays and from 8:00 A.M. to 1:00 P.M. on Saturdays.

The selection of places to dine and to drink is impressive. The Cafe-in-the-Park is open twenty-four hours and has a daily breakfast buffet and lunch and dinner buffets on Saturdays.

The Unkai Japanese Restaurant is on the second floor, and is open for lunch and dinner. It has three sections—the à la carte section features Japanese cuisine and seasonal delicacies; the shushi bar is among the best in town; and the *teppanyaki* section serves meat, seafood, and vegetables prepared on a griddle.

Also on the second floor is the Hubertus Grill, styled after a European hunter's lodge. Featured is game in season, charcoal-grilled prime American beef, and local seafood. *My favorite* is the selection of flambé desserts. Lunch, dinner, and Sunday brunch are served here.

Other places of interest include the Black Velvet and Gold discotheque, with laser light shows, open from 9:00 P.M.

until 2:00 A.M. and to 3:00 A.M. on weekends. There is a poolside snack bar, and the Fountain Lounge on the first floor is open from 11:00 A.M. until 1:00 A.M. and until 2:00 A.M. on weekends, with musical entertainment in the evening.

THE DYNASTY SINGAPORE
320 Orchard Road
Singapore 0923
P.O. Box 176
Orchard Point Post Office
Singapore 9123
Telephone: 734-9900
Telex: DYNTEL RS 36633
Cable: DYNASTY SINGAPORE
Fax: 733-5251
Reservations:
    In Singapore call 734-9900
    In New York call (212) 757-2981
    Elsewhere in the USA call Utell International at
        1-800-223-9868
All major credit cards
Managing Director: Tang Wee Chang
General Manager: Richard Oon
Front Office Manager: Andrew Low
Director of Sales and Marketing: Benjamin Chua
Rates (approx.):
    Standard room $71
    Super deluxe room $85
    Suite $165–$1,033
400 rooms, 22 suites
Service charge 10%; tax 3%

The Dynasty Singapore, one of the most spectacular buildings on the Singapore skyline, is also on the famous Orchard Road. Besides being a deluxe hotel, it is an arresting landmark. Its octagonal tower, reminiscent of the pagodas of Imperial China, is thirty-three stories high.

The impressive design continues inside. Don Ashton, world-renowned interior designer, created the spectacular interiors throughout the hotel, from *my favorite*, the palatial lobby, to all the glamorous public rooms and to the opulent guest rooms and suites. The three-story atrium lobby has two great walls of Thai teakwood carvings. Each of twenty-four panels is about four feet wide and forty-two and a half feet high. Three central themes are depicted in relief—major wars in Chinese history, famous historical personalities, and well-known legends. Continuity of design has been achieved by having the heroes, the activities, and skyline on the same level of each panel.

Mr. Tang Wee Cheng, the chairman and the managing director of the hotel, is a persistent man. He was told it was impossible to create these huge teakwood carvings. He went to Hong Kong, where no space big enough could be found. Finally, he went to the Dongyang Wood Carving Factory in Shanghai, known as the home of the world's finest wood-workers and cabinetmakers, to get the job done. Mr. Tang had to go to the Thai border to find trees large enough for the project.

After they were received in Shanghai, the raw panels were matched by color and grain, numbered, and shipped to a village where there was a Dongyang factory. The entire village worked on the hotel's massive carvings for two years. Some of the villagers were master carvers, mostly sixty to seventy-five years old. More of them were brought from other parts of China to add their expertise.

The result was a Chinese *War and Peace*, portrayed on these panels depicting scenes of four hundred to four thousand years ago. They were shipped to Singapore in December 1981, and carpenters were brought from Hong Kong to put them in place.

So immense are these panels that special equipment is needed to clean them. They are vacuumed once every six months from 2:00 until 6:00 A.M.

The four gigantic Chinese-lantern-style chandeliers are cleaned with a dry mop, each taking four hours to clean. Each of the 156 bulbs must be cleaned, too.

Each of the hotel guest rooms are beautifully furnished with lacquered paintings and fine-detailed carvings—camouflage for a mini-bar and a radio with piped-in music. Each room has color TV and direct-dial telephones.

The guest rooms and suites have double-glazed windows to limit the loss of cool air from the rooms and keep out exterior heat. They also cut down on noise.

Every guest-room door has a lock that is reprogrammed in seconds to a new set of keys for each new guest. There are up to seventy-five hundred different key combinations. It is believed that the Dynasty was the first hotel in the world to provide these costly locks to protect its guests.

The Willow Garden pool is at the fifth level of the hotel.

Guests can relax, sip a cup of jasmine or chrysanthemum tea in quiet, beautiful surroundings, swim, sunbathe, or enjoy a thirst-quencher from the pool-side bar.

All of the restaurants are beautiful. *My favorites* are the Tang Court, said to be the most beautiful Chinese restaurant in Singapore, and Le Vendome, which features a delightful French cuisine in a truly elegant setting. Others include the Golden Dew Coffee House, which is open on the first level twenty-four hours for a snack or a meal, and, also on the first level, Bill Bailey's Bar, "named for an American who never went home." On the same level is the Stroller's Side-walk Cafe, with garden views. In the basement is Twilight, the executive club, a private entertaining hideaway available to guests of the hotel.

The hotel has a health club and secretarial help. There are telephone, cable, and telex services as well. The hotel has its own house physician on call twenty-four hours a day.

Next to the hotel is a new Tangs Superstore, which is a high-quality department store.

THE GOODWOOD PARK HOTEL
22 Scotts Road
Singapore 0922
Telephone: 737-7411
Telex: RS24377 GOODTEL
Cable: GOODWOOD
Fax: 732-8558
Reservations:
   In California call 1-800-922-1344
   Elsewhere in the USA call 1-800-247-6435
All major credit cards
General Manager: Mavis Oei
Sales Manager: Felix Yeo
Goodwood Group
Rates (approx.):
   Deluxe room $95 single, $110 double
   Suite $140–$1,500
4 rooms, 231 suites
Service charge 10%; tax 3%

The Goodwood Park Hotel is the most elegant of that fine group of four hotels in Singapore known as the Goodwood Group. Each of the four has a different character, catering to the various personalities and budgets of those who visit Singapore.

Perhaps some of the grand elegance of the Goodwood Park is due to the heritage of the place. On September 21, 1900, an imposing private club was opened on Scotts Road. Called the Teutonia Club, it was the gathering place for the German mercantile community of Singapore. A newspaper account of the event stated that "the unanimous opinion last night was that the German community possess in their new Club house a building which is a distinct addition to the buildings of Singapore, and is better than all of them."

The building had an exciting life, not only as a club. After World War I it was renovated to become a restaurant, then a cafe, then an entertainment palace—a hall where the lords and ladies of this crown colony gathered in their finery, and a place where the great ballerina Anna Pavlova danced before it became a hotel in April of 1929. One of the first visitors was the late duke of Windsor, then the prince of Wales.

The hotel became a Japanese officers' club during World War II, and after that a war crimes court. In 1948 it became a hotel again. It added more rooms, but never became a high-rise. And again it attracted illustrious guests—William Holden, Noel Coward, British prime ministers Edward Heath and Harold Macmillan, the king of Malaysia, and the sultans of neighboring countries.

In 1983 all of the rooms were totally refurbished, and today it again is a residence to kings, queens, presidents, and statesmen and stateswomen as well as guests who wish the comforts of a super-deluxe hotel. It has retained its grand nineteenth-century tower, which offers the ultimate in luxury and is the location of the delicately opulent Brunei Suite, which has its own private elevator.

The hotel's 235 deluxe rooms and suites are built around two pools and flowering gardens. The rooms are extravagantly furnished and have combined Old World charm with the most modern of amenities. The rooms are all air-conditioned and equipped with direct-dial telephones, color TVs, and mini-bars.

The quality of the cuisine is equal to the surroundings. Considered by local food critics as serving the best meat dishes on the island of Singapore, the Gordon Grill, with its Highland Bar, is a favorite meeting place for both guests and local business people. The Coffee Lounge offers authentic local dishes and Taiwan porridge, as well as carefully prepared Western meals. At L'Espresso, coffees of the world are served. It is also a favorite spot for afternoon tea. The favorites for many connoisseurs are the Min Jiang Sichuan Restaurant and the Garden Seafood Restaurant. Local food critics say they serve the best in Sichuan cooking and seafood specialities.

My favorite spot is the Brunei Suite, which is in the old tower of the hotel. It is acclaimed as the most luxurious suite in Asia. We were impressed with the delicacy of the decor and the opulence of the setting. It has nineteenth-century floral wall carvings, fluted columns, and graceful archways. The lounge, the dining room, the drawing room, and the bedroom are furnished most extravagantly and dominated by soft, warm colors.

The ultimate joy is having breakfast in the roof garden of the suite, or, at the end of the day, relaxing in the suite's sauna. There are gold-plated fittings in the bathroom. You have a choice of fifteen other tower suites, all furnished in an eighteenth-century Robert Adam style. For those taking up residence for a while in Singapore, there are split-level apartment suites with balconies and kitchenettes.

There is a modest shopping arcade in the hotel; the most fascinating shop is the Gourmet Market. On the lower ground floor of the tower, you find here a wide selection of cakes, pies, and pastries prepared by a French patissier and confectioner. There are freshly made sausages and breads as well.

And if it is shopping you enjoy, you are in the right location. The hotel is on Scotts Road, which has a very large indoor shopping mall a short distance from the hotel. Just a bit further down Scotts Road you come to Orchard Road, with its prestigious shops, boutiques, and exciting atrium malls.

The hotel quietly caters to those who wish to hold conferences or seminars in a luxurious setting. From time to time haute couture shows from Paris are presented here in the lovely Tudor Ballroom, which can hold as many as four hundred people. There are four other small meeting rooms.

HILTON INTERNATIONAL SINGAPORE
581 Orchard Road
Singapore 0923
P.O. Box 115
Singapore 9123
Telephone: 737-2233

Telex: RS21491
Cable: HILTELS SINGAPORE
Fax: 732-2917
Reservations:
  In Singapore call 737-2233
  In the USA call Hilton Reservation Service at
    (212) 697-9370
All major credit cards
Owner: Ong Beng Seng
General Manager: Oskar Von Kretschmann
Director of Marketing: Mohd Rafin
Hilton International
Rates (approx.):
  Standard room $65 single, $75 double
  Superior room $75 single, $85 double
  Deluxe room $85 single, $95 double
  Suite $150–$582
435 rooms, 29 suites
Service charge 10%; Tax 3%

The Hilton International was in Singapore before the recent spate of new hotels, having opened in 1970. It is still one of the city's more modern and efficient hotels and a favorite of many business and independent travelers. By mid-1987 a major renovation and refurbishment program was completed, and a great job was done.

The hotel is conveniently situated on the fashionable and busy Orchard Road. From many of the rooms there are splendid views of the city and its famous harbor.

My favorite spot is on top of the hotel, the twenty-fourth floor, where there is a tropical roof garden, a swimming pool, and a guaranteed sunburn.

The guest rooms have all you need—individually controlled air conditioning, private, spacious bathrooms, direct-dial telephones, radios, color TVs with free Teletext information service, digital bedside clocks, executive writing desks, multiple telephone jacks so you can move your phone to any convenient spot, mini-bars, refrigerators, and even more. There are two nonsmoking floors. The rooms have the UNIQEY security system.

On the twenty-second floor are the famous Givenchy Suites, found in some of the better Hilton International hotels around the world. Designed by Hubert deGivenchy, they have private balconies overlooking the city, whirlpool baths and steam shower stalls, and crystal decanters of selected liquor. The floor is served by a concierge and a team of butlers and maids who even pack and unpack your luggage.

There are four fine restaurants. Two of them are *my favorites* partly because they are on the top floor of the building and offer great views to dine by. One is the Inn of Happiness, which features Cantonese cuisine in a setting reminiscent of the courtyard of a Chinese inn. The other is the Tradewinds Foodstalls, which offers pool-side snacks such as *murtabak, roti prata*, curries, and *satays*. In the evenings there is the "Golden Steamboat treat and entertainment," with a full-length movie on Sunday nights at no extra charge. And when the weather cooperates this is the best vantage point for viewing a Singapore sunset. The Tradewinds Bar is also on the twenty-fourth floor, with entertainment in the evenings.

For gourmets there is the Harbour Grill on the third floor, which features French cuisine accentuating contemporary, lighter dishes made of natural, fresh ingredients. Lunch and dinner are served, and you might want to try the "Cuisine en Evolution," the five-course Chef's surprise gourmet dinner. The final preparation of all dishes served is in the dining room so you can watch.

Very popular is the modestly priced Orchard Cafe, on the lobby level. The buffet corner is open for breakfast, lunch, and dinner. There are fountain treats, a local and Western menu, and a large selection of pastries. There is a nonsmoking area.

The freshwater outdoor pool, on the top floor, is the highest hotel swimming pool in Singapore. On the floor below (23) is the Hilton Fitness Centre with sauna, massage, steam bath, whirlpool bath, and gymnasium.

The Executive Business Centre is on the second floor. Open from 9:00 A.M. to 7:00 P.M. on weekdays and until 1:00 P.M. on Saturdays, it has complete secretarial services, communications equipment, a library, word processing, and overnight film development.

The Shopping Gallery occupies two floors and has a separate entrance. It is a fine shopping area, with high-quality shops and merchandise and the products of internationally famous designers.

Even if you do not attend an event in it, you should sneak a look at the Grand Ballroom of this hotel. It has also been beautifully refurbished. Note especially the sixty-four hand-crafted stained-glass panels on the ceiling. They are magnificent.

HOLIDAY INN PARKVIEW
11 Cavenagh Road
Singapore 0922
Telephone: 733-8333
Telex: RS55420HIPV
Cable: HOINPAVIEW
Fax: 734-4593
Reservations:
  In Singapore call 733-8333
  In the USA call 1-800-HOLIDAY
All major credit cards
General Manager: Andreas Obrist
Concierge: Mohd Arman
Director of Sales: Roy Yan
Holiday Inn Asia-Pacific
Rates (approx.):
  Superior/King Leisure room $80 single, $90 double
  King Leisure Deluxe room $90 single, $100 double
  Executive/Parlour Suite $150
  Presidential Suite $400
320 rooms, 21 suites
Service charge 10%; tax 3%

This Holiday Inn opened on August 27, 1985, at the junction of Cuppage and Cavenagh roads, just off Orchard Road. Living up to its name, it is lavishly landscaped both inside and outside. It is the first Holiday Inn in Asia to have an atrium, which is glass-roofed and air-conditioned. It has a peaceful and relaxing indoor garden lounge and a dramatic four-story-high waterfall. This Atrium Garden, as it is called, is reserved for the exclusive use of hotel guests.

Most of the hotel's guest rooms and suites have views of the adjoining park and the Stana grounds, which is why the hotel is called the Holiday Inn Parkview. The inner balconies of the hotel are the corridors, which surround and overlook the Atrium Garden. Plantings cascade from these balconies of the six guest-room floors, giving the area a greenhouse look.

The rooms are spacious—designed for relaxing or working, with comfortable seating and a table or desk with well-designed lighting. Each has three telephones (in the bathroom, on the desk, and by the bed). There are bedside controls for lighting and radio, and remote control for TV and Teletext as well. All rooms have unique built-in wall safes, which can be set to respond only to a guest's credit card.

There is a delightful selection of restaurants. The New Orleans Restaurant and Bar, open for dinner only, at 7:00 P.M. every night except Sunday, is an elegant dining room specializing in traditional New Orleans cuisine as well as continental specialties. It has a true New Orleans look and feeling enhanced by live entertainment featuring light jazz and blues.

The Fragrant Blossom Restaurant serves Cantonese cuisine and seafood, and Tandoor is a delightful Indian dining room featuring North Indian cuisine. Cleamenceau's is the comfortable cocktail lounge at lobby level, with live entertainment in the evening.

Very popular and *my favorite* is the Window on the Park, which is much more than a coffee shop. It has a light and airy setting enhanced by lots of greenery and natural wood tones. Large windows provide a pleasant view of trees and landscaped gardens. This dining room has a wide variety of continental and Asian dishes on its menu along with special "gourmet health dishes." The dinner buffet features cuisine from a different country each night. A buffet of local foods is available at lunch. This dining room is open from 7:00 A.M. until midnight, except on Friday and Saturday nights, when it is open until 1:00 A.M.

HOTEL NEW OTANI SINGAPORE
177A River Valley Road
Singapore 0617
Telephone: 338-3333
Telex: RS 20299 SINOTA
Fax: 339-2854
Reservations:
   In Singapore call 338-3333
   In New York call (212) 308-7491
   In California call 1-800-252-0197 or (213) 629-1200 (Los Angeles)
   Elsewhere in the USA and Canada call 1-800-421-8795
All major credit cards
General Manager: Masasto Nakada
Hotel Manager: Chester Tket
Resident Manager: William Wong
New Otani Group
Rates (approx.):
   Regular room $70 single, $80 double
   Superior room $80 single, $90 double
   Deluxe room $90 single, $100 double
   Suite $165–$350

386 rooms, 22 suites
Service charge 10%; tax 3%

There are a lot of special things about this hotel. For example, every Friday evening at 5:30 the general manager goes on a two-and-a-half-mile easy run through nearby Fort Canning Park. Guests are invited to join him for the run and have a cold beer afterward at the hotel's pool. Many of the staff run after work, including the assistant manager, who wrote a free leaflet entitled *Jogger's Survival Guide*.

The Hotel New Otani has been open since the end of 1984. Located on the banks of the historic Singapore River along River Valley Road, the hotel is within easy reach of commercial, shopping, and entertainment areas. Yet it's not in the midst of the hustle and bustle.

It is about ten minutes from Orchard Road, and about the same time from the commercial district. It takes about twenty-five minutes by taxi to get to the Changi International Airport.

The New Otani Singapore is a part of the Liang Court Complex. This consists of twin twenty-five-story towers linked together by a shopping complex. The hotel occupies one of the towers, and apartments are in the other.

Unlike in other hotels in Singapore, the lobby is on the seventh floor, and this is for good reason. The hotel was designed so that shoppers visiting the complex do not annoy the hotel guests. From the fourth to the seventh floor are the banquet and convention rooms, the restaurants, the disco, and the lounge.

The Liang Court Shopping Centre has a large number of shops, fast food outlets, and the popular Daimaru Department Store and Supermarket. Here shopping can really be done under one roof.

The hotel is in an interesting area. The Singapore River is rich with the city-state's history. It was at the mouth of this river that Sir Stamford Raffles landed and found Singapore in 1819. This was the first commercial hub of the city.

Just opposite the hotel is the lush and quiet Fort Canning Park, ideal for strolling and for jogging. It is pleasant to stroll past the quaint buildings along the Singapore River, which have been long vacated, and enjoy the unique architecture of the past. (From the hotel rooms, guests have an enchanting view of the unique façades of old shophouses and warehouses, which are in stark contrast to the modern skyscrapers behind them.) Other attractions nearby are a huge public pool and the Van Kleef Aquarium, both just across from the hotel, an Indian temple, and a Catholic Church.

The Istana, which is the president's residence, is nearby, as are the National Museum, the National Archives, the National Library, and, of course, the important Orchard Road. Fifteen minutes' walk away is Chinatown.

The hotel rooms all have air conditioning, direct-dial phones, mini-bars and refrigerators, color TVs, and radios. In some rooms are AM/FM stereo cassette recorders. All rooms have large work desks and vanity tables. The bathrooms are all in Italian marble.

Every room has a *yukata*, a cool, comfortable cotton lounging robe often worn as pajamas. When the hotel opened, the managers planned to have heavy terry towel robes. But, Singapore being in the tropics, they found that the light cotton *yukatas*, found in most Japanese hotels, were better.

There is a nonsmoking floor, and the Golden Tower Service Floor has more luxurious rooms and butler services for a higher rate.

Among the places to eat are the Taikan En Chinese restaurant, the Senbazuru Japanese restaurant, Trader Vic's Restaurant and Boathouse Bar, and, *my favorite*, the River Terrace Coffeehouse, overlooking the lovely pool and sunbathing deck on the seventh floor, with a bonus view of Singapore. It is open from 6:30 A.M. to 2:00 A.M. On the fourth floor is the pulsating Mystery Disco.

Most Americans seem to head for Trader Vic's of San Francisco, a restaurant and bar on the hotel's fifth floor. It has a South Seas decor and an international menu featuring a variety of curries and some local surprises. It is open for lunch and dinner as are the Chinese and Japanese dining rooms on the sixth floor.

Every room has a hot-water maker as well as a complimentary supply of coffee, tea, and instant soup. The hotel found that the instant soup was ideal for guests suffering from jet lag hunger pangs in the middle of the night, and even for the flu and what they call "travelers' tummy." This is the only hotel in Singapore to provide instant soup in all guest rooms.

HYATT REGENCY SINGAPORE
10–12 Scotts Road
Singapore 0922
Telephone: 733-1188

Cable: HYATT SINGAPORE
Telex: RS 24415
Fax: 7321696
Reservations:
 In Singapore call 733-1188
 In Alaska and Hawaii call 1-800-228-9005
 In Nebraska call 1-800-228-9001
 Elsewhere in the USA call Hyatt Worldwide
  Reservations at 1-800-228-9005
All major credit cards
Managing Director: Rajan Retnam
General Manager: Andre Pury
Executive Assistant Manager Rooms: Daniel Studer
Executive Assistant Manager Marketing: Michael Oh
Hyatt International
Rates (approx.):
 Superior room $66
 Deluxe room $89
 Regency Club room $108
 Suite $188–$1,179
1,016 rooms, 72 suites
Service charge 10%; tax 3%

Scotts Road might be called the second main shopping boulevard in Singapore, second only to Orchard Road, which it meets only a two-minute walk from the Hyatt Regency Singapore.

This is a big hotel, or perhaps I should say pair of hotels, for in 1985 another beautiful wing was added. Now the gardens and swimming pool are within the partial circle formed by the buildings, providing a tranquility that contrasts with the activity of Scotts Road.

The Main Tower, the older portion, has twenty-one floors and 791 rooms and suites. The new building is eleven floors high and is called the Regency Terrace. Rooms in both hotels are very much Hyatt in their modern furnishings, spaciousness, and amenities.

The Regency Club rooms are in both the Main Tower and the Regency Terrace. Seven Regency Club floors have lounges providing complimentary breakfast in the morning and complimentary cocktails and hors d'oeuvres in the evening.

When I saw it, I could understand why the Hyatt Fitness Centre is the pride of the hotel. It is a spacious operation on the first level of the Regency Terrace. Among its facilities are its gym, spa, aerobic studio, sauna, steam room, tennis and squash courts, and two swimming pools.

For meetings and groups of all sizes and types, the hotel has function space spread out over three levels, dividable into eighteen different rooms.

My favorite spot, I admit, is the bathroom. It has wall-to-wall mirrors and separate areas for the bathtub and shower. With these separate areas, more than one person can use the bathroom at the same time. There is a telephone in the toilet area. The bathroom also features a dressing area with a luggage rack and a spacious wardrobe. But—this is best —the bath can be filled with water up to twenty-two inches deep (compared to the normal depth of sixteen to eighteen inches). Arabescato marble from Italy is laid in the bathroom. It is creamy white with gray running through it.

Food and beverage spots are excellent. My favorite is Nutmegs, the American specialty restaurant. The decor is reminiscent of the thirties, in beautiful art deco style. It has an elevated cocktail lounge for drinks, and Mondays through Saturdays there is a jazz band in the evening, from 8:30 until 1:00 A.M. In the main dining room you can watch the chefs prepare the meals through glass panels. This dining room is open for lunch and dinner (until 1:00 A.M.). In the center of the dining room is a magnificent display of desserts. Specialties of Nutmegs are charcoal-grilled meats and spit-roasted crisp duckling. There is a large selection of seafood, served steamed, charcoal-grilled, or pan-fried. The beautiful sight at lunchtime is the gourmet buffet. Guests can pick from an astounding array of appetizers before ordering a main course.

Pete's Place is basically an Italian dining room featuring hot pizzas and tasty pastas. It also has a delicatessen, with gourmet foods from around the world, and a bake shop whose aroma is enough to stir up any appetite. This restaurant in the cellar also has a wine bar. It is open for lunch and dinner.

Plum's is on the lobby level, serving as a cafe restaurant in a sunken area. It is open daily around the clock, and it is dominated by a huge rectangular table with arrowed thrusts at each end. The center of the very impressive food display, on several levels, is a magnificent arrangement of flowers. Kids love the place not only because child's portions can be ordered, but because of the special coloring book–menu provided.

I love the Lounge. On the lobby level, it is bordered by a picturesque glass wall through which can be seen waterfalls cascading four stories from the adjacent garden of the new Regency Terrace. It is pleasant to have traditional English tea here in the afternoon—there's a fine selection from eight different blends along with delicate sandwiches, hot scones with homemade jams, and French pastries. A string quartet is on hand from 3:00 to 6:00 P.M. on Tuesdays through Saturdays. Other live entertainment is here from 6:00 P.M. until 1:00 A.M. The Lounge is open from 11:00 A.M. until 2:00 A.M.

The hotel's discotheque, called Chinoiserie, is unique. It has a collection of remarkable works of art—unusual Chinese artifacts, elegant Chinese antique screens and remarkably preserved scrolls, and delicate paintings in Chinese brush style. A computerized light bank operates like a grand piano, producing lighting effects that intensify or soften the atmosphere. It is linked with a superb sound system. Chinoiserie is open from 8:00 P.M. until 3:00 A.M.

The Hyatt Business Centre is open from 8:00 A.M. to 11:00 P.M. Monday through Friday and until 5:00 P.M. on Saturday, as well as from 9:00 A.M. until 1:00 P.M. on Sunday and holidays. A complete center, it houses two private offices, a conference room, and two lounge areas where complimentary tea and coffee are available at all times. Secretarial and other services, equipment, and research library facilities are all the best. This is one of the top business centers in a hotel.

Within a minute's walk to Scotts Road are over a thousand shops and restaurants.

LADYHILL HOTEL
1 Ladyhill Road
Singapore 1025
Telephone: 737-2111
Telex: RS 23157
Cable: LEHOTEL
Reservations:
    In California call 1-800-922-1344
    Elsewhere in the USA call 1-800-247-6435
All major credit cards
General Manager: Alfred Low
Assistant Sales and Marketing Manager: Serene Kong
Goodwood Group
Rates (approx.):
    Standard room $37 single, $46 double
    Superior room $46 single, $55 double
    Deluxe room $55 single, $64 double
    Suite $87

172 rooms, 2 suites
Service charge 10%; tax 3%

This Goodwood Group hotel is set in country-estate surroundings with lush tropical flora. It is a tranquil and peaceful setting in bustling Singapore, yet a five-minute walk
brings you to the shopping and entertainment area found
on Orchard and Scotts roads.

There are 180 rooms, 80 of them chalet-style, clustered
around a swimming pool. Each room is very pleasant and
offers coffee- and tea-making supplies. Because the Ladyhill
is a comparatively small hotel, the staff seems to have more
time to attend to you. They remember your name and to
which room you belong.

My favorite spot, Le Chalet, has won the "World Famous
Restaurant Award" for its superb Swiss specialties and fon-
dues. The Swiss community in Singapore loves it.

Adjoining Le Chalet is the cozy and intimate split-level
Cocktail Lounge, where drinking is accompanied by music
of a band. At the pool-side coffee shop local dishes are
featured. The pool-side Barbecue Ranch serves meat or seafood barbecue as well as the best *satay* in town.

The hotel has two modest-sized meeting rooms.

LE MERIDIEN SINGAPOUR
100 Orchard Road
Singapore 0923
Telephone: 733-8855
Telex: RS 50163 HOMERI
Cable: HOMERI
Fax: 732-7886
Reservations:
　In Singapore call (65) 732-2878
　In the USA call (212) 956-4390
All major credit cards
General Manager: Jean-Claude Bailly
Concierge: Morgan Raj
Director of Marketing and Sales: Tony Cousens
Société des Hotels Meridien
Rates (approx.):
　Standard room　$67 single
　Superior room　$67 single, $81 double
　Deluxe room　$81 single, $95 double
　Executive room　$119
　Suite　$143–$857

407 rooms, 16 suites
Service charge 10%; tax 3%

Continental elegance is always a delight, and Le Meridien Singapour prides itself in being "the only Asian hotel with European service and French flair." It is among the fine hotels and shops and restaurants on the famous Orchard Road. Somewhat more modest than others, it is a nine-story hotel with a shopping center.

Most exciting is the atrium lobby of the hotel, with its glass-enclosed elevators and its sparkling crystal sculpture hanging from the skylighted top of the atrium. The gleaming white marble floor and the tasteful arrangement of furnishings and plants gives it a richness and elegance that is exceptional, even in Singapore.

Each room and suite is an exhibit of good taste, too. Furnished in soothing hues of salmon, pink, and blue, the design blends East and West. Touches of the East are the silk-screened fabric wall murals of delicate Chinese art and the faintly Oriental furniture fittings, giving a *chinoiserie* effect that is part French and part Chinese. Everything needed is here—a direct-dial phone with an extension in the bathroom, a digital alarm clock in the bedside table, a key tag device that turns the lights on and off. More than a hundred of the rooms have private balconies with landscaping. There are two rooms designed for the handicapped.

The suites are resplendent, particularly the Opal Suite on the eighth floor and the Jade Suite on the ninth. On the seventh floor is Le Club President, where for an additional charge guests receive numerous additional amenities, including a private dining room on the floor with video facilities, a library, and an office with an adjoining conference room.

The hotel's excellent business center is in the lobby, with a private meeting room available free of charge to guests on a first-come, first-served basis. There is something very special here: the China Trade Information and Consultancy Services (CTICS) has a desk here with a library of materials on Hong Kong and China. There is also a Quick Response Referral Service, with a charge of $100 per referral.

As with most Meridien hotels, there is Le Restaurant de France, a fine French dining room presenting the cuisine of Louis Outhier, the master chef. Le Brasserie Georges serves provincial European fare, and Café La Terrasse is the twenty-four-hour café offering snacks during the day and a selection of local and Western food at night. Le Lagon is a pool-side restaurant on the fourth floor, with air-conditioned and open-air sections. Charming Garden is an elegant Chinese dining room serving Cantonese cuisine. Le Rendezvous is the hotel's piano bar.

On the fourth floor is the hotel's swimming pool, health center, and sauna facilities. Eighteen boutiques and shops are on the lobby level. Two floors below are seventy more shops, including Printemps, a leading French department store, which has a whole floor in the basement.

My favorite spot is the terrace of Le Restaurant de France. You feel as if you are sitting on a verandah of a chateau with a view of a park. But here, the "park" is actually a huge wall mural hand-painted by Count Bernard de Petyhuis.

LE MERIDIEN SINGAPOUR CHANGI
1 Netheravon Road
Singapore 1750
Telephone: 542-7700
Telex: RS 36042
Reservations:
    In Singapore call 542-7700
    In New York call (212) 265-4494
    Elsewhere in the USA and Canada call 1-800-543-4300
All major credit cards
Meridien Hotels
Rates (approx.):
    Standard room $62 single, $78 double
    Superior room $78 single, $93 double
    Deluxe room $93 single, $108 double
    Executive suite $125
    Executive superior suite $140
    Executive deluxe suite $400
276 rooms, 4 suites
Service charge 10%; tax 3%

This is another Meridien unit in Singapore, but away from the city center. Located at Changi Point, one of the few remaining countryside enclaves in Singapore, this seven-story resort hotel is only ten minutes' drive from the Changi Airport and a five-minute walk from the nearby Changi Beach. The hotel is next to the Changi Golf Club, and a short distance from the Changi Village.

The dominant feature in this triangular-shaped building

is the atrium lobby. What is especially interesting about it is the "layering" of the floors. Someone standing on the fifth floor would, for instance, see part of the coffee house at the lobby level, a little of the Lotus Lounge on the second floor and a mass of the foliage on yet another level. Almost overwhelming are the fountains and the waterfalls and the masses of plantings that are weaved into the interior design of this hotel.

The lobby floor itself has a series of levels. One is a sprawling seating lounge designed to resemble the exotic lotus flower. The Changi Café, the coffeehouse, flows from one level to two others. Slightly higher is The Verandah, a specialty restaurant serving French cuisine, and on the second level is the Lotus Lounge, open from 5:00 P.M. to midnight, which has live band entertainment.

Rising majestically from the heart of the lobby is an imposing seven-story column built to support the round swimming pool and sun deck at the top of the building.

The rooms are attractively furnished with much use of rattan and pine. Each of the rooms is equipped with a mini-bar, international direct-dial telephone service, a digital alarm clock, and other amenities. The suites—four of them—all face the sea. Each has a master bedroom and a twin-bedded room, two bathrooms, a living room, and a dining room.

The hotel has a discotheque, health club with a sauna, and boutiques. There is a shuttle service between Changi Airport and the hotel and between the hotel and Orchard Road.

A fun thing to do is to hop on a bumboat off nearby Changi Jetty and take a cruise to the nearby islands, visit kelongs and fish farms, and discover some of the old charm of Singapore.

Be sure to ask for the free leaflet *Track Meridien—Your Jogging Guide to Four Scenic Runs in Changi*. Each of the runs shown is described (tough, uphill and downhill; plain sailing, flat route; and lots to see but tough, hilly yet enjoyable).

THE MANDARIN SINGAPORE
333 Orchard Street
Singapore 0923
Telephone: 737-4411
Telex: RS 21528 MANOTEL
Cable: MANRINOTEL
Fax: 732-2361

Reservations:
  In Singapore call 737-4411, ext. 646, 647, 648, or 649, or
    737-2200
  In the eastern USA call (212) 838-7874
  In the western USA call (213) 627-0185
All major credit cards
General Manager: Sonnie T. W. Lien
Concierge: Harry Chen
Director of Sales and Marketing: Michael Tan
Mandarin Singapore International
Rates (approx.):
  Deluxe room $64
  Super deluxe room $74
  Grand deluxe room $84
  VIP deluxe room $93
  Executive suite $119
  Senior executive suite $152 or $167
  1-bedroom Regency Suite $190
  2-bedroom Regency Suite $276
  Presidential Suite $571
1,200 rooms, 59 suites
Service charge 10%; tax 3%

One of a few very special hotels in the city, the Mandarin Singapore provides superb service, the best of Western-style conveniences, and a beautiful Oriental setting.

Before building this $52 million edifice in 1972, Lien Ying Chow, a Singapore banker, traveled three times around the earth with his wife just to study all the world's best hotels. From these they chose for their own hotel the features they liked best: spacious guest rooms (each is over four hundred feet square) and, for each room, a sofa, a soft, handwoven Taiping carpet, and a beautiful view of the harbor.

The hotel's twin towers, one thirty-nine floors, the other thirty-six, are right in the center of the fashionable Orchard Road. The building's magnificence is amplified by its lobby, so big it is called Mandarin Square.

Occupying an entire wall of this huge lobby, a mural, etched in marble and streaked with gold, tells the story of the eighty-seven Taoist Immortals. A masterpiece by the famous Chinese sculptor Yuyu Yang, the mural is based on an eighth-century scroll now in the Palace Museum in Beijing.

Other works of Professor Yang appear throughout the hotel—as part of the main pillars of the hotel entrance; as plaques in the Mandarin Court, the hotel's banquet hall; in

Act I, the cocktail lounge adjoining the lobby; and on the Jade Terrace. Try to see them all.

The guest rooms and suites provide both a luxurious Oriental setting and thoroughly modern amenities. For example, all electrical power is controlled by inserting your key tag into a module in the room; when you leave you remove the key tag, and everything electrical except for the air conditioner is turned off. The rooms are furnished with radio, color TV, mini-bars, sofas, push-button phones, and supplies for making tea and coffee. The bathrooms have telephone extensions, both tubs and stall showers, bidets, and bathroom scales.

Business travelers love the Mandarin, and not only for the fully equipped Mandarin Executive Service salon, on the second floor. A 15 to 20 percent discount is available for frequent business travelers, and the hotel often offers an available higher-priced room, or even a suite, at no extra charge to an executive who has reserved a lower-priced room. Additionally, regular guests are made members of the Kuan Dai Club, which offers many special privileges (in Mandarin, *kuan dai* means hospitality of the highest order).

Among the hotel's seven restaurants, five specialize in Western cuisine, one in Chinese, and another in Japanese. Charles Benz, the hotel's executive chef, is from Zurich. He and his four Swiss assistants and their staff of two hundred use fresh foods flown in from around the world to provide exceptional meals.

On the thirty-ninth floor is my favorite dining room, the Top of the M. Singapore's highest revolving restaurant, it offers spectacular views of Singapore, Indonesia, and Malaysia at lunch and dinner. At night, the continental meals are served under low lights so diners can fully appreciate the continuously changing panorama.

Other places to eat include the thirty-fifth-floor Pine Court, featuring excellent Beijing cuisine at lunch and dinner, and the New Tsuru-no-ya, serving Japanese breakfast, lunch, and dinner. On the fifth floor, the Belvedere serves excellent French dinners and buffet breakfast and lunch, and the Stables, in the style of an English country inn, features U.S. prime roast beef and steaks and charcoal-broiled seafood at lunch and dinner. The first-floor Chatterbox serves snacks and meals around the clock. Snacks and cool drinks are also served at the Sandbar, on the fifth floor alongside the pool. Here too is a barbecue-cum-cultural show, offered nightly except Mondays.

The hotel has several bars and lounges as well. With its wonderful views, the Observation Lounge, on the thirty-eighth floor, is a good place for cocktails at sundown. The Mezzanine Lounge and the Clipper Bar are on the second floor. Act I, on the lobby floor, has music nightly. The fifth-floor Kasbah nightclub has an Arabian Nights decor, and the Library, in the basement, is the hotel's disco.

The Mandarin Singapore's three floors of shops include the boutiques of such internationally famous designers as Hermes, Emanual Ungaro, Courreges, and Givenchy, as well as several good local emporiums.

MARCO POLO SINGAPORE
247 Tanglin Road
Singapore 1024
Telephone: 474-7141
Telex: BEDTEL RS21476
Cable: HOMARCPOLO
Fax: 4710521 MARCPOLO FAX
Reservations:
  In Singapore call 474-7141
  In New York call (212) 757-2981
  Elsewhere in the USA call 1-800-223-9868
All major credit cards
General Manager: Han Oldenburger
Rooms Division Manager: Edwin Cho
Director of Sales and Marketing: Elizabeth Lee
Marco Polo International
Rates (approx.):
  Superior room $66 single, $76 double
  Deluxe room $85 single, $94 double
  Terrace room $118
  Executive room $118 single, $142 double
  Executive suite $179 single, $198 double
  Deluxe suite $212
  Singapore Suite $259
  Presidential Suite $401
  Marco Polo Suite $566
573 rooms, 30 suites
Service charge 10%; tax 3%

Another of Singapore's luxurious hotels is the Marco Polo. Situated as it is on four acres of lush landscaped grounds in the fashionable Tanglin district, it is isolated from but close to the hustle and bustle of the commercial and tourist areas of the city. It is just opposite the fascinating Singapore Handicraft Centre, and within easy walking distance of the beautiful Botanic Gardens.

This is a fine hotel, with a choice of thirty suites, from the truly fantastic Marco Polo and Presidential suites to those favored by the business persons visiting Singapore. Rooms and suites are well-equipped, with headboard controls for air conditioning, lighting, four-channel sound, and color TV with free in-house movies, built-in hair dryers, and massage showers. There is one floor reserved for non-smokers.

Cabaña-style terrace rooms are available, and these open onto a private patio from which you can walk directly to the swimming pool.

The hotel provides beautiful places to relax, dine, and drink. One of the city's popular meeting places is the Marco Polo Lounge. Leading up to it is a five-paneled batik mural by one of Singapore's foremost artists, Seah Kim Joo. It vividly portrays its title, *The Joy of Living*. There is a pianist and other live entertainment in the evening.

To the right of the lobby is the Brasserie la Ronde, which is a replica of a Parisian boulevard-style restaurant. There are French accordion medleys, gleaming copper, and even red-checked tablecloths. It is open for lunch and dinner. One of *my favorite spots* in the hotel and that of many others is La Pinta Coffee Shop, which has a Spanish decor and serves international food from 6:00 A.M. until 1:00 A.M. Built on split levels with intimate alcoves, white walls, and intricate handworked iron and rustic furniture, it has garden views. Also having views is El Patio, where guests may dine in a setting of exotic tropical flowers under canopies. It's open from 7:00 A.M. until 10:00 P.M. Specialties include sizzling *satay*, steamboat, Hokkien spring rolls, and fresh seafood Singapore-style.

In the basement is a luxurious discotheque called the Club. It is open only to hotel guests and its own members, from 9:00 P.M. until 3:00 A.M. every night.

The hotel has a fine shopping arcade with fashion boutiques and the famous Marco Polo Cake Shop.

The hotel has three function rooms, the largest of which, the San Marco Room, can hold two hundred for cocktails. And there is a boardroom for intensive work sessions or corporate pow-wows. The Marco Polo Business Centre is a fully equipped service center for business people. It has a good reference library.

On the second floor, the recreational complex has a wading pool, a children's pool, and a large pool for adults, with an island bar where guests may swim up to for snacks and refreshments. On the ground floor is the Clark Hatch Fitness Centre, with a fully equipped gymnasium, sauna and massage, and a juice bar. There is a jogging area on the hotel grounds. In the landscaped garden area, guests often do some sunbathing. There are also concerts and parties in this garden area.

In 1987, the British publication *Executive Travel* selected the Marco Polo Singapore as one of the top ten hotels in the world for the fifth consecutive year. It was also selected as the "best value hotel" as well as "the hotel with the best cuisine." Other recognition includes *Business Traveller*'s selection of it as the fifth "Best Business Hotel in the World," in 1986.

MARINA MANDARIN SINGAPORE
6 Raffles Boulevard
01–100 Marina Square
Singapore 0103
P.O. Box 0003
Singapore 9103
Telephone: (65) 338-3388
Telex: 22299 MARINA
Cable: MARINAMAND
Fax: 339-3977
Reservations:
  In Singapore call 339-0933
  In the USA call (212) 838-7874 (New York) or
    (213) 627-0185 (Los Angeles)
All major credit cards
General Manager: Achim Ihlenfeld
Concierge: Lawrence Wee
Director of Sales: Doreen Poh
Mandarin Singapore International
Rates (approx.):
  Deluxe room $71
  Superior deluxe room $80
  Marina Club room $90
  Marina View I Suite $130
  Marina View II Suite $200
  Marina Club I Suite $165
514 rooms, 43 suites
Service charge 10%; tax 3%

The Marina Mandarin Singapore opened on January 14, 1987, at Marina Square, a great spot right on the waterfront of the world's second busiest port.

At its opening this hotel, designed by John Portman of the United States, became an immediate local attraction. Singaporeans came to see its expansive twenty-one-story atrium lobby, claimed to be the largest in Southeast Asia.

Built on reclaimed land, this hotel offers its guests an unimpeded view of Marina Bay and the city skyline. The Marina Mandarin is only five minutes away from the business and financial district of Shenton Way, ten minutes from the busy Orchard Road, and within walking distance of some of the major tourist spots—the Singapore River, the National Library, the National Museum, Chinatown, and the symbol of the city, the Merlion. But it is also very much self-contained. Within the hotel's shopping arcade and the Marina Square complex are four department stores and a two-story landscaped mall with 250 shops, all ready for delightful browsing.

The rooms combine the elegance of the East with the modern comforts of the West. The TVs in all rooms not only provide Teletext services but also flight information. Coffee- and tea-making facilities come with the room, a feature that hotels in the Far East are just beginning to offer. Each room has its own balcony, with great unobstructed views of the sea or the city. All rooms have fully-marbled bathrooms with twin wash basins, shower stall and long bathtubs, telephones, and hair dryers.

On the fifth floor is a large outdoor swimming pool. Other recreational facilities include a fully equipped gymnasium, steam room, sauna, and Jacuzzi. There are two squash and four tennis courts as well.

The restaurants are showplaces. On the fourth level is the Cricketer, a typical English pub that serves imported ales, lunches and snacks, and bar items from noon until midnight. Also on the fourth floor is the Ristorante Bologna, designed in the style of an Italian nobleman's villa, with murals in the style of Raphael and Leonardo da Vinci as a backdrop for Italian cuisine.

Probably most popular is the Brasserie Tatler, with light oak beams, old-fashioned brass lamps, quaint fireplaces, and shelves lined with French provincial culinary artifacts and chinaware. The cuisine includes Singaporean favorites, popular Japanese dishes, and Western fare.

My favorite is the Atrium Lounge, set amidst one of the world's largest open-air art galleries. Large trees, lush greenery and sculptures by Richard Lippold and Van Lau enrich the setting. Lippold has become the most famous of the Marina Square artists. Born in Milwaukee, Wisconsin, he is responsible for the impressive hanging sculpture of the twenty-one-story atrium. It is made up of hundreds of anodized metal discs that fall gracefully from the skylight, and is accentuated at the base with sweeping plumes of a reddish prismatic material. Bringing up the ends are a series of wing-like hoops giving a feeling of flight. Lippold is seventy-two and has earned many awards. Among his famous pieces are *Orpeus and Apollo* in Lincoln Center in New York and *Flight* in the lobby of New York's Pan Am building.

On the fifth floor is the pretty House of Blossoms, the hotel's Chinese restaurant, which is a series of private dining rooms separated by intricately-carved screens. Rich silk wallcoverings, created in the imperial style of Old Cathay, feature birds of all types. Lunch and dinner are prepared by chefs from Hong Kong.

On the hotel's fourth floor is a complete business center, open from 8:00 A.M. to 11:00 P.M. on weekdays and until 10:00 P.M. on Saturday. It has everything, including private offices that can be rented for less than five dollars an hour.

Make it your business to see the Reading Room. From the imposing wall murals depicting scholarly days of Imperial China to the mother-of-pearl inlay along the edges of the book shelves, this area is stately and rich in decor. It is a masterpiece created by David Tan, a local interior designer. It has many exciting things to see—a bird watcher's stand, a games room, a billiards room, a dining room, and a small theater, and there are even book shelves in the toilet rooms, behind the cisterns. There is a high ceiling that can be raised or lowered, a gold statue of a scholar, and a pair of emperor's robes stretched out on a lacquered pole on the wall. And you will discover more.

Be sure to asked for the hotel's *Shopping Guide*, which tells you where to find what on Marina Square. It is very helpful.

NOVOTEL ORCHID INN SINGAPORE
214 Dunearn Road
Singapore 1129
Telephone: 250-3322
Telex: INN RS 21756
Cable: HOTORCHID
Fax: (65) 250-9292

Reservations:
 In Singapore call 250-3322
 In the USA call 1-800-221-4542
Major credit cards
General Manager: Pierre Eber
ACCOR Group
Novotel
Rates (approx.):
 Standard room $61 single, $71 double
 Superior room $66 single, $76 double
 Deluxe room $76 single, $84 double
 Apartment $118
Service charge 10%; tax 3%
321 rooms, 18 suites

The ambiance at this off-the-beaten-track hotel is a combination of friendly Asian hospitality and gracious French refinement. The hotel is situated in a quiet residential area, yet it's only five minutes away from Orchard Road, fifteen minutes from the business district, and twenty minutes from the airport. Here are no skyscrapers, and the grounds, with a swimming pool, are spacious and landscaped.

The rooms are all air-conditioned, and there is radio, TV, a mini-bar, a refrigerator, direct-dial telephone service, and tea- and coffee-making supplies in each. The hotel has a health center and a shopping arcade. There are nonsmoking floors and rooms for the handicapped. There is a free shuttle bus every hour to Orchard Road from 8:30 A.M. until 9:00 P.M., every day.

In a French-run hotel like this, of course, the restaurants are good. There is Le Pescadou Restaurant Provençal, featuring south-of-France cuisine. The Moby Dick Coffee House is open twenty-four hours, with luncheon buffets and barbecue grill specialties in the evening. There are two Chinese restaurants—the Dragon City Sichuan Restaurant and the Charming Garden Restaurant. The Vanda Bar has live music at night, and the Plymouth Lounge is a quiet watering spot.

There are also five function rooms and a health center, and golf, tennis, squash, and boating not far from the hotel.

THE ORIENTAL SINGAPORE
6 Raffles Boulevard
01–200 Marina Square
Singapore 0103
Telephone: 338-0066

Telex: RS 29117 ORSIN
Cable: ORSINHOTEL
Fax: 339-9537
Reservations:
  In Singapore call 338-0066
  In Los Angeles call (213) 649-1634
  In Chicago call (312) 346-7663
  In New York call (212) 752-9710
  Elsewhere in the USA call 1-800-663-0787
  In Toronto call (416) 860-1513
All major credit cards
General Manager: Michael Williams
Concierge: Jerry Soh
Director of Sales: Joseph Toh
Mandarin Oriental Hotel Group
Rates (approx.):
  Deluxe room $80
  Executive deluxe room $95
  Suite $160–$790
459 rooms, 62 suites
Service charge 10%; tax 3%

The Oriental is the eighth property in the Mandarin Oriental Hotel group, which includes two of the world's best hotels, the Oriental in Bangkok and the Mandarin in Hong Kong. The Oriental opened in February 1987 as a part of the unique Marina Square, an entirely new section of Singapore designed by the American architect John Portman.

Marina Square covers an area the size of twelve football fields, or more than one-and-a-half times the size of Madison Square Garden in New York. This spaciousness has allowed the opportunity for innovations in design and creative landscaping. The square's promenades and water gardens uniquely integrate the Oriental Singapore, the Marina Mandarin, and the Pan Pacific Singapore hotels with four international department stores, a shopping mall, a supermarket, two movie houses, and 240 specialty shops, boutiques, and restaurants.

The Oriental is a triangular-shaped hotel, with its rooms built around an eighteen-story atrium. The imaginative decor of the restaurants, lounges, and meeting areas is the work of famed interior designer Don Ashton. The views are of the harbor on one side and landscaped gardens on the other. The rooms with the harbor view also overlook Marina Bay, with its light seacraft and Chinese junks, as well as the Singapore city skyline. The Benjamin Sheares

Bridge, a historical landmark, can also be seen. The hotel is adjacent to the central downtown commercial area, with a direct expressway to the Changi International Airport and to the World Trade Centre of Singapore.

You enter the hotel from a driveway that sweeps past the waterfront. You then cross the entrance lobby to one of six "observation" elevators and ascend to the fourth-floor lobby in the heart of the hotel. This floor contains all the service counters and desks as well as the concierge, the Executive Centre, and some of the hotel's restaurants and bars.

Curving up from the fourth story across the Atrium are two elevated walkways, leading to the fifth-floor Chinese Sichuan restaurant, the Cherry Garden, two private banquet suites, L'Aperitif Bar, and *my favorite spot*, the Atrium Lounge.

As is typical in Mandarin Oriental hotels, each guest room is beautifully decorated and includes original works of art. There are international direct-dial telephones and a remote-controlled color TV with up-to-date news and information services including stock market reports and flight information. There is a bedside panel controlling the lights and radio and for calling the valet. There also is individually controlled air conditioning. The three telephones are at the bed and the desk and in the bathroom. The marble bathroom is particularly luxurious, with a shower in addition to a king-sized tub, and a large vanity area with a built-in hair dryer and volume control for entertainment programs.

The hotel's sixty-two suites are magnificent. They range from executive suites to large two-bedroom suites, each individually designed and named after classical Chinese painters, Asian flowers, birds, or maritime themes. All have handcrafted furniture, original works of art, the finest of Chinese silks, carpets, and marble. Each of the paintings in the guest rooms is one of a kind. They are the work of Singaporean artist Peh Eng Send, known for his meticulous watercolor renderings of old Chinese domestic, street, and river scenes. He is a graduate of the Nanyang Academy of Fine Arts, and his works have been exhibited around the world, including the United States. His watercolors in the rooms have captured old Singapore on canvas and—in my opinion—have delightfully ignored the modern.

This hotel is dedicated to the individual traveler. If he or she is on business, the Executive Centre off the fourth-floor lobby is available to serve with staff and equipment. It also provides a fully equipped private office for business meetings and interviews.

As is the case at other Mandarin Oriental hotels, the dining facilities are spectacular in design and decor and excellent in cuisine. The top dining room is Fourcheets on the fourth floor, serving continental cuisine. There is an open grill and an excellent wine cellar. From time to time, there are guest chefs from Europe.

The Gallery runs along one side of the fourth-floor lobby and has magnificent views of the Atrium above and below. This spot is popular for morning coffee, afternoon tea, and cocktails. Behind The Gallery is the Captain's Bar, in the evening featuring light entertainment and dancing. Also off the main lobby is the Cafe Palm, open from early morning breakfast until late night supper. This snack and meal spot overlooks a landscaped terrace. The Cherry Garden features spicy Sichuan cuisine, and the decor recreates the inner courtyard of a Ming dynasty nobleman's house. It is on the fifth floor. Next to it is L'Aperitif Bar.

The fifth floor is mostly devoted to recreation, health, and leisure. The Health Centre has separate facilities for women's and men's massage, sauna, and steam baths as well as hot and cold Jacuzzi pools. Outside is a landscaped pool deck with the Marina Pool Bar and Barbeque, two squash courts, and the swimming pool with its unique underwater sound system. I love the luxuriant plants and tropical flowers of the pool deck. There are two tennis courts on one side of the hotel.

The hotel has excellent and beautiful function facilities. The Oriental Ballroom can accommodate up to eight hundred guests in its spectaular fan-shaped space, and five other function suites are available for meetings, conferences, or banquets.

Be sure to see *The Tales of Wenji*, eighteen magnificent panels describing a Han Dynasty poem, on the walls around the Atrium lobby. The originals are on display at the Metropolitan Museum of Art in New York.

PAN PACIFIC SINGAPORE
01-300 Marina Square
6 Raffles Boulevard
Singapore 0103
Telephone: 336-8111
Telex: RS 38821 PPSH
Fax: 339-1861
Reservations:
    In Singapore call 336-8111, ext. 4227

In the USA call Pan Pacific Hotels at (213) 452-7736
  (California) or 1-800-663-1515
All major credit cards
General Manager: Manfred Haeger
Director of Marketing: Mark Greedy
Pan Pacific Hotels
Rates (approx.):
  Promenade Floor room $70–$84
  Pacific Floor room $86–$100
  Panoramic Floor room $102–$116
  Kingfisher $134
  Executive suites $191–$268
  Presidential Suite $1,250
  Other suites vary
800 rooms, 37 suites
Service charge 10%; tax 3%

The Pan Pacific Singapore was the first of the three big
hotels to open in the John Portman–designed Marina Square,
and it is the biggest of the three.

This deluxe business hotel faces the waterfront of Marina
Square and has its main access from Bras Basah Road. It is
thirty-seven stories high, taller than the other two and unique
in having a two-story restaurant and lounge at the top. Since
this is the highest structure in the Marina Square development, the panoramic views from the top are outstanding.

The hotel is actually divided into four sections, according
to height. The popular Promenade Floors are the fifth to
the thirteenth floors, where the deluxe rooms are claimed
to be the best accommodations buy in Singapore. The Pacific
Floors, from the fourteenth to the twenty-fifth, offer what
the hotel calls first-class service and international hotel–
class luxury. The Kingfisher Floor is the twenty-sixth. It has
an exclusive lounge, twenty-four-hour butler service, and
a host of other amenities, including a card-operated elevator
reserved for the Kingfisher Floor guests. There is even a
private library, and secretarial service is available twenty-
four hours a day. A chauffeured limousine whisks you from
and back to the airport. And all hotel facilities, wine with
meals in some of the fine dining rooms, and many other
things are complimentary to Kingfisher guests. Kingfisher
guests even get complimentary shark's fin soup when dining at Hai Tien Lo, the hotel's Chinese restaurant.

But my favorite section is the Panoramic Floors, from the
twenty-seventh to the thirty-fifth. It has extraordinary views
of the city, the bay, and the harbor, and super-deluxe ser-

vice. And at the top of it all, on the thirty-sixth and thirty-seventh floors, is Hai Tien Lo, *one of my favorite places*. This dining room can be reached by only one of the four exterior glass-enclosed bubble elevators. When you leave the elevator you see an enormous Chinese mural especially commisioned for this spot by the hotel. The dining room is built as a circle and has a 360-degree view of Singapore. It is open for lunch, tea, and dinner, and there is entertainment from 10:00 P.M. until 2:00 A.M.

The biggest suite of the hotel is the Presidential Suite, on the thirty-third and thirty-fourth floors. The lower level of this six-room suite has an entry hall, a pantry with a stove and bar, a huge living room and sitting area, an open space with a grand piano, a dining room with a large balcony overlooking the sea, and two bedrooms with large marble bathrooms. A spiral staircase leads to the second floor, which has an enormous master bedroom, a sitting area, and an opulent marble bathroom with Jacuzzi, sauna, huge shower stall, and bath. A butler stands by to serve the guests of this palatial suite.

Another of *my favorite places* in this hotel is the Pearl of Casablanca, the atrium lounge on the third floor. It is built like an arena, with a two-story ceiling. It is both grand and intimate, decorated in shades of green and gold, with beautiful marble bar and tables. It has unique chandeliers made of links of gold leaves. Large picture windows show the beautifully landscaped terrace garden. This atrium lounge features Middle Eastern cuisine for lunch and dinner, cocktails, or hors d'oeuvres, and daily entertainment. It is open until 1:00 A.M.

Opposite is the hotel's premier grill restaurant, Chateaubriand. It has a timber ceiling, Burmese teak woodwork, Japanese stone surroundings, and comfortable leather chairs. It features steaks, seafood, and accompaniments at lunch and dinner, and closes at midnight.

Also on the third floor is the Five Domes, which is the twenty-four-hour coffee shop featuring international and Asian meals. Next to it is the Veranda, a sidewalk café for a snack or a light meal (a good spot to watch passersby). Also next door is La Patisserie, selling pastries and delicatessen items.

On the fourth floor terrace is Keyaki, the Japanese garden restaurant designed by Ishikatsu, a world-renowned landscape architect. It has a well, a river, a bridge, a waterfall, a bamboo grove, and a small pavilion. Guests cross the bridge to get to the restaurant, which is designed as a traditional seventeenth-century Japanese farm house. Served are *robatayaki*, sushi, *teppanyaki*, and tempura at lunch or dinner. Also on this floor is the Summer House, a trellis-covered café that offers snacks and local specialities from 8:00 A.M. until 10:00 P.M, and, next to the pool-side cafe, the Summer House Bar.

The Tiki is a Polynesian restaurant open from noon to midnight on the second floor.

The hotel's Business Executive Centre, on the second floor, is in business twenty-four hours a day. The Health Club, open from 7:00 A.M. until 11:00 P.M., is on the fourth floor. It has a large gymnasium, sauna, spa pool, massage shower, solarium, exercise-aerobics room, and physiotherapy rooms. The pool on the fourth floor has an underwater sound system and is also open from 7:00 A.M. until 11:00 P.M. There are two hard tennis courts near the pool.

The Elite is the discotheque on the first floor, open from 8:00 P.M. until 2:00 A.M. Sundays to Thursdays and until 3:00 A.M. on Fridays and Saturdays.

THE PAVILION INTER-CONTINENTAL
One Cuscaden Road
Singapore 1024
Telephone: (65) 733-8888
Telex: SINIHC RS 37248
Cable: INHOTELOR
Fax: 732-8838
Reservations:
  In Singapore call (65) 733-8888
  In the USA call 1-800-327-0200
All major credit cards
General Manager: D. Andrew Quinlan
Concierge: Peter Silas
Director of Sales: P. K. Chia
Inter-Continental Hotels
Rates (approx.):
  Rooms $86 single, $100 double
  Suite $238–$829
441 rooms, 44 suites
Service charge 10%; tax 3%

It sounds like Paris: Maxims, Lapidus, Cartier, Givenchy, Hermes, Celine. Or maybe Italy: Ferragamo, Testoni, Fendi. Of course, it is Singapore, and they are the names of the shops and a restaurant in the Pavilion Inter-Continental.

It is another spanking modern hotel, fourteen stories high, designed by John Portman and Associates of Atlanta in the futuristic atrium design pioneered by Portman in the United States.

The hotel has nine guest room floors, three floors of public facilities, and two floors of below-ground parking. The guest rooms and public areas are built around a skylit atrium. East and west walls slope upward, adding to the dramatic effect created on the interior and exterior. To conform with Signapore's reputation as a "garden city," the hotel has spectacular landscaping both inside and out. Four glass-walled elevators in the center of the atrium serve all floors and offer guests a stunning view.

As you go up the elevators you pass *Singapore Rainshower*, a five-story piece of modern art by Portman hanging from the ceiling of the atrium. It has thousands of shimmering particles suspended in a unique gold-on-stainless-steel mobile of gigantic proportions. You can see in it a rainshower, a flight of migratory birds, a wind song.

On the second floor is the Tea Garden, an informal restaurant overlooking the atrium on one side and the pool terrace on the other. It has a wide selection of continental and Asian specialities, plus great pastries and cakes. Within it is the Pavilion Steak Corner, serving U.S. beef with a selection of salads. Opposite the dining room is the Lower Bar, with the Upper Bar just above it. There is chamber music here every evening.

At the third level is the Summer Palace Chinese restaurant, designed to look like a Chinese emperor's summer retreat. It has three skilled Hong Kong chefs who are masters in the preparation of Cantonese cuisine. Lunch and dinner are served.

The hotel's Royal Pavilion Ballroom can accommodate up to five hundred people. It is richly paneled in rosewood, with large crystal chandeliers. There are six other function rooms available.

The Business Center, well directed by an executive secretary, is designed to handle all business travelers' needs. It is open from 8:45 A.M. until 6:45 P.M., except on Saturday when it closes at 1:00 P.M.

The hotel's guest rooms and suites are modern and have a quiet ambiance. In addition to the usual mini-bar, refrigerator, direct-dial phones, and radio and TV control panel there are special amenities like plump terry cloth robes, personalized stationery, and daily ice bucket service.

You should ask for a room on the sloping east and west

sides, for they have large balconies. The seventh is the non-smoking floor. Ask early if you want to stay there.

The Pavilion Health Center, next to the swimming pool terrace, has saunas, a steam room, exercise machines, and massage rooms.

Be sure to notice *Harmony*, a gigantic piece of modern art created by an American artist, Stephanie Scuris of Baltimore, for the exterior of the hotel. Fashioned from stainless steel tubing, this futuristic sculpture has a feeling of endless movement. When viewed from different angles, the sculpture shifts into exquisite kaleidoscopic patterns. The waters springing from the fountain in which the sculpture has been set reflect on its shimmering surfaces.

Here Maxim's de Paris is a replica of the original one at 3 Rue Royale in Paris. There are red velvet seats, banquettes, massive cut-glass mirrors surrounded by arabesques of copper and carved wood, and rococo paintings. On the tables, petite, pink-shaded lamps cast the roseate glows that are supposed to flatter the diners and enhance the table settings. We suggest you order the sole Albert, by master chef Bertrand, who has served at Lasserre and the Oustau de Baumaniere. *My favorite spot*, this restaurant is a delight!

RAFFLES HOTEL
1–3 Beach Road
Singapore 0718
Telephone: 337-8041
Cable: RAFLOTEL
Telex: RS 21586 RAFFLES
Fax: 339-7650
Reservations:
   In Singapore call 336-0448
   In the USA call Utell International at (212) 757-2981 or
      1-800-223-9868
Visa, American Express, Diners, MasterCard
General Manager: Roberto Pregarz
Rates (approx.):
   Standard room $60 single, $65 double
   Superior room $80 single, $85 double
   Writers Suite $90 single, $95 double
   Family suite $210
   Executive suite $250–$260
100 rooms, 27 suites
Service charge 10%; tax 3%

Raffles is a part of the history of the city of Singapore and of the Colonial British society in this part of the world. In 1986, it celebrated its one hundredth anniversary as the Grand Old Lady of the city. Despite the skyscraper hotels offering state-of-the-art facilities that have sprung up around it—and just across the street is the tallest hotel in the world—Raffles is still the proud and well-preserved custodian of the memories of the great who have lived and wrote here.

Rudyard Kipling, who visited the hotel in 1889, wasn't completely happy. He wrote, "Providence conducted me along a beach in full view of five miles of shipping—five solid miles of masts and funnels—to a place called Raffles Hotel, where the food is excellent as the rooms are bad." Well, the rooms have been improved, and the food is still good.

Other writers who have stayed here include W. Somerset Maugham, who wrote, "Raffles stands for all the fables of the exotic East," and Ilsa Sharp, who wrote, "There is only one Raffles."

The list of the famous who have stayed at Raffles is endless. Here are just a few: Joseph Conrad, Herman Hesse, Elizabeth Taylor, Charlie Chaplin, Haille Selassie, Noel Coward, William Holden, John Lennon, Alfred Hitchcock, Bruce Boxleitner, Richard Chamberlain, Henry Ford, Douglas Fairbanks, Ginger Rogers, Xavier Cugat, Frank Buck, Orson Wells, Otto Preminger, Ingrid Bergman, Edmund de Rothschild, Peter Bogdanovich, Mike Todd, Marlon Brando, James Michner, Ben Gazzara, Abbe Lane, and Richard Burton.

Raffles is named for Sir Stamford Raffles, the founder of Singapore. Its history begins in the 1880s as a *tiffin-house* within a private residence. It was mainly concerned with serving luncheons, and it gradually became a kind of hostel. By 1886 the Raffles Hotel came into being as one of a chain of hotels run by the Sarkies Brothers, three Armenian expert hoteliers who came to Singapore to seek fame and fortune. By the 1890s the modest building was too small, so extensions were added, and in 1896 the "new" Raffles was formally opened. In the early 1900s, the hotel was one of the centers of social life—a London paper called it "The Savoy of Singapore." It was here that the famous Singapore Gin Sling was created in the hotel's Long Bar. In the 1930s, when depression hit Singapore, most hotels were forced to close, but Raffles retained its position as the town's leading hotel and stayed open.

In 1941, Singapore suffered bombings day and night. The hotel perfected a successful blackout for its large ballroom, and the orchestra played every night until midnight. When the Japanese invaded Singapore, the lobby filled with refugees, while the staff fled with their families for safety. From 1942 to 1945, high-ranking Japanese officers occupied the hotel. At that time the main entrance of the hotel was changed from the front of the building to its present location.

On September 12, 1945, Raffles gave temporary shelter to hundreds of people rescued from internment camps in Java and other islands of the East Indies. In 1946, the doors were opened to the public again.

Today, in the hustle and bustle of the late twentieth century, Raffles stands unique, combining the charm of a gracious age with the efficiency of a modern hotel. Because it is so important in Singapore's history it is a major tourist attraction, and busloads of visitors come to explore the hotel. It is positioned on busy Beach Road, just minutes away from the financial district, and across the street from Raffles City, with its multilevel atrium shopping mall and convention center.

The grand old hotel is set in two acres of tropical gardens, and its rooms now have air conditioning, sitting rooms, dressing rooms, bathrooms, color TV, mini-bars, and refrigerators. For business travelers, function rooms can accommodate from a dozen to a hundred people.

The Elizabethan Grill, decorated in Tudor fashion, serves international fare highlighted by English specialties such as roast beef and yorkshire pudding from the hotel's famous silver wagon. Another spot to eat is the Palm Court, where you can enjoy Italian meals by candlelight. The Tiffin Room offers informal dining from the *tok panjang* buffet.

To keep with the old tradition, if you drink, you must have a Singapore Sling at the hotel's Long Bar.

When you have breakfast, lunch, or dinner at the Palm Court, overlooking the enclosed gardens of the hotel, you will see a lot of bird cages. They contain a collection of birds from the north of China, Indonesia, West Malaysia, and Singapore. This collection started years ago when the wife of Hoh Hee Yong, a cook at Raffles, told him that the twenty-three birds he had collected had to be removed from their home. Raffles Palm Court became their home, and birds have been singing there happily every morning since. Now there are nearly fifty birds, the pets of a number of the employees of the hotel.

SHANGRI-LA SINGAPORE
22 Orange Grove Road
Singapore 1025
Telephone: 737-3644
Telex: RS 21505
Cable: SHANGRILA
Fax: 733-7220 or 733-1029
Reservations:
  In Singapore call 338-3300
  In Los Angeles call (213) 417-3483
  Elsewhere in the USA call Shangri-La International at
    1-800-457-5050
All major credit cards
General Manager: Randolph F. Guthrie
Director of Marketing: Paul Pei
Shangri-La International Hotels
Rates (approx.):
  Tower room $64–73 single, $75–84 double
  Garden Wing room $96–105 single, $109–118 double
  Valley Wing room $120 single, $134 double
  Suite $159–$989
Service charge 10%; tax 3%
750 rooms, 60 suites

Since its opening in 1971, the Shangri-La has won accolade after accolade for its fine services and luxurious accommodations. It has grown better through the years, with its Garden Wing addition in 1978 and the Valley Wing addition in 1985. It has been rated among the world's top hotels in surveys conducted by various publications of their readers. In 1987, *Euromoney*'s readers selected it as "the best hotel you've stayed at," and in 1986 readers of *Business Traveller* selected it as the "Best business hotel" in the world. In *Institutional Investor*'s annual poll, readers have always included it among the top ten in the world. It ranked seventh in 1986.

Situated in a quiet, prestigious area of the city, the hotel is away from the hustle and bustle that is Singapore. Yet, not too far—it is only a five-minute walk from Orchard Road, the "Champs Élysées of Singapore." Spread across twelve and a half acres of landscaped greenery, the hotel is a lush private garden within the city.

The three buildings of the Shangri-La are stunning, particularly the Garden Wing, with rounded balconies from which spill a riot of deep pink bougainvillaeas.

Accommodations are in three structures. The first is the

original Tower, with 520 rooms and suites that have been refurbished during the past few years. Then there is the nine-story Garden Wing, which was opened in 1978 with 165 rooms, and finally the seventeen-story Valley Wing, having 114 rooms and 22 suites.

One of *my favorite places* in this hotel complex is the atrium of the Garden Wing. The building is designed to enclose a spectacular open-air garden where over one hundred varieties of palms and trees, other tropical shrubs, ferns, and vines are planted. The garden not only blooms outdoors but indoors as well—right on the rooms' rounded balconies, where vibrant pink bougainvillaea are watered by an automatic sprinkler system. The rhythmic splash of water tripping over the rocks and falls creates a tranquil setting.

The suites in the Main Building are fabulous. Among them is the Singapore Suite, one of the hotel's best, with three luxurious bedrooms. There is also a choice of five special Chinese, Indonesian, Japanese, Malaysian, and Thai suites. These two-bedroom suites are decorated in the fashion of the countries for which they are named.

The Valley Wing is really another separate hotel, designed to be the ultimate in luxury. It appears that no expense had been spared in creating it. It has its own entrance and driveway, and a separate lobby and registration area. It is linked to the main building by a sky bridge, which offers spectacular views of the Shangri-La grounds. The rooms are tastefully appointed in formal European style, and they have large marble-tiled bathrooms with separate showers, private tea-making facilities, and safes.

On its top floor is the fabulous Shangri-La Suite, with three bedrooms. It even has its own private elevator. There are two other superb suites in this wing, each having two bedrooms.

Also in the Valley Wing is the new Health Club, having all the latest in exercise equipment, sauna and steam rooms, an indoor swimming pool, and a convenient health bar.

The Valley Wing lobby is thirty-three feet high and is magnificent. It has exquisite crystal chandeliers. Impressive Chinese murals of gold-matted characters depict longevity in different ancient calligraphic styles. The lobby, with its sparkling white marble floor, is grand yet simple. Next to the lobby is the semicircular Summit Room, overlooking beautiful gardens. This room is for top-level meetings and conferences of up to sixty people.

The settings for dining and drinking are as elegant and beautiful as the rest of the hotel and its grounds. For fine

Chinese cuisine there is the Shang Palace. Here, in the ambiance reminiscent of a Shang emperor's palace, Cantonese cooking can be enjoyed. During lunch more than a hundred dim sum items are available.

The Restaurant Latour was designed by Don Ashton. It is the spot for guests who enjoy gourmet Western fare in a refined and relaxed setting. The decor features salmon-colored walls with white lattice skylight ceilings, hand-painted batik art with Austrian gold chandeliers, and Christofle silverware. It has a wine cellar worthy of the famous vineyard for which it is named.

The Nadaman restaurant in this hotel specializes in *ka-iseki*, a 150-year-old culinary tradition. It is one of the finest Japanese restaurants outside of Japan. The tatami and the *teppanyaki* rooms have spectacular views of the city.

The Waterfall Cafe is the spot for quick or unhurried meals in a garden setting, not far from the main swimming pool. You dine to the sound of cascading waterfalls. The café is open from 7:30 A.M. until 10:30 P.M., with Western, Chinese, Malay, and Indian dishes.

The Coffee Garden is the popular twenty-four-hour coffeehouse, where guests and visitors enjoy tasty snacks. The lunch buffet, featuring specialties of Singapore, is very popular and is available daily except Sunday and public holidays. I like the freshly baked bread and pralines.

The hotel's lounges include *my favorite*, the Lobby Court, with its towering columns and chandeliers. The other popular drinking spots are the Poolside Bar and the Peacock Bar, next to the Restaurant Latour.

Xanadu is the hotel's discotheque in the lower lobby of the hotel. It is open from 9:00 P.M. until 3:00 A.M. daily.

On the fourth floor of the hotel is the Business Centre, and not only is it well equipped and well staffed, but it is managed by a team who are there twenty-four hours a day to cater to the needs of business executives.

Within the grounds are tennis and squash courts, a swimming pool, an outdoor spa pool, and a three-hole pitch and putt green. For the jogger, nothing is more invigorating than a morning or evening run around the nearby Botantic Gardens. A complimentary shuttle bus service takes guests to the Gardens and back in the morning.

There are some special things you should know about the Shangri-La. One is that it has a staff of twelve hundred which assures excellent service. The hotel has installed a video movie system in all of the rooms, with twenty-eight different movies every month, two available each day. There are four TV channels as well. There is a fleet of Mercedes Benz 300 SELs, which provide transportation to and from the airport as well as the Central Business District and Jurong areas. In the limos are newspapers, weekly publications, and telephones. If you reserve a Valley Wing room, the chauffeur will be looking for you when you arrive at the airport. You can arrange for this service if you reserve a room elsewhere in the hotel for about fourteen dollars.

The best views are from the Garden Wing and Valley Wing pool-view rooms. From these rooms you can see the entire hotel grounds and gardens.

SHERATON TOWERS SINGAPORE
39 Scotts Road
Singapore 0922
Telephone: 737-6888
Telex: RS 37750 SHNSIN
Fax: 737-1072
Reservations:
    In Singapore call 732-6000
    In the USA call 1-800-325-3535
All major credit cards
General Manager: Carl Kono
Concierge: Brian Wieder
Sales Manager: Roger Foster
Sheraton Hotels
Rates (approx.):
    Deluxe room $83 single, $103 double
    Cabaña $98 single, $122 double
356 rooms, 22 suites,
16 pool-side cabañas
Service charge 10%; tax 3%

This hotel is well situated, near Orchard Road yet in a residential area away from the traffic and crowds. When I was last here, the city was building a subway entrance not far from the hotel, so the neighborhood was not as attractive as usual. But when I entered the hotel I was in a different world—of waterfalls, fountains, and greenery.

At the Terazza, the hotel's coffeehouse, marble columns rise from the ground to the third floor. Just beyond are two waterfalls, a reflecting pool at their feet. The waterfalls blend into the backdrop of Goodwood Hill, visible through the thirty-foot-high glass screen behind them. (A government-owned property, Goodwood Hill is covered with well-preserved bungalows, built as British clubs).

The hotel's main public area is an elegant open space of crystal, subtle lighting, and vertically veined marble that draws the eye up to the high ceiling and down to a black marble fountain, which spills water down four steps to the basement.

The Sheraton Corporation usually uses the name *Towers* to designate certain floors of a hotel that offer greater elegance and service than the rest. Now, for the first time, the Towers are an entire hotel, not just a few floors. The Sheraton Towers Singapore is grand throughout, with crystal in place of glass, porcelain and bone china in place of crockery, silver in place of stainless steel, and the finest furnishings everywhere.

All the rooms are beautifully decorated. TV, radio, and temperature are controlled from a panel beside the bed. There are direct-dial telephones, and this is the first Singapore hotel to provide complimentary in-house movies.

Another special feature is the butler provided for each of the seventeen guest floors. Instead of trying to figure out which button to press for a specific service or an answer to a question, all you do is call your butler. He goes to work as soon as you arrive—unpacking bags, hanging clothes, and handling all laundry and valet needs. He sees to it that wrinkles are steamed out and shoes are shined, at no charge. He also checks to see that the room is properly cleaned, amenities replenished, and so on. You'll wish you could take him home with you.

Also very helpful is Brian Wieder, the first and only American concierge in Asia.

The hotel has three restaurants: Domus (Latin for *home*), with modern elegance and a continental menu, serves dinner only; Li Bali serves authentic Cantonese meals; and my favorite, the Terazza, with its view of the waterfalls, is grand yet very comfortable.

The luxurious ballroom can accommodate five hundred people. The hotel has three other, smaller function rooms as well.

In the lower lobby is the 43 Scotts disco, and just off the lobby is the Aurum Bar, providing drinks and background music.

The hotel's Business Centre has a staff of executive secretaries, three private offices, a conference room, and all the services you'll need.

The Health Club has a full gym, saunas, massage services, and trained physical therapists. The large, fifth-floor swimming pool has a snack bar and a view of Goodwood Hill, scattered with its bungalows.

THE WESTIN PLAZA/THE WESTIN STAMFORD
2 Stamford Place
Raffles City
Singapore 0617
Telephone: 338-8585
Telex: RS 22206 RCHTLS
Fax: 338-2862
Reservations:
  In Singapore call 338-8585
  In the USA call 1-800-228-3000
All major credit cards
Managing Director: William W. McCreary
General Manager: Richard C. Helfer
Senior Assistant Manager: Inge Kreig
Director of Sales: Peter Davies
Westin Hotels and Resorts
Rates (approx.):
  Plaza room $78–$112 single, $93–$127 double
  Plaza suite $224–$732
  Stamford room $68–$98 single, $83–$112 double
  Stamford suite $224–$1,464
Plaza: 749 rooms, 47 suites
Stamford: 1,173 rooms, 80 suites
Service charge 10%; tax 3%

The Westin Stamford and its smaller sister hotel, the Westin Plaza, are part of the enormous Raffles City. This complex includes the most comprehensive meeting and convention facilities in Singapore, able to accommodate five thousand persons, and the colorful Raffles City Shopping Center, whose seventy-five shops on four levels include Sogo, a trilevel Japanese department store and supermarket.

Together, the Stamford and the Westin promise the ultimate in hotel facilities. The Westin is a particularly amazing structure. It is the world's tallest hotel; seventy-three stories high, it measures 746 feet from street level to its highest point. Designed by I. M. Pei, it was built over six years, from 1980 to 1986.

Although under the same management, the two hotels serve somewhat different clienteles. Whereas the Stamford caters to groups, the Plaza specializes in serving individuals. This is not to say individual travelers won't enjoy the Stamford—my wife and I did, with our lovely room forty-five floors above the earth. The Plaza is a bit more luxurious and a bit quieter than the Stamford, but its rooms do not offer the magnificent views of Singapore. And I found the Stamford's public level to be no less tranquil than the Plaza's, except possibly when groups are checking in or out.

The dining facilities, shared by both hotels, feature seventeen restaurants and lounges. They include Sichuan, Italian, Cantonese, Japanese, French, and American cuisines. I found the Palm Grill, which features haute cuisine, and Prego, with authentic Italian cuisine, to be delightful.

But *my favorite spot* is the highest hotel restaurant in the world—the Compass Rose, on the sixty-ninth, seventieth, and seventy-first floors of the Stamford. Its huge windows provide spectacular views on all sides—of clouds floating over the world's second largest port, of all of Singapore, and, on clear days, of Malaysia and Indonesia as well. Tables are arranged so no diner's view is obstructed. The wonderful menu features fresh, seasonal specialties from around the world, as well as local favorites prepared in a Western style. Very popular is the luncheon buffet in the Compass Rose Lounge, which seems to be becoming a favorite meeting place of local business people and visitors alike. My wife and I enjoyed the huge selection of fresh seafood and salads here.

The two hotels provide more than ample recreational facilities, including four squash courts, six tennis courts, two swimming pools, and a fully equipped health center staffed with fitness specialists.

Although not in the center of the city, the Stamford and the Plaza are in easy reach of everything. Close by are Marina Square, the historic green playing fields, and the harbor. And but a few minutes' ride away are Orchard Street, Chinatown, Arab Street, Little India, and the financial district.

Conveniently set between the two hotels is the Raffles City Shopping Center. For a taste of Singapore's culture, visit the mall's center. There is always something going on here—an art exhibition, a bazaar, a demonstration of some new product, a handicrafts sale, or a traditional performance. The mall also has what it claims is the world's largest full-color animated sign, to announce cultural events, sales, and so on. The locals, especially, like to just stand and watch the show put on by this sign.

Be sure to get your free copy of *Westin's Walking Tours Around Raffles City*. Featuring an excellent map, this brochure describes six tours that include the majority of Singapore's most interesting sights.

YORK HOTEL
21 Mount Elizabeth
Singapore 0922
Telephone: 737-0511
Telex: RS 21683 YOTEL
Cable: YORKHOTEL
Fax: 732-1217
Reservations:
  In California call 1-800-922-1344
  Elsewhere in the USA call 1-800-247-6435
All major credit cards
General Manager: Elizabeth Lin
Sales Manager: Lynn Yeo
Goodwood Group
Rates (approx.):
  Superior room $60 single, $67.50 double
  Deluxe room $70 single, $77.50 double
  Cabaña $70–$90 single, $90 double
  Suite $90–$220
400 rooms and suites
Service charge 10%; tax 3%

Sitting atop Mount Elizabeth, just off Orchard Road, is another of the Goodwood Group of hotels. The York Hotel is a modern two-tower hotel that prides itself in "offering the comforts of home with a touch of extravagance."

One of the towers has only suites, just four to a floor to ensure privacy. Then there is a pool-side wing, which features luxurious split-level cabañas and spacious rooms.

The hotel was recently renovated, and as a result the rooms are very attractive. The floors are covered by carpets in soft, relaxing colors of brown and green. The walls are in a soothing beige, and the pastel floral quilted bedspreads are very pretty. The furniture was custom-made, and the white glass lampshades on gold stands or porcelain bases add a feel of modern elegance. The rooms all are extra large and air-conditioned. They have direct-dial phones, color TVs, and stocked mini-bars.

The wining and dining spots are delightful. The White Rose Cafe, which is the hotel's coffee shop, offers both

Chinese and western food, and has such exotic dishes as Thai *tom yam kung* and Indonesian *satay istemewa*. *My favorite spot* is the Balalaika Room, which has a dramatic Russian decor and serves unique Russian specialties. Also featured is fine continental cuisine. The Carriage Bar is plush and cozy, and in the evening there is live entertainment.

There is a delightful outdoor swimming pool and the fully equipped Nautilus Health Centre, staffed with professional instructors.

The York has five function rooms of different sizes, for meetings of ten to four hundred fifty persons. The hotel is linked by a driveway to the luxurious Goodwood Park Hotel, and many of its facilities are available to the York's guests.

Those in the medical profession favor this hotel because it is in the area of Singapore where some of its best medical centers are located.

SRI LANKA

This is the country most of us once knew as Ceylon. An independent country since 1948, the country took its ancient name, Sri Lanka—"resplendent land"—in 1972.

Twenty-five thousand miles square, it is the ancient island of the great Hindu legend, the Ramayana. Later, the Arabs called it Serendib, a word that Horace Walpole took and reworked it into *serendipity*, or what Webster's dictionary calls the "art of making happy discoveries by accident."

Populated originally by the Sinhalese, it witnessed the arrival of Buddhism in 247 B.C. It was about this time that many of its great cities were built.

Nearly 16 million people live in this country, including Sinhalese, Tamils, Moors, Burghers (of Dutch and Portuguese origin), Eurasians, Malays, Europeans, and Veddhas (the descendants of Sri Lankan aborigines).

The country is covered by tropical forests, mountains, and flat, sandy plains. The sun shines for months on end, and there are over a thousand miles of beaches, lots of resorts, and modest but enjoyable resort hotels.

The country's economy is mostly agricultural. Tea, rubber, and coconut, which are all grown on plantations, represent 90 percent of the island's exports.

The favorite resorts are Negombo, Mount Lavinia, Beruwela, Bentota, and Hikkaduwa on the southwestern coast, and Trincomalee, Nilaweli, and Kalkudah on the eastern coast.

For the energetic visitor there is water-skiing, sailing, surfing, scuba diving, and deep-sea fishing. The coral gardens of Hikkaduwa, the Great and Little Basses off the southern coast, and Trincomalee, the area around Pigeon Island on the east coast, are a few of the places for the underwater enthusiasts.

Sri Lanka is the world center of Theravada Buddhism. The sacred city of Anuradhapura, founded in the fifth century B.C., is honored as the capital city of this religion. Here is found the sacred Bo Tree, grown from a sapling from the very Bo Tree under which Gautama, the Buddha, attained enlightenment. The oldest living tree in documented history, it is more than two thousand years old. In the vicinity of the Bo Tree is a fabulous array of Buddhist architectural masterpieces, created as tributes to the faith. The towering Ruwanwelisaya stupa, the remains of the one-time nine-story Brazen Palace, and the calm features of the face of the Samadhi Buddha statue all bear testimony to the religion's rich past.

Kandy, the last capital of the Sinhala kings, is a living record of this past. Dominating the city, which is set in one of the most picturesque valleys of the island, is the Sacred Temple of the Tooth, the Dalada Maligawa, enshrining the Tooth Relic of the Buddha, Buddhism's most sacred shrine. The Kandy Lake has beautiful reflections of the Sacred Temple.

Visitors love to discover precious and semiprecious stones here—rubies, sapphires, zircons, garnets, amethyst, topaz, and cat's eyes—for which Sri Lanka has been famous since the days of Sinbad the Sailor. But be sure you know what you are purchasing. Check with the State Gem Corporation at 24 York Street in Colombo and at the Hotel Ceylon Inter-Continental. They sell fine gem stones and will be pleased to examine, at no charge, gems bought anywhere in the country, to certify whether they are genuine.

Sri Lankan tea is considered by many the best in the world and is easily found in many shops.

Ahungalla

TRITON HOTEL
Ahungalla
Sri Lanka

Telephone: 09-27218
09-27228
Telex: 21788 AIR ACE
Cable: AITKEN COLOMBO
Reservations:
   In Colombo Aitken Colombo call 01-547161 or 01-26767
   In Ahungalla call 09-27218
All major credit cards
General Manager: Mahinda Ratnayake
Sales Manager: Amal Weerasinghe
Ahungall Hotels
Rates (approx.):
   Room $54–$68 single, $67–$97 double
   Suite $90–$103
125 rooms, 6 suites
Service charge 10%; no tax

Nestled amidst the coconut groves of the sleepy little village of Ahungalla, one of Sri Lanka's southern beaches, is this attractive beach resort hotel.

Each of the suites and many of the rooms have views of the sea, and those that do not have views of the countryside. The suites have balconies. Each room has a telephone, piped-in music, hot and cold water, and twenty-four-hour room service. The hotel's swimming pool, one of the largest in Sri Lanka, is right by the sea.

The hotel's main restaurant features international cuisine and exotic Sri Lankan seafood. It is open for all three meals. The Coffee Shop has round-the-clock service. The air-conditioned Supper Club is open from 8:00 P.M. until 2:00 A.M. and has dancing. There are three bars—the Poolside Bar, the air-conditioned Bacchus Bar, and the Lobby Bar. There is a pool-side Bar-Be-Que night and a Sri Lanka night once every week.

The hotel has tennis and badminton courts and table tennis tables, but the beach and the sea are the favorite places for the guests.

Beruwela

CONFIFI BEACH HOTEL
Moragalle
Beruwela
Sri Lanka

Telephone: 034-75217 or 034-75317
Telex: 22033 CONFIFI CE
Reservations:
  In Colombo call 92325, 598534, 93042, or 597996
  Telex: 22033 CONFIFI CE
All major credit cards
Chairman: M. T. A. Furkhan
Manager: F. H. Ansar
Concierge: Bandula Ekanayke
Director of Sales: A. S. T. Furkhan
Confifi Group
Rates (approx.):
  Room only $25 single, $30 double
  Room with breakfast $28 single, $36 double
  Room with half board $33 single, $46 double
  Room with full board $37 single, $54 double
  Suite surcharge $10
68 rooms, 1 suite
Service charge 10%; no tax

The Confifi Beach Hotel was the first hotel in Beruwela, and one of the pioneer resort properties in Sri Lanka.

Although small, the hotel is well known and is very popular with the Germans, Austrians, and Swiss. The hotel is supposed to have the highest rate of repeat clients among the Sri Lankan resort hotels.

It's fun when you arrive. Sri Lankan girls clad in the charming saris greet you and help you check in. The Sunday buffet, the Barbecue in the Garden, Sri Lanka Night, Flambé Night, and Lobster Night are among the popular events put on at this resort hotel.

The hotel is a two-and-a-half-hour drive from the international airport. It is only a fifteen-minute walk to the fishing village of Beruwela and other interesting places in the area.

It has two floors and is very close to the beach, directly facing the sea. It is situated at a bay surrounded by a coral reef, which makes the waters in front of the hotel ideal for snorkeling and swimming.

The hotel was refurbished in 1985, and the new facilities include a lounge bar that leads to a completely open garden terrace right on the beach. In the summer of 1987 a new beach patisserie-bar was constructed, and the garden was beautifully relandscaped.

On the first floor is a circular dining room with excellent views of the sea, the bay, and the reefs. Often you see guests sitting in the dining room taking pictures of the sun setting.

The rooms are comfortable, with balconies or terraces and with sea views. All of the rooms have showers, toilets, hot and cold water, ceiling ventilators, balconies or terraces, piped-in music, and telephones. Seventeen rooms are air-conditioned.

The fresh-water swimming pool is in the garden right on the sea. The sandy beach is lovely under the moonlight and the palm trees.

Also on the first floor are the indoor recreation facilities, which include a billiard and snooker room and a games room that includes a number of the more popular indoor games. This room is often converted into a miniature conference hall. On the ground floor, facing the pool, with the sea on one side and a beautiful garden on the other, is a sunken, split-level restaurant that is being beautifully refurbished in the summer of 1988.

The sports facilities include two floodlit tennis courts, a full eighteen-hole mini–golf course, a mini–cricket pitch, a volleyball court, and a badminton court. Water sports include water-skiing, windsurfing, sailing, diving, and, in season, deep-sea fishing.

The hotel is ideal for young, active travelers.

RIVERINA HOTEL
Kaluwa Modera
Beruwela
Sri Lanka
Telephone: 034-75377/9
Telex: 22033 CONFIFI CE
Reservations:
   In Columbo call 597996, 598534, 93042, or 92325
American Express, Visa
Chairman: M. T. A. Furkhan
General Manager: Srilal Miththapala
Concierge: Mohan Anthonypillai
Sales Manager: Stefan Furkhan
Confifi Group of Hotels
Rates (approx.):
   Room only $40 single, $45 double
   Room with breakfast $45 single, $55 double
   Room with half board $53 single, $71 double
   Room with full board $59 single, $83 double
   Suite $20 surcharge

190 rooms, 3 suites
Service charge 10%; no tax

The Riverina Hotel, about thirty-five miles south of Colombo, is on the famous Beruwela Beach, next to the Palm
Garden Hotel.

This is one of the better hotels of the resort, with all of
its rooms air-conditioned as of November 1987. They are
pleasantly furnished, tasteful, and clean. Each of them has
a balcony or terrace overlooking the hotel's garden or the
sea. There are private bathrooms, with hot and cold water
and showers, and some have bathtubs as well. All of the
rooms have telephones and in-house music.

The garden is a delight. It has everything, it seems—
palm trees, temple trees, palmyrah trees, and tropical flowers. The large swimming pool is free-form, like a meandering pond, with a peninsula extending to its center.
Adjoining the pool is a bar and nearby is the Fruit Stall,
where all the Sri Lankan fruits can be purchased in season.

This hotel has five bars! The Lounge Bar is beautifully
designed in the style of a pub, with a barrel entrance and
matching barrel-style seats, in polished teak and brass. There
is soft piano music.

The Restaurant Bar is in *my favorite spot*, the beautiful
split-level dining room of the hotel. The three levels have
unobstructed views through a high glass wall of the garden
and the pool. The Pool Bar is at the center of the garden,
next to the pool. And there are bars in the Discotheque and
the Konditorei, open in the evenings.

Other places to eat include the Coffee Shop on the first
floor, with attractive timber decor enhanced with delicate
cane furniture. It is open for snacks and light meals. The
Konditorei is situated right on the beach. This is the favorite
spot for afternoon tea, snacks, a quick bite, and some of
the best cakes and pastries in Sri Lanka. In the evenings,
guests like to sit here looking at the sea and the beach while
enjoying a drink or a snack.

There are plenty of things to do for the more active. There
are floodlit tennis courts, table tennis, miniature golf, an
indoor games room, and billiard and pool tables. There are
a gymnasium and a sauna and massage parlor as well as a
beauty parlor.

On the beach there is a windsurfing school, and sailing
and water-skiing can be arranged during the winter season.

Because of its popularity the hotel hosts exciting events,
like the Miss Sri Lanka competition. Popular are the theme

nights, such as Lobster Night, Sri Lankan Night, Bar-B-Cue Night, and Flambé Night. Sundown dances are popular in the Lounge Bar, but also at sundown a favorite pastime is watching the sun set into the Indian Ocean over a drink.

The Discotheque is very popular, even attracting visitors from as far as Colombo for an evening of fun.

Meetings are held in the air-conditioned conference rooms on the hotel's first and second floors, with the main conference hall accommodating up to 225.

Colombo

The largest city and capital of Sri Lanka, this port on the Indian Ocean, near the mouth of the Kelani River, has a population of nearly one million.

The city's more important sections are the old area of narrow streets and colorful market stalls; the modern commercial, business, and governmental area built up around a sixteenth-century Portuguese fort; and the Cinnamon Gardens, which is the city's wealthy residential and recreational area.

Colombo has one of the world's largest constructed harbors. And the city as a whole is gracious, dotted with small parks and gardens, temples, museums, and many Victorian houses and administrative buildings. The streets are always crowded with ox carts, buses, barefoot children, women in bright saris, and Englishmen in tweed jackets. It is a world of old and new, East and West.

Gem cutting and ivory carvings are among the city's specialties. Among the industries are food and tobacco processing, metal fabrication, engineering, and the manufacture of textiles, chemicals, glass, leather goods, cement, clothing, jewelry, and furniture.

Colombo was an open anchorage for oceangoing ships of traders more than two thousand years ago. Moslems settled here in the eighth century. The Portuguese arrived in the sixteenth century and built a fort to protect their spice trade. The Dutch gained control in the seventeenth century. In 1796, the British took over; they made Colombo the capital of their colony of Ceylon in 1802. In the 1880s Columbo replaced Galle as Ceylon's chief port. In 1948, it became the capital of an independent Ceylon.

Among the important and interesting places to see are the National Gardens Museum, the Zoological Gardens (which are among the best in the world, with beautiful landscaping, a walk-in aviary, and an elephant circus), the Aquarium (the best of its kind in Asia), and the Raja Maha Vihare Temple at Kelaniya (particularly rewarding in January, when a colorful procession takes place in honor of the visit of Buddha).

THE GALLE FACE HOTEL
2 Kollupitiya Road
P.O. Box 63
Colombo 3
Sri Lanka
Telephone: 541010/6
Telex: 21281 GFH CE
Cable: SUNSEASAND
Reservations:
  In Colombo call 541010
  In the USA call Golden Tulip Reservation System at
    (212) 247-7950 or 1-800 numbers in each state
All major credit cards
Chairman: Cyril Gardiner
General Manager: Lalith Rodrigo
Sales Director: Brigadier M. A. Jayaweera
KLM Golden Tulip Hotels
Rates (approx.):
  Room $60–$90
  Suite $60–$100
52 rooms, 13 suites
Service charge 10%; no tax

The Galle Face Hotel is one of those special treasures. It is one of the oldest hotels in the world, having started business about a century and a quarter ago. It has been written about in publications around the world as one of the few elegant colonial-style hotels in Asia that has survived the ravages of time. It has been described as a hotel that takes its guests back to the time of the British Raj—the kind of hotel known by Somerset Maugham. *Newsweek*, in 1986, selected the Veranda Bar of the hotel as "one of the truly old British colonial 1850s bars."

It occupies a magnificent location along the principal boulevard of Colombo, with the Indian Ocean at its western terrace and its North Wing looking out on one of the most famous promenades of the East, the Galle Face Green.

The hotel has two ornate banquet halls with high ceilings

and classical architecture. There are thirteen elegant suites in the hotel, of which one, the King Emperor Suite, is among the largest and most luxurious in the world. The hotel's Royal Suites all have elegant marble bathrooms and panoramic views of the Indian Ocean.

The hotel has continually had renovations and improvements during the past twenty years. All of its rooms were air-conditioned by 1970.

Despite its air conditioning, its electronic telephone system, and other modern amenities, it has not lost its Old World character. The high ceilings, the antique-style furniture, the wooden floors, the ceiling fans, and the old-fashioned "lift" (elevator) are still all there. Room service from a butler on each floor has an unbroken tradition from the early days. The hotel has a staff averaging three employees to a room.

Chairman Cyril Gardiner has been striving since the beginning of the eighties to make the Galle Face the best of its kind in the world. He is dedicated to the concept of what he calls "rugged splendor." There are no crystal chandeliers, only wooden ones. There is no wall-to-wall carpeting, just gleaming marble and polished wood floors, and brass instead of chrome. The shops that were once in the lobby have been re-established around the corner. The foyer has been opened up to let in air and light. There are two bird baths in this foyer to encourage local bird life into the hotel. Gardiner wants guests to hear only the sounds of the birds and of the sea, and for that reason musical entertainment is carefully planned not to interrupt the natural serenity.

The entrance tells of the elegance to come. You go to the lobby up marble steps and through beautifully carved doors. On the wall at one end of the lobby is a striking mural showing aspects of Sri Lankan life and culture. The ornate lobby furniture makes all guests feel that they are potentates.

The restaurants are part of the Old World setting, too. The Terrace Restaurant overlooks the pool and is popular for cool drinks as well as meals. The guests are served by barefoot Sri Lankan waiters in long white sarongs. The Royal Room is the fine room for dinner, and it was once the hotel's grand ballroom.

The rooms are delightfully spacious, and the bathrooms are as big as the guest rooms found in many other hotels.

The hotel is right on the beach, and the Galle Face Green, now a promenade, was once used by the British for horse races.

The hotel is concerned for guests' wellbeing. One bit of proof is a sign in a corridor that reads "Don't smoke in bed or the ashes we find may be yours."

In this hotel, as well as the others in Colombo, because there are simply too many hotel rooms in the city, it is advisable to ask for the 50 percent discount on your room. You very likely will get it.

HOTEL CEYLON INTER-CONTINENTAL
48 Janadhipathi Mawatha
P.O. Box 408
Colombo 1
Sri Lanka
Telephone: 21221 or 26880 or 26881
Telex: COLUMBO 21188
Cable: INHOTELCOR COLOMBO
Reservations:
  In Colombo call 20836
  In the USA call 1-800-33-AGAIN
All major credit cards
General Manager: Max Brechbuhl
Inter-Continental Hotels
Rates (approx.):
  Special room $62 single, $68 double
  Standard room $70 single, $76 double
  Superior room $80 single, $86 double
  Standard suite $160
  Superior suite $220
  250 rooms and suites
Service charge 10%; no tax

When it opened in 1973, this hotel represented the first international hotel chain in Sri Lanka. It is in a good spot, for while it overlooks the ocean, it is still in the heart of the city's commercial and administrative center. Nearby are all the airline offices, international banks, business buildings, and shopping centers.

All of the rooms and suites are air-conditioned and equipped with telephones, color TV with in-house movies, radios, and refrigerators with mini-bars. There is same-day laundry service and twenty-four-hour room service.

My favorite spot is the Palms Roof Top Restaurant because of its fine view. It has a luncheon buffet Monday through Friday and serves international fare at night, with live music. The Emerald Tea and Coffee Shop serves snacks and meals from an international menu that includes Sri Lankan specialties. The Pearl Seafood Restaurant is an open-air spot for dinner, served to the accompaniment of Calypso music. There are two bars in the hotel: the Aquamarine, in the lobby, has piano music; and the Palms Bar, on the roof, has a great view of the ocean.

The hotel has a modest business center, and the Sapphire Ballroom is large enough to host eight hundred at conferences. In the main lobby are a jewelry shop and batik, handloom, and clothing shops. There are a beauty parlor and a newsstand.

The hotel has a swimming pool, a tennis and a squash court, and sauna and massage services.

HOTEL LANKA OBEROI
77 Steuart Place
Colombo 3
Sri Lanka
Telephone: 20001 or 21171
Telex: 21201 OBEROI CE or 21369 OBEROI CE
Cable: OBHOTEL
Fax: COLOMBO 549280
Reservations:
  In Colombo call 20001, ext. 2239
  In the USA call Oberoi at 1-800-223-1474 or
    (212) 682-7655, or call Loews Representatives at
    1-800-223-0888 or (212) 841-1111
All major credit cards
General Manager: Kaval Nain
Sales Director: Palitha Wijesuriya
Oberoi Hotels International
Rates (approx.):
  Room $70 single, $80 double
  Junior suite $100
  Deluxe suite $150
  Presidential Suite $200
  Penthouse Suite $350
520 rooms, 66 suites
Service charge 10%; no tax

This is a truly beautiful hotel. It operates as the luxury hotel in town, with beautiful interiors, discreet and quiet professional service by the staff, and an atmosphere within the high standards of the Oberoi hotels everywhere. It is also well located, barely five minutes from the heart of the city.

It is really a garden resort hotel in the city itself, near the sea.

My favorite spot is right where you enter. It is a magnificent eight-story atrium lobby, with three majestic batik sixty-foot banners hanging from the ceiling. As you walk up the several stairs to the richly red-carpeted central lounge of the lobby, you are a bit overwhelmed by the massiveness of it all.

Every one of the rooms and suites overlooks the Beira Lake or the Indian Ocean, and each is beautifully decorated with fine handwoven furnishings and rosewood furniture. I particularly like the fine latticework sliding screens over the floor-to-ceiling windows, and the spacious marble bathrooms. The rooms are large, too, with fitted wardrobes, color TVs, international direct-dial telephones, individually controlled air conditioning, and twenty-four-hour room service.

The hotel is well equipped to serve the needs of the business traveler. The Business Club is especially well set up as a self-contained wing of the hotel. It includes dining and bar facilities with meeting and conference rooms, a library, and full secretarial services. The Club is a popular meeting place for Sri Lankan business leaders. In the hotel are conference and banquet facilities for as many as a thousand people.

The hotel has nine restaurants and bars. The Araliya is the place for an international menu, while Ranmalu features the fresh seafood of Sri Lanka as well as Chinese and Indian cuisine.

The favorite is the Supper Club on the rooftop, which also has a good international menu and selection of wines, as well as views of the sea and the city.

Many like the club atmosphere of the London Grill for its setting and its selection of fine grilled meats. It is also popular as the place for a drink or snack in the afternoon or early evening. The Arcade Bar is the intimate place for the cocktail hour or after dinner.

The hotel has facilities for squash and tennis and it has a huge open pool with a sun deck. There is a well-equipped health club as well as a shopping arcade where you can find gems, batiks, and handloomed textiles.

The place I most remember is the Lobby Lounge. Here is the glass-ceilinged Lounge Bar, with its spectacular batik banners and lush foliage. While you have your favorite drink, you relax and listen to a pianist in the morning, or a string orchestra in the evening. It is open at 10 A.M. The piano music is from 11:45 A.M. until 1:45 P.M., and the string orchestra plays from 6:30 until 8:30 P.M.

RAMADA RENAISSANCE HOTEL
115 Sir Chittampalam
A. Gardiner Mawatha
Colombo 2
Sri Lanka
Telephone: 544200
Telex: 22386 RAMADA CE
Fax: 549184
Reservations:
   In Colombo call 544200
   In the USA call 1-800-228-9898
All major credit cards
General Manager: Felix Nypels
Director of Sales: Milinda Hettiarachchi
Ramada International Hotels
Rates (approx.):
   Standard room $39 single, $44 double
   Executive Floor Rooms $52 single, $58 double
   Asean Suite $88
   Asean Deluxe Suite $165
   Presidential Suite $300
356 rooms, 26 suites
Service charge 10%; no tax

This hotel was designed by a Singaporean team of architects to reflect traditional Sri Lankan art and still have all the most modern facilities.

The hotel is on the bank of Lake Beira, just a short distance from the ocean. It is a horseshoe-shaped structure with wings terraced in the direction of the lake, which gives guests a good view of the water and surroundings. A unique feature of the hotel is a thirty-foot-high *cabook* base, which strengthens and gives color to the design. Local raw materials, like granite and timber, have been used in the overall design. A number of well-known Sri Lankan artists participated in adding beautiful features to the hotel.

The hotel is set in seven acres of landscaped gardens. Bordering the entrance is a "jungle" of bamboo, through which visitors drive to the hotel lobby. There they have a view of seemingly endless expanses of water—the largest swimming pool in Colombo and, beyond it, Lake Beira.

Two terraces overlook the pool and serve as connecting walkways to the hotel's public areas and restaurants.

The Long Feng Chinese restaurant serves Hokkien and Sichuan specialties, which may be enjoyed along with a view of the lake. The Noblesse Bar and Restaurant provides continental nouvelle cuisine and vintage wines. Summer-fields is the round-the-clock restaurant, which serves continental and Oriental specialities, including such items as an "All-American burger," Indonesian *nasi goreng*, Italian spaghetti, and a Spanish omlette. Then there is the Ibn Batuta Spicy Corner, featuring specialties from India, Indonesia, Singapore, Malaysia, Philippines, Thailand, the Middle East, and, of course, Sri Lanka.

The Beira Lounge and Terrace is for cocktails and specialty coffees. Looking much like a private club is the Library Executive Lounge and Music Room. It is an elite membership club with fine cuisine, where hotel guests can feel right at home.

Very popular is the Pool Bar and Terrace. You may get a long cool drink or a sizzling snack from the swim-up bar.

The hotel has a good Business Centre with Reuters and Fax services, memory typewriters, word processors and other business equipment and a secretarial staff.

The King's and Queen's Court are function rooms. The hotel can arrange for meetings and events for from five to 500. They provide sophisticated audio-visual equipment.

The Sports Centre and Health Club has tennis, squash, boating, Finnish Sauna and Turkish baths. The Shopping Mall has jewelry, handicrafts and fashion boutiques. And very important is Goodies, the hotel's take-out shop with an array of delicacies.

When reserving your room be sure to remember that every room has a view. If you want the Beira Lake view, that is to the east, and the Indian Ocean view is to the west.

TAJ SAMUDRA HOTEL
25 Galle Face Centre Road
Colombo 3
Sri Lanka
Telephone: 54662
Telex: 21729 TAJ LANCE
Cable: PALACE
Reservations:
    In Colombo call 546622
    In the USA call 1-800-I LUV TAJ

All major credit cards
General Manager: Yezdi Katrak
Sales Manager: Selvakumar Selvathurai
Taj Group of Hotels
Rates (approx.):
   Standard room $45 single, $50 double
   Executive suite $60–$75
   Deluxe suite $75–$120
400 rooms, 28 suites
Service charge 10%; no tax

The Taj Samudra is not in the heart of busy Colombo, but just five minutes away from its commercial district.

It is set on eleven acres of landscaped gardens, with a leaf-motif door opening onto an ornately furnished lobby featuring lush tropical decor.

On the property is the Old Colombo Club, one of the oldest buildings in Colombo. It is a sturdy red tile–roofed structure facing the sea on the edge of the hotel gardens. It is now used by the hotel as its banquet and convention center. This brings the activities away from the hotel itself and thereby benefits the hotel guests and those attending events as well.

The hotel enjoys fine views. From the front there is an unobstructed view of the beach and the sea, and from the back guests see the swimming pool, the garden, and the city.

The Ports of Call, which is the hotel's coffee shop, has the best view of any dining spot in the hotel, and is a delightful twenty-four-hour restaurant. As its name implies, the cuisine features the best of delicacies from Southeast Asian ports that were once part of the spice trade routes, as well as continental food from the nations who owned ships on the trade route. The decor of the Ports of Call is an attractive blend of a Dutch roof, Buddhist rafters, and intricate trellis work.

Another attractive spot in the hotel is its Lobby Bar, which affords an excellent view of the beautiful lobby and the gigantic lantern-style chandeliers.

The rooms in this hotel on the Galle Face Green and on the Indian Ocean all are pleasant and comfortable, with twenty-four-hour room service and valet and laundry service.

The hotel has a health club and squash and tennis courts on the grounds.

There is a shopping arcade with all the necessities. The

city's shops and entertainment spots are within walking
distance.

Galle

Galle is a town of nearly one hundred thousand, and is the
capital of the southern province. On the Indian Ocean, it
was famous as a trade center for the Chinese and Arabs by
100 B.C. It rose to its prominence under Portuguese rule
from 1057 until 1640, when it became the chief port of Sri
Lanka. It was the capital of Sri Lanka under the Dutch from
1640 to 1656.

THE NEW ORIENTAL HOTEL
10 Church Street Fort
Galle
Sri Lanka
Telephone: 09-22059
Cable: ORIENTAL
Reservations:
   In Galle call 09-22059
Visa, American Express, MasterCard
Managing Proprietress: A. E. Brohier
General Manager: A. Amunugama
Rates (approx.):
   Room $9 single, $14 double
   Suite $13 single, $18 double
24 rooms, 12 suites
Service charge 10%; no tax

The New Oriental Hotel is an old building. It was built in
1684 by the Dutch as quarters for their commanders and
officers. It became a hotel in 1865, when the British took
over. In 1902 it was purchased by the grandfather of the
present owner, Nesta Brohier.
   It was a hotel long before the southern coast of Sri Lanka
got so many hotels at the island's lovely beach resorts.
Affectionately called "N.O.H.," the hotel is a three-story
building and the tallest structure within the Fort. It overlooks the harbor that was the main port of call until the
1860s. In the background are the Deniyaya mountains.
   The two upper stories of the hotel have wooden floors
(connected by the original wooden stairway) with twelve

large, airy rooms with hot and cold running water. From these rooms there is a panoramic view of the natural harbor and the city of Galle through arched, swiveling, wooden-slatted windows typical of the colonial Dutch architecture.

The ground floor has fourteen rooms with wooden floors, overlooking the garden and its abundance of flowers and greenery. You may not see the swimming pool at the far end of the garden, for it is hidden by the lush foliage. These rooms also have private bathrooms and are furnished with antiques in keeping with the heritage of the establishment.

A dining room serves delicacies of the East and the West, especially seafood such as crabs, lobsters, and prawns, along with a favorite, Sri Lankan curried rice.

There is a bar next to the dining room. You may want to try the Sri Lanka Cocktail flavored with arrack, the spirits of the coconut Palm. An interesting taste sensation.

There are fans in the rooms, but no air conditioning, the better to experience a bit of the ancient past of Galle.

Kandy

With a population of over one hundred thousand, Kandy is situated in the lush green hilly tea country, seventy-two miles northeast of Colombo and sixteen hundred feet above sea level. It is one of Sri Lanka's most beautiful towns and is very popular with visitors to the country.

The Sinhala monarchy, one of the oldest in the world, was more than two thousand years old when Kandy was taken by the British in 1815. The last of the Sinhala kings, Sri Wickrema Rajasinghe, built the city's beautiful lake in 1806.

Set in low hills, with valleys, lakes, cascading waterfalls, and the island's longest river, the Mahaveli, Kandy remains a marvelous center of arts and crafts, music, and dance, as it has been for centuries.

The main attraction of Kandy is the Dalada Maligawa, the Temple of the Tooth, where the sacred Tooth Relic of the Buddha is enshrined. Thousands of visitors from the Buddhist world visit this shrine each year, and thousands more come to enjoy the magnificent ancient pageant, the Esala Perahera, in which a replica of the casket enshrining the sacred Tooth Relic is taken in procession through the streets of Kandy. The procession is led by dancers, drummers, whip-crackers, jugglers, torch bearers, Kandyan chiefs in their colorful traditional costumes, and nearly a hundred elephants, led by the majestic Temple Tusker carrying the jeweled relic casket. The festival continues ten nights and a day, and is held some time during July or August.

The Temple of the Tooth dates from the sixteenth century, and the Octagon, which was added to the temple in the nineteenth century by the last king of Kandy, is a much-photographed building.

Other photogenic temples include the Malwatte (Flower Garden) and the Asgiriya, with a gigantic statue of the Recumbent Buddha. Both are monasteries.

The artificial lake built in 1806 should be visited between 2:00 and 4:00 any afternoon. It is the thrill of a lifetime! The mahouts bring their elephants to bathe here. You will want to take pictures, and for a small fee you can ride one of the pachyderms.

Another great place is the Royal Botanic Gardens, Peradeniya, which is less than four miles from Kandy. It was built as a pleasure garden by a Sinhala king, and has 147 acres of a wide variety of flowers and trees. It is a nice place to drive through, with places to stop and sit—garden seats, pavilions, gazebos, and a restaurant. Among the highlights are the Orchid House, Palm Avenue, and the spiced Medicinal Herb Garden.

The town is a market center for an area that produces tea, rubber, rice, and cacao. Shopping is best in the government-run Laksala or the Kandyan Arts Association store, for quality and value in wood, copper, silver, brass, ivory, ebony, bronze, ceramics, lacquer, handloomed items, batiks, jewelery, filigree, antiques, and rush and reed ware. For fun and pictures go to the Kandy Bazaar.

HOTEL SUISSE
Sangaraja Mawatha
P.O. Box 13
Kandy
Sri Lanka
Telephone: 08-22637, 08-22671 or 08-22672
Reservations:
   In Kandy call 32083 or 22672
Diners Club
General Manager: Nihal Perera
Sales manager: Leslie Zoysa
Kandy Hotels

Rates (approx.):
  Room $20 single, $21 double
  Room with breakfast $24 single, $27 double
  Room with American plan $32 single, $43 double
  Suite $37 single, $40 double
95 rooms, 5 suites
Service charge 10%; no tax

This is another of the historic hotels of Sri Lanka. In the seventeenth century it was the residence of the chief minister of the royal granary. In 1818, it was taken over by the British and was occupied by an officer of the British administration, who called it Haramby House.

Some years later, it was sold to a Swiss woman who ran it as a simple guest house. This was the beginning of what developed into the Hotel Suisse.

During the second world war, from 1943 to 1945, it was used as the Headquarters of the South East Asia Command, and Lord Mountbatten presided as the supreme allied commander.

Its one hundred rooms and suites are nicely appointed, all having hot and cold water, telephones, and piped-in music.

There is plenty to do here. The hotel has a big swimming pool, with a pool-side bar. There are indoor games, including a billiard room. Outside there are floodlit tennis courts.

The hotel has a barbecue terrace, a beer garden, a bar, and a nightclub. There is a shopping arcade, and even a helicopter landing pad. Guests of the hotel enjoy jogging around Kandy Lake.

Nuwara Eliya

SAINT ANDREW'S HOTEL
10 Saint Andrew's Drive
Nuwara Eliya
Sri Lanka
Telephone: 052-2445
Telex: 21815 JETRA CE
Cable: ANDREWS
For reservations:
  In Sri Lanka call (01) 052-2445

No credit cards
Chairman: G. E. B. Milhuisen
General Manager: Gemunu Karunaratne
Blue Oceanic Group of Hotels
Rates (approx.):
  Room $18 single, $22 double
  Room with breakfast $20 single, $26 double
  Room with half board $24 single, $35 double
  Room with full board $27 single, $42 double
  Suite (meals excluded) $35
27 rooms, 4 suites
Service charge 10%; tax 1%

If you want low prices and a picturesque setting, this hotel is for you. The Saint Andrew's Hotel is over a century old; it was built during the British colonial period. It has been renovated recently but the same style of antique furnishings has been used to maintain the original atmosphere.

This modest inn is in a very beautiful spot at the foot of Sri Lanka's highest mountain, Pidurutalagala. It overlooks the Nuwara-Eliya Golf Course, situated sixty-two hundred feet above sea level.

The rooms are a bit spartan—each has a bathtub, a wash basin, a commode, and hot and cold running water. There are a dressing table, a room heater, a double bed, and a set of chairs. Each room has either a private garden or private balcony.

A short distance from the hotel is the Nuwara Eliya Shopping Arcade. There is a jewelry shop in the hotel.

The hotel has a restaurant open from 6:00 A.M. until 10:00 P.M., a TV set, a billiard room, and a fully equipped bar.

Tangalla

TANGALLA BAY HOTEL
Tangalla
Sri Lanka
Telephone: 0416-246
Telex: 21803 INTENT CE
Cable: TANGALLA BAY
Reservations:
  In Colombo call 598383 or 598047
  In Tangalla call 0416-246

American Express, Visa
Chairman: Sunil Wickremasuriya
General Manager: Upail Jayalath
Sales Director: Gilbert Jayasuriya
Rates (approx.):
  Room $14 single, $15 double
  Room with breakfast $15 single, $17 double
  Room with half board $18 single, $23 double
  Room with full board $22 single, $28 double
36 rooms
Service charge 10%; no tax

This is certainly one of the most dramatically designed resort hotels in Sri Lanka. It reminds me of the unique architecture used in some Mexican hotels. The theme the
architect used here is that of a land-based ship, with its
bedrooms honeycombed into a cliff fringed with coconut
palms, all set right at the water's edge.

There is no air conditioning in the rooms, although, as
the sales director points out, "the bedrooms are served with
nature's finest natural year-round air conditioning—which
are the ocean breezes."

The rooms are attractive and spacious and have showers,
toilets, and washbasins, plus attractive ceiling fans. The
hotel has a large swimming pool right on the sea. There is
an attractive high-ceilinged dining room right off the lobby.

The view from the hotel is of the Indian Ocean, with its
many fishing sailboats seen against the horizon in the morning, and at night with their distant lights.

Wattala

PEGASUS REEF HOTEL
Santa Maria Mawatha
Hendala
Wattala
Sri Lanka
Telephone: 530206/8 or 530734
Telex: 21168
Cable: REGASUS WATTALA
Reservations:
  In Wattala call 530734 or 530403

All major credit cards
Manager: Clarence Perera
General Manager: Eraj Abeywardana
Golden Tulip International
Rates (approx.):
  Room $33 single, $44 double
  Suite $66
144 rooms, 6 suites
Service charge 10%; no tax

This resort hotel is actually closer to the Colombo International Airport than the hotels in Colombo. It is about fifteen miles from the airport and less than eight miles from the center of Colombo. There is an air-conditioned shuttle coach to the city three times a day with reserved seating.

The hotel is well situated amidst a luxurious tropical garden, right on the shores of the Indian Ocean. The rooms are modern and air-conditioned, with big windows open to the garden, the beach, or both. The rooms' amenities include adjacent bathrooms with English baths, hot and cold running water, and individual balconies or terraces. Guests have a bedside telephone and piped-in music channels. There is twenty-four-hour room service.

There are two dining rooms at this resort—the Ruwanara, the Sri Lankan-style dining room, and the more informal Garden Cafe. This is the place where, on Sundays, you find the guests crowding around the sumptuous buffet luncheon display while the calypso band plays. Fresh seafood is the specialty here, and there is both Western and Sri Lankan cuisine.

Designed for the active guest, the hotel has a floodlit tennis court, a putting green, an immense open-air swimming pool, indoor games, and a well-equipped Health Club and sauna.

The hotel is set up to handle meetings and events, including conventions of up to three hundred guests. The pillarless Shobena Ballroom can also hold three hundred people. All audio-visual aids are available.

TAIWAN

Formosa, now called Taiwan, is about one hundred miles off the coast of southeast China.

It is a lovely island, only about 90 miles wide and about 250 miles long. It is divided by a mountain chain running north and south. The eastern or Pacific Ocean side is mountainous, and there are miles of cliffs rising as high as eight thousand feet. Many travelers consider them among the most magnificent in the world. On the western half of Taiwan are the rather flat and fertile lowlands.

This island has been under continuous occupation for the past five centuries by one nation or another. The Chinese are there now, as they were before. After the Sino-Japanese War in 1895, Taiwan was supposedly given to Japan "in perpetuity," but the islands went back to China in 1945 when Japan surrendered to the Allied forces.

Today it is the only remaining bastion of the Nationalist Government of China, which moved to Formosa in 1949 when the Chinese Communists took over the mainland. Since then, over two million Chinese who were loyal to Chiang Kai-shek (who died in 1975) have left the mainland for Formosa, increasing the island's population to more than 16 million.

Its most important crop is sugar, followed by pineapples, bananas, sweet potatoes, jute, and rice. There is a lot of forest land, and more than a quarter million of the Taiwanese fish for a living.

Taiwan has one of the highest standards of living in the

Far East. In the past it received important aid from the United States, but in recent years it has become more independent and is achieving great success in the development of its industry. There are numerous mills to refine sugar, the country's most valuable export. Other industries include papermaking, textiles, aluminum, building materials, petroleum, electronics, and a wide range of consumer goods.

Taipei is the capital and the best-known city. There are other cities of interest to travelers, among them Kaohsiung, Taichung, and Tainan.

Taipei

Taipei is considered by many to be a true miracle of a city. Thirty years ago, it was little known except as the provisional capital of the Republic of China. Sugar was its major concern and livelihood. There wasn't a single international-class hotel on the city's dusty, unpaved streets. In 1956 the city had about fifteen thousand tourists. In 1986, it had 1.6 million visitors, more than half its population of three million.

By the 1970s, the economists of the world were astounded by the city's rapidly growing economy and called Taiwan an economic miracle. Electronics, plastics, pharmaceuticals, and machinery soon rivaled sugar and textiles as important exports. Taiwan's economy grew at a rate of 10 percent a year, an extraordinary figure.

Yet in Taipei, despite the powerful veneer of steel and glass skyscrapers, fancy boutiques, and luxurious limousines, the people still live according to timeless Chinese patterns established by Confucius more than twenty-five hundred years ago. Their way of life is best described by the Chinese phrase renching-wei—"the flavor of human feeling."

Because of this feeling, there is much to see in Taipei. The city's most popular tourist attraction since it was opened in 1965 is the National Palace Museum, which holds treasures brought from the mainland in 1949. The ten thousand–item display is rotated every three months from more than six hundred thousand objects d'art stored in tunnels that had been drilled into the mountain behind the museum. Other sights to see include the National Revolutionary Martyr's Shrine, the elaborate Lung Shan Temple, and the gigantic, classically designed Chiang Kai-shek Memorial Hall (which, by the way, can be seen from the Roof Garden of the Taipei Hilton).

Other places to visit include the Botantical Gardens, which contains the National Museum of History, the National Taiwan Arts Hall, the Central Library, and the New National Science Hall of Taiwan. Another major park is called the New Park. Try to get here early; every morning at 6:30 the flag of the Republic is raised, the band plays, and everything—even the taxis—comes to a halt.

Stroll around the area near the Lungshan Temple in Wanhua after dark and visit the colorful night markets. Although the city is certainly not the prettiest in the world, it does have great character. Walking shoes and a good map (one is available at the Lai Lai Sheraton) are helpful. But what is beautiful is the courtesy and friendliness of the people. Confucius wrote in the Lun Yü (The Analects), "When friends visit from afar, is this not indeed a pleasure?" Perhaps this explains the obvious pleasure the local people take in extending gracious hospitality to visitors.

HILTON INTERNATIONAL TAIPEI
38 Chung Hsiao West Road
Section 1
Taipei
Taiwan, Republic of China
Telephone: (02) 311-5151
Telex: 11699 or 22413
Cable: HILTELS TAIPEI
Fax: (02) 331-9944
Reservations:
   In Taipei call 331-5151
   In the USA call the Hilton International Reservation
      Service at 1-800-445-8667 (California), 1-800-325-4620
      (Illinois), 1-800-462-1083 (New York), or a local Hilton
      number
All major credit cards
General Manager: Philip Paxton
Sales Manager: Jimmy Shun
Hilton International
Rates (approx.):
   Room $103–$125 single, $120–$138 double
   Suite $210–$645
456 rooms, 50 suites
Service charge 10%; tax 5%

It was the Year of the Ox, 1973, when Hilton opened, in Taipei's tallest building, the city's first hotel managed by an international chain.

Fifteen years later, the skyline has several taller buildings and several very fine hotels. But the Hilton is still one of the best.

Phil Paxton has been the Hilton's manager for more than six years. He has overseen two renovations and built a staff so proficient the chain often sends trainees from European Hiltons to learn the ancient art of Chinese hospitality. During Paxton's reign the staff has become almost entirely Chinese, including the executive chef, the first Chinese to run a kitchen for Hilton.

The hotel strives constantly to keep ahead of the competition. For example, just completed are the thirty-six luxurious Executive Guest Rooms, which occupy the ninth and tenth floors. Created by combining two regular rooms, each occupies the space of a suite, although its price is lower. Besides the usual amenities, each of these rooms has a cassette player, an electric trouser press, and a walk-in closet. The roomy bathrooms include full-sized tubs, separate glass-enclosed showers, heated racks for bath towels, electric hair dryers, and magnifying shaving and cosmetic mirrors.

Also in this section of the hotel is the Executive Lounge— a library, game room, and business center. Buffet breakfast, coffee and tea, and cocktails are served here free of charge to ninth- and tenth-floor guests.

Since it was opened fifteen years ago, the hotel's elegant Trader's Grill has been the most popular Western dining room in town, for business luncheons and leisurely gourmet dinners. If an entire lunch is not served to the guest's complete satisfaction in fifty minutes, there is no bill. Dinner is served to piano music except on Sundays.

The Golden China, a Hunan-style dining room, earned Taipei's Golden Wok award for its cuisine. The restaurant's decor is enhanced by replicas of ancient Chinese art treasures.

In a cheerful bistro atmosphere, La Pizzeria provides pizzas baked to ideal crispness in a brick oven.

The Coffee Garden, popular for snacks, looks out on a bright and luxuriant tropical garden. It is a favorite rendezvous in Taipei. The attached pastry shop sells fresh breads, cakes, pies, and pastries.

For drinks there are the Galleon Pub, with a nautical decor, and the elegant Lobby Lounge, my favorite place to unwind and watch the world go by, under gigantic twin crystal chandeliers. Tiffany's, a private function room by day, changes to a swinging disco at night.

On the fourth floor are five function rooms, recently decorated with rich, custom-made Chinese carpets, temple carvings, ceramic figures, and other works of art.

The hotel's excellent range of facilities includes the Health Club, with a sauna, gymnasium equipment, and massage services, and the Roof Garden, where guests may relax in a Jacuzzi, lie in the sun, and order snacks from a figure-conscious menu. The lobby staff can arrange for guests to golf, play tennis, ride horses, or visit a hot springs resort nearby.

Within the hotel are neccessities shops, and right next door is a shopping mall with popular-priced food stalls in its basement.

HOTEL ROYAL TAIPEI
37–1 Chungshan North Road
Section 2
Taipei
Taiwan, Republic of China
Telephone: (02) 542-3266
Telex: 23915
Cable: ROYAL HTL
Fax: 5434897 (02) 543-4897
Reservations:
    In Taipei call 543-3827
    In the USA call Nikko Hotels at (212) 484-5100 or
        1-800-NIKKO-US
All major credit cards
Chairman: Lin Chin Po
General Manager: Satoru Wakairo
Sales Manager: Larry Ian
Nikko Hotels International
Rates (approx.):
    Regular room $89 single, $116 double
    Deluxe room $105
    Junior suite $168
    Corner suite $205
    Executive suite $221
    Deluxe suite $342
    Royal Suite $447
203 rooms, 20 suites
Service charge 10%; tax 5%

Opened in early 1984, this twelve-story modern hotel is in the heart of the city, less than an hour's drive from the Chiang Kai-shek International Airport.

Designed by Parisian as well as Taiwanese specialists, the Hotel Royal seems much like an elegant and stately European residence. In the beautiful lobby are Italian white marble floors and glittering Austrian chandeliers, which hang from a ceiling three floors above. On the mezzanine, white, columned archways and wicker chairs create a comfortable place to relax or to meet. The Lobby Lounge, to the right of the main entrance, overlooks one of Taipei's busiest streets. *My favorite spot*, the lounge combines the comfort of European furnishings with the refinement of Ching Dynasty porcelain. It is an ideal place to relax with a cup of tea and a pastry.

Another favorite spot is the Café, an elegant, turn-of-the-century-style coffeehouse next to the Lobby Lounge. A popular place for snacks and all meals, it has a display of pastries and breads for takeout as well.

Perhaps the finest dining place here is Les Célébrités, reached by the staircase from the main lobby to the second floor. Considered by many the best French restaurant in Taiwan, it features a garden-style decor and magnificent gastronomic creations by Jean-Louis Mermet, executive chef.

Also on the second floor is Nakayama, a Japanese dining room open for lunch and dinner.

On the third floor is the Ming Court. This elegant Chinese restaurant is decorated with intricately carved wood window frames and subtle tones recalling the classical period of the Ming Dynasty. Featuring Cantonese cuisine, it is open for lunch and *yum-cha*, and later for dinner.

The Doré Bar, open in the evenings on the second floor, features music from the grand piano.

In the first basement are a health club and sauna, a beauty parlor, a barbershop, and necessities shops.

On the roof is a large swimming pool with a panoramic view of Taipei.

The hotel has a well-equipped executive lounge.

The guest rooms are on the fourth through the twelfth floors. Each room has a refrigerator, color TV and in-house movies, three phones, and complimentary Chinese tea on request. The French-style suites are magnificently furnished.

LAI LAI SHERATON HOTEL
12 Chung Hsiao East Road
Section 1
Taipei
Taiwan, Republic of China
Telephone: (02) 321-5511
Telex: 23939
Cable: SHANGTEL
Fax: (02) 3944240 LAI LAI TPE
Reservations:
    In Taipei call 321-5511
    In the USA call 1-800-325-3535
All major credit cards
Chairman: H. C. Chang
General Manager: C. H. Lai
Sales Manager: Victor Chou
Sheraton Hotels
Rates (approx.):
    Superior room $150 single, $158 double
    Deluxe room $183 single, $183 double
    Junior suite $287
    Standard suite $380
    Deluxe suite $493
    Executive suite $653
    Lai Lai Suite $913
    Shangri-La Suite $913
    Presidential Suite $2,670
705 rooms, 72 suites
Service charge 10%; tax 5%

The ultramodern yet very Chinese Lai Lai Sheraton is an eighteen-story hotel right in the heart of the business, banking, and shopping area of Taipei, and just a few minutes from the freeway leading to the Chiang Kai-shek International Airport and to central and southern Taiwan.

It is the kind of hotel you don't ever have to leave. Occupying a part of the lobby floor and the first basement level are the opulent Champs Élysées and Shangri-La shopping arcades. The sixty shops include the fine emporiums of Dunhill, A. Testoni, Gucci, Givenchy, Mario Valentino, and Issey Miyake. There are shops for everyone and every need, selling everything from books to pottery, coral, antiques, art pieces, and handicrafts.

As in most of the Sheraton hotels in Asia, the rooms are simple and elegant. And there are some special things, such as six in-house movies each day, twenty-four-hour room service, same-day free laundry service, complimentary English newspapers and magazines, private doorbells, and an automatic computerized wake-up service. The decor is modern Chinese with fine furnishings. The suites are fancier, more spacious, and richer in their furnishings. Most luxurious, of course, is the hotel's Presidential Suite. This spacious duplex apartment has private quarters for a secretary and a guard. It features an international decor enriched with stunning Chinese antiques and has a grand piano, a sauna, and a whirlpool bath, as well as a fully equipped kitchen and a private bar, all within its nine rooms. Other suites are especially designed for Japanese and for Middle Eastern guests of the hotel.

Catering to the traveling business person, this hotel has set up what it calls the Distinguished Customer Service (DCS) program. If you arrange for this service, a DCS team member meets you at the door and takes you to your room to handle check-in formalities and to discuss any arrangements you wish. There is also the Business Service Center, which is open from 7:00 A.M. until 10:30 P.M. every day. It has individual offices that may be rented for a day (for about one hundred dollars) or for an hour (for about thirteen dollars). There is a conference room, a lounge, and secretarial and translation services. A full range of business equipment is available as well as fresh-off-the-wire UPI and Dow Jones reports. There is a large reference library as well.

The Lai Lai Sheraton has more dining spots than any other hotel in the city. There are four Chinese, two Japanese, one Italian, and one French dining room, and a Western-style coffee shop. There are four lounges, including the British Pub.

Among the most delightful of the places to dine in this hotel is the Antoine Room, featuring classical French cuisine in truly elegant nineteenth-century surroundings. The Hunan Garden is a first-of-its-kind Chinese dining room in Taipei, serving Hunan foods Western style. Equally elegant is the Cantonese Jade Garden, with *yum cha* at breakfast and lunch. Momoyama has a sushi bar and private tatami rooms, while Teppan Yaki serves sizzling steaks, seafood, and vegetable specialties made at the table. In the Happy Garden guests are served authentic Taiwanese dishes, and in the Shangri-La Garden Shanghai meals are provided. Certainly one of the favorite spots at almost any hour is the Four Seasons Cafe, the Western-style coffee shop where all meals are available, including three different buffets a day.

Le Bar is the hotel's watering hole, and the Lai Lai Night-club is the center of disco activity until early morning.

The hotel claims that the Lai Lai Executive Club has the most extensive facilities of any health club in any hotel in Taipei. It has a fully equipped gymnasium, squash courts, a 260-foot rooftop jogging track, tennis and golf practice areas, a rooftop swimming pool, a sauna, and a massage service.

I meant it when I said you really don't have to leave the hotel. But of course you should. Within ten to fifteen minutes by taxi are all of the sights worth seeing in Taipei. Or walk, but before you do be sure to get your free copy of the pocket-sized *Tourist Map*. It is a large very clear map of the city, the island, and Kaohsiung, and Taichung. Information is in both English and Chinese. Don't go anywhere without it.

THE RITZ TAIPEI
155 Minn Chuan East Road
Taipei
Taiwan, Republic of China
Telephone: (02) 597-1234
Telex: 27345 THE RITZ
Cable: THERITZ
Fax: (02) 596222-3
Reservations:
   In Taipei call 597-1234, ext. 255 or 288
   In the USA call Leading Hotels of the World at
      1-800-223-6800
All major credit cards
President: Stanley Yen
General Manager: Andre A. Joulian
Concierge: Joseph Hsieh
Sales Manager: Lily Duann
Leading Hotels of the World
Rates (approx.):
   Standard room $136
   Deluxe room $181
   Junior suite $245
   Corner suite $265
   Manet Suite $355
   Renoir Suite $516
   Ritz Suite $774
195 room, 91 suites
Service charge 10%; tax 5%

This is a truly luxurious hotel. When the limousine picks up guests at the airport, it is stocked with local newspapers, soft drinks, and cold, damp towels. There is no front desk; guests are shown straight to their rooms and greeted with flowers, a cake with their name on it, and a bottle of good burgundy. In the room are bathrobes and silk-covered clothes hangers.

You'll appreciate the Ritz's art deco decor as soon as the doormen in gray uniforms open the smoky-gray glass doors. Etched glass, displays of fresh flowers, and rich 1930s-style furnishings are everywhere.

The guest rooms are delightful. Beardsley art on screens, mirrors, and chairs and tables are all reminiscent of the thirties in Europe. The rooms have all the amenities of the eighties, however, including individual temperature control, a central dehumidifying system, radio, and color TV with complimentary in-house movies. The luxurious and spacious bathrooms, with walls and floors of marble, have both tubs and stall showers as well as hair dryers and makeup mirrors.

With ninety-one suites, this hotel is dedicated to serving the affluent, which it does very well. It also has a nonsmoking floor.

Dining by candlelight in Paris 1930, an intimate French restaurant with an art deco decor, is a pleasurable trip into another world. The other dining rooms include the Chinese Restaurant, featuring top Hunan cuisine and a Ching Dynasty decor, and *my favorite*, La Brasserie. The fare is delightful any time of day at this French Tiffany-style bistro.

One of the hotel's great features is its Matisse Suite. Resembling a library in a manor house, it is a sort of private club for business guests. On the second floor, it offers a full range of business services.

The well-equipped Ritz Health Centre includes a gymnasium and a jogging track. There is no swimming pool, but a Swedish sauna and an open-air Jacuzzi are on a sun deck.

So it can assure the best services for individual travelers, the Ritz Taipei does not accept groups.

In keeping with its elegant European atmosphere, the hotel doesn't contain many shops. It does have a bookshop, and a contemporary hair salon. Other good shops are nearby on Chung-Shan North Road.

THAILAND

*T**hai* means "free," and Thailand has managed to exist for more than seven centuries as an independent country.

Today, it is a constitutional monarchy occupying nearly two hundred thousand square miles in southeast Asia. It has a population of nearly 50 million. The capital is Bangkok.

Thailand is bordered by Burma on the west and northwest, Laos on the north and east, Cambodia on the southeast, and the Gulf of Siam and Malaysia on the south. A southward extension into the Malay Peninsula gives Thailand a long coastline on the Gulf of Siam and the Andaman Sea.

The fertile and thickly populated central plain in the heart of the country is actually one vast rice paddy, entirely flat and never more than a few feet above sea level. It is watered by the Chao Phraya and smaller rivers and has a system of canals for irrigation and drainage. Both Bangkok and Ayutthaya, the old capital, are situated within this basin.

The northern area is mountainous, having peaks as high as eighty-five hundred feet. Extensive forests in this area include teak, which is cut, hauled by elephants to the rivers, and floated to the market. Rice is grown in the northern river valleys. Peninsular Thailand in the south includes the famous resort area Phuket and other offshore islands. The area is covered with jungles and is mostly mountainous. It is an important source of rubber and tin, making Thailand third in the world in the production of these materials.

Thai, the official language, is related to Chinese. English is the predominant Western language spoken. Hinayana Buddhism is the state religion, and more than 93 percent of the people are Bhuddists.

The former kingdom of Siam is full of color and excitement. There are truly magnificent gold-crested temples, ancient cities, ornate religious artifacts, classical dancing, elephants, deep jungles, the best rice in the world, and a capital, Bangkok, with streets of water. This vibrant metropolis has some of the world's best hotels.

Thailand is most impressive for its gentle people, who are well mannered, friendly, always smiling, and very hospitable to visitors. The people love to dress well and neatly, and seem to savor being neat in all things. They love their food, and as a result Thai cuisine is known around the world. They work hard, too: you see them always busy, carrying great loads of wood, food, and whatever in their small boats or in baskets on their heads. While 80 percent of the people are farmers, those in Bangkok are very much city people and enjoy the good things a city has to offer.

Rama IX, a direct descendant of Rama I (who governed from 1782 to 1809), is the king of Thailand now. The most famous of Thai kings was Rama IV, who was the subject of *The King and I*, a story based on an autobiography by an English teacher, Anna Leonowens (because the movie distorts the character of their truly great king, *The King and I* has been forbidden to be shown in Thailand). Rama IV, who is known as King Mongkut, was the first of the nation's rulers to truly understand Western culture and science, and he endeavored to bring the two cultures together to serve his nation.

Thailand had nearly 3 million visitors in 1986, and by the year 2,000 it expects to have 15 million. The Thais are building grand new hotels and keeping up their older hotels by constant renovation and redecoration. They are enlarging their air terminals and improving their airlines, and more international carriers are arriving at Bangkok's beautiful modern international airport. Only Japan sends more visitors to Thailand than the United States.

Bangkok

Bangkok, also known as Krung Thep, or the City of Angels, is the capital of Thailand and is on the east bank of the Chao Phraya River, not far from the Gulf of Siam.

It is a confusing, poorly laid-out city, and you should have a guide at first to help you orient yourself. Fortunately, the principal things to see are in its Inner Center, which you can tour on foot if you have good walking shoes.

There is so much to see in Bangkok. When my wife and I first saw such things as the Grand Palace (built in 1782), the Temple of the Emerald Buddha, the Wat Po of the Reclining Buddha, and all of the others in the Royal Palace compound, we were speechless. It was the first time I was so impressed with something that I forgot I had a camera in hand. It seemed impossible to absorb all we saw of the remarkable architecture and skilled craftsmanship.

Although many of the canals have been filled in and made into boulevards, some of them are left from the days when Bangkok was called the Venice of the East. Now West is becoming more a part of this East, with modern high-rises on wide streets. Fortunately, none of the grand and exotic richness of Bangkok has been harmed.

After the unforgettable sights in the Grand Palace compound, the second best tourist attraction is the Floating Market at Thonbari—at least it was until it became too popular. Now tourists are encouraged to travel about an hour southwest of the city to see the more attractive, unspoiled Floating Market at Damnern Saduak in the Ratchaburi province.

Most attractive are many of the three hundred temples in Bangkok. In addition to the two already mentioned, the most outstanding are the Temple of the Golden Buddha, or Wat Trimitr, with a ten-foot-high statue of solid gold, and the Temple of the Dawn, or Wat Arun, whose five towers sit on a series of terraces supported by statues of demons and angels.

Among the many other places to see are the National Museum, the Jim Thompson House (former home of the American who helped the Thais develop their silk industry), and the Suan Pakkard Palace. If you can, on Saturday or Sunday, visit the Sunday Market at the Pramane Ground, where everything from antiques to exotic food and wild animals are sold from hundreds of stalls.

Thirty-five miles from Bangkok is the famous Rose Garden at Nakon Pathom, and about twenty miles away is the ancient city at Samut Prakarn.

Shopping is a pastime of importance to visitors to Bangkok. The greatest bargains found by my wife and I were in the fine silk fabrics. We bought such things as colorful silk-covered pillows and luxurious soft silk blouses. We found that the shops in the hotels and the Jim Thompson Shop were the best and most reliable for silks. The same goes for the fine gems. The shops in the better hotels are trustworthy, as are the several fine government-approved gem shops in mid-city. It is interesting to visit the gem shops and watch the stones being polished and the jewelery being created. The tailors, as in Hong Kong, are very good in the hotel tailor shops, and here, too, the prices are good.

You'll find that you can buy watches with all the famous names, from Cartier to Rolex. They look great, and some of them keep good time, but at twenty to thirty dollars apiece they are fakes. Remember two things about shopping: Don't buy in a hurry, shop around; and do bargain. It is expected.

It is wise to get a copy of the *Official Shopping Guide*, issued by the Tourism Authority of Thailand. This helpful one hundred–page booklet is free from the tourist office and, often, at the concierge desk in your hotel. It has the advertisements and listings of all the lapidaries (gem shop-factories) and other businesses—many of which will provide free transportation to get you into their shops. All of the shops in the booklet are recommended by the Authority and checked for fair trading practices.

ASIA HOTEL
296 Phayathai Road
Bangkok 10400
Thailand
Telephone: (02) 215-0808
Telex: 82722 ASIATEL TH
Cable: ASIAHOTEL
Fax: (662) 215-4360
Reservations:
   In Bangkok call 215-0808
   In the USA call Utell International at (212) 397-1560
All major credit cards
Property Manager: Peeruch Chotigapugana
General Manager: Robert Thein Pe
Sales Manager: Amphai Areephongsa

Rates (approx.):
  Standard room $72 single, $80 double
  Deluxe room $80 single, $88 double
  2-room suite $152
  3-room suite $220
650 rooms, 20 suites
Service charge 10%; tax 11%

The Asia Hotel is in the heart of Bangkok and has been there for more than twenty years. It is close to all business and shopping centers and about a half hour from the Don Muang International Airport. It provides shuttle service or a limousine to carry guests from and to the airport.

In 1985, the hotel underwent extensive renovation to meet rising standards in this city of many fine hotels. Its rooms are excellent for a modestly priced hotel. It has TV with in-house movies, four-channel music, direct-dial telephones, refrigerators, individually controlled air conditioning, and marble bathrooms. The rooms in the older, original buildings have been enlarged and upgraded so they are as nice as those in the hotel's new wings.

Something very nice about this hotel is its two swimming pools, on the fifth and twelfth floors. Both have extensive lounge areas and landscaped gardens. Recently opened are the hotel's Health Club and Business Center. The Club has a fully equipped gymnasium with sauna and massage. The Business Center offers translating, secretarial, and other business services.

The hotel's Japanese dining room, Kagetsu, reflects the city's heavy inflow of Japanese visitors. This excellent place has two private rooms as well as tempura counters and sushi bars. The Great Wall is the Chinese restaurant, featuring Cantonese cuisine. It has ten private rooms, and its chefs are from Hong Kong. On the hotel's third floor, it is an elegant spot with traditional Chinese decor.

Bonanza is the hotel's Steak House. This grill room has a rustic design, charcoal spits, and modest prices. The Tivoli is the popular coffee shop for snacks and lunches and dinners. It is a nice place, overlooking the lobby.

For nighttime excitement, the hotel's basement nightclub is the spot. A new addition to the hotel, it is called Cabaret, and it really lives up to its name. It features one of three live bands every evening, and the disco sounds are selected by the town's leading disc jockeys. In front of the stage is a circular dance floor, surrounded by easy chairs. The lighting is surprisingly tasteful. The bar is one of the longest in

Thailand, and from it you have a view of the dance floor. There are international shows as well.

Another popular spot is the Velvet Cocktail Lounge, which has a buffet at lunch and dinner. In the lobby area is the cocktail spot, the Lobby Bar. Both have live entertainment. On the top floor of a parking complex is the hotel's Beer Garden, which serves draught and bottled beer, snacks, and barbecue in a garden setting with views of the city twelve stories below.

DUSIT THANI HOTEL
946 Rama IV Road
Bangkok 10500
Thailand
Telephone: 233-1130 or 236-0450
Telex: TH 81170 or TH 81027
Cable: DUSITOTEL
Fax: (662) 236400
Reservations:
   In Bangkok call 233-1130, ext. 2872, or 236-0450/9
   In New York state call (212) 593-2988 collect or
      1-800-221-4862
   Elsewhere in the USA call 1-800-223-5652 or
      1-800-221-4862
All major credit cards
Managing Director: Chanut Piyaoui
General Manager: Daniel McCafferty
Director of Sales: Surakarn Kitchakarn
Rates (approx.):
   Standard room $100 single, $110 double
   Superior room $115 single, $125 double
   Deluxe room $135 single, $150 double
   Suite $240 single, $275 double
   Deluxe suite $550–$700
488 rooms, 37 suites
Service charge 10%; tax 11%

In ancient times, the Thais believed that Dusit Thani was a town in heaven. In adopting the name, the hotel accepted quite a challenge. It is a challenge it handles very well.

Opened in 1970, the Dusit Thani is an elegantly designed building. The hotel is at one of Bangkok's most important junctions. Immediately opposite is the city's lovely Lumpini Park, with acres of tropical trees and flowers, and the business and entertainment district of Silom Road is just a few minutes' walk away.

Realizing that bigness is not necessarily greatness, this hotel reduced its size in 1983 from 800 rooms to the present 525 rooms and suites. This made it possible for the hotel to create what it calls its Landmark Rooms, which are among the largest standard-price rooms in the area.

As luxurious as these rooms are, the hotel has even more luxurious accommodations, including four sumptuous deluxe suites—Majesty, Regent, Royal, and Presidential—and an Executive Wing as well.

Each of the hotel's rooms is superbly decorated with Thai paintings, silks, and ceramics. The modern amenities are all there, including individually controlled air conditioning, in-house TV and video, mini-bars, and beautiful bathrooms. The Landmark Rooms are divided into two areas—the sitting area and the sleeping area. The beds are twin doubles or king-sized. There is a separate dressing area adjacent to the marble bathroom. Each of the deluxe suites has a unique decor.

The lineup of dining spots is most impressive. Hamilton's is the gourmet dining room, featuring imported steaks, beef, and lobsters. The menu was created by former White House chef Rene Verdon, who is the culinary advisor for this restaurant. There are views of the hotel's beautiful gardens.

The Mayflower is the Chinese restaurant, serving everything from dim sum or a bowl of noodles to rare Taechieu duck's feet in jelly. Shogun has Japanese master chefs preparing sushi, tempura, sukiyaki, and Kobe steaks.

My favorite is the the Tiara. It is a rooftop dining room with breathtaking views of Bangkok on all sides. In the evening it has an international floor show with a superb French menu. In charge is Joel Diouet of Gault and Millau–starred Le Bocage of Bordeaux. The international buffet at lunch is sumptuous.

Dusit-Bussaracum is an elegant dining room serving the Royal Thai-style cuisine at lunch and dinner. The Pavilion Cafe on the ground floor is a moderate-priced dining room serving Oriental and continental dishes. The Library 1918 is a combination reading room and cocktail lounge, where afternoon tea and evening drinks are served and there is a lovely view of the garden. The Lobby Lounge is popular for drinks and has live entertainment. The Landmark Lounge is limited to the use of the hotel's Landmark guests and provides continental breakfast, cocktails and snacks throughout the day. There are writing desks, reading materials and a garden view.

Bubbles is the exciting disco with a resident deejay. It's one of the city's popular spots.

The Health Center, operated by Fitness International, has a fully air-conditioned gymnasium, a squash court and a floodlit outdoor tennis court. There are separate saunas for men and women, whirlpools and aerobic dancing. The swimming pool, surrounded by the hotel garden, is large and attractive.

The Executive Center has a full range of services for business people, with a fully-equipped conference room, library and a Reuters wire link-up to world-wide stock, business and commodity information. It is open every day including Sunday.

On the ground floor is the hotel's Shopping Arcade, featuring modern clothing and tailormade garments, souvenirs, silks, jewelry, books and necessity shops.

The hotel is one of the city's leading convention hotels, with ample facilities for meetings. The largest is the Napalai Ballroom, which can hold up to 2,000 people. New and very nice is the small luxurious Vimarnman Room, for high-level meetings and parties.

One of the pleasures of this hotel are the surprise guests of honor. They have among them writers, singers, artists, etc. Guests of the hotel are invited to come and meet them, and often an evening of entertainment begins at 7:30 of a designated day. There are recitals, exhibitions and sometimes just discussions. They are held in Library 1918, where, in addition, you may enjoy a splendid view of the hotel's hanging gardens.

HILTON INTERNATIONAL BANGKOK
AT NAI LERT PARK
2 Wireless Road
Bangkok 10500
Thailand
Telephone: 253-0123
Telex: TH 72206 HILBKK
Cable: HILTELS
Fax: (662) 253-6509
Reservations:
In Bangkok call 250-0999 or 253-0123, ext. 8671
In the USA call Hilton Reservation Service at
1-800-445-8667

All major credit cards
General Manager: Bernard E. Brack
Concierge: Thavorn Puttan
Sales Director: Piyasak Jaroonpipatkul
Hilton International
Rates (approx.):
   Superior room $93 single, $100 double
   Deluxe room $112 single, $120 double
   Suite $196–$905
352 rooms, 37 suites
Service charge 10%; tax 11%

This might be called the garden hotel of Bangkok. It is a beautifully designed hotel sitting amidst beautiful gardens. It is on Bangkok's "embassy row" and just minutes away from the major business and shopping districts. Fairly new, it was opened in 1983.

It occupies a magnificent eight-and-a-half-acre landscaped park with fragrant gardens, waterfalls, and lily ponds. It is only a twenty-minute drive from the airport and fifteen minutes from the railway station.

The building is a five-story crescent giving more of an appearance of a resort hotel than a city hotel. Its exterior is softened by bougainvillaea-draped balconies, which help it to blend into the lush tropical gardens.

The hotel is named after Nai Lert, a prominent Bangkok businessman who loved plants and was the creator of one of the city's few green spaces. The hotel occupies part of Nai Lert Park and therefore can boast of having not only one of the largest gardens in modern Bangkok but also one filled with an exceptionally varied collection of plants.

The hotel's design has created its own views, and this is apparent when you enter. You see bright fresh greenery all around and the cool deep blue of the swimming pool. The wall facing the main entrance is of sheer glass rising two stories.

The spaciousness of the hotel is enhanced by its three atrium wings, providing more public space than is usually found in a hotel of this size. The atriums are naturally illuminated by skylights, and their outstanding decor features beige Italian marble, a wealth of indoor plants, cascading greenery from the atrium balconies, and, in one wing, an indoor water garden.

Directly opposite the main entrance is a Thai *sala* built over a lotus pond. Traditional in design, it is a symbol of shade, relaxation, and hospitality. Its message is repeated inside, with another *sala* just left of the entrance.

Do see the unusual and eye-catching mural in the hotel's grand ballroom. Executed on a piece of sold teak measuring four by twenty feet, it depicts through scenes of festivals and work the life and culture of people in the various regions of Thailand. It took four months for the artist, Somyos Traiseni, to complete it. Also be sure to see the striking tapestry in the hotel's Saranrom Garden restaurant. It shows many flowers of Thailand and was created by twelve women working 2,147 hours.

The rooms are spacious and delightfully Thai in decor, with soft pastels and all modern appointments, including individual temperature control, direct-dial telephones, color TV, refrigerator and mini-bar, large writing desk, and, in the spacious bathroom, hair dryer and scale. The Royal and Presidential apartments were designed by Valentino of Rome and have large balconied windows with wide views over landscaped gardens. Each suite has individual decor with exceptional furniture, Italianate in design for the most part. For example, the dining and the occasional tables are made of hand-painted and lacquered wood that looks like marble or lapis lazuli. The bathrooms are resplendent in marble. The Royal Suites are particularly delightful in their luxurious Thai decors.

As in Hilton International hotels around the world there is an Executive Floor here, a hotel within a hotel with upgraded rooms and services designed for the business traveler. There is a butler, an exclusive lounge with complimentary continental breakfast, afternoon tea and cocktails, and an executive floor manager waiting to be of service.

The dining rooms are delightful. In the elegant Ma Maison, diners may enjoy French haute cuisine and wines in a sophisticated Thai-style decor characterized by teakwood paneling and rare antiques in display cases. For more informal dining, the Suan Saranrom garden restaurant serves both Thai and European favorites in a room with a glass wall, permitting a view of the lush gardens and the pool. The Genji restaurant serves Japanese lunch and dinner cuisine in an elegant setting. It has seven traditional-style private dining rooms with panoramic views of the park.

The magnificent Lert Wanalai Grand Ballroom can accommodate up to 850 people, and there are six more function rooms for business meetings and other events.

A very nice place is the Lobby Lounge, where you may

enjoy a cocktail and a string quartet in the evening. There is also a Thai-style shopping village offering antiques, handicrafts, and other Thai products.

The swimming pool is surrounded by flowering shrubs and trees, and there is the Chuan Chom Pool Pavilion for drinks and snacks. Two floodlit tennis courts for all-weather play are operated by Peter Burwash International. There's also a sports complex of two squash courts, a gymnasium, and a sauna, whirlpool, and massage service operated by the Clark Hatch Fitness Center. The winding garden pathways are excellent jogging tracks.

The Executive Business Center is well staffed and well equipped to handle the needs of the business traveler. Most helpful are the translating and appointment-making services available on request.

HOTEL SIAM INTER-CONTINENTAL
967 Srapatum Palace Property
Rama One Road
P.O. Box 2052
Bangkok 10500
Thailand
Telephone: (662) 253-0355/7
Telex: TH 81155 SIAMINT
Cable: INHOTELCOR BANGKOK
Fax: (662) 253-2275
Reservations:
   In Bangkok call 253-0355/7
   In the USA call Inter-Continental Hotels at
      1-800-327-0200
All major credit cards
General Manager: Daniel Desbaillets
Front Office Manager: Sompan Usahapanich
Marketing Director: Naphalai Areesorn
Inter-Continental Hotels
Rates (approx.):
   Standard room $100 single, $107 double
   Superior room $115 single, $123 double
   Junior suite $230
   Executive suite $288
   Deluxe suite $327
   Royal Suite $615–$960
400 rooms, 23 suites
Service charge 10%; tax 11%

This delightful hotel is a beautiful sight. Located in the center of Bangkok, it is within the twenty-six acres of tropical landscaped gardens that are a part of the Srapatum Royal Palace estate. It is next to the city's largest commercial center, and within easy reach of the cultural, shopping, and entertainment areas of Bangkok.

A few years ago the hotel spent about $7 million on a renovation program that improved not only its guest rooms but its public areas as well. You enter a lobby of lush landscaped gardens with water cascading into pools, reflecting the look of the gardens surrounding the hotel. This lobby is decorated with marble, exquisite Thai silks, and intricate wood carvings. The decor is a continuation of the beauty of the exterior. The hotel's architecture features a classic sweep of its pagoda-style roof, which is reflected in the waters of the lotus pond in front of it.

With the surrounding parklands the largest of any hotel in Bangkok, sports enthusiasts get added pleasure as they swim in the outdoor pool, play tennis on the night-lighted courts, or do a turn around the hotel's half-mile jogging track.

Here is a hotel that makes a special effort to serve the business traveler. In addition to improving facilities to serve the business person, the hotel upgraded services as well. The Executive Recognition Service (ERS) pre-registers the guest, guarantees garden-wing accommodations, and provides a basket of fruit or a bottle of imported whiskey, a selection of business publications, a free pressing for the first suit or dress, and a free drink at the hotel's Terrace Bar. Other benefits are described in a folder given to the ERS guest on arrival.

Also available for the use of the business traveler is a well-staffed and -equipped business center. The hotel was the first to install the UPI hotel news service, which is available at all times on the room TV.

The hotel's rooms are equipped with large work desks, direct-dial telephones, color TV with two channels of video movies, and refrigerators with mini-bars. All of the bathrooms have teakwood paneling, radio and telephone extensions, and built-in hair dryers.

Avenue One is the hotel's top dining room, and Chef Warren Pearson has introduced what he calls Thai nouvelle cuisine, which has lighter versions of the favorite Thai dishes. Here, both Oriental and Western dishes are served.

My favorite spot is the Talay Tong Seafood Inn, which was one of the first seafood dining rooms in a hotel when it was opened about twenty years ago. It has on the menu every-thing from fish from the Gulf of Siam to mussels, clams, and lobsters from Phuket—all from the same day's catch. Each is prepared to the guest's specifications.

But the best deal is the luncheon buffet, which features Thai dishes from all parts of the country. The knowledge-able diner will start, in the Thai manner, with noodles, then choose from spicy entrees of *yums*, a variety of curries or *kaeng ped*, a selection of vegetable dishes, *nam prik*, the famed Thai preparation eaten with rice, *kanom jeen*, the Thai an-swer to pasta, and an exciting array of scrumptious seafoods steamed on the spot. Then comes the dessert—with a range of Thai desserts, or *kanom*, from *ruam mitr* to *foy thong*, as well as fresh fruits. Some people come to this restaurant for the desserts alone.

The hotel has a coffee shop called Sivalai, a terrace bar, and a pool-side snack bar. The Tea Garden, which recently opened at the terrace to the left of the lobby entrance, is an outdoor restaurant that serves afternoon tea from 2:30 until 6:00 P.M., with a wonderful selection of cakes, pastries, pancakes, waffles, and scones. Between 11:30 A.M. and 2:30 P.M. the Tea Garden serves noodles dry or with soup— thin, wide, *bahmee*, or vermicelli along with pork, chicken, beef, fish balls, or shrimp balls—and more.

In 1987, the hotel reproduced a Thai village in its gardens. An authentic setting, it is made up of Thai houses built over the lake that winds around the gardens. Here are presented shows of Thai classical and folk dances and martial arts, and a buffet of dishes from all parts of the country—and there is a handicrafts bazaar for shoppers. Some guests hold receptions and events in the Thai Village.

HYATT CENTRAL PLAZA BANGKOK
P.O. Box 10-182
1695 Phaholyothin Road
Bangkhen
Bangkok 10900
Thailand
Telephone: (02) 541-1234
Telex: 20173 HYATTBK TH
Fax: (662) 541-1087
Reservations:
   In Bangkok call 541-1234, ext. 2116 or 2118
   In Nebraska call 1-800-228-9001
   In Alaska and Hawaii call 1-800-228-9005

Elsewhere in the USA call Hyatt International at
    1-800-228-9000
All major credit cards
General Manager: Frank S. W. Kuhn
Director of Sales: Danai Wansom
Hyatt International
Rates (approx.):
    Standard room $68 single, $80 double
    Superior room $88 single, $104 double
    Deluxe room $100 single, $116 double
    Regency Club room $120 single, $136 double
Suite $132–$736
607 rooms, 104 suites
Service charge 10%; tax 11%

This Hyatt hotel is about midway between the International Airport and the center of the city. It calls itself a "hotel and convention centre," and it does a good job of being both. Opposite the hotel is the Railway Golf Course. It takes ten minutes to get to the Bangkok International Airport via the nearby expressway. There is a scheduled shuttle service that runs from the hotel to the Central Department Store on Ploenchit and Silom roads at regular intervals. A fleet of luxury cars based at the hotel is available for service.

There is good reason the hotel is so popular for conventions. It adjoins both the Bangkok Convention Centre and the Bangkok International Exposition Centre. Within the same large complex is a shopping mall and the Central Department Store. The convention center is Thailand's largest, with state-of-the-art technology. It has Thailand's largest pillarless auditorium, which can accommodate up to three thousand people.

The Hyatt Business Centre was recently voted to be the best of its kind in Bangkok by *Business Traveller* magazine. It has an efficient staff, a range of business equipment and conference rooms, and a library and reading lounge with up-to-date business publications. All facilities are open until 7:00 P.M.

The Fitness Centre is on the lower lobby floor and has exercise rooms, separate saunas and plunge pools for men and women, lounges with TV and in-house movies, and a massage service. The Fitness Centre facilities also include three tennis courts, a swimming pool, a jogging track, and access to the Railway Golf Course across the street, which has an excellent driving range.

All of the hotel rooms have individually controlled air

conditioning, private bathrooms and showers, color TV with in-house movies, in-house music, direct-dial telephones, and telephone handsets in bathrooms. There are two floors devoted to the Regency Club, with complimentary continental breakfast and cocktails in the evening. These floors have upgraded rooms and service and a concierge on duty.

Hugo's is the elegant ninety-six-seat gourmet dining room for lunch and dinner, with seafood from the Gulf of Thailand and prime steaks from the United States and New Zealand. The Dynasty Restaurant has windows overlooking a Chinese garden, and it serves Cantonese cuisine with dim sum at lunch. The Suan Bua Thai Restaurant is in the poolside garden and serves authentic Thai dishes in an air-conditioned room or on a sheltered verandah. It overlooks a lotus pond. In the cool months, guests also sit in the garden.

The Chatuchak Cafe is the twenty-four-hour restaurant that serves local and Western favorites. It has an attractive blue-and-white tiled decor.

The Lobby Lounge opens at noon and from 5:00 P.M. until very late offers live entertainment. The first "videotheque" to be set up in Bangkok is the hotel's Hollywood Discotheque. Vibrant and fun, it is open from 9:00 P.M. until 1:00 A.M.

THE IMPERIAL HOTEL
Wireless Road (Vitayu Road)
Patumwan
Bangkok 10500
Thailand
Telephone: 252-0450/7, 252-4730/7, or 252-4744/9
Telex: 84418 IMPER TH
82301 IMPER TH
Cable: IMPERHOTEL
Fax: (662) 253-3190
Reservations:
   In Bangkok call 254-0023 or 254-0111
All major credit cards
General Manager: Chompunute Hoontrakul
Imperial Family of Hotels
Rates (approx.):
   Room $85 single, $95 double
   Suite $160–$400
400 rooms, 20 suites
Service charge 10%; tax 11%

The Imperial had major expansion in 1980 and as a result has attracted many clients from abroad. Six brothers and one sister share the ownership and management, and it is apparent that there is a personal concern for their guests.

The hotel is on six acres right on tree-lined Wireless Road. Within ten minutes' walk are about ten foreign embassies, five major department stores, two shopping arcades, and the head offices of four major Thai banks. It is a garden hotel, surrounded by lawns and tropical plants. It has a beautiful lobby, decorated with a huge handmade teak carving across the high wall. The hotel's rooms have private bathrooms with showers, central air conditioning, international direct-dial telephones with bathroom extensions, mini-bars, refrigerators, piped-in music, and color TV with free video movies.

The hotel claims to have the largest hotel swimming pool in Bangkok, and it is beautifully surrounded by the landscaped grounds. There are a tennis court, two air-conditioned squash courts, and a putting green. There's a small gymnasium with workout machines and saunas.

Among the five restaurants is Teikoku, the Japanese gourmet dining room open for lunch and dinner, and Tai Pan, featuring Cantonese cuisine for lunch and dinner. The Garden Room has an international buffet at lunchtime and serves sukiyaki and *shabu-shabu* at dinner. The twenty-four-hour restaurant is Jarmjuree, which serves Thai, Chinese, and European dishes. Jim's House, the hotel's European dining room, serves lunch and dinner, and high tea from 3:30 until 5:30 P.M. The Poolside Bar has drinks and snacks, and The Peep Inn Cocktail Lounge has drinks and a live band.

There are ten function rooms for meetings and other events, accommodating from ten to a thousand people.

Right next door is the Big Bell Department store, which can take care of most shopping needs.

THE ORIENTAL HOTEL
48 Oriental Avenue
Bangkok 10500
Thailand
Telephone: 236-0400 or 236-0420
Telex: TH 82997
Cable: ORIENHOTEL
Fax: (662) 236-1939
Reservations:
  In Bangkok call 236-0400 or 236-0420

In the USA call Mandarin Oriental Hotels at
  1-800-663-0787 or Leading Hotels of the World at
  1-800-223-6800
All major credit cards
General Manager: Kurt Wachtveitl
Director of Sales and Marketing: Savas Rattakunjara
Mandarin Oriental Hotel Group
Rates (approx.):
  Superior room $152 single, $166 double
  Deluxe room $214 single, $233 double
  Suite $275–$997
368 rooms, 30 suites
Service charge 10%; tax 11%

If you've stayed here you can justifiably say you've stayed
in the best hotel in the world. Readers of *Institutional Investor
Magazine* have judged it as such every year since 1981. The
Oriental has rated well in many other surveys too, and on
my visit here I discovered why.

All of the physical amenities are provided, and they are
certainly top-notch. But the staff is truly exceptional. The
boy who brought breakfast to our room gave us a weather
report, then suggested we try some breakfast rolls made in
a new European oven. So it went throughout the hotel;
everyone honestly tried to please and be helpful.

Opened in 1876, the hotel still stands on its original site
by the Chao Phraya (also called Chao Phya) River. The
original building, which can now be seen only from the
river, contains shops; the delightful Authors' Lounge, *my
favorite spot* for tea; and some fantastic suites, named for
some of the famous authors who have stayed and worked
here.

Modern wings, added in 1958 and 1976, retain much of
the old hotel's charm. Among the beautiful rooms and suites
in the new wings is the Jim Thompson Suite, named for
the American who returned after military duty in Thailand
to help the Thais develop their silk industry. The suite is
magnificiently furnished, using Jim Thompson silks.

While the suites are magnificent, the superior and deluxe
rooms are also delightful. In the modern wings they are
especially large, with silk-covered walls and teak paneling.
The TV is hidden in a teak and polished brass cabinet, and
the other furnishings are also made of teak and brass. Two
sinks are in the bathroom, and a dressing room is provided.
All rooms and suites have great river views.

The lobby is big, but not as massive as so many Asian

hotel lobbies. It is simple yet luxuriant, with white marble and floor-to-ceiling windows looking out on the garden, the pool, and the river. Huge Thai temple bells hanging from the ceiling serve as lighting fixtures. The lobby, too, is a nice place for tea, with a string quartet providing background music.

One of *my favorite* restaurants in the world is the Normandie, on the Oriental's rooftop. I like it not only for the impeccable service and the superb French cuisine of Jean Bardet at both lunch and dinner, but for the spectacular view down and across the river. Long and narrow and beautiful, the dining room is like an elegant Orient Express dining car, only better.

Other restaurants here include Lord Jim's, where we enjoyed an astounding variety of Thai seafoods, and the Verandah, a busy but pleasant place providing Thai and international foods and prompt service. At night steak and seafood barbecues take place on the Terrace, right by the river. The newest dining room, Ciao, serves pizza, pasta, and other Italian dishes along with a view.

Just across the Chao Phraya, by a five-minute ferry, is the Oriental's big tourist attraction, the Oriental Rim Naam. This large, Thai-style dining pavilion features exotic Thai cuisine and traditional Thai dances. Within the Rim Naam complex is the Thai Cooking School at the Oriental, where guests may take a course from Chalie Amatyakul.

At the Oriental Plaza is Diana's, said to be the city's most sophisticated discotheque.

The Oriental Sports Centre has two tennis courts, a jogging track, golf nets, indoor air-conditioned squash courts, and a fully equipped health club across the river.

Staying at the Oriental is one of life's great adventures. As I strolled the gardens, walked along the river promenade, sat in the Authors' Lounge, and relaxed in the Somerset Maugham Suite, I thought of all the famous people who had been here—from the Russian court jeweler Carl Faberge, who came for the coronation of King Vajiravudh in 1911, to John Steinbeck, Joseph Conrad, and other great writers, to kings and queens and princes and prime ministers, to, in recent years, Danny Kaye, Roger Moore, William Holden, Lauren Bacall, Peter Ustinov, and Robert de Niro. Perhaps they enjoyed it as much as I.

THE REGENT OF BANGKOK
155 Rajadamri Road
Bangkok 10500
Thailand
Telephone: 251-6127
Telex: TH20004 REGBKK
Cable: REGHO
Fax: (662) 253-9195
Reservations:
   In Bangkok call 250-0805 or 251-6127, ext. 115, 116, or
      122
   In the USA call 1-800-545-4000
All major credit cards
General Manager: William D. Black
Concierge: Yudhadanai Vesarach
Director of Sales and Marketing: Malcolm McKenzie-Vass
Regent International Hotels
Rates (approx.):
   Standard room $104
   Superior room $116
   Deluxe room $128
   1-bedroom suite $220
   2-bedroom suite $336
   Rajadamri Suite $1,200
368 rooms, 32 suites
Service charge 10%; tax 11%

Although only five years old, the Regent seems like one of
the long-established grand hotels. This is partly because of
its construction. Like a set of interconnecting Thai houses,
the hotel is made up of a central building of nine floors
flanked by two hollow-core blocks of seven and eight floors,
which surround landscaped gardens.

The Regent seems like a masterpiece on the inside, too.
Past lotus ponds and hand-carved sandstone elephants is
the lobby, whose broad, tall columns soar to a ceiling of
silk hand-painted in spectacular detail. Rich marble and teak
are all around, and over the landing of the wide staircase
is a wonderful mural of Thai scenery. On a balcony above,
an orchestra provides soft background music. In this setting
guests and locals meet for breakfast, coffee, lunch, tea, cocktails, or light evening meals.

The hotel's spacious guest rooms overlook the Royal
Bangkok Sports Club, the pool-side terrace, or the fashionable diplomatic, residential, and business section of Bangkok. Every room and suite is equipped with individually

controlled air conditioning, a mini-bar, color TV with in-house movies, in-house multichannel radio, a bedside control panel, a telephone, a large desk, a sitting area, and a dressing area. Large silkscreen prints are above the headboards.

In the suites, the decor ranges from stylishly functional to Thai magnificent. The luxurious Rajadamri Suite consists of a dining room seating eighteen people, a large sitting room, a library, and a master bedroom with a dressing room, Jacuzzi, and massage shower.

For business travelers, the Business Executive Centre offers offices, a private meeting room, a library, multilingual secretaries, and state-of-the-art equipment.

Dining and drinking places here are top-notch. La Brasserie, open for lunch and dinner, features French provincial cuisine. Le Cristal, the hotel's premier dining room features haute cuisine, with an emphasis on top-quality beef, in a sophisticated Thai setting. The Spice Market features the best of Thai cooking, including many desserts and exotic fruits. The Rimsra Terrace, next to the hotel swimming pool, serves a range of light snacks with an Italian flavor, such as pizza, charcoal-grilled meats and fish, fresh salads, sandwiches, and fruits.

The Medifit Club, on the ground floor, has two air-conditioned squash courts, a fully equipped gymnasium, Jacuzzi, sauna, and massage rooms, and an excellent professional staff. The Regent's swimming pool is one of the largest in Bangkok, eighty-five by forty-one feet.

Besides necessities shops, the shopping arcade has a gift shop, a jewelry shop, a tailor, an art gallery, an antique shop, and a leather shop.

Completed in 1987 is the Regent Conference Center, in its own building on the hotel's property. It contains four banquet rooms and three other function rooms.

Nice things happen at the Regent. For example, after you arrive there is a knock at your door. A smiling Thai housekeeper will introduce herself and offer to serve you a fragrant Chinese tea she has brought, and to help you unpack. This is the kind of personal attention that is such a pleasant part of the Regent experience.

ROYAL ORCHID SHERATON HOTEL AND TOWERS
2 Captain Bush Lane
Siphya Road
Bangkok 10500
Thailand

Telephone: 234-5599
Telex: 84491 ROYORCH TH or 84492 ROYORCH TH
Cable: ROYORCH BKK
Fax: (02) 236-8320
Reservations:
   In Bangkok call 235-2400/1
   In the USA call 1-800-325-3535
All major credit cards
General Manager: Peter B. Hollaus
Front Office Manager: Sawang Phoompoung
Marketing Director: Bert van Walbeek
Sheraton Hotels
Rates (approx.):
   Hotel room $78–90 single, $90–102 double
   Towers room $102 single, $114 double
   Business suite $118–$137
   Executive 1-bedroom suite $157
   Executive 2-bedroom suite $263
   1-bedroom theme suite $216 single, $216 double
   2-bedroom theme suite $302 single, $333 double
   Krungthep Suite $588
   Royal Orchid Suite $588
701 rooms, 74 suites
Service charge 10%; tax 11%

The magnificent twenty-eight-story Royal Orchid is one of
the more popular hotels in Bangkok with Americans, and
many are surprised to find it to be more luxurious than
some of the Sheratons they've seen and lived in at home.

Not only is it a beautiful hotel, but it is well situated on
the eastern bank of the River of Kings, the Chao Phraya,
in the heart of Bangkok's business center.

The Y-shaped building is connected by a bridge to the
adjacent River City Shopping Centre. The Y-shape gives all
guest rooms a view of the river.

Those who know Sheraton hotels are familiar with the
company's Towers concept. It is the Sheraton effort to cater
exclusively to top corporate executives and VIP travelers.
Here in Bangkok, the Sheraton Towers is the hotel's top
three floors, twenty-six to twenty-eight, an exclusive and
elegant hotel within a hotel. It offers upgraded facilities and
services, including being met at the airport by a Towers
representative and being taken by express elevator to an
exclusive reception area on the twenty-sixth floor. In the
Towers is a private executive boardroom with audio-visual
facilities. Private luncheons and dinners may be served there.

In the private lounge, guests have a magnificent panoramic view, and they can meet informally to talk business, play chess, backgammon, or cards, or read some of a large selection of magazines and newspapers. Here, too, are complimentary breakfast, tea, coffee and light snacks throughout the day, and drinks in the evening. A butler attends to guests' needs.

All of the hotel's rooms are spacious and beautifully appointed, and, while the Towers rooms are bigger and fancier, most guests do as well to stay in the rooms on the lower floors.

The suites are in both the hotel and Towers. All of the suites are quite elegant, but the two larger suites, the Krungthep and the Royal Orchid, are fantastic, with spacious angular rooms and grand furnishings. The master bedrooms and bathrooms are the ultimate in luxury.

The hotel's Business Centre is well conceived, having a full range of services and facilities. Set on the first floor, it is open from 10:00 A.M. to 7:00 P.M. Monday through Friday and from 8:30 A.M. until noon on Saturday.

Among the places to eat is the very popular Rim Nam Coffee Shop, which has a river view. It is on the ground floor and open from 6:00 A.M. until 11:30 P.M. Light meals and snacks are available. Giorgio's is the Italian restaurant on the first floor (both indoors and outdoors), serving all three meals and Sunday brunch. Also on the first floor is the Captain Bush Grill, named after the nineteenth-century Harbor Master of Bangkok, whose house was on the site of the hotel. The menu features grilled meats with possibly the widest variety of cuts of prime beef to be found in Asia. Also from the charcoal grill and open roasting spit are fish, poultry, veal, and lamb, much of it imported. With its teakwood, black and white marble, and rich furnishings it is like a British gentleman's club.

Delightful, too, is the Benkay Restaurant on the hotel's second floor. It has a river view and fine Japanese cuisine, with private tatami rooms. The decor is reminiscent of the famed Kawaramachi Street of Kyoto.

From November through May, the Bho Tree Terrace on the ground floor is the place of the Rivernight Market, which features traditional Thai entertainment and classical dances.

But *my favorite spot* is the Garden Cafe, the twenty-four-hour French-style cafe where you can get continental breakfast, French pastries, gateaux, quiche, sandwiches, and light snacks whenever you want them, along with a delightful view of the river.

Bars? Of course: the Pool Bar is open from 7:00 A.M. until 9:00 P.M., and the intimate Suralai Bar on the ground floor is open from 10:00 A.M. until 1:00 A.M. with live entertainment.

SHANGRI-LA HOTEL
89 Soi Wat Suan Plu
New Road
Bangrak
Bangkok 10500
Thailand
Telephone: 236-7777
Telex: TH 84265
Cable: SHANGRILA BANGKOK
Fax: (662) 236-8579
Reservations:
  In Bangkok call 236-7777
  In the USA call 1-800-457-5050 or, in Los Angeles,
    (213) 551-1121
All major credit cards
General Manager: Franz X. Wyder
Concierge: Sanit Boonthong
Assistant Direct of Sales: Voraphon Udomchokpiti
Shangri-La International
Rates (approx.):
  Room $102–$118 single, $114–$129 double
  Deluxe room $133 single, $145 double
  Club 21 room $141 single, $153 double
  Suite $157–$1,333
650 rooms, 47 suites
Service charge 10%; tax 11%

Opened in 1986, this is the newest of the city's top hotels. Like some of the other fine hotels in Bangkok, it is on the banks of the busy Chao Phraya River. It is conveniently situated next to the Sathorn Bridge and another grand hotel, the Oriental, and a short walk from the Royal Orchid Sheraton.

The spaciousness of the hotel is impressive, beginning with the vast lobby and its full views of the river. The lobby is dominated by polished marble, crystal chandeliers, and lush green plants.

This is a busy place. The Shangri-La encourages conventions and meetings in its splendid function rooms, which can accommodate from ten to two thousand guests. Another attraction for business people is the well-equipped Executive Centre.

The hotel's attractive guest rooms all have uninterrupted views of the river. The better rooms, for "the traveling executive," are in Club 21 and on the Executive Floor. Most opulent, of course, are the suites, some of which have private balconies.

The Health Club, open to both men and women, has a gymnasium, a sauna, a steam bath, a whirlpool bath, aerobic dance classes, and massage. Two tennis courts and squash courts are on the top floor of the parking garage. The freeform swimming pool, between the hotel and the river, has a tiny island with a palm tree on it. Manicured lawns with more palm trees surround the pool.

The hotel offers French meals at La Tache and Chinese meals at Shang Palace. Most pleasant is the Coffee Garden, which has river views and is open twenty-four hours a day, with an international buffet at lunch. *My favorite spot* is the Maenam Terrace, right on the river, where a nightly barbecue takes place. Another favorite is the Salathip Pavilion; also next to the river, it is open daily for dinner with classical Thai entertainment. The Palm Court has a pleasant river view, too, along with light meals and refreshments. The Captain's Bar, good for pre-dinner or after-dinner drinks, has live entertainment.

Not far from the hotel are the Silom Shopping Arcade, the Silom Village Trade Centre, and the Central Department Store. A few shops are in the hotel as well.

Chiang Mai

DUSIT INN
112 Chang Klan Road
Chiang Mai 50000
Thailand
Telephone: (053) 251-0337
Telex: 49325 DUSITINN
Fax: (053) 251-0337
Reservations:
  In Chiang Mai call 251-0336
  In Bangkok call Dusit Thani Hotel at (02) 233-1130
All major credit cards

General Manager: Sangworn Suntisuk
Sales Manager: Yupin Kuptavanich
Dusit Thani Hotel Group
Rates (approx.):
  Rooms $42–$52 single, $54–$64 double
  1-bedroom suite $120
  2-bedroom suite $180
200 rooms, 9 suites
Service charge 10%; tax 11%

The Dusit Inn is a delightful, modestly priced hotel situated in the heart of town, next to the fascinating Night Bazaar.

The rooms are reasonably sized, with tasteful decor and attractive furnishings. They have amenities that include mini-bars, color TV, and daily video movies.

There's a selection of places to dine. The Jasmine restaurant claims to serve the finest Chinese food in the city. The Garden Cafe, open from early morning until late night, features Thai and international dishes, either for a meal or snack. In the evening, there is piano music at the Lobby Bar and more upbeat music at the hotel's sophisticated Music Room.

During the day, the swimming pool is the popular spot either for a refreshing dip, sunbathing, or a cool drink.

The hotel's ballroom can hold up to three hundred for seminars and business meetings.

Hua Hin

Hua Hin is one of the most charming resorts on the southern coast of Thailand, known for its pleasant tropical climate, beautiful beaches, crystal-clear water, bountiful marine life, picturesque fishing villages, and sugarcane and pineapple plantations.

Hua Hin's beauty, first discovered by King Rama VII in the late 1920s, is as pleasant and preserved as ever, in what is known to be the oldest seaside resort town in Thailand.

Hua Hin is a fascinating mixture of coastline, hills, and valleys, all about an hour and a half from Bangkok and not too far from two interesting and old provincial capitals— Prachuab Khiri Khan and Petchaburi. Its soft white beach stretches for nearly three miles, making it popular for family outings. There is swimming and sunbathing, riding on little ponies, and leisurely strolls to the southern end of the beach—a rocky point called Hua Hin (Stone Head), for which the resort is named. The town is is dominated by the picturesque Khao Takiab hill, with its Buddhist temple on top. Here also is Khao Krilas, another hill that has a grand panoramic view of the surrounding coast.

The town is a busy fishing port with reminders of its great regal past. It was here that King Rama VII built his summer palace on the northern edge of town. It is called Klai Kangwon, which means "Far From Worries," and it is where the railway station with its royal waiting room is situated. There is the beach promenade, where old-fashioned deck chairs remind visitors of old seaside movie scenes.

Hua Hin also has one of the best standard golf courses in the country, called the Royal Golf Course.

In the evening, visitors wander to the fishing pier and watch the return of the fishing boats from their daily run. Big baskets of fish are unloaded and distributed to buyers under large floodlights—just like a nighttime sporting event back in the United States.

A popular resort, it has three first-class hotels and fourteen small tourist hotels and inns, not including a number of hotels at other nearby beach towns.

HOTEL SOFITEL CENTRAL
1 Damnerkasem Road
Hua-Hin, Prachuap 77110
Khirikhan
Thailand
Telephone: (032) 511-012/14
Telex: 78313 CETRAC TH
Reservations:
    In Hua-Hin call (032) 511012
    In Bangkok call (02) 233-0256
    In the USA call 1-800-221-4548
All major credit cards
Managing Director: Suthikisti Chirativat
General Manager: J. Y. Cottard
Assistant Sales Manager: Tanyalak Suvanapat
Sofitel Hotels
Rates (approx.):
    Standard room $58
    Superior room $70
    Deluxe room $81
    Suite $138

142 rooms, 8 suites, 45 villas
Service charge 10%; tax 11%

Hua Hin's State Railway Hotel was opened in 1923 as Thailand's first beach hotel. It has been charming visitors for more than sixty years with its restful, Old World atmosphere and its beautiful location amidst a profusion of carefully tended gardens and finely sculptured topiary.

The State Railway Hotel was built with royal guests in mind, complete with tennis courts and an eighteen-hole golf course. In 1986, it became the Hotel Sofitel Central, and renovation and enlargement was started. The new management preserved and enhanced the original colonial architectural style and decorations. Completed late in 1987, the addition of a three-story oblong concrete structure added a hundred new air-conditioned rooms, in a modern version of the original building.

In constructing the new addition, the use of plastic and chrome was forbidden. Brass and wood were the components. Teak was the most important material when the original building was constructed, so it was the main material in the addition. Every detail was important in the new construction, even down to old-style brass light switches.

The new rooms are fully appointed, with mini-bars, color TV, telephones, private terraces, and air conditioning—which is still not in the original building. Those rooms are still fan-cooled, in some cases by fans put there in the 1920s. New bathrooms, as well as TV and other modern amenities, have been added in the old building.

With the additions, the hotel grounds extend down to the beach. The hotel has substantially improved the landscaped gardens and put in magnificent swimming pools as well.

The hotel's original Thai and seafood restaurant along the beach now has a sister restaurant in the new section of the hotel, as well as a bar and a meeting room to hold as many as two hundred people.

ROYAL GARDEN RESORT
107/1 Petkasem Beach Road
Hua Hin 77110
Thailand
Telephone: (032) 511-881/4 or 512-410/9
Telex: 78309 ROGAHUA TH

Reservations:
  In Hua Hin call (032) 511881/4
  In Bangkok call 251-8659
  In the USA call Steigenberger Reservation Service at
    1-800-223-5652 or, in New York state, at
    (212) 593-2988
Most major credit cards
General Manager: Chaiporn Mahakan
Sales Manager: Boonrak Preedarat
Royal Garden Resorts
Rates (approx.):
  Standard room $58 single, $62 double
  Superior room $69 single, $73 double
  Deluxe room $81 single, $85 double
  Suite $192–$308
222 rooms, 5 suites
Service charge 10%; tax 11%

The crescent-shaped Royal Garden Resort is a complex of modern low-rise buildings in six acres of beautiful lush gardens. It is a bit more than fifteen hundred feet from the town of Hua Hin—about 118 miles from Bangkok and just a bit more from the Bangkok International Airport. It is situated on the Gulf of Thailand, directly across from its sister hotel at Pattaya.

The Royal Garden's rooms and suites are beautifully furnished with wicker furniture and other Thai decorative pieces, and they have all the amenities of a first-class hotel. Some of its guests like to use the hotel for their headquarters in Thailand, even visiting Bangkok from here.

The hotel has three sections: the Tower building, which contains the well-designed entrance and lobby and the music room; the South Wing, with guest rooms, restaurants, and the cocktail lounge; and the North Wing, with fifty-four guest rooms and suites. The hotel's recently completed forty-room extension gave it five new suites, two of which are penthouses.

All rooms and suites are arranged in a circular fashion around the hotel's large swimming pool, beyond which are the gardens and the beach. The arrangement provides all rooms with a splendid view of the Gulf. All rooms have full bathtubs, hot and cold water, individually controlled air conditioning, mini-bars, piped-in music, telephones, and color TV with video movies. Each penthouse features a living room, a bedroom, a kitchen and dining area, a bathroom, a guest room, and huge picture windows on a private terrace with a spectacular ocean view.

The hotel has a conference room that can hold up to two hundred people for meetings and exhibitions.

The resort's Petchburi and Pranburi rooms are used for painting and handicraft exhibitions during the winter season.

The Garden Coffee Shop serves breakfast and quick snacks, seafood specials, salads, steaks, chicken, sandwiches, and hamburgers. Open throughout the day and evening, it has both indoor and outdoor seating in a garden. Other places to eat include the Market Seafood Restaurant, with musicians from the Philippines in the evening; the Barbeque Terrace, with Thai and European barbecue dishes at lunch and dinner on the terrace with a view of the Gulf; the Rooftop Cocktail Terrace, on the fourth floor, with drinks and buffet dinners; The Poolside, in the gardens next to the pool, with drinks and snacks; the Nautilus Cocktail Lounge, with daily video programs; and the Jungle Disco, the only disco in town, with a striking decor and lighting, and its own deejay. Just opened is a new Thai Restaurant, which features native performances.

Next to the lobby is a shopping arcade having all the necessities. It also has the Khomapastr cotton and silk shop, with high-quality cloth and gift items made from Thai cotton. It has been in business for more than thirty years.

The hotel also has delightful large seawater aquariums showing off the exotic and colorful marine creatures of the gulf.

In addition to the swimming pool, the hotel has two floodlit all-weather tennis courts. There are boats for hire, and there is windsurfing, water-skiing, and other water sports. The hotel has recently added the modern Gym Centre, complete with weights, a power-pack, an exercise bicycle, rowing machines, and an abdominal conditioner.

Pattaya

Called the international pleasure capital of Thailand, Pattaya is about ninety-five miles east of Bangkok and directly across the Gulf of Siam (Thailand) from Hua Hin. It is linked with the Thai capital by every means of modern transportation, air-conditioned public and private coaches among them.

Pattaya has a population of about one hundred thousand, and the city's major source of income is its tourist visitors.

The climate is semitropical. Mild temperatures from November through February during the northwest monsoon season make that the best time to visit. It is generally warm and humid from May through July, with temperatures in the nineties. Rain squalls generally occur from September through October. However, rain usually lasts only one or two hours in the early morning or around sundown.

There are more than sixty-five tailor shops in Pattaya, mostly along Beach Road, that offer reasonable prices and twenty-four-hour service. Thai silk, guaranteed by the Thai Silk Association, is sold in the three Tai Pan shops in town. Gem dealers will cut sapphires, rubies, and emeralds to your taste. Handicrafted products can be found at the Royal Patronage shop, Chitralada, near the PK Villa on Beach Road. Local artists do paintings—your portrait or copies of your favorite snapshot—within twenty-four hours.

GRAND PALACE HOTEL
Pattaya Beach Resort
Cholburi
Thailand
Telephone: (038) 429901/3, 428541, or 428239
Telex: 85917 GRANPAT TH
Cable: GRANDPAT
Reservations:
  In Pattaya call (038) 429901
  In Bangkok call Ramada Hotel at 233-2305/6
American Express, MasterCard, Visa
Managing Director: Thanes Telan
General Manager: Anusak Rodboonmee
Sales Manager: William Ha
Rates (approx.):
  Garden-view room $69
  Sea-view room $86
  Suite $131–$166
  Duplex suite $235
500 rooms, 42 suites
Service charge 10%; tax 11%

This hotel is set right on the beach at the Pattaya Strip, having perhaps the most spectacular view of Pattaya Bay.

Its rooms are very open and attractive, all having marble

bathrooms, refrigerators, color TV, and an in-house video program. All of the rooms have balconies with great views.

Dining choices include casual meals in the hotel's Oriental Food Market and grand-style dining in the Grill Room. There are a cozy cocktail lounge and a very popular swinging discotheque.

Recreational activities include bowling, tennis, billiards, and all kinds of water sports, including sailing, scuba diving, parasailing, and windsurfing. The Grand Palace Convention Centre is the biggest in Thailand, with a seating capacity of four thousand.

Most striking is the hotel's interior water garden, with inside rooms overlooking it from an open-air atrium.

There are a few shops in the hotel, mostly for necessities.

NOVOTEL TROPICANA
Pattaya Beach Resort
Thailand
Telephone: (038) 418645/8
Telex: 85910 TH
Reservations:
  In Pattaya call (038) 418645
  In Bangkok call (662) 252-9187 or (662) 251-5514
  In the USA call 1-800-221-4542 or (212) 752-7430
All major credit cards
General Manager: Gaston Frechet
ACCOR Group
Rates (approx.):
  Cabaña $33 single, $37 double
  Superior room $39 single, $42 double
  Deluxe room $46 single, $50 double
186 rooms
Service charge 10%; tax 11%

The Novotel Tropicana is certainly an attractive resort. It is one of the medium-sized modern hotels of Pattaya, set in seven acres of tropical gardens.

Unlike some others at this resort, the rooms are spacious and attractively furnished, with large windows offering views of the gardens, the pool and the estate. All rooms are cabaña-style or have a private terrace, and all have a private bath and shower, wall-to-wall carpet, telephone, radio, minibar with refrigerator, and individually controlled air conditioning. Family and executive suites are available, and the conference room can accommodate up to eighty people for a business meeting or seminar. The hotel now provides a limousine transfer service to and from Bangkok for its corporate guests.

The South Seas Cafe has an all-day menu of Thai and international snacks, crisp salads, seafood, fruits, and ices. The Mai Kai Grill is for steaks, traditional grills, and Thailand's famous fish and shellfish. The open-air Boat Bar, by the pool and overlooking the garden, has live music every evening. Dancing is at the Seahorse Disco.

There is plenty to do, including giant chess, miniature golf, and tennis on asphalt courts. There's a children's playground, and there are two pools surrounded by terraces with lounge chairs for sunbathing and palm gardens for shade. The hotel has an attractive atrium lobby with greenery hanging from the upper floors.

You may catch your own fish and have it prepared for dinner.

ROYAL CLIFF BEACH RESORT
Near Pattaya City
Thailand
Telephone: (038) 421421/30
Telex: CLIFFEX TH 85907
Cable: CLIFFTATTAYA
Fax: (038) 428511
Reservations:
   In Pattaya call (038) 421421/30
   In Bangkok call 282-0999
   In the USA call Pan Pacific Hotel at (213) 452-7736
All major credit cards
General Manager: A. X. Fassbind
Sales Director: Athuk Pramoj
Pan Pacific Hotels
Rates (approx.):
   Superior room $78
   Deluxe room $98
   Mini-suite $120
   Honeymoon Suite $120
   Executive Suite (1 bedroom) $170
   Family Suite (2 bedrooms) $194
550 rooms, 195 suites
Service charge 10%; tax 11%

The Royal Cliff Beach Resort is acclaimed as the most comprehensive seaside development in Southeast Asia. It is near Pattaya City and about two hours' drive from Bangkok. It is, in reality, three hotels in one. Each wing of the hotel is special in its own way and is set up to appeal to a different kind of guest.

The Royal Cliff Beach Hotel, with its 550 spacious rooms and suites, is designed to appeal to holiday makers, conference delegates, and incentive groups.

Sweeping down to the sea is the Royal Cliff Terrace, with its twenty-seven family suites and sixty-four mini- or honeymoon suites.

The third and the most recent addition to the resort estate is the luxurious Royal Wing, with its beautiful one-bedroom executive suites and two Presidential Suites, each with three bedrooms, a boardroom, and a dining room.

In addition to the guest rooms, the resort has a great choice of restaurants, both indoor and outdoor, a shopping arcade, three swimming pools, two private beaches, an all-weather tennis complex, a mini–golf course, a jogging track, and acres of park lands and tropical gardens.

Magnificence is the word for this resort. It begins at the hotel, with its extraordinary lobby, and continues into the extensive gardens, with their walks and sports facilities.

Dining here is delightful. One of *my favorite spots* is the Panorama Restaurant and Terrace, which overlooks the sea and the gardens. This is the place where parties are usually held. My other *favorite spot* is the Palm Terrace Cafe, open from 7:00 A.M. until 10:00 P.M. for breakfast, a light lunch, or dinner by candlelight in a tropical garden. The Grill Room features an à la carte international menu for dinner, and the Benjarong Restaurant also serves dinner, featuring delicacies from land and sea in an intimate setting. From 10:00 A.M. to 7:00 P.M. you can have food and drink at the Poolside. There is also a swim-up bar. The Supper Club is open from 8:00 P.M. until 1:00 A.M. and has live music for dancing in an elegant candlelit atmosphere. In the high season, there are shows.

In the Beach Hotel there is a majestic Siam Ballroom, which can hold fifteen hundred people, and seven smaller meeting rooms. On Royal Cliff Avenue there are fifteen Thai *sala* shops offering a variety of items for shoppers.

The Royal Cliff Terrace building has spacious family suites with lounge areas and balconies, color TV, mini-bars, and separate toilets for each room. The honeymoon suites each offer a choice of a four-poster bed or twin beds, a raised lounge area, a marble bathroom, and a large balcony overlooking Royal Cliff Bay.

The Royal Wing is a grand hotel in itself, with panoramic views across the beautiful Gulf of Thailand. Located on its own beach in acres of landscaped gardens, it is a self-contained refuge for those who demand the highest levels of service, comfort, and privacy.

The Royal Wing provides personal butler service from arrival to check-out. The butlers deliver luggage to the suites, prepare and serve breakfast in the guest rooms, reserve lounge chairs by the pool, and are available throughout the day to serve drinks and snacks.

Guests consider the huge temperature-controlled swimming pool and sun patio (reserved for the exclusive use of Royal Wing guests) as the most exciting of the amenities. This area has beautifully landscaped gardens and one of Southeast Asia's largest free-form swimming pools. At no point is the pool deeper than five feet, so it is considered safe for bathers of all ages and abilities. There are two Jacuzzi spas located within the pool, plus A Ronde, a swim-up bar.

The Lobby Lounge on the eighth floor has live music and great views of the bay. Another favorite spot of ours is the Royal Wing lobby, with its spread of white marble, white columns and white ceiling, and even a white baby grand piano.

While here, be sure to visit the statue of Phra Aphai Mani playing his flute while he guards the resort. A hero of Thai literature, Phra Aphai Mani is to Thailand as Orpheus is to Greece and Neptune to Rome. He left his father's palace at the age of thirteen, and a forest hermit taught him to play the flute so well that he could use it to hypnotize or destroy anyone. On returning to his home he was captured by a female giant who took him off to sea and soon presented him with a son. Eventually he disposed of his giantess with his lethal flute and happily married a mermaid. Now he is on duty, protecting the Royal Wing of the Royal Cliff Beach Resort and its guests. This should be comforting.

SIAM BAYVIEW HOTEL
Pattaya Beach
Cholburi Province
Thailand

Telephone: (038) 428728/9 or 423325/9
Telex: 82820 BAYVIEW TH
Reservations:
   In Pattaya call (038) 428728
   In Bangkok call 221-1004/5 or 223-1784
All major credit cards
Resident Manager: Philippe Delaloye
General Manager: Hans Ruedi Frutiger
Concierge: Prachan Soonponsri
Sales Manager: Khun Kamala Sukosol
Siam Bay Hotels
Rates (approx.):
   Bayside Wing room $46
   Bayside Tower room $58
   Bayside Tower room with sea view $70
   1-bedroom suite $135
   2-bedroom suite $174
   3-bedroom suite $210
   Deluxe 1-bedroom suite $230
245 rooms, 15 suites
Service charge 10%; tax 11%

This attractive resort hotel is right in the heart of Pattaya, facing the Gulf of Siam. It has lushly landscaped tropical gardens, and the interior design of the hotel is a tasteful combination of antique and contemporary.

The guest rooms are modern and comfortably appointed. Each has contemporary, locally made furniture and fabrics in colorful arrangements. The rooms all have modern bathrooms, refrigerators, and mini-bars, and color TV and free movies are provided in the Tower Wing.

There are three dining places, including the Garden Terrace Cafe, where snacks, lunches, and full meals are served by the pool. There is a weekly pool-side barbecue, with live music for dancing. Narissa is the Oriental specialty restaurant, with a menu of Chinese and Thai dishes ranging from a simple bowl of noodles for lunch to an imperial-style banquet. The elegant dining room is the Exotica, with European-style cuisine. The menu features well-known international dishes as well as some new and innovative taste delights. This is the place for special occasions.

In addition to swimming pools and tennis courts on the grounds, the hotel also has a video lounge, and it provides guided tours of the Pattaya area. Sporting activities include windsurfing, parasailing, water-skiing, boat excursions, fishing, and golf. Hydrofoil service to the islands and hot-air ballooning (during the winter months) provide unusual excursions.

The hotel has three conference rooms with complete audio-visual equipment for groups from 20 to 350. In April the resort of Pattaya celebrates with a colorful spring festival featuring a floral float procession, an international beauty pageant, an Asian song festival, international food fairs, and tennis, golf, windsurfing, speedboat, and boxing competitions. The Siam Bayview is heavily involved in many of these events.

Be sure to ask for a copy of the hotel booklet called *Destination Pattaya*. It tells all there is to do and see at this resort and nearby areas. There is an excellent centerfold map of Pattaya.

Phuket

A little more than an hour's flying time from Bangkok is Phuket, Thailand's most spectacular destination outside of the capital. This idyllic southern isle is a tropical paradise of unspoilt and rarely surpassed beauty. An island on the Andaman Coast, Phuket is also Thailand's most recently developed oceanside resort. It is known for its delicious seafood in addition to its perfect beaches.

Phuket town was founded in the first century B.C. by colonists from India. European merchants came here in the sixteenth century. The Siamese and the Burmese fought over the island in the eighteenth century, and it finally became a part of Thailand in the nineteenth century.

The island is the size of Singapore but has a fraction of its population. It has dozens of fine beaches washed by the clear, clean waters of the Andaman Sea. There are lush rolling hills and endless groves of rubber trees. Offshore there are scores of beautiful islands, many uninhabited, surrounded by seas filled with tropical fish and gorgeous coral.

In this setting, sports of all kinds are popular—scuba diving, island-hopping by sailboat, deep-sea fishing for tuna and barracuda, and tennis. Visitors should make a point of joining one of the island's festivals and trying the fresh seafood.

DUSIT LAGUNA RESORT HOTEL
Phuket
Thailand
Reservations:
   In Bangkok call the Dusit Thani at 233-1130 or 233-1140
All major credit cards
Dusit Thani Hotels
Rates (approx.):
   Room $60 single, $68 double
   1-bedroom suite $128
   2-bedroom suite $168
   Executive suite $240
240 guest rooms and suites
Service charge 10%; tax 11%

The Dusit Laguna, sister hotel of the luxury Dusit Thani in Bangkok and the Dusit Inn in Chiang Mai, opened in October of 1987. Situated on Bang Tao Bay, at one of the fine beaches of Phuket, it is fifteen minutes from the airport and twenty minutes from the center of the town. It is on a large landscaped estate, facing the Andaman Sea.

All of the rooms and suites are nicely furnished, with modern amenities including mini-bars, color TV, large bathrooms and private balconies.

There is a fine specialty dining room and the Lagunda Cafe, with casual dining. There is a seafood barbecue corner for feasting alfresco under the stars.

The site contains two large inland lagoons for all-season water sports. There are also a large swimming pool, a separate children's pool, tennis courts, and putting greens. There is room for seminars or conferences of up to four hundred people.

HOLIDAY INN PHUKET
86/11 Thaweewong Road
Patong Beach
P.O. Box 158
Phuket
Thailand
Telephone: (076) 321020/21
Telex: 69545 PHUKET TH
Cable: HOLIDAYINN
Fax: (076) 321435
Reservations:
   In Phuket call (076) 321020

In Bangkok call (02) 236-7245 or 233-2385
In the USA call 1-800-HOLIDAY
All major credit cards
General Manager: Udo Jaritz
Sales Director: Ittivudh Sumongkol
Holiday Inns Asia-Pacific
Rates (approx.):
  Standard room $60 single, $68 double
  Studio suite $112
  Executive suite $160
  Presidential Suite $240
  Surcharge in peak season (Dec. 20 to Feb. 20) $12
280 rooms, 23 suites
Service charge 10%; tax 11%

Opened in the late summer of 1987, the Holiday Inn Phuket is beautifully situated on the white crescent of Patong Beach, a little more than six miles from Phuket town. The hotel is charming in its decor, and well set up for the enjoyment of the beach and water sports.

The guest rooms and suites are spacious, with the amenities of color TV, mini-bars and refrigerators, and direct-dial telephones. The rooms have views and balconies. The views of the beach and the tiny rock islands covered with trees are most delightful.

The landscaped grounds of the hotel have pretty lagoons, lots of palm trees, and a large free-form swimming pool. There are tennis courts on the grounds, too.

The Lobby PalmCourt Lounge, with its wicker furnishings, is an attractive and relaxing spot. But the favorite is bound to be the Sea Breeze Cafe, with its terrace overlooking the pool. The hotel's specialty dining room, the Baron's Table and Tavern, is an attractive and elegant grill room. Most fun is swimming up to Treasure Island, the bar in the middle of the swimming pool.

The hotel has a banquet hall that can hold up to three hundred people and can be divided into three small rooms for events. There are a jewelry shop and a boutique in the hotel along with necessity shops.

LE MERIDIEN PHUKET
P.O. Box 277
8/5 Moo 1 Tambol Karon
Amphur Muang
Phuket 83000
Thailand

Telephone: (076) 321480/5
Telex: 69542 MERIHKT TH
69543 RELAX TH
Fax: (076) 321479
Reservations:
  In Phuket call (076) 321480/5, ext. 1806 or 1807
  In Bangkok call 252-9328
  In the USA call 1-800-543-4300 or any Air France or
    Meridien Hotel office
All major credit cards
General Manager: Didier Tourneboeuf
Concierge: Khun Soyyukol Bhanomjaya
Sales Manager: Mr. Duncan Jamieson
Le Meridien
Rates (approx.):
  Standard room $75 single, $82 double
  Superior room $82 single, $90 double
  Standard suite $216
  Royal Suite $353
450 rooms, 14 suites
Service charge 10%; tax 11%

Set in forty acres of tropical gardens on what is very appropriately called Relax Bay, this is the first hotel in Phuket to provide superior accommodations as well as extensive conference facilities. The resort's attractive contemporary Thai architecture blends beautifully with the tropical gardens and the wide private beach, providing a feeling of seclusion and privacy.

The rooms and suites all have sea views and private balconies, deluxe bathrooms, air conditioning, mini-bars, color TV, in-house video, and international direct-dial telephones. Each has a personal safe and an elaborate fire protection system. The rooms have such amenities as a hair dryer, shampoo, hair conditioner, suntan lotion, and foam bath packets. The suites have large balconies with beautiful views.

The area of the pool and the lagoons is beautifully designed and spacious. You have a choice of going swimming in the hotel's huge salt-water lagoon or in the free-form fresh-water pools and Jaccuzi.

There is Le Meridien Phuket Health Club, with a complete gymnasium and sauna. You may play tennis or squash on the hotel's private courts.

Dining is delightful at this French-run hotel. There is an international dining room for steaks, salads, and roasts, with an extensive selection of wines. *My favorite spot* is the Seafood Pavilion, set in its own lagoon, with delicacies cooked in either Western or Oriental style. There is the Buffet Restaurant for breakfast, lunch, or dinner, and the Coffee Shop for round-the-clock dining, indoors or outdoors. And there are the Lounge and the Poolside bars, providing drinks and musical entertainment.

For large gatherings, the hotel has the Karon Ballroom, which can accommodate up to a thousand people. There are four rooms for smaller meetings, each holding as many as a hundred people.

PEARL VILLAGE
Nai Yang Beach and National Park
P.O. Box 93
Phuket 83000
Thailand
Telephone: (076) 311338 or (076) 311378
Telex: 65539 VILLAGE TH
Cable: VILLAGE
Fax: (076) 212911
Reservations:
  In Phuket call (076) 311378, ext. 616
  In Bangkok call (02) 252-5245 or (02) 252-5340
All major credit cards
Managing Director: Wichit Na-Ranong
General Manager: Franco Romagnoli
Sales Manager: Vina Suvagondha
Golden Tulip Hotels
Rates (approx.):
  Room $58 single, $66 double
  Executive Family room $81
  Village Suite $212
  Pearl Suite $346
163 rooms, 6 suites
Service charge 10%; tax 11%

This is Thailand's only beach resort within a national park. It is set in twenty acres of landscaped tropical gardens facing the beach at Nai Yang National Park.

The design concept is delightful. The resort has as its center a central clubhouse of generous proportions, with magnificent Thai-style chandeliers hanging from the high arched ceiling in the lobby area.

Within the central clubhouse are the wining, dining, and entertainment facilities. There is an excellent dining room serving Thai and international specialties, a choice of bars, and music in the evening.

Other activities include a barbecue corner, a game room, and a conference room that can hold as many as two hundred people.

Year-round activities center on a variety of water sports such as boating, windsurfing, snorkeling, and scuba diving. The coral beds off Nai Yang beach are fascinating. In the park, there is horseback riding and bicycle riding. There is tennis and pitch-and-putt golf. The children have a playground, and there is a swimming pool in a natural setting.

The rooms have the amenities of color TV, video, radio, mini-bars, refrigerators, telephones, and even scales. The Pearl Suite has a living room, a dining area, a Jacuzzi, a telephone in the bathroom, and other luxuries.

In the hotel is the Chitrladda Souvenir Shop, which is fun for browsing.

One of the more beautiful spots is the setting for the large swimming pool. It is surrounded by large lush palm trees and has a rock at the end of it with a waterfall. Sunbathing is very popular here.

RECOMMENDED GUIDEBOOKS

I recommend these books as excellent sources of information on sightseeing and restaurants. This chapter was excerpted from Going Places: The Guide to Travel Guides *by Greg Hayes and Joan Wright, to be published by the Harvard Common Press.*

Asia as a Whole

ABC Air Asia, Australia and New Zealand
ABC International, monthly editions, 250 pages, paper, $7.00.
This airline schedule is a must for travelers making many connections and compelled to play travel agent.

All-Asia Guide
Charles E. Tuttle Co., 1986 (14th ed.), 704 pages, paper, $12.95.
The *All-Asia Guide*, produced by the *Far Eastern Economic Review*, has been a standard for many years. The guide covers twenty-six different countries and includes history, the practicalities and idiosyncrasies of each country, and sightseeing tips. Clear detail maps of major cities and a separate hotel guide supplement the work. Restaurant and hotel comments are brief, but still reasonably informative. This is the best single guide for travelers visiting a multitude

of countries, but the use of additional guides for individual countries should be considered if they are available.

Asia 101: History, Art and Culture for the Traveler
By John Gottberg, John Muir Publications, 1988, 352 pages, paper, $11.95. This new guide, released after press time, is produced in the same format as the classic *Europe 101*.

Asia through the Back Door
By Rick Steves and John Gottberg, John Muir Publications, 1986, 319 pages, paper, $11.95. Rick Steves has adapted his classic *Europe through the Back Door* concept to the Asian continent. The result is an excellent strategy book especially useful for those wishing to travel cheaply. Included among the many practical subjects are separate sections on transportation, budget eating and sleeping, health, attitude adjustment, and eighteen suggested "back doors"—ways to enter and experience the *real* Asia.

Fielding's Far East
By Antoinette DeLand, William Morrow and Co., 1986, 592 pages, paper, $14.95. Typical of a number of other Fielding titles, this one is written in a somewhat uncomfortable omniscient style. Nonetheless, it contains plenty of information, especially on shopping, entertainment, and night life. The hotel write-ups are often too "brochure-like" and are rated with the well-known Fielding five-star system. This book is part of the Fielding's Travel Guide series, which is reviewed in more detail under "Series Reviews."

International Herald Tribune Guide to Business Travel in Asia
Edited by Robert McCage, Passport Books, 1988, 208 pages, paper, $14.95. In this book, the *International Herald Tribune* expands on the theme of its popular European guide for the business traveler. Addressing the stated needs of the business person, the reporters and editors of this famous newspaper cover all the topics of importance for each of the sixteen major business cities in considerable detail. This title was released after press time, but the European version is well known and well done. The cities and colonies covered are: Bangkok, Beijing, Brunei, Canton, Hong Kong, Jakarta, Kuala Lumpur, Macau, Manila, Osaka, Seoul, Shanghai, Sherzhen, Singapore, Taipei, and Tokyo.

Sunset Orient Travel Guide
Lane Publishing, 1986, 160 pages, paper, $9.95. This large-format guide is spotty in its coverage of the Orient and

should only be used for vacation ideas. It is part of the Sunset Travel Guide series, which is reviewed in more detail under "Series Reviews."

The Traveler's Guide to Asian Customs and Manners
By Elizabeth Devine and Nancy Braganti, St. Martin's Press, 1986, 315 pages, paper, $9.95. This useful book covers myriad topics from greetings, dress, meals, hotels, and business concerns to transportation needs, health issues, and helpful phrases for the traveler. Note that the authors have included Australia and New Zealand as well.

Travel With Children: A Survival Kit for Travel in Asia
By Maureen Wheeler, Lonely Planet Publications, 1985, 96 pages, paper, $4.95. This guide is full of information for those contemplating traveling in Asia with children. Wheeler deals with myriad cultural issues and kid-related problems beginning with the most immediate ones of culture shock, health, food, and even diaper resources ("nappies" are not readily available everywhere; Wheeler lists the realities specific to each country). She then moves on to ways to keep the kids entertained. It may seem like an overwhelming idea to take a child to Asia, but it can be done, and this little book will certainly help.

Southeast Asia

The Economist Business Traveller's Guides: Southeast Asia
Prentice Hall Press, 1988, 250 pages, paper, $17.95. This is a new, expected addition to the excellent Economist Business Traveller's Guide series, which is reviewed in more detail under "Series Reviews." Since it was released after press time, the number of pages is approximate.

Fodor's Southeast Asia
Fodor's Travel Guides, 1987, 439 pages, paper, $15.95. This well-regarded volume of the Fodor series covers Hong Kong, the Philippines, Thailand, Singapore, Malaysia, Indonesia, Macau, Brunei, and Burma, as well as Taiwan. It is part of the Fodor's Country/Regional Guides series, which is reviewed in more detail under "Series Reviews." The series is updated annually.

South-East Asia Handbook
By Stefan Loose and Renate Ramb, Riverdale Co., 1985 (2nd ed.), 558 pages, paper, $12.95. This well-done, comprehensive guide

covers all price ranges and travel topics, but is especially useful for those traveling on a budget. Good detail maps are an added bonus. Countries covered are: Brunei, Burma, Indonesia, Malaysia, Singapore, and Thailand. (Note: Those traveling to Malaysia, Singapore, or Brunei will find more detail in his *Malaysia, Singapore, Brunei Traveller's Handbook.*)

South-East Asia on a Shoestring
By Tony Wheeler, Lonely Planet Publications, 1985 (5th ed.), 574 pages, paper, $9.95. This is one of the books that made Lonely Planet famous although, at this point, it is looking for its next update. Therefore, be sure to confirm all the details until the 6th edition arrives. The countries covered are Brunei, Burma, Hong Kong, Indonesia, Macau, Malaysia, Papua New Guinea, The Philippines, Singapore, Thailand, and, briefly, Vietnam, Laos, and Kampuchea. This is part of the budget-oriented "On A Shoestring Guide" series, which is reviewed in more detail under "Series Reviews." The series is generally updated every two to three years.

Sunset Southeast Asia Travel Guide
Land Publishing, 1982, 160 pages, paper, $9.95. This particular member of the Sunset Travel Guide series (reviewed in more detail under "Series Reviews") is pretty spotty in its coverage and is best used for ideas only.

Bangladesh

Bangladesh: A Travel Survival Kit
By José Santiago, Lonely Planet Publications, 1985, 136 pages, paper, $7.95. This book is part of the popular Travel Survival Kit series, which is reviewed in more detail under "Series Reviews." Most titles in this series are updated every two to three years.

West Asia on a Shoestring
By Tony Wheeler, Lonely Planet Publications, 1986 (5th ed.), 368 pages, paper, $8.95. Describing the overland route from Bangladesh to Turkey, this book is part of the budget-oriented On a Shoestring Guide series, which is reviewed in more detail under "Series Reviews." This series is updated every two to three years.

China

All China
Passport Books, 1986, 143 pages, paper, $8.95
Beijing
Passport Books, 1987, 144 pages, paper, $8.95
These two titles are in the Passport China Guide series, which is reviewed in more detail under "Series Reviews."

Beijing Old and New
By Zhou Shachen, China Books, 1984, 404 pages, paper, $7.95. Written and published in Beijing, this is a historical guide to the city's interesting sights and the areas within one day's journey of the famous city. Included are color photos and good detail maps of some of the points of interest.

Berlitz: China
Macmillan Publishing, 1986, 256 pages, paper, $8.95. This is one of the larger volumes in the Berlitz Country Guide series, which is reviewed in more detail under "Series Reviews."

China: A Travel Survival Kit
By Alan Samagalski and Robert Strauss, Lonely Planet Publications, 1988 (2nd ed.), 820 pages, paper, $17.95. This book is one of the popular Travel Survival Kit series, which is reviewed in more detail under "Series Reviews." The series is updated every two to three years. This edition was released after press time; the number of pages is approximate.

The China Business Handbook
By Arne de Keijzer, China Books, 1986, 217 pages, paper, $16.95. One of the authors of the highly regarded *China Guidebook* has written this excellent, concise guide to doing business in China. It is considered a valuable resource to those expert in China trade.

China Companion: A Guide to 100 Cities, Resorts, and Places of Interest in the People's Republic
By Evelyne Garside, Farrar, Straus, and Giroux, 1981, 276 pages, cloth, $14.95. While this superbly done guidebook, winner of the prestigious Thomas Cook Guide Book Award in 1981, is clearly out-of-date on the specifics of hotels, restaurants, and shopping, its excellent sections on history, geography, art, and architecture make it a good choice as a "companion guide."

China Guidebook
By Frederic Kaplan, et al., Eurasia Press, 1987 (8th ed.), 768 pages, paper, $15.95. Long the best-selling guide to China, this book is considered one of the best guides available by those knowledgable in the travel industry and *the* best guide to take on a tour. It is authoritative, comprehensive, and well organized. No subject is neglected, and special sections on cuisine, archaeology, shopping, and arts are included. This book is updated annually.

China in 22 Days
See *22 Days in China* below.

China, Solo: A Guide to Independent Travel in the People's Republic of China
By Barbara Letson, Jadetree Press, 1984, 213 pages, paper, $9.95. This excellent book is a delight to read. Letson, who has been through it all, shares her mistakes and the wisdom she has gleaned from her solo travels. This really is a strategy book on "how to do it." Even sections on hotels and food deal primarily with the peculiarities facing travelers away from more familiar, Western hotels. Combined with another standard guide, *China, Solo* will more than pay for itself in helpful time-saving and headache-saving hints.

The Economist Business Traveller's Guides: China
Prentice Hall Press, 1988, 250 pages, paper, $17.95. This book is a new addition to the respected Economist Business Traveller's Guide series, which is reviewed in more detail under "Series Reviews." Since it was released after press time, the number of pages is approximate.

Fielding's People's Republic of China
By Ruth Malloy and Priscilla Hsu, William Morrow and Co., 1988, 400 pages, paper, $13.95. This book is part of the Fieldings Travel Guide series, which is reviewed in more detail under "Series Reviews." The series is updated annually.

Fodor's Beijing, Guangzhou, and Shanghai
Fodor's Travel Guides, 224 pages, 1988, paper, $7.95. This book is one of Fodor's City Guide series, which is reviewed in more detail under "Series Reviews." The series is updated annually.

Fodor's People's Republic of China
By John Summerfield, Fodor's Travel Guides, 1987, 595 pages, paper, $15.95. This book is one of Fodor's Country/Regional Guide series, which is reviewed in more detail under "Series Reviews." The series is updated annually.

Fujian
Passport Books, 1988, 144 pages, paper, $9.95
Guilin, Canton, Guangdong
Passport Books, 1988, 208 pages, paper, $9.95
Hangzhou and Zhejiang
Passport Books, 1987, 144 pages, paper, $8.95
These are three titles in the Passport China Guide series, which is reviewed in more detail under "Series Reviews."

Hildebrand's Travel Guide: China
Hunter Publishing, 1985, 336 pages, paper, $11.95. This book is part of the Hildebrand's Guide series, which is reviewed in more detail under "Series Reviews."

How to Tour China: The Newest Comprehensive Guidebook
China Books, 1986, 197 pages, paper, $9.95. Written in China, this small guidebook covers all the standard tourist bases briefly, but adequately. Plenty of color photos highlight the sights described. At press time, Kampmann and Company was listing a new edition at $12.95.

Insider's Guide to China
Hunter Publishing, 1987, 224 pages, paper, $12.95. This book is part of the Hunter Insider's Guide series, which is reviewed in more detail under "Series Reviews."

Magnificent China: A Guide to Its Cultural Treasures
By Petra Haring-Kuan and Kuan Yu-Chien, China Books, 1987, 425 pages, cloth, $34.95. The outstanding aspect of this well-done hardback book is its excellent descriptions of the important cultural sites throughout China. It provides an encyclopedic look at China's history, literature, religion, philosophy, art, and architecture. The detailed maps of towns and historic sites are superb, and good color photos supplement the text. As a sightseeing guide it is excellent. The book contains some practical information as well, but this is brief.

Nagel's China
Passport Books, 1984, 1504 pages, cloth, $49.95. This classic, comprehensive cultural guide is part of the Nagel's Guide series, which is reviewed in more detail under "Series Reviews."

Nanjing and Jiangsu
Passport Books, 1988, 160 pages, paper, $8.95. This book is part of the Passport China Guide series, which is reviewed in more detail under "Series Reviews."

North-East Asia on a Shoestring
Edited by Tony Wheeler, Lonely Planet Publications, 1985, 288 pages, paper, $7.95. Covering China, Hong Kong, Japan, Macau, South Korea, and Taiwan, with short notes on visiting North Korea, this book is part of the budget-oriented On a Shoestring Guide series, which is reviewed in more detail under "Series Reviews." The series is generally updated every two to three years. At press time, a new edition had not yet been announced.

Rough Guide to China
By Catherine Sanders, Chris Stewart, and Rhonda Evans, Routledge and Kegan Paul, 1987, 595 pages, paper, $12.95. Already considered by many to be the best guide for independent travel in China, especially by the younger, more adventurous crowd, this book is part of the Rough Guides series, which is reviewed in more detail under "Series Reviews." The series is updated every two to three years.

Shanghai
Passport Books, 1987, 144 pages, paper, $8.95. This book is part of the Passport China Guide series, which is reviewed in more detail under "Series Reviews."

Shopping in China: Arts, Crafts and the Unusual
By Roberta Stalberg, China Books, 1986, 230 pages, paper, $9.95. This is a well-organized book that is fascinating to read; it covers twelve major cities and explains what to look for and where to look. It also offers detailed discussions on each "highly recommended" or "recommended" store. Widely praised, this book is recommended for the traveling shopper.

Southwest China Off the Beaten Track
By Mark Stevens and George Wehrfritz, Passport Books, 1988, 224 pages, paper, $12.95. Released after press time, this is the first title in a new series for "the adventuresome and independent traveler." It covers large cities, wilderness areas, small villages, and such practicalities as hitchhiking and the etiquette of crossing through closed areas. Numerous maps, including one large fold-out map of the four-province area, are provided.

Tibet
Passport Books, 1986, 208 pages, paper, $9.95. This book is part of the Passport China Guide series, which is reviewed in more detail under "Series Reviews."

Tibet: A Travel Survival Kit
By Michael Buckley and Robert Strauss, Lonely Planet Publications, 1986, 256 pages, paper, $7.95. This book is part of the

popular Travel Survival Kit series, which is reviewed in more detail under "Series Reviews." The series is updated every two to three years.

22 Days in China: The Itinerary Planner
By Gaylon Duke and Zenia Victor, John Muir Publications, 1987, 141 pages, paper, $6.95. One of the series of books modeled after the well-known *Europe In 22 Days* (now called *22 Days in Europe*). The Itinerary Planner series is reviewed in more detail under "Series Reviews." Note that the title change is recent; this book may also be entitled *China in 22 Days*.

Xi'an
Passport Books, 1988, 128 pages, paper, $7.95
The Yangzi River
Passport Books, 1985, 208 pages, paper, $9.95
Yunnan
Passport Books, 1987, 208 pages, paper, $9.95
These are three titles in the Passport China Guide series, which is reviewed in more detail under "Series Reviews."

Hong Kong

The American Express Pocket Guide to Hong Kong, Singapore, and Bangkok
Prentice Hall Press, 1988, 200 pages, cloth, $9.95. This book is part of the respected American Express Pocket Guide series, which is reviewed in more detail under "Series Reviews." Since it was released after press time, the number of pages is approximate.

Baedeker's Hong Kong
Prentice Hall Press, 1987, 168 pages, paper, $10.95. This is part of Baedeker's City guide series, which is reviewed in more detail under "Series Reviews."

Berlitz: Hong Kong
Macmillan Publishing, 1979, 128 pages, paper, $6.95. This book is part of the small-format Berlitz Guide series, which is reviewed in more detail under "Series Reviews."

Born to Shop: Hong Kong
By Suzy Gershman and Judith Thomas, Bantam Books, 1986, 240 pages, paper, $8.95. This book is one of the well-done Born to Shop Guide series, which is described in more detail under "Series Reviews."

The Complete Guide to Hong Kong Factory Bargains
By Dana Goetz, Delta Dragon Books, 1987, 234 pages, paper,
$9.95. This is a tiny, handy shopping guide to Hong Kong,
although it is not as extensive as other guides now available.
What is covered has informative write-ups. Clear maps are
also provided. Published in Hong Kong, this book has no
American distributor at present.

Fodor's Hong Kong and Macau
Fodor's Travel Guides, 1987, 271 pages, paper, $10.95. This
book is part of Fodor's Country/Regional Guide series, which
is reviewed in more detail under "Series Reviews." The
series is updated annually.

Frommer's Dollarwise Guide to Japan and Hong Kong
by Beth Reiber, Prentice Hall Press, 1988, 384 pages, paper,
$13.95. This book is part of Frommer's Dollarwise Guide
series, which is reviewed in more detail under "Series Reviews." These series guides emphasize selections in the
moderate price range and are updated every two years.

Hong Kong
Passport Books, 1986, 144 pages, paper, $8.95. This book is
part of the Passport China Guide series, which is reviewed
in more detail under "Series Reviews."

Hong Kong in Your Pocket
Barron's Educational Series, 1987, 176 pages, paper, $3.95. This
small-format guide is part of the In-Your-Pocket Guide series, which is reviewed in more detail under "Series Reviews."

Hong Kong, Macau and Canton: A Travel Survival Kit
By Carol Clewlow and Alan Samagalski, Lonely Planet Publications, 1986 (4th ed.), 256 pages, paper, $7.95. This book is one
of the popular Travel Survival Kit series, which is reviewed
in more detail under "Series Reviews." The series is updated every two to three years.

Insider's Guide to Hong Kong
Hunter Publishing, 1987, 176 pages, paper, $12.95. This book
is part of Hunter's Insider's Guide series, which is reviewed
in more detail under "Series Reviews."

Insight Guides: Hong Kong (with Macau)
By APA Productions, Prentice Hall Press, 1986, 338 pages, paper,
$16.95. This book is one of the widely praised Insight Guide
series, which is reviewed in more detail under "Series Reviews."

Post Guide: Hong Kong
Hunter Publishing, 1987, 144 pages, paper, $8.95. This book is part of the Post Guide series, which is reviewed in more detail under "Series Reviews."

Shopping in Exotic Hong Kong: Your Passport to Asia's Most Incredible Shopping Mall
By Ronald Krannich, et al., Impact Publications, 1988, 180 pages, paper, $9.95
Shopping in Exotic Places: Your Passport to Exciting Hong Kong, Korea, Thailand, Indonesia, and Singapore
by Ronald Krannich, et al., Impact Publications, 1987, 469 pages, paper, $13.95
Both of these titles are part of the excellent Shopping in Exotic Places series, which is reviewed in more detail under "Series Reviews." The Hong Kong volume is an anticipated addition to the series that will expand on the Hong Kong section of the second title. The series is updated every two years. The Hong Kong volume was released after press time, so the number of pages is approximate.

Shopwalks: Hong Kong
By Corby Kukmmer, Crown Publishing, 1987, fold-out map-guide, paper, $5.95. This book is part of the Shopwalks series, which is reviewed in more detail under "Series Reviews."

India

Berlitz: India
Macmillan Publishing, 1986, 256 pages, paper, $8.95. This is a larger title in the Berlitz County Guide series, which is reviewed in more detail under "Series Reviews."

The Best of India, from Budget to Luxury
By Paige Palmer, Pilot Books, 1987, 196 pages, paper, $7.95. In a succinct, well-organized style, this book covers all the traveler's bases in less than two hundred pages. A wide choice of lodging and restaurants in every price category, including choices appropriate for the backpacker, are included. From shopping to sightseeing, the book moves rapidly through the topics—with just enough detail to point travelers in the right direction. The author's considerable experience in almost every corner of India is evident in this book.

Cadogan Guides: India
By Frank Kusy, Globe Pequot Press, 1987, 406 pages, paper, $12.95. This book is one of the highly regarded Cadogan Guide series, which is reviewed in more detail under "Series Reviews." The series is updated every two years.

Fodor's India, Nepal, and Sri Lanka
Fodor's Travel Guides, 1987, 520 pages, paper, $16.95. This book is part of Fodor's Country/Regional Guide series, which is reviewed in more detail under "Series Reviews." The series is updated annually.

Frommer's India on $25 a Day
By Jan Aaron, Prentice Hall Press, 1988, 375 pages, paper, $10.95. This book is part of the budget-oriented Frommer's Dollar-a-Day Guide series, which is reviewed in more detail under "Series Reviews." The series is updated every two years. This edition was released after press time so the number of pages is approximate.

Guide to Rajasthan
By Kim Naylor, Hippocrene Books, 1988, 160 pages, paper, $11.95. This may be the only guide to the mystical, magical land of Rajasthan.

Hildebrand's Travel Guide: India and Nepal
Hunter Publishing, 1985, 224 pages, paper, $10.95. This book is part of the Hildebrand's Guide series, which is reviewed in more detail under "Series Reviews."

India: A Travel Survival Kit
By Geoff Crowther, et al., Lonely Planet Publications, 1987 (3rd ed.), 801 pages, paper, $17.95. This is a huge, highly-regarded title in the popular Travel Survival Kit series, which is reviewed in more detail under "Series Reviews." The series is updated every two to three years.

India in 22 Days
See *22 Days in India.*

India, Nepal and Sri Lanka: The Traveller's Guide
By Peter Meyer and Barbara Rausch, Riverdale Co., 1987, 656 pages, paper, $14.95. Brought to America for the first time in early 1988, this book is the fourth edition of a popular German travel guide. The focus of the book is on the young adventurer who wants to get by as cheaply as possible with a reasonable measure of cleanliness and safety. The information presented is solid and thorough. Careful attention

has been paid to all the important details, and clear maps are provided.

Insight Guides: India
By APA Productions, Prentice Hall Press, 1987, 359 pages, paper, $16.95. This book is part of the acclaimed Insight Guide series, which is reviewed in more detail under "Series Reviews."

Kashmir, Ladakh and Zanskar: A Travel Survival Kit
By Margaret and Rolf Schettler, Lonely Planet Publications, 1985 (2nd ed.), 204 pages, paper, $7.95. This book is part of the popular Travel Survival Kit series, which is reviewed in more detail under "Series Reviews." Generally, titles in this series are updated every two to three years. At press time, a new edition had not yet been announced.

Nagel's India and Nepal
Passport Books, 1983, 831 pages, cloth, $49.95. This classic, cultural guide is part of the Nagel's Guide series, which is reviewed in more detail under "Series Reviews."

The Traveler's Key to Northern India: A Guide to the Sacred Places of Northern India
By Alistair Shearer, Alfred Knopf, 1983, 546 pages, paper, $18.95. This book is an exploration of the legends, art, and architecture of Northern India. It is part of the finely crafted Traveler's Key Guide series, which is reviewed in more detail under "Series Reviews."

Trekking in the Indian Himalaya
By Gary Weare, Lonely Planet Publications, 1986, 160 pages, paper, $6.95. This is the first edition of a guide to this somewhat less popular trekking area of the Himalaya. Plans are already being made to add other trekking routes and regions, and to improve the current information in the next edition. This guide, however, appears well done, with clear, concise coverage of all the essential topics of importance to the trekker.

22 Days in India: The Itinerary Planner
By Anurag Mather, John Muir Publications, 1988, 136 pages, paper, $6.95. This book is a new title in the Itinerary Planner series, which is reviewed in more detail under "Series Reviews." Note that there has been a recent title change; this book may also be entitled *India in 22 Days.*

Visiting India
By Allan Stacey, Hippocrene Books, 1987, 192 pages, paper, $9.95. This is an illustrated guide focusing on the background

information of use to the traveler: regional customs, the various religions of the country, the realities of transportation, and flora and fauna, as well as suggestions for various side trips.

West Asia On a Shoestring

By Tony Wheeler, Lonely Planet Publications, 1986 (5th ed.) 368 pages, paper, $8.95. Describing the overland route from Bangladesh to Turkey, this book is part of the budget-oriented On a Shoestring Guide series, which is reviewed in more detail under "Series Reviews." The series is updated every two to three years.

Indonesia

Bali and Lombok: A Travel Survival Kit

By Mary Covernton and Tony Wheeler, Lonely Planet Publications, 1986, 208 pages, paper, $6.95. This book is one of the popular Travel Survival Kit series, which is reviewed in more detail under "Series Reviews." The series is updated every two to three years.

Hildebrand's Travel Guide: Indonesia

Hunter Publishing, 1985, 333 pages, paper, $10.95. This book is one of the Hildebrand's Guide series, which is reviewed in more detail under "Series Reviews."

Indonesia: A Travel Survival Kit

By Ginny Bruce, Mary Covernton, and Alan Samagalski, Lonely Planet Publications, 1986, 768 pages, paper, $14.95. This book is part of the well-known Travel Survival Kit series, which is reviewed in more detail under "Series Reviews." The series is updated every two to three years.

Indonesia Handbook

By Bill Dalton, Moon Publications, 1988 (4th ed.), 900 pages, paper, $17.95. One of the best travel guides ever written, this book is part of the first-rate Moon Handbooks series, which is reviewed in more detail under "Series Reviews." The series is updated every two years.

Insight Guides: Bali

By APA Productions, Prentice Hall Press, 1986, 275 pages, paper, $16.95

Insight Guides: Indonesia

By APA Productions, Prentice Hall Press, 1986, 418 pages, paper, $16.95.

These two titles are in the acclaimed Insight Guide series, which is reviewed in more detail under "Series Reviews."

Post Guide: Indonesia
Hunter Publishing, 1987, 144 pages, paper, $8.95. This book is one of the Post Guide series, which is reviewed in more detail under "Series Reviews."

Shopping in Exotic Indonesia
by Ron Krannich, et al., Impact Publications, 1988, 180 pages, paper, $9.95
Shopping in Exotic Places: Your Passport to Exciting Hong Kong, Korea, Thailand, Indonesia, and Singapore
by Ronald Krannich, et al., Impact Publications, 1987, 469 pages, paper, $13.95
Both of these titles are part of the excellent Shopping in Exotic Places series, which is reviewed in more detail under "Series Reviews." The Indonesian volume is an anticipated addition to the series that will expand on the Indonesian section of the second title. The series is updated every two years. The Indonesian volume was released after press time, so the number of pages is approximate.

The Times Travel Library: Bali
Hunter Publishing, 1987, 104 pages, paper, $10.95
The Times Travel Library: Jakarta
Hunter Publishing, 1987, 104 pages, paper, $10.95
These two titles are in a new large-format series Times Travel Library Guides, which is reviewed in more detail under "Series Reviews."

Japan

The American Express Pocket Guide: Tokyo
Prentice Hall Press, 1988, 200 pages, cloth, $9.95. This book is part of the American Express Pocket Guide series, which is reviewed in more detail under "Series Reviews." Since it was released after press time, the number of pages is approximate.

Baedeker's Japan
Prentice Hall Press, undated, 352 pages, paper, $15.95. This book is part of the Baedeker's Guide series, which is reviewed in more detail under "Series Reviews."

Baedeker's Tokyo
Prentice Hall Press, 1987, 153 pages, paper, $10.95. This book
is part of the Baedeker's City Guide series, which is reviewed in more detail under "Series Reviews."

Berlitz: Japan
Macmillan Publishing, 1986, 256 pages, paper, $8.95. This book
is one of the small-format Berlitz Country Guide series,
which is reviewed in more detail under "Series Reviews."

A Bird Watcher's Guide to Japan
*By Mark Brazil, Kodansha International, 1988, 220 pages, paper,
$13.95.* This new title, released after press time, highlights
the sixty best bird-watching areas of Japan.

Born to Shop: Tokyo
*By Suzy Gershman and Judith Thomas, Bantam Books, 1987, 329
pages, paper, $9.95.* This book is part of the well-done Born
to Shop Guide series, which is reviewed in more detail
under "Series Reviews."

Crown Insider's Guide: Japan
*Edited by Robert Fisher, Crown Publishers, 1987, 328 pages,
paper, $10.95.* This book is part of the Crown Insider's Guide
series, which is reviewed in more detail under "Series Reviews."

Discovering Cultural Japan
*By Boye De Mente, Passport Books, 1988, 152 pages, paper,
$12.95.* This book covers a wide variety of important topics
such as crossing cultural barriers, the traditions of hospitality, the special joys of Japan, and the unique "faces" of
the Japanese.

**Eating Cheap in Japan: The Gaijin Gourmet's Guide to Or-
dering in Non-Tourist Restaurants**
*By Kimiko Nagasawa and Camy Condon, Charles E. Tuttle Co.,
1972, 104 pages, paper, $9.95.* This "old" book is definitely
not out of date. Now in its nineteenth printing, this is not
a book on specific restaurants but rather contains the information necessary to dine in many wonderful (and relatively cheap) restaurants where English is neither on the
menu nor spoken. Compact, with copious color photos of
specific dishes, this little guide will greatly expand any traveler's culinary horizons.

The Economist Business Traveller's Guide: Japan
Prentice Hall Press, 1987, 256 pages, paper, $17.95. This book
is part of the excellent Economist Business Traveller's Guide

series, which is reviewed in more detail under "Series Reviews."

Fisher's World: Japan
By Robert Fisher, Fisher's World, 1988, 367 pages, paper, $14.95. This book is one of the Fisher's World Guide series, which is reviewed in more detail under "Series Reviews." The series is updated annually.

Fodor's Japan
Fodor's Travel Guides, 1988, 544 pages, paper, $15.95. This book is part of Fodor's Country/Regional Guide series, which is reviewed in more detail under "Series Reviews." The series is updated annually.

Fodor's Great Travel Values: Japan
Fodor's Travel Guides, 1988, 192 pages, paper, $6.95. This book is part of Fodor's Great Travel Values Guide series, which is reviewed in more detail under "Series Reviews." The series is updated annually.

Fodor's Tokyo
Fodor's Travel Guides, 1988, 144 pages, paper, $6.95. This book is one of the Fodor's City Guide series, which is reviewed in more detail under "Series Reviews." The series is updated annually.

Frommer's Dollarwise Guide to Japan and Hong Kong
By Beth Reiber, Prentice Hall Press, 1988, 384 pages, paper, $13.95. This book is part of Frommer's Dollarwise Guide series, which is reviewed in more detail under "Series Reviews." The series is updated every two years.

Good Tokyo Restaurants
By Rick Kennedy, Kodansha International, 1985, 268 pages, paper, $7.95. From among Tokyo's seventy-seven thousand restaurants Kennedy has chosen some of the best, including various price ranges and many different cuisines. The full range of Japanese foods is offered in thirty-nine of these choices. Others offer Swiss, Swedish, French, and other types of food. Each restaurant chosen is given an informative, well-written, two-page review, including a hand-drawn map on which important buildings appear in three-dimensions.

A Guide to Food Buying in Japan
By Carolyn Krouse, Charles E. Tuttle Co., 1986, 191 pages, paper, $9.50. This is an excellent guide to shopping for foodstuffs,

not for what to eat in a restaurant. It is very helpful for those wishing to do their own cooking.

The Guide to Japanese Food and Restaurants
By Russel Marcus and Jack Plimpton, Charles E. Tuttle Co., 1984, 263 pages, paper, $12.95. In this well-organized guide containing excellent detail maps, the authors describe over seven hundred restaurants. Different types of cuisine are arranged by section, and special tab markers are used for easy reference. Recommended restaurants are tied to specific maps. The Restaurant Finder inside the front cover is an added feature, and the section on how to spot different types of restaurants is always handy in a crowded and unfamiliar place.

Hildebrand's Travel Guide: Japan
Hunter Publishing, 1985, 352 pages, paper, $10.95. This book is part of the Hildebrand's Guide series, which is reviewed in more detail under "Series Reviews."

How to Get Lost and Found in Japan
By John McDermott, Hunter Publishing, 1984, 271 pages, paper, $9.95. This book is part of the delightful Lost and Found Guide series.

Insider's Guide to Japan
Hunter Publishing, 1987, 212 pages, paper, $12.95. This book is part of the Hunter's Insider's Guide series, which is reviewed in more detail under "Series Reviews."

Japan: A Travel Survival Kit
By Ian McQueen, Lonely Planet Publications, 1986 (2nd ed.), 520 pages, paper, $12.95. This book is one of the popular Travel Survival Kit series, which is reviewed in more detail under "Series Reviews." The series is updated every two to three years.

Japan At Night: A Complete Guide to Entertainment and Leisure in Japan
By Boye De Mente, Passport Books, 1987, 307 pages, paper, $7.95. This compact little book is crammed with information. It takes a little getting used to, but the write-ups are informative and the variety of topics is truly incredible for such a small book. Areas covered include recreational activities, spectator sports, personal services, spas, discos, and pleasure baths.

Japan for Westerners
Yes!, 1986, 88 pages, paper, $5.95. This is a resource guide to books on Japan, including the topics of arts, music, literature, history, martial arts, cuisine, business, language, and travel. An update addendum is expected in 1988-89.

Japan Handbook
By J.D. Bisignani, Moon Publications, 1983, 505 pages, paper, $12.95. The new edition of this guide is due out in 1989. It is part of the superb Moon Handbook series, which is reviewed in more detail under "Series Reviews." Moon Publications has recently made a commitment to updating their various titles every two years.

Japan in 22 Days
See *22 Days in Japan.*

Japan: Land of Many Faces
By Alan Booth, Passport Books, 1988, 288 pages, paper, $9.95. This book is part of the Passport Asian Guide series, which is reviewed in more detail under "Series Reviews."

Japan Solo: A Practical Guide for Independent Travelers
By Eiji Kanno and Constance O'Keefe, Warner Books, 1988, 400 pages, paper, $14.95. The authors of this book, both of whom have had considerable experience with the Japan National Tourist Organization, have created a book of great and lasting value for independent travelers. It is well organized and includes many walking tours, much sightseeing information, and a large number of excellent detail maps. This edition covers the north and south islands and is printed in a small, manageable size. Hotels in all price ranges are briefly described, and restaurant picks are selected to fit into various itineraries.

Japan Today! A Westerner's Guide to the People, Language, and Culture of Japan
By Theodore Welch and Hiroki Kato, Passport Books, 1986, 115 pages, paper, $7.95. This title covers essential cultural information in an A-to-Z format. It is a handy reference work and includes a special language section.

Japan Unescorted: A Practical Guide to Discovering Japan on Your Own
By James Weatherly, Kodansha International, 1986, 200 pages, paper, $6.95. This delightful little guide is one of several well-done books on independent travel in Japan. It is full of helpful descriptions of hotels and restaurants in all price

ranges, although the focus of the book is on "practicality and budget." The detail maps are helpful.

Kyoto: Seven Paths to the Heart of the City
By Diane Durston, Kodansha International, 1988, 64 pages, paper, $9.95. This large-format book, due for release after press time, focuses on seven districts "that best exemplify Japan's old imperial capital." Carefully drawn maps allow travelers to explore the narrow back streets of Kyoto even though most, in typical Japanese style, are nameless. Additional sections on cuisine, festivals, customs, and practical facts are also included. This author has also produced the excellent *Old Kyoto: A Guide to Traditional Shops, Restaurants, and Inns*.

National Parks of Japan
By Mary Sutherland and Dorothy Dritton, Kodansha International, 1980, 148 pages, cloth, $19.95. Containing great descriptions of Japan's twenty-seven national parks, this is the kind of book that belongs on the coffee table. Combining clear maps and some fantastic photographs, the book will encourage even the most itinerary-oriented traveler to allow a visit to some of these magnificent spots.

North-East Asia on a Shoestring
Edited by Tony Wheeler, Lonely Planet Publications, 1985, 288 pages, paper, $7.95. Covering China, Hong Kong, Japan, Macau, South Korea, and Taiwan, with short notes on visiting North Korea, this book is part of the budget-oriented On a Shoestring Guide series, which is reviewed in more detail under "Series Reviews." Titles in this series are generally updated every two to three years. At press time, a new edition had not yet been announced.

Old Kyoto: A Guide to Traditional Shops, Restaurants, and Inns
By Diane Durston, Kodansha International, 1986, 240 pages, paper, $11.95. This is a thoroughly classy guide to the old section of this ancient city: its history; its shops of food goods, textiles, incense, tea, sweets, dolls; its traditional inns and restaurants. This book will allow all travelers, even armchair ones, to experience the real Kyoto.

Passport's Japan Almanac
By Boye De Mente, Passport Books, 1987, 319 pages, paper, $17.95. This large-format book takes Passport Books' other A-to-Z "compendium of all things Japanese" (*Japan Today!*) a step further. It is well written and pleasantly laid out, and

it covers almost one thousand subjects, including art, education, social customs, and history. Too large to carry comfortably, this book will answer after the trip questions the guidebooks didn't cover.

Post Guide: Japan

Hunter Publishing, 1987, 144 pages, paper, $8.95. This is one of the Post Guide series, which is reviewed in more detail under "Series Reviews."

Tokyo/Access

By Richard Saul Wurman, Prentice Hall Press, 1987, 225 pages, paper, $11.95. This is part of the Access Guide series, which is reviewed in more detail under "Series Reviews."

Tokyo City Guide

By Judith Conner and Mayumi Yoshida, Kodansha International, 1987 (revised ed.), 363 pages, paper, $15.95. This beautifully laid-out and thoroughly comprehensive *Tokyo City Guide* contains information on accommodations; places to eat; the best shopping, entertainment, and night life; the arts; sightseeing; and health and beauty resources. The multicolored map section is particularly excellent in this wonderful resource.

Tokyo in Your Pocket

Barron's Education Series, 1987, 160 pages, paper, $3.95. This is one of the small-format In-Your-Pocket Guide series, which is reviewed in more detail under "Series Reviews."

Top Shopping in Japan

Charles E. Tuttle Co., 1984, 303 pages, paper, $19.95. Produced in Japan for the tourist trade, this book is full of photos, good detail maps, and the occasional advertisement. It covers a little bit of everything, including eating spots, hotels, and sightseeing along the shopping trail. Its biggest plus is that it covers shopping areas not generally covered elsewhere. For Tokyo, it is a useful complement to the more detailed Born to Shop guide.

22 Days in Japan: The Itinerary Planner

By David Old, John Muir Publications, 1987, 133 pages, paper, $6.95. Rick Steves' famous *Europe in 22 Days* (now called *22 Days in Europe*) has spawned a whole Itinerary Planner series, which is reviewed in more detail under "Series Reviews." Note that the change in title is quite recent; this book may also be entitled *Japan in 22 Days*.

What's What in Japanese Restaurants
By Robb Satterwhite, Kodansha International, 1988, 144 pages, paper, $9.95. This new title, released after press time, delves into the specific cuisines of the Japanese, many of which are unfamiliar to Westerners. The book contains a section on the Japanese menu, designed to let travelers know what they are ordering, and some very helpful chapters on beer, sake, and tourist traps.

Malaysia

Insight Guides: Malaysia
By APA Producitons, Prentice Hall Press, 1986, 350 pages, paper, $16.95. This is one of the highly regarded Insight Guide series, which is reviewed in more detail under "Series Reviews."

Malaysia, Singapore and Brunei: A Travel Survival Kit
By Geoff Crowther and Tony Wheeler, Lonely Planet Publications, 1988 (3rd ed.), 320 pages, paper, $9.95. This is an excellent title in the popular Travel Survival Kit series, which is reviewed in more detail under "Series Reviews." The series is updated every two to three years. This edition was released after press time, so the number of pages is approximate.

Malaysia, Singapore, Brunei Traveller's Handbook
By Stefan Loose and Renate Ramb, Riverdale Co., 1986, 331 pages, paper, $9.95. Translated from the German, this little book focuses on the budget-minded traveler, but covers price ranges from "luxurious to super cheap" in hotels, restaurants, and transportation. The layout is strictly utilitarian, but the information on practicalities and pleasures is as enjoyable to read as it is helpful. Good detail maps are a plus.

Post Guide: Malaysia
Hunter Publishing, 1987, 144 pages, paper, $8.95. This book is part of the Post Guide series, which is reviewed in more detail under "Series Reviews."

Shopping in Exotic Singapore and Malaysia
By Ronald Krannich, et al., Impact Publications, 1988, 170 pages, paper, $9.95. This new book, released after press time, is part of the Shopping in Exotic Places series, which is re-

viewed in more detail under "Series Reviews." The series is updated every two years; the number of pages is approximate.

Time Travel in the Malay Crescent
By Wayne Stier, Meru Publishing, 1985, 312 pages, paper, $10.00.
This enjoyable, informative book provides some real insight into the lands of Malaysia, Singapore, Borneo, and Brunei. It makes a terrific companion to a standard guide to this fascinating region of the world.

Nepal

Berlitz: Nepal
Macmillan Publishing, 1988, 128 pages, paper, $6.95. This book is one of the small-format, Berlitz Guide series, which is reviewed in more detail under "Series Reviews."

A Guide to Trekking in Nepal
By Stephen Bezruchka, The Mountaineers, 1985 (5th ed.), 352 pages, $10.95. This well-organized, well-written guide describes the best trekking routes in detail and provides additional notes on history and natural history. It is perfect for those trekking alone or with a group, offering excellent information on preparations, health care, and interacting with the Nepalese (including a good section on language and useful phrases for the trekker).

Insight Guides: Nepal
by APA Productions, Prentice Hall Press, 1986, 351 pages, paper, $16.95. This book is part of the excellent Insight Guide series, which is reviewed in more detail under "Series Reviews."

Kathmandu and the Kingdom of Nepal: A Travel Survival Kit
By Prakash A Ray, Lonely Planet Publications, 1985 (5th ed.), 144 pages, paper, $7.95. This book is part of the popular Travel Survival Kit series, which is reviewed in more detail under "Series Reviews." The titles in this series are generally updated every two to three years. At press time, a new edition had not yet been announced.

The Times Travel Library: Kathmandu
Hunter Publishing, 1987, 104 pages, paper, $10.95. This book is part of the new large-format, photo-filled Times Travel

Library Guide series, which is reviewed in more detail under "Series Reviews."

The Trekker's Guide to the Himalaya and Karakoram
By Hugh Swift, Sierra Club Books, 1982, 352 pages, paper, $10.95. This fine guide is done in typical Sierra Club fashion, but is not as up-to-date on some issues as other guides to the area.

Trekking in the Nepal Himalaya
By Stan Armington, Lonely Planet Publications, 1985 (4th ed.), 200 pages, paper, $7.95. This solid guide emphasizes trek organization. It includes suggestions on routes, equipment needs, maps, and more.

West Asia on a Shoestring
By Tony Wheeler, Lonely Planet Publications, 1986 (5th ed.), 368 pages, paper, $8.95. Describing the overland route from Bangladesh to Turkey, this book is part of the budget-oriented On a Shoestring Guide series, which is reviewed in more detail under "Series Reviews." The series is updated every two to three years.

Pakistan

Pakistan: A Travel Survival Kit
By José Santiago, Lonely Planet Publications, 1987 (3rd ed.), 240 pages, paper, $8.95. This book is part of the well-known Travel Survival Kit series, which is reviewed in more detail under "Series Reviews." The series is updated every two to three years.

Philippines

Hildebrand's Travel Guide: Philippines
Hunter Publishing, 1988, 240 pages, paper, $10.95. This book is a new member of the Hildebrand's Guide series, which is reviewed in more detail under "Series Reviews."

Insight Guides: the Philippines
By APA Productions, Prentice Hall Press, 1986, 335 pages, paper, $16.95. This book is part of the acclaimed Insight Guide series, which is reviewed in more detail under "Series Reviews."

Nagel's Philippines
Passport Books, 1982, 367 pages, cloth, $39.95. This classic, cultural guide is part of the Nagel's Guide series, which is reviewed in more detail under "Series Reviews."

Philippines: A Travel Survival Kit
By Jens Peters, Lonely Planet Publications, 1987 (3rd ed.), 372 pages, paper, $8.95. This book is part of the popular Travel Survival Kit series, which is reviewed in more detail under "Series Reviews." The series is updated every two to three years.

Singapore

Baedeker's Singapore
Prentice Hall Press, 1986, 112 pages, paper, $10.95. This book is part of Baedeker's City Guide series, which is reviewed in more detail under "Series Reviews."

Berlitz: Singapore
Macmillan Publishing, 1979, 128 pages, paper, $6.95. This book is part of the small-format Berlitz Guide series, which is reviewed in more detail under "Series Reviews."

Fodor's Singapore
Fodor's Travel Guides, 1987, 176 pages, paper, $7.95. This book is one of Fodor's City Guide series, which is reviewed in more detail under "Series Reviews." The series is updated annually.

Insight Guides: Singapore
By APA Productions, Prentice Hall Press, 1986, 342 pages, paper, $16.95. This book is part of the acclaimed Insight Guide series, which is reviewed in more detail under "Series Reviews."

Post Guide: Singapore
Hunter Publishing, 1983, 144 pages, paper, $8.95. This book is part of the Post Guide series, which is reviewed in more detail under "Series Reviews."

South Korea

Fodor's Korea
Fodor's Travel Guides, 1988, 192 pages, paper, $10.95. This book is part of Fodor's Country/Regional Guide series, which is reviewed in more detail under "Series Reviews." The series is updated annually.

Hildebrand's Travel Guide: South Korea
Hunter Publishing, 1987, 255 pages, paper, $10.95. This book is part of the Hildebrand's Guide series, which is reviewed in more detail under "Series Reviews."

Insider's Guide to Korea
Hunter Publishing, 1987, 196 pages, paper, $12.95. This book is part of the Hunter Insider's Guide series, which is reviewed in more detail under "Series Reviews."

Insight Guides: Korea
By APA Productions, Prentice Hall Press, 1986, 321 pages, paper, $16.95. This book is one of the acclaimed Insight Guide series, which is reviewed in more detail under "Series Reviews."

Korea: A Travel Survival Kit
By Geoff Crowther, Lonely Planet Publications, 1988, 200 pages, paper, $8.95. This new title, released after press time, is half of what used to be the old "Survival Kit" on Korea and Taiwan. This title is now part of the popular Travel Survival Kit series, which is reviewed in more detail under "Series Reviews." The series is updated every two to three years; the number of pages is approximate.

Korea Guide
By Edward Adams, Charles E. Tuttle Co., 1986, 360 pages, cloth, $19.50. This attractive, hard-bound volume, replete with many beautiful photos, is an excellent planning tool. At the back of the book is a Directory that offers practical information and hotel selections (without detailed comment). However, the real strengths of this book are its coverage of history and cultural attributes and the many suggested sightseeing tours described by a man who has lived and worked in Korea for several decades.

The Korea Guidebook
By Kyung Cho Chung, et al., Eurasia Press, 1987, 528 pages, paper, $14.95. This comprehensive, well-written guide covers all the classic tourist bases. Major sections on practicalities, doing business, history and culture, and various

tours—each with recommended things to see, places to stay in different price ranges, and a few select restaurants—make this a great resource.

Korea: The Land of Morning Calm
By Daniel Reid, Passport Books, 1988, 208 pages, paper, $9.95. This book is one of the Passport Asian Guide series, which is reviewed in more detail under "Series Reviews."

Seoul, 1988 Olympic Site
By Edward Adams, Charles E. Tuttle Co., 1984, 57 pages, paper, $4.00. Although the hotel recommendations certainly need updating, this little paperback remains a useful, compact guide to the capital city. Information includes a subway guide, what to see, what to eat (general strategies and suggested dishes), shopping, and entertainment. Detail maps are only adequate.

Shopping in Exotic Korea
By Ronald Krannich, et al., Impact Publications, 1988, 180 pages, paper, $9.95.
Shopping in Exotic Places: Your Passport to Exciting Hong Kong, Korea, Thailand, Indonesia, and Singapore
By Ronald Krannich, et al., Impact Publications, 1987, 469 pages, paper, $13.95.
Both of these titles are part of the excellent Shopping in Exotic Places series, which is reviewed in more detail under "Series Reviews." The Korean volume is an anticipated addition to the series and expands on the Korean section of the second title. The series is updated every two years. The Korean volume was released after press time, so the number of pages is approximate.

South Korea Handbook
By Robert Nilsen, Moon Publications, 1988, 600 pages, paper, $14.95. This is a new edition, released after press time, to the superb Moon Handbook series, which is reviewed in more detail under "Series Reviews." The series is updated every two years.

The Times Travel Library: Seoul
Hunter Publishing, 1987, 104 pages, paper, $10.95. This book is part of the large-format, photo-filled Times Travel Library series, which is reviewed in more detail under "Series Reviews."

Sri Lanka

Berlitz: Sri Lanka and the Maldives
Macmillan Publishing, 1981, 128 pages, paper, $6.95. This book is one of the small-format Berlitz Guide series, which is reviewed in more detail under "Series Reviews."

Hildebrand's Travel Guide: Sri Lanka
Hunter Publishing, 1985, 143 pages, paper, $8.95. This book is one of the Hildebrand's Guide series, which is reviewed in more detail under "Series Reviews."

Insight Guides: Sri Lanka
By APA Productions, Prentice Hall Press, 1985, 367 pages, paper, $16.95. This book is part of the widely praised Insight Guide series, which is reviewed in more detail under "Series Reviews."

Nagel's Ceylon
Passport Books, 1983, 271 pages, cloth, $39.95. This classic, cultural guide is part of the Nagel's Guide series, which is reviewed in more detail under "Series Reviews."

Post Guide: Sri Lanka
Hunter Publishing, 1983, 144 pages, paper, $8.95. This book is part of the Post Guide series, which is reviewed in more detail under "Series Reviews."

Sri Lanka: A Travel Survival Kit
By Tony Wheeler, Lonely Planet Publications, 1984 (4th ed.), 240 pages, paper, $8.95. This book is part of the popular Travel Survival Kit series, which is reviewed in more detail under "Series Reviews." Titles in this series are generally updated every two to three years. At press time, a new edition had not yet been announced.

Taiwan

Guide to Taipei and Taiwan
By Joseph Nerbonne, W. S. Heinman-Imported Books, 1988 (9th ed.), 330 pages, paper, $12.00. In perhaps the single best guide to Taiwan, Nerbonne, a long-time resident, provides a truly massive amount of sightseeing information, hotel and restaurant choices, and all sorts of practical facts and figures. This is a particularly helpful guide both for its excellent maps and for its inclusion of the Chinese and English lan-

guage words for important streets, trains, etc. What this means is that travelers who are totally stuck can show the written word for the place or street they are seeking to the person they are asking directions of. The price and number of pages for the 1988 edition, not yet released at press time, are approximate.

Hildebrand's Travel Guide: Taiwan
Hunter Publishing, 1986, 190 pages, paper, $10.95. This book is part of the Hildebrand's Guide series, which is reviewed in more detail under "Series Reviews."

Insight Guides: Taiwan
By APA Productions, Prentice Hall Press, 1986, 355 pages, paper, $16.95. This book is part of the acclaimed Insight Guide series, which is reviewed in more detail under "Series Reviews."

Taiwan: A Travel Survival Kit
By Robert Storey, Lonely Planet Publications, 1987, 250 pages, paper, $8.95. This book is one of the well-known Travel Survival Kit series, which is reviewed in more detail under "Series Reviews." The series is updated every two to three years.

Thailand

Baedeker's Bangkok
Prentice Hall Press, 1987, 144 pages, paper, $10.95. This book is part of Baedeker's City Guide series, which is reviewed in more detail under "Series Reviews."

Bangkok's Back Streets
By Bob Todd, Excogitations, 1986, 72 pages, paper, $9.95. This "guide to the pleasure of the world's most open city" is only for those seeking help surviving and enjoying Bangkok's "red light" district.

Berlitz: Thailand
Macmillan Publishing, 1979, 128 pages, paper, $6.95. This book is one of the small-format Berlitz Guide series, which is reviewed in more detail under "Series Reviews."

Cadogan Guides: Thailand and Burma
By Frank Kusy and Frances Capel, Globe Pequot Press, 1988, 350 pages, paper, $14.95. This is an expected new title in the

highly regarded Cadogan Guide series, which is reviewed in more detail under "Series Reviews." The price and number of pages are approximate. The series is updated every two years; this title is due out in late 1988.

Frommer's Touring Guide to Thailand
Prentice Hall Press, 1988, 175 pages, paper, $9.95. This book is a new title in the latest Frommer series, Frommer's Touring Guides, which is reviewed in more detail under "Series Reviews."

Guide to Chiang Mai and Northern Thailand
By John Hoskin, Charles E. Tuttle Co., 1984, 180 pages, paper, $4.95. This book is considered by many to be the best guide to this region. It is written in an enjoyable style and is full of information on how to get there and what to see and do. The hotel listing is long and covers all price ranges, but additional comments are scant. The publication date means that some details need updating, so be sure to confirm all time-sensitive information.

Hildebrand's Travel Guide: Thailand
By Dieter Rumpf, Hippocrene Books, 1985, 300 pages, paper, $10.95. This book is one of the Hildebrand's Guide series, which is reviewed in more detail under "Series Reviews."

Insight Guides: Thailand
By APA Productions, Prentice Hall Press, 1987, 343 pages, paper, $16.95. This book is part of the excellent Insight Guide series, which is reviewed in more detail under "Series Reviews."

Nagel's Thailand
Passport Books, 1982, 383 pages, cloth, $39.95. This classic, cultural guide is part of the Nagel's Guide series, which is reviewed in more detail under "Series Reviews."

Post Guide: Thailand
Hunter Publishing, 1987, 144 pages, paper, $8.95. This book is part of the Post Guide series, which is reviewed in more detail under "Series Reviews."

Shopping in Exotic Places: Your Passport to Exciting Hong Kong, Korea, Thailand, Indonesia, and Singapore
By Ronald Krannich, et al., Impact Publications, 1987, 469 pages, paper, $13.95.

Shopping in Exotic Thailand
By Ronald Krannich, et al., Impact Publications, 1988, 200 pages, paper, $10.95.

Both of these titles are part of the excellent Shopping in Exotic Places series, which is reviewed in more detail under "Series Reviews." The Thailand volume is an anticipated addition to the series and expands on the Thailand section of the first title. The Thailand volume was released after press time, so the number of pages is approximate. The series is updated every two years.

Thailand: A Travel Survival Kit
By Joe Cummings, Lonely Planet Publications, 1987 (3rd ed.), 284 pages, paper, $8.95. This book is one of the popular Travel Survival Kit series, which is reviewed in more detail under "Series Reviews." The series is updated every two to three years.

Thailand: The Kingdom of Siam
By John Haskins, Passport Books, 1988, 224 pages, paper, $9.95. This book is part of the Passport Asian Guide series, which is reviewed in more detail under "Series Reviews."

The Traveler's Complete Guide to Pattaya and Southeastern Thailand
By Steve Van Beek, Charles E. Tuttle Co., 1981, 150 pages, paper, $4.95. This guide is in need of an update, but is still useful for sightseeing and providing ideas for enjoying this popular place. Hotel selections are probably still useful—at least for the larger chains—although price ranges are undoubtedly higher now. The section on foods of the area will point out delicacies not to miss, but a few of the restaurants that are singled out may not exist anymore.

Series Reviews

Access Guides
Prentice Hall Press. The Access series has its ardent fans and those who find it perhaps a little too strange to use. Peruse it yourself, and decide if this unique, award-winning design fits your needs. Its developer, Richard Saul Wurman, is a cartographer and graphic designer, as evidenced throughout each book. Wurman uses different colors to represent each particular category of tourist attraction. So, by color alone you can tell at a glance whether the information is on sightseeing, restaurants, or hotels. In addition, the books are designed to be used by the walker as he or she moves down the avenue. All shops, parks, points of interest, and

so forth, show up in a logical color-coded pattern. The descriptions are nicely done, and there are plenty of tips, practical facts, and maps.

American Express Pocket Guides

Prentice Hall Press. The print is small and, for some, a small reading glass may be in order. Those who read on will be rewarded with an amazing amount of information packed into a small, convenient-sized book. Most titles in this series concentrate on cities or small regions where a small guide can do great justice. Inside is information on walks, sightseeing (with gallery and museum information in considerable detail), lodging, restaurants, night life, and excursions to the areas nearby. As with other books that pack a lot of information in, you will have to get used to a number of hieroglyphic symbols to learn some of the details. The maps, too, are excellent—particularly the finedetail maps.

Baedeker's City Guides

Prentice Hall Press. Of the several Baedeker's series, the City Guides work best. The reason is the large, fold-out map that is keyed to references in the text. The text provides practical information on shopping, night life, tours, and, briefly, restaurants and hotels. But you don't buy a Baedeker for these kinds of facts; you buy it as a sightseeing guide. Descriptions of the sights, including color photos and public transportation options, are arranged in an A-to-Z format. The format is easy to use because the large, excellent map lets you get oriented geographically. There are also detail maps and museum floor plans.

Berlitz Country Guides

Macmillan Publishing. Most of the Country Guides are recent additions to the Berlitz series. While the Berlitz Guides (below) have focused almost exclusively on single cities or regions, the Country Guides have taken on much larger areas, although the number of pages is only double those of the other series. The structure and content are similar, but the amount of detail is less than in the classic Berlitz Guides. The overview provided, however, is practical and helpful.

Berlitz Guides

Macmillan Publishing. For tiny, pocket-sized books, these guides are quite informative. If you put a premium on small size, and want just the essentials, Berlitz can help. These guides are not updated frequently, and they make only general comments on lodging and food (although several newer editions now have a separate sixteen-page supplement at the back specifically on these more quickly dated subjects). However, these books provide a good review of the history of the region and a practical facts section, plus much information on where to go, when to go, what to do, sports, and other activities. These are handy little guides and, if the trend toward a hotel and restaurant supplement spills over into more titles, they will be all the better. Our listings reflect the price increase of 1988. However, you should be able to find most titles at a lesser price for some time to come.

Born to Shop Guides
Bantam Books. Slick and uptown, these guides generally appeal to wealthier travelers. But there are bargain shopping tips as well. As a matter of fact there is a whole, lengthy section devoted to the "business of bargains." Well researched, these little guides contain a good deal of the practical details on what to watch out for, how to find fakes, hot merchandise, customs, etc. Selections are arranged by district and cover the gamut: clothing, home furnishing, antiques, collectibles, etc. Well organized and solidly prepared.

Cadogan Guides
Globe Pequot Press. The quality of writing in this British series is exceptional, producing results that are always solid, and usually excellent. Several of the guides are updates of books that were first part of the Island Hopping Guide series (some titles of which are still available). From practical facts to history, customs, sightseeing, food, and lodging, the Cadogan Guides can be counted on for interesting detail and informed recommendations. Aimed at the "discerning traveler," the guides are strongly weighted toward history and cultural information. Each guide is updated biannually.

Crown Insiders' Guides
Crown Publishers. This fairly new series, edited by Robert Fisher, (who also produces his own series, Fisher's World Guides) is written by numerous writers who have lived or studied in each area, but who are also Americans and familiar with what interests Americans. They are both insiders and outsiders. As such, they offer a great many inside tips on managing in and appreciating the lands you are visiting. They also provide itineraries, coupled with detailed text and a five-star rating system for hotels and restaurants in a wide range of prices (mostly moderate and up.) Com-

ments on hotels and restaurants are fairly brief, but informative. The overall result is a solid, well-produced series that has a growing number of fans. We have other favorites for some regions, but the Crown series is definitely a good choice for the well-heeled traveler.

The Economist Business Traveller's Guides
Prentice Hall Press. This rapidly expanding series of superb, business-oriented guides is getting top reviews from those business travelers already using them. You will find information on business practices and local etiquette, some historical notes, a rundown of the economic scene by business category in each country or region, and a discussion of the industrial scene (cars, food, drink, etc.), including prospects for the future. Each major business area is covered. Included are hotel and restaurant reviews, which are well done and of moderate length. You'll also find specifics on transportation, shopping, sightseeing, and entertainment. The focus is always on the needs of the business person on the go, and some titles provide details on less frequently covered areas like the Arabian Peninsula or Southeast Asia.

Fielding's Travel Guides
William Morrow and Co. Among the titles of this series, only *Fielding's Caribbean* receives high grades, but all are more than adequate travel guides. Plenty of good information on shopping and sightseeing is included, and hotel and restaurant ratings use a star system of 1 to 5. Selections cover the moderate to very expensive, with a heavy leaning toward the more expensive. A problem we found with these guides is the author's condescending tone of voice. So while the information may be good, it may be difficult to assimilate due to a feeling of being talked down to. However, Fielding plans a "total redesign" with the 1989 editions. If this affects form as well as substance, these books may become more palatable.

Fodor's City Guides
Fodor's Travel Guides/Random House. Fodor is showing some distinct signs of improvement (see comments under Fodor's Country/Regional Guides). For years they have seemed to rest on the laurels earned by Eugene Fodor, even though he sold the company in the late 1960s. The guides follow such a strict formula that they seem to cramp the style of even the most talented of travel writers. Nevertheless, the city guides are solid, with selections in every price range, some good sightseeing information, and other practical facts. In general, these guides are predictable and unexciting.

Fodor's Country/Regional Guides

Fodor's Travel Guides/Random House. If you speak with people who make their livelihood selling travel books, you will discover that very few Fodor's titles are strongly recommended. A few specific titles are mentioned as exceptions to the rule, and we have noted these accordingly. A few others have been severely criticized. It's certain not that these guides offer nothing of value. Far from it. They are very popular—partly because of the name Eugene Fodor created for the series. But most knowledgeable travelers find the Fodor titles stodgy and a bit boring. However, there are signs of significant change. Random House now owns Fodor and recently brought in Michael Spring as the editorial director. Spring, who has a reputation as a fine travel writer in his own right, has said that he anticipates a significant change in the look and format of this series in 1989. If that happens, these guides will be on their way to the top. For now, Fodor still covers all the bases more than adequately in most titles. Yearly updates, however, are fairly limited, and major updates have traditionally occurred about every four years. A few titles are updated only occasionally.

Fodor's Great Travel Values Guides

Fodor's Travel Guides/Random House. This is the new name for Fodor's budget series (*Budget Europe* has retained its old title so far). The style and format is, to date, the style of old: plenty of information on practical issues and sightseeing; cryptic notes on hotels and restaurants. Some good detail maps are included, but the overall tone remains lifeless. As with other traditional guides, updates are minimal on a yearly basis; full updates occur about every four years.

Frommer's Dollar-a-Day Guides

Prentice Hall Press. The Dollar-a-Day Guides are one of the better budget guide series. Each receives an extensive biennial update. And although it is difficult to stay under the daily dollar figure that is part of the title, there are plenty of bargains here. Each book provides a good introduction to the area, including history, a discussion of the people, festivals, sports, and foods. Transportation options are covered extensively—there is no assumption that you have your own vehicle. Selections of lodging and restaurants are given full coverage so you can make an informed choice. This is one of several top-quality budget series.

Frommer's Dollarwise Guides

Prentice Hall Press. If your budget is a bit bigger, but you don't want to use one of the guides that may overemphasize the more expensive choices, this is a good series. Emphasis is on moderately priced selections, although all price ranges are included. Each guide has a good orientation section, some fine choices of hotels and restaurants with extensive evaluations, and good sightseeing information. The guides concentrate on major cities and tourist areas. Smaller towns and other, more rural destinations away from the travel mainstream are briefly mentioned. As with every Frommer title, these are significantly updated every other year.

Frommer's Touring Guides
Prentice Hall Press. This newer series offers a different focus from the other Frommer series—on culture and history, with essays on art, architecture, and traditions. Although they include photographs, maps, suggested itineraries, and practical information on hotels, restaurants, etc., these books make better "companion guides" than primary travel guides.

Hildebrand's Guides
Hunter Publishing. This German series, now in a new, somewhat larger format, covers most travel topics but is especially good on history and impressions that will add significantly to your sightseeing pleasure. You will also find a full range of hotel choices, travel maps, lots of practical details, and plenty of color photographs. The food sections offer more an orientation to local cuisine than specific selections. These are compact, useful guides.

Hunter Insider's Guides
Hunter Publishing. Slickly produced, this Insider's series from Hunter Publishing has a look a bit like the more famous Insight Guides. With numerous, beautiful color photographs and an informative text, the books present a good overview of each area and its many sightseeing options. Details on hotels, restaurants, and specific activities are merely listed, with price ranges noted. We much prefer more detail when it comes to hotels and restaurants, but for good general, mainstream touring guides, these work quite well. Pretty to look at, they also come with large, fold-out maps.

In-Your-Pocket Guides
Barron's Educational Series. If you put a premium on the size of your guide, one series that packs a considerable amount of information into a small space is the Barron's In-Your-Pocket series. For a mere $3.95 you get a very handy directory to restaurants, hotels, museums, theaters, stores, night life, sightseeing, and important services. Obviously, there isn't as much in one of these small guides as in one

ten times its weight, but for the money they have a lot to offer. If small is beautiful to you, take a look at one of these city guides and see if it doesn't meet your needs.

Insight Guides
Prentice Hall Press. The Insight Guides are simply wonderful. Produced by a Singapore company, they weave an interesting text through a potpourri of spectacular photographs. When we first saw the Insight Guides years ago, we thought they were simply picture books. Not so. There is a vast amount of information inside as well. They dedicate a good, meaty fifty pages or so to the history, geography, and people of each area. Then they take you on a guided tour of all the major areas—the backcountry too—and provide special features on areas of unusual interest, parks, etc. The "guide in brief" at the back does a commendable job with practical details, including respectable lists of lodgings. In general, these guides seem to be updated every two or three years, so information is kept quite current.

Itinerary Planners
John Muir Publications. The number of titles in this series is expanding rapidly—all because of the runaway success of Rick Steves's *Europe in 22 Days*. Steves is a veteran guide, having led tours, primarily in Europe, for almost fifteen years. The intent of this series is to help you lead your own tour by providing clear, well-planned itineraries for classic three-week vacations. Optional side trips are included to allow you to expand your trip even further. The itineraries are also designed to let you begin or end a trip at any point in the schedule. Generally, these trips are for energetic souls with some "get-up-and-go," although some "R & R" days are planned. And, in spite of the assumption that you have your own vehicle, the books are for the budget-minded, with good picks for lodging and restaurants. The whole idea is to let the experts lead the way, but not to pay someone to actually be there. Note that the title of each guide in this series was changed in 1988; you may find either title on the bookstore shelf for some time to come.

Moon Handbooks
Moon Publications. The orientation of this series is for the young and adventurous, but every traveler can glean tremendous value from it. Most people using the Moon guides rely on public transportation, bicycles, or their thumbs, but there is always information for those who wish to rent a car. (Remember, though, that these books are certainly not

focused on auto travel.) Each guide offers an incredible amount of background information on history, natural history, the people, arts and crafts, events, etc. If you read and study this section before you go, you will be a *very* well-educated traveler. Sightseeing notes are offered in copious detail, and there are always good maps of important areas. Food and lodging recommendations are not neglected; numerous well-described choices generally cover the price ranges of budget to moderate. The occasional guide, such as the *Japan Handbook*, offers a much wider range. The series is comprehensive and, in a word, superb.

Exciting announcements have reached us at press time: the long awaited arrival of the *Japan Handbook* update will appear in 1989; the company has now made a commitment to thorough revisions every two years (it will take a while to put this policy into effect); and new books on Southeast Asia and the Philippines are due out in late 1988.

Nagel's Guides

Passport Books/National Textbook Co. This vintage Swiss series is meant for the sophisticated traveler who would like more than the typical amount of detail on history, physical geography, economy, literature, the theater, philosophy, science, art, music, and the cinema. These and similar topics make up the first part of each book. What follows are detailed itineraries through the various regions of each country, including copious notes on history and activities for each town and point of interest. Detail maps are numerous. The Nagel guides are often a thousand pages or more— small, thick, sturdy, hardbound volumes. If the label "sophisticated" sounds correct for you, take the time to evaluate the Nagel Guides for yourself. Though sometimes a little old, they make wonderful companions to more practical, primary guidebooks.

On a Shoestring Guides

Lonely Planet Publications. These are the super budget guides—to cheap hotels, local food, touring, and everything on a shoestring. The Southeast Asia guide has long been very popular, and it is largely responsible for Lonely Planet's rise to fame. On the other hand, *South America On a Shoestring* is criticized for its inaccuracy. Such difficulties are undoubtedly part of Lonely Planet's decision to focus more on individual countries in their Travel Survival Kit series (which covers a broader range of price ranges but is still useful to the budget traveler). The other Shoestring titles are well respected; they are very thorough, touching on all the necessary topics. The detail maps are clear and carefully drawn. Lonely Planet prides itself in its responsiveness to the criticism of those who use their books, so we look for significant improvement in the South America title in its next edition.

Passport Asian Guides

Passport Books/National Textbook, Co. This new series for 1988 was released after we went to press. It appears to be a twin of the existent Passport China Guide series (see below).

Passport China Guides

Passport Books/National Textbook, Co. Although they offer some specific hotel and restaurant choices, the main thrust of these handsome, illustrated guides concerns orientation, learning the ropes, cultural topics specific to the region, historical notes, and the important sights. In this they succeed admirably. The color photographs are nothing short of exceptional. Quite a few orientation maps, plus the occasional detail map of a larger city, are included.

Post Guides

Hunter Publishing. These fairly compact guides emphasize background information, practical survival tips, and sightseeing. The general information section is quite good and runs the gamut (weather, customs, tipping, dos and don'ts, festivals, transportation, etc.). Sightseeing is adequately covered and aimed at the mainstream tourist. There are some eating and sleeping tips for the major cities, with brief notes or none at all. Numerous color photos and the occasional maps are also included. These books are solid and reasonably thorough, but not particularly exciting.

Rough Guides

Routledge and Kegan Paul/Methuen. The Rough Guides are another one of those rare collections of travel guides able to maintain top quality throughout their titles. The guides have a definite low-budget orientation and, because they are a British series, prices are usually noted in pounds instead of dollars. Aimed toward the traveler using public transportation, they are excellent at pointing in the right direction for sights, lodging, or food. There are some hotel suggestions, but restaurant ideas are few; however, the books provide a good orientation to the local cuisine and offer a challenge to explore dining options. The maps are excellent, directions clear, and the survival section on "the basics" very well done. But check the publication date. These titles are updated regularly, but editions may be as long as three years apart. As with any other guide that is a few years old or more, be sure to check things out. Independent travelers with a sense of adventure, even if they have a large budget, will find much of value in the *Rough Guides*.

Shopping in Exotic Places
Impact Publications. This is a truly excellent shopping guide series. Each guidebooks is replete with information on what to buy and where to buy it as well as specific practical points for each geographic location: when to go, customs, food, lodging, shipping, and how to survive the peculiarities of each location. There are good detail maps of major locations. This comprehensive series is for the serious shopper and is updated every two years.

Shopwalks
Crown Publishers. The Shopwalks series is made up of several two-page map-guides, one for each important shopping district in the city. Each includes a large detail map of the area, on which the recommended shops are plotted. Color coding is used to facilitate quick perusal. Also plotted are "miscellaneous stores," which may sell anything from jewelry to antiques. Other things, like transportation points, are shown as well. Colored dots are numbered to match with brief descriptions of the stores selected. These little maps don't provide the detailed analysis of other shopping guides, but they are lightweight and convenient, and may be all you need if more specific information is not important.

Sunset Travel Guides
Lane Publishing. These large-format guides from the publishers of *Sunset* magazine are best used as planning tools. The guides contain some specific suggestions on tours, lodging, activities, restaurants, etc., but information on these subjects is available in more detail elsewhere. The real strength of the books is the feel they give of an area, at least from the point of view of the typical "mainstream" traveler. They contain nicely written overviews and oodles of color photographs.

Times Travel Library Guides
Hunter Publishing. These large-format guides with a heavy emphasis on color photography provide practical tips, local trivia, do-it-yourself walks, excursions, and other useful details.

Travel Survival Kits
Lonely Planet Publications. Lonely Planet, an Australian publisher, has burst on the travel scene, mainly on the strength

of its Travel Survival Kit series. More recently, the books have tried to broaden their focus, leaving true budget travel to its other series, On a Shoestring Guides. But the Travel Survival Kits still have a flavor most appropriate for the moderately young and adventurous, although any traveler can find much of value in them. They are almost always solidly done and sometimes simply wonderful. The guides written by Tony Wheeler, the founder of the company, are among the best. The company seems to be moving toward a stricter schedule of revisions—every two years—but some titles may wait three years or more before updating. Since even two years can be a very long time in some of the volatile countries on Lonely Planet's list, be careful to confirm details, especially with an older publication date. The guides are comprehensive: history, natural history, sightseeing, getting there and getting around (public transportation data is always included), hotels and restaurants are all well covered. The "what to see, what to do" sections are especially thorough. Price ranges are inexpensive to moderate. Plenty of detail maps are included as well. Lonely Planet welcomes comments and criticisms, and publishes many in a quarterly book, *Lonely Planet Update* ($3.95). This excellent series will be made even better as updates become more frequent.

APPENDIX

HOTELS WITH CASINOS

Korea

Cheju	Hyatt Regency Cheju
Kangwon-do	Hotel Sorak Park
Seoul	Sheraton Walker Hill

Macau

Hotel Lisboa
Mandarin Oriental
Oriental Macau

The Philippines

Baguio	Hyatt Terraces Baguio
Manila	Manila Hilton International

HOTELS WITH REVOLVING RESTAURANTS

China

Beijing	Kunlun Hotel
	Xi Yuan Hotel
Guangdong	Zhongshan International Hotel
Guangzhou	The Garden Hotel

Hong Kong

Furama Inter-Continental

India

Bombay   Welcomgroup Sea Rock

Malaysia

Kuala Lumpur   Federal Hotel

Singapore

The Mandarin

HOTELS WITH EXTRAORDINARY LOBBIES

China

Beijing   Kunlun Hotel
                        Xi Yuan Hotel
Guangdong   Zhongshan International Hotel
Guangzhou   The Garden Hotel
                        White Swan Hotel
Shanghai   Hua Ting Sheraton
                        Shanghai Hotel
Tianjin   Crystal Palace Hotel
                        Hyatt Tianjin

Hong Kong

Kowloon   The Regent
                        The Peninsula
                        Shangri-La

India

Bangalore   Holiday Inn Bangalore
Bombay   Taj Mahal Inter-Continental
New Delhi   The Oberoi
                        Taj Mahal Hotel
                        Taj Palace Hotel
                        Welcomgroup Maurya Sheraton Hotel

The Philippines

Manila   Century Park Sheraton Manila
                        The Oriental Mandarin

Singapore

The Dynasty Singapore
Hyatt Regency Singapore
Le Meridien Singapour
Le Meridien Singapour Changi
The Mandarin Singapore
Marina Mandarin Singapore

Sri Lanka

Colombo   Hotel Lanka Oberoi

Taiwan

Taipei   Hotel Royal Taipei

Thailand

Bangkok   Regent of Bangkok
                             Hotel Siam Inter-Continental
                             The Oriental Hotel

RESORTS

China

Beijing   Great Wall Sheraton Hotel
Guangdong   Nan Hai Hotel
Guangzhou   The Garden Hotel
Shanghai   Cypress Hotel

Hong Kong

Cheung Chau   Hotel Warwick

India

Cochin   Malabar Hotel
Goa   The Fort Aguada Beach Resort
                             The Taj Holiday Village
                             Welcomgroup Cidade de Goa
Srinagar   Alexandra Palace Group of Houseboats
Udaipur   The Lake Palace

Indonesia

Bali   Bali Hyatt
                             Hotel Bali Oberoi
                             Hotel Club Bualu
                             Nusa Dua Beach Hotel
Jakarta   Hotel Borobudur Inter-Continental
                             Jakarta Hilton International

Japan

Ibusuki   Ibusuki Kanko Hotel
Ito   Kawana Hotel
Niseko   Hotel Nikko Annupuri
Tokyo   Sheraton Grande Tokyo Bay Hotel
                             Shinagawa Prince Hotel
                             Sunshine City Prince Hotel

Korea

Cheju	Hyatt Regency Cheju
Kangwon-do	Dragon Valley Hotel
	Hotel Sorak Park
Kyongju	Kyongju Tokyu Hotel
Pusan	The Westin Chosun Beach
Seoul	Hyatt Regency Seoul
	Sheraton Walker Hill
Taejeon	Yousoung Tourist Hotel

Macau

Hyatt Regency Macau

Malaysia

Kuala Lumpur	Hyatt Saujana Hotel and Country Club
	Kuala Lumpur Hilton
	Petaling Jaya Hilton
Kuantan	Hyatt Kuantan
	Ramada Beach Resort
Penang	Golden Sands Hotel
	Holiday Inn Penang
	Penang Mutiara Beach Resort
	Rasa Sayang Hotel
Sarawak	Damai Beach Resort

Nepal

Kathmandu	Everest Sheraton Hotel
Pokhara	Fish Tail Lodge

Pakistan

Lahore	Pearl-Continental Hotel Lahore

The Philippines

Batangas	Punta Baluarte Inter-Continental
Cavite	Puerto Azul Beach Hotel
Davao City	Davao Insular Inter-Continental Inn
Manila	The Westin Philippine Plaza

Singapore

Le Meridien Singapour Changi

Sri Lanka

Ahungalla	Triton Hotel
Beruwela	Confifi Beach Hotel
	Riverina Hotel
Colombo	Hotel Lanka Oberoi
	Ramada Renaissance Hotel
Tangalla	Tangalla Bay Hotel
Wattala	Pegasus Reef Hotel

Thailand

Bangkok	Hilton International Bangkok
	at Nai Lert Park
	Hotel Siam Inter-Continental
	The Imperial Hotel
	The Oriental Hotel
	Hotel Sofitel Central
Hua Hin	Royal Garden Resort
Pattaya	Novotel Tropicana
	Royal Cliff Beach Resort
	Siam Bayview Hotel
Phuket	Dusit Laguna Resort Hotel
	Holiday Inn Phuket
	Le Meridien Phuket
	Pearl Village

A-A TRAVEL INFORMATION OFFICES

Bangladesh

Bangladesh Parjatan Corporation
National Tourist Organization
 of Bangladesh
233 Old Airport Road
Tejgaon, Dhaka-15
Bangladesh

China

Kowloon China International Travel Service
 (Hong Kong) Ltd.
6/F, Tower II, South Seas Centre,
75 Mody Road
Tsimshatsui, Kowloon
Hong Kong

Hong Kong

Hong Kong Central Hong Kong Tourist Association
Connaught Centre, 35th floor
Connaught Road, Central
Hong Kong

San Francisco Suite 200, 421 Powell Street
San Francisco, CA 94102-1568

Chicago Suite 2323
333 North Michigan Avenue
Chicago, IL 60601-3966

New York 548 Fifth Avenue
New York, NY 10036-5092

India

New York

Government of India Tourist Office
15, 30 Rockefeller Plaza
New York, NY 10112

Indonesia

Los Angeles

Indonesia Tourist Promotion Office
Indonesia Consulate
3457 Wilshire Boulevard
Los Angeles, CA 90010

Japan

New York

Japan National Tourist Organization
630 Fifth Avenue
New York, NY 10111

Korea

Los Angeles

Korea National Tourism Corporation
Suite 323, 510 West Sixth Street
Los Angeles, CA 90014

New York

Korea Center Building, Suite 400
460 Park Avenue
New York, NY 10022

Macau

Los Angeles

Macau Tourist Information Center
3133 Lake Hollywood Drive
Los Angeles, CA 90068

Malaysia

Los Angeles

Malaysia Tourist Information Center
818 West Seventh Street
Los Angeles, CA 90017

Nepal

Kathmandu

Nepal Department of Tourism
Tripureswore
Kathmandu
Nepal

Pakistan

New York

Pakistan Tourism Development
    Corporation Ltd.
c/o Pakistan Airlines
545 Fifth Avenue
New York, NY 10017

The Philippines

Los Angeles

Philippine Ministry of Tourism
Suite 1212
3460 Wilshire Boulevard
Los Angeles, CA 90010

Singapore

Beverly Hills

Singapore Tourist Promotion Board
8484 Wilshire Boulevard, Suite 510
Beverly Hills, CA 90211

Sri Lanka

Sri Lanka

Celyon Tourist Board
P.O. Box 1504, 228 Havelock Road
Colombo 5
Sri Lanka

Taiwan

San Francisco

Tourism Bureau of the Republic of
     China
Suite 1605, 166 Geary Street
San Francisco, CA 94108

New York

Chinese Information Service
159 Lexington Avenue
New York, NY 10016

Thailand

New York

Tourism Authority of Thailand
5 World Trade Center, Suite 2449
New York, NY 10048

Los Angeles

Suite 101, 3440 Wilshire Boulevard
Los Angeles, CA 90010

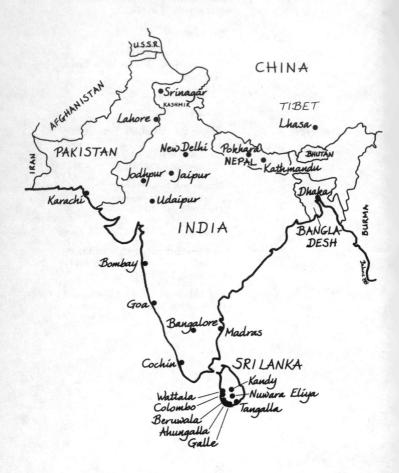

SOUTH ASIA

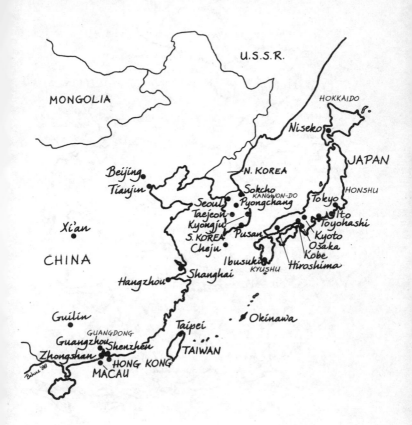

EAST ASIA

SOUTHEAST ASIA

Index

BEST PLACES REPORT

Have we overlooked a hotel you'd recommend? We would appreciate any information you can supply about the quality of the lodgings. Details about the building, furniture, service, food, and setting are most important. Describe as many rooms as you can, including dining rooms, other common rooms, and of course guest rooms. A note about activities and nearby sights would be helpful. Finally, how did you hear about the place, and how long have you been going there?

We will be happy to send you a free copy of the next edition of the book if we use your suggestion.

To: Chris Paddock
        Best Places to Stay in Asia
        The Harvard Common Press
        535 Albany Street
        Boston, Massachusetts 02118

Name of hotel: _____

Telephone: _____

Address: _____

_____

_____

Description: _____

_____

_____

_____

_____

_____

_____

Your Name: _____

Telephone: _____

Address: _____

_____

_____ Zip: _____

BEST PLACES REPORT

Have we overlooked a hotel you'd recommend? We would appreciate any information you can supply about the quality of the lodgings. Details about the building, furniture, service, food, and setting are most important. Describe as many rooms as you can, including dining rooms, other common rooms, and of course guest rooms. A note about activities and nearby sights would be helpful. Finally, how did you hear about the place, and how long have you been going there?

We will be happy to send you a free copy of the next edition of the book if we use your suggestion.

To: Chris Paddock
      Best Places to Stay in Asia
      The Harvard Common Press
      535 Albany Street
      Boston, Massachusetts 02118

Name of hotel: _____

Telephone: _____

Address: _____

_____

_____

Description: _____

_____

_____

_____

_____

_____

_____

Your Name: _____

Telephone: _____

Address: _____

_____

_____ Zip:_____

BEST PLACES REPORT

Have we overlooked a hotel you'd recommend? We would appreciate any information you can supply about the quality of the lodgings. Details about the building, furniture, service, food, and setting are most important. Describe as many rooms as you can, including dining rooms, other common rooms, and of course guest rooms. A note about activities and nearby sights would be helpful. Finally, how did you hear about the place, and how long have you been going there?

We will be happy to send you a free copy of the next edition of the book if we use your suggestion.

To: Chris Paddock
      Best Places to Stay in Asia
      The Harvard Common Press
      535 Albany Street
      Boston, Massachusetts 02118

Name of hotel: _____

Telephone: _____

Address: _____

_____

_____

Description: _____

_____

_____

_____

_____

_____

_____

Your Name: _____

Telephone: _____

Address: _____

_____

_____ Zip:_____

BEST PLACES REPORT

Have we overlooked a hotel you'd recommend? We would appreciate any information you can supply about the quality of the lodgings. Details about the building, furniture, service, food, and setting are most important. Describe as many rooms as you can, including dining rooms, other common rooms, and of course guest rooms. A note about activities and nearby sights would be helpful. Finally, how did you hear about the place, and how long have you been going there?

We will be happy to send you a free copy of the next edition of the book if we use your suggestion.

To: Chris Paddock
         Best Places to Stay in Asia
         The Harvard Common Press
         535 Albany Street
         Boston, Massachusetts 02118

Name of hotel: _____

Telephone: _____

Address: _____

_____

_____

Description: _____

_____

_____

_____

_____

_____

_____

Your Name: _____

Telephone: _____

Address: _____

_____

_____ Zip:_____

BEST PLACES REPORT

Have we overlooked a hotel you'd recommend? We would appreciate any information you can supply about the quality of the lodgings. Details about the building, furniture, service, food, and setting are most important. Describe as many rooms as you can, including dining rooms, other common rooms, and of course guest rooms. A note about activities and nearby sights would be helpful. Finally, how did you hear about the place, and how long have you been going there?

We will be happy to send you a free copy of the next edition of the book if we use your suggestion.

To: Chris Paddock
        Best Places to Stay in Asia
        The Harvard Common Press
        535 Albany Street
        Boston, Massachusetts 02118

Name of hotel: _____

Telephone: _____

Address: _____

_____

_____

Description: _____

_____

_____

_____

_____

_____

_____

Your Name: _____

Telephone: _____

Address: _____

_____

_____ Zip:_____